HISTORY AND RELATED DISCIPLINES
SELECT BIBLIOGRAPHIES
GENERAL EDITOR: R. C. RICHARDSON

BRITISH ECONOMIC AND SOCIAL HISTORY

This is the third edition of a bibliographical guide which has become firmly established in its field. The new edition is much revised and enlarged. Its 7400 entries begin with items on Historiography and Methodology and then are divided into four principal sections on England covering the periods 1066–1300, 1300–1500, 1500–1700, and 1700–1980.

There are separate extended sections on Wales, Scotland and Ireland. In all cases annotations are given where appropriate and cross references guide the user from one section to another. The bibliography also forms a kind of map of its field. The much more substantial treatment given here than in earlier editions to the history of the family, women, leisure, recreation, popular culture, crime, law and order, and to the social effects of war eloquently testifies to the changing contours of British economic and social history as a discipline.

HISTORY AND RELATED DISCIPLINES
SELECT BIBLIOGRAPHIES
GENERAL EDITOR: R. C. RICHARDSON

Bibliographical guides designed to meet the needs of undergraduates, postgraduates and their teachers in universities and colleges of higher education. All volumes in the series share a number of common characteristics. They are selective, manageable in size, and include those books and articles which are most important and useful. All volumes are edited by practising teachers of the subject and are based on their experience of the needs of students. The arrangement combines chronological with thematic divisions. Most of the items listed receive some descriptive comment.

Already published in the series:

EUROPEAN ECONOMIC AND SOCIAL HISTORY

THE STUDY OF HISTORY

SOCIETY AND ECONOMY IN EARLY MODERN EUROPE

BRITISH AND IRISH ARCHAEOLOGY

AFRICA, ASIA AND SOUTH AMERICA SINCE 1800

WESTERN POLITICAL THOUGHT: POST-WAR
RESEARCH

ANCIENT GREECE AND ROME

BRITISH WOMEN'S HISTORY

RUSSIA AND EASTERN EUROPE

JAPANESE STUDIES FROM PREHISTORY TO 1990

UNITED STATES HISTORY

BRITISH ECONOMIC AND SOCIAL HISTORY
A BIBLIOGRAPHICAL GUIDE
THIRD EDITION

COMPILED BY

R. C. RICHARDSON
AND W. H. CHALONER

MANCHESTER UNIVERSITY PRESS
Manchester and New York

Distributed exclusively in the USA and Canada by
St. Martin's Press, New York

Copyright © R. C. Richardson and W. H. Chaloner 1996
First published 1976, second edition 1984

Published by
MANCHESTER UNIVERSITY PRESS
Oxford Road, Manchester M13 9NR, UK
and Room 400, 175 Fifth Avenue, New York
NY 10010, USA

Distributed exclusively in the USA and Canada by
St. Martin's Press, Inc., 175 Fifth Avenue, New York,
NY 10010, USA

British Library Cataloguing-in-Publication Data
A catalogue record for this book is available from the
British Library

Library of Congress Cataloging-in-Publication Data applied for
ISBN 0 7190 3600 3 *hardback*

Photoset in Plantin
by Northern Phototypesetting Co. Ltd., Bolton
Printed in Great Britain
by Cromwell Press Ltd, Melksham

CONTENTS

General editor's preface—ix
Editorial preface—x
List of abbreviations—xii

CONTENTS

CONTENTS

GENERAL EDITOR'S PREFACE

History, to an even greater extent than most other academic disciplines, has developed at a prodigious pace in the twentieth century. Its scope has extended and diversified, its methodologies have been revolutionized, its philosophy has changed, and its relations with other disciplines have been transformed. The number of students and teachers of the subject in the different branches of higher education has vastly increased, and there is an ever-growing army of amateurs, many of them taking adult education courses. Academic and commercial publishers have produced a swelling stream of publications – both specialist and general – to cater for this large and expanding audience. Scholarly journals have proliferated. It is no easy matter even for the specialist to keep abreast of the flow of publications in a particular field. For those with more general academic interests the task of finding what has been written on different subject areas can be time-consuming, perplexing, and often frustrating.

It is primarily to meet the needs of undergraduates, postgraduates and their teachers in universities, and colleges of higher education, that this series of bibliographies is designed. It will be a no less valuable resource, however, to the reference collection of any public library, school or college.

Though common sense demands that each volume will be structured in the way which is most appropriate for the particular field in question, nonetheless all volumes in the series share a number of important common characteristics. First – quite deliberately – all are *select* bibliographies, manageable in size, and include those books and articles which in the editor's judgement are most important and useful. To attempt an uncritically comprehensive listing would needlessly dictate the inclusion of items which were frankly ephemeral, antiquarian, or discredited and result only in the production of a bulky and unwieldy volume. Like any select bibliography, however, this series will direct the reader, where appropriate, to other more specialised and detailed sources of bibliographical information. That would be one of its functions. Second, all the volumes are edited not simply by specialists in the different fields but by practising teachers of the subject, and are based on their experience of the needs of students in higher education. Third, there are common features of arrangement and presentation. All volumes begin with listings of general works of a methodological or historiographical nature, and proceed within broad chronological divisions to arrange their material thematically. Most items receive some descriptive comment. Each volume, for ease of reference, has an index of authors and editors.

R. C. RICHARDSON

EDITORIAL PREFACE

The first edition of this bibliographical guide appeared in 1976. Having gone out of print a second, much extended version came out to replace it in 1984. Since that too has been unavailable for some time an enlarged, updated third edition is now called for. The case for a publication of this kind is as strong as ever. No competitor has appeared and new material on British economic and social history continues to be published at a startling rate. The annual list of new publications in the *Economic History Review* – running at 40 pages in November 1994 – provides ample testimony to that fact.

Like its predecessors this enlarged third edition opens with Historiography and General Works and is then chronologically divided at 1300, 1500 and 1700. Items are arranged thematically and numbered separately within each of the eight major sections. Each book or article is numbered only once; further mentions of it are cross-referenced.

The first edition of this work contained 4200 items and the second 5800. For this third edition many existing items were deleted to make way for new ones. Even so the third edition now contains 7400 items. But there are other changes as well as increased size. The chronological end point of the period coverage now becomes 1980, not 1970. The sections on Wales, Scotland and Ireland are greatly strengthened – that on Ireland, for example

goes up by a third. In sections 2 to 5 on England the changing priorities of economic and social history are reflected in the much more substantial treatment given to the family, women, leisure, recreation, popular culture, crime, law and order, and to the social history of war.

Many scholars have suggested items for inclusion in this new edition and I have drawn freely on their expertise. Jane Thorniley-Walker of Manchester University Press has waited patiently for this volume to appear and Joan Chaloner has maintained a keen interest in its progress. Stephen Lehec assisted me in the early stages of preparation and without the invaluable contribution made in the summers of 1994 and 1995 by Michael Martin to the final stages of compilation, checking, assembling and indexing, this volume would never have been completed. I could not have wished for a more enthusiastic, industrious, resilient and good-humoured research assistant.

The first two editions of this bibliographical guide were compiled in collaboration with W. H. Chaloner. Though he died in 1987 his inimitable style and encyclopaedic knowledge still live on in the third edition which is dedicated, affectionately, to his memory.

RCR
July 1995

PRINCIPAL
ABBREVIATIONS

Though this is not a complete list of abbreviations
used in the text, all others should be self-explanatory.
Ass.: Association, Ec.: Economic, J.: Journal,
Proc.: Proceedings, R.: Review, Soc.: Society, throughout.

Ag.H.   **Agricultural History**
Ag.H.R.   **Agricultural History Review**
A.H.R.   **American Historical Review**
Arch.Cant.   **Archaeologia Cantiana**
Arch.J.   **Archaeological Journal**
B.I.H.R.   **Bulletin of the Institute of Historical Research**
B. John Rylands Lib.   **Bulletin of the John Rylands Library**
B.Bd.Celtic Studs.   **Bulletin of the Board of Celtic Studies**
Brit.J.Soc.   **British Journal of Sociology**
Bus.H.   **Business History**
Bus.H.R.   **Business History Review**
Canadian J.Ec.&Pol. Science   **Canadian Journal of Economics and Political Science**
Chet.Soc.   **Chetham Society**
Church H.   **Church History**
Comp.Studs.Soc.&H.   **Comparative Studies in Society and History**
East Yorks.Loc.H.Soc.   **East Yorkshire Local History Society**
Ec.H.R.   **Economic History Review**
E.J.Ec.H.Supp.   **Economic Journal Economic History Supplement**
E.H.R.   **English Historical Review**
Essex R.   **Essex Review**
Expl.Entrepren.H.   **Explorations in Entrepreneurial History**
Geog.   **Geography**
Geog.R.   **Geographical Review**
Hist.   **History**
H.Today   **History Today**
Hist.Ass.   **Historical Association**

H.Educ.   **History of Education**
H.& Theory   **History and Theory**
Hist.Studs.   **Historical Studies**
Hug.Soc.   **Huguenot Society**
Ind.Arch.R.   **Industrial Archaeology Review**
Internat.R.Soc.H.   **International Review of Social History**
Irish Hist.Studs.   **Irish Historical Studies**
J.Brit.Studs.   **Journal of British Studies**
J.Contemp.H.   **Journal of Contemporary History**
J.Ec.H.   **Journal of Economic History**
J.Ec.& Bus.H.   **Journal of Economic and Business History**
J.Eccles.H.   **Journal of Ecclesiastical History**
J.Educ.Admin.& H.   **Journal of Educational Administration and History**
J.Europ.Ec.H.   **Journal of European Economic History**
J.H.Geog.   **Journal of Historical Geography**
J.H.Ideas   **Journal of the History of Ideas**
J.Interdis.H.   **Journal of Interdisciplinary History**
J.Peasant Studs.   **Journal of Peasant Studies**
J.Pol.Econ.   **Journal of Political Economy**
J.Roy.Stat.Soc.   **Journal of the Royal Statistical Society**
J.Soc.H.   **Journal of Social History**
J.Trans.H.   **Journal of Transport History**
Lit.& H.   **Literature and History**
Loc.Historian   **Local Historian**
Loc.Pop.Studs.   **Local Population Studies**
Nat.Lib.WalesJ.   **National Library of Wales Journal**

Northern H. **Northern History**
Northern Scot. **Northern Scotland**
P.P. **Past and Present**
Pop.Studs. **Population Studies**
Proc.Brit.Acad. **Proceedings of the British Academy**
Proc.Dorset Nat.H. & Arch.Soc. **Proceedings of the Dorset Natural History and Archaeological Society**
Proc.Hug.Soc. **Proceedings of the Huguenot Society**
Renaiss. & Mod.Studs. **Renaissance and Modern Studies**
Scand.Ec.H.R. **Scandinavian Economic History Review**
Scot.H.R. **Scottish Historical Review**
Scot.J.Pol.Econ. **Scottish Journal of Political Economy**
Soc.R. **Sociological Review**
Southern H. **Southern History**
Studs.Med.& Renaiss.H. **Studies in Medieval and Renaissance History**
T.H.S.L.C. **Transactions of the Historic Society of Lancashire and Cheshire**
T.L.C.A.S. **Transactions of the Lancashire and Cheshire Antiquarian Society**
T.Cumb.& West.Antiq.& Arch.Soc. **Transactions of the Cumberland and Westmorland Antiquarian and Archaeological Society**
T.Hon.Soc.Cymmrod. **Transactions of the Honourable Society of Cymmrodorion**
T.I.B.G. **Transactions of the Institute of British Geographers**
T.Jewish H.Soc. **Transactions of the Jewish Historical Society**
T.R.H.S. **Transactions of the Royal Historical Society**
Trans.H. **Transport History**
Urban H.Yearbook **Urban History Yearbook**
V.C.H. **Victoria County History**
Vict.Studs. **Victorian Studies**
Welsh H.R. **Welsh History Review**
Worcs.H.Soc. **Worcestershire Historical Society**
Yorks.B. **Yorkshire Bulletin**

In memory of W. H. Chaloner
(1914–1987)

1

GENERAL WORKS

HISTORIOGRAPHY AND METHODOLOGY

1.1 **Abelove**, H. et al., eds., *Visions of History*, 1983. Interviews with leading historians, including E. P. Thompson, Eric Hobsbawm, Sheila Rowbotham, and Natalie Zemon Davis.

1.2 **Abrams**, P., 'History, Sociology, Historical Sociology', *P.P.*, 87, 1980, 3–16.

1.3 **Aitken**, H. G. J., 'On the present state of economic history', *Canadian J. Ec. and Pol. Science*, XXVI, 1960, 87–95.

1.4 **Andreano**, R., ed., *The New Economic History. Recent Papers on Methodology*, N.Y., 1970.

1.5 **Angerman**, A. et al., *Current Issues in Women's History*, 1989. Ranges widely in terms of period and geography and situates the different essays within a clearly defined conceptual framework.

1.6 **Arnstein**, W. L., ed., *Recent Historians of Great Britain*, Ames, Iowa, 1990.

1.7 **Ashley**, W. J., *Surveys, Historic and Economic*, 1900. Includes two chapters on the study of economic history (1–30).

1.8 —— 'The place of economic history in university studies', *Ec.H.R.*, I, 1927–8, 1–11. On Ashley see: Scott, W. R., 'Memoir: Sir William Ashley', *Ec.H.R.*, I, 1927–8, 319–21.

1.9 **Ashplant**, T. G. and Wilson, A., 'Present-centred history and the problem of historical knowledge', *Hist.J.*, XXXI, 1988, 253–74.

1.10 **Ashton**, T. S., 'The relation of economic history to economic theory', 1946. In Harte, ed. (1.124). On Ashton *see* John, A. H., 'Thomas Southcliffe Ashton, 1889–1968', *Ec.H.R.*, 2nd ser., XXI, 1968, iii–v; Sayers, R. S., 'Thomas Southcliffe Ashton, 1889–1968', *Proc.Brit.Acad.*, LVI, 1972, 263–81.

1.11 **Ashworth**, W., 'The study of modern economic history', 1958. In Harte, ed. (1.124).

1.12 **Aydelotte**, W. O., *Quantification in History*, Reading, Mass., 1971.

1.13 **Baker**, R. H. and Billinge, M., eds., *Period and Place. Research Methods in Historical Geography*, 1982.

1.14 **Ballard**, M., ed., *New Movements in the Study and Teaching of History*, 1970.

1.15 **Banks**, J. A., 'From universal history to historical sociology', *Brit.J.Soc.*, XL, 1989, 521–43.

1.16 **Barker**, T. C., 'The beginnings of the Economic History Society', *Ec.H.R.*, 2nd ser., XXX, 1977, 1–19.

1.17 **Barzun**, J., *Clio and the Doctors: Psycho-history, Quanto-history and History*, Chicago, 1974.

1.18 **Basmann**, R. L., 'The role of the economic historian in the productive testing of proffered "economic laws" ', *Expl. Entrepren. H.*, 2nd ser., II, 1965, 159–86.

1.19 **Beales**, D., *History and Biography*, 1981.

1.20 **Bedarida**, F., 'The modern historian's dilemma: conflicting pressures from sciences and society', *Ec.H.R.*, 2nd ser.,

XL, 1987, 349–79.

1.21 **Beresford**, M. W., 'Time and place', 1960. In Harte, ed. (1.124).

1.22 —— *History on the Ground*, 2nd ed., 1971.

1.23 **Berg**, Maxine, 'The first women economic historians', *Ec.H.R.*, 2nd ser., XLV, 1992, 308–29.

1.24 **Bertaux**, D., ed., *Biography and Society: the life history approach in the social sciences*, 1982.

1.25 **Birkos**, A. S., *Historiography, Method, History Teaching: A Bibliography of Books and Articles in English, 1965–73*, Hamden, Conn., 1975.

1.26 **Blaug**, M., *Economic History and the History of Economics*, 1986.

1.27 —— *The History of Economics*, 1991.

1.28 **Bloch**, M., *The Historian's Craft*, 1954.

1.29 **Borsay**, P., 'History or heritage?: perceptions of the urban past', *Urban H. Yearbook*, XVIII, 1991, 32–40.

1.30 **Bottigheimer**, K., 'The new Irish history', *J.Brit.Studs.*, XXVII, 1988, 72–79.

1.31 **Bridbury**, A. R., *Historians and the Open Society*, 1972.

1.32 **Bryman**, A., *Quantity and Quality in Social Research*, 1988.

1.33 **Buchanan**, R. A., *History and Industrial Civilisation*, 1970.

1.34 —— 'Technology and History', *Soc.Studs. in Science*, V, 1975, 488–99.

1.35 **Burke**, P., ed., *New Perspectives on Historical Writing*, 1989. A spirited collection dealing with 'History from below', women's history, oral history, history of reading habits, history of images, and the history of the body.

1.36 **Burke**, P., *Sociology and History*, 1980.

1.37 **Butt**, J., 'Achievement and Prospect: Transport History in the 1970s and 1980s', *J.Trans.H.*, 3rd ser., II, 1981, 1–24.

1.38 **Cairncross**, A. K., 'In praise of economic history', *Ec.,H.R.*, 2nd ser., XLII, 1989, 173–85.

1.39 **Cameron**, R., 'Economic history: pure and applied', *J.Ec.H.*, XXXVI, 1976, 3–27.

1.40 **Campbell**, R. H., 'Scottish economic and social history: past developments and future prospects', *Scot.Ec. & Soc.H.*, X, 1990, 5–20.

1.40a **Cannadine**, D., *The Pleasures of the Past*, 1989. An engagingly written collection of essays which includes studies of urban history, London's urban fabric, socialist history, and of the histories of food, poverty and sex.

1.40b **Cannon**, J., ed., *The Blackwell Dictionary of Historians*, 1988. An invaluable reference tool which includes accounts of the Annales School, Philippe Ariès, Asa Briggs, T. S. Ashton, H. J. Dyos, R. W. Fogel, E. P. Thompson, R. H. Tawney and C. Hill.

1.41 **Cantor**, N. F., *Perspectives on the European Past: Conversations with Historians*, N. Y., 2 vols., 1971. Amongst the historians included in this collection of interviews are R. M. Hartwell on 'The Industrial Revolution', D. S. Landes on 'Labour and the Labour Movement', A. P. Thornton on 'Imperialism' and A. Briggs on 'Modern Britain'.

1.42 **Cardwell**, D. S. L., 'The history of technology: now and in the future', *Ind.Arch.R.*, II, 1978, 103–10.

1.43 **Carus-Wilson**, Eleanora M. *See* Youings, Joyce, 'Eleanora M. Carus-Wilson, 1897–1977', *Ec.H.R.*, 2nd ser., XXX, 2, 1977, iii–v.

1.44 **Chambers**. J. D., 'The place of economic history in historical studies', 1960. In Harte, ed. (1.124). On Chambers *see*: Mingay, G. E., 'The contribution of a regional historian: J. D. Chambers 1898–1970', *Studs. in Burke and his Time*, XIII, 1972, 2002–2010.

1.45 **Chandler**, J. D. and Galambos, J., eds., *Economic History: Retrospect and Prospect. Papers Presented at the Thirteenth Annual Meeting of the Economic History Association*, 1971 (A special issue of the *J.Ec.H.*, XXXI, 1, 1971). Contains papers by W. N. Parker, A. Fishlow and R. W. Fogel, J. Swanson and J. Williamson, P. Temin and D. C. North.

1.46 **Cherry**, G. E., 'Planning history: recent developments in Britain', *Planning Perspectives*, VI, 1991, 33–45.

1.47 **Church**, C. H., 'Disciplinary dynamics', *Studs.Higher Ed.*, I, 1976, 101–18.

1.48 **Church**, R. A., 'Business history in England', *J.Europ.Ec.H.*, V, 1976, 209–28.

1.49 **Cipolla**, C. M., *Between Two Cultures: An Introduction to Economic History*. 1991. Deals with the nature, methods and the sources of economic history.

1.50 **Clapham**, J. H., 'The study of economic history', 1929. In Harte, ed. (1.124). On

Clapham *see*: Heaton, H., 'Clapham's contribution to economic history', *Pol. Sci. Quart.*, LIII, 1938, 599–602; Postan, M. M., 'Sir John Clapham', *Univ. Leeds.R.*, XVII, 1974, 129–36, and Court (1.63).

1.51 **Clark**, C. M., 'Trouble at t'mill: industrial archaeology in the 1980s', *Antiquity*, LXI, 1987, 169–79.

1.52 **Clark**, G. N., 'The study of economic history', 1932. In Harte, ed. (1.124).

1.53 **Clive**, J., *Not by Fact Alone. Essays on the Writing and Reading of History*, 1989. A collection focussed chiefly on nineteenth-century historiography but with an afterward on the great historians in the age of cliometrics.

1.54 **Coats**, A. W., 'Economic growth. The economic and social historian's dilemma', 1966. In Harte, ed.

1.55 —— 'The historical context of the "New Economic History" ', *J.Europ.Ec.H.*, IX, 1980, 185–207.

1.56 **Coleman**, D. C., *History and the Economic Past. An Account of the Rise and Decline of Economic History in Britain*, 1987. Charts the main trends in the growth of economic history as a discipline, highlighting the rival tendencies of the twentieth century.

1.57 —— *Myth, History and the Industrial Revolution*, 1992. Traces the history of the term 'Industrial Revolution' and, more generally, changing patterns in the study of economic history and business history.

1.58 **Cohen**, J. S., 'The achievements of economic history: the Marxist School', *J.Ec.H.*, XXXVIII, 1978, 29–57.

1.59 **Cohn**, B. S., 'History and Anthropology: the state of play', *Comp.Studs. Soc. & H.*, XXII, 1980, 198–221.

1.60 **Cole**, W. A., *Economic History as a Social Science*, 1967.

1.61 **Conrad**, A. H., 'Economic theory, statistical inference and economic history', *J.Ec.H.*, XVII, 1957, 524–44.

1.62 —— and Meyer, J. R., *Studies in Economic History*, 1965.

1.63 **Court**, W. H. B., *Scarcity and Choice in History*, 1970. A collection of essays, including a valuable study of 'Two economic historians: R. H. Tawney and Sir John Clapham', 127–50.

1.64 **Crafts**, N. F. R. et al., *Quantitative Economic History*, 1991.

1.65 **Cruise**, H. F., 'The economic historian and the growth debate', *Austral. Ec.H.R.*, XV, 1975, 83–106.

1.66 **David**, P., 'Economic history through the looking glass', *Econometrica*, XXXII, 1964, 694–6.

1.67 **Davidoff**, Leonore, *Life is Duty, Praise and Prayer. Some Contributions of New Women's History*, 1991.

1.68 **Davis**, H. E., *History and Power. The Social Relevance of History*, 1983.

1.69 **Davis**, L. E., 'Professor Fogel and the new economic history', *Ec.H.R.*, 2nd ser., XIX, 1966, 657–63.

1.70 —— ' "And it will never be literature": the new economic history: a critique', *Expl.Entrepren.H.*, 2nd ser., VI, 1969, 75–92.

1.71 —— et al., 'Aspects of quantitative research in economic history', *J.Ec.H.*, XX, 1960, 539–47.

1.72 **Davis**, R., 'History and the social sciences', 1965. In Harte ed. (1.124).

1.73 **Degler**, C. N., *Is there a History of Women?*, 1975.

1.74 **Delzell**, C. F., ed., *The Future of History*, Nashville, Tenn., 1977. Includes essays on the new urban history and on history and the social sciences.

1.75 **Denley**, P. et al., eds., *History and Computing*, I, 1987, II, 1989, III, 1990. Collections of essays dealing with different varieties of work in progress and with general issues of methodology.

1.76 **Desai**, M., 'Some issues in econometric history', *Ec.H.R.*, 2nd ser., XXI, 1968, 1–16.

1.77 **Dickson**, T., 'Marxism, nationalism and Scottish history', *J.Contemp.H.*, XX, 1985, 323–36.

1.78 **Dobb**, M., 'Historical materialism and the role of the economic factor', *Hist.*, XXXVI, 1951, 1–11.

1.79 **Dockes**, P. and Rosier, B., 'Histoire raisonée et économie historique', *Revue Economique*, XLII, 1991, 181–210.

1.80 **Dollar**, C. M., and Jewsen, R. J. N., *Historian's Guide to Statistics: Quantitative Analysis and Historical Research*, N. Y., 1971.

1.81 **Douring**, F., *History as a Social Science*, The Hague, 1960.

1.82 **Drake**, M., ed., *Applied Historical Studies: An Introductory Reader*, 1973. Contains a general introductory chapter on 'Sociology and the historical perspective'.

1.83 **Duberman**, M. et al., *Hidden from History. Reclaiming the Gay and Lesbian Past*, 1991. An extensive collection of articles which includes sections on the preindustrial period, the nineteenth century, early twentieth century, and on the Second World War and after.

1.84 **Dyer**, C. C., 'The past, the present, and the future in medieval rural history', *Rural Hist.*, I, 1990, 37–49.

1.85 **Dymond**, D., *Writing Local History. A Practical Guide*, 1981.

1.86 **Edington**, S., *Micro-History. Local History and Computing Projects*, 1985.

1.87 **Ellis**, S. G., 'Historiographical debate: representations of the past in Ireland. Whose past and whose present?', *Irish Hist.Studs.*, XXVII, 1991, 289–308.

1.88 **Elton**, G. R., 'The historian's social function', *T.R.H.S.*, 5th ser., XXVII, 1977, 197–211.

1.89 **Erickson**, Charlotte, 'Quantitative history', *A.H.R.*, LXXX, 1975, 351–65.

1.90 **Farnie**, D. A., 'Three historians of the cotton industry: Thomas Ellison, Gerhart von Schulze-Gaevernitz and Sydney Chapman', *Textile H.*, IX, 1978, 75–89.

1.91 **Federn**, K., *The Materialist Conception of History: A Critical Analysis*, 1939.

1.92 **Feinstein**, C., and Digby, Anne, *New Directions in Economic and Social History*, 1989.

1.93 **Finberg**, H. P. R., *The Local Historian and his Theme*, 1952.

1.94 —— *Local History in the University*, 1964.

1.95 —— ed., *Approaches to History: A Symposium*, 1962. Includes essays on economic, social and local history.

1.96 **Fisher**, F. M., 'On the analysis of history and the interdependence of the social sciences', *Philosophy of Science*, XXVII, 1960, 147–58.

1.97 **Fishlow**, A., and Fogel, R. W., 'Quantitative economic history. An interim evaluation; past trends and present tendencies', *J.Ec.H.*, XXXI, 1971, 15–42.

1.98 **Floud**, R., *An Introduction to Quantitative Method for Historians*, 1973.

1.99 —— 'Quantitative history: evolution of methods and techniques', *J.Soc.Archivists*, V, 1977, 407–17.

1.100 **Fogel**, R. W., 'The specification problem in economic history', *J.Ec.H.*, XXVII, 1967, 283–308.

1.101 —— 'The new economic history: its findings and methods', *Ec.H.R.*, 2nd ser., XIX, 1966, 642–56.

1.102 —— 'The limits of quantitative methods in history', *A.H.R.*, LXXX, 1975, 329–50.

1.103 —— and Elton, G. R., *Which Road to the Past? Two Views of History*, 1983. Two very different conceptions of history are paraded here with Elton, as ever, resolutely defending the traditional line.

1.104 **Fussell**, G. E., 'Agricultural history: its recent development', *Loc.Historian*, XV, 1982, 157–60.

1.105 **Fraser**, D. and Sutcliffe, A., eds., *The Pursuit of Urban History*, 1983. A memorial volume for H. J. Dyos. As well as subject-specific chapters there are several essays dealing expressly with the historiography, rationale, and methodologies of urban history.

1.106 **Gallman**, R. E., ed., *Recent Developments in the Study of Business and Economic History*, Greenwich, Conn., 1977.

1.107 **Gilbert**, C. L., *The Development of British Econometrics, 1945–85*, 1986.

1.108 **Glynn**, S., 'Approaches to urban history: the case for caution', *Austral. Ec.H.R.*, X, 1970, 218–25.

1.109 **Gluck**, S. B. and Patai, D., eds., *Women's Worlds: the Feminist Practice of Oral History*, 1991.

1.110 **Goodrich**, C. L., 'Economic history: one field or two?', *J.Ec.H.*, XX, 1960, 531–8.

1.111 **Gordon**, P. and Szreter, R., eds., *History of Education: The Making of a Discipline*, 1989.

1.112 **Gordon**, S., *The History and Philosophy of Social Science*, 1991.

1.113 **Gottschalk**, L., ed., *Generalization in the Writing of History*, Chicago, 1963. Contains a very good bibliography on historiography, 213–48.

1.114 **Gras**, N. S. B., *Introduction to Economic History*, 1922.

1.115 —— 'The rise and development of economic history', *Ec.H.R.*, I, 1927–8, 12–34.

1.116 **Grele**, R., *Envelopes of Sound. The Art of Oral History*, 1986.

1.117 **Gunderson**, G., 'The nature of social saving', *Ec.H.R.*, 2nd ser., XXIII, 1970, 207–20. A consideration of the 'new economic history'.

1.118 **Habakkuk**, H. J., 'Economic history and

1.119 **Hale**, J. R., *The Evolution of British Historiography*, 1967. A substantial introductory essay followed by representative extracts.

1.120 **Hammond**, J. L. *See* the obituary notice by R. H. Tawney, 'J. L. Hammond, 1872–1949', *Proc.Brit.Acad.*, XLVI, 1960, 267–94.

1.121 **Hancock**, W. K., 'Economic history at Oxford', 1946. In Harte, ed. (1.124).

1.122 **Hannah**, L., 'New issues in British business history', *Bus.H.R.*, LVII, 1983, 165–93.

1.123 **Harrison**, R., 'Marxism as nineteenth-century critique and twentieth-century ideology', *Hist.*, LXVI, 1981, 208–20.

1.124 **Harte**, N. B., ed., *The Study of Economic History*, 1971. An extremely useful collection of reprinted inaugural lectures with an introduction by the editor.

1.125 —— 'Trends in publications on the economic and social history of Great Britain and Ireland', *Ec.H.R.*, 2nd ser., XXX, 1977, 20–41.

1.126 **Harvey**, C. E., ed., *Business History: Concepts and Measurements*, 1989.

1.127 —— and Jones, G., 'Business history in Britain into the 1990s', *Bus.H.*, XXXII, 1990, 267–80.

1.128 **Hawke**, G. R., *Economics for Historians*, 1980.

1.129 **Hawthorn**, G., *Plausible Worlds. Possibility and Understanding in History and the Social Sciences*, 1991.

1.130 **Hayek**, F. A., ed., *Capitalism and the Historians*, 1954.

1.131 **Heater**, D., 'History and the social sciences'. In Ballard (1.14), 134–46.

1.132 **Heckscher**, E. F., 'A plea for theory in economic history', *Ec.J.Ec.H.Supp.*, I, 1929, 525–34.

1.133 **Henige**, D., *Oral Historiography*, 1982.

1.134 **Hexter**, J. H., *Doing History*, 1972.

1.135 —— 'A new framework for social history', in the same author's *Reappraisals in History*, 1961, 14–25.

1.136 **Hicks**, J., *A Theory of Economic History*, 1969.

1.137 **Hill**, C., Hilton, R. H., and Hobsbawm, E. J., 'Past and Present: origins and early years', *P.P.*, X, 1983, 3–13. *See also* (1.179)

1.138 **Hilden**, P., 'Women's history: The Second Wave. Review article', *Hist.J.*, XXV, 1982, 501–12.

1.139 **Himmelfarb**, Gertrude, *The New History and the Old*, 1987. A somewhat jaundiced view of new trends in history.

1.140 **Hirst**, P. Q., *Marxism and Historical Writing*, 1985. Includes critiques of E. P. Thompson and P. Anderson.

1.141 **Hobsbawm**, E. J., 'The contribution of History to social science', *Internat.Soc. Sci.J.*, XXXIII, 1918, 624–41.

1.142 —— 'Karl Marx's contribution to historiography', in R. Blackburn, ed., *Ideology in Social Science*, 1972, 265–83.

1.143 —— 'The social function of the past', *P.P.*, LV, 1972, 3–17.

1.144 —— 'From social history to the history of society' in Flinn and Smout (1.327), 1–22.

1.145 —— 'The Historians' Group of the Communist Party' in Cornforth (5.1995), 21–48.

1.146 **Holloway**, S. J. F., 'Sociology and history', *Hist.*, XLVIII, 1963, 154–80.

1.147 **Holton**, R. J., *The Transition from Feudalism to Capitalism*, 1985. Largely historiographical in approach.

1.148 **Hoskins**, W. G., *Local History in England*, 1959, 2nd ed., 1973.

1.149 **Houston**, R. and Smith, R., 'A new approach to family history?', *Hist.Workshop J.*, XIV, 1982, 120–32.

1.150 **Hughes**, H. S., 'The historian and the social scientist', in A. V. Riasanovsky and B. Riznik, eds., *Generalizations in Historical Writing*, Philadelphia, 1963, 18–59.

1.151 **Hughes**, J. R. T., 'Fact and theory in economic history', *Expl. Entrepren. H.*, III, 1966, 75–100.

1.152 —— 'Measuring British economic growth', *J.Ec.H.*, XXIV, 1964, 60–82.

1.153 **Humphries**, S., *The Handbook of Oral History*, 1984.

1.154 **Hunt**, E. H., 'The new economic history', *Hist.*, LIII, 1968, 3–18.

1.155 **Hunt**, Lynn, *The New Cultural History*, 1989. Divided into two parts – models and new approaches – which consider the impact of feminism, post structuralism and anthropology to the redefinition of cultural history.

1.156 **Igartua**, J. E., 'The computer and the historian's work', *Hist. & Computing*, III, 1991, 73–83.

1.157 **Iggers**, G. G. and Parker, H. T., eds., *International Handbook of Historical*

economic theory', *Daedalus*, 1971, 305–22.

Studies, 1980.

1.158 **Innes**, Joanna, 'Jonathan Clark, social history and England's "Ancien Regime"', *P.P.*, CXVIII, 1987, 165–200.

1.159 **John**, E., 'Some questions on the materialist interpretation of history', *Hist.*, XXXVIII, 1953, 1–10.

1.160 **Johnson**, R. et al., eds., *Making Histories. Studies in History Writing and Politics*, 1982. Eight essays divided into three principal categories: historians and the people, Marxist theory and historical analysis, and autobiography/memory/tradition.

1.161 **Jones**, G. S., 'History: the poverty of empiricism', in R. Blackburn, ed., *Ideology in Social Science*, 1972, 96–118.

1.162 —— 'From historical sociology to theoretic history', *Brit.J.Soc.*, XXVII, 1976, 295–305.

1.163 **Jude**, T., 'A clown in regal purple: social history and the historians', *Hist.Workshop*, VII, 1979, 66–94.

1.164 **Kadish**, A., *Historians, Economists, and Economic History*, 1989.

1.165 **Kain**, R. J. P., 'Extending the agenda of historical enquiry: computer processing of the tithe survey data', *Hist. & Computing*, III, 1991, 23–35.

1.166 **Kammen**, M., ed., *The Past Before Us*, Ithaca, N. Y., 1980. An invaluable collection whose twenty chapters include discussions of new trends in social history, labour history, women's history, oral history, and quantitative social scientific history.

1.167 **Kaye**, H. J., *The British Marxist Historians. An Introductory Analysis*, 1984. Useful historiographical case studies of Maurice Dobb, R. H. Hilton, Christopher Hill, Eric Hobsbawm, and E. P. Thompson.

1.168 —— *The Powers of the Past. Reflections on the crisis and the Promise of History*, 1991.

1.169 —— *The Education of Desire. Marxists and the Writing of History*, 1992. Contains chapters on Rudé, Kiernan, Thompson and Morton.

1.170 **Kent**, C., 'The establishment of British social history', *Canadian J.Hist.*, XXVI, 1991, 267–76.

1.171 **Kent**, R. A., *A History of British Empirical Sociology*, 1981. Covers the period from the 1830s, focusing particularly on the contributions of Engels, Mayhew, Booth and the Webbs.

1.172 **Kenyon**, J., *The History Men. The Historical Profession in England since the Renaissance*, 1983, 2nd ed., 1993. Not principally concerned with the economic and social history though R. H. Tawney is discussed at some length and others in the economic history field are mentioned.

1.173 **King**, J. E., 'Marx as a historian of economic thought', *Hist. Pol.Econ.*, XI, 1979, 382–94.

1.174 **Koot**, G. M., *English Historical Economics, 1870–1926. The Rise of Economic History and Neo-Mercantilism*, 1988. A limited, idiosyncratic study of Toynbee, Ashley, Cunningham, Hewins, Rogers, Ingram, and the Webbs.

1.175 **Kuznets**, S., 'Statistics and economic history', *J.Ec.H.*, I, 1941, 26–41.

1.176 **Landes**, D. S. and Tilly, C., *History as Social Science*, Englewood Cliffs, N. J., 1971.

1.177 **Laslett**, P., 'The wrong way through the telescope', *Brit.J.Soc.*, XXVII, 1976, 319–42.

1.178 **Lee**, C. H., *The Quantitative Approach to Economic History*, 1977.

1.179 **Le Goff**, J., 'Past and Present: later history', *P.P.*, C, 1983, 14–28. *See also* Hill (1.137).

1.180 **Lennard**, R., 'Agrarian history: some vistas and pitfalls', *Ag.H.R.*, XII, 1964, 83–90.

1.181 **Lewis**, C., *Particular Places: An Introduction to English Local History*, 1989.

1.182 **Lloyd**, C., *Explanation in Social History*, 1986. Draws on the work of leading twentieth century social historians and examines questions relating to methodology and philosophy.

1.183 **Lythe**, S. G. E., 'The historian's profession', 1963. In Harte, ed. (1.124).

1.184 **McClelland**, P. D., *Causal Explanation and Model Building in History, Economics and the New Economic History*, 1975.

1.185 **McCloskey**, D. N., *Econometric History*, 1987.

1.186 **Macfarlane**, A., *Reconstructing Historical Communities*, 1977.

1.187 **McGregor**, O. R., *Social History and Law Reform*, 1981.

1.188 **McLennan**, G., *Marxism and the Methodologies of History*, 1981. A useful overview dealing with philosophy, methodology and historiography.

1.189 **Manuel**, F. E., 'The use and abuse of

psychology in history', *Daedalus*, CXVII, 1988, 119–42.

1.190 **Marczewski**, J., 'Quantitative history', *J.Contemp.H.*, III, 1968, 179–92.

1.191 **Marwick**, A., *The Nature of History*, 1970. 2nd ed. 1981.

1.192 **Mathias**, P., 'Economic history – direct and oblique'. In Ballard (1.14), 76–92.

1.193 **Mayfield**, D. and Thorne, S., 'Social history and its discontents. Gareth Stedman Jones and the politics of language', *Soc.Hist.*, XVII, 1992, 165–88.

1.194 **Meyer**, J. R., 'Economic theory, statistical inference and economic history', *J.Ec.H.*, XVII, 1957, 545–53.

1.195 **Morazé**, C., 'The application of the social sciences to history', *J.Contemp.H.*, III, 1968, 207–16.

1.196 **Murphy**, G. G. S., 'The "new" history', *Expl.Entrepren.H.*, 2nd ser., II, 1965, 132–46.

1.197 **Neale**, R. S., *Writing Marxist History. British Society, Economy and Culture since 1700*, 1985. Assesses and implements Marxist perspectives on a variety of socio-economic topics.

1.198 **Newton**, J. L. et al., eds, *Sex and Class in Women's History*, 1983. A reprint collection of essays combining theoretical approaches with detailed empirical research.

1.199 **Nield**, K. and Seed, J., 'Versions of historiography. Marxism and the methodologies of history', *Econ. & Soc.*, XII, 1983, 276–85.

1.200 **Nordahl**, R., 'Marx and the use of history in the analysis of capitalism', *Hist.Pol.Econ.*, XIV, 1982, 342–66.

1.201 **Norris**, C., 'Post-modernising history, right-wing revisionism, and the uses of history', *Southern Review* (Adelaide), XXI, 1988, 123–40.

1.202 **North**, D. C., 'The state of economic history', *American Ec.R.*, LV, 1965, Supplement, 86–91.

1.203 —— 'Economic history', *Internat. Encyc.Soc.Sci.*, VI, 1968, 468–74.

1.204 —— 'Institutional change and economic growth', *J.Ec.H.*, XXXI, 1971, 118–25.

1.205 —— 'Structure and performance: the task of economic history', *J.Ec.Lit.*, XVI, 1978, 963–78.

1.206 **Offen**, K. et al., eds, *Writing Women's History: International Perspectives*, 1991.

1.207 **Parker**, W. N., *Economic History and the Modern Economist*, 1986.

1.208 —— 'From old to new to old in economic history', *J.Ec.H.*, XXXI, 1971, 3–14.

1.209 **Payne**, P. L., 'The uses of business history', *Bus.H.*, V, 1962, 11–21.

1.210 **Perkin**, H. J., 'What is social history?', *B. John Rylands Lib.*, XXXVI, 1953, 56–74.

1.211 **Perrot**, Michelle, ed., *Writing Women's History*, 1992. A collection of essays translated from the French illustrating different aspects of the current state of French feminist historiography.

1.212 **Phythian-Adams**, C., 'Hoskins' England: a local historian of genius and the realisation of his theme', *Loc.Hist.*, XX, 1992, 170–83.

1.213 —— 'Local history and national history: the quest for the peoples of England', *Rural Hist.*, II, 1991, 1–24.

1.214 —— *Re-thinking English Local History*, 1987.

1.215 **Pollard**, S., 'Economic history. A science of Society?', *P.P.*, 30, 1965, 3–22. In Harte, ed. (1.124).

1.216 —— *The Idea of Progress. History and Society*, 1968.

1.217 **Portelli**, A., 'The Peculiarities of Oral History', *Hist. Workshop*, XII, 1981, 96–108.

1.218 **Postan**, M. M., 'The historical method in social science', 1939. In Harte, ed. (1.124).

1.219 —— *Fact and Relevance: Essays on Historical Method*, 1971.

1.220 —— 'Function and dialectic in economic history', *Ec.H.R.*, 2nd ser., XIV, 1961–2, 397–407. On Postan *see* the obituary in *Ec.H.R.*, 2nd ser., XXXV, 1982, iv–vi.

1.221 **Power**, Eileen, 'On medieval history as a social study', 1933. In Harte, ed. (1.124).

1.222 **Powicke**, F. M., 'The economic motive in politics', *Ec.H.R.*, XVI, 1946, 85–92.

1.223 —— *Modern Historians and the Study of History*, 1955. Includes a study of the Manchester School of historians.

1.224 **Price**, L. L., 'The position and prospects of the study of economic history', 1908. In Harte, ed. (1.124).

1.225 **Price**, R., 'The future of British labour history', *Internat.R.Soc.H.*, XXXVI, 1991, 249–60.

1.226 **Rabb**, T. K., 'The historian and the climatologist', *J.Interdis.H.*, X, 1980, 831–7.

1.227 —— and Rothberg, R. I., eds, *The New*

History. The 1980s and Beyond. Studies in Interdisciplinary History, 1982. A collection of reprinted articles, featuring developments in family history, quantitative history, demographic history, and anthropologically based social history.

1.228 **Redlich**, F., 'New and traditional approaches to economic history and their interdependence', *J.Ec.H.*, XXV, 1965, 480–95.

1.229 —— 'Potentialities and pitfalls in economic history', *Expl.Entrepren.H.*, 2nd ser., VI, 1969, 93–108.

1.230 **Richardson**, R. C., ed., *The Study of History. A Bibliographical Guide*, 1988. Economic and social history are well represented.

1.231 **Robbins**, M., 'The progress of transport history', *Trans.Hist.*, XII, 1992, 74–87.

1.232 **Roberts**, H., ed., *Doing Feminist Research*, 1981.

1.233 **Roskill**, M., 'History and the uses of photography', *Vict.Studs.*, XXII, 1979, 335–44.

1.234 **Rostow**, W. W., 'The interrelation of theory and economic history', *J.Ec.H.*, XVII, 1957, 509–23.

1.235 **Rowney**, D. K. and Graham, J. Q., eds., *Quantitative History: Selected Readings in the Quantitative Analysis of Historical Data*, Homewood, Ill., 1969. Includes sections on 'Social history and social change', 'Historical demography', 'Cliometrics: the new economic history'. Bibliography.

1.236 **Samuel**, R., 'British marxist historians, 1880–1980', *New Left, R.*, CXX, 1980, 21–96.

1.237 —— ed., *People's History and Socialist Theory*, 1981. A collection of *History Workshop* essays which question and explore the concept of socialist history.

1.238 **Saville**, J., *Marxism and History*, 1974. Inaugural lecture.

1.239 **Schlatter**, R., ed., *Recent Views on British History. Essays on Historical Writing since 1966*, 1984. Includes chapters on the different periods of English history, and on Scotland, Ireland and the British Empire/Commonwealth.

1.240 **Schofield**, R. S., 'Historical demography: some possibilities and some limitations', *T.R.H.S.*, 5th ser., XXI, 1971, 119–32.

1.241 **Schurer**, K., 'The future for local history: boom or recession?', *Loc.Hist.*,

XXI, 1991, 99–108.

1.242 **Sée**, H., *The Economic Interpretation of History*, trans. and intro. by M. M. Knight, N. Y., 1929.

1.243 **Seldon**, A., ed., *Contemporary History: Practice and Method*, 1988.

1.244 —— and Papworth, J., *By Word of Mouth*, 1983. Deals with the pros and cons of oral history and scrutinises, partly through case studies, its characteristic methodologies.

1.245 **Seligman**, E. R. A., *The Economic Interpretation of History*, N. Y., 1902, 2nd ed., 1922.

1.246 **Shafer**, R. J., *A Guide to Historical Method*, Homewood, Ill., 1969.

1.247 **Shorter**, E., *The Historian and the Computer: a practical guide*, Englewood Cliffs, N. J., 1971.

1.248 **Skipp**, V., 'Local History: a new definition', *Loc.Hist.*, XIV, 1981, 325–31, 392–99.

1.249 **Smith**, Bonnie, 'The contribution of women to modern historiography in Great Britain, France, and the United States, 1750–1940', *Am.H.R.*, LXXXIX, 1984, 708–33.

1.250 **Smith**, D., *The Rise of Historical Sociology*, 1991. A general survey which includes discussion of Smelser, Lipset, Talcott Parsons, Bloch and Elias.

1.251 **Smith**, P., ed., *The Historian and Film*, 1976.

1.252 **Sombart**, W., 'Economic theory and economic history', *Ec.H.R.*, II, 1929–30, 1–19.

1.253 **Speck**, W. A., 'Clio and the Computer', *University of Leeds R.*, XXIX, 1986/7, 175–89.

1.254 **Spiegel**, H. W., 'Theories of economic development: history and classification', *J.H.Ideas*, XVI, 1955, 518–39.

1.255 **Stanley**, L., 'Recovering women in history from feminist deconstruction', *Women's Stud. Internat.Forum*, XIII, 1990, 151–58.

1.256 **Stephens**, W. B., *Sources for English Local History*, 1973.

1.257 **Stern**, F., ed., *The Varieties of History from Voltaire to the Present*, Cleveland, Ohio, 1956; London, 1971. A collection of extracts from writings on the nature of history with critical notes and introduction. On economic history Unwin, Clapham and Cochran are represented.

1.258 **Stone**, L., 'Family history in the 1980s. Past achievements and future trends', *J.Interdis.H.*, XII, 1981, 51–88.

1.259 —— *The Past and the Present*, 1981. A stimulating collection of essays including a major one on 'History and the social sciences in the twentieth century'.

1.260 —— *The Past and the Present Revisited*, 1987. Includes chapters on history and the social sciences, and on historical approaches to madness, crime, childhood, sexuality, old age and death.

1.261 **Strauss**, G., 'The dilemma of popular history', *P.P.*, CXXXII, 1991, 130–49.

1.262 **Supple**, B. E., 'Economic history and economic growth', *J.Ec.H.*, XX, 1960, 548–68.

1.263 —— 'Economic history in the 1980s: old problems and new directions', *J.Inderdis.H.*, XII, 1981–2, 199–215.

1.264 **Sutch**, R., 'All things reconsidered: the life cycle perspective and the third task of economic history', *J.Ec.H.*, LI, 1991, 271–88.

1.265 **Sutcliffe**, A., 'The condition of urban history in England', *Local H.*, XI, 1975, 278–84.

1.266 **Swanson**, J. and Williamson, J., 'Explanations and issues; a prospectus for quantitative economic history', *J.Ec.H.*, XXXI, 1971, 43–57.

1.267 **Tawney**, R. H., 'The study of economic history', 1932. In Harte (1.124).

1.268 —— 'Social history and literature' in Rita Hendon, ed., *The Radical Tradition*, 1966, 191–219. On Tawney *see* Court, and: Stone, L., in *P.P.*, 21, 1962, 73–7; Ashton, T. S., in *Proc.Brit.Acad.*, XLVII, 1963, 461–82; Chambers, J. D., 'The Tawney Tradition', *Ec.H.R.*, 2nd ser., XXIV, 1971, 355–69; Winter, J. M., and Joslin, D. M., eds., *R. H. Tawney's Commonplace Book*, 1972. Deals with the years 1912–14; Ormrod, D., 'R. H. Tawney and the origins of English capitalism', *Hist.Workshop J.*, XVII, 1984, 138–60.

1.269 **Temin**, P., ed., *New Economic History*, 1973.

1.270 —— 'General equilibrium models in economic history', *J.Ec.H.*, XXI, 1971, 58–75.

1.271 —— 'The future of "new economic history"', *J.Interdis.H.*, XII, 1981–2, 179–197.

1.272 **Thane**, Pat et al., eds., *The Power of the Past. Essays for Eric Hobsbawm*, 1984. A wide-ranging collection of essays which includes studies of English landed society, late nineteenth-century banking, industrial relations, together with an historiographical appreciation of Hobsbawm's work.

1.273 **Thomas**, K., 'History and anthropology', *P.P.*, 24, 1963, 3–24.

1.274 **Thompson**, E. P., 'On history, sociology and historical relevance', *Brit. J.Soc.*, XXVII, 1976, 387–402.

1.275 —— *The Poverty of Theory*, 1978.; *See* Warde, A., 'E. P. Thompson and "poor theory"', *Brit.J.Soc.*, XXXIII, 1982, 222–36.

1.276 **Thompson**, F. M. L., 'Agricultural history', *Hist.*, XLVIII, 1963, 28–33.

1.277 —— F. M. L., 'Dyos and the urban past', *London J.*, IX, 1983, 67–70.

1.278 **Thompson**, P., *The Voice of the Past: Oral History*, 1978.

1.279 **Tonkin**, E., *Narrating our Pasts. The Social Construction of Oral History*, 1992.

1.280 **Trevor-Roper**, H. R., 'The past and the present; history and sociology', *P.P.*, XLII, 1969, 3–17.

1.281 **Tuma**, E. H., *Economic History and the Social Sciences*, 1971.

1.282 **Tunzelmann**, G. N. von, 'The new economic history: an econometric appraisal', *Expl.Entrepren.H.*, 2nd ser., V, 1968, 175–200.

1.283 **Unwin**, G., *Studies in Economic History: The Collected Papers of George Unwin*, with an introductory memoir by R. H. Tawney, 1927. Part One of the book is taken up with papers on 'The Study and teaching of economic history'. On Unwin *see also*: Daniels, G. W., *George Unwin. A Memorial Lecture*, 1926.

1.284 **Uselding**, P. J., 'Business history and the history of technology', *Bus.H.R.*, LIV, 1980, 443–52.

1.285 **Vicinus**, Martha, 'The Study of Victorian Popular Culture', *Vict.Studs.*, XVIII, 1975, 473–83.

1.286 **Webb**, S. and Beatrice, *Methods of Social Study*, 1932.

1.287 **Wickham**, C., 'Historical materialism, historical sociology', *New Left R.*, CLXXI, 1988, 63–80.

1.288 **Williams**, G., *George Ewart Evans*, 1991. A biography of one of the pioneers of oral history.

1.289 **Wilson**, A., ed., *Re-thinking Social*

History. English Society, 1570–1920 and its interpretation, 1993. A significant, theoretically oriented collection of essays which takes stock of what is considered to be the current impasse in social history. A firm commitment to a totalising history of society is evinced.

1.290 **Wilson**, B. R., 'Sociological methods in the study of history', *T.R.H.S.*, 5th ser., XXI, 1971, 101–18.

1.291 **Wilson**, C., 'History in special and in general'. In Wilson (4.97), 201–16.

1.292 **Winter**, J. M., 'The economic and social history of war', in Winter (1.332), 1–10.

1.293 **Wrigley**, E. A., 'The prospects for population history', *J.Interdis.H.*, XII, 1981–2, 207–20.

1.294 **Young**, J. D., 'Nationalism, marxism and Scottish history', *J.Contemp.H.*, XX, 1985, 337–56.

1.295 **Youngson**, A. J., 'Progress and the individual in economic history', 1959. In Harte, ed. (1.124).

1.296 **Zagorin**, P., 'Historiography and postmodernism: reconsiderations', *Hist. & Theory*, XXIX, 1990, 263–74.

1.297 **Zeitlin**, J., 'From labour history to the history of industrial relations', *Ec.H.R.*, 2nd ser., XL, 1987, 159–84.

1.298 **Zeldin**, T., 'Personal history and the history of emotions', *J.Soc.H.*, XV, 1982, 339–48.

GENERAL WORKS

(a) Bibliographies

1.299 **Denman**, D. R., Switzer, J. F. Q. and Sawyer, O. H. M., eds., *Bibliography of Rural Land Economy and Landownership, 1900–57. A Full List of the Works relating to the British Isles and Selected Works from the U.S. and Western Europe*, 1958.

1.300 **Elton**, G. R., *Modern Historians on British History, 1485–1945. A Critical Bibliography, 1945–69*, 1970.

1.301 —— ed., *Annual Bibliography of British and Irish History*, 1976–.

1.302 **Furber**, E. C., ed., *Changing Views on British History: Essays on Historical*

Writing Since 1939, Cambridge, Mass., 1966.

(b) Source material

1.303 **Bland**, A. E., Brown, P. A. and Tawney, R. H., eds., *English Economic History. Select Documents*, 1914. Several times reprinted. Covers the period 1000 to 1846.

1.304 **Clapp**, B. W., Fisher, H. E. S. and Jurica, A. R. J., eds., *Documents in English Economic History. I: 1000–1760*; II: *England since 1760*, 1976.

1.305 **Flinn**, M. W., ed., *readings in Economic History*, 1964.

(c) General surveys

1.306 **Buckatzch**, E. J., 'The geographical distribution of wealth in England, 1086–1843', *Ec.H.R.*, 2nd ser., III, 1951, 180–202.

1.307 **Burstall**, A. F., *History of Mechanical Engineering*, 1963. A survey from prehistoric to modern times.

1.308 **Clapham**, J. H., *Concise Economic History of Britain from the Earliest Times to 1750*, 1949.

1.309 **Darby**, H. C., ed., *Historical Geography of England Before A.D. 1800*, 1936, new ed., 1973.

1.310 **Dodgshon**, R. A. and Butlin, R. A., eds., *An Historical Geography of England and Wales*, 1978. Extends from prehistoric times to 1900, partly chronological partly thematic in coverage.

1.311 **Flinn**, M. W., *An Economic and Social History of Britain, 1066–1939*, 1961.

1.312 **Harding**, A., *A Social History of English Law*, 1966.

1.313 **Hechter**, M., *Internal Colonialism. The Celtic Fringe in British National Development, 1536–1966*, 1975.

1.314 **Hoskins**, W. G., *The Making of the English Landscape*, 1955, 3rd ed., 1984.

1.315 **Jenkins**, R., *Links in the History of Engineering and Technology from Tudor Times*, 1936. A useful collection of miscellaneous papers.

1.316 **King**, P., *The Development of the English Economy to 1750*, 1971. A useful textbook with extended bibliography.

1.317 **Laslett**, P., ed., *Household and Family*

Past Time, 1972.

1.318 **Murphy**, B., *A History of the British Economy, 1066–1970*, 1973.

1.319 **Musson**, A. E., *The Growth of British Industry*, 1978. Surveys the period 1500–1939.

1.320 **Pollard**, S., and Crossley, D. W., *The Wealth of Britain 1085–1966*, 1968. A valuable, one-volume survey of English economic history. Good bibliography.

1.321 **Rostow**, W. W., *The Stages of Economic Growth*, 1960, 2nd ed. 1971.

1.322 **Wallerstein**, I., *The Modern World System. I: Capitalist Agriculture and the Origins of the European World Economy in the Sixteenth Century*, N. Y., 1974.

1.323 —— *The Modern World System. II: Mercantilism and the Consolidation of the European World Economy, 1600–1750*, 1980.

1.324 —— *The Capitalist World Economy*, 1979. Elaborates some of the implications of his 'World System' perspective.

1.325 **Zupco**, R. E., *A Dictionary of English Weights and Measures from Anglo-Saxon Times to the Nineteenth Century*, Madison, Milwaukee, 1968.

(d) Collections of essays

1.326 **Carus-Wilson**, Eleanora M., ed., *Essays in Economic History*, 3 vols., 1954–62. A reprint collection of important articles. Indispensable.

1.327 **Flinn**, M. W. and Smout, T. C., eds., *Essays in Social History*, 1974.

1.328 **Floud**, R., ed., *Essays in Quantitative Economic History*, 1974. An extensive collection of articles which range from the fourteenth to the twentieth century.

1.329 **McGrath** , P. and Cannon, J. eds., *Essays in Bristol and Gloucestershire History*, 1976. Includes chapters on Bristol under the Normans, economic projects in the Vale of Tewkesbury in the early seventeenth century, the Gloucestershire spas, and the economic development of Bristol in the nineteenth century.

1.330 **Minchinton**, W. E., ed., *Essays in Agrarian History*, 2 vols., 1968. Covers both the medieval and modern periods.

1.331 **Winter**, J. M., ed., *History and Society. Essays by R. H. Tawney*, 1978. Includes a long introduction, four of Tawney's most important essays, and six shorter reviews and revaluations.

1.332 —— *War and Economic Development. Essays in Memory of David Joslin*, 1975.

2

ENGLAND 1066–1300

GENERAL WORKS

(a) Bibliographies

2.1 **Altschul**, M., ed., *Bibliographical Handbooks: Anglo-Norman England 1066–1154,* 1969. A useful compilation covering all aspects of the period.

2.2 **Bonser**, W., ed., *An Anglo-Saxon and Celtic Bibliography, 450–1087,* 1957.

2.3 **Graves**, E. B., ed., *A Bibliography of English History to 1485,* 1975. A revised and expanded version of Gross, C., *The Sources and Literature of English History,* 1900, 2nd ed., 1915.

2.4 **Hall**, H., ed., *Select Bibliography for the Study, Sources and Literature of English Medieval Economic History,* 1914.

(b) Sources

2.5 **Bagley**, J. J., *Historical Interpretation: Sources of English Medieval History, 1066–1540,* 1965.

2.6 **Douglas**, D. C. and Greenaway, G. W., eds., *English Historical Documents, 1042–1189,* 1955.

2.7 **Hennings**, Margaret, A., ed., *England under Henry III, 1216–72,* 1924. Section Four, 249–69, is on social and economic aspects of the period.

2.8 **Rothwell**, H., ed., *English Historical Documents. III: 1189–1327,* 1975. Economic history is not well represented in this selection.

2.9 **Stenton**, F. M., ed., *Documents Illustrative of the Social and Economic History of the Danelaw,* 1920.

(c) General works on the Medieval English economy and on post-conquest society

2.10 **Baker**, T., *The Normans,* 1966.

2.11 **Barlow**, F., *The Feudal Kingdom of England, 1042–1216,* 1955, 2nd ed., 1962.

2.12 —— *The Norman Conquest and Beyond,* 1983.

2.13 —— *William I and the Norman Conquest,* 1965.

2.14 **Barraclough**, G., ed., *Social Life in Early England,* 1960. A varied collection of essays originally issued as Hist.Ass. pamphlets.

2.15 **Barrow**, G. W. S., *Feudal Britain: The Completion of the Medieval Kingdoms, 1066–1314,* 1956. More attention than usual is given to Wales, Scotland and Ireland.

2.16 **Bloch**, M., *Feudal Society,* 2 vols., Paris, 1939–40, English trans., 1960. For background.

2.17 **Brooke**, C. N. L., *From Alfred to Henry III, 871–1272,* 1961.

2.18 **Brown**, R. A., *The Norman Conquest,* 1969.

2.19 —— *The Origins of English Feudalism,* 1973.

2.20 **Cantor**, L., ed., *The English Medieval*

12

Landscape, 1982.

2.21 **Chevalier**, C. T., ed., *The Norman Conquest*, 1966. Includes essays by Whitelock and Barlow.

2.22 **Chibnall**, Marjorie, *Anglo-Norman England, 1066–1166*, 1986.

2.23 **Coss**, P. R., *Lordship, Knighthood, and Locality. A Study in English Society, c.1180–c.1280*, 1991.

2.24 **Cronne**, H. A., *The Reign of Stephen, 1135–54*, 1970

2.25 **Darlington**, R. R., *The Norman Conquest*, 1963. (Creighton Lecture in History for 1962.) A very useful summary.

2.26 **Denholm-Young**, N., 'Feudal society in the thirteenth century', *Hist.*, XXIX, 1944, 107–19.

2.27 **Dickinson**, J. C., *The Great Charter*, Hist.Ass. pamphlet, 1955. A readiy accessible text of Magna Carta with notes on its background and significance.

2.28 **Douglas**, D. C., *William the Conqueror: The Norman Impact upon England*, 1964.

2.29 —— 'The Norman Conquest and English Feudalism', *Ec.H.R.*, IX, 1938–9, 128–43.

2.30 **Ganshof**, F., *Feudalism*, English trans., 1952, 3rd ed., N. Y. and London, 1964. For background.

2.31 **Hollings**, M., 'The survival of the Five Hide unit in the west Midlands', *E.H.R.*, LXIII, 1948, 435–87.

2.32 **Hollister**, C. W., *The Making of England, 55 B.C. to 1399*, Boston, Mass., 1966.

2.33 —— *The Military Organisation of Norman England*, 1965.

2.34 —— 'The irony of English Feudalism', *J.Brit.Studs.*, II, 1963, 1–26.

2.35 —— 'The Norman Conquest and the genesis of English Feudalism', *A.H.R.*, LXVI, 1961, 641–63.

2.36 —— 'The significance of scutage rates in eleventh and twelfth-century England', *E.H.R.*, LXXV, 1960, 577–88.

2.37 —— '1066: the "Feudal Revolution"', *A.H.R.*, LXX, 1968, 708–23.

2.38 —— 'The Five Hide unit and military obligation', *Speculum*, XXXVI, 1961, 61–74.

2.39 —— 'The knights of Peterborough and the Anglo-Norman fyrd', *E.H.R.*, LXXVII, 1962, 417–36.

2.40 —— and Holt, J. C., 'Two comments on the problem of continuity in Anglo-Norman feudalism', *Ec.H.R.*, 2nd ser., XVI, 1963, 104–18.

2.41 **Holt**, J. C., *Magna Carta*, 1965. A major work on the subject.

2.42 —— 'The barons and the Great Charter', *E.H.R.*, LXIX, 1955, 1–24.

2.43 —— 'Feudalism re-visited', *Ec.H.R.*, 2nd ser., XIV, 1961, 333–40.

2.44 —— 'Politics and property in early medieval England', *P.P.*, LVII, 1972, 3–52.

2.45 **John**, E., 'English feudalism and the structure of Anglo-Saxon society', *B. John Rylands Lib.*, XLVI, 1963, 14–41. For background.

2.46 **Jones**, R. J., 'Economic organisation and policies in the Middle Ages', *Ec.H.R.*, 2nd ser., XVII, 1965, 570–78. A review article on Postan, Rich and Miller (2.66).

2.47 **Kapelle**, W. E., *The Norman Conquest of the North. The Region and its Transformation, 1100–1135*, 1979.

2.48 **King**, E., *England, 1175–1425*, 1979. Includes chapters on population and settlement, lordship and wealth, trade and industry.

2.49 **Lopez**, R. S., 'Agenda for medieval studies', *J.Ec.H.*, XXXI, 1971, 165–71.

2.50 **Loyn**, H. R., *Anglo-Saxon England and the Norman Conquest*, 1962. A valuable economic and social history. Good bibliography.

2.51 —— *The Norman Conquest*, 1965.

2.52 **McKechnie**, W. S., *Magna Carta: A commentary*, 1905, 2nd ed., 1914. Still a standard authority.

2.53 **Maitland**, F. W., *Domesday Book and Beyond*, 1897. A classic, but one which is preferably read in the light of a modern introduction. Two recent paperback editions of Maitland's book are available: (1) with an introduction by E. Miller, 1960; (2) with an introduction by B. D. Lyon, N. Y., 1966.

2.54 **Matthew**, D. J. A., *The Norman Conquest*, 1966.

2.55 **Miller**, E. and Hatcher, J., *Medieval England. Rural Society and Economic Change, 1086–1348*, 1978.

2.56 **Milsom**, S. F. C., *The Legal Framework of English Feudalism*, 1976.

2.57 **Painter**, S., *Studies in the History of the English Feudal Barony*, Baltimore, 1943.

2.58 **Platt**, C., *Medieval England. A Social History and Archaeology from the Conquest to A.D. 1600*, 1978. Includes chapters on the Anglo-Norman settlement, economic growth, the Black Death, conspicuous consumption, and reorientation under the Tudors.

2.59 **Poole**, A. L., *From Domesday Book to Magna Carta, 1087–1216*, 1951, 2nd ed., 1955. Good bibliography.

2.60 —— *Obligations of Society in the Twelfth and Thirteenth Centuries*, 1946.

2.61 —— ed., *Medieval England*, 2 vols., 1958.

2.62 **Postan**, M. M., ed., *Cambridge Economic History of Europe (1) The Agrarian Life of the Middle Ages*, 2nd ed., 1966.

2.63 —— *The Medieval Economy and Society. An Economic History of Britain, 1100–1500*, 1972.

2.64 —— 'The rise of a money economy', *Ec.H.R.*, XIV, 1944, 123–34. Reprinted in Carus-Wilson, ed. (1.326), II, 1–12.

2.65 —— and Rich, E. E., eds., *Cambridge Economic History of Europe II: Trade and Industry in the Middle Ages*, 1952.

2.66 —— Rich, E. E., and Miller, E., eds., *Cambridge Economic History of Europe III: Economic Organization and Policies in the Middle Ages*, 1963.

2.67 **Pounds**, N. J. G., *An Economic History of Medieval Europe*, 1974. For background.

2.68 **Powicke**, F. M., *The Thirteenth Century, 1216–1307*, 1953. A useful survey, though hardly a readable one. Good bibliography.

2.69 **Powicke**, M., *Military Obligation in England: A Study in Liberty and Duty*, 1962.

2.70 **Roehl**, R., *Patterns and Structure of Demand, 1000–1500*, 1970. (Fontana Economic History of Europe, vol. I, section 3.) For background.

2.71 **Rowley**, T., *The Norman Heritage*, 1983.

2.72 **Saunders**, I. J., *Feudal Military Service in England: A study of the Constitutional and Military Powers of the Barones in Medieval England*, 1956.

2.73 **Sawyer**, P. H., 'The wealth of England in the eleventh century', *T.R.H.S.*, 5th ser., XV, 1965, 145–64. Argues that England was wealthier than often supposed and that the chief source of this wealth was wool.

2.74 **Sayles**, G. O., *The Medieval Foundations of England*, 1948, 2nd ed., 1950. A well-known textbook.

2.75 **Skelton**, R. A. and Harvey, P. D. A., *Local Maps and Plans from Medieval England*, 1987.

2.76 **Southern**, R. W., *The Making of the Middle Ages*, 1953.

2.77 **Stafford**, Pauline, *Unification and Conquest. England in the Tenth and Eleventh Centuries*, 1989.

2.78 **Stanley**, M., 'The geographical distribution of wealth in medieval England', *J.H.Geog.*, VI, 1980, 315–24.

2.79 **Stenton**, Doris M., *English Society in the Early Middle Ages, 1066–1307*, 1951, 4th ed., 1965.

2.80 —— ed., *Preparatory to Anglo-Saxon England: The Collected Papers of F. M. Stenton*, 1970. A useful collection which includes Stenton's essays on 'Norman London', on 'The development of the castle in England and Wales', and on 'The road system of medieval England'.

2.81 **Stenton**, F. M., *Anglo-Saxon England, c.550–1087*, 1943, 3rd ed., 1971. Good bibliography.

2.82 —— *The First Century of English Feudalism, 1066–1166*, 1932, 2nd ed., 1961.

2.83 **Tomkieff**, O. G., *Life in Norman England*, 1966.

2.84 **Vinogradoff**, P., *English Society in the Eleventh Century*, 1908. Reprinted 1968. *See also* Bean (3.8), and Clapham (1.308), and Pollard and Crossley (1.320).

(d) Monographs and regional studies

2.85 **Alschul**, M., *A Baronial Family in Medieval England: The Clares, 1217–1314*, Baltimore, 1965.

2.86 **Barker**, Juliet R., *The Tournament in England, 1000–1400*, 1986. Examines tournaments as costly, chivalric court spectacles.

2.87 **Darby**, H. C., *The Medieval Fenland*, 1940.

2.87a —— *Medieval Cambridgeshire*, 1977.

2.88 **Gelling**, Margaret, *The West Midlands in the Early Middle Ages*, 1992.

2.89 **Hoskins**, W. G., 'The wealth of medieval Devon'. In Hoskins and Finberg (4.118), 212–49.

2.90 **Kermode**, J. I., *Medieval Cheshire*, T.H.S.L.C., CXXVIII, 1979. Includes chapters on manorial demesnes, social mobility, and on relations between the Earl of Chester and the gentry.

2.91 **Palmer**, R. C., *The County Courts of Medieval England, 1150–1350*, 1982.

2.92 **Wightman**, W. E., *The Lacy Family in England and Normandy, 1066–1194*, 1966.

2.93 **Witney**, K. P., *The Jutish Forest. A Study of the Weald of Kent from 450 to 1380*, 1976.

DOMESDAY STUDIES

Although many of the entries in this section could quite logically have been placed in other parts of the bibliography – under *Agriculture*, for example – it has been thought most useful to collect most of them under this heading.

The text of the Domesday Book was printed by the Record Commission as follows:

2.94 **Ellis**, H., ed., *Libri Censualis vocati Domesday Book Additamenta*, 1816. This contains the texts of the Exon Domesday, the Inquisitio Eliensis and the Winchester and Boldon Book surveys.

2.95 —— *Libri Censualis vocatus Domesday Book Indices*, 3 vols., 1816–33.

2.96 **Farley**, A., ed., *Liber Censualis vocatus Domesday Book*, 2 vols., 1783.

2.97 **Ballard**, A., *The Domesday Borough*, 1904.

2.98 **Bishop**, T. A. M., 'The Norman settlement of Yorkshire', in R. W. Hunt, W. A. Pantin, and R. W. Southern, eds., *Studies in Medieval History Presented to F. M. Powicke*, 1948, 1–14. Reprinted in Carus-Wilson, ed. (1.326), II, 1–11.

2.99 **Bridbury**, A. R., 'Domesday Book: a re-interpretation', *E.H.R.*, CV, 1990, 284–309.

2.100 **Brooks**, F. W., *Domesday Book and the East Riding*, East Yorks.Loc.H.Soc., 1966.

2.101 **Darby**, H. C., ed., *The Domesday Geography of Eastern England*, 1952, 2nd ed., 1957. The first instalment of a massive historical enterprise.

2.102 —— *Domesday England*, 1977.

2.103 —— and Terrett, I. B., eds., *The Domesday Geography of Midland England*, 1954, 2nd ed., 1971.

2.104 —— and Campbell, E. M., eds., *The Domesday Geography of South-East England*, 1962.

2.105 —— and Maxwell, I. S., eds., *The Domesday Geography of Northern England*, 1962.

2.106 —— and Finn, R. W., eds., *The Domesday Geography of South-West England*, 1967.

2.107 —— 'Domesday woodland', *Ec.H.R.*, 2nd ser., III, 1950–1, 21–43.

2.108 —— and Versey, G. R., *Domesday Gazetteer*, 1975.

2.109 **Dodwell**, Barbara, 'The making of the Domesday Survey in Norfolk: The Hundred and a Half of Clacklose', *E.H.R.*, LXXXIV, 1969, 79–84.

2.110 **Ellis**, H., *A General Introduction to Domesday Book*, 1833. Reprinted 1972.

2.111 **Finn**, R. W., *The Domesday Inquest and the Making of Domesday Book*, 1961. *See also* Galbraith (2.124).

2.112 —— *Domesday Studies: The Liber Exoniensis*, 1964.

2.113 —— *Domesday Studies: The Eastern Countries*, 1967.

2.114 —— *Domesday Studies: The Norman Conquest and its Effect on the Economy, 1066–86*, 1971.

2.115 —— 'The immediate sources of the Exchequer Domesday', *B. John Rylands Lib.*, XL, 1958, 47–78.

2.116 —— 'The making of the Dorset Domesday', *Proc.Dorset Nat.H. & Arch.Soc.*, LXXXI, 1960, 50–7.

2.117 —— 'The Exeter Domesday and its construction', *B. John Rylands Lib.*, XLI, 1959, 360–87.

2.118 —— 'The making of the Wiltshire Domesday', *Wilts. Arch. & Nat.H. Mag.*, LII, 1948, 318–27.

2.119 —— 'Some reflections on the Cambridgeshire Domesday', *Proc. Cambridge Antiq.Soc.*, LIII, for 1959, 29–38.

2.120 —— 'The teamland of the Domesday Inquest', *E.H.R.*, LXXXIII, 1968, 95–101. A reply to Moore (2.133).

2.121 **Foster**, C. W. and Longay, T., eds., *The Lincolnshire Domesday and the Lindsey Survey* (Linc.Rec.Soc., XIX), 1924.

2.122 **Fowler**, G. H., *Bedfordshire in 1086*, 1922.

2.123 **Fraser**, H. M., eds., *The Staffordshire Domesday*, 1936.

2.124 **Galbraith**, V. H., *The Making of Domesday Book*, 1961.

2.125 **Harvey**, Sally, 'Royal revenue and Domesday terminology', *Ec.H.R.*, 2nd ser., XX, 1967, 221–8.

2.126 —— 'Domesday Book and Anglo-

Norman governance', *T.R.H.S.*, 5th ser., XXV, 1975, 175–93.

2.127 **Hoskins**, W. G., 'The highland zone in Domesday Book'. In Hoskins (4.116), 15–52.

2.128 **Hoyt**, R. S., 'Farm of the manor and community of the vill in Domesday Book', *Speculum*, XXX, 1955, 147–69.

2.129 **Kapelle**, W. E., 'Domesday Book: F. W. Maitland and his successors'. *Speculum*, LXIV, 1989, 62–40.

2.130 **Lennard**, R. V., *Rural England, 1086–1135*, 1959.

2.131 **MacDonald**, J. and Snooks, G. D., 'The suitability of Domesday Book for cliometric analysis', *Ec.H.R.*, 2nd ser., XL, 1987, 252–61.

2.132 —— *Domesday Economy. A New Approach to Anglo Norman History*, 1987. An analysis – heavily statistical – based on the Domesday returns for Essex and Wiltshire.

2.133 **Moore**, J. S., 'The Domesday teamland: a reconsideration', *T.R.H.S.*, 5th ser., XIV, 1964, 109–30. *See* Finn (2.120).

2.134 **Postan**, M. M., 'The Maps of Domesday', *Ec.H.R.*, 2nd ser., VII, 1954, 98–100.

2.135 **Roffe**, D., 'Domesday Book and northern society: a re-assessment', *E.H.R.*, CV, 1990, 310–36.

2.136 **Sawyer**, P., ed., *Domesday Book. A Re-assessment*, 1985. Includes studies of the Domesday 'ploughlands' and the secular ministers.

2.137 —— 'The "original returns" and Domesday Book', *E.H.R.*, LXX, 1955, 177–97.

2.138 **Tait**, J., ed., *Domesday Survey of Cheshire*, Chet.Soc., n.s., LXXV, 1916.

POPULATION

(a) General works

2.139 **Arnold**, C. J. and Wardle, P., 'Early medieval settlement patterns in England', *Med.Arch.*, XXV, 1981, 145–49.

2.140 **Hallam**, H. E., 'Population density in medieval Fenland', *Ec.H.R.*, 2nd ser., XIV, 1961, 71–81.

2.141 —— 'Some thirteenth-century censuses', *Ec.H.R.*, 2nd ser., X, 1958, 340–61.

2.142 —— 'Further observations on the Spalding serf lists', *Ec.H.R.*, 2nd ser., XVI, 1963, 338–50.

2.143 **Harvey**, J. B., 'Population trends and agricultural developments from the Warwickshire hundred rolls of 1279', *Ec.H.R.*, 2nd ser., XI, 1958–9, 8–18.

2.144 **Hoskins**, W. G., 'The population of an English village, 1086–1801. A study of Wigston Magna', *Trans.Leics.Arch.Soc.*, XXXIII, 1957, 15–35. Reprinted in Hoskins (4.116), 181–208.

2.145 **Kealey**, E. J., *Medieval Medicus: A Social History of Anglo-Norman Medicine*, Baltimore, 1982. A scholarly study which approaches its subject by way of art, archaeology, biography, ecclesiology and economics.

2.146 **Roberts**, B. K., *Rural Settlement in Britain*, 1979.

2.147 —— 'A study of medieval colonisation in the Forest of Arden, Warwickshire', *Ag.H.R.*, XVI, 1968, 101–13.

2.148 **Russell**, J. C., *British Medieval Population*, Albuquerque, New Mexico, 1949 The main work on the subject, though its conclusions do not command general assent.

2.149 —— 'The clerical population of medieval England', *Traditio*, II, 1944, 177–212.

2.150 —— 'Recent advances in medieval demography', *Speculum*, XL, 1965, 84–101.

2.151 —— 'The pre-Plague population of England', *J.Brit.Studs.*, V, 1966, 1–21.

2.152 —— 'A quantitative approach to medieval population change', *J.Ec.H.*, XXIV, 1964, 1–21.

2.153 —— *Population in Europe, 500–1500*, (Fontana Economic History of Europe, vol. I, section I), 1969. Useful for the general background.

2.154 —— 'Demographic limitations of the Spalding serf lists', *Ec.H.R.*, 2nd ser., XV, 1962, 138–44. A comment on Hallam (2.140).

2.155 **Titow**, J. Z., 'Some evidence of the thirteenth-century population increase', *Ec.H.R.*, 2nd ser., XIV, 1961, 218–33. *See also* Hollingsworth (4.170) and Wrigley (4.187).

(b) The family

2.156 **Helmholz**, R. H., *Marriage Litigation in Medieval England*, 1975.
2.157 **Krause**, J. T., 'The medieval household, large or small?', *Ec.H.R.*, 2nd ser., IX, 1957, 420–32.
2.158 **Painter**, S., 'The family and the feudal system in twelfth-century England', *Speculum*, XXXV, 1960, 1–16. An important study of family solidarity in this period.

AGRICULTURE AND RURAL SOCIETY

2.159 **Lamond**, Elizabeth, ed., *Walter of Henley's Husbandry*, 1890. Written in the thirteenth century.
2.160 **Oschinsky**, Dorothea, ed., *Walter of Henley: and Other Treatises on Estate Management and Accounting*, 1971. On Walter of Henley, *see:*
2.161 **Denholm-Young**, N., 'Walter of Henley', *Medievalia et Humanistica*, XV, 1962, 61–8.
2.162 **McDonald**, D., *Agricultural Writers from Walter of Henley to Arthur Young, 1200–1800*, 1908.

For other source material in this field, *see* Bland, Brown and Tawney (1.303), and Titow (2.194).

(a) General

2.163 **Ashley**, W. J., *The Bread of our Forefathers: An Inquiry in Economic History*, 1928.
2.164 **Bennett**, M. K., 'British wheat yield per acre for seven centuries', *Ec.J.Ec.Hist.Supp.*, III, 1935, 12–29. Reprinted in Minchinton (1.330), I, 53–72.
2.165 **Beresford**, M. W. and Joseph, J. K. St., *Medieval England. An Aerial Survey*, 1958.
2.166 **Beveridge**, W. H., 'The yield and price of corn in the Middle Ages', *Ec.J.Ec.H.Supp.*, I, 1927, 155–67.

Reprinted in Carus-Wilson, (1.326), I, 13–25.
2.167 **Cronne**, H. A., 'The Royal Forest in the reign of Henry I', in Cronne, Moody and Quinn (4.788), 1–23.
2.168 **Dewindt**, A. R., 'Re-defining the peasant community in medieval England: regional perspectives', *J.Brit.Studs.*, XXVI, 1987, 163–207.
2.169 **Duby**, G., *Rural Economy and Country Life in the Medieval West*, English trans., 1968.
2.170 —— *Medieval Agriculture, 900–1500* (Fontana Economic History of Europe, Vol. I, section 5), 1969. For background.
2.171 **Ernle**, Lord (R. E. Prothero), *English Farming Past and Present*, 1912, 6th ed., 1961, with valuable new introductions by G. E. Fussell and O. R. McGregor. A pioneer work of considerable historiographical interest.
2.172 **Fussell**, G. E., *Farming Technique from Prehistoric to Modern Times*, 1966.
2.173 **Hallam**, H. E., *Rural England, 1066–1272*, 1981.
2.174 —— *The Agrarian History of England and Wales. II: 1042–1348*, 1988. Organised geographically and thematically with substantial sections on Domesday, prices and wages, agrarian life, and rural buildings.
2.175 **Homans**, G. C., *English Villagers of the Thirteenth Century*, Harvard, Mass., 1942. Reprinted 1960. An important book.
2.176 —— 'The rural sociology of medieval England', *P.P.*, IV, 1953, 32–43.
2.177 —— 'Men and the land in the Middle Ages', *Speculum*, XI, 1936, 338–51.
2.178 **Hoskins**, W. G., 'Sheep farming in Saxon and medieval England'. In Hoskins (4.116), 1–14.
2.179 **Hyams**, P. R., *King, Lords and Peasants in Medieval England. The Common Law of Villeinage in the Twelfth and Thirteenth Centuries*, 1980.
2.180 **Jones**, A., 'Land measurement in England, 1150–1350', *Ag.H.R.*, XXVII, 1979, 10–18.
2.181 **Kershaw**, I., 'The Great Famine and agrarian crisis in England, 1315–1322', *P.P.*, LIX, 1973, 3–50.
2.182 **Kosminsky**, E. A., *Studies in the Agrarian History of England in the Thirteenth Century*, 1956. The work of a Marxist historian in which the peasantry receive most attention.

2.183 **Lennard**, R. V., 'Statistics of sheep in medieval England. A question of interpretation', *Ag.H.R.*, VII, 1959, 75–81.

2.184 **Long**, W. H., 'The low yields of corn in medieval England', *Ec.H.R.*, 2nd ser., XXXII, 1979, 459–69.

2.185 **Neilson**, Nellie, 'Early English woodland and waste', *J.Ec.H.*, II, 1942, 54–62.

2.186 **Parain**, C., 'The evolution of agricultural technique'. In Postan (2.62), 126–79.

2.187 **Poole**, A. L., 'Livestock prices in the twelfth century', *E.H.R.*, LV, 1940, 284–95.

2.188 **Postan**, M. M., *Essays on Medieval Agriculture and General Problems of the Medieval Economy*, 1973.

2.189 —— 'Medieval agrarian society in its prime: England'. In Postan (2.62), 549–632.

2.190 —— 'Investment in medieval agriculture', *J.Ec.H.*, XXVII, 1967, 576–87. A pioneer article.

2.191 —— 'Village livestock in the thirteenth century', *Ec.H.R.*, 2nd ser., XV, 1962, 219–49.

2.192 **Sawyer**, P. H., ed., *Medieval Settlement. Continuity and Change*, 1977.

2.193 **Slicher van Bath**, B. M., *Yield Ratios 810–1820*, Wageningen, 1963.

2.194 **Titow**, J. Z., *English Rural Society, 1200–1350*, 1969. Half the book consists of documents.

2.195 —— *Winchester Yields. A Study in Medieval Agricultural Productivity*, 1972. Covers the period 1208–1350.

2.196 **Young**, C. R., *The Royal Forests of Medieval England*, 1979.

(b) Regional studies

2.197 **Slade**, C. F., ed., *The Leicestershire Survey, c.1130*, University of Leicester, Department of English Loc.H., Occ. Papers, 7, 1956.

2.198 **Chibnall**, A. C., *Sherington: Fiefs and Fields of a Buckinghamshire Village*, 1965. A survey from the twelfth to the eighteenth century.

2.199 **Finberg**, H. P. R., *West Country Historical Studies*, 1969.

2.200 **Gras**, N. S. B. and E. C., *The Economic and Social History of an English Village (Crawley, Hants), 909–1928*, Cambridge, Mass., 1930. Very well documented.

2.201 **Hallam**, H. E., *Settlement and Society: A Study of the Early Agrarian History of South Lincolnshire*, 1965. An interesting study which examines land and people in the period between the eleventh century and 1307.

2.202 **Harvey**, P. D. A., *A Medieval Oxfordshire Village: Cuxham, 1240–1400*, 1965.

2.203 **Hilton**, R. H., *The Social Structure of Rural Warwickshire in the Middle Ages*, Dugdale Soc.Occ. Papers, IX, 1956.

2.204 —— *A Medieval Society: the West Midlands at the End of the Thirteenth Century*, 1967.

2.205 —— 'Medieval agrarian history', *V. C. H. Leics.*, ed. W. G. Hoskins and R. A. McKinley, II, 1954, 145–98.

2.206 **Hoskins**, W. G., 'The making of the agrarian landscape'. In Hoskins and Finberg (4.118), 289–333. A general survey from medieval times to the nineteenth century.

2.207 **Lennard**, R. V., 'The destruction of woodland in the eastern counties under William the Conqueror', *Ec.H.R.*, XV, 1945, 36–43.

2.208 **Madicott**, J. R., 'Magna Carta and the local community', *P.P.*, CII, 1984, 25–65.

2.209 **Moore**, J. S., *Laughton: A Study in the Evolution of the Wealden Landscape*, University of Leicester, Department of English Loc.H.Occ. Papers, 19, 1966.

2.210 **Naughton**, K. S., *The Gentry of Bedfordshire in the Thirteenth and Fourteenth Centuries*, 1976.

2.211 **Postles**, D., 'Markets for rural produce in Oxfordshire, 1086–1350', *Midland H.*, XII, 1987, 14–26.

2.212 **Raftis**, J. A., *Assart Data and Land Values. Two Studies in the East Midlands, 1200–1350*, Toronto, 1974.

2.213 **Ravensdale**, J., *Liable to Floods. Village Landscape on the Edge of the Fens, 450–1850*, 1974.

2.214 **Scott**, Richenda, 'Medieval Agriculture', In *V. C. H. Wilts.*, ed. R. B. Pugh, IV, 1959, 7–42.

2.215 **Siddle**, D. J., 'The rural economy of medieval Holderness', *Ag.H.R.*, XV, 1967, 40–5.

2.216 **Summerson**, H., 'Crime and society in thirteenth-century Devon', *Rep. and Trans. Devon Ass.*, CXIX, 1987, 67–84.

2.217 **Sylvester**, Dorothy, *The Rural Landscape*

of the Welsh Borderland: A Study in
Historical Geography, 1969.

2.218 **Thomas**, C., 'Thirteenth-century farm
economies in North Wales', *Ag.H.R.*,
XVI, 1968, 1–14.

2.219 **Vollans**, E. C., 'The evolution of farm
lands in the central Chilterns in the
twelfth and thirteenth centuries',
T.I.B.G., XXVI, 1959, 197–241.

2.220 **Whitney**, K. P., 'The woodland economy
of Kent, 1066–1348', *Ag.H.R.*, XXXVIII,
1990, 20–39.

(c) The Manor

2.221 **Page**, F. M., ed., *Wellingborough Manorial
Accounts, A.D. 1258–1323*, Northants.
Rec.Soc., 1936.

2.222 **Redwood**, B. C. and Wilson, A. E., eds.,
*Custumals of the Sussex Manors of the
Archbishops of Canterbury*, Sussex
Rec.Soc., LVII, 1957.

2.223 **Wilson**, A. E., ed., *Custumals of the
Manors of Laughton, Willingdon and
Goring*, Sussex Rec.Soc., LX, 1961.

2.224 **Aston**, T. H., 'The origins of the manor
in England', *T.R.H.S.*, 5th ser., VIII,
1958, 59–83. Reprinted in Minchinton, I,
9–35. An important article which
considers the development of the manor
in the Anglo-Saxon period and in the
years following the Norman Conquest.

2.225 **Bennett**, H. S., *Life on the English Manor*,
1937.

2.226 **Bishop**, T. A. M., 'The distribution of
manorial demesne in the Vale of
Yorkshire', *E.H.R.*, XLIX, 1934, 386–406.

2.227 **Coleman**, M. Clare, *Downham in the Isle.
A Study of an Ecclesiastical Manor in the
Thirteenth and Fourteenth Centuries*, 1984.
Exploits the uneven records of the
fenland manor controlled in the Middle
Ages by the Bishops of Ely. The leasing
out of demesne land and commutation of
labour services are among the themes
considered.

2.228 **Davenport**, F. G., *The Economic
Development of a Norfolk Manor,
1086–1565*, 1906.

2.229 **Drew**, J. S., 'Manorial accounts of St.
Swithun's Priory, Winchester', *E.H.R.*,
LXII, 1947, 20–41. Reprinted in Carus-
Wilson, ed. (1.326), II, 12–30. Covers the
period from 1248 to 1400.

2.230 **Hilton**, R. H., 'Winchcombe Abbey and
the Manor of Sherborne'. In Finberg
(4.109), 89–113.

2.231 —— 'Kibworth Harcourt, a Merton
College manor in the thirteenth and
fourteenth centuries', In Hoskins (4.117),
17–40.

2.232 **Latham**, L. C., 'The manor and the
village'. In Barraclough (2.14), 29–50.
Originally published as an Hist.Ass.
pamphlet.

2.233 **Levett**, Ada E., *Studies in Manorial
History*, 1938. Reprinted 1962.

2.234 **Sylvester**, Dorothy, 'The manor and the
Cheshire landscape', *T.L.C.A.S.*, LXX,
for 1960, 1961, 1–15.

2.235 **Ugawa**, K., 'The economic development
of some Devon manors in the thirteenth
century', *T.Devonshire Assoc.*, XCIV,
1962, 630–83.

2.236 **Vinogradoff**, P., *The Growth of the Manor*,
1905, 2nd ed., 1911. Book 3, 291–379,
covers the feudal period. Needs to be
read in the light of Aston (2.224). *See also*
Titow (2.194).

(d) Land tenure and the land market

Many titles relevant in this connection are listed
in the section *General Works*.

2.237 **Denman**, D. R., *Origins of Ownership: A
Brief History of Land Ownership and
Tenure in England from Earliest Times to
the modern Era*, 1958.

2.238 **Harvey**, P. D. A., ed., *The Peasant Land
Market in Medieval England*, 1984. A
collection of local studies from Norfolk,
Berkshire, Bedfordshire and Durham
which explores the fluctuating size and
fortunes of peasant holdings.

2.239 **Homans**, G. C., 'Partible inheritance of
villagers' holdings', *Ec.H.R.*, VIII,
1937–8, 48–56.

2.240 **Hoyt**, R.S., *The Royal Demesne in English
Constitutional History, 1066–1272*, Ithaca,
N. Y., 1950.

2.241 **Hyams**, P. R., 'The origins of a peasant
land market in England', *Ec.H.R.*, 2nd
ser., XXIII, 1970, 18–31.

2.242 **King**, E., *Peterborough Abbey, 1086–1310.
A Study in the Land Market*. 1973.

2.243 **Roden**, D., 'Inheritance customs and
succession to land in the Chiltern hills in
the thirteenth and fourteenth centuries',

J.Brit.Studs., VII, 1967, 1–11.

(e) Estates

2.244 **Stitt**, F. B., ed., *Lenton Priory Estate Accounts, 1296–1298*, Thoroton Soc.Rec. series, XIX, 1959.

2.245 **Chibnall**, Marjorie, *The English Lands of the Abbey of Bec*, 1946.

2.246 **Dyer**, C., *Lords and Peasants in a Changing Society. The Estates of the Bishopric of Worcester, 680–1540*, 1980.

2.247 **English**, B., *The Lords of Holderness, 1086–1260*, 1980.

2.248 **Harvey**, Barbara, *Westminster Abbey and its Estates in the Middle Ages*, 1977.

2.249 **Hilton**, R. H., 'Gloucester Abbey leases of the late thirteenth century', *Birm.Hist.Jnl.*, IV, 1953–4, 1–17.

2.250 **Lennard**, R. V., 'The demesnes of Glastonbury Abbey in the eleventh and twelfth centuries', *Ec.H.R.*, 2nd ser., VIII, 1956, 355–63. A critique of Postan (2.254).

2.251 **May**, Teresa, 'The estates of the Cobham Family in the later thirteenth century', *Arch.Cant.*, LXXXIV, 1970, 211–29. Presents a profit and loss account of a large lay manor.

2.252 **Miller**, E., *The Abbey and Bishopric of Ely: The Social History of an Ecclesiastical Estate from the Tenth to the Early Fourteenth Century*, 1951. Reprinted 1969.

2.253 **Oschinsky**, Dorothea, 'Medieval treaties on estate management', *Ec.H.R.*, 2nd ser., VIII, 1955–6, 296–309. See also Oschinsky (2.160).

2.254 **Postan**, M. M., 'Glastonbury estates in the twelfth century', *Ec.H.R.*, 2nd ser., V, 1953, 358–67. *See also* Lennard (2.250).

2.255 —— 'Glastonbury estates in the twelfth century: a reply', *Ec.H.R.*, 2nd ser., IX, 1957, 106–18. A reply to Lennard (2.250).

2.256 **Raban**, S., *The Estates of Thorney and Crowland. A Study in Medieval Monastic Land Tenure*, 1977.

2.257 **Stansfield**, J., ed., 'Rent roll of Kirkstall Abbey (1459)', *Thoresby Soc., Miscellanea* I, 1891, 1–21.

2.258 **Ward**, J. C., 'The estates of the Clare family, 1066–1317', *B.I.H.R.*, XXXVII, 1964, 114–17.

(f) Rent

2.259 **Hilton**, R. H., 'Rent and capital formation in feudal society', *International Conference of Economic History*, Aix, 1962, 33–68.

2.260 **Kosminsky**, E. A., 'The evolution of feudal rent in England from the eleventh to the fifteenth centuries', *P.P.*, VII, 1955, 12–36.

(g) Field systems

2.261 **Baker**, A. R. H. and Butlin, R. A., (eds.), *Studies of Field Systems in the British Isles*, 1973. A standard work of reference on the development of British field systems from Anglo-Saxon times to the breakup of the medieval pattern.

2.261a **Bishop**, T. A. M., 'Assarting and the growth of the open fields', *Ec.H.R.*, VI, 1935, 13–29. Reprinted in Carus-Wilson, ed. (1.326), I, 26–40.

2.262 **Dodgshon**, R. A., *The Origin of British Field Systems*, 1980.

2.263 **Homans**, G. C., 'The explanation of English regional differences', *P.P.*, 42, 1969, 18–34. A critique of Thirsk (2.266) in this section.

2.264 **Pocock**, E. A., 'The first fields in an Oxfordshire village', *Ag.H.R.*, XVI, 1968, 85–100.

2.265 **Rowley**, T., ed., *The Origins of Open Field Agriculture*, 1981. Ten essays of varying value.

2.266 **Thirsk**, Joan, 'The common fields', *P.P.*, XXIX, 1964 3–25. An important article arguing that the growth of the three-field system was slower and less widespread than often assumed.

2.267 —— 'The origins of the common fields', *P.P.*, XXXIII, 1966, 142–7. A reply to Titow (2.268).

2.268 **Titow**, J. Z., 'Medieval England and the open-field system', *P.P.*, 32, 1965, 86–102. Takes issue with Thirsk (2.266).

(h) Place-name studies

No attempt is made here to provide a comprehensive list of works on this subject. The reader is referred to Altschul's bibliography (2.1), for details of the publications of the English Place Name Society. Only three items of a general nature are listed below.

2.269 **Cameron**, K., *English Place Names*, 1961.
2.270 **Ekwall**, E., *Studies on English Place Names*, Stockholm, 1936. A work by the leading authority on the subject.
2.271 **Sawyer**, P. H., 'The place names of Domesday Book', *B. John Rylands Lib.*, XXXVIII, 1956, 483–506.

INDUSTRY

(a) General

2.272 **Carus-Wilson**, Eleanora M., 'An industrial revolution of the thirteenth century', *Ec.H.R.*, XI, 1941, 39–60. Reprinted in Carus-Wilson, ed. (1.326), I, 41–60. The claims for this industrial revolution rest on evidence relating to water-powered fulling mills.
2.273 **Salzman**, L. F., *English Industries of the Middle Ages*, 1913, 2nd ed., 1923.
2.274 **White**, L., *Medieval Technology and Social Change*, 1962. Chapters 2 and 3 on 'The agrarian revolution of the early Middle Ages' and 'The medieval expansion of mechanical power' are useful.

(b) Textiles

2.275 **Carus-Wilson**, Eleanora M., 'The English cloth industry in the late twelfth and early thirteenth centuries', *Ec.H.R.*, XIV, 1944, 32–50.
2.276 —— 'The woollen industry', in Postan and Rich, eds. (2.65), 355–429.
2.277 **Gerrers**, M., 'The textile industry in late twelfth and thirteenth century Essex: a study based on occupational names in charter sources', *Essex Arch. & Hist.*, XX,

1989, 34–73.
2.278 **Miller**, E., 'The fortunes of the English textile industry during the thirteenth century'. *Ec.H.R.*, 2nd ser., XVIII, 1965, 64–82.

(c) Metals

2.279 **Schubert**, H. R., *History of the British Iron and Steel Industry from c.450 B.C. to A.D. 1775*, 1957. Particularly useful on the technical aspects.
2.280 **Waites**, B., 'Medieval iron-working in N. E. Yorkshire', *Geography*, XLIX, 1964, 33–43. See also Gough (4.481), Lewis (4.535), Raistrick and Jennings (4.538) and Straker (4.542).

(d) Building

2.281 **Colvin**, H. M., ed., *Building Accounts of King Henry III*, 1971.
2.282 —— ed., *History of the King's Works, I and II, The Middle Ages* (by R. A. Brown, H. M. Colvin and A. J. Taylor), 1963.
2.283 **Johnson**, H. T., 'Cathedral building and the medieval economy', *Expl.Entrepren.H.*, 2nd ser., IV, 1967, 191–210.
2.284 **Knoop**, D., and Jones, G. P., 'The English medieval quarry', *Ec.H.R.*, IX, 1939, 17–37. See the section on *Labour* (p. 23) for other titles by Knoop and Jones. See also Salzman (3.275).

(e) Miscellaneous

2.285 **Kilmurray**, K., *The Pottery Industry of Stamford, Lincolnshire, c.850–1250; Its Manufacture, Trade and Relationship with Continental Wares, with a Classification and Chronology*, 1980.
2.286 **McDonnell**, J., *Inland Fisheries in Medieval Yorkshire, 1066–1300*, Borthwick Papers, 60, 1981.
2.287 **Murray**, Kathleen M. E., 'Shipping'. In Poole (2.61), I, 168–95.

MONEY, PRICES AND PUBLIC FINANCE

(a) Money and Prices

2.288 **Brooke**, G. C., *English Coins from the Seventh Century to the Present Day*, 1932. Reprinted 1966.

2.289 **Craig**, J., *The Mint. A History of the London Mint from A.D. 287 to 1948*, 1953.

2.290 **Dolley**, R. H. M., *The Norman Conquest and the English Coinage*, 1966.

2.291 —— 'Coinage'. In Poole (2.61), I, 264–99.

2.292 **Farmer**, D. L., 'Some price fluctuations in Angevin England', *Ec.H.R.*, 2nd ser., IX, 1956–7, 34–43.

2.293 —— 'Some grain price movements in thirteenth-century England', *Ec.H.R.*, 2nd ser., X, 1957–8, 207–20.

2.294 **Feavearyear**, A. E., *The Pound Sterling*, 1931, 2nd ed., revised by E. V. Morgan, 1963.

2.295 **Harvey**, P. D. A., 'The English inflation 1180–1220', *P.P.*, LXI, 1973, 3–30.

2.296 **Homer**, S., *A History of Interest Rates*, New Brunswick, 1963.

2.297 **Lloyd**, T. H., *The Movement of Wool Prices in Medieval England*, 1973. Covers the period from the thirteenth to the fifteenth century.

2.298 **Oman**, C., *The Coinage of England*, 1931.

2.299 **Spufford**, P., 'Coinage and currency'. In Postan, Rich and Miller, eds. (2.66), 576–602. *See also* the book by E. H. Phelps Brown (4.1186).

(b) Public finance

2.300 **Johnson**, C., ed., *Dialogus de Scaccario: the Discourse of the Exchequer, by Richard son of Nigel*, 1950.

2.301 —— *The De Moneta of Nicholas Oresme, and English Mint Documents*, 1956.

2.302 **Brown**, R. A., 'The Treasury of the later twelfth-century'. In J. C. Davies, ed., *Studies Presented to Sir Hilary Jenkinson*, 1957, 35–49.

2.303 **Davies**, J. C., 'The memoranda rolls of the Exchequer to 1307'. In J. C. Davies, ed., *Studies Presented to Sir Hilary Jenkinson*, 1957, 97–154.

2.304 **Kaeuper**, R. W., *Bankers to the Crown. The Riccardi of Lucca and Edward I*, Princeton, N. J., 1973.

2.305 **Mitchell**, S. K., *Studies in Taxation under John and Henry III*, New Haven, Conn., 1914.

2.306 —— *Taxation in Medieval England*, ed. S. Painter, New Haven, Conn., 1951.

2.307 **Poole**, R. L., *The Exchequer in the Twelfth Century*, 1912.

2.308 **Prestwich**, J. O., 'War and finance in the Anglo-Norman state', *T.R.H.S.*, 5th ser., IV, 1954, 19–44.

2.309 **Prestwich**, M., 'Edward I's monetary policies and their consequences', *Ec.H.R.*, 2nd ser., XXII, 1969, 406–16.

2.310 **Roseveare**, H. G., *The Treasury; The Evolution of a British Institution*, 1969.

2.311 **Stacey**, R., *Politics, Policy and Finance under Henry III, 1216–45*, 1987. Looks at the various ways in which royal revenue was increased. Based chiefly on the Exchequer records.

2.312 **White**, G. H., 'Financial administration under Henry I', *T.R.H.S.*, 4th ser., VIII, 1925, 56–78.

2.313 **Whitwell**, R. J., 'Italian bankers and the English Crown', *T.R.H.S.*, n.s., XVII, 1905, 175–233. Deals with the thirteenth century.

LABOUR

2.314 **Beveridge**, W. H., 'Wages on the Winchester manors', *Ec.H.R.*, VII, 1936, 22–43. Covers the period from the early thirteenth to the mid-fifteenth century.

2.315 —— 'Westminster wages in the manorial era', *Ec.H.R.*, 2nd ser., VIII, 1955–6, 18–35.

2.316 **Dodwell**, Barbara, 'The free tenantry of the hundred rolls', *Ec.H.R.*, XIV, 1944, 163–71.

2.317 —— 'The free peasantry of East Anglia in Domesday', *Norfolk Arch*, XXVII, 1940, 145–57.

2.318 **Gray**, H. L., 'The commutation in villein services in England before the Black Death', *E.H.R.*, XXIX, 1914, 625–56.

2.319 **Hilton**, R. H., 'Peasant movements in England before 1381', *Ec.H.R.*, 2nd ser., II, 1949, 117–36. Reprinted in Carus-Wilson, ed. (1.326), II, 73–90.

2.320 —— 'Freedom and villeinage in England', *P.P.*, XXXI, 1965, 3–19. This and the previous article are valuable contributions to medieval labour history.

2.321 —— 'Lord and peasant in Staffordshire in the Middle Ages', *North Staffs. J. Field Studs.*, X, 1970, 1–20.

2.322 **Jones**, G. R. J., 'The distribution of bond settlements in N. W. Wales', *Welsh H.R.*, II, 1964, 19–36.

2.323 **Knoop**, D., and Jones, G. P., *The Medieval Mason*, 1933.

2.324 —— 'The impressment of masons in the Middle Ages', *Ec.H.R.*, VIII, 1937–8, 57–67.

2.325 **Kosminsky**, E. A., 'Services and money rents in the thirteenth century', *Ec.H.R.*, V, 1935, 24–45. Reprinted in Carus-Wilson, ed. (1.326), II, 31–48. Important.

2.326 **Lennard**, R. V., 'The economic position of the Domesday villani', *Ec.J.*, LVI, 1946, 244–64.

2.327 —— 'The economic position of the Domesday sokemen', *Ec.J.*, LVII, 1947, 179–95.

2.328 —— 'The economic position of the bordars and cottars of Domesday Book', *Ec.J.*, LXI, 1951, 342–71.

2.329 —— 'The composition of the demesne plough teams in twelfth-century England', *E.H.R.*, LXXV, 1960, 193–207.

2.330 —— 'Domesday plough teams: the south-west evidence', *E.H.R.*, LXXX, 1965, 217–33.

2.331 **Lloyd**, T. H., 'Ploughing services on the demesnes of the Bishop of Worcester in the late thirteenth century', *Birm.Hist.J.*, VIII, 1962, 189–96.

2.332 **Postan**, M. M., 'The chronology of labour services', *T.R.H.S.*, 4th ser., XX, 1937, 169–93. Reprinted in a revised form in Minchinton (1.330), I, 73–91.

2.333 —— *The Famulus: The Estate Labourer in the Twelfth and Thirteenth Centuries*, supplement to *Ec.H.R.* 1954. Demonstrates the importance of the hired labourer.

2.334 —— and Titow, J. Z., 'Heriots and prices on Winchester manors', *Ec.H.R.*, 2nd ser., XI, 1959, 392–411.

2.335 **Richardson**, H. G., 'The medieval plough team', *Hist.*, XXVI, 1942, 287–96.

2.336 **Shelby**, L. R., 'The role of the master mason in medieval English building', *Speculum*, XXXIX, 1964, 387–403.

2.337 **Stenton**, F. M., *The Free Peasantry of the Northern Danelaw*, 1969.

2.338 **Titow**, J. Z., 'Some differences between manors and their effects on the condition of the peasant in the thirteenth century', *Ag.H.R.*, X, 1962, 1–13. Reprinted in Minchinton, (1.330), I, 37–51.

TOWNS

2.339 **Gross**, C., *A Bibliography of British Municipal History*, Cambridge, Mass., 1897. Reprinted with a new introduction by G. H. Martin, 1966. The main bibliography for older histories of towns. It is brought up to date in:

2.340 **Martin**, G. H. and MacIntyre, Sylvia, *A Bibliography of British and Irish Municipal History I: General Works*, 1971.

(a) Sources

2.341 **Ballard**, A., ed., *British Borough Charters, 1042–1216*, 1913.

2.342 —— and Tait, J., eds., *British Borough Charters, 1216–1307*, 1923.

2.343 **Bateson**, Mary, ed., *Records of the Borough of Leicester, 1103–1327*, 1899.

2.343a —— *Borough Customs*, Selden Soc., XVIII and XXI, 2 vols., 1904–6.

2.344 **Biddle**, M., ed., *Winchester in the Early Middle Ages. An Edition and Discussion of the Winton Domesday*, 1976.

2.345 **Coss**, P. R. and Jones, T., eds., *The Early Records of Medieval Coventry, with the Hundred Rolls of 1280*, 1986.

2.346 **Le Patourel**, J., *Documents Relating to the Manor and Borough of Leeds, 1066–1400*, Thoresby Soc., 1956.

2.347 **Martin**, G. H., *The Early Court Rolls of the Borough of Ipswich*, University of Leicester, Department of English Loc.H., Occ. Papers, 5, 1954.

2.348 **Palmer**, W. M., ed., *Cambridge Borough Documents*, 1931.

(b) Surveys and monographs

2.349 **Beresford**, M. W., *New Towns of the Middle Ages: Town Plantation in England, Wales and Gascony*, 1967. An important study of a significant aspect of urban history in the medieval period.

2.350 **Billson**, C. J. *Medieval Leicester*, 1920.

2.351 **Brooke**, C. N. L., *London, 800–1216. The Shaping of a City*, 1975.

2.352 **Carus-Wilson**, Eleanora, 'Towns and Trade'. In Poole (2.61), I, 209–63.

2.353 —— 'The first half century of the borough of Stratford upon Avon', *Ec.H.R.*, 2nd ser., XVIII, 1965, 46–63.

2.354 **Corfield**, Penelope, and Keene, D., eds., *Work in Towns, 850–1850*, 1990. A wide-ranging collection of essays which includes chapters on individual towns as well as more general studies of interactions between town and countryside, patterns of women's work, and on mobility.

2.355 **Davis**, R. H. C., *The Early History of Coventry*, Dugdale Soc.Occ. Papers, XXIV, 1976.

2.356 **Finberg**, H. P. R., 'The genesis of the Gloucestershire towns'. In Finberg (4.109), 52–88.

2.357 **Fox**, L., 'The early history of Coventry', *Hist.*, XXX, 1945, 21–37.

2.358 **Hibbert**, A., 'The economic policies of towns'. In Postan, Rich and Miller (2.66), 157–229.

2.359 **Hill**, J. W. F., *Medieval Lincoln*, 1948.

2.360 **Hollaender**, A. E. J. and Kellaway, W., eds., *Studies in London History Presented to Philip Edmund Jones*, 1969. A festschrift which includes essays on London history from medieval to modern times.

2.361 **Hoskins**, W. G., 'The origin and rise of Market Harborough', *Trans.Leics.Arch.Soc.*, XXV, 1949, 56–68. Reprinted in Hoskins (4.116), 53–67.

2.362 **Lobel**, Mary D., *The Borough of Bury St. Edmunds: A Study in the Government and Development of a Monastic Town*, 1935.

2.363 **Martin**, G. H., 'The English borough in the thirteenth century', *T.R.H.S.*, 5th ser., XIII, 1963, 123–44.

2.364 **Miller**, E., 'Medieval York. The twelfth and thirteenth centuries'. In *V.C.H. Yorks.*, ed. P. M. Tillot. *The City of York*, 1961, 25–116.

2.365 **Murray**, Katherine M. E., *The Constitutional History of the Cinque Ports*, 1935.

2.366 **Platt**, C., *The English Medieval Town*, 1975. Particularly valuable on the topography of medieval towns.

2.367 **Redford**, A., 'The emergence of Manchester', *Hist.*, XXIV, 1939, 32–49.

2.368 **Reynolds**, Susan, 'The rulers of London in the twelfth century', *Hist.*, LVII, 1972, 337–57.

2.369 —— *An Introduction to the History of English Medieval Towns*, 1977. Surveys the period from the fifth to the early sixteenth centuries.

2.370 **Salter**, H. E., *Medieval Oxford*, 1936.

2.371 **Simmons**, J., *Leicester Past and Present I: The Ancient Borough*, 1974.

2.372 **Stenton**, F. M., 'Norman London'. In Barraclough, ed. (2.14), 179–207. Originally issued as an Hist.Ass. pamphlet.

2.373 **Stephenson**, C., *Borough and Town: A Study of Urban Origins in England*, Cambridge, Mass., 1933. Contended that the process of urbanisation was only fully developed in England after 1066.

2.374 **Tait**, J., *The Medieval English Borough*, 1936. Refuted Stephenson's claims. Tait demonstrated the importance of towns in the Anglo-Saxon period.

2.375 —— *Medieval Manchester and the Beginnings of Lancashire*, 1904.

2.376 **Urry**, W., *Canterbury under the Angevin Kings*, 1967. A significant contribution to urban studies.

2.377 **Werveke**, H. van, 'The Rise of the Towns'. In Postan, Rich and Miller (2.66), 3–41.

2.378 **Williams**, G. A., *Medieval London from Commune to Capital*, 1963. A well-documented study of the constitutional and social history of London between c.1200 and 1337.

2.379 **Young**, C. R., *The English Borough and Royal Administration 1130–1307*, Durham, N. C., 1961.

COMMERCE

2.380 **Baker**, J. N. L., 'Medieval trade-routes'. In Barraclough, ed. (2.14), 224–46.

2.381 **Brutzkus**, J., 'Trade with eastern Europe, 800–1200', *Ec.H.R.*, XIII, 1943, 31–41. For background.

2.382 **Carus-Wilson**, Eleanora M., 'The English cloth trade in the late twelfth and early, thirteenth centuries, *Ec.H.R.*, XIV, 1944, 32–50.

2.383 **Davies**, J. C., 'Shipping and trade in Newcastle upon Tyne, 1294–1296', *Arch.Aeliana*, 4th ser., XXXI, 1953, 175–204.

2.384 **Postan**, M. M., 'The trade of medieval Europe: the north'. In Postan and Rich, eds. (2.65), 119–256.

2.385 **Salzman**, L. F., *English Trade in the Middle Ages*, 1931. *See also* Carus-Wilson and Coleman (3.301), Kerling (3.320) and Postan (3.332).

2.386 **Titow**, J. Z., 'The decline of the fair of St Giles, Winchester, in the thirteenth and fourteenth centuries', *Nottingham Med.Studs.*, XXXI, 1987, 58–75.

GOVERNMENT

2.387 **Cam**, Helen M., *Liberties and Communities in Medieval England*, 1944, 2nd ed., corrected, 1963.

2.388 —— *The Hundred and the Hundred Rolls*, 1930.

2.389 **Chrimes**, S. B., *Introduction to the Administrative History of Medieval England*, 1952, 3rd ed., 1966.

2.390 **Hoyt**, R. S., 'Royal taxation and the growth of the realm in medieval England', *Speculum*, XXV, 1950, 36–48.

2.391 **Miller**, E., 'The economic policies of governments: France and England'. In Postan, Rich and Miller (2.66), 290–339.

2.392 —— 'The state and landed interests in thirteenth century France and England', *T.R.H.S.*, 5th ser., II, 1952, 109–29.

2.393 **Morris**, W. A., *The Medieval Sheriff to A.D. 1300*, 1927.

2.394 **Richardson**, H. G. and Sayles, G. O. *The Governance of Medieval England from the Conquest to Magna Carta*, 1963.

2.395 **Sayles**, G. O., *The King's Parliament of England*, 1975.

2.396 **Tringham**, N. J., 'The 1260 Staffordshire tallage assessment', *Staffs.Rec.Soc.*, XIII, 1988, 1–18.

THE JEWS IN ENGLAND

2.397 **Adler**, M., *The Jews of Medieval England*, 1939.

2.398 **Elman**, P., 'Jewish finance in thirteenth-century England', *Trans. Jewish H.Soc.*, XVI, 1945–51, 89–96.

2.399 —— 'Economic causes of the expulsion of the Jews in 1290', *Ec.H.R.*, VII, 1936–7, 145–54.

2.400 **Grayzel**, S., *The Church and the Jews in the Thirteenth Century*, Philadelphia, 1933. Useful for the general background.

2.401 **Lipman**, V. D., *The Jews of Medieval Ipswich*, Jewish H.Soc., 1967.

2.402 **Richardson**, H. G., *The English Jewry under the Angevin Kings*, 1960.

2.403 **Roth**, C., *History of the Jews in England*, 1941.

STANDARDS OF LIVING

2.404 **Calthrop**, D. C., *English Costume from William I to George IV, 1066–1830*, 1937.

2.405 **Colvin**, H. M., 'Domestic architecture and town planning'. In Poole (3.61), I, 37–97.

2.406 **Cunnington**, Phillis and Lucas, C., *Occupational Dress in England from the Eleventh Century to 1914*, 1967.

2.407 **Faulkner**, P. A., 'Domestic planning from the twelfth to the fourteenth century', *Arch. J.*, CXV, 1958, 150–83.

2.408 **Hassall**, W. O., *How They Lived, 55 B.C.–1485*, 1962.

2.409 **Holmes**, D. T., Jnr., *Daily Living in the Twelfth Century*, Madison, Wis., 1962.

2.410 **Labarge**, Margaret W., *A Baronial Household of the Thirteenth Century*, London and N. Y., 1965. Based on the accounts of Eleanor, wife of Simon de

Montfort.

2.411 **Nevinson**, J. C., 'Civil costume'. In Poole (2.61), I, 300–13.

2.412 **Wood**, Margaret E., *Thirteenth-century Domestic Architecture in England*, 1950 (supplement to *Arch. J.*, CV).

COMMUNICATIONS AND INTERNAL TRADE

2.413 **Britnell**, R. H., 'The proliferation of markets in England, 1200–1349', *Ec.H.R.*, 2nd ser., XXXIV, 1981, 209–21.

2.414 **Coates**, B. E., 'The origin and distribution of markets and fairs in medieval Derbyshire', *Derbyshire Arch. J.*, LXXXV, 1966, 92–111.

2.415 **Richardson**, H., *The Medieval Fairs and Markets of York*, Borthwick Papers, 20, 1961.

2.416 **Stenton**, Doris M., 'Communications'. In Poole (2.61), I, 196–208.

2.417 **Stenton**, F. M., 'The road system in medieval England', *Ec.H.R.*, VII, 1936, 1–21. Reprinted in Doris M. Stenton, ed. (2.80), 234–52.

2.418 **Tupling**, G. H., 'The origin of markets and fairs in medieval Lancashire', *T.L.C.A.S.*, XLIX, 1933, 75–94.

2.419 **Verlinden**, O., 'Markets and Fairs'. In Postan, Rich and Miller, eds. (2.66), 119–53.

THE MONASTERIES

No attempt is made here to list the printed sources for this subject. The reader is referred to Altschul's bibliography, listed above, 49–56.

2.420 **Constable**, G., *Monastic Tithes from their Origins to the Twelfth Century*, 1964.

2.421 **Day**, L. J. C., 'The early monastic contribution to medieval farming', *Lincs. Historian*, 5, 1950, 200–14.

2.422 **Dickinson**, J. C., *Monastic Life in Medieval England*, 1961.

2.423 **Donkin**, R. A., 'Settlement and depopulation on Cistercian estates during the twelfth and thirteenth centuries, especially in Yorkshire', *B.I.H.R.*, XXXIII, 1960, 141–65.

2.424 —— 'Cistercian sheep farming and wool sales in the thirteenth century', *Ag.H.R.*, VI, 1958, 2–8.

2.425 —— 'Cattle on the estates of medieval Cistercian monasteries in England and Wales', *Ec.H.R.*, 2nd ser., XV, 1962, 31–53.

2.426 —— 'The Cistercian order in medieval England: some conclusions', *T.I.B.G.*, 33, 1963, 181–98.

2.427 —— *The Cistercian Settlement and the English Royal Forests*, 1960.

2.428 —— 'The Cistercian Order and the settlement of northern England', *Geog.Rev.*, LIX, 1969, 403–16.

2.429 **Harvey**, Barbara, *Living and Dying in England, 1100 to 1540. The Monastic Experience*, 1993. Based on the author's Ford lectures the book utilises the copiously full records of Westminster Abbey.

2.430 **Hill**, B. D., *English Cistercian Monasteries and their Patrons in the Twelfth Century*, Urbana, Illinois, 1968.

2.431 **Knowles**, D., *The Monastic Order in England: A History of its Development, 943–1216*, 1940, 2nd ed., 1963.

2.432 —— *The Religious Orders in England*, vol. I, 1948. Covers the period 1216–1340.

2.433 **Madden**, J. E., 'Business monks, banker monks, bankrupt monks: the English Cistercians in the thirteenth century', *Catholic H.R.*, XLIX, 1963, 341–64.

2.434 **Matthew**, D., *The Norman Monasteries and their English Possessions*, 1962.

2.435 **Robinson**, D. M., *The Geography of Augustinian Settlement in Medieval England and Wales*, 1980.

2.436 **Waites**, B., *Moorland and Vale-land Farming in N. E. Yorkshire: The Monastic Contribution in the Thirteenth and Fourteenth Centuries*, Borthwick Papers, 32, 1967.

2.437 —— 'The monastic grange as a factor in the settlement of N. E. Yorkshire', *Yorks.Arch. J.*, XL, 1959–62, 627–56.

2.438 —— 'The monastic settlement of N. E. Yorkshire', *Yorks.Arch. J.*, XL, 1959–62, 478–95.

2.439 **Wood**, S. M., *English Monasteries and their Patrons in the Thirteenth Century*, 1955.

CULTURE

2.440 **Thomson**, R. M., 'England and the Twelfth Century Renaissance', *P.P.*, CI, 1983, 3–21.

3

ENGLAND 1300–1500

GENERAL WORKS

(a) Bibliographies

3.1   **Guth**, D. L., ed., *Late Medieval England, 1377–1485. Bibliographical Handbooks*, 1976. *See also* Graves (2.3).

(b) Sources

3.2   **Du Boulay**, F. R., ed., *Documents Ilustrative of Medieval Kentish Society*, Kent Archaeological Society, Kent Records, XVIII, 1964.

3.3   **Flemming**, Jessie H., ed., *England under the Lancastrians*, 1921.

3.4   **Gairdner**, J., ed., *The Paston Letters*, 6 vols., 1904. There is a one-volume selection of the *Letters*, ed. N. Davis, 1958.

3.5   **Myers**, A. R., ed., *English Historical Documents IV; 1327–1485*, 1969. An invaluable collection. *See* especially Part 4 on economic and social developments, Part 2 on the government of the realm, and Part 3 on the Church and education.

3.6   **Thornley**, Isobel, D., ed., *England under the Yorkists*, 1920.

(c) General surveys

3.7   **Bailey**, M., 'The concept of the margin in the medieval English economy',

Ec.H.R. 2nd ser., XLII, 1989, 1–17.

3.8   **Bean**, J. M. W., *The Decline of English Feudalism, 1215–1540*, 1968.

3.9   **Beer**, M., *Early British Economics from the Thirteenth to the Middle of the Eighteenth Century*, 1938. Reprinted 1967.

3.10   **Bellamy**, J. G., *Bastard Feudalism and the Law*, 1989.

3.11   **Bennett**, H. S., *The Pastons and their England*, 1922, 2nd ed., 1932. Reprinted 1968.

3.12   **Bolton**, J. L., *The Medieval English Economy, 1150–1500*, 1980.

3.13   **Bradac**, J., 'Czech visitors to fifteenth-century England', *H.Today*, XV, 1965, 320–7.

3.14   **Bridbury**, A. R., *Economic Growth: England in the Later Middle Ages*, 1962. As its title makes clear, this stimulating little book does not share the traditional view of the period. *See also* Du Boulay (3.22).

3.15   **Britnell**, R. H. *The Commercialisation of British Society, 1000–1500*, 1992. An up to date survey of five hundred years of economic and social development between technical, institutional and demographic factors.

3.16   **Cam**, Helen M., 'The decline and fall of English Feudalism', *Hist.*, XXV, 1940, 216–33.

3.17   **Carter**, J. M., *Medieval Games: Sports and Recreation in Feudal Society*, 1992.

3.18   **Carus-Wilson**, Eleanora M., *Medieval Merchant Venturers*, 1954.

3.19   **Coss**, P. R., 'Bastard Feudalism revised',

P.P., CXXV, 1989, 27–65.

3.20 **Day**, J., *The Medieval Market Economy*, 1987. Stresses the importance of bullion shortages and rebuts 'crisis of feudalism' theories.

3.21 **Denholm-Young**, N., *The Country Gentry in the Fourteenth Century*, 1969.

3.22 **Du Boulay**, F. R. H., *An Age of Ambition: English Society in the Late Middle Ages*, 1970. Shares Bridbury's rejection of the traditional view of decline and decay in the later Middle Ages. Good bibliography.

3.23 —— and Baron, Caroline, M., eds., *The Reign of Richard II*, 1972. A *festschrift* for Profesor May McKisack which includes essays by V. H. Galbraith on the Peasants' Revolt and J. A. Tuck on aspects of the patronage system.

3.24 **Fussell**, G. E., 'Social change but static technology: rural England in the fourteenth century', *Hist.Studs.*, I, 1968, 23–32.

3.25 **Given-Wilson**, C., *The English Nobility in the Middle Ages: the Fourteenth Century Political Community*, 1987.

3.26 —— *The Royal Household and the King's Affinity, Service, Politics, and Finance in England, 1360–1413*, 1986. Looks at the organisation of the household and the practice and regulation of livery.

3.27 **Griffiths**, R. A., ed., *Patronage, the Crown and the Provinces in Later Medieval England*, 1981.

3.28 **Hanawalt**, Barbara A., *Crime and Conflict in English Communities, 1300–48*, 1979. Explores the incidence of crimes such as homicide and robbery within village communities.

3.29 —— 'Fur collar crime: the pattern of crime among the fourteenth-century nobility', *J.Soc.H.*, VIII, 1975, 1–17.

3.30 **Hilton**, R. H. ed., *Peasants, Knights and Heretics, Studies in Medieval English Social History*, 1976.

3.31 —— *The Transition from Feudalism to Capitalism*, 1976.

3.32 **Hodgett**, G. A. J., *A Social and Economic History of Medieval Europe*, 1972. For background.

3.33 **Holmes**, G. A., *The Later Middle Ages, 1272–1485*, 1962.

3.34 **Jacob**, E. F., *The Fifteenth Century, 1399–1485*, 1961. A comprehensive study. Good bibliography.

3.35 **Jarrett**, B., *Social Theories of the Middle*

3.36 *Ages, 1200–1500*, 1926. Reprinted 1968.

Kingsford, C. L., *Prejudice and Promise in Fifteenth Century England*, 1925. Reprinted 1962.

3.37 **Lander**, J. R., *Conflict and Stability in Fifteenth Century England*, 1970.

3.38 —— *Crown and Nobility, 1450–1509*, 1976.

3.39 **MacFarlane**, K. B., 'Bastard feudalism', *B.I.H.R.*, XX, 1945, 161–80.

3.40 —— *England in the Fifteenth Century*, 1981.

3.41 **McKisack**, May, *The Fourteenth Century 1307–1399*, 1959. Good bibliography.

3.42 **Mertes**, Kate, *The English Noble Household, 1250–1650. Good Governance and Politic Rule*, 1988. Based particularly on household accounts the book considers the organisation, membership, income and expenditure of the household and its impact on local society and economy.

3.43 **Miskimin**, H. A., *The Economy of Early Renaissance Europe, 1300–1460*, 1975. For background.

3.44 **Myers**, A. R., *England in the Late Middle Ages, 1307–1536*, 1952. Reprinted with revisions 1956, 1959.

3.45 **Postan**, M. M., 'The fifteenth century', *Ec.H.R.*, IX, 1938, 160–7.

3.46 **Raftis**, J. A., 'Social structures in five East Midland villages: a study of possibilities in the use of court roll data', *Ec.H.R.*, 2nd ser., XVIII, 1965, 83–99.

3.47 **Rawcliffe**, C., *The Staffords, Earls of Stafford and Dukes of Buckingham, 1394–1521*, 1978.

3.48 **Robinson**, W. C., 'Money, population and economic change in late medieval Europe', *Ec.H.R.*, 2nd ser., XII, 1959, 63–76. For background.

3.49 **Rosenthal**, J. H., *The Purchase of Paradise*, 1972. An examination of medieval charity highlighting the importance of the self-interest motive.

3.49a —— *Nobles and Noble Life, 1295–1500*, 1976.

3.50 **Schofield**, R. S., 'The geographical distribution of wealth in England, 1334–1649', *Ec.H.R.*, 2nd ser., XVIII, 1965, 483–510. Suggests that it was mainly concentrated, as in the twentieth century, in the south-east and Midlands.

3.51 **Thomson**, J. A. F., *The Transformation of Medieval England, 1370–1529*, 1983.

3.52 **Tuck**, J. A., *Richard II and the English*

Nobility, 1974.

3.53 **Tydeman**, W., *English Medieval Theatre, 1400–1500*, 1986.

3.54 **Ullman**, W., *The Individual and Society in the Middle Ages*, Baltimore, 1966. For background.

3.55 **Watts**, D. G., 'A model for the early fourteenth century', *Ec.H.R.*, 2nd ser., XX, 1967, 543–7.

3.56 **Wilkinson**, B., *The Later Middle Ages in England 1216–1485*, 1969. Mainly political in emphasis though social and economic aspects are covered. *See also* Clapham (1.308) and Pollard and Crossley (1.320).

POPULATION

(a) Sources

3.57 **Ekwell**, E., ed., *Two Early London Subsidy Rolls*, Lund, 1951.

3.58 **Erskine**, A. M., ed., *The Devonshire Lay Subsidy of 1332*, Devon and Cornwall Rec.Soc., n.s., XIV, 1969.

3.59 **Glasscock**, R. E., ed., *The Lady Subsidy of 1334*, 1975.

(b) Secondary works

3.60 **Attreed**, L. C., 'From Pearl Maiden to Tower Princess: towards a new history of medieval childhood'. *J.Med.H.*, IX, 1983, 43–58.

3.61 **Bailey**, M., 'Blowing up bubbles: some new demographic evidence for the fifteenth century?', *J.Med.H.*, XV, 1989, 347–58.

3.62 **Bean**, J. M. W., 'Plague, population and economic decline in England in the later Middle Ages', *Ec.H.R.*, 2nd ser., XV, 1963, 423–37.

3.63 **Bennett**, Judith M., 'The tie that binds: peasant marriages and families in late medieval England', *J.Interdis.H.*, XV, 1984, 111–29.

3.64 **Beresford**, M. W., *Lay Subsidies and Poll Taxes*, 1964.

3.64a **Boucher**, C. E., 'The Black Death in Bristol', *Trans.Bristol and Gloucs.Arch.Soc.*, LX, 1938, 31–46.

3.65 **Bridbury**, A. R., 'The Black Death', *Ec.H.R.*, 2nd ser., XXVI, 1973, 557–92.

3.66 —— 'Before the Black Death', *Ec.H.R.*, 2nd ser., XXX, 1977, 393–410.

3.67 **Brooke**, C. N. L., *The Medieval Idea of Marriage*, 1989.

3.68 **Campbell**, B. M. S., ed., *Before the Black Death. Studies in the 'Crisis' of the Early Fourteenth Century*, 1991. A collection of six essays which examine the general movement of population trends, their regional variations and their impact on economy and society.

3.69 **Clark**, E., 'The decision to marry in thirteenth and early fourteenth century Norfolk', *Med.Studs.*, XLIX, 1987, 495–516.

3.70 **Ekwall**, E., *Studies on the Population of Medieval London*, Stockholm, 1956. Concentrates on the period 1250–1350 and is mainly a detailed study of immigration into the capital.

3.71 **Fraser**, C. M., 'Population density in medieval fenland', *Ec.H.R.*, 2nd ser., XIV, 1961, 71–81.

3.72 **Gottfried**, R. S., *Doctors and Medicine in Medieval England, 1340–1530*, 1986.

3.73 —— *Epidemic Disease in Fifteenth-Century England. The Medical Response and the Demographic Consequences*, 1978.

3.74 **Hanawalt**, Barbara A., 'Childbearing among the lower classes of late medieval England', *J.Inter-dis.H.*, VIII, 1977, 1–22.

3.75 —— *The Ties that Bind. Peasant Families in Medieval England*, 1986. Stresses the significance of the conjugal family using evidence from coroners' wills.

3.76 **Hanham**, Alison, *The Celys and their World. An English Merchant Family of the Fifteenth Century*, 1985.

3.77 **Harvey**, Barbara, 'The population trend in England, 1300–48', *T.R.H.S.*, 5th ser., XVI, 1966, 23–42. Contends that there was no dramatic change during this period.

3.78 **Hatcher**, J., *Plague, Population and the English Economy, 1348–1530*, 1977.

3.79 **Helleiner**, K. F., 'Population movements and agrarian depression in the later Middle Ages', *Canadian J.Ec.& Pol. Science*, XV, 1949, 368–77.

3.80 **Ives**, E. W., *The Common Lawyers of Pre-Reformation England. Thomas Kebell. A Case Study*, 1983.

3.81 —— and Manchester, A. H., eds., *Law, Litigants and the Legal Profession*, 1983.

3.82 **Jacquart**, D., *Sexuality and Medicine in the Middle Ages*, 1988.

3.83 **Jones**, E. D., 'Going round in circles: some new evidence for population in the later Middle Ages', *J.Med.Hist.*, XV, 1989, 329–45.

3.84 **Langford**, A. W., 'The Plague in Herefordshire', *Trans. Woolhope Nat.Hist. Field Club*, XXXV, 1956, 146–53.

3.85 **Levett**, Ada E., 'The Black Death on the St Albans manors'. In Levett (2.233), 248–86.

3.86 —— *The Black Death on the Estates of the See of Winchester*, 1916.

3.87 **Lucas**, H. S., 'The great European famine, 1315, 1316 and 1317', *Speculum*, V, 1930, 343–77.

3.88 **McClure**, P., 'Patterns of migration in the late Middle Ages: the evidence of English place name surnames', *Ec.H.R.*, 2nd ser., XXXII, 1979, 167–82.

3,89 **Mullett**, C. F., *The Bubonic Plague and England: An Essay in the History of Preventive Medicine*, Lexington, Ky., 1956.

3.90 **Newman**, Charlotte, *The Anglo-Norman Nobility in the Reign of Henry I. The Second Generation*, 1989. A social and political study which considers marriage, women, and the family.

3.91 **Nohl**, J., *The Black Death: A Chronicle of the Plague Compiled from Contemporary Sources*, 1961.

3.92 **Pelham**, R. A., 'The urban population of Sussex in 1340', *Sussex Arch.Collns.*, LXXVIII, 1938, 211–23.

3.93 **Postan**, M. M., 'Some economic evidence of declining population in the later Middle Ages', *Ec.H.R.*, 2nd ser., II, 1949–50, 221–46.

3.94 **Raftis**, J. A., 'Changes in an English village after the Black Death', *Medieval Studs*, XXIX, 1967, 158–77. Looks at Upwood, Hampshire.

3.95 **Razi**, Z., *Life, Marriage and Death in a Medieval Parish, Economy, Society and Demography in Halesowen, 1270–1400*, 1980.

3.96 **Robo**, E., 'The Black Death in the Hundred of Farnham', *E.H.R.*, XLIV, 1929, 560–72.

3.97 **Rubin**, S., *Medieval English Medicine*, 1974.

3.98 **Russell**, J. C., 'Late medieval population patterns', *Speculum*, XX, 1945, 157–71.

3.99 —— 'Effects of pestilence and plague, 1315–85', *Comp.Studs.Soc.& H.*, VIII, 1966, 464–73.

3.100 **Saltmarsh**, J., 'Plague and economic decline in England in the later Middle Ages', *Cambridge H. J.*, VII. 1941, 23–41.

3.101 **Scammell**, Jean, 'Freedom and marriage in medieval England', *Ec.H.R.*, 2nd ser., XXVII, 1974, 523–37.

3.102 **Shahar**, Shulamith, *Childhood in the Middle Ages*, 1990. A general survey concentrating principally on theories of childhood.

3.103 **Shrewsbury**, J. F. D., *A History of Bubonic Plague in the British Isles*, 1970.

3.104 **Talbot**, C. H., *Medicine in Medieval England*, 1967.

3.105 **Thrupp**, Sylvia, 'The problem of replacement rates in late medieval English population', *Ec.H.R.*, 2nd ser., XVIII, 1965, 101–19. Based mainly on court roll data.

3.106 —— 'Plague effects in medieval Europe', *Comp.Studs.Soc.H.*, VIII, 1966, 474–83.

3.107 **Walker**, Sue S., 'Free consent and marriage of feudal wards in medieval England', *J.Med.H.*, VIII, 1982, 123–34.

3.108 **Ziegler**, P., *The Black Death*, 1969. *See also* Hoskins (4.116), Hollingsworth (4.170), Wrigley (4.187), and Russell (2.148).

AGRICULTURE AND RURAL SOCIETY

(a) General

3.109 **Astill**, G. and Grant, A., eds., *The Countryside of Medieval England*, 1988.

3.110 **Aston**, Margaret, Austin, D., and Dyer, C., eds., *The Rural Settlements of Medieval England*, 1989.

3.111 **Aston**, T. H. et al., eds., *Social Relations and Ideas. Essays in Honour of R. H. Hilton*, 1983. A *festschrift* predominantly based in the period of the Middle Ages explored by Hilton himself. Joan Thirsk takes the collection into the seventeenth century and there are essays on rural life in Germany, France and Russia.

3.112 **Ault**, W. O., *The Self-directing Activities of Village Communities in Medieval England*, Boston, Mass., 1952.

3.113 —— *Open Field Farming in Medieval England*, 1972.

3.114 —— 'By-laws of gleaning and the problem of harvest', *Ec.H.R.*, 2nd ser., XIV, 1961, 210–17. Deals with the situation in England in the fourteenth century.

3.115 **Baker**, A. R. H., 'Evidence in the Nonarum Inquisitiones of contracting arable land in the early fourteenth century', *Ec.H.R.*, 2nd ser., XIX, 1966, 518–32.

3.116 —— 'Some evidence of a reduction in the acreage of cultivated lands in Sussex during the early fourteenth century', *Sussex Arch.Collns.*, CIV, 1966, 1–5.

3.117 **Bean**, J. M. W., *From Lord to Patron. Lordship in late Medieval England*, 1989. A technical account of the complexities of bastard feudalism.

3.118 **Beresford**, M. W., 'The Poll Tax and the census of sheep', *Ag.H.R.*, I, 1953, 9–15; *ibid.*, II, 1954, 15–29.

3.119 **Biddick**, K. A., 'Malthus in a straitjacket? Analysing agrarian change in medieval England', *J.Interdis.H.*, XX, 1989, 623–36.

3.120 —— 'Missing links: taxable wealth, markets and stratification among medieval peasants,' *J.Interdis.H.*, XVIII, 1987, 277–98.

3.121 **Britnell**, R. H., 'Production for the market on a small fourteenth-century estate', *Ec.H.R.*, 2nd ser., XIX, 1966, 380–7. Deals with Langenhoe, Essex.

3.122 **Britton**, E., *The Community of the Vill. A Study in the History of the Family and Village Life in Fourteenth-Century England*, 1977.

3.123 **Campbell**, B. M. S., 'The diffusion of vetches in medieval England', *Ec.H.R.*, 2nd ser., XLI, 1988, 193–208. *See also* Currie (3.124).

3.124 **Currie**, C. R., 'Early vetches in medieval England', *Ec.H.R.*, 2nd ser., XLI, 1988, 114–16. *See also* Campbell (3.123).

3.125 **Dyer**, C. C., 'English peasant buildings in the later Middle Ages (1200–1500), *Med.Arch.*, XXX, 1986, 19–45.

3.126 —— 'A redistribution of incomes' in fifteenth-century England', *P.P.*,

XXXIX, 1968, 11–13. Explores the relationship between a lord and his tenants as an agency of social and agrarian change in the fifteenth century.

3.127 **Fussell**, G. E., 'The classical tradition in west European farming: the fourteenth and fifteenth centuries', *Ag.H.R.*, XVII, 1969, 1–8.

3.128 **Gatrell**, P., 'Historians and peasants: studies of medieval English society in a Russian context', *P.P.*, XCVI, 1982, 22–50.

3.129 **Gray**, H. L., 'Incomes from land in England in 1436', *E.H.R.*, XLIX, 1934, 607–39.

3.130 **Hilton**, R. H., 'The content and sources of English agrarian history before 1500', *Ag.H.R.*, III, 1955, 3–19. *See also* Thirsk (4.325), a companion article for the later period.

3.131 —— *The English Peasantry in the Later Middle Ages*, 1975. Provocatively original treatment of the peasantry as a social class.

3.132 —— *Class Conflict and the Crisis of Feudalism. Essays in Medieval Social History*, 1986. Marxist inspired, pathfinding essays addressing the 'crisis' in feudal relations between landlords and tenants and the complexities of small-town society.

3.133 **Hodgett**, G. A. J., *Agrarian England in the Later Middle Ages* (Hist.Ass., Aids for Teachers series, 13), 1966. A useful summary with a bibliographical note.

3.134 **Hoskins**, W. G., 'Regional farming in England', *Ag.H.R.*, II, 1954, 3–11.

3.135 **Howell**, Cecily, 'Stability and change, 1300–1700: the socio-economic context of the self-perpetuating family farm in England', *J.Peasant Studs.*, II, 1975, 468–82.

3.136 **Kosminsky**, E. A., *Studies in the Agrarian History of England in the Thirteenth Century*, 1956.

3.137 **Langdon**, J., 'The economics of horses and oxen in medieval England', *Ag.H.R.*, XXX, 1982, 31–41.

3.138 **Maddicott**, J. R., 'The county community and the making of public opinion in fourteenth-century England', *T.R.H.S.*, 5th ser., XXVIII, 1978, 27–43.

3.139 —— *The English Peasantry and the Demands of the Crown, 1294–1341*, 1975.

3.140 **Miller**, E., ed., *The Agrarian History of England and Wales. III: 1348–1500*, 1991.

A massive volume which explores population trends, farming techniques and changing tenures in the countryside. Chapters are also included on marketing, prices, wages, landlords, and peasant discontent.

3.141 **Taylor**, E. G. R., 'The Surveyor', *Ec.H.R.*, XVII, 1947, 121–33.

3.142 **Trow-Smith**, R., A *History of British Livestock Husbandry to 1700*, 1957.

3.143 **Ward**, J. C., *The Essex Gentry and the County Community in the Fourteenth Century*, 1991.

(b) Regional studies

3.144 **Aldred**, D., and Dyer, C. C., *A Medieval Cotswold Village, Roel, Gloucestershire*, 1991.

3.145 **Bailey**, M., *A Marginal Economy? East Anglian Breckland in the Later Middle Ages*, 1989.

3.146 **Bennett**, M. J., *Community, Class and Careerism. Cheshire and Lancashire Society in the Age of Sir Gawain and the Green Knight*, 1983.

3.147 **Cracknell**, B. E., *Canvey Island: The History of a Marshland Community*, University of Leicester, Department of English Loc.H., Occ. Papers, 12, 1959.

3.148 **Dyer**, C., *Warwickshire Farming 1349–1520. Preparations for Agricultural Revolution*, Dugdale Soc.Occ. Papers, XXVII, 1981.

3.149 **Fisher**, P. and W. B., 'The medieval land surveys of County Durham', *Research Paper No. 2*, University of Durham, 1959.

3.150 **Glasscock**, R. E., 'The distribution of wealth in East Anglia in the early fourteenth century', *T.I.B.G.*, XXXII, 1963, 113–23.

3.151 **Halcrow**, Elizabeth M., 'The decline of demesne farming on the estates of Durham cathedral priory', *Ec.H.R.*, 2nd ser., VII, 1955, 345–56.

3.152 **Hallam**, H. E., 'The agrarian economy of medieval Lincolnshire before the Black Death', *Hist.Studs. Australia & New Zealand*, XI, 1964, 163–69.

3.153 —— 'The agrarian economy of south Lincolnshire in the mid-fifteenth century', *Nottingham Med.Studs.*, XI, 1967, 86–95.

3.154 **Hatcher**, J., *Rural Economy and Society in the Duchy of Cornwall, 1300–1500*, 1970.

3.155 **Hewitt**, H. J., *Medieval Cheshire. An Economic and Social History of Cheshire in the Reigns of the Three Edwards*, Chet.Soc., n.s., 88, 1929.

3.156 **Hogan**, M. Patricia, 'Medieval villainy. A study in the meaning and control of crime in an English village', *Studs.Med & Renaiss.H.*, n.s., II, 1979, 121–215.

3.157 **Lythe**, S. G. E., 'The organisation of drainage and embankment in medieval Holderness', *Yorks.Arch.J.*, XXXIV, 1939, 282–95.

3.158 **Newton**, K. C., *Thaxted in the Fourteenth Century*, 1960.

3.159 **Poos**, L. R., *A Rural Society after the Black Death, Essex, 1350–1525*, 1991.

3.160 **Ruston**, A. G., and Witney, D., *Hooton Pagnell: The Agricultural Evolution of a Yorkshire Village*, 1934.

3.161 **Saul**, N., *Knights and Esquires. The Gloucestershire Gentry in the Fourteenth Century*, 1981.

3.162 —— *Scenes from Provincial Life, Knightly Families in Sussex, 1280–1400*, 1986. Looks chiefly at three well documented families in an unusual county.

3.163 **Smith**, A., 'Regional differences in crop production in medieval Kent', *Arch.Cant.*, LXXVIII, 1964, 147–60.

3.164 **Smith**, R. B., *Blackburnshire: A Study in Early Lancashire History*, University of Leicester, Department of English Loc.H., Occ. Papers, 15, 1961. The first part of the essay is a general survey of landholding and of the economy of the area in the early fourteenth century.

3.165 **Spufford**, Margaret, *A Cambridgeshire Community: Chippenham from Settlement to Enclosure*, University of Leicester, Department of English Loc.H., Occ. Papers, 20, 1965.

3.166 **Winchester**, A. J. L., *Landscape and Society in Medieval Cumbria*, 1987.

3.167 **Wright**, S. M., *The Derbyshire Gentry in the Fifteenth Century*, 1983.

See also Gras (2.200), Harvey (2.202), Hoskins (2.206), Postan (2.62), and Hoskins (4.115).

(c) The Manor

3.168 **Dale**, M. K., eds., *Court Roll of Chalgrave Manor, 1278–1313*, Beds.Hist.Rec.Soc., XXVIII, 1948.

3.169 **Salzman**, L. F. ed., *Ministers' Accounts of the Manor of Petworth, 1374–53*, Sussex

Rec.Soc., LV, 1955. *See also* Le Patourel (2.346), and Bland, Brown and Tawney (1.303).

3.170 **Ault**, W. O., 'Manor court and parish church in fifteenth-century England: a study of English by-laws', *Speculum*, XLII, 1967, 53–67. *See* the other titles by Ault (3.112–14).

3.171 **Bridbury**, A. R., 'The farming out of manors', *Ec.H.R.*, 2nd ser., XXI, 1978, 503–20.

3.172 **Hatcher**, J., 'Non-manorialism in medieval Cornwall', *Ag.H.R.*, XVIII, 1970, 1–16.

3.173 **Lloyd**, E., 'The farm accounts of the manor of Hendon, 1316–1416', *Trans. London and Middx.Arch.Soc.*, XXI, 1967, 157–63.

3.174 **McIntosh**, Marjorie K., *Autonomy and Community, The Royal Manor of Havering, 1200–1500*, 1986. Examines the prosperous community of a royal manor which enjoyed fixed rents and services, the benefits of proximity to London, and nearby woodland for expansion.

3.175 **Mate**, Mavis, 'Agrarian economy after the Black Death: the manors of Canterbury cathedral priory, 1348–91', *Ec.H.R.*, 2nd ser., XXXVII, 1984, 341–54.

3.176 **Post**, J. B., 'Some manorial amercements and peasant poverty', *EC.H.R.*, 2nd ser., XXVIII, 1975, 304–11.

For other material on this subject, *see also* Davenport (2.228) and Hodgett (3.32).

(d) Estate management

3.177 **Denney**, A. H., ed., *The Sibton Abbey Estates: Select Documents, 1325–1509*, Suffolk Rec.Soc., II, 1960.

3.178 **Hilton**, R. H., ed., *Ministers' Accounts of the Warwickshire Estates of the Duke of Clarence, 1479–80*, Dugdale Soc., XXI for 1944, 1952.

3.179 **Bean**, J. M. W., *The Estates of the Percy Family, 1416–1537*, 1958.

3.180 **Biddick**, K., *The Other Economy, Pastoral Husbandry on a Medieval Estate*, 1989.

3.181 **Britnell**, R. H., 'Minor landlords in England and medieval agrarian capitalism', *P.P.*, LXXXIX, 1980, 3–22.

3.182 **Denholm-Young**, N., *Seigneurial Administration in England*, 1937.

3.183 **Du Boulay**, F. R. H., *The Lordship of Canterbury: An Essay on Medieval Society*, 1966. A valuable study of the economic, social, legal and military organisation of the lordship.

3.184 —— 'Who were farming the English demesnes at the end of the Middle Ages?', *Ec.H.R.*, 2nd ser., XVII, 1965, 443–55.

3.185 —— 'A rentier economy in the later Middle Ages: the archbishopric of Canterbury', *Ec.H.R.*, 2nd ser., XVI, 1964, 427–38.

3.186 **Harvey**, Barbara, 'The leasing of the Abbot of Westminster's demesnes in the later Middle Ages', *Ec.H.R.*, 2nd ser., XXII, 1969, 17–27.

3.187 **Hassall**, W. and Beauroy, N., eds., *Lordship and Landscape in Norfolk, 1250–1350*, 1993.

3.188 **Hilton**, R. H., *The Economic Development of Some Leicestershire Estates in the Fourteenth and Fifteenth Centuries*, 1947.

3.189 **Holmes**, G. A., *The Estates of the Higher Nobility in Fourteenth-Century England*, 1957.

3.190 **Jack**, I. R., 'Entail and descent: the Hastings inheritance, 1370–1436', *B.I.H.R.*, XXXVIII, 1965, 1–19.

3.191 **Keil**, I., 'Farming on the Dorset estates of Glastonbury Abbey in the early fourteenth century', *Proc.Dorset Nat.H. & Arch.Soc.*, LXXXVII, 1966, 234–50.

3.192 **Kershaw**, I., *Bolton Priory: The Economy of a Northern Monastery 1286–1325*, 1973.

3.193 **Page**, F. M., *The Estates of Crowland Abbey*, 1934.

3.194 **Raftis**, J. A., *The Estates of Ramsey Abbey: A Study in Economic Growth and Organisation*, Toronto, 1957.

3.195 **Roberts**, A. K. B., *St George's Chapel, Windsor Castle, 1348–1416. A Study in Early Collegiate Administration*, 1947. Includes a discussion of estate management.

3.196 **Rosenthal**, J. T., 'The estates and finances of Richard, Duke of York, 1411–60'. In W. M. Bowsky, ed., *Studs.Med. & Renaiss.H.*, II, 1965, 115–204.

3.197 **Ross**, C., *The Estates and Finances of Richard Beauchamp, Earl of Warwick*, Dugdale Soc.Occ. Papers, XII, 1956.

3.198 **Searle**, Eleanor, *Lordship and Community. Battle Abbey and its Banlieue 1066–1538*,

Toronto, 1974.

3.199 **Smith**, R. A. L., *Canterbury Cathedral Priory: A Study in Monastic Administration*, 1943.

3.200 **Wolffe**, B. P., 'The management of English royal estates under the Yorkist kings', *E.H.R.*, LXXI, 1956, 1–27. *See also* the book by the same author listed below (4.383).

3.201 —— 'Acts of Resumption in the Lancastrian parliaments, 1399–1456', *E.H.R.*, LXXIII, 1958, 583–613.

(e) Land tenure

3.202 **Dodwell**, Barbara, 'Holdings and inheritance in medieval East Anglia', *Ec.H.R.*, 2nd ser., XX, 1967, 53–66.

3.203 **Faith**, R. J., 'Peasant families and inheritance customs in medieval England', *Ag.H.R.*, XIV, 1966, 77–95.

3.204 **Pitkin**, D. S., 'Partible inheritance and the open fields', *Ag.H.*, XXXV, 1961, 65–9.

3.205 **Raftis**, J. A., *Tenure and Mobility: Studies in the Social History of the Medieval English Village*, Toronto, 1964.

3.206 **Razi**, Z., 'Family land and the village community in later medieval England', *P.P.*, 93, 1981, 3–36.

(f) Field systems

3.207 **Ault**, W. O., 'Open field husbandry and the village community: a study of agrarian by-laws in medieval England', *Trans.American Phil.Soc.*, n.s., LV, 1965.

3.208 **Baker**, A. R. H., 'Open fields and partible inheritance on a Kent manor', *Ec.H.R.*, 2nd ser., XVII, 1964, 1–23. Looks at the manor of Gillingham in 1285 and 1447.

3.209 —— 'Observations on the Open Fields. The present position of studies in British field systems', *J.H.Geog.*, V, 1979, 315–26.

3.210 **Beresford**, M. W., 'Glebe terriers and open fields', *Yorks.Arch.J.*, XXXVII, 1951, 325–68.

3.211 —— 'Ridge and furrow and the open fields', *Ec.H.R.*, 2nd ser., I, 1948, 34–45.

3.212 —— 'Lot acres', *Ec.H.R.*, XIII, 1943, 74–9. Discusses the practice of dividing up the arable from the waste by lot.

3.213 **Butler**, R. M., 'The common lands of the borough of Nottingham', *Trans. Thoroton Soc.*, LIV, 1950, 45–62.

3.214 **Chapman**, V., 'Open fields in West Cheshire', *T.H.S.L.C.*, 104, 1952, 35–60.

3.215 **Cromarty**, D., *The Fields of Saffron Walden in 1400*, 1966.

3.216 **Fox**, H. S. A., 'The alleged transformation from two-field to three-field systems in medieval England', *Ec.H.R.*, 2nd ser., XXXIX, 1986, 526–49.

3.217 **Dahlman**, C. J., *The Open Field System and Beyond*, 1980. Applies the techniques of the 'New Economic History' to the problems surrounding the origins and survival of the open field system.

3.218 **Finberg**, H. P. R., 'The open field in Devon'. In Hoskins and Finberg (4.118), 265–88.

3.219 **Harris**, A., *The Open Fields of East Yorkshire*, East Yorks.Loc.Hist.Soc., pamphlet series, 9, 1959.

3.220 **Hilton**, R. H., 'A study in the pre-history of English enclosure in the fifteenth century'. In *Studi in Onore di Armando Sapori*, Milan, 1957, I, 675–85.

3.221 **Hoskins**, W. G., and Stamp, L. D., *The Common Lands of England and Wales*, 1963.

3.222 **Kerridge**, E., *The Common Fields of England*, 1992.

3.223 **Lennard**, R. V., 'The alleged exhaustion of the soil in medieval England', *Ec.J.*, XXXII, 1922, 12–27. Refuted the views put forward by Harriet Bradley in *The Enclosures in England: An Economic Reconstruction*, 1918.

3.224 **Orwin**, C. S., and Christabel S., *The Open Fields*, 1954, 3rd ed., 1967, with an introduction by Joan Thirsk.

3.225 **Postgate**, M. R., 'The field systems of Breckland', *Ag.H.R.*, X, 1962, 80–101. Points to the variations occurring in traditional field patterns as a response to local soil conditions.

3.226 **Roden**, D., 'Field systems in Ibstone: a township of the S. W. Chilterns during the later Middle Ages', *Recs. of Bucks.*, XVIII, 1966, 43–57

3.227 —— and Baker, A. R. H., 'Field systems of the Chiltern hills and parts of Kent from the late thirteenth to the early seventeenth century', *T.I.B.G.*, XXXVIII, 1966, 73–88.

3.228 **Saltmarsh**, J. and Darby, H. C., 'The

infield-out-field system on a Norfolk manor', (West Wretham), *Ec.J.Ec.H.Supp.*, III, 1935, 30–44.

3.229 **Sylvester**, Dorothy, 'The open fields of Cheshire', *T.H.S.L.C.*, 108, 1956, 1–34.

3.230 **Yelling**, J. A., 'Rationality in the Common Fields', *Ec.H.R.*, 2nd ser., XXXV, 1982, 409–15.

3.231 **Youd**, G., 'The common fields of Lancashire', *T.H.S.L.C.*, 113, 1962, 1–42.

(g) Deserted villages

3.232 **Allison**, K. J., Beresford, M. W. and Hurst, J. G., *The Deserted Villages of Northamptonshire*, University of Leicester Department of English Loc.H., Occ. Papers, 18, 1966.

3.233 —— *The Deserted Villages of Oxfordshire*, University of Leicester, Department of English Loc.H., Occ. Papers, 17, 1965.

3.234 —— 'The lost villages of Norfolk', *Norfolk Arch.*, XXXI, 1955, 116–62.

3.235 **Beresford**, M. W., *The Lost Villages of England*, 1954. The main work on the subject. Beresford stresses the medieval stages in the history of deserted villages and rejects an oversimplified monocausal explanation based on sixteenth-century enclosures. Reprinted 1965.

3.236 —— and Hurst, J. G., eds., *Deserted Medieval Villages*, 1971. Brings together essays on the most recent historical and archaeological work on the subject. Gazetteers of deserted sites are appended.

3.237 **Dyer**, C. C., 'Deserted medieval villages in the West Midlands', *Ec.H.R.*, 2nd ser., XXXV, 1982, 19–35.

3.238 —— 'Population and agriculture on a Warwickshire manor in the later Middle Ages', *Birm.H.J.*, XI, 1968, 113–27. A local study of a village which was only gradually deserted.

3.239 —— 'Deserted medieval villages in the West Midlands', *Ec.H.R.*, 2nd ser., XXXV, 1982, 19–34.

3.240 **Gould**, J. D., 'Mr Beresford and the lost villages', *Ag.H.R.*, III, 1955, 107–13.

3.241 **Hoskins**, W. G., 'The deserted villages of Leicestershire', in Hoskins, (4.116) 67–107.

(h) Forests

3.242 **Birrell**, J., 'The forest and the chase in medieval Staffordshire', *Staffs.Studs.*, III, 1991, 23–50.

3.243 —— 'The forest economy of the honour of Tutbury in the fourteenth and fifteenth centuries', *Birm.H.J.*, VIII, 1962, 114–34.

3.244 **Cantor**, L. M., 'The medieval forests and chases of Staffordshire', *North Staffs. J. Field Studies*, VIII, 1968, 39–53.

3.245 **Husain**, B. M. C., 'Delamere forest in later medieval times', *T.H.S.L.C.*, 107, 1955, 23–39.

3.246 **Schumer**, B., *The Evolution of Wychwood to 1400. Pioneers, Frontiers and Forests*, 1984.

3.247 **Shaw**, R. C., *The Royal Forest of Lancaster*, 1957.

3.248 **Taylor**, C. C., 'The pattern of medieval settlement in the Forest of Blackmoor', *Proc.Dorset Nat.H. & Arch.Soc.*, LXXXVII, 1966, 251–4.

3.249 —— 'Whiteparish: a study of the development of a forest edge parish', *Wilts.Arch & Nat.H.Mag.*, LXII, 1967, 79–102.

See also Roberts (2.147), and Tupling (4.129).

INDUSTRY

(a) General

3.251 **Blair**, J. and Ramsay, N., eds., *English Medieval Industries*, 1991. Designed as a successor to Salzman's book. Includes chapters on stone, tin, lead and pewter, pottery, leather, textiles, horn and bone, and wood.

3.252 **Carus-Wilson**, Eleanora M., 'Evidence of industrial growth on some fifteenth-century manors', *Ec.H.R.*, 2nd ser., XII, 1959, 190–205.

3.253 **Crossley**, D. W., *Medieval Industry*, 1981.

3.254 **Salzman**, L. F., *English Industries of the Middle Ages*, 1913, 2nd ed., 1923. Covers – *inter al.* mining, building and cloth-making. Illustrated. *See also* White (2.274).

(b) Industrial organisation

The literature on individual companies is too enormous to list here. The reader is referred to Kahl's bibliography, and to his introduction to Unwin's *Gilds and Companies of London*, both of which are listed below.

3.255 **Gross**, C., *The Gild Merchant*, 2 vols., 1890. Reprinted, 1965. Still an important work on the subject.

3.256 **Hibbert**, F. A., *The Influence and Development of English Gilds, as Illustrated by the History of the Craft Gilds of Shrewsbury*, 1891.

3.257 **Imray**, Jean M., 'Les Bones Gentes de la Mercerye de Londres: a study of the membership of the medieval Mercers' Company'. In Hollaender and Kellaway (2.360), 155–78.

3.258 **Thrupp**, Sylvia, 'The gilds'. In Postan, Rich and Miller (2.66), 155–78.

3.259 ——— 'Medieval gilds reconsidered', *J.Ec.H.*, II, 1942, 164–73.

For source material on this subject, *see* the useful section on 'Towns and gilds' in Bland, Brown and Tawney (1.303), 114–50.

(c) Textiles

3.260 **Bridbury**, A. R., *Medieval English Clothmaking. An Economic Survey*, 1982.

3.261 **Gray**, H. L., 'The production and exportation of English woolens in the fourteenth century', *E.H.R.*, XXXIX, 1924, 13–35.

3.262 **McClenaghan**, B., *The Springs of Lavenham and the Suffolk Cloth Trade in the Fifteenth and Sixteenth Centuries*, 1924.

3.263 **Power**, Eileen, *The Paycockes of Coggeshall*, 1920. A short study of a family of clothiers.

See also Carus-Wilson. Studies of the wool trade are listed below under *Commerce*, (pp. 38–9).

(d) Mining and metallurgy

3.264 **Giuseppi**, M. S., 'Some fourteenth-century accounts of iron works at Tudely, Kent', *Archaeologia*, LXIV,

1912–13, 145–64.

3.265 **Lapsley**, G. T., 'The account roll of a fifteenth-century ironmaster', *E.H.R.*, XIV, 1899, 509–28.

3.266 **Hatcher**, J., *English Tin Production and Trade Before 1550*, 1973.

3.267 ——— and Barker, T. C., *A History of British Pewter*, 1974.

3.268 **Mott**, R. A., 'English bloomeries, 1329–1589', *J.Iron and Steel Institute*, CXCVIII, 1961, 149–61.

3.269 **Nef**, J. U., 'Mining and metallurgy in medieval civilisation'. In Postan and Rich (2.65), 430–92.

3.270 **Simpson**, J. B., 'Coal mining by the monks', *Trans. Institute of Mining Engineers*, XXXIX, 1910, 572–98.

See also Gough (4.481), Lewis (4.535), Nef (4.508), and Schubert (2.279) and Waites (2.280).

(e) Salt

3.271 **Berry**, E. K., 'The borough of Droitwich and its salt industry, 1215–1700', *Birm.H.J.*, VI, 1957, 39–61.

3.272 **Hallam**, H. E., 'Salt making in the Lincolnshire fenlands during the Middle Ages', *Lincs. Architectural & Arch.Soc.*, n.s., VIII, 1959–60, 85–112.

3.273 **Rudkin**, E. H. and Owen, Dorothy M., 'The medieval salt industry in the Lindsey marshland', n.s., VIII, 1959–60, 76–84.

See also Bridbury's book on the salt trade (3.305).

(f) Miscellaneous

3.274 **Harvey**, J., *The Master Builders of the Middle Ages*, 1972.

3.275 **Salzman**, L. F., *Building in England down to 1540: A Documentary History*, 1952, 3rd ed., 1967.

3.276 **Saul**, A., 'The herring industry at Great Yarmough, c.1280–1400', *Norfolk Arch.*, XXXVIII, 1981, 33–43.

3.277 **Turton**, R. B., *The Alum Farm*, 1938. The alum trade in N. E. Yorkshire.

3.278 **Veale**, Elspeth M., 'Craftsmen and the economy of London in the fourteenth century'. In Hollaender and Kellaway (2.360), 133–51.

3.279 **Wright**, Jane A., *Brick Building in England from the Middle Ages to 1550*, 1972.

See also Colvin (2.282), Johnson (2.283), and Knoop and Jones (2.284).

(g) Sources of power for industry

3.280 **Adams**, J. W. R., *Windmills in Kent*, 1955.
3.280a **Atkinson**, F., 'The horse as a source of rotary power', *Trans. Newcomen Soc.*, XXXIII, 1962, 31–55.
3.281 **Dewar**, H. S. L., 'The windmills, watermills and horse mills of Dorset', *Proc.Dorset Nat.H. & Arch.Soc.*, LXXXII, for 1960, 109–32.
3.282 —— 'The windmills, watermills and horsemills of Dorset – new evidence', *Proc.Dorset Nat.Hist. & Arch.Soc.*, LXXXVI, 1965, 179–81.
3.283 **Freese**, S., *Windmills and Millwrighting*, 1957. Reprinted 1971.
3.284 **Holt**, R., *The Mills of Medieval England*, 1988.
3.285 **Pelham**, R. A., *Fulling Mills: A Study of the Application of Water Power to the Woollen Industry*, 1958 (Society for the Protection of Ancient Buildings: Wind and Watermill section, publications, 5).
3.286 **Pratt**, D., 'The medieval watermills of Denbighshire', *Denbighshire H.Soc.Trans.*, XIII, 1964, 22–37.
3.287 **Reid**, K. C., 'The watermills of London', *Trans. London and Middx.Arch.Soc.*, n.s., XI, 1954, 227–36.
3.288 **Wailes**, R., *Windmills in England: A Study of Their Origin, Development and Future*, 1948.
3.289 —— *The English Windmill*, 1954.
3.290 —— *Tidemills, Parts 1 and 2*, 1956 (Society for the Protection of Ancient Buildings. Wind and Watermill section, publication 2–3).
3.291 **Wilson**, P. N., *Watermills: An Introduction*, 1956 (Society for the Protection of Ancient Buildings. Wind and Watermill section, publication, 1).

COMMERCE

(a) Sources

3.292 **Childs**, Wendy R., ed., *The Customs Accounts of Hull, 1453–90*, Yorks.Arch. Soc.Rec.Ser., CXLIV, 1984.
3.293 **Cobb**, H. S., ed., *The Local Port Book of Southampton, 1439–40*, Southampton Records Series, V, 1961. *See also* Foster (3.295).
3.294 **Coleman**, Olive, ed., *The Brokage Book of Southampton, 1443–44*, Southampton Records Series, IV, 1960.
3.295 **Foster**, B., ed., *The Local Port Book of Southampton for 1435–6*, Southampton Records Series, VII, 1963. *See also* Cobb (3.293).
3.296 **Lister**, J., ed., *The Early Yorkshire Woollen Trade: Extracts from the Hull Customs Rolls and Complete Transcripts of the Ulnagers' Rolls*, Yorks.Arch.Soc.Rec.Ser., LXIV, 1924. Deals with the fourteenth and fifteenth centuries.
3.297 **Quinn**, D. B., ed., *The Port Books or Local Customs Accounts of Southampton for the Reign of Edward IV, vol. 1: 1469–71*. Southampton Rec.Soc., XXXVII, 1938.
3.298 **Rowe**, M. M. and Draisey, J. M., eds., *The Receivers' Accounts of the City of Exeter, 1304–53*, Devon & Cornwall Rec.Soc., XXXII, 1989.
3.299 **Sellers**, Maud, ed., *The York Mercers and Merchant Adventurers, 1356–1917*, Surtees Soc., CXXIX, 1918.
3.300 **Warner**, G. F., ed., *The Libelle of Englyshe Policye (1436)*, 1926. A contemporary tract which emphasised the opportunities which English merchants were missing in South-west Europe. *See* the article by Holmes (3.318).
3.301 **Wilson**, K. P., ed., *Chester Customs Accounts, 1301–1565*, Rec.Soc.Lancs. & Ches., CXI, 1969. *See* the article by Wilson (3.348).

(b) General and miscellaneous

3.302 **Baker**, R. L., 'The establishment of the English wool staple in 1313', *Speculum*, XXXI, 1956, 444–53.
3.303 **Blake**, J. B., 'The medieval coal trade of N. E. England: some fourteenth-century evidence', *Northern H.*, II, 1967, 1–26.

3.304 —— Medieval smuggling in the N. E. Some fourteenth-century evidence', *Arch.Aeliana*, 4th ser., XLIII, 1965, 243–60. On medieval smuggling, *see also* Williams (3.347).

3.305 **Bridbury**, A. R., *England and the Salt Trade in the Later Middle Ages*, 1965.

3.306 **Carus-Wilson**, Eleanora M., 'The ulnage accounts: a criticism', *Ec.H.R.*, II, 1929, 114–23.

3.307 —— 'Trends in the export of English woollens in the fourteenth century', *Ec.H.R.*, 2nd ser., III, 1950, 162–79.

3.308 —— 'The effects of the acquisition and of the loss of Gascony on the English wine trade', *B.I.H.R.*, XXI, 1947, 145–54.

3.309 —— 'The medieval trade of the ports of the Wash', *Med.Arch.*, VI–VII, 1962–3, 182–201.

3.310 —— *The Overseas Trade of Bristol in the Later Middle Ages*, 1937, 2nd ed., 1967. The later edition contains a supplement to the bibliography.

3.311 —— and Coleman, Olive, *England's Export Trade, 1275–1547*, 1963.

3.312 **Childs**, Wendy R., *Anglo-Castilian Trade in the Later Middle Ages*, 1978.

3.313 **Dulley**, A. J. F., 'The level and port of Pevensey in the Middle Ages', *Sussex Arch.Collns.*, CIV, 1966, 26–45.

3.314 **Flenley**, R., 'London and foreign merchants in the reign of Henry VI', *E.H.R.*, XXV, 1910, 644–55.

3.315 **Fraser**, C. M., 'The N. E. coal trade until 1421', *Trans.Durham and Northumberland Architectural and Arch.Soc.*, XI, 1962, 209–20.

3.316 **Fryde**, E. B., *Studies in Medieval Trade and Finance*, 1982. Uses royal and foreign (especially Italian) archives to explore international patterns of trade and finance.

3.317 **Girling**, F. A., *English Merchants' Marks: A Field Survey of Marks Used by Merchants and Tradesmen in England Between 1400 and 1700*, 1964.

3.318 **Holmes**, G. A., 'The Libel of English Policy', *E.H.R.*, LXXVI, 1961, 193–216. *See* Warner, ed.

3.319 **James**, Margaret K., *Studies in the Medieval Wine Trade*, ed. Elspeth Veale, 1971.

3.320 **Kerling**, Nellie J. M., *Commercial Relations of Holland and Zeeland with England from the Late Thirteenth Century to the Close of the Middle Ages*, Leiden, 1954.

3.321 **Kermode**, J. I., 'Merchants, overseas trade and urban decline. York, Beverley and Hull, c.1380–1500', *Northern H.*, 1987, 51–73.

3.322 **Kinsford**, C. L., 'The beginnings of English maritime enterprise in the fifteenth century', *Hist.*, XIII, 1928–9, 97–106, 193–203.

3.323 **Lloyd**, T. H., *The English Wool Trade in the Middle Ages*, 1977. The first full-length treatment of the subject. Looks at the production, internal marketing of and overseas trade in wool. *See also* Power (3.337).

3.324 —— *England and the German Hanse, 1157–1611. A Study of their Trade and Commercial Diplomacy*, 1991.

3.325 **McCusker**, J. J., Jnr., 'The wine prise and medieval mercantile shipping', *Speculum*, XLI, 1966, 279–96.

3.326 **Mace**, F. A., 'Devonshire ports in the fourteenth and fifteenth centuries', *T.R.H.S.*, 4th ser., VIII, 1925, 98–126.

3.327 **Mallett**, M. E., 'Anglo-Florentine commercial relations, 1465–1491', *Ec.H.R.*, 2nd ser., XV, 1962, 250–65.

3.328 **Martin**, G. H., 'Shipments of wool from Ipswich to Calais, 1399–1402', *J.Trans.H.*, II, 1956, 177–81.

3.329 **Mollat**, M., 'Anglo-Norman trade in the fifteenth century', *Ec.H.R.*, XVII, 1947, 143–50.

3.330 **Munro**, J. H. A., *Wool, Cloth and Gold: The Struggle for Bullion in Anglo-Burgundian Trade, 1340–1478*, Brussels and Toronto, 1973.

3.331 **Palais**, H., 'England's first attempt to break the commercial monopoly of the Hanseatic League, 1377–80', *A.H.R.*, LXIV, 1959, 852–65.

3.332 **Postan**, M. M., *Medieval Trade and Finance*, 1973. Collected essays.

3.333 —— 'Credit in medieval trade', *Ec.H.R.*, I, 1927–8, 234–61. Reprinted in Carus-Wilson, ed. (1.326), I, 61–87.

3.334 —— 'Italy and the economic development of England in the Middle Ages', *J.Ec.H.*, XI, 1951, 339–46.

3.335 —— 'The economic and political relations of England and the Hansa from 1400 to 1475', in Power and Postan (3.338), 91–153.

3.336 **Pounds**, N. J. G., 'The ports of Cornwall in the Middle Ages', *Devon and Cornwall Notes and Queries*, XXIII, 1947, 65–73.

3.337 **Power**, Eileen, *The Wool Trade in English*

Medieval History, 1941. An important study of England's major export in the fourteenth and fifteenth centuries.

3.338 —— and Postan, M. M., *Studies in English Trade in the Fifteenth Century*, 1933. Reprinted 1951.

3.339 **Richardson**, H., 'Medieval trading restrictions in the N. E.', *Arch.Aeliana*, 4th ser., XXXIX, 1961, 135–50.

3.340 **Ruddock**, A. A., *Italian Merchants and Shipping in Southampton, 1270–1600*, Southampton Records, Series, 1951.

3.341 —— 'Italian trading fleets in medieval England', *Hist.*, XXIX, 1944, 192–202.

3.342 —— 'John Day of Bristol and the English voyages across the Atlantic before 1497', *Geog.J.*, CXXXII, 1966, 225–32.

3.343 **Sherbourne**, J. W., *The Port of Bristol in the Middle Ages*. Bristol branch of the Hist.Ass., 1965.

3.344 **Simon**, A. L., *The History of the Wine Trade in England*, 3 vols., 1906–9.

3.345 **Veale**, Elspeth M., *The English Fur Trade in the Later Middle Ages*, 1966.

3.346 **Wee**, W. Van der, *The Growth of the Antwerp Market and the European Economy from the Fourteenth to the Sixteenth Centuries*, 3 vols., The Hague, 1963. An important study of an entrepôt which was growing in significance throughout this period.

3.347 **Williams**, N., *Contraband Cargoes: Seven Centuries of Smuggling*, 1959.

3.348 **Wilson**, K. P., 'The port of Chester in the fifteenth century', *T.H.S.L.C.*, 117, 1966, 1–16. *See also* Wilson's edition of the Chester customs accounts (3.301).

3.349 **Wolff**, P., 'English cloth in Toulouse, 1380–1450', *Ec.H.R.*, 2nd ser., II, 1950, 290–4.

(c) The mercantile community

3.350 **Carus-Wilson**, Eleanora M., *The Merchant Adventurers of Bristol in the Fifteenth Century*, 1962.

3.351 —— 'The origins and early development of the Merchant Adventurers' organisation in London as shown in their own medieval records', *EC.H.R.*, IV, 1932, 147–76.

3.352 **James**, Margaret K., 'A London merchant of the fourteenth century',

Ec.H.R., 2nd ser., VIII, 1956, 364–76.

3.353 **Postan**, M. M., 'Partnership in English medieval commerce'. In *Studi in Onore di Armando Sapori*, Milan, 1957, I, 522–49.

3.354 **Thrupp**, Sylvia, *The Merchant Class of Medieval London*, 1948.

3.355 **Ward**, G. F., 'The early history of the Merchant Staplers', *E.H.R.*, XXXIII, 1918, 297–319.

PRICES, PUBLIC FINANCE, USURY AND THE ORIGINS OF BANKING

(a) Prices

3.356 **Ames**, E., 'The sterling crisis of 1337–39', *J.Ec.H.*, XXV, 1965, 496–522.

3.357 **Burnett**, J., *History of the Cost of Living*, 1969. A work of popularisation.

3.358 **Herlitz**, L., 'The medieval theory of the just price', *Scand.Ec.H.R.*, VIII, 1960, 71–76. *See also* Roover (3.363).

3.359 **Hughes**, A., Crump, C. G. and Johnson, C., 'The debasement of the coinage under Edward III', *Ec.J.*, VII, 1897, 185–97.

3.360 **Mate**, Mavis, 'High prices in fourteenth-century England: causes and consequences', *Ec.H.R.*, 2nd ser., XXVIII, 1975, 1–16.

3.361 **Miskimin**, H. A., 'Monetary movements and market structure forces for contraction in fourteenth- and fifteenth-century England', *J.Ec.H.R.*, XXIX, 1964, 470–90.

3.362 **Reddaway**, T. F., 'The King's Mint and Exchange in London, 1343–1543', *E.H.R.*, LXXXII, 1967, 1–23.

3.363 **Roover**, R. de, 'The concept of the just price', *J.E.H.*, XVIII, 1958, 418–34. *See* Herlitz (3.358).

3.364 **Schreiner**, J., 'Wages and prices in England in the later Middle Ages', *Scand.Ec.H.R.*, II, 1954, 61–73. *See also* Feavearyear (2.294), Beveridge (4.887) and Phelps Brown (4.1186).

(b) Public finance

3.365 **Spufford**, P., *Money and its Use in Medieval Europe*, 1988. For background.

3.366 **Bolton**, J. L., 'The City and the Crown, 1456–61', *London J.*, XII, 1986, 11–24.

3.367 **Bryant**, W. N., 'The financial dealings of Edward III with the county communities, 1330–60', *E.H.R.*, LXXXIII, 1968, 760–71.

3.367A **Buck**, M. C., 'The Reform of the Exchequer, 1316–26', *E.H.R.*, XCVIII, 1983, 241–61.

3.368 **Fryde**, E. B., 'Materials for the study of Edward III's credit operations, 1327–48', *B.I.H.R.*, XXIII, 1950, 1–30.

3.369 —— 'Loans to the English Crown, 1328–31', *E.H.R.*, LXIX, 1955, 198–211.

3.370 **MacFarlane**, K. B., 'Loans to the Lancastrian kings: the problem of inducement', *Cambridge H. J.*, IX, 1947, 51–68.

3.371 **Mayhew**, N. J. ed., *Edwardian Monetary Affairs, 1279–1344*, 1977.

3.372 **Ramsay**, J. H., *A History of the Revenues of the Kings of England 1066–1399*, 2 vols., 1925.

3.373 **Steel**, A., *The Receipt of the Exchequer, 1377–1485*, 1954.

3.374 **Unwin**, G., ed., *Finance and Trade under Edward III*, 1918. Reprinted 1962.

3.375 **Virgoe**, R., 'The Parliamentary Subsidy of 1450', *B.I.H.R.*, LV, 1982, 125–39.

3.376 **Willard**, J. F., *Parliamentary Taxes on Personal Property, 1290–1334: A Study in Medieval English Financial Administration*, Cambridge, Mass., 1934.

See also Roseveare (2.310).

(c) Usury and the origins of banking

3.377 **Kermode**, J. I., *Money and Credit in the Fifteenth Century. Some Lessons from Yorkshire*, 1991.

3.378 **McIntosh**, Marjorie K., 'Money lending on the periphery of London, 1300–1600', *Albion*, XX, 1988, 557–71.

3.379 **Nelson**, N., *The Idea of Usury*, Princeton,, N. J., 1949.

3.380 **Noonan**, J. T., *The Scholastic Analysis of Usury*, Cambridge, Mass., 1957.

3.381 **Pugh**, R. B., 'Some medieval moneylenders', *Speculum*, XLIII, 1968, 274–89.

3.382 **Usher**, A. P., 'The origins of banking: the primitive bank of deposit, 1200–1600', *Ec.H.R.*, IV, 1932–4, 399–428.

WAR: ITS IMPACT ON MEDIEVAL SOCIETY AND ECONOMY

3.383 **Allmand**, C. T., 'War and profit in the late Middle Ages', *H.Today*, 15, 1965, 762–69.

3.384 **Barnie**, J., *War in Medieval Society*, 1974.

3.385 **Fowler**, K., ed., *The Hundred Years War*, 1971. A collection of essays.

3.386 **Gillingham**, J., *The Wars of the Roses. Peace and Conflict in Fifteenth-Century England*, 1981.

3.387 **Goodman**, A., *The Wars of the Roses. Military Activity and English Society, 1452–97*, 1981. Argues that the probable effect of the wars was to increase local allegiances at the expense of an embryonic nationalism.

3.388 **Hale**, J. R., 'War and public opinion in the fifteenth and sixteenth centuries', *P.P.*, 22, 1962, 18–33.

3.389 **Haward**, W. I., 'Economic aspects of the Wars of the Roses in East Anglia', *E.H.R.*, XLI, 1926, 170–89.

3.390 **Hay**, D., 'The division of the spoils of war in fourteenth-century England', *T.R.H.S.*, 5th ser., IV, 1954, 91–109.

3.391 **Hewitt**, H. J., *The Organisation of War under Edward III*, 1966.

3.392 **Keen**, M., *The Laws of War in the Late Middle Ages*, 1965.

3.393 **Lander**, J. R., *The Wars of the Roses*, 1965.

3.394 **MacFarlane**, K. B., 'The investment of Sir John Fastolf's profits in war', *T.R.H.S.*, 5th ser., VII, 1957, 91–116.

3.395 —— 'England and the Hundred Years' War', *P.P.*, 22, 1962, 3–13.

3.396 **Miller**, E., 'War, taxation and the English economy in the late thirteenth and early fourteenth centuries'. In Winter (1.332).

3.397 **Morgan**, P., *War and Society in Cheshire, 1277–1403*, Chet.Soc. 3rd ser., XXXIV, 1987.

3.398 **Nef**, J. U., *War and Human Progress*, Cambridge, Mass., 1950.

3.399 **Postan**, M. M., 'Some social consequences of the Hundred Years' War', *Ec.H.R.*, XII, 1942, 7–12.

3.400 —— 'The costs of the Hundred Years' War', *P.P.*, 27, 1964, 34–53.

3.401 **Sherborne**, J. W., 'The Hundred Years' War: The English navy, shipping and manpower, 1369–89', *P.P.*, 37, 1967, 163–75. Comments on the previous article by Postan.

3.402 **Steel**, A., 'The financial background of the Wars of the Roses', *Hist.*, XL, 1955, 18–30.

3.403 **Vale**, M. G. A., ed., *War and Chivalry. Warfare and Aristocratic Culture in England, France and Burgundy at the end of the Middle Ages*, 1981. *See also* Coleman and John (4.42).

LABOUR

(a) General and miscellaneous

3.404 **Cheney**, E. P., 'The disappearance of English serfdom', *E.H.R.*, XV, 1900, 20–38.

3.405 **Clark**, Alice, 'Serfdom on an Essex manor, 1308–78', *E.H.R.*, XX, 1905, 479–83.

3.406 **Dale**, M. K., 'The London silkwomen of the fifteenth century', *Ec.H.R.*, IV, 1932–3, 324–35.

3.407 **Davenport**, F. G., 'The decay of villeinage in East Anglia', *T.R.H.S.*, n.s., XIV, 1900, 123–42.

3.408 **Harvey**, I. M. W., *Jack Cade's Rebellion of 1450*, 1991. Though primarily a political revolt Cade's rebellion – as this study makes clear – had economic ramifications. Using a wide range of sources the author examines the social composition of the revolt.

3.409 **Hatcher**, J., 'English serfdom and villeinage: towards a re-assessment', *P.P.*, 90, 1981, 3–39.

3.410 **Hilton**, R. H., *The Decline of Serfdom in Medieval England*, 1969. (Studies in Economic History pamphlet series.) A

very useful survey with a bibliographical guide.

3.411 **Knoop**, D., and Jones, G. P., 'Masons' wages in medieval England', *Ec.J.Ec.H.Supp.*, II, 1933, 473–99.

3.412 **Ritchie**, Nora, 'Labour conditions in Essex in the reign of Richard II', *Ec.H.R.*, IV, 1932–4, 429–51. Reprinted in Carus-Wilson, ed. (1.326), II, 91–111.

3.413 **Swanson**, H., *Medieval Artisans. An Urban Class in Late Medieval England*, 1989. *See also* Beveridge (2.314–15).

(c) The peasants' revolt

3.414 **Dobson**, R. B., ed., *The Peasants' Revolt of 1381*, 1970. A valuable collection of documents.

3.415 **Fryde**, E. B., *The Peasants' Revolt of 1381*, 1981. Hist.Ass. pamphlet.

3.416 **Harvey**, Barbara, 'Draft letters patent of manumission and pardon for the men of Somerset in 1381', *E.H.R.*, LXXX, 1965, 89–91.

3.417 **Hilton**, R. H., *Bond Men Made Free. Medieval Peasant Movements and the English Rising of 1381*, 1973.

3.418 **Hilton**, R. H. and Aston, T. H. eds., *The English Rising of 1381*, 1984. A collection of conference papers re-assessing the various dimensions of the revolt and drawing on both royal and manorial records. Towns as well as the countryside are discussed.

3.419 —— and Fagan, H., *The English Rising of 1381*, 1950. A Marxist account.

3.420 **Kesteven**, G., *The Peasants' Revolt*, 1964.

3.421 **Lyle**, H. M., *The Peasants' revolt, 1381*, 1950.

3.422 **Ormrod**, W. M., 'The Peasants' Revolt and the government of England', *J.Brit.Studs*, XXIX, 1990, 1–30.

3.423 **Warren**, W. L., 'The Peasants' Revolt of 1381', *H.Today*, 12, 1962, 845–53.

3.424 **Wilkinson**, B., 'The Peasants' Revolt of 1381', *Speculum*, XV, 1940, 12–35.

STANDARDS OF LIVING

3.425 **Aston**, T. H., ed., *Medieval Fish, Fisheries and Fishponds in England*, 1988.

3.426 **Drummond**, J. C. and Wilbraham, Anne, *The Englishman's Food. A History of Five Centuries of English Diet*, 1939, 2nd ed., revised and enlarged by Dorothy Hollingsworth, 1958.

3.427 **Dyer**, C. C., *Everyday Life in Medieval England*, 1994. Focuses on real people in local contexts.

3.428 —— *Standards of Living in the Later Middle Ages. Social Change in England, c.1200–1520*, 1989.

3.429 **Jope**, E. M., 'Cornish houses, 1400–1700'. In E. M. Jope, ed., *Studies in Building History*, 1961, 192–222.

3.430 **McLean**, T., *Medieval English Gardens*, 1989.

3.431 **Mead**, W. E., *The English Medieval Feast*, 1931. Reprinted 1968.

3.432 **Newton**, Stella M., *Fashion in the Age of the Black Price*, 1981.

3.433 **Pantin**, W. A., 'Medieval English town house plans', *Medieval Arch.*, VI–VII, for 1962–3, 202–39.

3.434 —— 'The merchants' houses and warehouses of King's Lynn', *Medieval Arch.*, VI–VII, for 1962–3, 173–81.

3.435 **Thompson**, A. H., 'The English house', in Barraclough, ed. (2.14), 139–78.

3.436 **Wilson**, C. Anne, *Food and Drink in Britain from the Stone Age to Recent Times*, 1973.

3.437 **Wood**, Margaret E., *The English Medieval House*, 1965. *See also* Barley (4.1184), and Ashley (2.163).

GOVERNMENT AND ADMINISTRATION

3.438 **Baker**, R. L., *The English Customs Service, 1307–43. A study of Medieval administration*, Trans. American Phil.Soc., n.s. LVI, Part 6, 1966.

3.439 **Baldwin**, J. F., *The King's Council*, 1913.

3.440 **Booth**, P. H. W., *The Financial Administration of the Lordship and County of Chester, 1272–1377*, Chet.Soc., 1981.

3.441 **Brown**, A. L., 'The authorisation of letters under the Great Seal', *BIHR*, XXXVII, 1964, 16–31.

3.442 **Chibnall**, A. C., *Early Taxation Returns: Taxation of Personal Property in 1332 and Later*, Bucks.Rec.Soc., XIV, 1966.

3.443 **Claydon**, D. J., *The Administration of the County Palatine of Chester, 1442–85*, 1990.

3.444 **Coleman**, Olive, 'The collectors of customs in London under Richard II'. In Hollaender and Kellaway (2.360), 181–94.

3.445 **Fryde**, E. B., 'The English farmers of the customs, 1343–51', *T.R.H.S.*, 5th ser., ix, 1959, 1–17.

3.446 **Given-Wilson**, C., *The Royal Household and the King's Affinity. Service, Politics and Finance in England, 1366–1413*, 1986.

3.447 **Griffiths**, R. A., 'Public and private bureaucracies in England and Wales in the fifteenth century', *T.R.H.S.*, 5th ser., XXX, 1980, 109–30.

3.448 **Hadwin**, J. F., 'The medieval lay subsidies and economic history', *Ec.H.R.*, 2nd ser., XXXVI, 1983, 200–17.

3.449 **Harriss**, G. L., *King, Parliament and Public Finance in Medieval England to 1369*, 1975. Concentrates on political theory rather than on the practicalities of finance.

3.450 **Highfield**, J. R. L. and Jeffs, R., eds., *The Crown and Local Communities in England and France in the Fifteenth Century*, 1982.

3.451 **Hunnisett**, R. F., *The Medieval Coroner*, 1961.

3.452 **James**, T. B., *The Palaces of Medieval England, c.1050–1550. Royalty, Nobility, the Episcopate and their Residences from Edward the Confessor to Henry VII*, 1990.

3.453 **Lapsley**, G. T., *Crown, Community and Parliament in the Later Middle Ages*, 1951.

3.454 **Levett**, Ada E., 'Notes on the Statute of Labourers', *Ec.H.R.*, IV, 1932–4, 77–80.

3.455 **Ormrod**, D. G., 'The English Crown and the customs, 1343–63', *Ec.H.R.*, 2nd ser., XL, 1987, 27–40.

3.456 **Pelham**, R. A., 'The provisioning of the Lincoln parliament of 1301', *Birm.H.J.*, III, 1952, 16–32.

3.457 **Prestwich**, M., 'Victualling estimates for English garrisons in Scotland during the early fourteenth century', *E.H.R.*, LXXXII, 1967, 536–43.

3.458 **Putnam**, Bertha, *The Enforcement of the*

Statute of Labourers, Columbia Studies in History, Economics and Public Law, XXXII, 1908.

3.459 **Steel**, A., 'The collectors of the customs at Newcastle upon Tyne in the reign of Richard II'. In J. C. Davies, ed., *Studies Presented to Sir Hilary Jenkinson*, 1957, 390–413.

TOWNS

For fuller bibliographical details, the reader is referred to Gross (2.339) and to Martin and MacIntyre (2.340).

3.460 **Dilks**, T. B., ed., *Bridgwater Borough Archives, 1445–68*, Somerset Rec.Soc., LX, 1947.

3.461 **Dobson**, R. B., ed., *York City Chamberlains' Account Rolls, 1396–1500*, Surtees Soc., CXCII, 1980.

3.462 **Prestwich**, M., ed., *York Civic Ordinances, 1301*, Borthwick Papers, 49, 1976.

3.463 **Weinbaum**, M., ed., *British Borough Charters, 1307–1660*, 1943. For further source material on this subject, *see* the section on 'Towns and gilds' in Bland, Brown and Tawney (1.303).

3.464 **Bartlett**, J. N., 'The expansion and decline of York in the later Middle Ages', *Ec.H.R.*, 2nd ser., XII, 1965, 17–33.

3.465 **Bonney**, Margaret, *Lordship and the Urban Community. Durham and its Overlords, 1250–1540*, 1990. Shows that the complex seigneurial division of Durham contributed to its lack of a communal identity and to its slow economic development.

3.466 **Bridbury**, A. R., 'English provincial towns in the later Middle Ages', *Ec.H.R.*, 2nd ser., XXXIV, 1981, 1–24.

3.467 **Britnell**, R. H., *Growth and Decline in Colchester, 1300–1525*, 1986. Sees the period 1350–1414 as the growth period followed by one of change and decay.

3.468 —— 'The towns of England and northern Italy in the early fourteenth century', *Ec.H.R*, 2nd ser., XLIV, 1991, 21–35.

3.469 **Butler**, R. M., *Medieval York*, 1982.

3.470 **Carus-Wilson**, Eleanora M., *The Expansion of Exeter at the Close of the Middle Ages*, 1963.

3.471 **Cronne**, H. A., *The Borough of Warwick in the Later Middle Ages*, Dugdale Soc.Occ. Papers, 10, 1951.

3.472 **Dobson**, R. B., 'Admissions to the Freedom of the City of York in the Later Middle Ages', *Ec.H.R.*, XXVI, 1973, 1–22.

3.473 —— 'Yorkshire towns in the late fourteenth century', *Thoresby Soc.Pub.*, LIX, 1985, 1–21.

3.474 **Dulley**, A. J. F., 'Four Kent towns at the end of the Middle Ages', *Arch.Cantiana*, LXXXI, 1966, 95–108.

3.475 **Finberg**,H. P. R., 'The borough of Tavistock'. In Hoskins and Finberg (4.118), 172–97.

3.476 **Fowler**, J., *Medieval Sherborne*, 1952.

3.477 **Gill**, C., 'Coventry in the fifteenth century'. In Gill, *Studies in Midland History*, 1930, 3–85.

3.478 **Goldberg**, P. J. P., 'Urban identity and the poll taxes of 1377, 1379, and 1381', *Ec.H.R.*, 2nd ser., XLIII, 1990, 6–11.

3.479 **Gottfried**, R. S., *Bury St Edmunds and the Urban Crisis, 1290–1539*, Princeton, NJ., 1982.

3.480 **Hilton**, R. H., 'Some problems of urban real property in the Middle Ages'. In Feinstein (4.1161), 326–37.

3.481 **Holt**, R., and Rosser, G., eds., *The English Medieval Town. A Reader in English Urban History, 1200–1540*, 1990. Twelve reprinted essays with a bibliographical introduction. General chapters deal with the development of boroughs, provincial culture and suburban growth. London, Gloucester, Exeter, Coventry, and Stratford upon Avon receive separate chapters.

3.482 **Keane**, D., 'Medieval London and its region', *London J.*, XIV, 1989, 99–111.

3.483 **Lobel**, M. D., ed., *Atlas of Historic Towns. London from Prehistoric Times to c.1520*, 1989.

3.484 **MacDonall**, K., *Medieval London Suburbs*, 1978.

3.484A **Mills**, A. D., 'Chester ceremonial: re-creation and recreation in an English medieval town', *Urban H. Yearbook*, 1991, 1–19.

3.485 **Phythian-Adams**, C., *Desolation of a City. Coventry and the Urban Crisis of the Late Middle Ages*, 1979.

3.486 **Rigby**, S. H., 'Late medieval urban prosperity: the evidence of the lay subsidies', *Ec.H.R.*, 2nd ser., XXXIX, 1986, 411–16.

3.487 —— 'Urban decline in the later Middle Ages. The reliability of the non-statistical evidence'. *Urban H. Yearbook*, 1984, 45–60.

3.488 —— 'Urban society in early fourteenth century England: the evidence of the lay subsidies', *B. J. Rylands Lib.*, LXXII, 1990, 169–84.

3.489 **Robertson**, D. W., *Chaucer's London*, N. Y., 1968.

3.490 **Rörig**, F.,*The Medieval Town*, English trans., 1967. For background.

3.491 **Rosser**, G., *Medieval Westminster, 1200–1500*, 1989.

3.492 **Rubin**, Miri, *Charity and Community in Medieval Cambridge*, 1987. Addresses the contributions made by the urban community as well as by individuals to the relief of poverty.

3.493 **Salusbury**, G. T., *Street Life in Medieval England*, 1939.

3.494 **Saul**, A., 'English towns in the late Middle Ages: the case of Great Yarmouth', *J.Med.H.*, VIII, 1982, 75–88.

3.495 **Smith**, B. S.,*A History of Malvern*, 1964.

3.496 **Tittler**, R., 'The end of the Middle Ages in the English country town', *Sixteenth Century J.*, XVIII, 1987, 471–88.

3.497 —— 'Late medieval urban prosperity', *Ec.H.R.*, 2nd ser., XXXVII, 1984, 551–55.

3.498 **Tout**, T. F., 'The beginnings of a modern capital: London and Westminster in the fourteenth century'. In Tout's *Collected Papers*, III, 1934, 249–75.

3.499 **Walker**, V. W., 'Medieval Nottingham: a topographical study', *Trans. Thoroton Soc.*, LXVII, 1963, 28–45.

3.500 **Woledge**, G., 'The medieval borough of Leeds', *Thoresby Soc.*, XXXVII, 1945, 288–309.

See also Williams (2.378).

COMMUNICATIONS AND INTERNAL TRADE

(a) Inland transport and communications

3.501 **Barley**, M. W., 'Lincolnshire rivers in the Middle Ages', *Lincs.Architectural and Arch.Soc.*, n.s., I, 1940, 1–21.

3.502 **Hill**, Mary C., *The King's Messengers, 1199–1377*, 1961.

3.503 **Massachaele**, J., 'Transport costs in medieval England', *Ec.H.R.*, 2nd ser., XLVI, 1993, 266–79.

3.504 **Willard**, J. F., 'The use of carts in the fourteenth century', *Hist.*, n.s., XVII, 1932, 246–50.

3.505 —— 'Inland transportation in England during the fourteenth century', *Speculum*, I, 1926, 361–74.

(b) Markets and fairs

3.506 **Addison**, W., *English Fairs and Markets*, 1953.

3.507 **Goodfellow**, P., 'Medieval markets in Northamptonshire', *Northants. P.P.*, VII, 1987, 305–24.

3.508 **Oliver**, J. G. 'Churches and wool: a study of the wool trade in fifteenth-century England', *H.Today*, I, 1951, 33–40.

3.509 **Pelham**, R. A., 'The early wool trade in Warwickshire and the rise of the merchant middle class', *Trans. Birmingham Arch.Soc.*, LXIII, for 1939–40, 1944, 41–62.

3.510 —— 'The cloth markets of Warwickshire during the Middle Ages', *Trans. Birmingham Arch.Soc.*, LXVI, for 1945 and 1946, 1950, 31–41.

3.511 —— 'The trade relations of Birmingham during the Middle Ages', *Trans. Birmingham Arch.Soc.*, LXII, for 1938, 1943, 32–40.

ALIEN IMMIGRANTS IN ENGLAND

3.512 **Allmand**, C. T., 'A note on denization in fifteenth-century England', *Medievalia et Humanistica*, XVII, 1966, 127–8.

3.513 **Beardwood**, Alice, *Alien Merchants in England, 1350–77, their Legal and Economic Position*, Medieval Academy of America Monographs, 3, Cambridge, Mass., 1931.

3.514 —— 'Alien merchants and the English crown in the later fourteenth century', *Ec.H.R.*, II, 1929–30, 229–60.

3.515 —— 'Mercantile antecedents of the English naturalisation laws', *Medievalia et Humanistica*, XVI, 1964, 64–77.

3.516 **Cohn-Sherbrook**, O., 'Medieval Jewish persecution in England: the Canterbury programs in perspective', *Southern H.*, III, 1981, 23–38.

3.517 **Holmes**, G. A., 'Florentine merchants in England, 1346–1436', *Ec.H.R.*, 2nd ser., XIII, 1960, 193–208.

3.518 **Lloyd**, T. H., *Alien Merchants in England in the High Middle Ages*, 1982. A partly statistical study. The author breaks new ground in his treatment of the role of the Italians.

3.519 **Kerling**, Nellie, J. M., 'Aliens in the county of Norfolk, 1436–1485', *Norfolk Arch.*, XXXIII, 1963, 200–15.

3.520 **Ruddock**, A. A., 'Alien hosting in Southampton in the fifteenth century', *Ec.H.R.*, XVI, 1946, 30–7.

3.521 **Rutledge**, E., 'Immigration and population growth in early fourteenth-century Norwich: evidence from the tithing roll', *Urban H. Yearbook*, 1988, 15–30.

3.522 **Thrupp**, Sylvia, 'A survey of the alien population of England in 1440', *Speculum*, XXXII, 1957, 262–73.

3.523 —— 'Aliens in and around London in the fifteenth century'. In Hollaender and Kellaway (2.360), 251–72.

RELIGION

3.524 **Aston**, Margaret, 'Lollardy and Literacy', *Hist.*, LXII, 1977, 347–71.

3.525 —— 'Lollardy and sedition, 1381–1431', *P.P.*, 17, 1960, 1–44.

3.526 **Buck**, M., *Politics, Finance and the Church in the Reign of Edward II*, 1983.

3.527 **Davies**, R. G., 'Lollardy and locality', *TRHS.*, 6th ser., I, 1991, 191–212.

3.528 **Duffy**, E., *The Stripping of the Altars. Traditional Religion in England, c.1400–1580*, 1992. A substantial but not altogether convincing account of late medieval religious practice and the impact of the Reformation. *See* the review by David Aers in *Literature & History*, 3.2, 1994.

3.529 **Gilchrist**, H., *The Church and Economic Activity in the Middle Ages*, 1969.

3.530 **Hall**, D. J., *The English Medieval Pilgrimage*, 1965.

3.531 **Hudson**, A., *Lollards and their Books*, 1985.

3.532 **Owen**, Dorothy M., *Church and Society in Medieval Lincolnshire*, 1971.

3.533 **Plumb**, D., 'The social and economic spread of rural Lollardy: a reappraisal', *Studs. Church H.*, XXIII, 1986, 111–30.

3.534 **Southern**, R. W., *Western Society and the Church in the Middle Ages*, 1970.

3.535 **Sumpton**, J., *Pilgrimage. An Image of Medieval Religion*, 1975.

3.536 **Swanson**, R. N., *Church and Society in Late Medieval England*, 1989.

3.537 **Thompson**, A. H., *The English Clergy and their Organisation in the Later Middle Ages*, 1947.

3.538 —— *The Later Lollards, 1414–1520*, 1965.

3.539 —— 'Piety and charity in late medieval London', *J.Eccles.H.*, XVI, 1965, 178–95.

3.540 **Vale**, M. G. A., *Piety, Charity and Literacy among the Yorkshire Gentry, 1370–1480*, Borthwick Papers, 50, 1976.

3.541 **White**, L., *Medieval Religion and Technology. Collected Essays*, Berkeley, Cal., 1978.

THE MONASTERIES

3.542 **Postan**, M. M. and Brooke, C. N. L., eds., *Carte Nativorum. A Peterborough Abbey Cartulary of the Fourteenth Century*, Northants. Rec.Soc., XX, 1950.

3.543 **Dobson**, R. B., *Durham Priory 1400–1450*, 1973.

3.544 **Donnelly**, J. S., 'Changes in the grange economy of English and Welsh Cistercian abbeys, 1300–1540', *Traditio*, X, 1954, 399–458.

3.545 **Finberg**, H. P. R., *Tavistock Abbey; A Study in the Social and Economic History of Devon*, 1951, 2nd ed., 1969, with minor corrections.

3.546 **Furniss**, D. A., 'The monastic contribution to medieval medical care: aspects of an earlier welfare state', *J. Royal College of General Practitioners*, LXIX, 1968, 244–50.

3.547 **Greene**, J. P., *Medieval Monasteries*, 1992.

3.548 **Hockey**, S. T., *Quarr Abbey and its Lands, 1132–1631*, 1970.

3.549 **Knowles**, D., *The Religious Orders in England*, vol. II: *The End of the Middle Ages*, 1955. Vol. I (2.432), is also relevant for the early part of this period.

3.550 **Lindley**, E. S., 'Kingswood Abbey, its lands and mills', *Trans. Bristol and Gloucs.Arch.Soc.*, LXXIII, 1955, 115–91, and *ibid.*, LXXIV, 1956, 36–59.

3.551 **Platt**, C., *The Monastic Grange in Medieval England: A Re-assessment*, 1969. An interesting and original study which makes use of the techniques of the archaeologist.

See also Cowley (6.77), Dickinson (2.422), and Williams (6.79).

EDUCATION AND LEARNING

For source material on this subject, *see* Sylvester (4.1439a).

3.552 **Alexander**, M. V. C., *The Growth of English Education, 1348–1648. A Social and Cultural History*, 1990. Based chiefly on secondary sources and heavily biographical in approach the book provides a general survey of developments in schools and universities and their changing social complexion in this period.

3.553 **Bender**, T., ed., *The University and the City: From Medieval Origins to the Present*, 1988. Oxford.

3.554 **Brand**, P., 'Courtroom and schoolroom: the education of lawyers in England prior to 1400', *Hist.Research*, LX, 1987, 147–65.

3.555 **Catto**, J. I., *The History of the University of Oxford. I: The Early Oxford Schools*, 1985. Includes chapters on endowments and on the estates of Merton College. *See also II: The Late Middle Ages*, 1992.

3.556 **Clough**, C. H., ed., *Profession, Vocation and Culture in Later Medieval England. Essays dedicated to the memory of A. R. Myers*, 1982.

3.557 **Cobban**, A. B., *The English Medieval Universities. Oxford and Cambridge to c.1500*, 1989. Re-assesses the nature of university education in the Middle Ages, the social composition of the student body, college resourcing, and the quality of teaching.

3.558 **Coleman**, J., *Medieval Readers and Writers*, 1981.

3.559 **Emden**, A. B., 'Learning and education'. In Poole (2.61), II, 515–40.

3.559a **Griffiths**, J. and Pearsall, D., eds., *Book Production and Publishing in Britain, 1375–1475*, 1989.

3.560 **Leach**, A. F., *The Schools of Medieval England*, 1915, 2nd ed., 1916. But *see* Parry (3.572) and Simon (3.576).

3.561 **Leader**, D. R., *A History of the University of Cambridge. I: the University to 1546*, 1989.

3.562 **Leff**, G., *Paris and Oxford Universities in the Thirteenth and Fourteenth Centuries: An Institutional and Intellectual History*, 1968.

3.563 **Lytle**, G. F., 'Patronage patterns and Oxford colleges, c.1300–c.1530' in Stone (4.1481), 111–49.

3.564 **McMahon**, C., *Education in Fifteenth-century England*, Baltimore, 1947.

3.565 **Moran**, Jo Ann, *Education and Learning in the City of York, 1300–1560*, Borthwick Papers, 55, 1979.

3.566 ——*The Growth of English Schooling, 1340–1548. Learning Literacy and Laicization in pre-Reformation York diocese*,

Princeton, N. J., 1985. Asks whether there was an Educational Revolution in the sixteenth century.

3.567 **Morgan**, J. A., *The Growth of English Schooling, 1340–1548*, 1985.

3.568 **Orme**, N., *Education and Society in Medieval and Renaissance England*, 1989.

3.569 —— *English Schools in the Middle Ages*, 1973.

3.570 —— *Education in the West of England, 1066–1548*, 1977.

3.571 —— *From Childhood to Chivalry: the Education of the English Kings and Aristocracy, 1066–1530*, 1985.

3.572 **Parry**, A. W., *Education in England in the Middle Ages*, 1920. A corrective to Leach (3.560).

3.573 **Rashdall**, H., *The Universities of Europe in the Middle Ages*, eds. F. M. Powicke and A. B. Emden, 3 vols., 1936. Vol. 3 deals with the English universities.

3.574 **Robson**, J. A., *Wyclif and the Oxford Schools*, 1961.

3.575 **Scattergood**, V. G. and Sherbourne, J. W., *English Court Culture in the Later Middle Ages*, 1983.

3.576 **Simon**, Joan, *The Social Origins of English Education*, 1971. A useful exploration of the medieval social background.

3.577 **Thompson**, J. W., *The Literacy of the Laity in the Middle Ages*, Berkeley, Calif., 1939.

3.579 **Barron**, Caroline and Sutton, Anne, eds., *Medieval London Widows*, 1994. A blend of general chapters and of individual portraits drawing chiefly on London probate records.

3.580 **Bennett**, Judith M., *Women in the Medieval English Countryside. Gender and Household in Brigstock before the Plague*, 1987.

3.581 **Goldberg**, P. J. P., *Women, Work and Life Cycle in a Medieval Economy. Women in York and Yorkshire, c.1300–1520*, 1992.

3.582 —— *Woman is a Worthy Wight. Women in English Society, c.1200–1500*, 1992.

3.583 **Jordan**, W. C., *Women and Credit in PreIndustrial Countries and Developing Societies*, 1993. Extraordinarily broad in its coverage, the book takes in early and medieval Europe and colonial and post colonial sub Saharan Africa and the Caribbean.

3.584 **McSheffrey**, S., 'Women and Lollardy: a reassessement', *Canadian J.H.*, XXVI, 1991, 199–224.

3.585 **Penn**, S. A. C., 'Female wage earners in late fourteenth-century England', *Ag.H.R.*, XXXV, 1987, 1–14.

3.586 **Power**, Eileen, *Medieval Women*, 1975.

3.587 **Rossiaud**, J., *Medieval Prostitution*, 1988.

3.588 **Shahar**, S., *The Fourth Estate. A History of Women in the Middle Ages*, 1983.

3.589 **Stenton**, Doris, *The Englishwoman in History*, 1957.

WOMEN

3.578 **Adams**, C., ed., *From Workshop to Warfare. The Lives of Medieval Women*, 1983.

4

ENGLAND 1500–1700

GENERAL WORKS

(a) Bibliographies

4.1 **Davies**, G., ed., *Bibliography of British History: Stuart Period 1603–1714*, 1928, 2nd ed., revised by Mary F. Keeler, 1970.

4.2 **Grose**, C. L., ed., *A Select Bibliography of British History 1660–1760*, Chicago, 1939. Reprinted N. Y., 1967.

4.3 **Levine**, M., ed., *Bibliographical Handbook: Tudor England 1485–1603*, 1968.

4.4 **Morrill**, J. S., *Seventeenth-Century Britain, 1603–1714*, 1980.

4.5 **Read**, C., ed., *Bibliography of British History: Tudor Period 1485–1603*, 1933, 2nd ed. 1959.

4.6 **Sachse**, W. L., ed., *Bibliographical Handbooks: Restoration England 1660–89*, 1971.

4.7 **Walcott**, R., 'The later Stuarts 1660–1741: significant work of the last twenty years (1939–59)', *A.H.R.*, LXVII, 1962, 352–70.

(b) Source material

4.8 **Alcock**, N. W., ed., *Warwickshire Glazier and London Skinner, 1532–55. The Account Book of Peter Temple and Thomas Heritage*, 1981.

4.9 **Beer**, E. S. de, *The Diary of John Evelyn*, 6 vols., 1955.

4.10 **Browning**, A., ed., *English Historical Documents, 1660–1714*, 1952. Part 3 on public finance, Part 4 on the Church and Part 5 on local government and social life are particularly useful.

4.11 **Burton**, Kathleen M., ed., *A Dialogue between Reginald Pole and Thomas Lupset by Thomas Starkey*, 1948.

4.12 **Byrne**, Muriel St. C., ed., *The Lisle Letters*, 6 vols., 1981. Correspondence of the period 1533–42.

4.13 **Dewar**, Mary, ed., *A Discourse of the Commonwealth of this Realm of England*, Washington, D.C., 1970. The editor argues persuasively that the author of the *Discourse* with Sir Thomas Smith.

4.14 **Dunham**, W. H. and Pargellis, S., eds., *Complaint and Reform in England 1436–1714*, N. Y., 1938. A miscellaneous collection of contemporary writings.

4.15 **Edelen**, G., ed., *William Harrison's Description of England*, Folger Shakespeare Library, 1968.

4.16 **Emmison**, F. G., *Elizabethan Life. Home, Work and Land*, 1976.

4.17 **Latham**, R. and Matthews, W. M. eds., *The Diary of Samuel Pepys. A New and Complete Transcription*, 9 vols., 1970–6.

4.18 **Macfarlane**, A., ed., *The Diary of Ralph Josselin, 1616–83*, 1976. A mine of information about rural economy and society as well as about religious affairs. *See also* Macfarlane (4.238).

4.19 **More**, Sir Thomas, *Utopia*. Numerous editions are available, for example the translation by P. Turner, 1967, and the

49

scholarly edition by E. Surtz and J. H. Hexter, New Haven, Conn., 1965.

4.20 **Morris**, C., ed., *The Journeys of Celia Fiennes*, 1947, 3rd ed., 1982.

4.21 **Phillips**, C. B., ed., *The Correspondence of Sir John Lowther of Whitehaven, 1693–98*, 1982.

4.22 **Spalding**, Ruth, ed., *The Diary of Bulstrode Whitelocke, 1605–75*, 1989. Impeccably prepared edition of the diary of a well known seventeenth-century landowner, lawyer, Parliamentarian, and ambassador. A companion volume – *Contemporaries of Bulstrode Whitelocke* – conveniently offers a biographical dictionary of individuals mentioned in the text.

4.23 **Tawney**, R. H. and Power, Eileen, *Tudor Economic Documents*, 3 vols., 1924. The standard collection.

4.24 **Thirsk**, Joan and Cooper, J. P., eds., *Seventeenth-century Economic Documents*, 1972. An invaluable source book. Sections on economic crises, agriculture, industries, inland and coastal trade and communications, overseas trade, finance and the coinage, aliens, wealth, population and land: some contemporary statistics.

4.25 **Williams**, C. H., ed., *English Historical Documents, 1485–1558*, 1967. Part 2 on the land, Part 3 on the commonweal, Part 5 on religion and Part 6 on daily life in town and country are particularly useful from the economic and social point of view.

4.26 **Wilson**, J. D., *Life in Shakespeare's England*, 1911. Several times reprinted.

4.27 **Wilson**, Thomas, *The State of England, 1600*, ed. F. J. Fisher, *Camden Miscellany*, XVI, 1936. *See also* Bland, Brown and Tawney (1.303), Part 2 of which, 231–476, covers the period 1485–1600.

(c) General surveys

4.28 **Appleby**, Joyce O., *Economic Thought and Ideology in Seventeenth-Century England*, Princeton, N. J., 1978.

4.29 **Ashley**, M., *Life in Stuart England*, 1964.

4.30 **Aston**, T. H., ed., *Crisis in Europe, 1560–1660*, 1965. A collection of reprinted articles from *P.P.*, several of which are directly concerned with English economic and social history in the period.

4.31 **Aylmer**, G. E., 'The meaning and definition of "property" in seventeenth-century England', *P.P.*, 86, 1980, 87–97.

4.32 **Beier**, A. L., Cannadine, D., and Rosenheim, J. M., eds., *The First Modern Society. Essays in English History in Honour of Lawrence Stone*, 1989. Sixteen essays grouped in three principal sections: (1) the Crown, aristocracy and gentry, (2) power and social relations, (3) urban society and social change.

4.32a **Bindoff**, S. T., Hurstfield, J. and Williams, C. H., eds., *Elizabethan Government and Society. Essays presented to Sir John Neale*, 1961.

4.33 **Braddick**, M., 'State formation and social change in early modern England: a problem stated and approaches suggested', *Soc.H.*, XVI, 1991, 1–18.

4.34 **Burke**, P., ed., *Economy and Society in Early Modern Europe. Essays from Annales*, 1971. For background.

4.35 **Byrne**, Muriel St. C., *Elizabethan Life in Town and Country*, 1925, 8th ed., revised, 1961.

4.36 **Chalklin**, C. W. and Havinden, M. A., eds., *Rural Change and Urban Growth: Essays in Regional History in Honour of W. G. Hoskins*, 1974.

4.37 **Chambers**, J. D., *Population, Economy and Society in Pre-industrial England*, 1972.

4.38 **Clark**, P., Smith, A. G. R., and Tyacke, N., eds., *The English Commonwealth. Essays in Politics and Society presented to Joel Hurstfield*, 1979.

4.38a **Clay**, C., *Economic Expansion and Social Change. England 1500–1700. I: People, Land and Towns. II: Industry, Trade and Government*, 1984.

4.39 **Clarkson**, L. A., *The Pre-industrial Economy in England, 1500–1750*, 1971. A concise analysis.

4.40 **Coleman**, D. C., 'Technology and economic history, 1500–1750', *Ec.H.R.*, 2nd ser., XI, 1958–9, 506–14.

4.41 —— *The Economy of England, 1450–1750*, 1977.

4.42 —— and John, A. H., eds., *Trade, Government and Economy in Pre-industrial England. Essays presented to F. J. Fisher*, 1976. A wide-ranging collection which includes esays on war and late medieval society, English cereal exports, 1660–1765, the sumptuary laws, urban development in the sixteenth and seventeenth centuries.

4.43 **Cooper**, J. P., *Land, Men and Beliefs*, 1983. Prefaced by an appreciation of the author, the volume brings together thirteen of Cooper's characteristically trenchant essays on sixteenth and seventeenth century economic history.

4.44 **Coward**, B., *The Stuart Age. A History of England 1603–1714*, 1980. Contains good general surveys of society and the economy in the period 1603–40 and of the co-existence of change and continuity later in the century.

4.45 —— *Social Change and Continuity in Early Modern England, 1550–1750*, 1988.

4.46 **Cornwall**, J., *Wealth and Society in Early Sixteenth Century England*, 1988. Has chapters dealing with status and wealth, the structure of personal wealth, landowning, the Commonweal, labourers and the poor.

4.47 **Davis**, J. C., *Utopia and the Ideal Society. A Study of English Utopian Writing, 1516–1700*, 1981. Includes some discussion of the lesser writers such as Samuel Gott as well as leading figures like More, Bacon, Winstanley, Chamberlen and Bellers.

4.48 **De Vries**, J., *The Economy of Europe in an Age of Crisis, 1600–1750*, 1976. For background.

4.49 **Dodd**, A. H., *Life in Elizabethan England*, 1961.

4.50 **Earle**, P., ed., *Essays in European Economic History, 1500–1800*, 1974.

4.51 **Everitt**, A. M., *Change in the Provinces: The Seventeenth Century*, University of Leicester, Department of English Loc.H.Occ. Papers, 2nd ser., 1, 1969.

4.52 **Fisher**, F. J., ed., *Essays in the Economic and Social History of Tudor and Stuart England in Honour of R. H. Tawney*, 1961. An invaluable collection of essays.

4.53 —— 'The sixteenth and seventeenth centuries: the dark ages in English economic history?', *Economica*, n.s., XXIV, 1957, 2–18. In Harte, ed. (1.124).

4.54 **Goring**, J., 'Social change and military decline in mid-Tudor England', *Hist.*, LX, 1975, 185–97.

4.55 **Hartwell**, R. M., 'Economic growth in England before the Industrial Revolution: some methodological issues', *J.Ec.H.*, XXIX, 1969, 13–31. In Hartwell (5.68).

4.56 **Hill**, C., *The Century of Revolution, 1603–1714*, 1961. 2nd ed. 1981. A stimulating textbook, untypical in its method of separating the narrative and analytical chapters.

4.57 —— *Reformation to Industrial Revolution: A Social and Economic History of Britain, 1530–1780*, 1967.

4.58 —— *Change and Continuity in Seventeenth-century England*, 1975. A stimulating collection of (mainly reprinted) essays.

4.59 **Holderness**, B. A., *Pre-industrial England. Economy and Society, 1500–1750*, 1976.

4.60 **Hoskins**, W. G., *The Age of Plunder. The England of Henry VIII, 1500–47*, 1976.

4.61 **Hurstfield**, J. and Smith, A. G. R., *Elizabethan People: State and Society*, 1972.

4.62 **Ives**, E. W., Knecht, R. J., and Scarisbrick, J. J., eds., *Wealth and Power in Tudor England, Essays presented to S. T. Bindoff*, 1978. A valuable collection which includes essays on 'Cardinal Wolsey and the Common Weal', 'Episcopal Palaces, 1535–1600', 'The East and West in Early Modern London', and on 'Antwerp and London'.

4.63 **James**, M., *Society, Politics and Culture. Studies in Early Modern England*, 1986. The author's collected essays, some of them very long ones – the Lincolnshire rebellion of 1536, (188–269) and 'English politics and the concept of honour, 1485–1642, (308–415).

4.64 **Jones**, W. R. D., *The Tudor Commonwealth, 1529–1559*, 1970.

4.65 **Kindleberger**, C. P., 'The economic crisis of 1619 to 1623', *J.Ec.H.*, LI, 1991, 149–75.

4.66 **Lachmann**, R., *From Manor to Market. Structural Change in England, 1536–1640*, Madison, Wis., 1987. A provocative re-exploration of England's transition from Feudalism to Capitalism.

4.67 **Lennard**, R. V., ed., *Englishmen at Rest and Play, 1558–1714*, 1931.

4.68 **Letwin**, W., *The Origins of Scientific Economics: English Thought, 1660–1776*, 1963.

4.69 **Levack**, B. P., *The Formation of the British State. England, Scotland, and the Union, 1603–1707*, 1987. Shows that economics were subordinate to political considerations.

4.70 **Macfarlane**, A., *The Origins of English Individualism*, 1978. Strident revisionism. see White, S. D. and Vann, R. T., 'The invention of English individualsm: Alan Macfarlane and the modernisation of pre-modern England', *Soc.H.*, VIII, 1983, 345–64.

4.71 **Mathew**, D., *The Social Structure in Caroline England*, 1948.

4.72 —— *The Age of Charles I*, 1951.

4.73 **Miskimin**, H. A., 'Agenda for early modern economic history', *J.Ec.H.*, XXXI, 1971, 172–83.

4.74 **Moir**, Esther A. L., *The Discovery of Britain: The English Tourists 1540–1840*, 1964.

4.75 **Nef**, J. U., 'War and economic progress 1540–1640', *Ec.H.R.*, XII, 1942, 13–38.

4.76 **Ogg**, D., *England in the Age of Charles II*, 2 vols., 1934, 2nd ed., 1955. A useful survey of the reign. Good bibliography.

4.77 —— *England in the Reigns of James II and William III*, 1955.

4.78 **Palliser**, D. M., *The Age of Elizabeth. England under the Later Tudors, 1547–1603*, 1983.

4.79 —— 'Tawney's century: Brave New World or Malthusian Trap', *Ec.H.R.*, 2nd ser., XXXV, 1982, 339–53.

4.80 **Pennington**, D. H. and Thomas, K., eds., *Puritans and Revolutionaries. Essays in Seventeenth-Century History presented to Christopher Hill*, 1978. The *festschrift* includes important essays on 'The Alehouse and the Alternative Society', 'Puritans and Poor Relief', 'The Puritans and Adultery', and on 'Social Mobility and Business Enterprise in Seventeenth-Century England'.

4.81 **Plumb**, J. H., *The Growth of Political Stability in England, 1675–1725*, 1967. A full discussion of the changing social foundations of politics.

4.82 **Ramsay**, P., *Tudor Economic Problems*, 1963. The best short introduction to sixteenth-century English economic history.

4.83 **Rich**, E. E. and Wilson, C., eds., *Cambridge Economic History of Europe IV: The Economy of Expanding Europe in the Sixteenth and Seventeenth Centuries*, 1967. The contributions are of varying usefulness.

4.84 **Rowse**, A. L., *The England of Elizabeth: The Structure of Society*, 1951.

4.85 **Russell**, C., *The Crisis of Parliaments: English History 1509–1660*, 1971. Mainly political, although there is some discussion of economic factors.

4.86 **Salzman**, L. F., *England in Tudor Times: An Account of its Social Life and Industries*, 1926.

4.87 **Seaver**, P. S., ed., *Seventeenth-Century England. Society in an Age of Revolution*, 1976. Reprints essays by Stone, Thirsk, Coleman, and Plumb with an editorial introduction.

4.88 **Sharpe**, J. A., *Early Modern England. A Social History, 1550–1760*, 1987. An excellent social history textbook, organised into three major sections (1) family, community and nation (2) social hierarchy and social change (3) spiritual and mental worlds.

4.89 **Smith**, A. G. R., ed., *The Reign of James VI and I*, 1973. A collection of essays dealing with various aspects of the reign.

4.90 **Stoye**, J. W., *English Travellers Abroad, 1604–67: Their Influence in English Society and Politics*, 1952. revised ed., 1989.

4.91 **Supple**, B. E., 'Economic history and economic underdevelopment', *Canadian J.Ec. and Pol.Science*, 27, 1961, 460–78.

4.92 **Thirsk**, Joan, *Economic Policy and Projects. The Development of a Consumer Society in Early Modern England*, 1978.

4.93 **Thomas**, K., 'Age and authority in early modern England', *Proc.Brit.Acad.*, LXII, 1977, 205–48.

4.94 **Williams**, P., *Life in Tudor England, 1964.*

4.95 **Williamson**, J. A., *The Tudor Age*, 1953. Good on maritime affairs.

4.96 **Wilson**, C., *England's Apprenticeship, 1603–1763*, 1965. Good bibliography.

4.97 —— *Economic History and the Historian. Collected Essays*, 1969. The main part of this useful book consists of reprints of the author's articles on the seventeenth century.

4.98 **Wrightson**, K., *English Society, 1580–1680*, 1982. A systematic, up-to-date social history which stresses the co-existence of change and continuity and the considerable social and local variations.

4.99 **Youings**, Joyce, *Sixteenth-century England*, 1984. Looks at the sixteenth century as a whole and is sceptical about placing undue reliance on statistics. The growth of the land market, changes in farming arrangements and trade, manufacture and towns are among the subjects discussed.

(d) Regional studies

4.100 **Beckett**, J. V., *Coal and Tobacco. The Lowthers and the Economic Development of West Cumberland, 1660–1760*, 1981.

4.101 —— *The East Midlands from AD 1000*, 1988.

4.102 **Blanchard**, I., 'Commercial crisis and change: trade and the industrial economy of the North East, 1509–32', *Northern H.*, VIII, 1973, 65–85.

4.103 **Bouch**, C. M. L. and Jones, G. P., *A Short Economic and Social History of the Lake Counties, 1500–1830*, 1961.

4.104 **Brent**, C. E., *The Maritime Economy of Eastern Sussex*, 1980.

4.105 **Chalklin**, C. W., *Seventeenth-century Kent*, 1965.

4.106 **Clark**, P., *English Provincial Society from the Reformation to the Revolution. Religion, Politics, and Society in Kent, 1500–1640*, 1977.

4.107 **Durston**, C. G., 'London and the provinces: the association between the capital and the Berkshire gentry of the seventeenth century', *Southern H.*, III, 1981, 39–54.

4.108 **Edwards**, A. C., *English History from Essex Sources, 1550–1750*, 1952.

4.109 **Finberg**, H. P. R., ed., *Gloucestershire Studies*, 1957.

4.110 **Gregson**, N., 'Tawney re-visited: custom and the emergence of capitalist class relations in N.E. Cumbria, 1600–1830', *Ec.H.R*, 2nd ser., XLII, 1989, 18–42.

4.111 **Hey**, D., *An English Rural Community: Myddle Under the Tudors and Stuarts*, 1974.

4.112 **Hirst**, D., 'Local affairs in seventeenth century England', *H.J.*, XXXII, 1989, 437–48.

4.113 **Hodgett**, G. A. J., *Tudor Lincolnshire*, 1975.

4.114 **Holmes**, C., *Seventeenth-Century Lincolnshire*, 1980.

4.115 **Hoskins**, W. G., *The Midland Peasant. The Economic and Social History of a Leicestershire Village*, 1957. A study of Wigston Magna.

4.116 —— *Provincial England: Essays in Social and Economic History*, 1963.

4.117 —— ed., *Essays in Leicestershire History*, 1950.

4.118 —— and Finberg, H. P. R., *Devonshire Studies*, 1952.

4.119 **James**, M. E., *Family, Lineage, and Civil Society. A Study of Society, Politics and Mentality in the Durham Region 1500–1640*, 1974.

4.120 **Johnson**, J., *Tudor Gloucestershire*, 1985.

4.121 **Marcombe**, D., *The Last Principality. Politics, Religion and Society in the Bishopric of Durham, 1494–1660*, 1987.

4.122 **Rollinson**, D., *The Local Origins of Modern Society. Gloucestershire, 1500–1800*, 1992. Concentrates on three principal themes: (1) demographic change (2) the decline of feudalism (3) the development of industrial capitalism. Much is said about the cultural identity of the region.

4.123 **Robson**, R., *The English Highland Clans. Tudor Responses to a Medieval Problem*, 1989.

4.124 **Rowlands**, Marie B., *The West Midlands from AD 1000*, 1987.

4.125 **Rowse**, A. L., *Tudor Cornwall*, 1941, 2nd ed., 1969.

4.126 **Rudden**, B., *The New River. A Legal History*, 1985. Examines the complex commercial structure and litigious early history of the company created to augment London's water supply.

4.127 **Slater**, T. R. and Jarvis, P. J., *Field and Forest. An Historical Geography of Warwickshire and Worcestershire*, 1982.

4.128 **Styles**, P., *Studies in Seventeenth-Century West Midlands History*, 1978. Includes essays on Worcester, Henley in Arden, Bewdley, and on the social structure of Kineton Hundred in the reign of Charles II.

4.129 **Tupling**, G. H., *The Economic History of Rossendale*, Chet.Soc., n.s., 87, 1927.

4.130 **Walker**, F., *The Historical Geography of South-West Lancashire before the Industrial Revolution*, Chet.Soc., n.s., 103, 1939.

4.131 **Watts**, S. J., *From Border to Middle Shire: Northumberland, 1586–1625*, 1975. Though primarily political, there is a full discussion of the distinctive social and economic environment of this turbulent region.

4.132 **Whetter**, J., *Cornwall in the Seventeenth Century. An Economic Survey of Kernow*, 1974.

4.133 **Wrightson**, K. and Levine, D., *Poverty and Piety in an English Village. Terling, 1525–1700*, 1979.

(e) Foreigners' views of England

A useful bibliographical introduction to the subject is:

4.134 **Fussell**, G. E., *The Exploration of England: A Selected Bibliography of Travel and Topography, 1570–1815*, 1935.

4.135 **Ballam**, H. and Lewis, R., eds., *The Visitors' Book: England and the English as Others Have Seen Them, 1500–1950*, 1950.

4.136 **Bülow**, G. von, ed., 'Journey through England and Scotland made by Leopold von Wedel in the years 1584 and 1585', *T.R.H.S.*, n.s, IX, 1895, 223–70.

4.137 —— 'Diary of the journey of Philip Julius, Duke of Stettin-Pomerania through England in the year 1602', *T.R.H.S.*, n.s., VI, 1897, 1–67.

4.138 **Letts**, M., *As the Foreigner Saw Us*, 1935. A survey of foreigners' impressions from c.1500 to c. 1830. Bibliography, 263–71.

4.139 **Malfatti**, C. V., ed., *Two Italian Accounts of Tudor England*, Barcelona, 1953.

4.140 **Palmer**, R. E., ed., *French Travellers in England, 1600–1900: Selections From Their Writings*, 1960.

4.141 **Rye**, W. B., ed., *England as Seen by Foreigners in the Days of Elizabeth and James I*, 1865. Reprinted 1967.

4.142 **Salter**, E. G., *Tudor England Through Venetian Eyes*, 1930.

4.143 **Scott**, W. D. R., *German Travellers in England, 1400–1800*, 1953.

4.144 **Smith**, E., *Foreign Visitors in England*, 1889.

4.145 **Sneyd**, C. A., ed., *A Relation, or Rather a True Account of the Island of England About the Year 1500*, Camden Soc., o.s., XXXVII, 1847.

4.146 **Williams**, C., ed., *Thomas Platter's Travels in England, 1599*, 1937.

4.147 **Wilson**, F. M., *Strange Island: Britain Through Foreign Eyes, 1395–1940*, 1955. See also Thirsk (4.322), xxix-xxxvi.

POPULATION

(a) Sources

4.148 **Allison**, K. J., ed., 'An Elizabethan village census', *B.I.H.R.*, XXXVI, 1963, 92–103.

4.149 **Cornwall**, J., 'An Elizabethan census', *Recs. of Bucks.*, XVI, 1959, 258–73.

4.150 **Faraday**, M. A., ed., *The Westmorland Protestation Returns 1641–42*, Cumb. and West.Antiq. and Arch.Soc. Tract Ser., XVII, 1971.

4.151 **Glass**, D. V., ed., *London Inhabitants Within the Walls, 1695*, London Rec.Soc., II, 1966.

4.152 **King**, Gregory, *Natural and Political Observations Upon the State and Condition of England* (1696), in G. Chalmers, ed., *Estimate of the Comparative Strength of Great Britain*, 1782, new ed., 1802.

4.153 **Levine**, D., 'The reliability of parochial registration and the representativeness of family reconstitution', *Pop.Studs.*, XXX, 1976, 107–22.

4.154 **Munby**, L., ed., *Hertfordshire Population Statistics, 1563–1801*, 1964.

4.155 **Petty**, William, *Political Arithmetick, or a Discourse Concerning the Extent and Value of Lands, People, Buildings, Husbandry, etc.*, 1690. The work is included in E. A. Aitken, ed., *Later Stuart Tracts* (An English Garner), 1903, 1–66.

4.156 **Whiteman**, Anne, ed., *The Compton Census of 1676. A Critical Edition*, 1986.

(b) General

4.157 **Appleby**, A. B., *Famine in Tudor and Stuart England*, 1978. A case study of Cumberland and Westmorland.

4.158 **Blanchard**, I., 'Population change, enclosure and the early Tudor economy', *Ec.H.R.*, 2nd ser., XXIII, 1970, 427–45.

4.159 **Bonar**, J., *Theories of Population from Raleigh to Arthur Young*, 1931. Reprinted 1966.

4.160 **Bonfield**, L., Smith, R., and Wrightson, K., eds., *The World We Have Gained. Histories of Population and Social Structure*, 1986. A *festschrift* for Peter Laslett containing essays which range chronologically from the fourteenth to the nineteenth century and which deal with migration, family patterns, household structure, marriage, illegitimacy, and inheritance.

4.161 **Cornwall**, J., 'English population in the early sixteenth century', *Ec.H.R.*, 2nd ser., XXIII, 1970, 32–44.

4.162 **Crawford**, Patricia, 'Attitudes to menstruation in seventeenth-century England', *P.P.*, 91, 1981, 47–73.

4.163 **Eccles**, Audrey, *Obstetrics and Gynaecology in Tudor and Stuart England*, 1982.

4.164 **Eshleman**, M. K., 'Diet during pregnancy in the sixteenth and seventeenth centuries', *J.H.Medicine & Allied Sciences*, XXX, 1975, 23–39

4.165 **Flinn**, M. W., *The European Demographic System,1500–1820*, 1981.

4.166 **Gittings**, Clare, *Death, Burial, and the Individual in Early Modern England*, 1984.

4.167 **Glass**, D. V. and Eversley, D. E. C., eds., *Population in History*, 1965. An important collection of comparative studies. On English population the book contains 'Two papers on Gregory King' by Professor Glass, 159–220.

4.168 **Habakkuk**, H. J., 'The economic history of modern Britain', *J.Ec.H.*, XVIII, 1958, 486–501.

4.169 **Hair**, P. E. H., 'Bridal pregnancy in rural England in earlier centuries', *Pop.Studs.*, XX, 1966, 233–43.

4.170 **Hollingsworth**, T. H., *Historical Demography*, 1969. A valuable discussion of the present state of historical demography and of the available sources. Excellent bibliography.

4.171 —— *Demography of the British Peerage*, Supplement to *Pop.Studs.*, XVIII, 1964.

4.172 **Houlbrooke**, R., ed., *Death, Ritual and Bereavement*, 1989.

4.173 **Houston**, R. A., *The Population History of Britain and Ireland, 1500–1750*, 1992. A compact discussion dealing with sources and methods, structures and trends, marriage and fertility, migration and death.

4.174 **Kerridge**, E., 'The returns of the Inquisition of Depopulation', *E.H.R.*, LXX, 1955, 212–28

4.175 **Laslett**, P., *The World We Have Lost*, 1965, 2nd ed., 1971.

4.176 —— Oosterveen, Karla, and Smith, R. M., eds., *Bastardy and its Comparative History*, 1980. Includes two chapters on illegitimacy and its context in early modern England.

4.177 **Levine**, D., *Reproducing Families. The Political Economy of English Population History*, 1987.

4.178 **MacDonald**, M. and Murphy, T. R., *Sleepless Souls. Suicide in Early Modern England*, 1990. Based on an examination of 20,000 cases, the study considers the incidence of suicide in this period, its significance, social reception and treatment under the law.

4.179 **Olney**, Martha L., 'Fertility and the standard of living in early modern England: in consideration of Wrigley and Schofield', *J.Ec.H.*, XLIII, 1983, 71–79.

4.180 **Patten**, J., 'The Hearth Taxes 1662–89', *Loc.Pop.Studs.*, 7, 1971, 14–27.

4.181 **Quaife**, G. R., *Wanton Wenches and Wayward Wives. Peasants and Illicit Sex in Early Seventeenth Century England*, 1979.

4.182 **Schnucker**, R. V., 'Elizabethen birth control and puritan attitudes', *J.Interdis.H.*, V, 1975, 655–67.

4.183 **Spengler**, J. J., 'Demographic factors and early modern economic development', *Daedalus*, XCVII, 1968, 433–46.

4.184 **Thirsk**, Joan, *Sources of Information on Population 1500–1760, and Unexplored Sources in Local Records*, 1965.

4.185 **Tucker**, G. S. L., 'English pre-industrial population trends', *Ec.H.R.*, XVI, 1963, 205–18.

4.186 **Utterström**, G., 'Climatic fluctuations and population problems in early modern history', *Scand.Ec.H.R.*, III, 1955, 3–37.

4.187 **Wrigley**, E. A., ed., *An Introduction to English Historical Demography*, 1966.

4.188 —— *Population and History*, 1969. Useful general survey. Good bibliography.

4.189 —— 'Family limitation in pre-industrial England', *Ec.H.R.*, XIX, 1966, 82–109. An important article using the Colyton evidence.

4.190 —— 'Mortality in pre-industrial England: the example of Colyton, Devon, over three centuries', *Daedalus*, XCVII, 1968, 246–80. *See also* F. J. Fisher (4.893).

(c) Internal population mobility and emigration

(i) INTERNAL MOBILITY

4.191 **Buckatzch**, E. J., 'The constancy of local populations and migration in England before 1800', *Pop.Studs.*, V, 1951–2, 62–9.

4.192 —— 'Places of origin of a group of immigrants into Sheffield, 1624–1799', *Ec.H.R.*, 2nd ser., II, 1950, 303–6.

4.193 **Clark**, P., 'Migration in England during the late seventeenth and early eighteenth centuries', *P.P.*, 83, 1979, 57–90.

4.194 —— and Souden, D., eds., *Migration and Society in Early Modern England*, 1987. A useful collection which includes essays on vagrancy, labour migration in East Anglia, social adaptation in English towns, and indentured servant migration to North America.

4.195 **Cornwall**, J., 'Evidence of population mobility in the seventeeth century', *B.I.H.R.*, XL, 1967, 143–52. Plays down the extent of internal mobility. But the type of source used – the deposition books of an ecclesiastical court – places a strict limit on the force of the argument.

4.196 **Patten**, J., *Rural–Urban Migration in Pre-Industrial England*, 1973.

4.197 **Pelham**, R. A., 'The immigrant population of Birmingham, 1686–1726', *Trans. Birmingham Arch.Soc.*, LX for 1936, 1940, 45–86.

4.198 **Rich**, E. E., 'The population of Elizabethan England', *Ec.H.R.*, 2nd ser., II, 1950, 247–65. Draws attention to the value of muster rolls as a source for the study of population mobility.

4.199 **Spufford**, P., 'Population movement in seventeenth-century England', *Loc.Pop.Studs.*, 4, 1970, 41–50.

4.200 **Wareing**, J., 'Changes in the geographical distribution of the recruitment of apprentices to the London companies, 1480–1750', *J.H.Geog.*, VI, 1980, 241–50.

(ii) EMIGRATION

4.201 **Banks**, C. E. and Morison, S. E., 'Persecution as a factor in emigration', *Proc. Massachusetts Hist.Soc.*, LXIII, 1930, 136–54.

4.202 **Bridenbaugh**, C., *Vexed and Troubled Englishmen, 1590–1642*, 1968. An important book. Its footnotes are a mine of information.

4.203 **Campbell**, Mildred, 'Of people either too few or too many. The conflict of opinion on population and its relation to emigration'. In W. A. Aiken and B. D. Henning, eds., (4.1209), 169–202.

4.204 **Crouse**, N. M., 'Causes of the great migration, 1630–40', *New England Quarterly*, V, 1932, 3–36.

4.205 **Newton**, A. P., *The Colonizing Activities of English Puritans*, 1914. Reprinted 1966.

4.206 **Salerno**, A., 'The social background of seventeenth-century emigration to America', *J.Brit.Studs.*, XIX, 1979, 31–52. *See also* Knorr (4.784) and Quinn (4.787), listed under the section on *Colonisation*.

(d) Disease

4.207 **Appleby**, A. B., 'Nutrition and disease. The case of London, 1550–1750', *J.Interdis.H.*, VI, 1975, 1–22.

4.208 **Beier**, Lucinda, *Sufferers and Healers. The Experience of Illness in Seventeenth Century England*, 1987. An interesting study of the different branches of the medical profession and of unofficial providers of remedies. The book also focuses on patients, especially women.

4.209 **Bell**, W. G., *The Great Plague in London in 1665*, 1924, 2nd rev. ed., 1951.

4.210 **Clarkson**, L. A., *Death, Disease and Famine in Pre-Industrial England*, 1975.

4.211 **Copeman**, W. S. C., *Doctors and Disease in Tudor Times*, 1960.

4.212 **Debus**, A. G., ed., *Medicine in Seventeenth-century England*, Berkeley, Calif., 1974.

4.213 **Levy**, H., 'The economic history of sickness and medical benefit before the Puritan Revolution' *Ec.H.R.*, XIII, 1943, 42–57.

4.214 —— 'The economic history of sickness and medical benefit since the Puritan Revolution', *Ec.H.R.*, XIV, 1944, 135–60.

4.215 **MacDonanald**, M., *Mystical Bedlam: Madness, Anxiety, and Healing in Seventeenth-Century England*, 1981. Based principally on the case-notes of an early seventeenth-century Buckinghamshire physician.

4.216 **Moore**, J. S., 'Jack Fisher's flu: a virus

still virulent', *Ec.H.R.*, 2nd ser., XLVII, 1994, 359–61. *See Fisher* (4.893) and Zell (4.228).

4.217 **Mullett,** C. F., 'Some neglected aspects of plague medicine in sixteenth-century England', *Scientific Monthly*, 44, 1937, 325–37.

4.218 —— 'The plague of 1603 in England', *Annals Med.H.*, n.s., 9, 1937, 230–47.

4.219 *The Plague Reconsidered. A New Look at its Origins and Effects in Sixteenth and Seventeenth Century England*, 1977. Deals primarily with the local history of plague with useful chapters on Bristol, Colyton and Eyam.

4.220 **Porter,** R., ed., *Patients and Practitioners. Lay Perceptions of Medicine in Pre-Industrial Society*, 1986. Essays stressing a new style patient oriented approach to the history of medicine.

4.221 **Roberts,** R. S., 'The personnel and practice of medicine in Tudor and Stuart England, Parts 1 and 2', *Medical H.*, 6, 1962, 363–82, *ibid.*, 8, 1964, 217–34.

4.222 **Slack,** P. A., 'The disappearance of plague an alternative view', *Ec.H.R.*, 2nd ser., XXXIV, 1981, 469–76.

4.223 —— *The Impact of Plague in Tudor and Stuart England*, 1985. Divided into three principal sections dealing with attitudes to plague, its chronology between 1485 and 1665, and with the social responses to its impact.

4.224 **Walter,** J. and Schofield, R., eds., *Famine, Disease and the Social Order in Early Modern Society*, 1989.

4.225 **Webster,** C., ed., *Health, Medicine and Mortality in the Sixteenth Century*, 1979.

4.226 *Wilshore*, J. E. O., 'Plague in Leicester, 1558–1665', *Trans.Leics.Arch.Soc.*, XLIV, for 1968–9, 1970, 45–71.

4.227 **Wilson,** F. P., *The Plague in Shakespeare's London*, 1927.

4.228 **Zell,** M., 'Fisher's flu and Moore's probates: quantifying the mortality crisis of 1556–60', *Ec.H.R.*, 2nd ser., XLVII, 1994, 354–358.

(e) The family

4.229 **Anderson,** M., *Approaches to the History of the Western Family, 1500–1914*, 1980.

4.230 **Carlton,** C., 'The widow's tale: male myths and female reality in sixteenth- and seventeenth-century England',

Albion, X, 1978, 118–27.

4.231 **Davies,** Kathleen M., 'The sacred condition of equality: how original were puritan doctrines of marriage?', *Soc.H.*, V, 1977, 563–80. *See also* Morgan (4.241) and Schücking (4.246).

4.232 **Goody,** J., Thirsk, Joan, and Thompson, E. P., eds., *Family and Inheritance. Rural Society in Western Europe, 1200–1800*, 1976. An indispensable volume which includes essays on England by Cecily Howell, Margaret Spufford, Joan Thirsk, J. P. Cooper and E. P. Thompson.

4.233 **Houlbrooke,** R., ed., *English Family Life, 1576–1716. An Anthology from Diaries*, 1988. A useful selection of source material though socially slanted towards the elite.

4.234 —— *The English Family, 1450–1700*, 1984. A well documented study utilising a wide variety of sources. Organised thematically around the institution of marriage and around relations between husband and wife and between parents and children.

4.235 **Laslett,** P., *Family Life and Illicit Love in Earlier Generations*, 1977.

4.236 **Leites,** E., 'The duty to desire: love, friendship, and sexuality in some puritan theories of marriage', *J.Soc.H.*, XV, 1982, 383–408.

4.237 **Levine,** D., *Family Formation in an Age of Nascent Capitalism*, 1977.

4.238 **Macfarlane,** A., *The Family Life of Ralph Josselin, a Seventeenth-century Clergyman: An Essay in Historical Anthropology*, 1970. *See also* (4.18).

4.239 **Michel,** R. H., 'English attitudes towards women, 1640–1700', *Canadian J.H.*, XIII, 1978, 35–60.

4.240 **Moran,** G. F., and Vinovskis, M. A., 'The puritan family and religion: a critical reappraisal', *William & Mary Quart.*, XXXIX, 1982, 29–63.

4.241 **Morgan,** E. S., *The Puritan Family*, Boston, Mass., 1944. Based on New England evidence.

4.242 **O'Day,** Rosemary, *The Family and Family Relationships, 1500–1900. England, France and the United States of America*, 1994. A comparative study with a pronounced methodological emphasis.

4.243 **Outhwaite,** R. B., ed., *Marriage and Society. Studies in the Social History of Marriage*, 1981.

4.244 **Pollock,** Linda A., *Forgotten Children.*

Parent–Child Relations, 1500–1900, 1983.

4.245 **Powell**, C. L., *English Domestic Relations, 1487–1653*, N. Y., 1917.

4.246 **Schücking**, L. L., *The Puritan Family: A Study from the Literary Sources*, 1929, English trans., 1969.

4.247 **Searle**, A., ed., *Barrington Family Letters, 1628–32*, Camden new ser., XXVIII, 1983.

4.248 **Slater**, Miriam, 'The weightiest business. Marriage in an upper gentry family in seventeenth-century England', *P.P.*, 72, 1976, 25–54.

4.249 **Smith**, R. M., ed., *Land, Kinship and Life Cycle*, 1985. Looks at the structure of kinship groups in England from the early modern period to 1850.

4.250 **Stone**, L., *The Family, Sex and Marriage in England, 1500–1800*, 1977. *See* the extended review by C. Hill, *Ec.H.R.*, 2nd ser., XXXI, 1978, 450–63.

4.251 —— *Broken Lives. Separation and Divorce in England, 1660–1857*, 1993.

4.252 —— *Road to Divorce. England, 1530–1987*, 1990. Considers the moral and cultural values displayed in attitudes to marital breakdown and the ways in which the law was manipulated and circumvented.

4.253 —— *Uncertain Unions. Marriage in England, 1660–1753*, 1992. A companion volume to *Road to Divorce* consisting of case studies drawn principally from the records of the Court of Arches.

4.254 **Thirsk**, Joan, 'Younger sons in the seventeenth century', *Hist.*, LIV, 1969, 358–78.

4.255 **Wrightson**, K., 'Infanticide in early seventeenth-century England', *Loc.Pop.Studs.*, XV, 1975, 10–22. *See also* the essay by Malcolmson on this subject in Cockburn (4.1009), *also* Hill (4.1383), ch. 13 on 'The spiritualization of the household', 443–81.

(f) Local and regional studies

4.256 **Brodskey**, V., *Mobility and Marriage. The Family and Kinship in Early Modern London*, 1989.

4.257 **Cornwall**, J., 'A Tudor Domesday. The musters of 1522', *J.Soc. Archivists*, III, 1965, 19–24.

4.258 —— 'The people of Rutland in 1522', *Trans.Leics.Arch.Soc.*, XXXVII, 1961–2,

7–28.

4.259 **Cowgill**, Ursula M., 'Life and death in the sixteenth century in the city of York', *Pop.Studs.*, XXI, 1967, 56–62.

4.260 **Dymond**, D. P., 'Suffolk and the Compton Census of 1676', *Suffolk R.*, III, 1966, 103–18.

4.261 **Eversley**, D. E. C., 'A survey of population in an area of Worcestershire, 1660–1850', *Pop.Studs.*, X, 1957, 253–79.

4.262 **Finlay**, R., *Population and Metropolis. The Demography of London, 1580–1650*, 1981.

4.263 **Fritze**, R. H., 'The role of the family and religion in the local politics of early Elizabethan England: the case of Hampshire in the 1560's', *H.J.*, XXV, 1982, 267–88.

4.264 **Glass**, D. V., 'Notes on the demography of London at the end of the seventeenth century', *Daedalus*, XCVII, 1968, 581–92.

4.265 **Gould**, J. D., 'The inquisition of depopulation of 1607 in Lincolnshire', *E.H.R.*, LXVII, 1952, 392–6.

4.266 **Harding**, V., 'The population of London, 1500–1700. A review of the published evidence', *London J.*, XV, 1990, 111–28.

4.267 **Hodgson**, R. I., *Demographic Trends in County Durham, 1560–1801*, 1978.

4.268 **Hoskins**, W. G., 'The population of an English village, 1086–1801: a study of Wigston Magna', in Hoskins (4.116), 181–208.

4.269 **Howson**, W. G., 'Plague, poverty and population in parts of N. W. England, 1580–1720', *T.H.S.L.C.*, CXII, 1960, 29–56.

4.270 **Husbands**, C., 'Regional change in a pre-industrial economy: wealth and population in England in the sixteenth and seventeenth centuries', *J.Hist.Geog.*, XIII, 1987, 345–59.

4.271 **James**, F. G., 'The population of the diocese of Carlisle in 1676', *Trans.Cumb. and West.Antiq. and Arch.Soc.*, LI, 1951, 137–41.

4.272 **Jones**, P. E. and Judges, A. V., 'London's population in the late seventeenth century', *Ec.H.R.*, VI, 1935, 45–63.

4.273 **Laslett**, P. and Harrison, J., 'Clayworth and Cogenhoe'. In H. F. Bell and R. L. Ollard, eds., *Historical Essays 1600–1750 presented to David Ogg*, 1962, 157–84. A pioneer study of English population and social structure using seventeenth-century census material.

4.274 **McKinley**, R. A., *Norfolk Surnames in the*

Sixteenth Century, University of Leicester, Department of English Loc.H., Occ.Papers, 2nd ser., II, 1969.

4.275 **Marshall**, Lydia M., *The Rural Population of Bedfordshire, 1671–1921*, Beds.Hist.Rec.Soc., XVI, 1934.

4.276 —— 'The levying of the Hearth Tax, 1662–88', *E.H.R.*, LI, 1936, 628–46.

4.277 **Morison**, E. J. D., 'The Hearth Tax in Chester', *J. Chester and N. Wales Architectural, Arch, and H.Soc.*, XXXVI, 1946, 31–43.

4.278 **Palliser**, D. M., 'Epidemics in Tudor York', *Northern H.*, VII, 1973, 45–63.

4.279 **Parker**, L. A., 'Depopulation returns for Leicestershire in 1607', *Trans.Leics.Arch.Soc.*, XXIII, 1947, 231–91.

4.280 **Patten**, J., 'Population distribution in Norfolk and Suffolk during the sixteenth and seventeenth centuries', *T.I.B.G.*, LXV, 1975, 45–65.

4.281 **Pickard**, R., *The Population and Epidemics of Exeter in Pre-Census Times*, 1947.

4.282 **Ralph**, E., and Williams, M. E., *The Inhabitants of Bristol in 1696*, Bristol Rec.Soc., XXV, 1968.

4.283 **Rogers**, C. D., *The Lancashire Population Crisis of 1623*, 1975.

4.284 **Slater**, Miriam, *Family Life in the Seventeenth Century. The Verneys of Claydon House*, 1984. A social study of this well documented family which examines the intricacies of its structure, interpersonal attitudes and relations.

4.285 **Smith**, C. T., 'Population'. In *V.C.H. Leicestershire*, ed. W. G. Hoskins and R. A. McKinley, III, 1955, 129–75.

4.286 **Spufford**, Margaret, 'The significance of the Cambridgeshire Hearth Tax', *Proc. Cambridge Antiq.Soc.*, LV, 1962, 53–64.

4.287 **Styles**, P., 'A census of a Warwickshire vilage in 1698', *Birm.H.J.*, III, 1951, 33–51.

4.288 **Wrathmell**, S., 'Village depopulation in the seventeenth and eighteenth centuries: examples from Northumberland', *Post.Med.Arch.*, XIV, 1980, 113–26.

AGRICULTURE AND RURAL SOCIETY

(a) Sources

4.289 **Bankes**, Joyce and Kerridge, E., eds., *The Early Records of the Bankes Family at Winstanley*, Chet.Soc., 3rd ser., 21, 1973. Contains the Memoranda book of James Bankes together with accounts and rentals.

4.290 **Eyre**, Adam, *A Dyurnall, or Catalogue of all my Accions and Expenses, etc*. In *Yorkshire Diaries*, Surtees Soc., LXV, 1877.

4.291 **Fussell**, G. E., ed., *Robert Loder's Farm Accounts 1610–1620*, Camden Soc., 3rd ser., LIII, 1936.

4.292 **Hartley**, Dorothy, ed., *Thomas Tusser: His Good Points of Husbandry*, 1931.

4.293 **Lodge**, Eleanor, *The Account Book of a Kentish Estate, 1616–1704* (Godminton), 1927.

4.294 **Robinson**, C. B., ed., *Rural Economy and Account Books of Henry Best of Elmeswell in the East Riding*, Surtees Soc., XXXIII, 1857.

4.295 **Skeat**, W. W., ed., *Fitzherbert's Book of Husbandry*, English Dialect Soc., XIII, 1882. *See also* Dewar (4.13) listed above. Additional source material will be found in Tawney and Power (4.23), Vol. 1, Section 1, 'Agriculture and rural society', 1–90 and Vol. III, section 1, 'Enclosures and the countryside', 12–81.

(b) General works

4.296 **Allison**, K. J., 'Flock management in the sixteenth and seventeenth centuries', *Ec.H.R.*, 2nd ser., XI, 1959, 98–112.

4.297 **Aston**, T. H. and Philpin, C. H. E., eds., *The Brenner Debate. Agrarian Class Stucture and Economic Development in Pre-industrial Europe*, 1985.

4.298 **Beckett**, J. V., 'The peasant in England: a case of terminological confusion', *Ag.H.R.*, XXXII, 1984, 113–24.

4.299 **Bridbury**, A. R., 'Sixteenth-century farming', *Ec.H.R.*, 2nd ser., XXVII, 1974, 538–56.

4.300 **Butlin**, R. A., *The Transformation of Rural England, c. 1580–1800. A Study in*

Historical Geography, 1982. Excellent bibliography, 68–74.

4.301 **Chartres**, J. and Hey, D., eds., *English Rural Society, 1500–1800. Essays in Honour of Joan Thirsk*, 1990. A significant collection which includes chapters on the use of particular sources, on land tenures, agricultural practice, rural industries, and on the structure of rural society.

4.302 **Clark**, G., 'Yields per acre in English agriculture, 1250–1860: evidence from labour inputs', *Ec.H.R.*, 2nd ser., XLIV, 1991, 445–60.

4.303 **Cooper**, J. P., 'In search of agrarian capitalism', *P.P.*, 80, 1978, 20–65.

4.304 **Fox**, H. S. A. and Butlin, R. A., eds., *Change in the Countryside. Essays on Rural England, 1500–1900*, 1979. A miscellaneous collection which includes essays on enclosure, mechanisation, and farmers' associations.

4.305 **Fussell**, G. E., *The English Dairy Farmer, 1500–1900*, 1966.

4.306 —— 'Agriculture from the Restoration to Anne', *Ec.H.R.*, IX, 1938–9, 68–74.

4.307 —— 'Crop nutrition in Tudor and Stuart England', *Ag.H.R.*, III, 1955, 95–106.

4.308 —— 'Crop nutrition in the late Stuart Age, 1660–1714', *Annals of Science*, XIV, 1958, 173–84.

4.309 —— and K. R., *The English Countrywoman: A Farmhouse Social History, 1500–1900*, 1953.

4.310 —— and K. R., *The English Countryman: His Life and Works, 1500–1900*, 1955.

4.311 **Hoskins**, W. G., 'Harvest fluctuations and English economic history, 1480–1619', *Ag.H.R.*, XII, 1964, 28–46, reprinted in Minchinton (1.330), I, 93–115.

4.312 —— 'Harvest fluctuations and English economic history, 1620–1759', *Ag.H.R.*, XVI, 1968, 13–31. Two useful articles which emphasise the crucial importance of the harvest in the pre-industrial economy.

4.313 **Jones**, E. L., ed., *Agriculture and Economic Growth in England, 1650–1815*, 1967. A useful collection of reprinted articles with an introduction and bibliography.

4.314 **Kain**, R., 'Tithe as an index of pre-industrial agricultural production', *Ag.H.R.*, XXVII, 1979, 73–81.

4.315 **Kerridge**, E., *Agrarian Problems in the Sixteenth Century and After*, 1969. An attack on Tawney (4.321). Half the book consists of documents.

4.316 —— 'Ridge and furrow in agrarian history', *Ec.H.R.*, 2nd ser., IV, 1951, 14–36.

4.317 **Kussmaul**, Anne, *A General View of the Rural Economy of England, 1538–1840*, 1990.

4.318 **Lennard**, R. V., 'English agriculture under Charles II', *Ec.H.R.*, IV, 1932, 23–45. Reprinted in Minchinton (1.330), I, 161–85.

4.319 **Leslie**, M. and Raylor, T., eds., *Culture and Cultivation in Early Modern England. Writing and the Land*, 1992. An interdisciplinary collection of essays which looks at the content, form and style of early modern agrarian writings.

4.320 **Overton**, M., 'Weather and agricultural change in England, 1660–1739', *Ag.H.*, LXIII, 1989, 77–88.

4.321 **Tawney**, R. H., *The Agrarian Problem in the Sixteenth Century*, 1912. Reprinted, N. Y., 1967 with an introduction by Lawrence Stone. A landmark in the writing of agrarian history.

4.322 **Thirsk**, Joan, ed., *The Agrarian History of England and Wales IV: 1500–1640*, 1967. Excellent bibliography. Includes chapters on the farming regions, on landowning and labour, agricultural improvement, rural housing, and marketing.

4.323 —— ed., *The Agrarian History of England and Wales. V: 1640–1750. Part One: Regional Farming Systems*, 1984; Part Two: *Agrarian Change*, 1985. A monumental study primarily grounded on local and regional studies which comprise the first volume. The study offers re-examinations of agricultural prices and profits, landlords and estate management, agricultural policy, marketing, and agricultural innovation and rural building. *See* the review by H. J. Habakkuk in *Ec.H.R.*, 2nd ser., XL, 1987, 281–96.

4.324 —— *Agricultural regions and Agrarian History in England, 1500–1750*, 1987. A compact distillation of volumes IV and V of the *Agrarian History of England and Wales*.

4.325 —— *The Rural Economy of England. Collected Essays*, 1984. Twenty one essays dealing with the sources for agrarian history, common fields and enclosures, agricultural practice, land sales and rural industrialisation.

4.326 —— ed., *Land Church and People. Essays Presented to Professor H. P. R. Finberg*, 1970. The collection contains an important and wide-ranging article by Dr Thirsk on 'Seventeenth-century agriculture and social change', 148–77, which attempts to place agricultural developments within the framework of the economic crises of the seventeenth century.

4.327 **Thomas**, K., *Man and the Natural World. Changing Attitudes in England, 1500–1800*, 1983. Analyses different aspects of the process described by the author as the 'dethronement of man'. Conservation, urbanisation, cultivation, hunting, garden cities and vegetarianism are among the impressively wide range of topics considered.

4.328 **Webber**, R., *The Early Horticulturalists*, 1968. *See also* Barnes (5.1215) and Russell (5.616), and Trow-Smith (3.142).

(c) Miscellaneous

4.329 **Chilton**, D., 'Land measurement in the sixteenth century', *Trans.Newcomen Soc.*, XXXI, 1957–9, 111–29.

4.330 **Fussell**, G. E., *The Old English Farming Books from Fitzherbert to Tull*, 1947.

4.331 —— *The Farmer's Tools, 1500–1900: The History of British Farm Implements, Tools, and Machinery Before the Tractor Came*, 1952.

4.331a **Hainsworth**, D. R., *Stewards, Lords and People. The Estate Steward and his World in Later Stuart England*, 1992.

4.332 **Hallam**, H. E., 'Fen by-laws of Spalding and Pinchbeck', *Trans. Lincs. Architectural & Arch.Soc.*, X, 1967, 40–56. Includes the text of by-laws of 1591.

4.333 **Hammersley**, G., 'The Crown Woods and their exploitation in the sixteenth and seventeenth centuries', *B.I.H.R.*, XXX, 1957, 136–61.

4.334 **Hoyle**, R. W., 'Lords, tenants and tenant right in the sixteenth century: four studies', *Northern H.*, XX, 1984, 38–63.

4.335 **Overton**, M., 'Estimating crop yields from probate inventories: an example from East Anglia, 1585–1735', *J.Ec.H.*, XXXIX, 1979, 363–78.

4.336 **Thick**, M., 'Garden seeds in England before the late eighteenth century. I: seed growing', *Ag.H.R.*, XXXVIII, 1990, 58–71.

(d) Regional studies

4.337 **Allen**, R. C., *Enclosure and the Yeoman. The Agricultural Development of the South Midlands, 1450–1850*, 1992. Based on a detailed statistical analysis of the Midland counties the author's conclusion is that large landlords were the only beneficiaries of enclosure.

4.338 **Brassley**, P., *The Agricultural Economy of Northumberland and Durham in the period 1640–1750*, 1985.

4.339 **Dyer**, C. C., *Hanbury. Settlement and Society in a Woodland Landscape*, 1991.

4.340 **Havinden**, M. A., ed., *Husbandry and Marketing in the South-West 1500–1800*, 1973.

4.341 **Hoskins**, W. G., ed., *Studies in Leicestershire Agrarian History*, 1949.

4.342 **Howell**, Cicely, *Land, Family and Inheritance in Transition. Kibworth Harcourt, 1280–1700*, 1983. A case study of a Leicestershire manor which examines manorial administration, changing patterns of landholding and agriculture, the impact of plague, household structure and inheritance customs.

4.343 **Kerridge**, E., 'Agriculture, 1500–1793', *V.C.H.Wilts.*, ed. E. Crittall. IV, 1959, 43–64.

4.344 **Nair**, Gwyneth, *Highley, The Development of a Community, 1550–1880*, 1988. Focuses on the breakdown of the manorial system, the enclosure of open fields and the development of industrialism.

4.345 **Pettit**, P. A. J., *The Royal Forests of Northamptonshire: A Study in Their Economy, 1558–1714*, Northants.Rec.Soc., XXIII, 1968.

4.346 **Phythian-Adams**, C., *Continuity, Fields, and Fission. The Making of a Midland Parish*, 1978.

4.347 —— ed., *Societies, Cultures and Kinship, 1580–1850. Cultural Provinces and English Local History*, 1993. A general introduction charts a new agenda for English local history. Case studies of S.W.Nottinghamshire in the seventeenth century, St Ives Huntingdonshire 1630–1740, and of S.E.Surrey 1750–1850 exemplify the overall approach.

4.348 **Rodgers**, H. B., 'Land use in Tudor Lancashire', *T.I.B.G.*, XXVII, 1955, 79–98.

4.349 **Rollison**, D., 'Property, ideology and popular culture in a Gloucestershire village, 1660–1740', *P.P.*, 93, 1981, 70–97.

4.350 **Skipp**, V. H. T., *Crisis and Development. An Ecological Case Study of the Forest of Arden, 1570–1674*, 1978.

4.351 **Smith**, R. B., *Land and Politics in the England of Henry VIII*, 1970.

4.352 **Spufford**, Margaret, *Contrasting Communities: English Villagers in the Sixteenth and Seventeenth Centuries*, 1974.

4.353 **Thirsk**, Joan, *English Peasant Farming; The Agrarian History of Lincolnshire from Tudor to Recent Times*, 1957.

4.354 —— 'Agrarian history, 1540–1950'. In *V.C.H.Leics.*, ed. W. G. Hoskins and R. A. McKinley, II, 1954, 199–264.

(e) Marketing

4.355 **Anderson**, B. L. and Latham, A. J. H., eds., *The Market in History*, 1986. A wide-ranging collection of essays, three of which cover markets and marketing in England from the Middle Ages to the Industrial Revolution.

4.356 **Bowden**, P. J., *The Wool Trade in Tudor and Stuart England*, 1962.

4.357 **Edwards**, P., *The Horse Trade of Tudor and Stuart England*, 1988.

4.358 **Everitt**, A. M., 'The marketing of agricultural produce'. In Thirsk (4.322), 466–592. An important general survey of the subject.

4.359 —— 'The food market of the English town, 1660–1760', *Third International Conference on Economic History*, Paris, 1968, 57–71.

4.360 **Fisher**, F. J., 'The development of the London food market, 1540–1640', *Ec.H.R.*, V, 1935, 46–64. Reprinted in Carus-Wilson (1.326), I, 135–51.

4.361 **Gras**, N. S. B., *The Evolution of the English Corn Market*, Cambridge, Mass., 1915.

4.362 **Kneisel**, E., 'The evolution of the English corn market', *J.Ec.H.*, XIV, 1954, 46–52.

4.363 **Outhwaite**, R. B., 'Dearth and government intervention in English grain markets, 1590–1700', *Ec.H.R.*, 2nd ser., XXXIV, 1981, 389–406.

4.364 **Ponko**, V., 'N. S. B. Gras and Elizabethan corn policy: a re-examination of the problem', *Ec.H.R.*, 2nd ser., XVII, 1964, 24–42. A critique of Gras's book.

4.365 **Skeel**, Caroline A. J., 'The cattle trade between Wales and England from the fifteenth to the nineteenth centuries', *T.R.H.S.*, 4th ser., ix, 1926, 135–58. *See also* the section on *Communications and internal trade* (pp. 81–82).

(f) The Manor

4.366 **Kerridge**, E., ed., *Surveys of the Manors of Philip, First Earl of Pembroke, 1631–32*, Wilts.Arch. and Nat.H.Soc., Records Branch, IX, 1953.

4.367 **Day**, R. H., 'Instability in the transition from manorialism: a classical analysis', *Expl.Entrepren.H.*, XIX, 1982, 321–39.

4.368 **Ellis**, M. J., 'A study in the manorial history of Halifax parish in the sixteenth and early seventeenth centuries', *Yorks.Arch. J.*, XL, 1960–1, 250–64, 420–42.

4.369 **Leconfield**, Lord, *Petworth Manor in the Seventeenth Century*, 1954.

4.370 —— *Sutton and Duncton Manors*, 1956. *See also* Davenport (2.228), and Kerridge (4.315), 17–31.

(g) Landholding

See also the separate section on *The gentry and their estates* (89–90).

(i) LANDHOLDING

4.371 **Batho**, G. R., 'Landlords in England: noblemen, gentlemen and yeomen'. In Thirsk (4.322), 276–305. A convenient survey.

4.372 **Beckett**, J. V., 'English landownership in the later seventeenth and eighteenth centuries: the debate and the problems', *Ec.H.R.*, 2nd ser., XXX, 1977, 567–81.

4.373 **Clay**, C., 'The greed of Whig bishops?

Church landlords and their lessees, 1660–1760', *P.P.*, 87, 1980, 128–57.

4.374 **Cross**, M. Claire, 'The economic problems of the see of York: decline and recovery in the sixteenth century'. In Thirsk (4.326), 64–83.

4.375 **Habakkuk**, H. J., 'Economic functions of English landowners in the seventeenth and eighteenth centuries', *Expl.Entrepren.H.*, VI, 1953, 92–102. Reprinted in Minchinton (1.330), I, 187–201.

4.376 **Thompson**, F. M. L., 'The social distribution of landed property in England since the sixteenth century', *Ec.H.R.*, 2nd ser., XIX, 1966, 505–17.

See also Stone (4.1070), and Campbell (4.1050).

(ii) THE CROWN LANDS

4.377 **Batho**, G. R., 'Landlords in England: the Crown', in Thirsk (4.322), 256–76.

4.378 **Gentles**, I., 'The management of the Crown lands, 1649–60', *Ag.H.R.*, XIX, 1971, 25–41.

4.379 —— 'The sales of Crown lands during the English Revolution', *Ec.H.R.*, 2nd ser., XXVI, 1973, 614–35.

4.380 **Grant**, R. K. J., *The Royal Forests of England*, 1991.

4.381 **Hoyle**, R. W., ed., *The Estates of the English Crown, 1558–1640*, 1993. An important volume of essays which provides a discussion of estate management, land reclamations, fiscal policy, fee farming, patronage, auditing, entrepreneurialism, social obligations and popular protests.

4.382 **Pugh**, R. B., *The Crown Estate: An Historical Essay*, 1960.

4.383 **Wolffe**, B. P., *The Crown Lands, 1461–1536*, 1970. A valuable examination of the subject. Half the book consists of documents.

4.384 —— 'Henry VIII's land revenues and chamber finance', *E.H.R.*, LXXIX, 1964, 225–54.

4.385 **Zell**, M., 'The mid Tudor market in crown land in Kent', *Arch.Cant.*, XCVII, 1981, 53–70.

Material relating to the disposal of the dissolved monastic lands is listed below in the sections on *The Land market* and on *The dissolution of the monastries.*

(h) The land market

4.386 **Allen**, R. C., 'The price of freehold land and the interest rate in the seventeenth and eighteenth centuries', *Ec.H.R.*, 2nd ser., XLI, 1988, 33–50.

4.387 **Clay**, C., 'The price of freehold land in the later seventeenth and eighteenth centuries', *Ec.H.R.*, 2nd ser., XXVII, 1974, 173–89.

4.388 **Coleman**, D. C., 'London scriveners and the estate market in the late seventeenth century', *Ec.H.R.*, 2nd ser., IV, 1951, 221–30.

4.389 **Gentles**, I., 'The sales of bishops' lands in the English Revolution, 1646–60', *E.H.R.*, XCV, 1980, 573–96.

4.390 **Habakkuk**, H. J., 'The market for monastic property', *Ec.H.R.*, 2nd ser., X, 1957–8, 362–80. *See also* the article by Outhwaite (4.393).

4.391 —— 'The long-term rate of interest and the price of land in the seventeenth century', *Ec.H.R.*, 2nd ser., V, 1952, 26–45.

4.392 **Hoyle**, R. W., 'Tenure and the land market in early modern England, or a contribution to the Brenner debate', *Ec.H.R.*, 2nd ser., XLIII, 1990, 1–20.

4.393 **Outhwaite**, R. B., 'The price of Crown land at the turn of the sixteenth century', *Ec.H.R.*, 2nd ser., XX, 1967, 229–40. *See also* Habakkuk (4.390).

4.394 —— 'Who bought Crown lands? The pattern of purchases 1589–1603', *B.I.H.R.*, XLIV, 1971, 18–33.

4.395 **Richardson**, W. C., *History of the Court of Augmentations, 1536–1554*, 1962. An authoritative study of the institution which handled the sales of monastic lands.

4.396 **Woodward**, G. W. O., 'A speculation in monastic lands', *E.H.R.*, LXXIX, 1964, 778–83. *See also* Thirsk (4.325).

(i) Rent

4.397 **Kerridge**, E., 'The movement of rent, 1540–1640', *Ec.H.R.*, 2nd ser., VI, 1953, 16–34. Reprinted in Carus-Wilson (1.326), II, 208–26.

4.398 **Rea**, W. F., 'The rental and accounts of Sir Richard Shireburn, 1571–77', *T.H.S.L.C.*, CX, 1959, 31–57. *See also* Bowden, listed under *Prices* (pp. 82–83).

(j) Field systems and enclosures

4.399 **Brewer**, J. G., *Enclosures and the Open Fields: A Bibliography*, 1972. Lists 355 items. *See also* two items by Thirsk (4.416), (4.417). For details of tracts and sermons on enclosures, *see* the list in Read (4.5), 169 *et. seq.*

4.400 **Hosford**, W. A., 'An eye witness's account of a seventeenth-century enclosure', *Ec.H.R.*, 2nd ser., IV, 1951, 215–20.

4.401 **Leadam**, I. S., ed., *The Domesday of Inclosures, 1517–18*, 2 vols, 1892. The information gathered by Wolsey's commission.

4.402 **Baker**, A. R. H., 'Field systems in the Vale of Holmesdale', *Ag.H.R.*, XIV, 1966, 1–24.

4.403 —— 'Howard Levi Gray and English field systems: an evaluation, *Ag.H.*, XXXIX, 1965, 86–91. Gray's book is listed below.

4.404 **Beresford**, M. W., 'Habitation versus improvement: the debate on enclosure by agreement'. In Fisher (4.52), 40–69.

4.405 **Butlin**, R. A., 'Northumberland field systems', *Ag.H.R.*, XII, 1964, 99–120

4.406 —— 'Enclosure and improvement in Northumberland in the sixteenth century', *Arch.Aeliana*, 3rd ser., XLV, 1967, 149–60.

4.407 **Curtler**, W. H., *The Enclosure and Redistribution of Our Land*, 1920.

4.408 **Elliot**, G., 'The system of cultivation and evidence of enclosure in the Cumberland open fields in the sixteenth century', *Trans.Cumb. & West.Antiq. & Arch.Soc.*, n.s., LIX, 1959, 85–104.

4.409 **Gay**, E. F., 'Inquisitions of depopulation in 1517 and the Domesday of Inclosures', *T.R.H.S.*, n.s., XIV, 1900, 231–303.

4.410 **Gray**, H. L., *English Field Systems*, Harvard Hist.Studs., XXII, Cambridge, Mass., 1915, reprinted 1959.

4.411 **Johnson**, A. H., *The Disappearance of the Small Landowner*, 1909. Reprinted with an introductory note by Joan Thirsk, 1963.

4.412 **Leonard**, Elizabeth M., 'The enclosure of common fields in the seventeenth century', *T.R.H.S.*, n.s., xix, 1905, 101–46. Reprinted in Carus-Wilson (1.326), II, 227–56.

4.413 **McCloskey**, D. N., 'The prudent peasant: new findings on open fields',

J.Ec.H., LI, 1991, 343–55.

4.414 **Parker**, L. A., 'The agrarian revolution at Cotesbach (Leics.)'. In Hoskins (4.341), 41–76.

4.415 **Tate**, W. E., 'An early record of open-field agriculture in Nottinghamshire', *Trans. Thoroton Soc.*, XLIII, for 1939, 1940, 33–48.

4.416 **Thirsk**, Joan *Tudor Enclosures*, Hist.Ass. pamphlet, 1959.

4.417 —— 'Enclosing and engrossing'. In Thirsk (4.326), 200–55.

4.418 **Yelling**, Joyce A., *Common Field and Enclosure in England, 1450–1850*, 1977. *See also* Kerridge's article (4.174), and Gonner (5.664) and Tate (5.669).

(k) Agricultural improvements

4.419 **Wood**, E. B., ed., *Rowland Vaughan, His Booke (1610)*, 1897. A seventeenth-century description by a pioneer of the floating of water-meadows.

4.420 **Allison**, K. J., 'The sheep-corn husbandry of Norfolk in the sixteenth and seventeenth centuries', *Ag.H.R.*, V, 1957, 12–30.

4.421 **Broad**, J., 'Alternate husbandry and permanent pasture in the Midlands, 1650–1800', *Ag.H.R.*, XXVIII, 1980, 77–89.

4.422 **Cornwall**, J., 'Agricultural improvement, 1560–1640', *Sussex Arch.Collns.*, XCVIII, 1960, 118–32.

4.423 **Darby**, H. C., *The Changing Fenland*, 1983. An updated version of Darby's earlier book on the draining of the fens. New chapters are added on the medieval and post 1930s fenland.

4.424 **Fussell**, G. E., 'The Low Countries' influence on English farming', *E.H.R.*, LXXIV, 1959, 611–22.

4.425 **Harris**, L. E., *Vermuyden and the Fens*, 1953.

4.426 **Havinden**, M. A., 'Agricultural progress in open-field Oxfordshire', *Ag.H.R.*, IX, 1961, 73–83. Reprinted in Minchinton (1.330), I, 147–59. Argues against the traditional view that open-field agriculture was backward and static.

4.427 —— 'Lime as a means of agricultural improvement: the Devon example'. In Chalklin and Havinden (4.36), 104–34.

4.428 **Hoskins**, W. G., 'The reclamation of the

waste in Devon, 1550–1800', *Ec.H.R.*, XIII, 1943, 80–92.

4.429 **Kerridge**, E., *The Agricultural Revolution*, 1967. An important and provocative book which argues that the main agricultural innovations belong, not to the eighteenth century, but to the period from about 1560 to 1690. For a balanced criticism of the book, *see* the review by Joan Thirsk in *Hist.*, LV, 1970, 259–62.

4.430 —— 'The sheepfold in Wiltshire and the floating of the water-meadows', *Ec.H.R.*, 2nd ser., VI, 1954, 282–9.

4.431 —— 'A reconsideration of some former husbandry practices', *Ag.H.R.*, III, 1955, 26–40.

4.432 **Simpson**, A., 'The East Anglian Foldcourse; some queries', *Ag.H.R.*, VI, 1958, 87–96. Comments on the article by Allison.

4.433 **Williams**, M., *The Draining of the Somerset Levels*, 1970.

4.434 **Yelling**, Joyce A., 'The combination and rotation of crops in east Worcestershire, 1540–1660', *Ag.H.R.*, XVII, 1969, 24–43.

(l) The dissolution of the monasteries

4.435 **Baskerville**, G., *English Monks and the Suppression of the Monasteries*, 1937. Takes a hostile view of the monks.

4.436 **Haigh**, C., *The Last Days of the Lancashire Monasteries and Pilgrimage of Grace*, Chet.Soc., 3rd ser., 17, 1969.

4.437 **Hodgett**, G. A. J., 'The dissolution of the religious houses in Lincolnshire and the changing structure of society', *Lincs. Architectural and Arch.Soc. Report and Papers*, IV, 1951, 83–99.

4.438 **Jack**, Sybil, 'Monastic lands in Leicestershire and their administration on the eve of the Dissolution', *Trans.Leics.Arch.Soc.*, XLI, 1967, 9–40.

4.439 **Kew**, J., 'The disposal of crown lands and the Devon land market, 1536–58', *Ag.H.R.*, XVIII, 1970, 93–105.

4.440 **Knowles**, D., *The Religious Orders in England III: The Tudor Age*, 1959.

4.441 **Oxley**, J. E., *The Reformation in Essex to the Death of Mary*, 1965. Chapters 6 and 7 deal with the Dissolution and its aftermath.

4.442 **Savine**, A., *English Monasteries on the Eve of the Dissolution*, Oxford Studs. in Social and Legal History, 1909. An important study based mainly on the *Valor Ecclesiasticus*.

4.443 **Snell**, L. S., *The Suppression of the Religious Foundations of Devon and Cornwall*, 1967.

4.444 **Swales**, T. H., 'The re-distribution of the monastic lands in Norfolk at the Dissolution. I: Value, gifts, leases and sales', *Norfolk Arch.*, XXXIV, 1966, 14–44.

4.445 **Woodward**, G. W. O., *The Dissolution of the Monasteries*, 1966. A clear and concise survey.

4.446 **Youings**, Joyce, 'The terms of the disposal of the Devon monastic lands, 1536–58', *E.H.R.*, LXIX, 1954, 18–38. Reprinted in Minchinton (1.330), I, 117–40.

4.447 —— 'Landlords in England: the Church'. In Thirsk (4.322), 306–56. A useful exploration of the subject. *See also* Finberg (4.109), 265–77, and Richardson (4.395).

INDUSTRY

(a) General works

4.448 **Clarkson**, L. A., *Proto-industrialization: The First Phase of Industrialization*, 1985.

4.449 **Coleman**, D. C., *Industry in Tudor and Stuart England*, 1975. A useful summary of the current state of research.

4.450 —— 'Proto-Industrialization. A concept too many', *Ec.H.R.*, 2nd ser., XXXVI, 1983, 435–48.

4.451 **Jack**, Sybil M., *Trade and Industry in Tudor and Stuart England*, 1977. Partly a collection of documents. Concentrates on the large-scale industries – such as coal and metals – though others, such as textiles and fishing, are included.

4.452 **Jones**, E. L., 'The agricultural origins of industry', *P.P.*, 40, 1968, 58–71.

4.453 **Nef**, J. U., 'English and French industry after 1540 in relation to the constitution'. In Conyers Read, ed., *The Constitution Reconsidered*, N. Y., 1938, 79–103.

4.454 **Sella**, D., *European Industries, 1500–1700*,

1970. Fontana Economic History of Europe, II, Section 5. Useful background.

4.455 **Thirsk**, Joan, 'Industries in the countryside'. In Fisher, ed. (4.52), 70–88.

(b) Industrial growth

4.456 **Coleman**, D. C., 'Industrial growth and industrial revolutions', *Economica*, n.s., XXIII, 1956, 1–20.

4.457 **Nef**, J. U., 'The progress of technology and the growth of large-scale industry in Great Britain, 1540–1640', *Ec.H.R.*, V, 1934, 3–24. Reprinted in Carus-Wilson, ed. (1.326), I, 88–107. Presents the famous 'Industrial revolution' thesis.

4.458 —— 'A comparison of industrial growth in France and England from 1540 to 1640', *J.Pol.Econ.*, XLIV, 1936, 289–317; 505–33, 643–66.

(c) Industrial Organisation

Histories of individual companies are too numerous to list in full and only a selection is given here. The reader is referred to the following, which provides a comprehensive bibliography of the subject:

4.459 **Kahl**, W. F., *The Development of the London Livery Companies: a bibliographical essay*, 1960.

4.460 **Alford**, B. W. E. and Barker, T. C., *A History of the Carpenters' Company*, 1968.

4.461 **Bindoff**, S. T., 'The making of the Statute of Artificers'. In Bindoff, Hurstfield and Williams (4.32a), 59–94.

4.462 **Blagden**, C., *The Stationers' Company: A History, 1403–1959*, 1960. An interesting and well-documented study. Chapters 1–11 deal with the pre-1700 period.

4.463 **Consitt**, F., *The London Weavers' Company, Vol. I: From the Twelfth Century to the Close of the Sixteenth*, 1933.

4.464 **Fisher**, F. J., 'Some experiments in company organisation in the early seventeenth century', *Ec.H.R.*, IV, 1932–4, 177–94.

4.465 **Foster**, E. R., 'The procedure of the House of Commons agaisnt Patents and Monopolies, 1621–24'. In Aiken and Henning eds. (4.1209), 57–87.

4.466 **Kellett**, J. R., 'The break-down of gild and corporation control over the handicraft and retail trade in London' (in the seventeenth and eighteenth centuries), *Ec.H.R.*, 2nd ser., X, 1958, 381–94.

4.467 **Kramer**, Stella, *The English Craft Gilds and the Government*, Columbia University Studies in History, Economics and Public Law, 23, N. Y., 1905.

4.468 —— *The English Craft Gilds: Studies in Their Progress and Decline*, N. Y., 1927.

4.469 **Marshall**, T. H., 'Capitalism and the decline of the English gilds', *Cambridge H.J.*, III, 1929, 23–33.

4.470 **Ramsay**, G. D., 'Industrial laissez-faire and the policy of Cromwell', *Ec.H.R.*, XVI, 1946, 93–110.

4.471 **Reddaway**, T. F., 'The Livery Companies of Tudor London', *Hist.*, LI, 1966, 287–99.

4.472 —— 'The London Goldsmiths c. 1500', *T.R.H.S.*, 5th ser., XII, 1962, 49–62.

4.473 **Thrupp**, Sylvia, *A Short History of the Worshipful Company of Bakers*, 1933.

4.474 **Unwin**, G., *Industrial Organisation in the Sixteenth and Seventeenth Centuries*, 1904, new ed., 1957, with an introduction by T. S. Ashton.

4.475 —— *The Gilds and Companies of London*, 1908. New ed., 1966.

4.476 **Youings**, Joyce, *Tuckers Hall, Exeter: The History of a Provincial City Company Through Five Centuries*, 1968. *See also* W. R. Scott (4.726).

(d) Investment and Entrepreneurship

4.477 **Coleman**, D. C., *Sir John Banks, Baronet and Businessman: A Study of Business, Politics and Society in Later Stuart England*, 1963. Banks (1627–99) was one of the richest businessmen of his day.

4.478 **Davies**, K. G., 'Joint stock investment in the later seventeenth century', *Ec.H.R.*, 2nd ser., IV, 1952, 283–301.

4.479 **Davis**, R., 'The earnings of capital in the English shipping industry, 1670–1730', *J.Ec.H.*, XVII, 1957, 409–25.

4.480 **Gough**, J. W., *Sir Hugh Myddleton: Entrepreneur and Engineer*, 1964. Not a biography of Myddleton (c. 1560–1631) but a study of aspects of his career including his part in the New River project.

4.481 —— *The Rise of the Entrepreneur*, 1969. Somewhat old-fashioned in approach, but the book usefully gathers together much material on the subject.

4.482 —— *The Superlative Prodigall: A Life of Thomas Bushell*, 1932. A case study of entrepreneurship.

4.483 **Robertson**, H. M., 'Sir Bevis Bulmer, a large-scale speculator of Elizabethan and Jacobean times', *J.Ec. & Bus.H.*, 4, 1931, 99–120.

4.484 **Stone**, L., 'The Nobility in business'. In *The Entrepreneur*, Cambridge, Mass., 1957, 14–21. *See also*, Stone (4.1070).

(e) Textiles

4.485 **Allison**, K. J., 'The Norfolk worsted industries in the sixteenth and seventeenth centuries. I: The traditional industry', *Yorks.B.*, 12, 1960, 73–83.

4.486 —— 'The Norfolk worsted industry in the sixteenth and seventeenth centuries. 2: The New Draperies', *Yorks.B.*, 13, 1961, 61–77.

4.487 **Chapman**, S. D., 'The genesis of the British hosiery industry 1600–1750', *Textile H.*, III, 1972, 7–50.

4.488 **Coleman**, D. C., 'An innovation and its diffusion: the New Draperies', *Ec.H.R.*, 2nd ser., XXII, 1969, 417–29.

4.489 **Elliott**, G., 'The decline of the woollen trade in Cumberland, Westmorland and Northumberland in the late sixteenth century', *Trans.Cumb. & West.Antiq. & Arch.Soc.*, LXI, 1961, 112–19.

4.490 **Heaton**, H., *The Yorkshire Woollen and Worsted Industries*, 1920, 2nd ed., 1965. The standard work.

4.491 **Kerridge**, E., *Textile Manufacture in Early Modern England*, 1985. Densely detailed study of the principal varieties of textile manufacture with supplementary chapters dealing with dyes, machinery, and with masters and servants.

4.492 **Lowe**, N., *The Lancashire Textile Industry in the Sixteenth Century*, Chet.Soc., 3rd ser., 20, 1972.

4.493 **Mann**, Julia de L., 'A Wiltshire family of clothiers: George and Hester Wansey, 1683–1714', *Ec.H.R.*, 2nd ser., IX, 1956, 241–53.

4.494 **Mendenhall**, T. C., *The Shrewsbury Drapers and the Welsh Wool Trade*, 1953.

4.495 **Moir**, Esther A. L., 'Benedict Webb, clothier', *Ec.H.R.*, 2nd ser., X, 1957, 256–64.

4.496 **Pilgrim**, J. E., 'The rise of the New Draperies in Essex', *Birm.H.J.*, 7, 1959, 36–59.

4.497 **Priestly**, U., ' "The fabric of stuffs". The Norwich textile industry, *c.* 1650–1750', *Textile H.*, XVI, 1985, 183–210.

4.498 **Ramsay**, G. D., 'The distribution of the cloth industry in 1561–2', *E.H.R*, LVII, 1942, 361–9.

4.499 —— 'The report of the Royal Commission on the clothing industry, 1640', *E.H.R.*, LVII, 1942, 482–93.

4.500 —— *The Wiltshire Woollen Industry in the Sixteenth and Seventeenth Centuries*, 1943.

4.501 —— *The English Woollen Industry, 1500–1700*, 1983. A concise survey which focuses on manufacture, marketing, and the general impact of the cloth industry on English society and politics during this period.

4.502 **Tann**, Jennifer, *Gloucestershire Woollen Mills*, 1967. The first three chapters are relevant to this period. The main part of the book consists of a gazetteer of woollen mills in the county.

4.503 **Thirsk**, Joan, 'The fantastical folly of fashion; the English stocking knitting industry 1500–1700'. In Harte and Ponting (5.808), 50–73.

4.504 **Wadsworth**, A. P. and Mann, Julia de L., *The Cotton Trade and Industrial Lancashire, 1600–1780*, 1931. Reprinted 1965.

See also Bowden (4.356), and Thirsk (4.455).

(f) Coal

4.505 **Hatcher**, J., ed., *History of the British Coal Industry. I: Before 1700*, 1993. Now the principal work in the field.

4.506 **Hopkinson**, G. G., 'The development of the South Yorkshire coalfield, 1500–1775', *Trans. Hunter Arch.Soc.*, VII, 1957, 295–319.

4.507 **Langton**, J., *Geographical Change and Industrial Revolution. Coalmining in South West Lancashire, 1590–1799*, 1979.

4.508 **Nef**, J. U., *The Rise of the British Coal Industry, 1550–1700*, 2 vols, 1932. Reprinted 1966.

4.509 **Smith**, R. S., *Early Coal Mining around Nottingham, 1500–1650*, 1989.

4.510 **Stone**, L., 'An Elizabethan coalmine', *Ec.H.R.*, 2nd ser., III, 1950–1, 97–106. Stone stresses the very modest scale of the undertaking and so questions Nef's claims for an Industrial Revolution in this period.

(g) Metals

5.511 **Collingwood**, W. G., *Elizabethan Keswick. Extracts from the Original Account Books, 1564–77, of the German Miners in the Archives of Augsburg*, Cumb. & West.Antiq. & Arch.Soc., Tract series, VIII, 1912.

4.512 **Crossley**, D. W., ed., *Sidney Iron Works Accounts, 1541–73*. Camden Soc., 4th ser., XV, 1975.

4.513 **France**, R. S. ed., *The Thieveley Lead Mines, 1629–1635*, Rec.Soc.Lancs. & Ches., CII, 1947.

4.514 **Schafer**, R. G., ed., *A Selection from the Records of Philip Foley's Stour Valley Ironworks, 1668–74*, Worcs.H.Soc., IX, 1978.

4.515 **Andrews**, C. B., *The Story of Wortley Iron Works: a record of its History, Traditions and eight centuries of Yorkshire Iron-Making*, 1950, 2nd rev. ed., 1956.

4.516 **Cleere**, H. and Crossley, D., *The Iron Industry of the Weald*, 1985.

4.517 **Court**, W. H. B., *The Rise of the Midland Industries, 1600–1838*, 1938. Deals with coal, chemical and glass as well as metals.

4.518 **Crossley**, D. W., 'The management of a sixteenth-century iron works', *Ec.H.R.*, 2nd ser., XIX, 1966, 273–88.

4.519 **Donald**, M. B., *Elizabethan Copper*, 1955.

4.519A —— *Elizabethan Monopolies: The History of the Company of Mineral and Battery Works*, 1961.

4.520 **Flinn**, M. W., 'Sir Ambrose Crowley, ironmonger, 1658–1713', *Expl.Entrepren. H.*, V, 1953, 162–80.

4.521 —— 'The growth of the English iron industry, 1660–1760', *Ec.H.R.*, 2nd ser., XI, 1958, 144–53. Bibliography.

4.522 —— 'Timber and the advance of technology: a reconsideration', *Annals of Science*, XV, 1959, 109–20. Concludes that the so-called timber famine has been much exaggerated.

4.523 **Gough**, J. W., *The Mines of Mendip*, 1930, rev. ed., 1967.

4.524 **Hamilton**, H., *The English Brass and Copper Industries to 1800*, 1926. Reprinted with a bibliographical introduction by J. R. Harris, 1967.

4.525 **Hammersley**, G., 'The charcoal iron industry and its fuel 1540–1750', *Ec.H.R.*, XXVI, 1973, 593–613.

4.526 —— 'The effect of technical change in the British copper industry between the sixteenth and the eighteenth centuries', *J.Europ.Ec.H.*, XX, 1991, 155–74.

4.527 **Hopkinson**, G. G., 'The charcoal iron industry in the Sheffield region, 1588–1755', *Trans.Hunter Arch.Soc.*, VIII, 1961, 122–51.

4.528 **Jenkins**, R., 'Notes on the early history of steelmaking in England', *Trans. Newcomen Soc.*, III, for 1922–3, 1924, 16–40.

4.529 —— 'Copper smelting in England: revival at the end of the seventeenth century', *Trans.Newcomen Soc.*, XXIV, for 1943–5, 1949, 73–80.

4.530 —— 'Ironfounding in England, 1490–1603', *Trans.Newcomen Soc.*, XIX, for 1938–9, 1940, 35–49.

4.531 **Johnson**, B. L. C., 'The Stour Valley iron industry in the late seventeenth century', *Trans.Worcs.Arch.Soc.*, n.s., XXVII, 1950, 35–46.

4.532 —— 'The Foley partnerships: the iron industry at the end of the Charcoal era', *Ec.H.R.*, 2nd ser., IV, 1952, 322–40.

4.533 —— 'The Iron industry of Cheshire and North Staffordshire, 1688–1712', *Trans.North Staffs. Field Club*, LXXXVIII, 1953–4, 32–55.

4.534 —— 'New light on the iron industry in the Forest of Dean', *Trans.Bristol and Gloucester Archaeological Society*, 72, for 1953, 1954, 129–43.

4.535 **Lewis**, G. R., *The Stannaries: A Study of the English Tin Miner*, Harvard Economic Series, III, Cambridge, Mass., 1906. *See also* Hatcher (3.266).

4.536 **Pelham**, R. A., 'The migration of the iron industry towards Birmingham during the sixteenth century', *Trans.Birm.Arch.Soc.*, 66, 1950, 192–9.

4.537 —— 'The establishment of the Willoughby iron works in N. Warwickshire in the sixteenth century', *Birm.H.J.*, 4, 1953, 18–29.

4.538 **Raistrick**, A. and Jennings, B., *A History of Leadmining in the Pennines*, 1965.

4.539 **Rees**, W., *Industry before the Industrial*

Revolution, 2 vols., 1968. Has chapters on coal and metal mining, on the Mines Royal and on the Mineral and Battery works.

4.540 **Rowlands**, Marie B., *Masters and Men in the West Midland Metalware Trades before the Industrial Revolution*, 1975. Usefully complements Court (4.517) by concentrating on the western part of the metalware region and explores the coexistence of small-scale industry and agriculture in this period.

4.541 **Smith**, R. S., 'Sir Francis Willoughby's ironworks, 1570–1610', *Renaiss. & Mod.Studs.*, XI, 1967, 90–140.

4.542 **Straker**, E., *Wealden Iron*, 1931. Reprinted 1969.

(h) Salt, leather, paper and glass

(i) SALT

4.543 **Calvert**, A. F., *Salt in Cheshire*, 1915.

4.544 **Chaloner**, W. H., 'Salt in Cheshire, 1600–1870', *T.L.C.A.S.*, LXXI, for 1961, 1963, 58–74.

4.545 **Ellis**, Joyce, 'The decline and fall of the Tyneside salt industry, 1660–1710; a re-examination', *Ec.H.R.*, 2nd ser., XXXIII, 1980, 45–58.

4.546 **Laver**, H., 'Salt works in Essex', *Essex R.*, LII, 1943, 184–8.

(ii) LEATHER

4.547 **Clarkson**, L. A., 'English economic policy in the sixteenth and seventeenth centuries: the case of the leather industry', *B.I.H.R.*, 38, 1965, 149–62.

4.548 —— 'The leather crafts in Tudor and Stuart England', *Ag.H.R.*, XIV, 1966, 23–39.

4.549 —— 'The organisation of the English leather industry in the late sixteenth and seventeenth centuries', *Ec.H.R.*, 2nd ser., XIII, 1960, 245–56.

4.550 **Woodward**, D. M., 'The Chester leather industry, 1558–1625', *T.H.S.L.C.*, 119, 1968, 65–112.

(iii) PAPER

4.551 **Coleman**, D. C., *The British Paper Industry, 1495–1860: A study in industrial growth*, 1958. The standard work on the subject.

4.552 **Shorter**, A. H., *Paper Mills and Paper Makers in England 1495–1800*, Hilversum, 1957. Chapter 1 deals with the period 1495–1700. A full list of known paper mills is given.

(iv) GLASS

4.553 **Crossley**, D. W., 'The performance of the glass industry in sixteenth-century England', *Ec.H.R.*, XXV, 1972, 421–33.

4.554 **Godfrey**, Eleanor S., *The Development of English Glassmaking, 1560–1640*, 1975.

4.555 **Kenyon**, G. H., *The Glass Industry of the Weald*, 1967.

4.556 **Smith**, R. S., 'Glass-making at Wollaton in the early seventeenth century', *Trans. Thoroton Soc.*, LXVI, 1963, 24–34.

(i) Shipping

4.557 **Albion**, R. G., *Forests and Sea Power: The Timber problem of the Royal Navy, 1652–1862*, Harvard Economic Studies, 29, Cambridge, Mass., 1926.

4.558 **Barbour**, V., 'Dutch and English merchant shipping in the seventeenth century', *Ec.H.R.*, II, 1930, 261–90. Reprinted in Carus-Wilson (ed. (1.326), I, 227–53.

4.559 **Burwash**, Dorothy, *English Merchant Shipping, 1460–1540*, Toronto, 1947. Reprinted 1969.

4.560 **Coleman**, D. C., 'The naval dockyards under the later Stuarts', *Ec.H.R.*, 2nd ser., VI, 1953, 134–155.

4.561 **Davis**, R., *The Rise of the English Shipping Industry in the Seventeenth and Eighteenth Centuries*, 1962. The standard work.

4.562 **Lane**, F. C., 'Tonnages, medieval and modern', *Ec.H.R.*, 2nd ser., XVII, 1964, 213–33.

4.563 **Scammell**, G. V., 'Ship-owning in England 1450–1550', *T.R.H.S.*, 5th ser., XII, 1962, 105–22.

4.564 —— 'English merchant shipping at the end of the Middle Ages: some East Coast evidence', *Ec.H.R.*, 2nd ser., XIII, 1960–1, 327–41.

(j) Miscellaneous

4.565 **Cheke**, V., *The Story of Cheesemaking in Britain*, 1959.

4.566 **Cutting**, C. L., *Fish Saving: A History of Fish Processing from Ancient to Modern Times*, 1955.

4.567 **Jones**, S. R. H., 'The development of needle manufacturing in the West Midlands before 1750', *Ec.H.R.*, 2nd ser., XXXI, 1978, 354–68.

4.568 **Lloyd**, G. I. H., *The Cutlery Trades: an Historical Essay in the Economics of Small-scale Production*, 1913. Reprinted 1968.

4.569 **Rowlands**, Marie B., 'Industry and Social change in Staffordshire, 1660–1760', *Lichfield and S.Staffs.Arch. and H.Soc.*, IX, 1967–8, 37–58.

4.570 **Singer**, C. J., *The Earliest Chemical Industry: an Essay in the Historical Relations of Economics and Technology Illustrated from the Alum Trade*, 1948. For developments in England, *see* 182–202.

4.571 **Swain**, J. T., *Industry before the Industrial Revolution. N.E. Lancashire, c.1500–1640*, Chet.Soc., 3rd ser., XXXIII, 1986. Against a background discussed in the introductory chapter on demography and agriculture the author deals with the cloth, coal and various craft industries.

4.572 **Tomlinson**, H., *Guns and Government. The Ordnance Office under the Later Stuarts*, 1979.

4.573 **Woodward**, D., 'Swords into ploughshares. Recycling in pre-industrial England', *Ec.H.R.*, 2nd ser., XXXVIII, 1985, 175–91.

TOWNS

Urban history has a voluminous literature. For a comprehensive guide to older histories of towns, *see* Gross (2.339), and Martin and MacIntyre (2.340).

(a) General

4.574 **Richardson**, R. C. and James, T. B., eds., *The Urban Experience. A Sourcebook – English, Scottish and Welsh Towns, 1450–1700*, 1983. A convenient collection of contemporary source material arranged chronologically and thematically.

4.575 **Abrams**, P. and Wrigley, E. A., eds., *Towns in Societies. Essays in Economic History and Historical Sociology*, 1978. A highly miscellaneous collection of essays extending from ancient times to 1914. Three are specifically concerned with England in the medieval and early modern periods. There is a general introduction to the theories and problems of the relationship between towns and economic growth and a consolidated bibliography.

4.576 **Barry**, J., ed., *The Tudor and Stuart Town. A Reader in English Urban History, 1530–1688*, 1990. Illustrates the changing trends in urban history in general essays on pre-industrial economies, urban development, and residential patterns. Cambridge, London, York, Gloucester, Newcastle and Bristol receive chapters of their own.

4.577 **Clark**, P., ed., *County Towns in Pre-Industrial England*, 1981. Comprises case studies of Warwick, Ipswich, Winchester and Bath.

4.578 —— *The Early Modern Town: A Reader*, 1976. A collection of reprinted articles with a substantial introduction.

4.579 —— and Slack, P., eds., *Crisis and Order in English Towns, 1500–1700: Essays in Urban History*, 1971.

4.580 —— *English Towns in Transition, 1500–1700*, 1976.

4.581 **Cornwall**, J., 'English country towns in the 1520s', *Ec.H.R.*, 2nd ser., XV, 1962, 54–69.

4.582 **De Vries**, J., *European Urbanisation, 1500–1800*, 1984. A wide-ranging statistical analysis which places the British urban experience in perspective.

4.583 **Dodd**, A. H., 'Elizabethan towns and cities', *H.Today*, 11, 1961, 136–44.

4.584 **Dyer**, A. D., 'Growth and decay in English towns, 1500–1700', *Urban H.Yearbook*, 1979, 60–72.

4.585 —— *Decline and Growth in English*

Towns, 1400–1640, 1991. A valuable brief overview the main emphasis being on the late Middle Ages. Excellent bibliography.

4.586 **Everitt**, A. M., ed., *Perspectives on English Urban History*, 1973. An interesting collection of essays, including one by the editor on 'The English urban inn, 1560–1760'.

4.587 **Goose**, N. R., 'In search of the urban variable; towns and the English economy, 1500–1650', *Ec.H.R.*, 2nd ser., XXXIX, 1986, 165–85.

4.588 **Hoskins**, W. G., 'English provincial towns in the early sixteenth century', *T.R.H.S.*, 5th ser., VI, 1956, 1–19. Reprinted in Hoskins (4.116), 68–85.

4.589 **Langton**, J., 'Residential patterns in pre-industrial cities: some case studies from seventeenth-century Britain', *T.I.B.G.*, LXV, 1975, 1–27.

4.590 **MacInness**, A., *The English Town, 1660–1760*, 1980. Hist.Ass. pamphlet.

4.591 **Patten**, J., *English Towns, 1500–1700*, 1978. A geographical approach. *See also* Dyos (5.1585).

(b) Specialised studies

4.592 **Farr**, M., ed., *The Great Fire of Warwick, 1694. The Records of the Commissioners appointed under an Act of Parliament for Rebuilding the Town of Warwick*, Dugdale Soc., XXXVI, 1992.

4.593 **Manley**, L., ed., *London in the Age of Shakespeare*, 1986. A useful sourcebook illustrating different dimensions of London's social and economic development.

4.594 **Martin**, G. H., ed., *The Royal Charters of Grantham, 1463–1688*, 1963.

4.595 **Riden**, P. and Blair, J., eds., *History of Chesterfield. V: Records of the Borough of Chesterfield and Related Documents 1204–1835*, 1980.

4.596 **Alexander**, H., 'The economic structure of the City of London at the end of the seventeenth century', *Urban H.Yearbook*, 1989, 47–62.

4.597 **Alldridge**, H. J., 'House and household in Restoration Chester', *Urban H.Yearbook*, 1983, 39–52.

4.598 **Archer**, I., *The Pursuit of Stability. Social Relations in Elizabethan London*, 1991.

Examines the solidarity of the city elite and the connections between oligarchy and community as in the crisis years of the 1590s.

4.599 **Atkinson**, T., *Elizabethan Winchester*, 1963.

4.600 **Beier**, A. L. and Finlay, R., eds., *London, 1500–1700. The Making of the Metropolis*, 1986. Three main sections deal with population and disease, commerce and industry, and with society and change.

4.601 **Boulton**, J., *Neighbourhood and Society. A London Suburb in the Seventeenth Century*, 1987.

4.602 **Brett-James**, N. G., *The Growth of Stuart London*, 1935.

4.603 **Burt**, S. and Grady, K., *War, Plague and Trade. Leeds in the Seventeenth Century*, 1985.

4.604 **Carr**, G., *Residence and Social Status. The Development of Seventeenth-Century London*, 1990.

4.605 **Clemens**, P. G. E., 'The rise of Liverpool, 1665–1750', *Ec.H.R.*, 2nd ser., XXIX, 1976, 211–25.

4.606 **Collier**, S., *Whitehaven, 1600–1800. A New Town of the late Seventeenth Century. A Study of its Buildings and Urban Development*, 1991.

4.607 **Cook**, A. J., *The Privileged Playgoers of Shakespeare's London, 1576–1642*, Princeton, NJ, 1981.

4.608 **Corfield**, Penelope and Harte, N. B., eds., *London and the English Economy, 1500–1700. Essays by F. J. Fisher*, 1990. The author's collected essays exploring different aspects of economic conditions in the capital and of conspicuous consumption. Due tribute is paid to Fisher's significance as a founding father of metropolitan history.

4.609 **Davies**, C. Stella, ed., *A History of Macclesfield*, 1961.

4.610 **Dickens**, A. G., 'Tudor York'. In *V.C.H.Yorks. The City of York*, ed. P. M. Tillott, 1961, 117–59. *See also* Forster (4.617).

4.611 **Dyer**, A. D., *The City of Worcester in the Sixteenth Century*, 1973.

4.612 —— 'The market towns of southern England, 1500–1700', *Southern H.*, I, 1979, 123–34.

4.613 —— 'Warwickshire towns under the Tudors and Stuarts', *Warwicks.H.*, III, 1977, 122–34.

4.614 —— 'Urban housing. A documentary

study of four Midland towns, 1530–1700', *Post.Med.Arch.*, XV, 1981, 207–18.

4.615 **Edie**, C. A., 'New buildings, new taxes and old interests: an urban problem of the 1670s', *J.Brit. Studs.*, VI, 1967, 35–63.

4.616 **Evans**, J. T., *Seventeenth-Century Norwich. Politics, Religion and Government, 1620–90*, 1979.

4.617 **Forster**, G. C. F., 'York in the seventeenth century'. In *V.C.H. Yorks. The City of York*, ed. P. M. Tillott, 1961, 160–206. *See also* Dickens (4.610).

4.618 **Foster**, F., *The Politics of Stability. A Portrait of the Rulers in Elizabethan London*, 1977.

4.619 **François**, Martha E., 'The social and economic development of Halifax, 1558–1640', *Proc.Leeds Phil. and Lit.Soc.*, XI, 1966, 217–80.

4.620 **Gill**, C., *History of Birmingham I: Manor and Borough to 1865*, 1952.

4.621 **Goose**, N. R., 'Decay and regeneration in seventeenth-century Reading. A study in a changing economy', *Southern H.*, VI, 1984, 53–74.

4.622 **Herbert**, N. M., ed., *V.C.H.Gloucestershire. IV: The City of Gloucester*, 1988.

4.623 **Hill**, J. W. F., *Tudor and Stuart Lincoln*, 1956.

4.624 **Holmes**, M., *Elizabethan London*, 1969.

4.625 **Hoskins**, W. G., 'An Elizabethan provincial town: Leicester'. In J. H. Plumb, ed., *Studies in Social History*, 1955, 33–67. Reprinted in Hoskins (4.116), 86–114.

4.626 **Kerridge**, E., 'Social and economic history of Leicester, 1509–1660'. In *V.C.H.,Leics.*, ed. W. G. Hoskins and R. I. McKinley, IV, 1958, 76–109.

4.627 **Kirby**, J. W., 'The rulers of Leeds. Gentry, clothiers, and merchants, c.1425–1626', *Thoresby Soc. Pub.*, LIX, 1985, 22–49.

4.628 **Levine**, D. and Wrightson, K., *The Making of an Industrial Society. Wickham, 1560–1765*, 1991.

4.629 **MacCaffrey**, W. T., *Exeter, 1530–1640: The Growth of an English County Town*, Cambridge, Mass., 1958.

4.630 **McIntosh**, Marjorie, *A Community Transformed. The Manor and Liberty of Havering, 1500–1620*, 1991.

4.631 **Marcombe**, D., *English Small Town Life. Retford, 1520–1642*, 1993. A detailed study of a small market town which looks at population, urban government, religion and education. The economic activities of the town are well documented.

4.632 **Marshall**, J. D., 'Kendal in the late seventeenth and eighteenth centuries', *Trans.Cumb. & West.Antiq. & Arch.Soc.*, LXXV, 1975, 186–257. Surveys the demographic structure and economic development of the town through this period.

4.633 **Mayhew**, G., *Tudor Rye*, 1987.

4.634 **Myers**, A. R., 'Tudor Chester', *J.Chester Arch.Soc.*, LXIII, 1980, 43–57.

4.635 **Palliser**, D. M., *Tudor York*, 1980. Explores the process of decline and recovery in the sixteenth century and analyses the demographic and occupational structure of the city, the distribution of wealth, and the ruling élite.

4.636 —— 'Civic mentality and the environment in Tudor York', *Northern H.*, XVIII, 1982, 78–115.

4.637 **Pearl**, Valerie, 'Change and stability in seventeenth-century London', *London J.*, V, 1979, 3–34.

4.638 **Pound**, J., *Tudor and Stuart Norwich*, 1988.

4.639 **Priestly**, U., *Shops and Shopkeepers in Norwich, 1660–1730*, 1985.

4.640 **Rappaport**, S., *Worlds within Worlds. Structures of Life in Sixteenth Century London*, 1989. Considers the members of the livery companies of the City of London and their social, economic and political role in the capital.

4.641 **Reddaway**, T. F., *The Rebuilding of London after the Great Fire*, 1940. Reprinted 1951.

4.642 **Rimmer**, W. G., 'The evolution of Leeds to 1700', *Thoresby Society*, 50, Part 2, 1967, 91–129.

4.643 **Ripley**, P., 'The economy of the city of Gloucester, 1660–1740', *Trans.Bristol & Gloucs.Arch.Soc.*, XCVIII, 1981, 135–53.

4.644 **Roy**, I. and Porter, S., 'The social and economic structure of an early moden suburb: the tithing at Worcester', *B.I.H.R.*, LIII, 1980, 203–17.

4.645 **Sacks**, D. H., *Trade, Society and Politics in Bristol, 1500–1640*, 1985.

4.646 —— *The Widening Gate. Bristol and the Atlantic Economy, 1450–1700*, 1991.

4.647 **Seaver**, P. S., *Wallington's World. A Puritan Artisan in Seventeenth-Century*

London, 1985. An intimate case study of the linkages between puritanism and economic life.

4.648 **Stephens**, W. B., *Seventeenth-Century Exeter. A Study in Industrial and Commercial Development, 1635–88*, 1958.

4.649 —— ed., *A History of Congleton*, 1970.

4.650 **Stone**, L., 'The residential development of the West End of London in the seventeenth century', in Barbara C. Malament, ed., *After the Reformation. Essays in Honour of J. H. Hexter*, 1981, 167–212.

4.651 **Thirsk**, Joan, 'Stamford in the sixteenth and seventeenth centuries'. In A. Rogers, ed., *The Making of Stamford*, 1965, 58–76.

4.652 **Underwood**, D., *Fire from Heaven. Life in an English Town in the Seventeenth Century*, 1992. A study of Dorchester beginning with the Great Fire of 1613. The book examines the changing social, economic, religious and political configuration of the town.

6.453 **Willan**, T. S., *Elizabethan Manchester*, Chet. Soc., 3rd ser., XXVII, 1980. Based principally on wills, inventories and the records of the Court Leet. Particularly strong on the trading and industrial activities of the town.

4.654 **Woodhead**, J. R., *The Rulers of London, 1660–1689: a Biographical Record of the Aldermen and Common Councilmen of the City of London*, London and Middx.Arch.Soc., 1966.

4.655 **Wrigley**, E. A., 'A simple model of London's importance in changing English society and economy, 1650–1750', *P.P.*, 37, 1967, 44–70. An important article.

4.656 **Youings**, Joyce, 'Tudor Barnstaple: new life for an ancient borough', *Rep. & Trans.Devons.Assoc.*, CXXI, 1989, 1–14. *See also* Redford (5.1689) on Manchester.

ALIEN IMMIGRANTS

(a) Dutch, Huguenots, Germans and Italians

4.657 **Cross**, F. W., ed., *History of the Walloon and Huguenot Church at Canterbury*, Hug.Soc., 1898.

4.658 **Kirk**, R. E. G. and E. F., eds., *Returns of Aliens Dwelling in the City and Suburbs of London from the Reign of Henry VIII to that of James I*, Hug.Soc., 4 vols., 1900–1908.

4.659 **Moens**, W. J. C., ed., *The Walloons and their Church at Norwich: Their History and Registers, 1565–1832*, Hug.Soc., 1888.

4.660 —— *Register of Baptisms in the Dutch Church at Colchester from 1645 to 1728*, Hug.Soc., 1905.

4.661 **Carter**, Alice C., 'The Huguenot contribution to the early years of the Funded Debt, 1694–1714', *Proc.Hug.Soc.*, XIX, 1955, 21–41.

4.662 **Coleman**, D. C., 'The early British paper industry and the Huguenots', *Proc.Hug.Soc.*, XIX, 1959, 210–25.

4.663 **Cottret**, B., *The Huguenots in England. Immigration and Settlement, c.1550–1700*, 1992. Three principal sections explore the establishment of the French communities in the second half of the sixteenth century, their consolidation in the seventeenth century, and the social and religious organisation of their groupings. The book also contains a selection of contemporary documents.

4.664 **Cunningham**, W., *Alien Immigrants to England*, 1897. Reprinted with a new introduction by C. Wilson, 1969. The best general survey of the period from the late fifteenth to the eighteenth century. The opening and closing sections of the book, however, are less valuable.

4.665 **Girouard**, M., 'Some alien craftsmen in sixteenth- and seventeenth-century England', *Proc.Hug.Soc.*, XX, 1959, 26–35.

4.666 **Gwynn**, R. D., *Huguenot Heritage. The History and Contribution of the Huguenots in Britain*, 1985. Published to coincide with the two hundredth anniversary of the Revocation of the Edict of Nantes.

The Huguenot contribution to textiles, paper-making, clock-making and other industries and professions is assessed.

4.667 **Hayward**, J. F., 'The Huguenot gunmakers of London', *Proc.Hug.Soc.*, XX, 1963–4, 649–63.

4.668 **Holmes**, M., 'Evil May Day 1517: the story of a riot', *H.Today*, 15, 1965, 642–50.

4.669 **Le Fanu**, W. R., 'Huguenot refugee doctors in England', *Proc.Hug.Soc.*, XIX, 1956, 113–27.

4.670 **Morant**, Valerie, 'The settlement of Protestant refugees in Maidstone during the sixteenth century', *Ec.H.R.*, 2nd ser., IV, 1951, 210–14.

4.671 **Murray**, J. J., 'The cultural impact of the Flemish Low Countries on sixteenth and seventeenth-century England', *A.H.R.*, LXII, 1957, 837–54.

4.672 **Pettegree**, A., *Foreign Protestant Communities in Sixteenth-Century London*, 1986. Principally a study of the religious organisation of the foreign communities. There are also chapters, however, on the inter-relationships between foreigners and Londoners and on other aspects of the social history of their churches.

4.673 **Ramsay**, G. D., 'The undoing of the Italian mercantile colony in sixteenth-century London, in Harte and Ponting (5.808), 22–49.

4.674 **Ransome**, D. R., 'The struggle of the Glaziers' Company with foreign glaziers, 1500–1550', *Guildhall Miscellany*, II, 1960, 12–20.

4.675 **Scouloudi**, Irene, 'Alien immigration into and alien communities in London, 1558–1640', *Proc.Hug.Soc.*, XVI, 1938, 27–49.

4.676 **Scouloudi**, Irene, ed., *Huguenots in Britain and their French Background, 1550–1800*, 1987.

4.677 **Scoville**, W. C., 'The Huguenots and the diffusion of technology', *J.Pol.Econ.*, LX, 1952, 294–311, 392–411.

4.678 **Shears**, P. J., 'Huguenot connections with the clockmaking trade in England', *Proc.Hug.Soc.*, XX, 1960, 158–76.

4.679 **Sheppard**, F. H. W., 'The Huguenots in Spitalfields and Soho', *Proc.Hug.Soc.*, XXI, 1969, 355–65.

4.680 **Statt**, D., 'The City of London and the controversy over immigration, 1660–1722', *H.J.*, XXXIII, 1990, 45–61.

4.681 **Taube**, E., 'German craftsmen in Tudor England', *Ec.J.Ec.H.Supp.*, 3, 1939,

167–78.

4.682 **Williams**, L., 'Alien immigrants in relation to industry and society in Tudor England', *Proc.Hug.Soc.*, XIX, 1956, 146–69.

4.683 —— 'The crown and the provincial immigrant communities in Elizabethan England' in H. Hearder and H. Loyn, eds. (1.303), *British Government and Administration*, 1974, 117–31.

4.684 **Wyatt**, T., 'Aliens in England before the Huguenots', *Proc.Hug.Soc.*, XIX, 1953, 74–94. *See also* Consitt (4.463), 33–60, on the Flemish weavers.

(b) Jews

4.685 **Giuseppi**, J. A., 'Sephardic Jews and the early years of the Bank of England', *Trans. Jewish H.Soc.*, XIX, 1960, 53–64.

4.686 **Hyamson**, A. M., *The Sephardim of England: a History of the Spanish and Portuguese Jewish Community, 1492–1951*, 1951.

4.687 **Katz**, D. S., *Philo-Semitism and the Re-admission of the Jews to England, 1603–55*, 1982.

4.688 **Osterman**, N., 'The controversy over the proposed readmission of the Jews to England (1655)', *Jewish Soc.Studs.*, III, 1941, 301–28.

4.689 **Rubens**, A., 'Portrait of Anglo-Jewry, 1656–1836. I: The Anglo-Jewish community, source material', *Trans. Jewish H.Soc.*, XIX, 1960, 13–52.

4.690 **Samuel**, E. R., 'Portuguese Jews in Jacobean London', *Trans. Jewish H.Soc.*, XVIII, sessions 1953–5, 1958, 171–230.

4.691 **Wolf**, L., 'The Jews in Tudor England'. In C. Roth, ed., *Essays in Jewish-History*, 1934, 73–90. *See also* Roth (2.403).

COMMERCE AND COLONISATION

4.692 **McCulloch**, J. R., ed., *Early English Tracts on Commerce*, 1856. Reprinted 1952. A very valuable collection which includes Lewes Roberts' *The Treasure of*

Traffike; or, A Discourse of Forraigne Trade
(1641) and Thomas Mun's *England's
Treasure by Forraign Trade* (1664).

4.693 **Willan**, T. S., ed., *A Tudor Book of Rates*,
1962.

For other documentary material on this subject,
see Bland, Brown and Tawney (1.303), and
Tawney and Power (4.23), II, 1–89.

(a) General works

4.694 **Andrews**, K. R., *Trade, Plunder and
Settlement. Maritime Enterprise and the
Genesis of the British Empire, 1480–1630*,
1984. Places English overseas expansion
in its European context and looks at the
country's resources for sustaining it.

4.695 **Bridenbaugh**, C. and Roberta, *No Peace
Beyond the Line: The English and the
Caribbean 1624–1690*, 1972.

4.696 **Connell-Smith**, G., *Forerunners of Drake:
A Study of English Trade With Spain in the
Early Tudor Period*, 1954.

4.697 **Cottrell**, P. L. and Aldcroft, D. H.,
*Shipping, Trade and Commerce. Essays in
Memory of Ralph Davis*, 1981. A
miscellaneous collection dealing with
trade in the Baltic, with Portugal and
with Asia, and with shipping and
shipbuilding in England and Scotland.

4.698 **Cressy**, D., *Coming Over. Migration and
Communication between England and New
England in the Seventeenth Century*, 1987.
An invaluable study of the waves of
migration across the Atlantic and of the
interconnections between colonies and
the homeland. Cressy emphasises the
wide range of migrants and plays down
the puritan contribution.

4.699 **Davis**, R., *English Oveseas Trade
1500–1700*, 1973.

4.700 —— 'English foreign trade, 1660–1700',
Ec.H.R., 2nd ser., VII, 1954, 150–166.
Reprinted in Minchinton (1.330),
99–120.

4.700A —— *A Commercial Revolution: English
Overseas Trade in the seventeenth and
eighteenth Centuries*, Hist.Ass. pamphlet,
1967. A valuable short survey.

4.701 **Fisher**, F. J., 'Commercial trends and
policy in sixteenth-century England',
Ec.H.R., X, 1940, 95-117. Reprinted in
Carus-Wilson, ed., (1.326), I, 152–72. A
valuable article.

4.702 **Friis**, Astrid, *Alderman Cockayne's
Project: the commercial policy of England in
its main aspects, 1603–25*, Copenhagen,
1927. A useful book. The wider subtitle
is justified.

4.703 **Gould**, J. D., 'Cloth exports, 1600–1640',
Ec.H.R., 2nd ser., XXIV, 1971, 249–52. A
comment on W. B. Stephens's article
(4.713). *See also* Stephens's rejoinder,
ibid., 253–7.

4.704 **Harper**, L. A., *The English Navigation
Laws*, N. Y., 1939.

4.705 **Kepler**, J. S., 'Fiscal aspects of the
English carrying trade during the Thirty
Years War', *Ec.H.R.*, 2nd ser., XXV,
1972, 261–83.

4.706 **McLachlan**, Jean M. O., *Trade and Peace
with Old Spain, 1607–1750*, 1940.

4.707 **Minchinton**, W. E., ed., *The Growth of
English Overseas Trade in the Seventeenth
and Eighteenth Centuries*, 1969. A
collection of reprinted articles with a
valuable introduction and critical
bibliography.

4.708 **Price**, J. M., 'Multilateralism and/or
bilateralism. The settlement of English
trade balance with "the North" c. 1700',
Ec.H.R., 2nd ser., XIV, 1961, 254–74.

4.709 **Priestley**, M., 'Anglo-French trade and
the "unfavourable balance" controversy,
1660–1685', *Ec.H.R.*, 2nd ser., IV, 1951,
37–52.

4.710 **Rabb**, T. K., *Enterprise and Empire:
Merchant and Gentry investment in the
expansion of England, 1575–1630*,
Cambridge, Mass., 1967. A computer-
based study. Good bibliography.

4.711 **Ramsay**, G. D., *English Overseas Trade
during the Centuries of Emergence*, 1957. A
good survey.

4.712 **Ramsey**, P., 'Overseas trade in the reign
of Henry VII: the evidence of customs
accounts', *Ec.H.R.*, 2nd ser., VI, 1953,
173–82.

4.713 **Stephens**, W. B., 'The cloth exports of
the provincial ports, 1600–1640',
Ec.H.R., 2nd ser., XXII, 1969, 228–48.

4.714 **Stone**, L., 'Elizabethan overseas trade',
Ec.H.R., 2nd ser., II, 1949, 30–58.

4.715 **Supple**, B. E., *Commercial Crisis and
Change in England 1600–1642: A Study in
the Instability of a Mercantile Economy*,
1959. A very important contribution to
seventeenth-century English economic
and social history.

4.716 **Taylor**, H., 'Trade neutrality and the
"English road", 1630–1648', *Ec.H.R.*,

2nd ser., XXV, 1972, 236–60.

4.717 **Waters**, D. W., *The Art of Navigation in England in Elizabethan and Early Stuart Times*, 1958.

4.718 **Willan**, T. S., *Studies in Elizabethan Foreign Trade*, 1959. An important collection of essays, particularly useful for English trade with Morocco. *See also* Carus-Wilson and Coleman (3.311).

4.719 **Zahedieh**, Nuala, 'London and the colonial consumer in the late seventeenth century', *Ec.H.R.*, XLVII, 1994, 239–61.

(b) England and the age of encounter

Many contemporary accounts of voyages of discovery have been published in modern editions. The reader is referred to the publications of the Hakluyt Society, London.

4.720 **Parry**, J. H., *The Age of Reconnaissance*, 1963. The best general introduction.

4.721 **Scammell**, G. V., 'The New Worlds and Europe in the sixteenth century', *H.J.*, XII, 1969, 389–412.

4.722 **Williamson**, J. A., *A Short History of British Expansion*, 1945.

(c) Trading companies and their organisation

4.723 **Carr**, C. T., ed., *Select Charters of Trading Companies, 1530–1707*, Selden Soc., XXVIII, 1913. A very useful collection which includes the charters of the Levant, Newfoundland and African Companies (1600, 1610 and 1618 respectively), and also the charters of major industrial undertakings.

4.724 **Rich**, E. E., ed., *Hudson's Bay Company Minutes (1671–84)*, 3 vols., 1942–60.

4.725 **Davies**, K. G., 'Joint stock investment in the late seventeenth century', *Ec.H.R.*, 2nd ser., IV, 1952, 283–301. Reprinted in Carus-Wilson, ed. (1.326), II, 273–90.

4.726 **Scott**, W. R., *The Constitution and Finance of English, Scottish and Irish Joint Stock Companies to 1720*, 3 vols., 1910–12. The scope of the work is as follows: volume 1 deals with the general development of the joint stock system to 1720; volume 2 surveys companies for foreign trade,

colonization, fishing and mining; volume 3 covers water supply, postal arrangements, street lighting, manufacturing, banking, finance and insurance.

(i) THE MERCHANT ADVENTURERS

4.727 **Lingelbach**, W. E., ed., *The Merchant Adventurers of England: Their Laws and Ordinances, With Other Documents*, Philadelphia, 1902.

4.728 **McGrath**, P. V., ed., *Records Relating to the Society of Merchant Venturers of Bristol in the Seventeenth Century*, Bristol Rec.Soc., XVII, 1952.

4.729 **Wheeler**, J. A., *Treatise of Commerce* (1601), ed. G. B. Hotchkiss, N. Y., 1931. Designed as a defence of the Merchant Adventurers' Company.

4.730 **Lingelbach**, W. E., 'The internal organisation of the Merchant Adventurers of England', *T.R.H.S.*, 2nd ser., XVI, 1902, 19–67.

4.731 **McGrath**, P. V., *The Merchant Venturers of Bristol*, 1975.

4.732 **Unwin**, G., 'The Merchant Adventurers' Company in the reign of Elizabeth'. In Unwin (1.283), 133–220.

(ii) THE RUSSIA COMPANY

4.733 **Willan**, T. S., *The Muscovy Merchants of 1555*, 1953.

4.734 —— *The Early History of the Russia Company, 1553–1603*, 1956. The standard works on the subject.

(iii) THE EASTLAND COMPANY AND TRADE WITH THE BALTIC

4.735 **Sellers**, Maud, ed., *The Acts and Ordinances of the Eastland Company of York*, Camden Soc., 3rd ser., XI, 1906.

4.736 **Aström**, S. E., *From Stockholm to St. Petersburg: Commercial Factors in the Political Relations between England and Sweden, 1675–1700*, Finnish H.Soc., Studia Historica, II, Helsinki, 1962.

4.737 —— *From Cloth to Iron. The Anglo-Baltic Trade in the Late Seventeenth Century. Part One: The Growth, Structure and*

4.738 *Organisation of the Trade*, Helsinki, 1963.

4.738 —— *From Cloth to Iron: The Anglo-Baltic Trade in the Late Seventeenth Century. Part Two*, Helsinki, 1965.

4.739 —— 'The English Navigation Laws and the Baltic trade 1660–1700', *Scand. Ec.H.R.*, VIII, 1960, 3–18.

4.740 **Deardorff**, N. R., 'English trade in the Baltic during the reign of Elizabeth', in *Studies in the History of English Commerce in the Tudor Period*, N. Y., 1912.

4.741 **Fedorowicz**, J. K., *England's Baltic Trade in the Early Seventeenth Century. A Study in Anglo-Polish Commercial Relations*, 1979.

4.742 **Hinton**, R. W. K., *The Eastland Trade and the Commonwealth in the Seventeenth Century*, 1959. The main work on England's trade with the Baltic. *See* the review article by R. H. Tawney, *Ec.H.R.*, 2nd ser., XII, 1959, 280–82.

4.743 **Zins**, H., *England and the Baltic in the Elizabethan Era*, 1972.

(iv) THE LEVANT

4.744 **Davis**, R., 'England and the Mediterranean, 1570–1670', in Fisher, ed. (4.52), 117–37.

4.745 **Foster**, W., *England's Quest of Eastern Trade*, 1933.

4.746 **Horniker**, A. L., 'Anglo-French rivalry in the Levant from 1583 to 1612', *J.M.H.*, XVIII, 1946, 289–305.

4.747 **Skilliter**, Susan A., *William Harborne and the Trade with Turkey, 1578–82. A Documentary study of the first Anglo-Ottoman Relations*, 1977.

4.748 **Willan**, T. S., 'Some aspects of English trade with the Levant in the sixteenth century', *E.H.R.*, LXX, 1955, 399–410.

4.749 **Wood**, A. C., *A History of the Levant Company*, 1935. Reprinted 1964.

(v) THE EAST INDIA COMPANY

4.750 **Bassett**, D. K., 'The trade of the East India Company in the Far East, 1623–1684', *J.Royal Asiatic Society*, 1960, 32–47.

4.751 **Chaudhuri**, K. N., *The English East India Company: The Study of an Early Joint Stock Company, 1600–1640*, 1965.

4.752 —— *The Trading World of Asia and the English East India Company 1660–1760*, 1978.

4.753 —— 'Treasure and trade balances: the East India Company's export trade', *Ec.H.R.*, 2nd ser., XXI, 1968, 480–502.

4.754 **Krishna**, B., *Commercial Relations Between India and England, 1601–1757*, 1924.

4.755 **Thomas**, P. J., *Mercantilism and the East India Trade*, 1926. Reprinted 1963.

(vi) MISCELLANEOUS

4.756 **Davies**, K. G., *The Royal Africa Company*, 1957.

4.757 **Preston**, R. A., 'The Laconia Company of 1629: an English attempt to intercept the fur trade', *Canadian H.R.*, XXXI, 1950, 125–44.

4.758 **Rich**, E. E., *The History of the Hudson's Bay Company I: 1670–1763*, Hudson's Bay Rec.Soc., 1958.

4.759 **Robbins**, W. G., 'The Massachusetts Bay Company: an analysis of motives', *Historian*, XXXII, 1969, 83–98. *See also* Rose-Troup (4.789).

(d) The mercantile community

4.760 **Dodd**, A. H., 'Mr Myddleton, the merchant of Tower St.'. In Bindoff, Hurstfield and Williams, eds. (4.32a), 249–81.

4.761 **Grassby**, R., 'The personal wealth of the business community in seventeenth-century England', *Ec.H.R.*, 2nd ser., XXIII, 1970, 220–34.

4.762 —— 'English merchant capitalism in the late seventeenth century: the composition of business fortunes', *P.P.*, 46, 1970, 87–107.

4.763 **Hoskins**, W. G., 'The Elizabethan merchants of Exeter'. In Bindoff, Hurstfield and Williams, eds. (4.32a), 163–87.

4.764 **Lang**, R. G., 'Social origins and social aspirations of Jacobean London merchants', *Ec.H.R.*, 1974, 28–47.

4.765 **Ramsey**, P., 'Some Tudor merchants' accounts'. In A. C. Littleton and B. S. Yamey, eds., *Studies in the History of Accounting*, Homewood, Ill., 1956, 185–201.

4.766 **Webb**, J., *Great Tooley of Ipswich: A Portrait of an Early Tudor Merchant*, Suffolk, Rec.Soc., 1963.

4.767 **Winchester**, *Barbara*, Tudor Family Portrait, 1955.

(e) Anglo-Dutch commercial relations

4.768 **Boxer**, C. R., *The Dutch Seaborne Empire, 1600–1800*, 1965.

4.769 —— 'Some second thoughts on the third Anglo-Dutch War, 1672–74', *T.R.H.S.*, 5th ser., XIX, 1969, 67–94.

4.770 **Clark**, G. N., *The Dutch Alliance and the War Against French Trade, 1688–1697*, 1923.

4.771 **Farnell**, J. E., 'The Navigation Act of 1651, the first Dutch War and the London merchant community', *Ec.H.R.*, 2nd ser., XVI, 1964, 439–54.

4.772 **Wilson**, C., *Profit and Power: A Study of England and the Dutch Wars*, 1957. The main work on the subject. For eighteenth-century developments in Anglo-Dutch relations, *see* (4.96), by the same author.

4.773 —— 'Cloth production and international competition in the seventeenth century', *Ec.H.R.*, 2nd ser., XIII, 1960, 209–21.

See also Barbour (4.558).

(f) Coastal trade

4.774 **Smith**, R. A., *Sea Coal for London: History of the Coal Factors in the London Market*, 1961. Nef (4.558), is also useful on this aspect.

4.775 **Willan**, T. S., *The English Coasting Trade, 1600–1750*, 1938. Reprinted with new preface, 1967. The standard work.

(g) Smuggling

4.776 **Ramsay**, G. D., 'The smugglers' trade: a neglected aspect of English commercial development', *T.R.H.S*, 5th ser., II, 1952, 131–57.

4.777 **Rive**, A., 'A short history of tobacco smuggling', *Ec.J.Ec.H.Supp.*, I, 1929, 554–69. *See also* Williams (3.347).

(h) Colonies

4.778 **Allen**, D. G., *In English Ways. The Movement of Societies and the Transferal of English Local Law and Custom to Massachusetts Bay in the Seventeenth Century*, Chapel Hill, N. C., 1981.

4.779 **Andrews**, C. M., *The Colonial Period of American History*, 4 vols., 1934.

4.780 —— British Committees, Commissions and Councils of Trade and Plantations, 1622–1675, Baltimore, 1908.

4.781 **Bailyn**, B., *The New England Merchants in the Seventeenth Century*, Harvard, Mass., 1955.

4.782 **Cell**, G. T., 'The Newfoundland Company: a study of subscribers to a colonizing venture', *William and Mary Quarterly*, XXII, 1965, 611–25.

4.783 **Gillespie**, J. E., *The Influence of Overseas Expansion on England to 1700*, Columbia University Studies in History, Economics and Public Law, N. Y., 1920.

4.784 **Knorr**, K. E., *British Colonial Theories, 1570–1850*, 1944. Reprinted 1963.

4.785 **Lucas**, C. P., *Religion, Colonising and Trade: The Driving Forces of the Old Empire*, 1930.

4.786 **Newton**, A. P., *The European Nations in the West Indies*, 1933.

4.787 **Quinn**, D. B., 'The first Pilgrims', *William and Mary Quarterly*, 3rd ser., XXIII, 1966, 359–90.

4.788 —— 'The failure of Raleigh's American colonies'. In H. A. Cronne, T. W. Moody and D. B. Quinn, eds., *Essays in British and Irish History in Honour of James Eadie Todd*, 1949, 61–85.

4.789 **Rose-Troup**, Frances, *The Massachusetts Bay Company and its Predecessors*, 1930.

4.790 **Wright**, L. B., *Religion and Empire: The Alliance Between Piety and Commerce in English Expansion, 1558–1625*, Chapel Hill N. C., 1943.

(i) Miscellaneous

4.791 **Hinton**, R. W. K., ed., *The Port Books of Boston, 1601–1640*, Lincs.Rec.Soc., L, 1956.

4.792 **Vanes**, Jean, ed., *Documents Illustrating the Overseas Trade of Bristol in the Sixteenth Century*, Bristol Rec.Soc., XXI, 1979.

4.793 **Jarvis**, R. C., 'Sources for the history of ports', *J.Trans.H.*, III, 1957–8, 76–93.

4.794 **Andrews**, K. R., *Elizabethan Privateering.*

English Privateering During the Spanish War, 1585–1603, 1964.

4.795 **Ashton**, R., 'The parliamentary agitation for free trade in the opening years of the reign of James I', *P.P.*, 38, 1967, 40–55.

4.796 **Croft**, Pauline, 'Free trade and the House of Commons 1605–1606', *Ec.H.R.*, 2nd ser., XXVIII, 1975, 17–27.

4.797 **Cullen**, L. M., *Anglo-Irish Trade, 1660–1800*, 1968. Extensive bibliography, 221–42. *See also* Longfield (4.811).

4.798 **Davis**, R., *The Trade and Shipping of Hull, 1500–1700*, East Yorks.Loc.H.Soc., pamphlet series, 17, 1964.

4.799 **Edler**, F., 'Winchcombe kerseys in Antwerp, 1538–44', *Ec.H.R.*, VII, 1936, 57–62.

4.800 **Gould**, J. D., 'The crisis in the export trade, 1586–7', *E.H.R.*, LXXI, 1956, 212–22.

4.801 ―― 'The trade depression of the early 1620s', *Ec.H.R.*, 2nd ser., VII, 1954, 81–90.

4.802 ―― 'The trade crisis of the early 1620s and English economic thought', *J.Ec.H.*, XV, 1955, 121–33.

4.803 **Gravil**, R., 'Trading to Spain and Portugal, 1670–1700', *Bus.H.*, X, 1968, 69–88.

4.804 **Innis**, H. A., *The Cod Fisheries*, 1940. Chapter 3 deals with the Spanish and English fisheries, 1550–1600.

4.805 **Jenkins**, J. T., *The Herring and the Herring Industries*, 1927. *See* 80–90 for some account of Stuart fishery companies.

4.806 **Jones**, D. W., 'The "Hallage" receipts of the London cloth markets 1562–c.1720', *Ec.H.R.*, 2nd ser., XXV, 1972, 567–87.

4.807 **Jones**, J. R., 'Some aspects of London mercantile activity during the reign of Queen Elizabeth'. In N. Downes, ed., *Essays in Honour of Conyers Read*, Chicago, Ill., 1953, 186–99.

4.808 **Jones**, W. J., 'Elizabethan marine insurance – the judicial undergrowth', *Bus.H.*, II, 1959, 53–66.

4.809 **Kepler**, J. S., *The Exchange of Christendom. The International Entrepôt at Dover, 1622–41*, 1976.

4.810 **Koenigsberger**, H., 'English merchants in Naples and Sicily in the seventeenth century', *E.H.R.*, LXII, 1947, 304–26.

4.811 **Longfield**, Ada K., *Anglo-Irish Trade in the Sixteenth Century*, 1929. *See also*

Cullen (4.797).

4.812 **Loomie**, A. J., 'Religion and Elizabethan commerce with Spain', *Cath.H.R.*, 50, 1964, 27–51.

4.813 **Lounsbury**, R. G., *The British Fishery at Newfoundland, 1634–1763*, New Haven, Conn. 1934.

4.814 **MacInnes**, C. M., *The Early English Tobacco Trade*, 1926.

4.815 **McGrath**, P. V., *Merchants and Merchandise in Seventeenth-Century Bristol*, Bristol Rec.Soc., 1955.

4.816 **Maloney**, F. X., *The Fur Trade in New England, 1620–1676*, 1931. Reprinted 1967.

4.817 **Miller**, L. R., 'New evidence on the shipping and imports of London, 1601–1602', *Quarterly J. of Econ.*, 1927, 740–60.

4.818 **Nash**, R. C., 'The English and Scottish tobacco trades in the seventeenth and eighteenth centuries: legal and illegal trade', *Ec.H.R.*, 2nd ser., XXXV, 1982, 354–72.

4.819 **Nettels**, C. P., 'England and the Spanish-American trade, 1680–1715', *J.M.H.*, III, 1931, 1–32.

4.820 **Parkinson**, C. N., *The Rise of the Port of Liverpool*, 1952.

4.821 **Rabb**, T. K., 'Free trade and the gentry in the parliament of 1604', *P.P.*, 40, 1968, 165–73. A rejoinder to Ashton (4.795).

4.822 ―― 'Sir Edwin Sandys and the Parliament of 1604', *A.H.R.*, LXIX, 1963, 646–70.

4.823 **Reynolds**, P., 'Elizabethan traders in Normandy', *J.M.H.*, IX, 1937, 289–303.

4.824 **Ruddock**, A. A., 'London capitalists and the decline of Southampton in the early Tudor period', *Ec.H.R.*, 2nd ser., II, 1949, 137–51.

4.825 **Stephens**, W. B., 'The overseas trade of Chester in the early seventeenth century', *T.H.S.L.C.*, 120, 1968, 23–34.

4.826 ―― 'The West Country ports and the struggle for the Newfoundland fisheries in the seventeenth century', *Trans Devonshire Assoc.*, LXXXVIII, 1956, 90–101.

4.827 ―― 'The foreign trade of Plymouth and the Cornish ports in the early seventeenth century', *Trans.Devonshire Assoc.*, CI, 1969, 125–37.

4.828 **Tawney**, R. H., *Business and Politics in the Reign of James I: Lionel Cranfield as Merchant and Statesman*, 1958.

4.829 **Williams**, N., 'England's tobacco trade in the reign of Charles I', *Virginia Magazine of History and Biography*, LXV, 1957, 403–49.

4.830 —— *The Maritime Trade of the East Anglian Ports, 1550–1590*, 1988. Basically the text of a 1952 Oxford DPhil thesis based on late sixteenth-century customs records.

4.831 **Woodward**, D. M., *The Trade of Elizabethan Chester*, University of Hull Occ. Papers in Ec. and Soc.H., No. 4, 1970. Deals with the port's overseas, coastal and home trade.

See also Ruddock (3.340) and van der Wee (3.346). For the English customs in this period, *see* Atton and Holland (4.958), listed in the section on *Government policy and administration*.

THE CONCEPT OF MERCANTILISM

4.832 **Biltz**, R. C., 'Mercantilist policies and the pattern of world trade, 1500–1750', *J.Ec.H.*, XXVII, 1967, 39–55.

4.833 **Coats**, A. W., 'In defence of Heckscher and the idea of Mercantilism', *Scand.Ec.H.R.*, V, 1957, 173–87. *See* Heckscher below (4.838).

4.834 **Coleman**, D. C., ed., *Revisions in Mercantilism*, 1969. A useful collection of reprinted articles, including Coleman's own essay 'Eli Heckscher and the idea of mercantilism', 92–117. Bibliography.

4.835 —— 'Mercantilism revisited', *H.J.*, XXIII, 1980, 773–91.

4.836 **Grampp**, W. D., 'The liberal elements in English Mercantilism', *Q. J.Econ.*, 66, 1952, 456–501.

4.837 **Heaton**, H., 'Heckscher on mercantilism', *J.Pol.Econ.*, 45, 1937, 370–93.

4.838 **Heckscher**, E. F., *Mercantilism*, 2 vols. English trans., 1935, 2nd ed., London and N. Y. 1956. A major work though one which has been criticised for its failure to distinguish between economic theory and economic practice. *See* Coleman (4.834).

4.839 —— 'Revisions in economic history: mercantilism', *Ec.H.R.*, VII, 1936–7, 44–54. Reprinted in Coleman (4.834), 19–34. Heckscher's second thoughts on the subject.

4.840 **Herlitz**, L., 'The concept of mercantilism', *Scand.Ec.H.R.*, XII, 1964, 101–20.

4.841 **Hinton**, R. W. K., 'The mercantile system in the time of Mun', *Ec.H.R.*, 2nd ser., VII, 1954–5, 277–90.

4.842 **Judges**, A. V., 'The idea of a mercantile state', *T.R.H.S.*, 4th ser., XXI, 1939, 41–70. Reprinted in Coleman (4.834), 35–60.

4.843 **Magnusson**, L., 'Eli Heckscher, Mercantilism and the favourable balance of trade', *Scand.Ec.H.R.*, XXVI, 1978, 103–27.

4.844 **Minchinton**, W. E., ed., *Mercantilism: system or expediency?*, Boston, Mass., 1969. A collection of brief extracts from the main contributions to the debate on the subject.

4.845 **Viner**, J., 'Power versus plenty as objectives of foreign policy in the seventeenth and eighteenth centuries', *World Politics*, I, 1948, 1–29. Reprinted in Coleman (4.834), 61–91.

4.846 **Wilson**, C., *Mercantilism*, Hist.Ass. pamphlet, 1958.

4.847 —— 'The other face of Mercantilism', *T.R.H.S.*, 5th ser., IX, 1959, 81–101, Reprinted in Wilson (4.97), 73–93.

4.848 —— 'Mercantilism. Some vicissitudes of an idea', *Ec.H.R.*, 2nd ser., X, 1957, 181–88. Reprinted in Wilson (4.97), 62–72.

4.849 —— 'Treasure and trade balances: the Mercantilist problem', *Ec.H.R.*, 2nd ser., II, 1949, 152–61. Reprinted in Wilson (4.97), 48–61.

4.850 —— 'Treasure and trade balances: further evidence', *Ec.H.R.*, 2nd ser., IV, 1951, 231–42.

4.851 —— 'Trade, society and the state'. In Wilson (4.97), 487–576.

COMMUNICATIONS AND INTERNAL TRADE

For fuller details of the literature of the subject, the reader is referred to the extensive bibliographies contained in Dyos and Aldcroft (5.1341) and Jackman (5.1343).

(a) River Navigation

4.852 **Chalklin**, C. W., 'Navigation schemes of the Upper Medway, 1600–1665', *J.Trans.H.*, V, 1961, 105–15.

4.853 **Duckham**, B. F., *The Yorkshire Ouse. The History of a River Navigation*, 1967.

4.854 **Skempton**, A. W., 'The engineers of the English river navigations, 1620–1760', *Trans. Newcomen Soc.*, XXIX, 1953–5, 24–54.

4.855 **Stephens**, W. B., 'The Exeter Lighter Canal, 1566–1698', *J.Trans.H.*, III, 1957, 1–11.

4.856 **Summers**, Dorothy, *The Great Ouse: The History of a River Navigation*, 1973.

4.857 **Willan**, T. S., *River Navigation in England, 1600–1750*, 1936. Reprinted 1964. The standard work.

4.858 —— *The Navigation of the Great Ouse between St Ives and Bedford in the Seventeenth Century*, Bed.Rec.Soc., 1946.

4.859 —— 'The navigation of the Thames and Kennet, 1600–1750', *Berks.Arch.J.*, XL, 1936, 144–56.

4.860 —— 'Yorkshire river navigation, 1600–1750', *Geog.*, XXII, 1937, 189–99.

4.861 —— 'River navigation and trade from the Witham to the Yare, 1600–1750', *Norfolk Arch.*, XXVI, 1938, 296–309.

4.862 —— 'The river navigation and trade of the Severn Valley, 1600–1750', *Ec.H.R.*, VIII, 1937–8, 68–79.

4.863 **Wood**, A. C., 'The history of the trade and transport on the river Trent', *Trans. Thoroton Soc.*, LIV, 1950, 1–44.

(b) Roads and their traffic

4.864 **Austen**, B., *English Provincial Posts, 1633–1840. A Study based on Kent Examples*, 1978.

4.865 **Cossons**, A., 'Warwickshire turnpikes', *Trans.Birm.Arch.Soc.*, LXIX, for 1941–2, 1946, 53–100.

4.866 **Crofts**, J. E. W., *Packhorse, Waggon and Post: Land Carriage and Communications under the Tudors and Stuarts*, 1967. A rather unsystematic treatment of the subject, based on literary evidence.

4.867 **Emmison**, F. G., 'The earliest Turnpike Bill (Biggleswade to Baldock road), 1622', *B.I.H.R.*, XII, 1935, 108–22.

4.868 —— '1555 and all that: a milestone in the history of the English road', *Essex R.*, 64, 1955, 15–25.

4.869 —— 'Was the highways Act of 1555 a success?', *Essex R.*, 64, 1955, 221–34.

4.870 **Fordham**, H. G., *The Road Books and Itineraries of Great Britain, 1570–1850*, 1924.

4.871 **Guttery**, D. R., 'Stourbridge market in Tudor times', *Trans.Worcs.Arch.Soc.*, n.s., XXX, 1954, 16–38.

4.872 **Parkes**, Joan, *Travel in England in the Seventeenth Century*, 1925. Reprinted 1968.

(c) Internal trade

See also the section on *Marketing* under *Agriculture.*

4.873 **Berger**, R. M., 'The development of retail trade in provincial England, c.1550–1700', *J.Ec.H.*, XL, 1980, 123–8.

4.874 **Chartres**, J. A., *Internal Trade in England, 1500–1700*, 1977.

4.875 —— 'Road carrying in the seventeenth century: myth and reality', *Ec.H.R.*, 2nd ser., XXX, 1977, 73–94.

4.876 **Edwards**, P. R., 'The horse trade of Chester in the sixteenth and seventeenth centuries', *J.Chester Arch.Soc.*, LXII, 1980, 91–106.

4.877 —— 'The horse trade of the Midlands in the seventeenth century', *Ag.H.R.*, XXVII, 1979, 90–100. *See also* (4.357).

4.878 **Hey**, D., *Packmen, Carriers and Packhorse Roads. Trade and Communications in North Derbyshire and South Yorkshire*, 1980.

4.879 **Hodgen**, Margaret J., 'Fairs of Elizabethan England', *Ec.Geog.*, XVIII, 1942, 389–400.

4.880 **Rodgers**, H. B., 'The market area of Preston in the sixteenth and seventeenth centuries', *Geog.Studs.*, III, 1956, 46–55.

4.881 **Simpson**, A., 'Thomas Callum, draper, 1587–1664', *Ec.H.R.*, 2nd ser., XI, 1958, 19–34.

4.882 **Spufford**, Margaret, *The Great Re-*

Clothing of Rural England. Petty Chapman and their Wares in the Seventeenth Century, 1983. Brings together much scattered information on petty trading activities.

4.883 **Tupling**, G. H., 'Lancashire markets in the sixteenth and seventeenth centuries, Parts 1 and 2', *T.L.C.A.S.*, LVIII, 1947, 1–34; *ibid.*, LIX, 1948, 1–34.

4.884 **Westerfield**, R. B., *Middlemen in English Business, Particularly between 1660 and 1760*, Trans. Connecticut Academy of Arts and Sciences, XIX, Connecticut, 1915. Reprinted N. Y., 1969.

4.885 **Willan**, T. S., *The Inland Trade. Studies in English Internal Trade in the Sixteenth and Seventeenth Centuries*, 1976. Has chapters on the wholesale and retail trades and on the movement of goods by land, river and sea.

4.886 **Williams**, N., *Tradesmen in Early Stuart Wiltshire*, Wilts.Arch. and Nat.H.Soc., Records branch, XV, 1960.

See also Everitt (4.358), Fisher (4.360) and Gras (4.361).

PRICES, PUBLIC FINANCE, BANKING AND FINANCIAL DEALINGS

(a) Prices

4.887 **Beveridge**, W. H., *Prices and Wages in England from the Twelfth to the Nineteenth Century I: Prices Tables: The Mercantile Era*, 1939. Reprinted 1966.

4.888 **Bowden**, P. J., 'Agricultural prices, farm profits and rents'. In Thirsk (4.322), 593–695. An important 'physical' interpretation of trends in agricultural prices.

4.889 **Brenner**, Y. S., 'The inflation of prices in early sixteenth-century England', *Ec.H.R.*, 2nd ser., XIV, 1961, 225–39.

4.890 —— 'The inflation of prices in England, 1551–1650', *Ec.H.R.*, XV, 1962, 266–84.

4.891 —— 'The price revolution reconsidered: a reply', *Ec.H.R.*, 2nd ser., XVIII, 1965, 392–6. A reply to Gould (4.896).

4.892 **Challis**, C. E., *The Tudor Coinage*, 1978.

A Comprehensive study dealing with the supply of bullion, with mints and minting, circulation, and the rôle of government.

4.893 **Fisher**, F. J., 'Influenza and inflation in Tudor England', *Ec.H.R.*, 2nd ser., XVIII, 1965, 120–29. Argues that a sharp fall in prices in 1558 was possibly the result of an influenza epidemic in the preceding year. *See* (4.216) and (4.228).

4.894 **Gould**, J. D., *The Great Debasement: currency and the economy in mid-Tudor England*, 1970.

4.895 —— 'The Royal Mint in the early seventeenth-century', *Ec.H.R.*, 2nd ser., V., 1952, 240–8.

4.896 —— 'Y. S. Brenner on prices: a comment', *Ec.H.R.*, 2nd ser., XVI, 1963, 351–60.

4.897 —— 'The price revolution reconsidered', *Ec.H.R.*, 2nd ser., XVII, 1964, 249–66.

4.898 **Hamilton**, E. J., 'American treasure and Andalusian prices, 1503–1660', *J.Ec.& Bus.H.*, I, 1928, 1–35. Related inflation to the influx of specie from the New World.

4.899 **Horsefield**, J. K., *British Monetary Experiments, 1650–1710*, 1960.

4.900 **Li**, M. H., *The Great Recoinage of 1696–9*, 1963.

4.901 **Monroe**, A. E., *Monetary Theory before Adam Smith*, 1923. Reprinted N. Y., 1966.

4.902 **Nef**, J. U., 'Prices and industrial capitalism in France and England, 1540–1640', *Ec.H.R.*, VII, 1937, 155–85. Reprinted in Carus-Wilson, ed. (1.326), I, 108–34.

4.903 **Outhwaite**, R. B., *Inflation in Tudor and Early Stuart England*, 1969. Studies in Economic History series (pamphlet). A valuable summary, with a bibliographical guide to the growing literature of the subject.

4.904 **Price**, J. M., 'Notes on some London price currents, 1667–1715', *Ec.H.R.*, 2nd ser., VII, 1954, 240–50.

4.905 **Ramsey**, P., ed., *The Price Revolution in Sixteenth-Century England*, 1971. Collects together several key articles.

4.906 **Schumpeter**, Elizabeth, 'English prices and public finance, 1660–1682', *Review of Economics and Statistics*, XX, 1938, 21–37.

4.907 **Supple**, B. E., 'Currency and commerce in the early seventeenth century', *Ec.H.R.*, 2nd ser., X, 1957, 239–55.

4.908 **Taylor**, H., 'Price revolution or price revision? The English and Spanish trade after 1604', *Renaiss.&Mod.Studs.*, XII, 1968, 5–32. *See also* Brown (4.1186), Burnett (3.357), Craig (2.289) and Feavearyear (2.294).

(b) Public finance: income and management

4.909 **Alsop**, J. D., *'The theory and practice of Tudor taxation'*, *E.H.R.*, XCVII, 1982, 1–31.

4.910 **Ashton**, R., *The Crown and the Money Market, 1603–40*, 1960.

4.911 'Charles I and the City'. In Fisher (4.52), 138–63.

4.912 —— 'Revenue farming under the early Stuarts', *Ec.H.R.*, 2nd ser., VIII, 1956, 310–22.

4.913 —— 'Deficit finance in the reign of James I', *Ec.H.R.*, 2nd ser., X, 1957, 15–29.

4.914 **Aylmer**, G. E., 'The last years of purveyance, 1610–60', *Ec.H.R.*, 2nd ser., X, 1957, 81–93.

4.915 —— 'Attempts at administrative reform, 1625–40', *E.H.R.*, LXXII, 1957, 229–59. *See also* Aylmer (4.959).

4.916 **Baxter**, S. B., *The Development of the Treasury, 1660–1702*, 1957.

4.917 **Bernard**, G. W., *War, Taxation and Rebellion*, 1986. A revisionist account – not altogether convincing – of the Amicable Grant of 1525.

4.918 **Chandaman**, C. D., *The English Public Revenue, 1660–88*, 1975. Has chapters on direct taxation and on customs and excise, the hearth tax, and casual receipts.

4.919 **Dietz**, F., *English Government Finance, 1485–1558*, Urbana, Ill., 1920. reprinted, with corrections, 1964.

4.920 —— *English Public Finance, 1558–1641*, N. Y., 1932. Reprinted 1964.

4.921 **Elton**, G. R., 'The Elizabethan Exchequer: war in the receipt'. In Bindoff, Hurstfield and Williams (4.32a), 213–48.

4.922 —— 'Taxation for war and peace in early Tudor England' in Winter (1.332), 33–48.

4.923 **Glassman**, D. and Reddish, A., 'Currency depreciation in early modern England and France', *Expl.Entrepren.H.*, XXV, 1988, 75–98.

4.924 **Harriss**, G. L., 'Aids, loans and benevolences', *H.J.*, VI, 1963, 1–19.

4.925 —— 'Fictitious loans', *Ec.H.R.*, 2nd ser., VIII, 1955–56, 187–99.

4.926 **Hurstfield**, J., *The Queen's Wards: Wardship and Marriage under Elizabeth I*, 1958. A scholarly investigation of the administration of wardships by the Court of Wards.

4.927 —— 'The profits of fiscal feudalism', *Ec.H.R.*, 2nd ser., VIII, 1955, 53–61.

4.928 **Mayes**, C. R., 'The sale of peerages in early Stuart England', *J.M.H.*, XXIX, 1957, 21–37.

4.929 **Richards**, R. D., 'The Exchequer in Cromwellian times', *Ec.J.Ec.H.Supp.*, II, 1931, 213–33.

4.930 —— 'The stop of the Exchequer', *Ec.J.Ec. H.Supp.*, II, 1930, 45–62.

4.931 **Richardson**, W. C., 'Some financial expedients of Henry VIII', *Ec.H.R.*, 2nd ser., VII, 1954, 33–58.

4.932 **Stone**, L., 'The inflation of honours, 1558–1641', *P.P.*, 1958, 45–70.

4.933 **Woodworth**, Allegra, 'Purveyance for the royal household in the reign of Queen Elizabeth', *Trans.American Phil.Soc.*, n.s., XXXV, 1945.

See also Dickson (5.1806) and Roseveare (2.310). *See also* the section on Crown Lands listed under *Agriculture and rural society* (p. 63).

(c) Banking and financial dealings

4.934 **Tawney**, R. H., ed. *Thomas Wilson's Discourse on Usury, 1572*, 1925. Reprinted 1962.

4.935 **Andréades**, A. M., *History of the Bank of England, 1640–1903*, 1909, 4th ed., with an introduction by P. Einzig, 1966.

4.936 **Ashton**, R., 'Usury and high finance in the age of Shakespeare and Jonson', *Renaiss.& Mod.Studs.*, IV, 1960, 14–43.

4.937 **Bisschop**, W. R., *The Rise of the London Money Market, 1640–1826*, 1910. Reprinted 1968.

4.938 **Buckley**, H., 'Sir Thomas Gresham and the foreign exchanges', *Ec. J.*, XXXIV, 1924, 589–601.

4.939 **Ehrenberg**, R., *Capital and Finance in the Age of the Renaissance*, N. Y., 1928.

4.940 **Grassby**, R., 'The rate of profit in seventeenth-century England', *E.H.R.*, LXXXIV, 1969, 721–51.

4.941 **Holden**, J. M., 'Bills of exchange in the seventeenth century', *Law Quarterly R.*,

LXVII, 1951, 230–48.

4.942 **Horsefield**, J. K., 'The Bank of England as mentor', *Ec.H.R.*, 2nd ser., II, 1949, 80–108.

4.943 **Kerridge**, E., *Trade and Banking in Early Modern England*, 1988. Includes chapters on commercial credit, bills of exchange, and the London money market. Excellent bibliography.

4.944 **Muldrew**, C., 'Credit and the courts: debt litigation in a seventeenth-century urban community', *Ec.H.R.*, XLVI, 1993, 23–38.

4.945 **Outhwaite**, R. B., 'The trials of foreign borrowing: the English Crown and the Antwerp Money Market in the mid-sixteenth century', *Ec.H.R.*, 2nd ser., XIX, 1966, 289–305.

4.946 —— 'Royal borrowing in the reign of Elizabeth I: the Aftermath of Antwerp', *E.H.R.*, LXXXVI, 1971, 251–63.

4.947 **Powell**, E. T., *The Evolution of the Money Market, 1385–1915*, 1915. Reprinted 1966.

4.948 **Richards**, R. D., *The Early History of Banking in England*, 1928. Reprinted 1958.

4.949 —— 'The pioneers of banking in England', *Ec.J.Ec.H.Supp.*, I, 1929, 485–502.

4.950 **Roover**, R. de, *Gresham on Foreign Exchange: An Essay on Early English Mercantilism, With the Text of Sir Thomas Gresham's Memorandum for the Understanding of the Exchange*, Cambridge, Mass., 1949. While the book as a whole is of considerable value, the question of the authorship of the *Memorandum* is less clear-cut than is suggested here.

4.951 **Rubini**, D., 'Politics and the battle for the banks, 1688–1697', *E.H.R.*, LXXXV, 1970, 693–714.

4.952 **Stone**, L., *An Elizabethan: Sir Horatio Palavicino*, 1956. Palavicino was an important source of loans to the crown.

4.953 **Tucker**, G. S. L., *Progress and Profits in British Economic Thought, 1650–1850*, 1960. Chapter 2 deals with 'The problem of interest in the seventeenth century'.

4.954 **Van der Wee**, H., *The Financial Revolution in Pre-industrial Europe*, 1988. For background.

4.955 **Yamey**, B. S., 'Scientific book-keeping and the rise of capitalism', *Ec.H.R.*, 2nd ser., I, 1948, 99–113.

4.956 ——, Edey, H. C. and Thomson, H. W.,

Accounting in England and Scotland, 1543–1800, 1963.

GOVERNMENT POLICY AND ADMINISTRATION

(a) The central government

4.957 **Ashley**, M., *Financial and Commercial Policy under the Cromwellian Protectorate*, 1934, 2nd ed., 1962.

4.958 **Atton**, H. and Holland, H. H., *The King's Customs, 1600–1706*, 2 vols., 1908–10. Reprinted 1968.

4.959 **Aylmer**, G. E., *The King's Servants: The Civil Service of Charles I, 1625–42*, 1961, 2nd ed., 1974.

4.960 —— *The State's Servants. The Civil Service of the English Republic 1649–1660*, 1973.

4.961 —— 'From officeholding to civil service: the genesis of modern bureaucracy', *T.R.H.S.*, 5th ser., XXX, 1980, 91–108.

4.962 **Baldwin**, F. E., *Sumptuary Legislation and Personal Regulation in England*, Johns Hopkins University Studies in Historical and Political Science, ser. 44, No. 1, Baltimore, 1926.

4.963 **Beresford**, M. W., 'The common informer, the penal statutes and economic regulation', *Ec.H.R.*, 2nd ser., X, 1957–8, 221–38.

4.964 **Bindoff**, S. T., 'The making of the Statute of Artificers'. In Bindoff, Hurstfield and Williams, ed. (4.32a), 59–94.

4.965 **Bush**, M. L., *The Government Policy of Protector Somerset*, 1975.

4.966 **Colvin**, H. M., 'Castles and government in Tudor England', *E.H.R.*, LXXXIII, 1968, 225–34.

4.967 **Cooper**, J. P., 'Economic regulation and the cloth industry in seventeenth-century England', *T.R.H.S.*, 5th ser., XX, 1970, 73–99.

4.968 **Davies**, C. S. L., 'The administration of the royal navy under Henry VIII', *E.H.R.*, LXXX, 1966, 268–86.

4.969 —— 'Provisions for armies, 1509–60: a

study in the effectiveness of early Tudor government', *Ec.H.R.*, 2nd ser., XVII, 1964, 234–48.

4.970 **Davis**, R., 'The rise of Protection in England, 1669–1786', *Ec.H.R.*, XIX, 1966, 306–17.

4.971 **Elton**, G. R., *Studies in Tudor and Stuart Politics and Government*, 2 vols., 1974.

4.972 —— *The Tudor Revolution in Government*, 1953. A controversial study which concentrates on Thomas Cromwell's administrative reforms and argues that they marked the end of the Middle Ages.

4.973 —— *Reform and Renewal: Thomas Cromwell and the Commonweal*, 1973.

4.974 —— *Policy and Police*, 1972. A study of the enforcement of the Henrician Reformation.

4.975 **Fox**, H. G., *Monopolies and Patents: A Study in the History and Future of the Patent Monopoly*, Toronto and London, 1947.

4.976 **Heinze**, R. W., *The Proclamations of the Tudor Kings*, 1976.

4.977 **Hughes**, E., *Studies in Administration and Finance, 1558–1825, With Special Reference to the History of Salt Taxation in England*, 1934.

4.978 —— 'The English Stamp Duties, 1664–1764', *E.H.R.*, XVI, 1941, 234–64.

4.979 **Hurstfield**, J., *Freedom, Corruption and Government in Elizabethan England*, 1973. Collects together the author's essays in this field.

4.980 **Lindquist**, E. N., 'The King, the people and the House of Commons: the problem of early Jacobean purveyance', *H.J.*, XXXI, 1988, 549–70.

4.981 **Nef**, J. U., *Industry and Government in France and England, 1540–1640*, Memoirs American Phil.Soc., XV, Philadelphia, 1940. Reprinted Ithaca, N. Y., 1957.

4.982 **Pearce**, B., 'Elizabethan food policy and the armed forces', *Ec.H.R.*, XII, 1942, 39–46.

4.983 **Pickthorn**, K., *Early Tudor Government I: Henry VII*, 1934, revised 1949; II: *Henry VIII*, 1934.

4.984 **Prestwich**, Menna, 'Diplomacy and trade in the Protectorate', *J.M.H.*, XXII, 1950, 103–21.

4.985 **Price**, W. H., *The English Patents of Monopoly*, Boston and Lond., 1906. Documentary appendix.

4.986 **Read**, C., 'Tudor economic policy', in R. L. Schuyler and H. Ausubel, eds., *The Making of English History*, N. Y., 1952, 195–201.

4.987 **Reid**, Rachel R., *The King's Council in the North*, 1921. Re-issued 1975.

4.988 **Riemersma**, J. C., 'Government influence on company organisation in Holland and England, 1550–1650', *J.Ec.H.*, supplement 10, 1950, 31–9.

4.989 **Slack**, P. A., 'The Book of Orders: the making of English social policy, 1577–1631', *T.R.H.S.*, 5th ser., XXX, 1980, 1–22.

4.990 **Smith**, A. G. R., *The Government of Elizabethan England*, 1967. A brief general survey with a guide to further reading.

4.991 **Stone**, L., 'State control in sixteenth-century England', *Ec.H.R.*, XVII, 1947, 103–20.

4.992 **Wilson**, C., 'Government policy and private interest in modern English history'. In Wilson, 129–39. *See also* Margaret G. Davies (4.1152).

(b) Local government

4.993 **Barnes**, T. G., *Somerset, 1625–40: A County's Government During the 'Personal Rule'*, 1961

4.994 **Gleason**, J. H., *The Justices of the Peace in England, 1558–1640*, 1969.

4.995 **Kent**, Joan R., *The English Village Constable, 1580–1642. A Social and Administrative Study*, 1986. Re-examines the powers and duties of the office of constable in this period, the increasing range of responsibilities and administrative burdens, and the social character of the office holders.

4.996 **Moir**, Esther A. L., *The Justice of the Peace*, 1969.

4.997 **Tate**, W. E., *The Parish Chest*, 1946, 3rd ed., 1969. The best introduction to the records of parochial government.

4.998 **Trotter**, Eleanor, *Seventeenth-century Life in the Country Parish, With Special Reference to Local Government*, 1919. Reprinted 1968.

4.999 **Webb**, S. and Beatrice, *English Local Government*, II vols., 1906–29. Reprinted 1963, with new introductions. The Webbs' major work.

4.1000 **Willcox**, W. B., *Gloucestershire: A Study in Local Government, 1590–1640*, New Haven, Conn., 1940.

LAW AND ORDER

4.1001 **Allan**, D. G. C., 'The rising in the west, 1628–31', *Ec.H.R.*, 2nd ser., V, 1952, 76–85.

4.1002 **Beier**, A. L., 'Vagrants and the social order in Elizabethan England', *P.P.*, 64, 1974, 3–29.

4.1003 **Bellamy**, J., *Criminal Law and Society in Late Medieval and Tudor England*, 1984.

4.1004 —— *The Tudor Law of Treason. An Introduction*, 1979.

4.1005 **Bindoff**, S. T., *Ket's Rebellion, 1549*, Hist.Ass. pamphlet, 1949, reprinted 1968.

4.1006 **Boynton**, L., *The Elizabethan Militia*, 1966.

4.1007 **Brewer**, J. and Styles, J., eds., *An Ungovernable People. The English and their Law in the Seventeenth and Eighteenth Centuries*, 1980. A collection of case studies exploring the connections and conflicts between popular justice and the law and its workings.

4.1008 **Cockburn**, J. S., *A History of English Assizes, 1558–1714*, 1972.

4.1009 —— ed., *Crime in England, 1550–1800*, 1977. A fascinating collection of eleven essays – many of them local in scope. Excellent critical bibliography.

4.1010 **Cornwall**, J., *The Revolt of the Peasantry, 1549*, 1977.

4.1011 **Davies**, C. S. L., 'The Pilgrimage of Grace reconsidered', *P.P.*, 41, 1968, 54–76.

4.1012 **François**, Martha E., 'Revolts in late medieval and early modern Europe: a spiral model', *J.Interdis.H.*, V, 1974, 19–43.

4.1013 **Friedeburg**, R., 'Reformation of Manners and the social composition of offenders in an East Anglian cloth village: Earls Colne, Essex, 1531–1642', *J.Brit.Studs.*, XXIX, 1990, 347–85.

4.1014 **Fuller**, L. B., *Turned to Account. The Forms and Functions of Criminal Biography in Late Seventeenth and Early Eighteenth-Century England*, 1987.

4.1015 **Gatrell**, V. A. C., Lenman, B. and Parker, G., eds., *Crime and the Law. The Social History of Crime in Western Europe since 1500*, 1980.

4.1016 **Gay**, E. F., 'The Midland Revolt and the Inquisitions of Depopulation of 1607', *T.R.H.S.*, n.s., XVIII, 1904, 195–244.

4.1017 **Harrison**, S. M., *The Pilgrimage of Grace in the Lake Counties, 1536–7*, 1981.

4.1018 **James**, M. E., 'Obedience and dissent in Henrician England: the Lincolnshire Rebellion, 1536', *P.P.*, 48 1970, 3–78.

4.1019 —— 'The concept of order and the Northern Rising of 1569', *P.P.*, 60, 1973, 49–83.

4.1020 **Ingram**, M., *Church Courts, Sex and Marriage in England, 1570–1640*, 1988. Based on court records from Wiltshire, Cambridgeshire, Leicestershire and West Sussex the book explores the activities of church courts and the local attitudes and responses they provoked.

4.1021 **Kerridge**, E., 'The revolts in Wiltshire against Charles I', *Wilts.Arch. & Nat.H.Mag.*, LVII, 1958–9, 64–75.

4.1022 **King**, W. J., 'Punishment for bastardy in early seventeenth-century England', *Albion*, X, 1978, 130–51.

4.1023 —— 'The regulation of alehouses in Stuart Lancashire: an example of discretionary administration of the law', *T.H.S.L.C.*, CXXIX, 1980, 31–46.

4.1024 **Lindley**, K. J., *Fenland Riots and the English Revolution*, 1982. Looks at the fenmen's resistance to enclosure and draining and relates it to the causes, course and aftermath of the English Revolution.

4.1025 —— 'Riot prevention and control in early Stuart London', *T.R.H.S.*, 5th ser., XXXIII, 1983, 109–27.

4.1026 **MacCulloch**, D., 'Ket's Rebellion in context', *P.P.* 84, 1979, 36–59.

4.1027 **Macfarlane**, A., *The Justice and the Mare's Ale. Law and Disorder in Seventeenth-Century England*, 1981. A case study of law and lawbreakers in Westmorland.

4.1028 **McGurk**, J. J. N., 'The clergy and the militia, 1580–1610', *Hist.*, LX, 1975, 198–210.

4.1029 **Manning**, R. B., *Village Revolts, Social Protests and Popular Disturbances in England 1509–1640*, 1988.

4.1030 **Roberts**, S. K., 'Alehouses, brewing, and government under the early Stuarts, *Southern H.*, XI, 1980, 45–73.

4.1031 **Salgado**, G., *The Elizabethan Underworld*, 1977.

4.1032 **Samaha**, J., *Law and Order in Historical Perspective: The Case of Elizabethan Essex*, 1974.

4.1033 **Sharp**, B., *In Contempt of all Authority.*

Rural Artisans and Riot in the West of England, 1586–1660, 1980.

4.1034 **Sharpe**, J. A., *Crime in Early Modern England, 1550–1750*, 1984. Discusses the sources, methods and statistics, and stresses the overwhelming predominance of theft in the gallery of crimes.

4.1035 —— *Crime in Seventeenth-Century England. A County Study*, 1983. An excellent pioneering study of patterns of crime in Essex. Property offences emerge as by far the largest single category of crime.

4.1036 —— *Defamation and Sexual Slander in Early Modern England. The Church Courts at York*, Borthwick Papers, 58, 1980.

4.1037 —— 'Domestic homicide in early modern England', *H.J.*, XXIV, 1981, 29–48.

4.1037a **Slack**, P., ed., *Rebellion, Popular Protest and the Social Order in Early Modern England*, 1984. A collection of important essays from the journal *Past and Present*. The coverage extends from the 1530s to the middle of the eighteenth century.

4.1038 **Stone**, L., 'Inter-personal violence in English society, 1300–1980', *P.P.*, CI, 1983, 22–33.

4.1038a **Thomas**, K. J. E., *House of Care. Prisons and Prisoners in England, 1500–1800*, 1988. A study which attempts to look at prisons and prison conditions from the inmates' point of view. The economics of imprisonment as well as the actual conditions of incarceration are considered.

4.1039 **Veall**, D., *The Popular Movement for Law Reform, 1640–60*, 1970.

4.1040 **Walter**, J. and Wrightson, K., 'Dearth and the social order in the early modern England', *P.P.*, 71, 1976, 22–42.

4.1041 **Walter**, J. A., 'A Rising of the People? The Oxfordshire Rising of 1596', *P.P.*, CVII, 1985, 90–144.

4.1042 **Williams**, N., 'The risings in Norfolk, 1569 and 1570', *Norfolk Arch.*, XXXII, 1959, 73–81.

See also Houlbrooke (4.1384).

CLASSES AND SOCIAL GROUPS

(a) General and miscellaneous

4.1043 **Barry**, J. and Brookes, C., eds., *The Middling Sort of People. Culture, Society and Politics in England, 1550–1800*, 1994. The essays examine the shifting definition and changing roles of the middle classes in English society.

4.1044 **Batho**, G. R., 'The finances of an Elizabethan nobleman: Henry Percy, ninth Earl of Northumberland (1564–1631)', *Ec.H.R.*, 2nd ser., IX, 1957, 433–50.

4.1045 **Bernard**, G. W., ed., *The English Nobility in the Sixteenth Century*, 1990.

4.1046 —— *The Power of the Early Tudor Nobility. A Study of the Fourth and Fifth Earls of Shrewsbury*, 1985. Chiefly political in scope but the economic foundations of the power base of the Earls are not neglected.

4.1047 **Brooks**, C. W., *Pettyfoggers and Vipers of the Commonwealth. The Lower Branch of the Legal Profession in Early Modern England*, 1986.

4.1048 **Bush**, M. L., *The English Aristocracy. A Comparative Synthesis*, 1984. Considers the character, development and impact of this group. Chaptes are devoted to privileges, functions, ethos, agrarian capitalism, and industrial investment. Extensive bibliography 217–30.

4.1049 —— *The European Nobility. I: Noble Privilege*, 1983. *II: Rich Noble, Poor Noble*, 1988. A comparative study looking at the character of political, fiscal, judicial and seigneurial privilege. Volume II has chapters on the size, structure, membership, wealth and residence patterns of this elite group.

4.1050 **Campbell**, Mildred, *The English Yeoman in the Tudor and Early Stuart Age*, New Haven, Conn, 1942. Reprinted 1960. A valuable and well-documented treatment of the subject.

4.1051 **Cressy**, D., 'Describing the social order of Elizabethan and Stuart England', *Lit. & H.*, III, 1976, 29–44. A critique of Stone (4.1072).

4.1052 **Coward**, B., *The Stanleys. Lords Stanley and Earls of Derby. The Origins, Wealth and Power of a Landowning Family*, Chet.Soc., n.s. XXX, 1983. A well-researched study of one of the dominant aristocratic families of the north of England. Economic and social as well as political in its coverage.

4.1053 **Davies**, K. G., 'The mess of the middle class', *P.P.*, 22, 1962, 77–83.

4.1054 **Doran**, S., 'The finances of an Elizabethan nobleman and royal servant: a case study of Thomas Radcliffe, third Earl of Sussex', *H.Res.*, LXI, 1988, 286–300.

4.1055 **Earle**, P., *The Making of the English Middle Class. Business, Society, and Family Life in London, 1660–1730*, 1989. Deals with the economic fortunes, social configuration, and lifestyle of this social group.

4.1056 **Everitt**, A. M., 'Social mobility in England, 1500–1700', *P.P.*, 33, 1966, 56–73. *See also* Stone (4.1072).

4.1057 **Grassby**, R., 'Social mobility and business enterprise in seventeenth-century England', in Pennington and Thomas (4.80), 355–81.

4.1058 **Habakkuk**, H. J., 'The rise and fall of English landed families, 1600–1800. Parts I, II and III', *T.R.H.S.*, 5th ser., XXIX, 1979, 187–207; XXX, 1980, 199–221; XXXI, 1981, 195–218.

4.1059 **Hexter**, J. H., 'The myth of the middle class in Tudor England'. In the same author's *Reappraisals in History*, 1961, 71–116.

4.1060 —— 'The English aristocracy: its crisis and the English Revolution', *J.Brit.Studs.*, VIII, 1968, 22–78.

4.1061 **Hill**, C., 'The many-headed monster in late Tudor and early Stuart political thinking'. In C. H. Carter, ed., *From Renaissance to Counter-Reformation*, 1966, 296–324. Reprinted in Hill (4.58), 181–204.

4.1062 **Holmes**, G. S., 'Gregory King and the social structure of pre-industrial England', *T.R.H.S.*, 5th ser., XXVII, 1977, 41–68.

4.1063 —— 'The professions and social change in England, 1680–1730', *Proc.Brit.Acad.*, LXV, 1981, 313–54.

4.1064 **Ives**, E. W., 'The reputation of the common lawyer in English society 1450–1550', *Birm.H.J.*, VII, 1960, 130–61.

4.1065 **Marshall**, J. D., 'Agrarian wealth and social structure in pre-industrial Cumbria', *Ec.H.R.*, 2nd ser., XXXIII, 1980, 503–21.

4.1066 **O'Day**, Rosemary, *The English Clergy. The Emergence and Consolidation of a Profession, 1558–1642*, 1979.

4.1067 **Prest**, W. R., ed., *The Professions in Early Modern England*, 1987. Chapters on the clergy, lawyers, doctors, schoolmasters, estate stewards, and soldiers within the context of a general discussion of the nature of the profesions in this period.

4.1068 —— *The Rise of the Barristers. A Social History of the English Bar, 1590–1640*, 1986. A deeply researched study of the composition and growth of the legal profession, looking at lawyers' career structures, wealth, social mobility, and religious outlook.

4.1069 **Ross**, D., 'Class privilege in seventeenth-century England', *Hist.*, XXVIII, 1943, 148–55.

4.1070 **Stone**, L., *The Crisis of the Aristocracy, 1558–1641*, 1965. A massive study which not only presents the 'crisis' thesis, but also comprehensively surveys the whole socio-economic setting and activities of the aristocracy. *See* the review articles on this book by D. C. Coleman in *Hist.*, LI, 1966, 165–78; by R. Ashton in *Ec.H.R.*, 2nd ser., XXII, 308–22; and by A. M. Everitt in *Ag.H.R.*, XVI, 1968, 60–7.

4.1071 —— *Family and Fortune. Studies in Aristocratic Finance in the Sixteenth and Seventeenth Centuries*, 1973. A series of case studies which supplement Stone's *Crisis of the Aristocracy*.

4.1072 —— 'Social mobility in England, 1500–1700', *P.P.*, 33, 1966, 16–55. *See also* Everitt (4.1056). Stone's book *Social Change and Revolution*, is also relevant in this connection.

4.1073 —— *An Open Elite? England 1540–1880*, 1984, extends chronologically from the Dissolution of the Monasteries to the late nineteenth-century agricultural depression and focuses on the landed elites of Hertfordshire, Northampton-shire, and Northumberland. A change in the composition of the landed elite is scrutinised and country houses receive detailed consideration. Bibliography, 523–44.

4.1074 **Styles**, P., 'The social structure of Kineton hundred in the reign of Charles II', *Trans.Birm.Arch.Soc.*, LXXVIII, 1962, 96–117.

4.1075 **Supple**, B. E., 'Class and social tension: the case of the merchant', in Ives (4.124),

131–43.

4.1076 **Williams**, G., *The General and Common Sort of People, 1540–1640*, 1977.

(b) The gentry and their estates

This section is not intended to be self-contained. It should, for example, be seen in conjunction with those of *Landholding* and the *Land market*.

4.1077 **Phillips**, C. B., ed., *Lowther Family Estate Books, 1617–75*, Surtees Soc., CXCI, 1979.

4.1078 **Smith**, A. H., Baker, Gillian, and Kenny, R. W., eds., *The Papers of Nathaniel Bacon of Stiffkey. I: 1556–77*, 1979.

4.1079 **Clay**, C., *Public Finance and Private Wealth. The Career of Sir Stephen Fox, 1627–1716*, 1978.

4.1080 —— 'Marriage, inheritance and the rise of large estates in England, 1660–1815', *Ec.H.R.*, 2nd ser., XXI, 1968, 503–18.

4.1081 **Cliffe**, J. T., *The Puritan Gentry. The Great Puritan Families of Early Stuart England*, 1984. Provides useful evidence of inter-marriage between gentry families and of family relations in this social group. The gentry's economic activities are also well documented.

4.1082 —— *Puritans in Conflict. Puritan Gentry during and after the Civil Wars*, 1988. A sequel to (4.1081) starting in 1641. The book documents the fortunes of this social group in the mid-seventeenth century upheavals. The losses and gains of both Parliamentarians and Royalists are analysed.

4.1083 —— *The Yorkshire Gentry from the Reformation to the Civil War*, 1969.

4.1084 **Cooper**, J. P., 'The counting of manors', *Ec.H.R.*, 2nd ser., VIII, 1956, 377–89. A significant contribution to the debate on the gentry which pointed out the statistical errors underlying Tawney's thesis.

4.1085 **Cornwall**, J., 'The early Tudor gentry', *Ec.H.R.*, 2nd ser., XVII, 1965, 456–71.

4.1086 **Finch**, Mary E., *The Wealth of Five Northamptonshire Families*, Northants.Rec.Soc., XIX, 1956. One of the first real attempts to approach the gentry controversy using the method of case-study rather than that of generalisation.

4.1087 **Heal**, Felicity and Holmes, C., eds., *The Gentry in England and Wales, 1500–1700*, 1994. Synthesises recent writing on this crucial social group.

4.1088 **Hexter**, J. H., 'Storm over the gentry'. In the same author's *Reappraisals in History*, 1961, 117–62. A very good – and witty – summary of the gentry controversy.

4.1089 **Hoskins**, W. G., 'The estates of the Caroline gentry'. In Hoskins and Finberg, eds. (4.118), 334–65.

4.1090 **Jenkins**, P., *The Making of a Ruling Class. The Glamorgan Gentry, 1640–1790*, 1983. Provides a useful overview of social and economic changes that took place prior to industrialisation. The activities and attitudes of the gentry are comprehensively investigated.

4.1091 **Laslett**, P., 'The gentry of Kent in 1640', *Cambridge H.J.*, IX, 1948, 148–64. *See also* the book by Everitt (4.1293).

4.1092 **Lavrovsky**, V. M., 'The Great Estate in England from the sixteenth to the eighteenth centuries', *First International Conference of Economic History, Contributions and Communciations*, Stockholm, 1960, 353–65.

4.1093 **Levy**, F. J., 'How information spread among the gentry, 1550–1640', *J.Brit.Studs.*, XXI, 1982, 11–34.

4.1094 **Mousley**, J. E., 'The fortunes of some gentry families of Elizabethan Sussex', *Ec.H.R.*, 2nd ser., XI, 1958, 467–83.

4.1095 **Roebuck**, P., *Yorkshire Baronets, 1640–1760. Families, Estates and Fortunes*, 1980.

4.1096 **Simpson**, A., *The Wealth of the Gentry, 1540–1660*, Chicago and Cambridge, 1961.

4.1097 **Stone**, L., *Social Change and Revolution in England, 1540–1640*, 1965. Summarises the gentry controversy, providing extracts from contemporary sources and from the main contributions to the historical debate. Useful bibliography.

4.1098 —— 'The fruits of office: the case of Robert Cecil, first Earl of Salisbury, 1596–1612'. In Fisher (4.52), 89–116.

4.1099 **Tawney**, R. H., 'The rise of the gentry, 1558–1640', *Ec.H.R.*, XI, 1941, 1–38. The famous article which initiated the gentry controversy. *See also* Tawney's 'Postscript', *Ec.H.R.*, 2nd ser., VII, 1954, 91–7. Both are reprinted in Carus-Wilson, ed. (1.326), I, 173–214.

4.1100 —— 'Harrington's interpretation of his

age', *Proc.Brit.Acad.*, XXVII, 1941, 199–223.

4.1101 **Thirsk**, Joan, 'The fashioning of the Tudor–Stuart gentry', *Bull.J.Rylands.Lib.*, LXXII, 1990, 69–86.

4.1102 **Trevor-Roper**, H. R., *The Gentry, 1540–1640 (Ec.H.R.* supplements, I), 1953. A vigorous attack on the Tawney thesis, arguing that the 'mere gentry', who lacked access to profitable offices in royal administration and whose income was derived entirely from the land, actually declined during this period.

4.1103 **Upton**, A. P., *Sir Arthur Ingram, c.1565–1642: A Study of the Origins of an English Landed Family*, 1961.

4.1104 **Wood**, A. C., 'The Holles Family', *T.R.H.S.*, 4th ser., XIX, 1936, 145–65.

POOR RELIEF: CHARITY AND THE POOR LAW

For the medieval background, *see:*

4.1105 **Clay**, Rotha M., *The Medieval Hospitals of England*, 1909. Reprinted, 1966.

4.1106 **Tierney**, B., *Medieval Poor Law: A Sketch of Canonical Theory and its Application in England*, Berkeley and Los Angeles, 1959.

4.1107 **Clarke**, G., ed., *John Bellers. His Life, Times and Writings*, 1987. Prefaced by a scholarly introduction the book provides a generous selection of the writings of this Quaker social reformer.

4.1108 **Melling**, Elizabeth, ed., *The Poor: A Collection of Examples from Original Sources in the Kent Archives Office from the Sixteenth to the Nineteenth Century*, 1964.

4.1109 **Slack**, P. A., ed., *Poverty in Early Stuart Salisbury*, Wilts.Rec.Soc., XXXI, 1976.

4.1110 **Webb**, J., ed., *Poor Relief in Elizabethan Ipswich*, Suffolk Rec.Soc., IX, 1966. A collection of documents with an introduction.

4.1111 **Arkell**, T., 'The incidence of poverty in England in the later seventeenth century', *Soc.H.*, XII, 1987, 23–48.

4.1112 **Aydelotte**, F., *Elizabethan Rogues and Vagabonds*, 1913. Reprinted 1967.

4.1113 **Beier**, A. L., *Masterless Men. The Vagrancy Problem in England, 1560–1640*, 1985. Unemployment is seen as the root cause of the increase in scale of vagrancy and the distances migrated.

4.1114 —— *The Problem of the Poor in Tudor and Early Stuart England*, 1983. A brief, thematic survey with a useful bibliography and summary of Poor Law legislation.

4.1115 —— 'Poor relief in Warwickshire, 1630–1660', *P.P.*, 35, 1966, 77–100. Argues that the Civil War did not bring about a general breakdown in poor relief.

4.1116 —— 'Social problems in Elizabethan London', *J.Interdis.H.*, IX, 1978, 203–21.

4.1117 **Bittle**, W. G. and Lane, R. I., 'Inflation and philanthropy in England: a re-assessment of W. K. Jordan's data', *Ec.H.R.*, 2nd ser., XXIX, 1976, 203–10. Argues against there being an increase in philanthropy in this period.

4.1118 **Carlton**, C., *The Court of Orphans*, 1974.

4.1119 **Davies**, C. S. L., 'Slavery and Protector Somerset: the Vagrancy Act of 1547', *Ec.H.R.*, 2nd ser., XIX, 1966, 533–49.

4.1120 **Elton**, G. R., 'An early Tudor Poor Law', *Ec.H.R.*, 2nd ser., VI, 1953, 55–67.

4.1121 **Fessler**, A., 'The official attitude towards the sick poor in seventeenth-century Lancashire', *T.H.S.L.C.*, 102, 1951, 85–114.

4.1122 **Gray**, B. K., *A History of English Philanthropy from the Dissolution of the Monasteries to the Taking of the First Census*, 1905. Reprinted 1967.

4.1123 **Hampson**, Ethel M., *The Treatment of Poverty in Cambridgeshire, 1597–1834*, 1934. An important regional study.

4.1124 **Herlan**, R. W., 'Poor relief in London during the English Revolution', *J.Brit.Studs.*, XVIII, 1979, 30–51.

4.1125 **Hill**, C., 'Puritans and the poor', *P.P.*, 2, 1952, 32–50. Reprinted in Hill (4.1236), as 'William Perkins and the poor', 215–38.

4.1126 —— 'The Poor and the parish'. In Hill (4.1383), 259–97.

4.1127 **James**, Margaret, *Social Problems and Policy During the Puritan Revolution*, 1930. Reprinted 1966.

4.1128 **Jones**, G. H., *History of the Law of Charity, 1532–1827*, 1969. The first five chapters deal with the pre-1700 period.

4.1129 **Jones**, G. P., 'The poverty of Cumberland and Westmorland', *Trans.Cumb. and West.Antiq. and Arch.Soc.*, LV, 1956, 198–208

4.1130 **Jordan**, W. K., *Philanthropy in England: A study of the Changing Pattern of English Social Aspirations, 1480–1660*, 1959.

4.1131 —— *The Charities of Rural England, 1480–1660*, 1961.

4.1132 —— *The Charities of London, 1480–1660*, 1961.

4.1133 —— *The Social Institutions of Lancashire*, Chet.Soc., 3rd ser., 11, 1962.

4.1134 —— *Social institutions in Kent, 1480–1660*, Arch.Cant., 75, 1961.

4.1135 —— *The Forming of the Charitable Institutions of the West of England*, American Philosophical Soc.Trans., n.s., 50, Part 8, Philadelphia, 1960. Altogether, Jordan's work amounts to a monumental study of the patterns of charitable giving in the early modern period. From a quantitative point of view, however, Jordan is less useful, since the Price Rise is not taken into account.

4.1136 **Judges**, A. V., *The Elizabethan Underworld*, 1930. Reprinted 1965.

4.1137 **Kiernan**, V. G., 'Puritanism and the poor', *P.P.*, 3, 1953, 45–54. A comment on Hill (4.1125).

4.1138 **Leonard**, Elizabeth M., *The Early History of English Poor Relief*, 1900. Reprinted 1965. Still the standard work though largely by default.

4.1139 **Pearl**, Valerie, 'Social policy in early modern London' in H. Lloyd-Jones, Valerie Pearl and B. Worden, eds., *History and Imagination. Essays in Honour of H. R. Trevor-Roper*, 1981, 115–31.

4.1140 **Pinchbeck**, Ivy and Hewitt, Margaret, *Children in English Society I: From Tudor Times to the Eighteenth Century*, 1969. Chapters 5–9 are particularly relevant in this connection. Good bibliography.

4.1141 **Pound**, J. F., *Poverty and Vagrancy in Tudor England*, 1971.

4.1142 —— 'An Elizabethan census of the poor. The treatment of vagrancy in Norwich, 1570–80', *Birm.H.J.*, VIII, 1962, 135–61.

4.1143 **Slack**, P., *The English Poor Law, 1531–1782*, 1990. A well organised, up-to-date survey which looks at the social and economic base and implementation of Poor Law legislation.

4.1144 —— *Poverty and Policy in Tudor and Stuart England*, 1988. A lucid account of the complexity of poverty in this period, the evolution of policy from Wolsey onwards, and the adaption of the parish unit to secular purposes.

4.1145 **Styles**, P., 'The evolution of the law of Settlement', *Birm.H.J.*, IX, 1963, 33–63.

4.1146 **Tonrud**, T. J., 'The response to poverty in three English towns, 1560–1640: a comparative approach', *Hist.Sociale*, XXXV, 1985, 9–28. *See also* Marshall (5.2638), Bruce (5.2693) and Owen (5.2678).

LABOUR

4.1147 **Allen**, R. C., 'The growth of labour productivity in early modern English agriculture', *Expl.Ec.H.*, XXV, 1988, 117–46.

4.1148 **Ben-Amos**, Ilana K., *Adolescence and Youth in Early Modern England*, 1994. Based chiefly on diaries and autobiographies of the period the book focuses on the experience of growing up. The favourite method used is that of the accumulation of individual case histories. Apprenticeship is the major topic considered.

4.1149 **Buckatzsch**, E. J., 'Occupations in the parish registers of Sheffield, 1655–1719', *Ec.H.R.*, 2nd ser., I, 1948–9, 145–50.

4.1150 **Coleman**, D. C., 'Labour in the English economy in the seventeenth century', *Ec.H.R.*, 2nd ser., VIII, 1956, 280–95. Reprinted in Carus-Wilson, ed. (1.326), II, 291–308. An important and wide-ranging article.

4.1151 **Corfield**, Penelope and Keene, D., eds., *Work in Towns, 850–1850*, 1990. Has useful chapters on the leather industry, East London in the seventeenth century, and a general chapter addresses the issues involved in defining urban work.

4.1152 **Davies**, Margaret G., *The Enforcement of English Apprenticeship 1563–1642: A Study in Applied Mercantilism*, Harvard, Mass., 1956. A useful study showing the gulf between the theory and practice of Tudor economic legislation.

4.1153 **Dunlop**, O. J. and Denham, R. D., *English Apprenticeship and Child Labour*, 1912.

4.1154 **Everitt**, A. M., 'Farm labourers'. In Thirsk (4.322), 396–465. A very valuable study of a neglected subject.

4.1155 **Furniss**, E. S., *The Position of the Labourer in a System of Nationalism*, Boston and N. Y., 1920. Reprinted N. Y., 1957.

4.1156 **Fussell**, G. E., *The English Rural Labourer*, 1949.

4.1157 **Glass**, D. V., 'Socio-economic status and occupations in the city of London at the end of the seventeenth century'. In Hollaender and Kellaway (2.360), 373–89.

4.1158 **Gregory**, T. E., 'The economics of employment in England, 1660–1713', *Economica*, I, 1921, 37–51.

4.1159 **Hart**, C. E., *The Free Miners of the Forest of Dean*, 1953.

4.1160 **Hasbach**, W., *History of the English Agricultural Labourer*, 1908. Reprinted 1966.

4.1161 **Hill**, C., 'Pottage for free-born Englishmen: attitudes to wage labour in the sixteenth and seventeenth centuries'. In C. H. Feinstein, ed., *Socialism, Capitalism and Economic Growth*, 1967, 338–50. Reprinted in Hill (4.58), 219–38. Considers the stigma which was attached to wage labour in the sixteenth and seventeenth centuries and suggests that this helps explain working-class reluctance to enter the early factories of the Industrial Revolution.

4.1162 **Hoskins**, W. G., 'The farm labourer through four centuries'. In Hoskins and Finberg (4.118), 419–41.

4.1163 **Jenkin**, A. K. H., *The Cornish Miner*, 1927, 3rd ed., 1962.

4.1164 **Kelsall**, R. K., *Wage Regulation under the Statute of Artificers*, 1938. The standard work. *See* Minchinton (4.1172).

4.1165 —— 'A century of wage assessment in Herefordshire', *E.H.R.*, LVII, 1942, 115–19.

4.1166 —— 'Statute wages during a Yorkshire epidemic 1679–81', *Yorks.Arch.J.*, XXXIV, 1939, 310–19.

4.1167 **Knoop**, D. and Jones, G. P., *The Sixteenth-century Mason*, 1937.

4.1168 —— *The London Mason in the Seventeenth Century*, 1935.

4.1169 —— 'Overtime in the age of Henry VIII', *Ec.J.Ec.H.Supp.*, 3, 1938, 13–20.

4.1170 **Kussmaul**, Anna S., *Servants in Husbandry in Early Modern England*, 1982.

4.1171 **Millward**, R., 'The emergence of wage labour in early modern England', *Expl.Ec.H.*, XVIII, 1981, 21–40.

4.1172 **Minchinton**, W. E., ed., *Wage Regulation in Pre-industrial England*, 1971. A valuable reprint of the works by Tawney and Kelsall, with a new introductory essay.

4.1173 **Norman**, F. A. and Lee, L. G., 'Labour exchanges in the seventeenth century', *Ec.J.Ec.H.Supp.*, 1, 1928, 399–404.

4.1174 **Ransome**, D. R., 'Artisan dynasties in London and Westminster in the sixteenth century', *Guildhall Miscellany*, II, 1964, 236–47.

4.1175 **Tawney**, R. H., 'The assessment of wages in England by the justices of the peace', *Vierteljahrschrift für Sozial-und Wirtschaftsgeschichte*, II, 1913, 307–37, 533–64. *See* Minchinton (4.1172).

4.1176 —— 'An occupational census of the seventeenth century', *Ec.H.R.*, V., 1934–5, 25–64. Analyses the occupational structure of Gloucestershire as revealed in the muster roll of 1608. Shows the intertwining of agriculture and industry.

4.1177 **Vanes**, J., *Education and Apprenticeship in Sixteenth-Century Bristol*, 1982.

4.1178 **Woodward**, D. M., 'The background to the Statute of Artificers: the genesis of labour policy, 1558–63', *Ec.H.R.*, 2nd ser., XXXIII, 1980, 32–44.

4.1179 —— 'The determination of wage rates in the early modern north of England', *Ec.H.R.*, 2nd ser., XLVII, 1994, 22–43.

See also the book by Phelps Brown and Hopkins (4.1186).

STANDARDS OF LIVING

4.1180 **Cash**, M., *Devon Inventories of the Sixteenth and Seventeenth Centuries*, Devon and Cornwall Rec.Soc., n.s., XI, 1966.

4.1181 **Harland**, J., ed., *The Household and Farm Accounts of the Shuttleworths of Gawthorpe Hall from September 1582 to October 1621*, Chet.Soc., o.s., 35, 41, 43, 46, 1856–8.

4.1182 **Havinden**, M. A., ed., *Household and Farm Inventories in Oxfordshire, 1550–1590*, 1965.

4.1183 **Ashmore**, O., 'Household inventories of the Lancashire gentry, 1550–1700', *T.H.S.L.C.*, 110, 1958–9, 59–105.

4.1184 **Barley**, M. W., *The English Farmhouse and Cottage*, 1961. Well illustrated.

4.1185 —— 'Rural housing in England'. In Thirsk (4.322), 696–766.

4.1186 **Brown**, E. H. P. and Hopkins, Sheila V., *A Perspective of Wages and Prices*, 1981. Brings together the well-known articles on the cost of living.

4.1187 **Cunnington**, C. W. and Phillis, *Handbook of English Costume in the sixteenth Century*, 1954, 2nd rev., ed., 1970.

4.1188 **Emmison**, F. G., *Tudor Food and Pastimes*, 1964.

4.1189 **Hole**, Christina, *English Home Life, 1500–1800*, 1947.

4.1190 **Hoskins**, W. G., 'The rebuilding of rural England, 1570–1640', *P.P.*, 4, 1953, 44–59. Reprinted in Hoskins (4.116), 131–48.

4.1191 **Lydall**, H. R. and Phelps-Brown, E. H., 'Seven centuries of real income per wage earner re-considered', *Economica*, XLIX, 1982, 201–06.

4.1192 **Machin**, R., 'The Great Rebuilding: a re-assessment', *P.P.*, 77, 1977, 33–56.

4.1193 **Mercer**, E., 'The houses of the gentry', *P.P.*, 5, 1954, 11–32.

4.1194 **Rive**, A., 'The consumption of tobacco since 1600', *Ec.J.Ec.H.Supp.*, I, 1926, 57–75.

4.1195 **Smith**, J. T., 'The evolution of the English peasant house in the late seventeenth century', *J.Brit.Architectural Ass.*, XXXIII, 1970, 122–47.

4.1196 **Thomas**, K., 'Work and Leisure in pre-industrial society. Conference paper and discussion', *P.P.*, 29, 1964, 50–66.

4.1197 **Thomson**, Gladys Scott, *Life in a Noble Household, 1641–1700*, 1937.

4.1198 **Willan**, T. S., 'Sugar and the Elizabethans'. In Willan (4.718), 313–32.

4.1199 **Wood-Jones**, R. B., *Traditional Domestic Architecture of the Banbury Region*, 1963.

4.1200 **Woodward**, D. M., 'Wage rates and living standards in pre-industrial England', *P.P.*, 91, 1981, 28–46.

See also Dover Wilson (4.26), Stone (4.1070) and Campbell (4.1050), all of which are relevant in this connection.

CIVIL WAR, INTERREGNUM, RESTORATION AND REVOLUTION, 1640–89

What follows is only a selection – though, it is hoped, a representative one – on the period 1640–89. It should, for example, be seen in conjunction with the sections on *Classes and social groups* and on *Religion*.

(a) Sources

4.1201 **Aylmer**, G. E., ed., *The Levellers in the English Revolution*, 1975. A documentary collection.

4.1202 **Hill**, C. and Dell, E. M., *The Good Old Cause*, 1949, 2nd ed., 1969.

4.1203 **James**, Margaret and Weinstock, Maureen, *England During the Interregnum, 1642–60*, 1935.

4.1204 **Morrill**, J. S., *The Revolt of the Provinces, 1630–50*, 1976. A useful collection of documents with an excellent introduction pointing out the strength of localism in this period.

4.1205 **Pocock**, J. G. A., ed., *The Political Works of James Harrington*, 1977. Pride of place is given to *Oceana*, Harrington's 'civil history of property' and subsequently a major element in the 'gentry controversy'.

4.1206 **Prall**, S. E., ed., *The Puritan Revolution, A Documentary History*, 1969. A well-chosen selection.

4.1207 **Thirsk**, Joan, ed., *The Restoration*, 1976. A useful sourcebook with an introduction and linking commentary.

4.1208 **Woodhouse**, A. S. P., ed., *Puritanism and Liberty, Being the Army Debates, 1647–49*, 1938, 3rd ed., 1974.

(b) General works

4.1209 **Aiken**, W. A. and Henning, B. D., eds., *Conflict in Stuart England. Essays in honour of Wallace Notestein*, 1960.

4.1210 **Ashton**, R., *The City and the Court, 1603–43*, 1979. A study of the economics and politics involved in the interplay between City, Parliament and Court.

4.1211 —— *The English Civil War. Conservatism and Revolution 1603–49*, 1978. Heavily thematic in treatment with chapters on 'monarchy and society', 'tradition and innovation', 'centralism and localism', 'gentlemen and bourgeois'.

4.1212 **Aylmer**, G. E., ed., *The Interregnum: The Quest for Settlement 1646–60*, 1972. Includes an important essay by J. P. Cooper on social and economic policy.

4.1213 **Brinton**, C., *The Anatomy of Revolution*, N. Y., 1938, 2nd ed., N. Y., 1952, London, 1953.

4.1214 **Brunton**, D. and Pennington, D. H., *Members of the Long Parliament*, 1954. Reprinted 1968. An analysis – on Namierite lines – of the social composition of the Long Parliament. The book threw doubts on some well-known generalisations about Royalists and Roundheads, but was itself much criticised. *See* Hill (4.1236) and Manning (4.1253).

4.1215 **Carlton**, C., *Going to the Wars. The Experience of the British Civil Wars, 1638–1651*, 1992. Partly psycho- history as well as social history, the book looks closely at conditions of military service, the incidence of violence, and desertion from the ranks.

4.1216 **Clark**, J. C. D., *Revolution and Rebellion. State and Society in England in the Seventeenth and Eighteenth Centuries*, 1986. A boldly right-wing reassessment of the early modern period arguing strongly against the notion of revolution as a component of seventeenth and eighteenth-century developments.

4.1217 **Coates**, W. H., 'An analysis of major conflicts in seventeenth-century England'. In Aiken and Henning (4.1209), 15–40.

4.1218 **Cust**, R. and Hughes, Ann, eds., *Conflict in Early Stuart England. Studies in Religion and Politics, 1603–42*, 1989. Includes chapters on property and the constitution and on local history and the origins of the Civil War.

4.1219 **Elton**, G. R., 'A high road to Civil War'. In C. H. Carter, ed., *From Renaissance to Counter-Reformation*, 1966, 325–47.

4.1220 **Engberg**, J., 'Royalist finances during the English Civil War, 1642–46', *Scand.Ec.H.R.*, XIV, 1966, 73–96.

4.1221 **Everitt**, A. M., 'The county community'. In Ives (4.1247).

4.1222 —— *The Local Community and the Great Rebellion*, Hist.Ass. pamphlet, 1969. *See*

also the two specialised studies by Everitt (4.1292–3).

4.1223 **Fletcher**, A., *The Outbreak of the English Civil War*, 1981. A narrative approach placing great stress on the interaction between the centre and the provinces.

4.1224 **Fletcher**, A. and Stevenson, J., eds., *Order and Disorder in Early Modern England*, 1985. Includes essays on puritanism and social control, patriarchal authority, the social tensions arising from Fenland drainage schemes, and on the 'moral economy' of the English crowd.

4.1225 **Frank**, J., *The Levellers*, Cambridge, Mass., 1955.

4.1226 **French**, A., *Charles I and the Puritan Upheaval: A Study of the Causes of the Great Migration*, 1955.

4.1227 **Gould**, M., *Revolution in the Development of Capitalism. The Coming of the English Revolution*, 1987. A complex, heavily economic analysis, not easily accessible to the average reader.

4.1228 **Habakkuk**, H. J., 'Landowners and the Civil War', *Ec.H.R.*, 2nd ser., XVIII, 1965, 130–51. *See also* Thirsk (4.325).

4.1229 —— 'Public finance and the sale of confiscated property during the Interregnum', *Ec.H.R.*, 2nd ser., XV, 1962–3, 70–88.

4.1230 —— 'The Parliamentary army and the crown lands', *Welsh H.R.*, 3, 1966–7, 403–26.

4.1231 —— 'English landownership, 1680–1740', *Ec.H.R.*, X, 1940, 2–17.

4.1232 —— 'The Land Settlement and the Restoration of Charles II', *T.R.H.S.*, 5th ser., XXVIII, 1978, 201–22.

4.1233 **Hammersley**, G., 'The revival of the Forest laws under Charles I', *Hist.*, XLV, 1960, 85–102.

4.1234 **Hardacre**, P. H., *The Royalists during the Puritan Revolution*, The Hague, 1956.

4.1235 **Hill**, C., *The English Revolution*, 1940, revised 1955.

4.1236 —— *Puritanism and Revolution: Studies in the Interpretation of the English Revolution of the Seventeenth Century*, 1958.

4.1237 —— *The Intellectual Origins of the English Revolution*, 1965.

4.1238 —— *God's Englishman: Oliver Cromwell and the English Revolution*, 1970.

4.1239 —— *The World Turned Upside Down. Radical Ideas During the English Revolution*, 1972.

4.1240 —— *Some Intellectual Consequences of the English Revolution*, 1980.

4.1241 —— *The Collected Essays of Christopher Hill*. I: *Writing and Revolution in Seventeenth-Century England*, 1985; II: *Religion and Politics in Seventeenth-Century England*, 1986; III: *People and Ideas in Seventeenth-Century England*, 1986. Conveniently brings together over forty of the author's characteristically illuminating essays.

4.1242 **Hirst**, D., *The Representative of the People? Voters and Voting in England under the Early Stuarts*, 1975. Argues that popular involvement in and awareness of politics were greater than commonly supposed.

4.1243 —— *Authority and Conflict. England, 1603–58*, 1986. Chiefly a political study but there are chapters on changes in the economy and society.

4.1244 **Hobsbawm**, E. J., 'The crisis of the seventeenth century', *P.P.*, 5, 6, 1954, 33–54, 44–65. Reprinted in Aston (4.30), 5–58. *See also* Trevor-Roper (4.1274).

4.1245 **Holiday**, P. G., 'Land sales and repurchases in Yorkshire after the Civil Wars, 1650–1670', *Northern H.*, V, 1970, 67–92.

4.1246 **Hutton**, R., *The Restoration. A Political and Religious History of England and Wales, 1658–1667*, 1985. The sub-title accurately describes the scope of the book.

4.1247 **Ives**, E. W., ed., *The English Revolution, 1600–1660*, 1968. A useful collection of short essays, originally broadcast talks, with guides to further reading.

4.1248 **Jones**, C., Newitt, M., and Roberts, S., eds., *People and Politics in Revolutionary England*, 1986. A distinguished collection of essays with contributions from C. Hill, P. R. Newman and J. A. Sharpe amongst others. Though politics is the main focus, subjects such as crime and popular religion find a place.

4.1249 **Keeler**, Mary F., *The Long Parliament: A Biographical Study of its Members*, American Phil.Soc., Philadelphia, 1954. *See also* Brunton and Pennington (4.1214).

4.1250 **Madge**, S. J., *The Domesday of Crown Lands: A Study of the Legislation, Surveys and Sales of Royal Estates Under the Commonwealth*, 1938. *See also* Thirsk (4.325).

4.1251 **Manning**, B., ed., *Politics, Religion and the English Civil War*, 1973.

4.1252 —— *The English People and the English Revolution, 1640–49*, 1976. Looks at the role of the 'middle sort of people' in the towns and of the peasantry in the countryside. Links with Hirst (4.1242).

4.1253 —— 'The Long Parliament', *P.P.*, 5, 1954, 71–6. *See also* Keeler (4.1249). Comments on Brunton and Pennington.

4.1254 **Morrill**, J. S., ed., *The Impact of the English Civil War*, 1991. Includes chapters on the military impact, on the ramifications of Puritanism, and on social dislocation.

4.1255 —— ed., *Revolution and Restoration. England in the 1650s*, 1992. Has chapters on the operation of the law, varieties of Puritanism, and patriarchalism.

4.1256 **Morse**, D., *England's Time of Crisis: From Shakespeare to Milton. A Cultural History*, 1988. A cultural history inadequately grounded in social history. The author's preference for treating the whole period as a unity has its drawbacks.

4.1257 **Mulligan**, Lotte, 'Property and parliamentary politics in the English Civil War, 1642–6', *Hist.Studs.*, XVI, 1975, 341–61.

4.1258 **Parry**, R. H., ed., *The English Civil War and After, 1642–1658*, 1970.

4.1259 **Pearl**, Valerie, 'The Royal Independents' in the English Civil War', *T.R.H.S.*, 5th ser., XVIII, 1968, 69–96.

4.1260 —— 'London's Counter-revolution'. In Aylmer (4.1212), 29–56.

4.1261 **Pennington**, D. H., 'The cost of the English Civil War', *H.Today*, 7, 1958, 126–33.

4.1262 —— 'The accounts of the Kingdom'. In Fisher (4.52), 182–203.

4.1263 **Pocock**, J. G. A., ed., *Three British Revolutions, 1641, 1688, 1776*, Princeton, N. J., 1980. A symposium which includes essays by Lawrence Stone on 'The results of the English Revolutions of the seventeenth century', Christopher Hill on 'A bourgeois revolution?', and by Robert Ashton on 'Tradition and innovation in the Great Rebellion'.

4.1264 **Porter**, S., *Destruction in the English Civil War*, 1994. A much needed analysis of the extent and forms of damage in the 1640s and of the processes of recovery and re-building.

4.1265 **Richardson**, R. C., *The Debate on the English Revolution Revisited*, 1988. Surveys the historiography of the English Revolution from the seventeenth century to the present day.

4.1266 —— ed., *Town and Countryside in the English Revolution*, 1992. Chapters on London, York, Coventry, Bristol, and Oxford together with discussions of agrarian problems in the English Revolution, the experience of the gentry, landlord–tenant relations and rural discontents. The editor provides a general introduction on the changing relations between town and countryside.

4.1267 —— and Ridden, G. M., eds., *Freedom and the English Revolution. Essays in History and Literature*, 1986. Includes chapters on Cromwell, Winstanley, London radicals, and on revolutionary pamphleteering.

4.1268 **Russell**, C., ed., *The Origins of the English Civil War*, 1973. Includes essays by Conrad Russell, 'Parliament and the King's finances', and by Penelope Corfield, 'Economic issues and ideologies'.

4.1269 **Schenk**, W., *The Concern for Social Justice in the Puritan Revolution*, 1948.

4.1270 **Stone**, L., *The Causes of the English Revolution, 1529–1642*, 1972. The longest section is on the causes of the Revolution which are sensibly discussed under the headings presuppositions, preconditions, precipitants, and triggers.

4.1271 —— 'The Bourgeois Revolution of seventeenth-century England revisited', *P.P.*, CIX, 1985, 44–54.

4.1272 **Taylor**, P. A. M., ed., *The Origins of the English Civil War: Conspiracy, Crusade or Class Conflict?*, Boston, Mass., 1960. A collection of extracts.

4.1273 **Trevor-Roper**, H. R., 'The social origins of the Great Rebellion', *H.Today*, 5, 1955, 376–82.

4.1274 —— 'The general crisis of the seventeenth century', *P.P.*, 16, 1959, 31–64. Reprinted in Aston (4.30), 59–96.

4.1275 **Underdown**, D., *Royalist Conspiracy in England, 1649–1660*, New Haven, Conn., 1960.

4.1276 —— 'The Independents again', *J.Brit.Studs.*, VIII, 1968, 83–93. Part of a debate on the subject. *See* Yule (4.1282).

4.1277 —— 'The problem of popular allegiance in the English Civil War', *T.R.H.S.*, 5th ser., XXXI, 69–94.

4.1278 —— *Revel, Riot and Rebellion. Popular Politics and Culture in England, 1603–1660*, 1985. Explores patterns of popular allegiance in the Civil War period in Dorset, Somerset, and Wiltshire using the methodologies of sociology as well as those of history. The book has much to say about fundamental cultural contrasts in the region studied and about the ways in which these contributed to political divisions.

4.1279 **Walzer**, M., *The Revolution of the Saints*, 1966. A sociological study which analyses the role of puritan ideology in the English Revolution.

4.1280 **White**, S. D., *Sir Edward Coke and the Grievances of the Commonwealth*, 1979. Includes a full treatment of the economic grievances which Coke articulated in Parliament.

4.1281 **Wilson**, C., 'Economics and politics in the seventeenth century', *Hist.J.*, V., 1962, 80–92. Reprinted in Wilson (4.97), 1–21.

4.1282 **Yule**, G., *The Independents in the English Civil War*, 1957.

4.1283 —— 'Independents and revolutionaries', *J.Brit.Studs.*, VII, 1967, 11–32.

4.1284 **Zagorin**, P., *The Court and the Country. The Beginning of the English Revolution*, 1969. Stresses the constitutional aspect of the Rebellion, but at the same time places it firmly in its socio-economic setting.

4.1285 —— 'The social interpretation of the English Revolution', *J.Ec.H.*, XIX, 1959, 376–401.

4.1286 —— 'The English Revolution', *J.World H.*, II, 1955, 667–81.

4.1287 —— *A History of Political Thought in the English Revolution*, 1954. Has chapters on Harrington, the Levellers, and the Diggers.

(c) Regional studies

4.1288 **Blackwood**, B. G., *The Lancashire Gentry and the Great Rebellion, 1640–60*, 1978. Heavily statistical in its approach to the numbers, distribution, status, allegiance and wealth of the county's gentry.

4.1289 **Coate**, Mary, *Cornwall in the Great Civil War and Interregnum, 1642–1660*, 1933. Reprinted 1963.

4.1290 **Dils**, J. A., 'Epidemics, mortality and the Civil War in Berkshire, 1642–46',

Southern H., II, 1989, 40–52.

4.1291 **Dore**, R. N., *The Civil Wars in Cheshire*, 1966.

4.1292 **Everitt**, A. M., *Suffolk and the Great Rebellion*, Suffolk Rec.Soc., III, 1960.

4.1293 —— *The Community of Kent and the Great Rebellion, 1640–60*, 1966. *See* the two shorter and more general works by Everitt on the same subject (4.1221), (4.1222).

4.1294 **Farrar**, W. J., *The Great Civil War in Shropshire, 1642–49*, 1926.

4.1295 **Fletcher**, A., *A County Community in Peace and War. Sussex, 1600–60*, 1975.

4.1296 **Guttery**, D. R., *The Great Civil War in Midland Parishes*, 1950.

4.1297 **Holmes**, C., *The Eastern Association in the English Civil War*, 1974. An interesting analysis of the interaction between local and national issues.

4.1298 —— 'The county community in Stuart historiography', *J.Brit.Studs.*, XIX, 1980, 54–73.

4.1299 **Howell**, R., *Newcastle-upon-Tyne and the Puritan Revolution: A Study of the Civil War in Northern England*, 1967.

4.1300 **Hughes**, Ann, *Politics, Society and Civil War in Warwickshire, 1620–1660*, 1987. Challenges Everitt's 'county community' model by insisting that the county boundaries did not contain separate sets of economic and social characteristics. The background to allegiance is considered as are the costs and impositions of Civil War and the social changes of the Interregnum.

4.1301 **Ketton-Cremer**, R. W., *Norfolk in the Civil War*, 1969. Looks old-fashioned in comparison with Everitt (4.1292).

4.1302 **Leach**, A. L., *The History of the Civil War, 1642–49, in Pembrokeshire and on its Borders*, 1937.

4.1303 **Lennard**, R. V., *Rural Northamptonshire under the Commonwealth*, Oxford Studies in Social and Legal History, 1916.

4.1304 **Lindley**, K., *Fenland Riots and the English Revolution*, 1982. Complex study of the ways in which the re-development of the Fenland and its social, economic and political consequences.

4.1305 **Morrill**, J. S., *Cheshire 1630–1660: County Government and Society During the English Revolution*, 1974.

4.1306 **Pearl**, Valerie, *London and the Outbreak of the Puritan Revolution*, 1961.

4.1307 **Phillips**, C. B., 'The Royalist North: the Cumberland and Westmorland gentry 1642–60', *Northern H.*, XIV, 1978, 169–92.

4.1308 **Roberts**, S. K., *Recovery and Restoration in an English County. Devon Administration, 1946–70*, 1985.

4.1309 **Sherwood**, R. E., *Civil Strife in the Midlands, 1642–51*, 1974.

4.1310 **Tennant**, P. E., 'Parish and people. South Warwickshire and the Banbury area in the Civil War', *Cake & Cockhorse*, XI, 1990, 122–52.

4.1311 **Tupling**, G. H., 'The causes of the Civil War in Lancashire', *T.L.C.A.S.*, LXV, 1955, 1–32.

4.1312 **Underdown**, D., *Somerset in the Civil War and Interregnum*, 1973.

4.1313 **Willan**, T. S., 'The parliamentary surveys for the North Riding of Yorkshire', *Yorks.Arch. J.*, XXXI, 1933, 224–89.

4.1314 **Wood**, A. C., *Nottinghamshire in the Civil War*, 1937.

(d) Miscellaneous

4.1315 **Aylmer**, G. E., 'Did the Ranters exist?', *P.P.*, CXVII, 1987, 208–19. A critique of Davis (4.1321).

4.1316 **Berens**, C. H., *The Digger Movement in the Days of the Commonwealth*, 1906. Reprinted 1961.

4.1317 **Brailsford**, H. N., *The Levellers and the English Revolution*, 1961.

4.1318 **Capp**, B., *Cromwell's Navy. The Fleet and the English Revolution, 1648–1660*, 1989. Examines the organisation, role and personnel of the fleet in this period.

4.1319 **Cole**, W. A., 'The Quakers and the English Revolution', *P.P.*, 9, 1956, 39–54. Reprinted in Aston (4.30), 341–58.

4.1320 **Davis**, J. C., 'The Levellers and Democracy', *P.P.*, 40, 1968, 174–80.

4.1321 —— *Fear, Myth and History. The Ranters and the Historians*, 1986. Argues that the Ranters were largely 'invented' by alarmed contemporaries and twentieth-century left-wing historians. *See* Aylmer (4.1315).

4.1322 **Durston**, C., *The Family in the English Revolution*, 1989. Based principally on case studies, the book suggests that the mid-century upheavals may have helped to strengthen, not weaken the family unit.

4.1323 **Friedman**, J., *Miracles and the Pulp Press during the English Revolution*, 1993. An interesting but unduly restrictive study which fails to explore the context of print culture and to do justice to popular mentalities.

4.1324 **Gaunt**, P., 'Interregnum governments and the reform of the Post Office', *Hist.Res.*, LX, 1987, 281–98.

4.1325 **Gentles**, I. J., *The New Model Army in England, Ireland and Scotland, 1645–53*, 1992. Includes a discussion of the fluctuating size of the army, its religious reputation, political role and ideological significance.

4.1326 —— and Sheils, W. J., *Confiscation and Restoration. The Archbishopric Estates and the Civil War*, 1981.

4.1327 **Gordon**, M. Dorothy, 'The collection of Ship Money in the reign of Charles I', *T.R.H.S.*, 3rd ser., 4, 1910, 141–62.

4.1328 **Gregg**, Pauline, *Free-born John: A Biography of John Lilburne*, 1961.

4.1329 **Grell**, O. P., Israel, J. and Tyacke, N., eds., *From Persecution to Toleration. The Glorious Revolution and Religion in England*, 1991. Fuller on the intellectual and political aspects than on the social.

4.1330 **Hornstein**, S. R., *The Restoration Navy and English Foreign Trade, 1674–88. A Study in the Peacetime Use of Sea Power*, 1991.

4.1331 **Kenyon**, T., *Utopian Communism and Political Thought in Early Modern England*, 1989. Concentrates on Thomas More and Gerrard Winstanley.

4.1332 **Lamont**, W. M., *Marginal Prynne, 1600–1669*, 1963.

4.1333 **Newman**, P. R., *The Old Service. Royalist Regimental Colonels in the Civil War, 1642–46*, 1993. Includes an account of the social and geographical origins of the Royalist army leaders.

4.1334 **Petegorsky**, D. W., *Left-wing Democracy in the English Civil War: A Study of the Social Philosophy of Gerrard Winstanley*, 1940.

4.1335 **Prall**, S. E., *The Agitation for Law Reform During the Puritan Revolution, 1640–60*, 1966. *See* Veall (4.1039).

4.1336 **Reay**, B., *The Quakers and the English Revolution*, 1985. Reassesses the dynamics of early Quakerism and presents a case for seeing this group as central to the mainstream of events.

4.1337 —— and McGregor, J. F., eds., *Radical Religion in the English Revolution*, 1986. A lively collection of essays which includes accounts of Baptists, Levellers, Seekers, Ranters, Quakers, Fifth Monarchists, and of the implications of radical irreligion.

4.1338 **Roy**, I., 'The English Civil War and English Society', in I. Roy and B. Bond, eds., *War and Society: A Yearbook of Military History*, 1975, 24–43.

4.1339 **Thomas**, K., 'Women and the Civil War sects', *P.P.*, 13, 1958, 42–62. Reprinted in Aston (4.30), 317–40.

4.1340 'The social origins of Hobbes' political thought'. In K. Brown, ed., *Hobbes Studies*, 1965, 185–236.

4.1341 **Yule**, G., *The Independents in the Civil War*, Melbourne and Cambridge, 1958.

4.1342 **Zatler**, R., 'The debate on capital punishment during the English Revolution', *Amer.J.Legal H.*, XXXI, 1987, 126–44.

RELIGION

(a) General and miscellaneous

4.1343 **Ashton**, R., 'Puritanism and progress', *Ec.H.R.*, 2nd ser., XVII, 1965, 579–87. A review article on Hill (4.1383).

4.1344 **Aston**, Margaret, *England's Iconoclasts, Laws against Images*, 1988.

4.1345 **Aveling**, J. H. C., *The Handle and the Axe. The Catholic Recusants in England from Reformation to Emancipation*, 1976.

4.1346 **Barbour**, H., *The Quakers in Puritan England*, Yale, 1964.

4.1347 **Bebb**, E. D., *Nonconformity and Social Life, 1660–1800*, 1935.

4.1348 **Blackwood**, B. G., 'Agrarian unrest and the early Lancashire Quakers', *J.Friends' Hist.Soc.*, LI, 1966, 72–6.

4.1349 **Bossy**, J., *The English Catholic Community, 1570–1850*, 1976. Particularly good on relations between priests and gentry.

4.1350 **Bouch**, C. M. L., *Prelates and People of the Lake Counties: A History of the Diocese of Carlisle, 1133–1933*, 1948.

4.1351 **Breslow**, M. A., *A Mirror of England, English Puritan Views of Foreign Nations, 1618–40*, Cambridge, Mass., 1970.

4.1352 **Brigden**, Susan, *London and the Reformation*, 1989. Considers the crucial role of London and Londoners in the Henrician and Edwardian Reformations.

4.1353 —— 'Youth and the English Reformation', *P.P.*, XCV, 1982, 37–67.

4.1354 **Capp**, B. S., *The Fifth Monarchy Men*, 1972.

4.1355 **Carlson**, E. J., *Clerical Marriage and the English Reformation*, 1992.

4.1356 **Cole**, W. A., 'The social origins of the early Friends', *J. Friends' Hist.Soc.*, XLVIII, 1957, 99–118. *See also* Vann (4.1406).

4.1357 **Collinson**, P., *The Elizabethan Puritan Movement*, 1967. The standard work.

4.1358 —— 'The beginnings of English Sabbatarianism'. In C. W. Dugmore and C. Duggan, eds., *Studies in Church History*, I, 1964, 207–21.

4.1359 —— *Godly People. Essays in English Puritanism and Protestantism*, 1983.

4.1360 —— *The Religion of Protestants. The Church in English Society, 1559–1625*, 1982.

4.1361 **Cressy**, D., *Bonfires and Bells. National Memory and the Protestant Calendar in Elizabethan and Stuart England*, 1989. Considers the high points of the Protestant calendar and their celebration. A wide range of contemporary source material is drawn on to explore patriotism, xenophobia, religious fervour and anti-Catholicism.

4.1362 **Cross**, M. Claire, *The Puritan Earl; The Life of Henry Hastings, Third Earl of Huntingdon, 1536–1595*, 1966. A study of influence and patronage.

4.1363 —— *Church and People, 1450–1660. The Triumph of the Laity in the English Church*, 1976.

4.1364 —— 'The genesis of a godly community: two York parishes, 1590–1640', *Studs.Church H.*, XXI, 1986, 92–106.

4.1365 **Curtis**, T. C. and Speck, W. A., 'The Societies for the Reformation of Manners: a case study in the theory and practice of moral reform', *Lit & H.*, III, 1976, 45–64.

4.1366 **Dickens**, A. G., *The English Reformation*, 1964.

4.1367 **Doran**, S. and Durston, C., *Princes, Pastors, and People. The Church and Religion in England, 1529–1689*, 1991. A basic introductory text which charts much contested territory. Social and economic aspects of ecclesiastical organisation and religious allegiance receive proper attention.

4.1368 **Everitt**, A. M., 'Nonconformity in country parishes'. In Joan Thirsk, ed., *Land, Church and People: Essays Presented to Professor H. P. R. Finberg*, 1970, 178–99. An interesting survey which examines the social and economic factors affecting the distribution of nonconformity.

4.1369 **Haigh**, C., *Reformation and Resistance in Tudor Lancashire*, 1975.

4.1370 **Hall**, B., 'Puritanism: the problem of definition'. In C. J. Cuming, ed., *Studies in Church History*, II, 1965, 283–96.

4.1371 **Haller**, W., *The Rise of Puritanism*, N. Y., 1938. A classic work by the doyen of historians of puritanism.

4.1372 —— *Liberty and Reformation in the Puritan Revolution*, N. Y., 1955. Reprinted 1963.

4.1373 **Hart**, A. T., *The County Clergy in Elizabethan and Stuart Times*, 1958.

4.1374 —— *The Man in the Pew*, 1966.

4.1375 —— *Studies in English Church Social History, 1558–1660*, 1989.

4.1376 **Havran**, M. J., *The Catholics in Caroline England*, 1962.

4.1377 **Heal**, Felicity, *Of Prelates and Princes. A Study of the Economic and Social Position of the Tudor Episcopate*, 1980.

4.1378 —— and O'Day, Rosemary, eds., *Church and Society in England. Henry VIII to James I*, 1977. Includes chapters on the economic problems of the clergy and on the disposal of monastic and chantry lands.

4.1379 **Heinemann**, Margot, *Puritanism and Theatre. Thomas Middleton and Opposition Drama under the Early Stuarts*, 1980. Argues that the conventional view of puritan hostility to drama is largely a myth.

4.1380 **Hembry**, Pauline M., *The Bishops of Bath and Wells, 1540–1640: Social and Economic Problems*, 1967.

4.1381 **Hill**, C., *A Turbulent, Seditious, and Factious People. John Bunyan and his Church*, 1988. Situates Bunyan firmly within the English Revolution.

4.1382 —— *Economic Problems of the Church from Archbishop Whitgift to the Long Parliament,*

1956.

4.1383 —— *Society and Puritanism in Pre-revolutionary England*, 1964. This and the previous book are essential reading on the social history of religion in the first half of the seventeenth century.

4.1384 **Houlbrooke**, R. A., *Church Courts and People during the English Reformation, 1520–70*, 1979.

4.1385 **Jordan**, W. K., *The Development of Religious Toleration in England*, 4 vols., 1932–40.

4.1386 **Knappen**, M. M., *Tudor Puritanism*, Chicago, Ill., 1939. Reprinted 1965. A standard work, which still supplements, and is not made redundant by, Collinson (4.1357).

4.1387 **Lloyd**, A., *Quaker Social History, 1669–1738*, 1950.

4.1388 **McGrath**, P. V., *Papists and Puritans under Elizabeth I*, 1967. A clear survey with a useful bibliography.

4.1389 **Merritt**, J., 'The social concept of the parish church in early modern Westminster', *Urban H. Yearbook*, XVIII, 1991, 20–31.

4.1390 **More**, E. S., 'Congregationalism and the social order. John Goodwin's gathered church, 1640–60', *J.Eccles.H.*, XXXVIII, 1987, 210–35.

4.1391 **Morton**, A. L., *The World of the Ranters*, 1971. *See also* Hill (4.1239).

4.1392 **O'Day**, Rosemary and Heal, Felicity, eds., *Continuity and Change. Personnel and Administration of the Church in England, 1500–1642*, 1976. Several of the chapters deal with economic and social aspects.

4.1393 —— *Princes and Paupers in the English Church, 1500–1800*, 1981. A collection of essays concerned with the economic foundations of the church in the early modern period and with the chronological, geographical and social variations which they displayed.

4.1394 **Reay**, B., 'The social origins of early Quakerism', *J.Interdis.H.*, XI, 1980, 55–72.

4.1395 **Richardson**, R. C., *Puritanism in Northwest England: A Regional Study of the Diocese of Chester to 1642*, 1972. A social approach examining the structure of puritanism in the region and the forces at work within it.

4.1396 **Scarisbrick**, J. J., *The Reformation and the English People*, 1984.

4.1397 **Schlatter**, R. B., *The Social Ideas of Religious Leaders, 1660–1688*, 1940.

4.1398 **Seaver**, P. S., *The Puritan Lectureships: The Politics of Religious Dissent, 1560–1662*, Stanford, Calif., 1970.

4.1399 **Solt**, L. F., *Saints in Arms: Puritanism and Democracy in Cromwell's Army*, Stanford, Calif., 1959.

4.1400 **Spurr**, J., *The Restoration Church of England, 1964–89*, 1991. A readable study drawing on a wide range of church records. The significance of the parish as a unit and the growth of dissent and of religious indifference are discussed.

4.1401 **Steffan**, T. G., 'The social argument against Enthusiasm, 1650–60', *Studies in English*, 21, 1941, 39–63.

4.1402 **Taylor**, S., 'Church and society after the Glorious Revolution', *H.J.*, XXXI, 1988, 973–88.

4.1403 **Trevor-Roper**, H. R., *Religion, the Reformation and Social Change*, 1967.

4.1404 **Trimble**, W. R., *The Catholic Laity in Elizabethan England*, Cambridge, Mass., 1964.

4.1405 **Tyacke**, N., 'Puritanism, Arminianism and Counter-Revolution'. In Russell (4.1268), 119–43.

4.1406 **Vann**, R. T., *The Social Development of English Quakerism, 1655–1755*, Harvard, Mass., 1969.

4.1407 —— 'Quakerism and the social structure in the Interregnum', *P.P.*, 43, 1969, 71–91.

4.1408 **Walsh**, J., Haydon, C., and Taylor, S., eds., *The Church of England c.1689–c.1833. From Toleration to Sectarianism*, 1993. Includes chapters on pastoral work, moral reform, patronage, and missionary activity.

4.1408a **Watts**, M. R., *The Dissenters from the Reformation to the French Revolution*, 1978.

4.1409 **Whitaker**, W. B., *Sunday in Tudor and Stuart Times*, 1933.

4.1410 **Whiting**, R., ' "Abominable idols": images and image breaking under Henry VIII', *J.Eccles.H.*, XXXIII, 1982, 30–47.

4.1411 —— *The Blind Devotion of the People. Popular Religion and the English Reformation*, 1989.

4.1412 **Whitney**, Dorothy W., 'London puritanism: the Haberdashers' Company', *Church H.*, XXXII, 1963, 298–321. A case study of the patronage wielded by bodies of merchants and tradesmen.

See also Walzer (4.1279).

(b) Religion and economic development

4.1413 **Birnbaum**, N., 'Conflicting interpretations of the rise of capitalism: Marx and Weber', *Brit.J.Soc.*, IV, 1953, 125–41.

4.1414 **Breen**, T. H., 'The non-existent controversy. Puritan and Anglican attitudes to work and wealth, 1600–1640', *Church H.* XXXV, 1966, 273–87. *See also* the book by the Georges (4.1420).

4.1415 **Burrell**, S. A., 'Calvinism, capitalism and the middle classes: some afterthoughts on an old problem', *J.M.H.*, 32, 1960, 129–41.

4.1416 **Collinson**, P., *The Birthpangs of Protestant England. Religious and Cultural change in Sixteenth and Seventeenth Centuries*, 1988.

4.1417 **Fanfani**, A., *Catholicism, Protestantism and Capitalism*, N. Y., 1935.

4.1418 **Fischoff**, E., 'The Protestant ethic and the spirit of capitalism: the history of a controversy' *Social Research*, XI, 1944, 61–77.

4.1419 **George**, C. H., 'English Calvinist opinion on usury, 1600–1640', *J.H. Ideas*, XVIII, 1957, 455–74.

4.1420 —— and Katherine, *The Protestant Mind of the English Reformation, 1570–1640*, Princeton, N. J., 1961. A useful book but by no means wholly convincing in its attempts to play down the distinctiveness of puritanism.

4.1421 **Greaves**, R. L., 'The origins of English sabbatarian thought', *Sixteenth Cen.J.*, XXI, 1981, 19–34.

4.1422 **Green**, R. W., ed., *Protestantism and Capitalism: The Weber Thesis and its Critics*, Boston, Mass., 1959. A collection of extracts from the main contributions to the debate.

4.1423 **Hill**, C., 'Protestantism and the rise of capitalism', in Fisher, ed. (4.52), 29–39. A stimulating essay by a distinguished defender of the Weber Thesis.

4.1424 **Hudson**, W. S., 'Puritanism and the spirit of capitalism', *Church H.*, XVIII, 1949, 3–16.

4.1425 **Kearney**, H. F., 'Puritanism, capitalism and the scientific revolution', *P.P.*, 28, 1964, 81–101.

4.1426 **Kitch**, M. J., ed., *Capitalism and the Reformation*, 1967. A collection of extracts from contemporary writings and from historians' interpretations, with an introduction and bibliography.

4.1427 **Luethy**, M., 'Once again: Calvinism and capitalism', *Encounter*, XXII, 1964, 26–38.

4.1428 **Morgan**, N. J., 'Lancashire Quakers and the tithe, 1660–1670', *Bull.J.Rylands Lib.*, LXX, 1988, 61–76.

4.1429 **Orme**, N., 'The dissolution of the Chantries in Devon, 1546–8', *T.Devonshire Ass.*, CXI, 1979, 75–123.

4.1430 **Parker**, K. L., *The English Sabbath. A Study of Doctrine and Discipline from the Reformation to the Civil War*, 1988.

4.1431 **Razzell**, P. E., 'The protestant ethic and the spirit of capitalism', *Brit.J.Soc.*, XXVIII, 1977, 17–37.

4.1432 **Reay**, B., 'Quaker opposition to tithes, 1652–60', *P.P.*, 86, 1980, 98–120.

4.1433 **Seaver**, P. S., 'The puritan work ethic revisited', *J.Brit.Studs.*, XIX, 1980, 35–53.

4.1433a **Supple**, B. E., 'The great capitalist manhunt', *Bus.H.*, VI, 1963, 48–62.

4.1434 **Tawney**, R. H., *Religion and the Rise of Capitalism*, 1926. Several times reprinted. A profound and wide-ranging study. One of the masterpieces of English historical writing.

4.1435 **Thomas**, K., *Religion and the Decline of Magic*, 1971.

4.1436 **Trevor-Roper**, H. R., 'The bishopric of Durham and the capitalist Reformation', *Durham Univ. J.*, XXXVIII, 1946, 45–58.

4.1437 **Weber**, M., *The Protestant Ethic and the Spirit of Capitalism*, 1904, English trans., N. Y. and London, 1930. One of the earliest attempts to explore the relationship between reformed religion and economic development. Its publication initiated a controversy amongst historians, economists, sociologists and theologians which has lasted for over sixty years. *See also* the chapter 'Religion and the social environment' in Thompson (5.121).

4.1438 **Wright**, Susan, ed., *Parish, Church and People. Local Studies in Lay Religion, 1350–1750*, 1988. A collection of essays looking at the social significance of parish, the links between the church and leisure activities, and the local influence of the clergy.

EDUCATION AND LEARNING

(a) Schools, schooling and higher education

4.1439 **Cressy**, D., *Education in Tudor and Stuart England*, 1975. Source material with extended commentary.

4.1439a **Sylvester**, D. W., ed., *Educational Documents, 800–1816*, 1970.

4.1440 **Turnbull**, G. L., ed., *Hartlib, Dury and Comenius*, 1947. The three most influential foreign intellectuals in the English Revolution.

4.1441 **Adamson**, J. W., *A Short History of Education*, 1919.

4.1442 —— *The Illiterate Anglo-Saxon and Other Essays on Education Medieval and Modern*, 1946.

4.1443 —— 'The extent of literacy in England in the fifteenth and sixteenth centuries: notes and conjuctures', *The Library*, 4th ser., X, 1929–30, 163–93.

4.1444 **Axtell**, J. L., 'Education and status in Stuart England: the London physician', *H.Educ. Quarterly*, X, 1970, 141–59.

4.1445 **Beales**, A. C. F., *Education under Penalty: English Catholic Education from the Reformation to the Fall of James II*, 1963.

4.1446 **Bok**, I., *The Social Thought of Francis Bacon*, 1989.

4.1447 **Brauer**, G. C., *The Education of a Gentleman: Theories of Gentlemanly Education in England, 1660–1775*, N. Y., 1959.

4.1448 **Brown**, J. H., *Elizabethan Schooldays*, 1933.

4.1449 **Caspari**, F., *Humanism and the Social Order in Tudor England*, Chicago and Cambridge, 1955.

4.1450 **Charlton**, K., *Education in Renaissance England*, 1965.

4.1451 **Conant**, J. B., 'The advancement of learning during the Puritan Commonwealth', *Proc. Massachusetts H.Soc.*, LXVI, for 1936–41, 1942, 3–31.

4.1452 **Costello**, W. T., *The Scholastic Curriculum at Early Seventeenth-century Cambridge*, Cambridge, Mass., 1958.

4.1453 **Cressy**, D., *Literacy and the Social Order, Reading and Writing in Tudor and Stuart England*, 1980. Combines a general outline of the subject with local case studies. Includes an extended discussion of the available sources and of the necessary research methods.

4.1454 **Curtis**, M. H., *Oxford and Cambridge in Transition*, 1959. A valuable study of the two universities in the early modern period.

4.1455 —— 'The alienated intellectuals of early Stuart England', *P.P.*, 23, 1962, 25–43. Reprinted in Aston (4.30), 295–316.

4.1456 **Galenson**, D. W., 'Literacy and age in pre-industrial England. Quantitative evidence and implications', *Econ.Dev. & Cult.Change*, XXIX, 1981, 813–31.

4.1457 **Graff**, H. J., ed., *Literacy and Social Development in the West*, 1982. A collection of reprinted essays dealing with the period from the eleventh to the twentieth centuries. The essays by Claunchy, Cressy, Spufford and Schofield specifically relate to England.

4.1458 **Greaves**, R. L., *The Puritan Revolution and Educational Thought*, Princeton N. J., 1969.

4.1459 **Green**, V. H. H., *The Universities*, 1969. A competent and readable general outline of their development.

4.1460 **Hadden**, R. W., 'Social relations and the content of early modern science', *Br.J.Sociol.*, XXXIX, 1988, 255–80.

4.1461 **Hexter**, J. H., 'The education of the aristocracy in the Renaissance'. In the same author's *Reappraisals in History*, 1961, 45–70.

4.1462 **Houston**, R. A., 'The development of literacy: Northern England, 1640–1750', *Ec.H.R.*, 2nd ser., XXXV, 1982, 199–216.

4.1463 —— 'Illiteracy in the diocese of Durham, 1663–89 and 1750–62: the evidence of marriage bonds', *Northern H.*, XVIII, 1982, 239–51.

4.1464 **Howell**, W. S., *Logic and Rhetoric in England, 1500–1700*, Princeton, N. J., 1958.

4.1465 **Hunter**, M., *Science and Society in Restoration England*, 1981.

4.1466 **Kearney**, H. F., *Scholars and Gentlemen: Universities and Society in Pre-industrial Britain, 1500–1700*, 1970. An important addition to the literature on the subject.

4.1467 **Lawson**, J., *A Town Grammar School Through Six Centuries* (Hull), 1963. One of the best examples of the large crop of local studies.

4.1468 **McConica**, J., ed., *The History of the University of Oxford*, III: *The Collegiate University*, 1986. Includes a discussion of the social origins and carers of students, the economic substructure of the university, curriculum and books.

4.1469 **Leach**, A. F., *English Schools at the Reformation*, 1896.

4.1470 **Morgan**, J., *Godly Learning. Puritan Attitudes towards Reason, Learning and Education, 1560–1640*, 1986.

4.1471 **O'Day**, Rosemary, *Education and Society, 1500–1800*, 1982.

4.1472 **Prest**, W. R., *The Inns of Court under Elizabeth I and the Early Stuarts, 1590–1640*, 1972.

4.1473 —— 'The legal education of the gentry at the Inns of Court, 1560–1640', *P.P.*, 38, 1967, 20–39.

4.1474 **Schofield**, R. S., 'The measurement of literacy in pre-industrial England'. In J. Goody, ed., *Literacy in Traditional Societies*, 1968, 311–25.

4.1475 **Seaborne**, M., *The English School, its Architecture and Organisation. I: 1370–1870*, 1971. Vol. 2 of this work is listed below (5.3165).

4.1476 **Simon**, B., ed., *Education in Leicestershire, 1540–1940*, 1968.

4.1477 **Simon**, Joan, *Education and Society in Tudor England*, 1966. Thorough bibliography.

4.1478 **Spufford**, Margaret, 'The schooling of the peasantry in Cambridgeshire, 1575–1700'. In Joan Thirsk, ed., *Land, Church and People: Essays Presented to Professor H. P. R. Finberg*, 1970, 112–47. An interesting local study of the availability of education facilities and of the extent of literacy. *See also* Spufford (4.352).

4.1479 **Stone**, L., 'The educational revolution in England, 1560–1640', *P.P.*, 28, 1964, 41–80.

4.1480 —— 'Literacy and education in England, 1640–1900', *P.P.*, 42, 1969, 69–139. These two articles along with Simon (4.1477), are essential reading on the history of education in this period.

4.1481 —— ed., *The University in Society*, 2 vols, Princeton, N. J., 1975. Includes chapters on the size and composition of the student body and on university links with the country opposition to Charles I.

4.1482 —— ed., *Schooling and Society. Studies in the History of Education*, 1976. Includes essays on book ownership in England, 1560–1640, and on English working-class education.

4.1483 **Thomas**, K., *Rule and Misrule in the Schools of Early Modern England*, 1976.

4.1484 —— 'Numeracy in early modern England', *T.R.H.S.*, n.s., XXXVII, 1987, 103–32.

4.1485 **Twigg**, J., *The University of Cambridge and the English Revolution*, 1990.

4.1486 **Vincent**, W. A. L., *The State and School Education 1640–1660 in England and Wales*, 1950.

4.1487 —— *The Grammar Schools. Their Continuing Tradition 1660–1714*, 1969.

4.1488 **Webster**, C., 'The curriculum of the grammar schools and universities, 1500–1660. A critical view of the literature', *H.Educ.*, IV, 1975, 51–68.

4.1489 —— *The Great Instauration. Science, Medicine and Reform 1626–1660*, 1976. The central figure in the book is Samuel Hartlib.

4.1490 —— ed., *The Intellectual Revolution of the Seventeenth Century*, 1975.

4.1491 **Wood**, N., *The Reformation and English Education*, 1931.

The various books by Professor Jordan on English philanthropy (p. 91), are also relevant in this connection. *See also* Lawson and Silver (5.3145).

(b) Books, newspapers and readers

4.1492 **Beer**, E. S. de., 'The English newspapers from 1695 to 1702'. In Ragnild Hatton and J. S. Bromley, eds., *William III and Louis XIV: Essays by and for Mark Thomson*, 1968, 117–29.

4.1493 **Bennett**, H. S., *English Books and Readers, 1485–1640*, 3 vols, 1952–70. A monumental study of patterns of production, distribution, and reception of books in this period.

4.1494 **Capp**, B. S., *Astrology and the Popular Press. English Almanacs 1500–1800*, 1979. A study of one of the most widely read forms of literature of the time and of its relevance to social, political, intellectual and religious life. *See also* Spufford (4.1505).

4.1495 **Chartier**, R. et al., *The Culture of Print. Power and the Uses of Print in Early Modern Europe*, 1989.

4.1496 **Clyde**, W. M., *The Struggle for the Freedom of the Press from Caxton to Cromwell*, 1934.

4.1497 **Cressy**, D., 'Books as totems in seventeenth-century England and New England', *J.Lib.Hist.*, XXII, 1987, 117–46.

4.1498 **Dukes**, G., 'The beginnings of the English newspaper', *H.Today*, 4, 1954, 197–204.

4.1499 **Eisenstein**, E. L., *The Printing Press as an Agent of Change: Communications and Cultural Transformations in Early Modern Europe*, 1979.

4.1500 **Frank**, J., *The Beginnings of the English Newspaper, 1620–1660*, Cambridge, Mass., 1961.

4.1501 **Fraser**, P., *The Intelligence of the Secretaries of State and their Monopoly of Licensed News, 1660–1688*, 1956.

4.1502 **Myers**, R., *The British Book Trade from Caxton to the Present Day*, 1973.

4.1503 **Rostenberg**, L., *The Minority Press and the English Crown 1558–1625*, Nieuwkoop, 1971.

4.1504 **Shaaber**, M. A., *Some Forerunners of the Newspaper in England, 1476–1622*, 1929. Reprinted 1966.

4.1504a **Siebert**, F. S., *Freedom of the Press in England, 1476–1776. The Rise and Decline of Government Control*, Urbana, Ill. 1965.

4.1505 **Spufford**, Margaret, *Small Books and Pleasant Histories. Popular Fiction and its Readership in Seventeenth Century England*, 1985. Fascinating exploration of seventeenth-century chapbooks which looks at their authorship, production, marketing and readership. The relationship between popular and elite culture is re-examined.

4.1506 **Sutherland**, J., *The Restoration Newspaper and its Development*, 1986.

4.1507 **Thompson**, R., *Unfit for Modest Ears. A Study of Pornographic, Obscene, and Bawdy Works written or published in the Second Half of the Seventeenth Century*, 1979.

4.1508 **Varley**, F. J., ed., *Mercurius Aulicus*, 1948. Extracts from the Royalist newspaper published at Oxford, 1643–5.

4.1509 **Watt**, Tessa, *Cheap Print and Popular Piety, 1550–1640*, 1991. A highly original and effective study wich shows how popular literature and prints figured in ordinary people's experience of sixteenth and seventeenth-century religious changes.

CULTURE AND LEISURE

4.1510 **Ashton**, R., 'Popular entertainment and social control in later Elizabethan and early Stuart London', *London J.*, IX, 1983, 3–20.

4.1511 **Burke**, P., 'From pioneers to settlers: recent studies of the history of popular culture', *Comp.Studs.Soc. & H.*, XXV, 1983, 181–87.

4.1512 **Clark**, P., *The English Alehouse. A Social History, 1200–1830*, 1983. A broad study of the place of the alehouse in local society which takes account of the drink trade, landlords and customers. The social functions of the alehouse are examined as are the issues relating to regulation and commercialisation.

4.1513 **Heal**, Felicity, *Hospitality in Early Modern England*, 1990. Deals with the theory, practice, and cultural significance of hospitality in the early modern period and with government concern for, and public interest in, the subject.

4.1514 **Henricks**, T. S., *Disputed Pleasures. Sport and Society in Preindustrial England*, 1991.

4.1515 **Howard**, Jean E., *The Stage and Social Struggle in Early Modern England*, 1994. Gives most weight to the material conditions – capital accumulation and the growth of London, for example – which facilitated the development of commercial drama.

4.1516 **Hutton**, R., *The Rise and Fall of Merry England. The Ritual Year, 1994.* Considers the ways in which religious and secular rituals of the Middle Ages were affected by the Reformation and by social and political changes of the sixteenth and seventeenth centuries.

4.1517 **Kiernan**, V. G., *The Duel in European History. Honour and the Reign of Aristocracy*, 1988.

4.1518 **Parry**, G., *The Golden Age Restor'd. The Culture of the Stuart Court, 1603–42*, 1981. A useful re-assessment of the significance of court masques in the early seventeenth century.

4.1519 **Reay**, B., ed., *Popular Culture in Seventeenth-Century England*, 1985. Has chapters on popular protest, religion, literature, the people and the law, and on sex and marriage. Case studies of London and Bristol are included.

4.1520 **Wright**, L. B., *Middle Class Culture in*

Elizabethan England, Chapel Hill, N.C., 1935. A famous study of late sixteenth-century reading habits.

4.1521 **Young**, A., *Tudor and Jacobean Tournaments*, 1987.

WOMEN

4.1522 **Blodgett**, Harriet, ed., *Centuries of Female Days. English Women's Private Diaries*, 1989.

4.1523 **Otten**, Charlotte F., ed., *English Women's Voices, 1540–1700*, Miami, Fla., 1992. A sourcebook containing 46 substantial extracts from contemporary writings. There are sections relating to abuse, persecution, love and marriage, health and sickness, childbirth, and death.

4.1524 **Asmussen**, Susan, D., *An Ordered Society. Gender and Class in Early Modern England*, 1988. Partly a local study drawing on Norfolk evidence, the book nonetheless ranges widely in its re-assessment of women's roles.

4.1525 **Brantt**, Clare and Purkiss, Diane, eds., *Women, Texts and Histories, 1575–1760*, 1992. An interdisciplinary collection which includes essays on the seventeenth century debate on women's place in society, on Restoration whores, and on women's experience of the law.

4.1526 **Briggs**, J., 'She preachers, widows, and other women: the feminine dimension in Baptist life since 1600', *Baptist Q.*, XXXI, 1986, 337–51.

4.1527 **Cahn**, S., *Industry of Devotion. The Transformation of Women's Work in England, 1500–1600*, 1987.

4.1528 **Cionik**, M. L., *Women and Law in Elizabethan England, with Particular Reference to the Court of Chancery*, 1985.

4.1529 **Charles**, L. and Duffin, L., eds., *Women and Work in Preindustrial England*, 1985.

4.1530 **Clark**, Alice, *The Working Life of Women in the Seventeenth Century*, 1919, rep. 1968 and 1982, with a new introduction by Miranda Chaytor.

4.1531 **Crawford**, Patricia, *Women and Religion, 1500–1720*, 1993. Embraces both Puritans and Roman Catholics and takes the English Revolution as its centrepiece. Women's roles as writers, preachers and prophets are discussed.

4.1532 **Cross**, Claire, 'Northern women in the early modern period: the female testators of Hull and Leeds, 1520–1650', *Yorks.Arch.J.*, LIX, 1987, 83–94.

4.1533 **Ezell**, Margaret, *The Patriarch's Wife. Literary Evidence and the History of the Family*, Chapel Hill, N.C., 1987. Based chiefly on manuscript sources and treatises on women, the book highlights how articulate women of the period could be, despite their prescribed submission to men.

4.1534 **Fraser**, Antonia, *The Weaker Vessel. Woman's Lot in Seventeenth Century England*, 1984. A wide ranging popular treatment of the subject.

4.1535 **George**, Margaret, *Women in the First Capitalist Society. Experiences in Seventeenth-Century England*, 1988. Chiefly a series of case studies, feminist in inspiration, of women writers and activists from the middling ranks.

4.1536 **Grundy**, Isobel, and Wiseman, Susan, *Women, Writing, History*, 1992. A collection of interdisciplinary essays in which individual women writers such as Aphra Behn, Mary Astell, and Margaret Cavendish figure prominently.

4.1537 **Hester**, M. *Lewd Women and Wicked Witches. A Study of the Dynamic of Male Domination*, 1992.

4.1538 **Hodgkin**, Katherine, 'The diary of Lady Anne Clifford: a study of class and gender in the seventeenth century', *H.Workshop J.*, XIX, 1985, 148–62.

4.1539 **Hoffer**, P. C. and Hull, N. E. H., *Murdering Mothers. Infanticide in England and New England, 1558–1803*, New York, 1981. A comparative study of the incidence of infanticide and of the ways in which crime was dealt with.

4.1540 **Hole**, Christina, *The English Housewife in the Seventeenth Century*, 1953.

4.1541 **Hufton**, Olwen, 'Women in history: early modern period', *P.P.*, CI, 1983, 125–40. Bibliographical survey.

4.1542 **Keeble**, N. H., 'Here is her glory, even to be under him'. The feminine in the thought and work of John Bunyan', *Baptist Q.*, XXXII, 1988, 380–92.

4.1543 **Lawrence**, Anne, *Women in England. A Social History, 1500–1760*, 1994.

4.1544 **Levack**, B. P., *The Witch Hunt in Early Modern Europe*, 1987. For background.

4.1545 **McMullen**, N., 'The education of English gentlewomen, 1540–1640', *H.Education*, VI, 1977, 87–101.

4.1546 **Mendelson**, Sarah, *The Mental World of Stuart Women. Three Studies*, 1988. Case studies of the lives of Margaret Cavendish, Duchess of Newcastle, of the playwright Aphra Behn, and of Mary Rich, Countess of Warwick.

4.1547 **Nadelhaft**, J., 'Englishwomen's sexual Civil War, 1650–1740', *J.Hist.Ideas*, XLIII, 1982, 555–80.

4.1548 **Prior**, Mary, ed., *Women in English Society, 1500–1800*, 1989. A useful collection of well-researched essays which includes studies of marital fertility, re-marriage, women's roles, and of women as diarists and authors.

4.1549 **Quaife**, G. R., *Godly Zeal and Furious Rage. The Witch in Early Modern Europe*, 1987. *See also* Levack (4.1544).

4.1550 **Rose**, S. O., 'Proto-industry, women's work, and the household economy in the transition to industrial capitalism', *J.Fam.H.*, XIII, 1988, 181–93.

4.1551 **Rushton**, P., 'Women, witchcraft and slander in early modern England: cases from the church courts of Durham, 1560–1675', *Northern H.*, XVIII, 1982, 116–32.

4.1552 **Shepherd**, S., *Amazons and Warrior Women. Varieties of Feminism in Seventeenth-Century Drama*, 1981.

4.1553 **Thompson**, R., *Women in Stuart England and America. A Comparative Study*, 1974. Examines the status and roles of women in the two countries commenting on the implications of sex ratios for the status of women and on the effects of Puritanism.

4.1554 **Warnicke**, R. M., *Women of the English Renaissance and Reformation*, 1983.

4.1555 **Willen**, D., 'Godly women in early modern England: Puritanism and gender', *J.Eccles.H.*, XLIII, 1992, 561–80.

5

ENGLAND 1700–1980

GENERAL WORKS
1700–1880

(a) Bibliographies and statistics

5.1 **Ashton**, T. S., *The Industrial Revolution: A Study in Bibliography*, 1937.

5.2 **Brown**, Lucy M. and Christie, I. R., eds., *Bibliography of British History, 1789–1851*, 1977.

5.3 **Cannery**, Margaret and Knott, D., eds., *Catalogue of Goldsmith's Library of Economic Literature*, I. 1970.

5.4 **Clark**, G. N., *The Idea of the Industrial Revolution*, 1953.

5.5 **Deane**, Phyllis and Cole, W. A., *British Economic Growth 1688–1959: Trends and Structure*, 1962, 2nd ed., 1967.

5.6 **Hanson**, L. W., ed., *Contemporary Printed Sources for British and Irish Economic History, 1701–1750*, 1963.

5.7 **Mitchell**, B. R., *British Historical Statistics*, 1988.

5.8 **Nicholls**, D., ed., *Nineteenth-century Britain, 1815–1914*, 1978.

5.9 **Pargellis**, S. and Medley, D., eds., *Bibliography of British History: The Eighteenth Century, 1717–89*, 1951.

(b) Sources and documentary collections

5.10 **Bastian**, F., 'Defoe's *Tour* and the

historian', *H.Today*, 1967, 845–51. A critical estimate.

5.11 **Bowditch**, J. and Ramsland, C., eds., *Voices of the Industrial Revolution. Selected Readings from the Liberal Economists and their Critics*, Ann Arbor, Mich., 1961.

5.12 **Brown**, A. F. J., ed., *English History from Essex Sources, 1750–1900*, 1952. Useful book of documents on many aspects of economic and social life.

5.13 **Cole**, G. D. H., ed., *Defoe's Tour through the Whole Island of Great Britain*, 2 vols., 1927. Another edition with introductions by G. D. H. Cole and D. C. Browning, 1974.

5.14 **Harrison**, J. F. C., *Society and Politics in England, 1780–1960: A Selection of Readings and Comments*, 1965. Largely economic in content.

5.15 **Harvie**, C., Martin, G. and Scharf, A., *Industrialisation and Culture, 1830–1914*, 1970. Documentary material with comments.

5.16 **Pike**, E. R., ed., *Human Documents of Adam Smith's Time*, 1974.

5.17 —— *Human Documents of the Industrial Revolution in Britain*, 1966. Editorial comments not well informed and often flippant; the extracts from documents are useful.

5.18 —— *Human Documents of the Victorian Golden Age, (1850–75)*, 1967.

5.19 **Smart**, W. *Economic Annals of the Nineteenth Century*, 1916–17, reprinted 1964. Vol 1 covers 1801–20, vol II, 1821–30. An economic epitome of

Hansard's Parliamentary Debates and *The Annual Register*.

5.20 **Tames**, R. L., ed., *Documents of the Industrial Revolution, 1750–1850*, 1971. The extracts tend to be short.

5.21 **Warburg**, J., ed., *The Industrial Muse: The Industrial Revolution in English Poetry*, 1958.

5.22 **Ward**, J. T., ed., *The Age of Change, 1770–1870. Documents in Social History*, 1975.

(c) General works

5.23 **Ashton**, T. S., *The Industrial Revolution, 1760–1830*, 1948.

5.24 —— *An Economic History of England: The Eighteenth Century*, 1955.

5.25 **Beales**, H. L., *The Industrial Revolution, 1750–1850: An Introductory Essay*, 1928, reissue with new introduction, 1958.

5.26 **Behagg**, C., *Politics and Production in the Early Nineteenth Century*, 1990. A case study of Birmingham and its transformation in the early nineteenth century. Industrial organisation and workplace culture are prominent themes.

5.27 **Beresford**, M. W., *Time and Place. Collected Essays*, 1984. Essays which deal with patterns of settlement, agricultural practice, taxation and urban development.

5.28 **Berg**, Maxine, *The Age of Manufacture. Industry, Innovation and Work in Britain, 1700–1820*, 1985. Challenges simplistic accounts of industrialisation and underlines the complexities, variety and contradictions in the process.

5.29 —— and Hudson, Pat, 'Rehabilitating the industrial revolution', *Ec.,H.R.*, XLV, 1992, 24–50.

5.30 —— Hudson, Pat, and Soneuscher, M., eds., *Manufacture in Town and Country before the Factory*, 1983.

5.31 **Best**, G. F. A., *Mid-Victorian Britain, 1851–75*, 1971.

5.32 **Black**, J. and Gregory, J., eds., *Culture, Politics and Society in Britain, 1660–1800*, 1991. Has chapters on patronage, the press, the social ramifications of Anglicanism, and on medicine.

5.33 **Bowden**, W., *Industrial Society in England towards the End of the Eighteenth Century*, 1925. 2nd ed. with new introduction and bibliography, 1965.

5.34 **Briggs**, A., *A Social History of England*, 1983. An impressive and highly readable distillation which makes sense of a long period of English history.

5.35 —— *Victorian Things*, 1988. The sequel to the same author's *Victorian People* and *Victorian Cities*. This is a learned and wide-ranging analysis of nineteenth-century material culture.

5.36 —— *Collected Essays and Reviews*. I: *Words, Numbers, Places, People*: II: *Images, Problems, Standpoints, Forecasts*, 1987. Brings together 25 of the author's essays.

5.37 **Brown**, R., *Society and Economy in Modern Britain, 1700–1850*, 1991.

5.38 **Butt**, J. and Clarke, I. F., eds., *The Victorians and Social Protest*, 1973. Contains chapters by H. J. Perkin on land reform and class conflict in Victorian Britain, and J. H. Treble on Irish immigrant attitudes to north of England Chartism. *See* Hollis (5.74).

5.39 **Cairncross**, A., *Society and Economy in Modern Britain, 1700–1850*, 1991.

5.40 **Cannadine**, D., 'The past and the present in the English Industrial Revolution, 1880–1980', *P.P.*, CIII, 1984, 131–72.

5.41 **Cannon**, J., *Aristocratic Century. The Peerage of Eighteenth-Century England*, 1984. Discounts the notion of a bourgeois revolution in the seventeenth century and calls into question the concept of an open aristocracy in the eighteenth.

5.42 **Chaloner**, W. H. and Ratcliffe, B. M., eds.,*Trade and Transport. Essays in Economic History in Honour of T. S. Willan*, 1977. A miscellaneous collection which extends chronologically and topically from seventeenth-century Yorkshire cattle droving and Cumbrian ironworks to the 1930s depression in Scotland.

5.43 **Chambers**, J. D., *The Workshop of the World: British Economic History from 1820–1880*, 2nd rev. ed., 1968.

5.44 **Chapman**, S. D. and Chambers, J. D., *The Beginnings of Industrial Britain*, 1970. Covers the period c. 1700–1830; good illustrations.

5.45 **Checkland**, S. G., *The Rise of Industrial Society in England, 1815–1885*, 1964. Valuable for footnote references to theses; good bibliography, 413–54.

5.46 **Church**, R. A., *The Great Victorian Boom, 1850–73*, 1975.

5.47 —— ed., *The Dynamics of Victorian Business. Problems and Perspectives in the 1870s*, 1980. Chapters on the coal, iron, engineering, cotton and woollen textiles, and shoe and leather industries.

5.48 **Clapham**, J. H., *An Economic History of Modern Britain*: Vol. I, *The Early Railway Age, 1820–1850*, 1926; Vol. II, *Free Trade and Steel, 1850–1886*, 1932; Vol. III, *Machines and National Rivalries (1886–1914) with an Epilogue (1914–29)*, 1938.

5.49 **Clark**, G. K., *The Making of Victorian England*, 1962. Covers the period 1830–60.

5.50 **Clark**, J. C. D., *English Society, 1688–1832. Ideology, Social Structure and Political Practice during the Ancien Regime*, 1985. A revisionist tract stressing the continuities from the seventeenth to the early nineteenth centuries focussing chiefly on the history of ideas.

5.51 **Coleman**, D. C., and Mathias, P., eds., *Enterprise and Industry. Essays in Honour of Charles Wilson*, 1984.

5.52 **Colley**, Linda, *Britons. Forging the Nation, 1707–1837*, New Haven, Conn., 1992. Examines the emergence of a distinctively 'British' nationalism in the eighteenth and early nineteenth centuries, the role of empire in its promotion, and its gender distinctions.

5.53 **Corrigan**, P. and Sayer, D., *The Great Arch. State Formation, Cultural Revolution and the Rise of Capitalism*, 1989. Demonstrates some of the strengths – especially the capacity for generalisation – and all of the weaknesses of historical sociology.

5.54 **Court**, W. H. B., *A Concise Economic History of Britain from 1750 to Recent Times*, 1954.

5.55 **Crafts**, N. F. R., 'English economic growth in the eighteenth century. A re-examination of Deane and Cole's estimates', *Ec.H.R.*, 2nd ser., XXIX, 1976, 226–35.

5.56 —— 'Industrial Revolution in England and France. Some thoughts on the question "Why was England first?" ', *Ec.H.R.*, XXX, 1977, 429–41.

5.57 —— *British Economic Growth during the Industrial Revolution*, 1985. Favours a gradualist interpretation of the changing industrial patterns of the period.

5.58 **Crouzet**, F., *The Victorian Economy*, 1982.

5.59 **Dabydeen**, D., *Hogarth, Walpole and Commercial Britain*, 1987. Uses visual evidence effectively.

5.60 **Deane**, Phyllis, *The First Industrial Revolution*, 1965. 2nd ed., 1980.

5.61 **Earle**, P., *The World of Defoe*, 1976. The best general introduction.

5.62 **Evans**, E. J., *The Forging of the Modern State. Early Industrial Britain*, 1983. A well organised textbook which addresses problems relating to the class structure of Britain in this period.

5.63 **Farnie**, D. A. and Henderson, W. O., eds., *Industry and Innovation. W. H. Chaloner: Selected Essays*, 1990. Reprints eighteen of the author's essays on industry, the growth of Manchester, and on social aspects of the Industrial Revolution. Bibliography of Chaloner's writings, 303–12.

5.64 **Flinn**, M. W., *The Origins of the Industrial Revolution*, 1966.

5.65 **Floud**, R. and McCloskey, D., eds., *The Economic History of Britain since 1700*. I: *1700–1860*, 1981. For Vol. II *see* (5.209).

5.66 **Fores**, M., 'The myth of a British Industrial Revolution', *Hist.*, LXVI, 1981, 181–98.

5.67 **Harrison**, J. F. C., *The Early Victorians, 1832–51*, 1971.

5.68 **Hartwell**, R. M., ed., *The Industrial Revolution*, 1970. A collection of essays.

5.69 —— *The Causes of the Industrial Revolution in England*, 1967. A collection of articles on various aspects of the subject by eminent economic historians.

5.70 —— *The Industrial Revolution*. Hist.Ass. Pamphlet; 1965.

5.71 —— *The Industrial Revolution and Economic Growth*, 1972. Collected essays.

5.72 **Hobsbawm**, E. J., *Industry and Empire: An Economic History of Britain*, 1968.

5.73 —— *The Age of Capital, 1848–75*, 1975.

5.74 **Hollis**, Patricia M. (ed.), *Pressure from Without in Early Victorian England*, 1974. *See also* Butt and Clarke (5.38).

5.75 **Holmes**, G. and Szechi, D., *The Age of Oligarchy. Pre-industrial Britain, 1722–1783*, 1994. A socio-economic survey which unduly neglects the politics of the period it covers.

5.76 **Hoppit**, J., *Risk and Failure in English Business, 1700–1800*, 1987. Considers the frequency of bankruptcy in the eighteenth century among merchants, wholesalers, industrialists, and bankers.

5.77 —— 'Counting the Industrial Revolution', *Ec.H.R.*, 2nd ser., XLIII, 1990, 173–93.

5.78 **Houston**, R. and Snell, K. D. M., 'Proto-industrialisation? Cottage industry, social change and the Industrial Revolution', *H.J.*, XXVII, 1984, 473–92.

5.79 **James**, J. A., 'Personal wealth distribution in late eighteenth-century Britain', *Ec.H.R.*, 2nd ser., XLI, 1988, 543–65.

5.80 **Jones**, D. W., *War and Economy in the Age of William III and Marlborough*, 1988.

5.81 **Jones**, E. L. and Mingay, G. E., *Land, Labour and Population in the Industrial Revolution: Essays Presented to J. D. Chambers*, 1967.

5.82 **Klingender**, F. D., *Art and the Industrial Revolution*, 1947. 2nd rev. and enlarged ed., 1968, by Sir Arthur Elton.

5.83 **Komlos**, J., 'Thinking about the Industrial Revolution', *J.Eur.Ec.H.*, XVIII, 1989, 191–206.

5.84 **Kovacevic**, I., *Fact into Fiction. English Literature and the Industrial Scene, 1750–1850*, 1975. *See also* Sussmann (5.119) and Warburg (5.21).

5.85 **Landes**, D. S., *The Unbound Prometheus: Technological Change and Industrial Development in Western Europe from 1750 to the Present*, 1969. Mainly about Britain.

5.86 **Langford**, P., *A Polite and Commercial People. England 1727–83*, 1989. Argues that the presence of the middle classes was the most important characteristic of eighteenth-century English society. Cultural developments are seen from this perspective and entrepreneurialism receives due attention.

5.87 —— *Public Life and the Propertied Englishman, 1689–1798*, 1991. An expanded version of the author's Ford Lectures at Oxford which, while accepting the commonplace that power was based on property in the eighteenth century, shows that the concept of property was broadened in the century after the Glorious Revolution.

5.88 **Langton**, J., 'The Industrial Revolution and the regional geography of England', *T.I.B.G.*, IX, 1984, 145–68.

5.89 **Lee**, C. H., *The British Economy since 1700. A Macro-economic perspective*, 1986.

Much more successful in its treatment of the eighteenth and nineteenth centuries than with the period after 1914.

5.90 **Lindent**, P. H., 'Who owned Victorian England? The debate over landed wealth and equality', *Ag.H.*, LXI, 1987, 25–51.

5.91 **Little**, A. J., *Deceleration in the Eighteenth-Century British Economy*, 1976.

5.92 **McCloskey**, D., *Enterprise and Trade in Victorian Britain. Essays in Historical Economics*, 1981. Deploys the techniques of the New Economic History to argue that the British economy in the late nineteenth century did not fail.

5.93 **Macfarlane**, A., *The Culture of Capitalism*, 1987. Speculative essays dealing with, inter al., peasants, violence, revolution, and concepts of nature, evil, and love.

5.94 **Marshall**, Dorothy, *English People in the Eighteenth Century*, 1956.

5.95 **Marshall**, Dorothy, *Industrial England, 1766–1851*, 1982.

5.96 **Mathias**, P., *The First Industrial Nation*, 1969.

5.97 —— *The Transformation of England. Essays in the Economic and Social History of England in the Eighteenth Century*, 1979. Useful on the role of science and technology, on the brewing industry, and on taxation and wages.

5.98 —— and Postan, M. M., eds., *Cambridge Economic History of Europe. VII: The Industrial Economies. Capital, Labour and Enterprise*, 1978.

5.99 **Melada**, I., *The Captain of Industry in English Fiction, 1821–1871*, Albuquerque, New Mexico, 1970.

5.100 **O'Brien**, P., *Economic Growth in Britain and France, 1780–1914*, 1978.

5.101 **Pawson**, E., *The Early Industrial Revolution. Britain in the Eighteenth Century*, 1979. A geographical perspective.

5.102 **Perry**, P. J., *A Geography of Nineteenth-Century Britain*, 1975.

5.103 **Pope**, R., ed., *An Atlas of British Social and Economic History since c.1700*, 1989.

5.104 **Porter**, R., *English Society in the Eighteenth Century*, 1982.

5.105 —— *Myths of the English*, 1992. Includes essays on 5 November celebrations, World War I remembrance, and the rival cults of Wellington and Napoleon.

5.106 **Presnell**, L. S., ed., *Studies in the Industrial Revolution Presented to T. S.*

Ashton, 1960.

5.107 **Ratcliffe**, B. M., ed., *Great Britain and her World, 1750–1914. Essays in Honour of W. O. Henderson*, 1975. A varied collection of essays dealing, for instance, with continental influences on British industrialisation, the legal framework of economic growth, and with the Anglo-French commercial treaty of 1860.

5.108 **Robbins**, K. G., *Nineteenth-century Britain. England, Scotland and Wales. The Making of a Nation*, 1989.

5.109 **Roebuck**, Janet, *The Making of Modern English Society*, 1982.

5.110 **Royle**, E., *Modern Britain. A Social History, 1750–1985*, 1987. A judicious survey which guides the reader through the controversies surrounding class, Industrial Revolution, enclosures, and entrepreneurialism.

5.111 —— *Radicalism and Reform, 1776–1848*, 1982.

5.112 **Rule**, J., *Albion's People. English Society, 1714–1815*, 1992.

5.113 —— *The Vital Century. England's Developing Economy, 1714–1815*, 1992.

5.114 **Slaven**, A., and Aldcroft, D. H., eds., *Business, Banking and Urban History. Essays in Honour of S. G. Checkland*, 1982.

5.115 **Smith**, R. A., *Late Georgian and Regency England, 1760–1837*, 1984. A representative sampling of recently published work with substantial sections on social and economic history and on science and technology.

5.116 **Smout**, T. C., ed., *The Search for Wealth and Stability. Essays in Economic and Social History presented to M. W. Flinn*, 1980. A useful, wide-ranging *festchrift* which includes important essays on research and development in British industry over the last century and on the 'property cycle' of the affluent middle class in the early nineteenth century.

5.117 **Spadafora**, D., *The Idea of Progress in Eighteenth-Century Britain*, New Haven, Conn., 1990. Examines the indigenous triumph of the idea of progress, particularly in the period 1730–80. Adam Smith is firmly placed within this context.

5.118 **Speck**, W. A., *Society and Literature in England, 1700–1760*, 1983. A historian's survey of the social resonances of literature.

5.119 **Sussmann**, H. L., *Victorians and the Machine: The Literary Response to Technology*, Cambridge, Mass., 1968. *See also* Warburg (5.21).

5.120 **Thomis**, M. I., *Responses to Industrialisation. The British Experience, 1780–1850*, 1976. Deals both with contemporary reactions to the process of industrialisation and its consequences, and also with the historiography of the subject.

5.121 **Thompson**, A., *The Dynamics of the Industrial Revolution*, 1973. Considers the interaction between the various factors which produced the industrial changes.

5.121a **Thompson**, F. M. L., ed., *The Cambridge Social History of Britain, 1750–1950. I: Regions and Communities; II: People and their Environment; III: Social Agencies and Institutions*, 1990. A bulky conflation exploring the different facets of this subject. Some unevenness of regional emphasis is noticeable. *See* the review by J. Stevenson, Hist., LXXVI, 1991, 418–32.

5.121b —— *The Rise of Respectable Society. A Social History of Victorian Britain, 1830–1900*, 1988.

5.122 **Trinder**, B., *The Making of the Industrial Landscape*, 1983. Explores the varied industrial topography of Britain's industrial past. But it raises too few questions and is at times overburdened with detail.

5.123 **Waller**, P. J., *Town, City and Nation. England, 1850–1914*, 1983.

5.124 **Wiener**, M. J., *English Culture and the Decline of the Industrial Spirit, 1850–1980*, 1981. Looks at some of the paradoxical attitudes to industrialism and the businessman and examines the ways in which these contributed to Britain's economic decline.

5.125 **Williamson**, J. G., 'Debating the British Industrial Revolution', *Expl.Ec.H.*, XXIV, 1987, 269–92.

5.126 —— *Did British Capitalism breed Inequality?*, 1985. An American economic historian looks at the British experience of industrialisation and the changes which occurred and at patterns of earnings and income inequality.

5.127 —— 'Why was British growth so slow during the Industrial Revolution?', *J.Ec.H.*, XLIV, 1984, 687–713.

5.128 **Wohl**, A. S., ' "Gold and mud": capitalism and culture in Victorian

Britain', *Albion*, XXIII, 1991, 275–84.

5.129 **Wrigley**, E. A., ed., *Nineteenth-Century Society. Essays in the Use of Quantitative Methods for the Study of Social Data*, 1972. Chiefly concerned with the problems arising from census material.

5.130 —— *Continuity, Chance and Change. The Character of the Industrial Revolution in England*, 1989. Challenges the notion that the Industrial Revolution was cumulative, progressive and unitary, and that it was dependent on earlier agrarian development.

5.131 —— *Peoples, Cities and Wealth. The Transformation of Traditional Society*, 1987. Reprints a number of the author's essays which are arranged in three major sections: the background to the Industrial Revolution; urban growth; population: marriage and reproduction.

(d) Regional studies

5.132 **Allen**, G. C., *The Industrial Development of Birmingham and the Black Country 1860–1927*, 1929.

5.133 **Ashmore**, O., *The Industrial Archaeology of North-West England*, 1982. Largely a gazetteer of sites.

5.134 **Aspin**, C., *Lancashire, the First Industrial Society*, 1969.

5.135 **Barnsby**, G. J., *Social Conditions in the Black Country, 1800–1900*, 1980.

5.136 **Booker**, F., *The Industrial Archaeology of the Tamar Valley*, 1967.

5.137 **Buchanan**, R. A. and Cossons, N., *The Industrial Archaeology of the Bristol Region*, 1969.

5.138 **Burt**, R., ed., *Industry and Society in the South West*, 1970. Useful for Cornwall during the Industrial Revolution.

5.139 **Chambers**, J. D., *The Vale of Trent, 1670–1800: A Regional Study of Economic Change, Ec.H.R. Supp.*, 3, 1957.

5.140 **Everitt**, A. M., *Landscape and Community in England*, 1985. The author's collected essays dealing with agrarian landscapes, marketing and communications, and town-countryside relations.

5.141 **Hall**, P. G., *The Industries of London since 1861*, 1962.

5.142 **Harris**, Helen, *The Industrial Archaeology of Dartmoor*, 1968.

5.143 **Harvey**, C. E. and Press, J., eds., *Studies in the Business History of Bristol*, 1988.

5.144 **Honeyman**, Katrina, *Origins of Enterprise. Business Leadership in the Industrial Revolution*, 1982. Looks at manufacturers in lead mining, cotton spinning and lace to determine how many of them were self-made men.

5.145 **Hudson**, K., *The Industrial Archaeology of Southern England (Hampshire, Wiltshire, Dorset, Somerset and Gloucestershire and the Severn)*, 1965.

5.146 **Hudson**, Pat, *Regions and Industries. A Perspective on the Industrial Revolution in Britain*, 1989.

5.147 **Jowitt**, J. A., ed., *Model Industrial Communities in Mid-Nineteenth-Century Yorkshire*, 1986.

5.148 **Kirby**, M. W., *Men of Business and Politics. The Rise and Fall of the Quaker Pease Dynasty of N.E.England, 1700–1943*, 1984. Discusses the different aspects of the family's entrepreneurialism and the ways in which these provided a foundation for nineteenth-century political careers.

5.149 **McCord**, N., *North East England. An Economic and Social History*, 1979. Covers the period 1760–1960.

5.150 **Marriner**, Sheila, *The Economic and Social Development of Merseyside*, 1982.

5.151 **Marshall**, J. D., *Furness and the Industrial Revolution*, 1958.

5.152 —— and Walton, J. K., *The Lake Counties from 1830 to the mid Twentieth Century. A Study in Regional Change*, 1981. Continues from the point at which Bouch and Jones (4.103) leave off. Deals with the continued industrialisation of the west coast, the growing emphasis on pasture farming, and with the development of tourism and conservation.

5.153 **Nixon**, F., *The Industrial Archaeology of Derbyshire*, 1969.

5.154 **Pollard**, S. and Holmes, C., eds., *Essays in the Economic and Social History of South Yorkshire*, 1976. Seventeen essays sectionalised under (1) economic conditions and employment, (2) the radical tradition, (3) housing, and (4) religion and culture.

5.155 **Preston**, J. M., *Industrial Medway. An Historical Survey*, 1977.

5.156 **Randall**, A. J., 'Industrial conflict and economic change. The regional context of the Industrial Revolution', *Southern H.*, XIV, 1992, 74–92.

5.157 **Raybould**, T. J., *The Economic Emergence of the Black Country: A Study of the Dudley Estate*, 1973.

5.158 **Rowe**, J., *Cornwall in the Age of the Industrial Revolution*, 1953. *See also* Todd and Laws (5.162).

5.159 **Singleton**, F., *The Industrial Revolution in Yorkshire*, 1970.

5.160 **Smith**, D. H., *The Industries of Greater London, Being a Survey of the Recent Industrialisation of the Northern and Western Sectors*, 1933. Useful for the period c. 1900–32.

5.161 **Smith**, D. M., *The Industrial Archaeology of the East Midlands (Nottinghamshire, Leicestershire and the Adjoining parts of Derbyshire)*, 1965.

5.162 **Todd**, A. C. and Laws, P., *The Industrial Archaeology of Cornwall*, 1972. *See also* Rowe (5.158).

5.163 **Trinder**, B., *The Industrial Revolution in Shropshire*, 1973.

5.164 **Walton**, J. K., *Lancashire. A Social History, 1558–1939*, 1987. An interesting survey by a leading social historian. The book is weighted towards the Industrial Revolution and after.

(e) Foreigners' impressions

There are numerous accounts of England, Wales and Scotland by foreign observers, from which the following are selected.

5.165 **Fussell**, G. E., and Goodman, Constance, 'Travel and topography in eighteenth-century England: a bibliography of sources for economic history', *The Library*, 4th ser., X, 1929–30, 84–103.

5.166 **Bell**, V., *To Meet Mr. Ellis: Little Gaddesden in the Eighteenth-Century*, 1956. Material on a Hertfordshire village, visited by the Swede Peter Kalm.

5.167 **Henderson**, W. O., *Industrial Britain under the Regency: The Diaries of Escher, Bodmer, May and le Gallois, 1814–18*, 1968.

5.168 —— *J. C. Fischer and his Diary of Industrial England, 1814–1851*, 1966.

5.169 **Kohl**, J. G., *England and Wales*, 1844. Reprinted 1968 (early 1840s).

5.170 **Ratcliffe**, B. M. and Chaloner, W. H., eds., *A French Sociologist looks at Britain. Gustave d'Eichthal and British Society in 1828*, 1977.

5.171 **Rochefoucauld**, F. de la, *A Frenchman in England, 1784*, ed. and trans. J. Marchand and S. C. Roberts, 1933.

5.172 **Svedenstierna**, E. T., *Svedenstierna's Tour: Great Britain, 1802–3: The Travel Diary of an Industrial Spy*, ed. M. W. Flinn, trans. E. M. Dellow, 1973.

5.173 **Taine**, H., *Taine's Notes on England*, trans. and ed. E. Hyams, 1957, (covers 1860–70).

1881–1980

(a) Bibliographies

5.174 **Hanham**, H. J., ed., *Bibliography of British History, 1851–1914*, 1976.

5.175 **Havighurst**, A., comp., *Bibliographical Handbooks. Modern England, 1901–70*, 1976.

(b) Documentary collections

5.176 **Breach**, R. W. and Hartwell, R. M., *British Economy and Society, 1870–1970: Documents, Descriptions, Statistics*, 1972.

5.177 **Court**, W. H. B., ed., *British Economic History, 1870–1914: Commentary and Documents*, 1965. Extracts from contemporary and secondary sources with useful bibliographical notes.

5.178 **Handcock**, W. D., ed., *English Historical Documents. XII, 2, 1870–1914*, 1977.

5.179 **Keating**, P., ed., *Into Unknown England, 1866–1913. Selections from the Social Explorers*, 1976. Includes essays from Booth, Rowntree, Gissing and others.

5.180 **Pike**, E. R., *Human Documents of the Age of the Forsytes*, 1969.

5.181 —— *Human Documents of the Lloyd George Era*, 1972. Suffers from the same defects as its predecessor.

5.182 **Read**, D., *Documents from Edwardian England, 1901–1915*, 1973.

(c) The changing structure of the economy

5.183 **Ackrill**, M., 'Britain's managers and the British economy, 1870s to the 1980s', *Oxford Rev.Ec.Policy*, IV, 1988, 59–73.

5.184 **Aldcroft**, D. H., ed., *The Development of British Industry and Foreign Competition, 1875–1914*, 1968.

5.184A —— *The Inter-War Economy, 1919–1939*, 1970.

5.184B —— and Fearon, P., eds., *Economic Growth in Twentieth Century Britain*, 1969. Thirteen articles by various hands with an introduction and bibliographical guide, 233–7.

5.184C —— and Richardson, H. W., *The British Economy 1870–1939*, 1969.

5.185 —— *The British Economy between the Wars*, 1983.

5.186 —— *The British Economy. I: Years of Turmoil, 1920–51*, 1986.

5.187 **Alford**, B. W. E., *British Economic Performance since 1945*, 1986.

5.188 **Allen**, G. C., *British Industries and their Organisation*, 2nd ed., 1935, 3rd ed., 1951.

5.189 **Armitage**, Susan M. H., *The Politics of Decontrol of Industry: Britain and the United States*, 1969.

5.190 **Arnold**, G., *Britain since 1945. Choice, Conflict and Change*, 1989.

5.191 **Ashworth**, W., *An Economic History of England, 1870–1939*, 1960.

5.192 **Bagwell**, P. S. and Mingay, G. E., *Britain and America, 1850–1939. A Study of Economic Change*, 1970. *See also* Holmes (5.219).

5.193 **Barry**, E. E., *Nationalisation in British Politics*, 1965 (Begins with the 1890s).

5.194 **Beckerman**, W., *The Labour Government's Economic Record, 1964–1970*, 1972.

5.195 **Berghoff**, H. and Moller, R., 'Tired pioneers and dynamic newcomers? English and German entrepreneurial history, 1870–1914', *Ec.H.R*, 2nd ser., XLVII, 1994, 262–87.

5.196 **Booth**, A. and Pack, M., *Employment, Capital and Economic Policy. Great Britain, 1918–39*, 1986. Deals with the views of the Labour movement, the Liberals, Conservatives, the TUC, the Webbs, Beveridge and Keynes.

5.197 **Boyce**, R. W. D., *British Capitalism at the Crossroads, 1919–32. A Study in Politics, Economics and International Relations*, 1988. Examines the shift from Free Trade to Protection, imperial preference, and monetary conservatism.

5.198 **Broadway**, F., *State Intervention in British Industry 1964–68*, 1969.

5.199 **Buxton**, N. K. and Aldcroft, D. H., eds., *British Industry between the Wars. Instability and Industrial Development, 1919–39*, 1980. A collection of essays covering both the old depressed industries and the new growth areas (motor manufacturing, rayon, etc.).

5.200 **Capie**, F., *Depression and Protectionism. Britain between the Wars*, 1983.

5.201 —— and Collins, M., *The Interwar British Economy. A Statistical Abstract*, 1983.

5.202 **Chandler**, A. D., 'The growth of the trans-national industrial firm in the United States and the United Kingdom: a comparative analysis', *Ec.H.R*, 2nd ser., XXXIII, 1980, 396–410.

5.203 **Chester**, N., *The Nationalisation of British Industry, 1945–51*, 1975.

5.204 **Childs**, D., *Britain since 1945*, 1983.

5.205 **Crafts**, N. F. R. and Woodward, N. W. C., eds., *The British Economy since 1945*, 1991.

5.206 **Davenport-Hines**, R. P. T. and Jones, G., eds., *Enterprise, Management and Innovation in British Business 1914–80*, 1988.

5.207 **Dow**, J. C. R., *The Management of the British Economy, 1945–60*, 1968.

5.208 **Elbaum**, B. and Lazonick, W., eds., *The Decline of the British Economy*, 1986.

5.208a **Feinstein**, C. H., *National Income, Expenditure and Output, 1855–1965*, 1972.

5.209 **Floud**, R. and McCloskey, D., eds., *The Economic History of Britain since 1700. II: 1860 to the 1970s*, 1981. For vol. I *see* (5.65).

5.210 **Foreman-Peck**, J., ed., *New Perspectives on the Late Victorian Economy. Essays in Quantitative Economic History, 1860–1914*, 1991.

5.211 **Gourvish**, T. R., ed., *Later Victorian Britain, 1867–1901*, 1988.

5.212 **Hannah**, L., *The Rise of the Corporate Economy*, 1976.

5.213 —— and Kay, J. A., *Concentration in Modern Industry*, 1977.

4.214 **Harlow**, C., *Innovation and Productivity under Nationalisation. The First Thirty Years*, 1977.

5.215 **Harrison**, B., *Peaceable Kingdom. Stability and Change in Modern Britain*, 1982.

5.216 **Harrison**, J. F. C., *Late Victorian Britain,*

1875–1901, 1991.

5.217 **Hart**, P. E. and Clark, R., *Concentration in British Industry, 1935–75. A Study of the Growth, Causes, and Effects of Concentration in British Manufacturing Industries*, 1980.

5.218 **Holland**, R. F., 'The Federation of British Industries and the International Economy, 1929–39', *Ec.H.R.*, 2nd ser., XXXIV, 1981, 287–300.

5.219 **Holmes**, G. M., *Britain and America. A Comparative Economic History, 1850–1939*, 1976. *See also* Bagwell and Mingay (5.192).

5.220 **Hudson**, J., 'The birth and death of firms in England and Wales during the interwar years', *Bus.H.*, XXXI, 1989, 102–21.

5.221 **Kelf-Cohen**, R., *British Nationalisation, 1945–1973*, 1974.

5.222 **Kennedy**, W. P., 'Economic growth and structural change in the U.K., 1870–1914', *J.Ec.H.*, XLII, 1982, 105–15.

5.223 **Kindleberger**, C. P., *Economic Growth in France and Britain, 1851–1950*, 1964. One of the few comparative studies; bibliography, 341–66.

5.224 **Kirby**, M. W., *The Decline of British Economic Power since 1870*, 1981.

5.225 **Langton**, J. and Morris, R. J., eds., *Atlas of Industrialising Britain, 1780–1914*, 1986. *See also* Pope (5.103).

5.226 **Law**, C. M., *British Regional Development since World War I*, 1980.

5.227 **Lee**, C. H., *Regional Economic Growth in the United Kingdom since the 1880s*, 1971.

5.228 —— 'Regional growth and structural change in Victorian Britain', *Ec.H.R.*, 2nd ser., XXXIV, 1981, 438–52.

5.229 **Levine**, A. L., *Industrial Retardation in Britain, 1880–1914*, 1967.

5.230 **Locke**, R. R., *The End of the Practical Man. Entrepreneurship and Higher Education in Germany, France and Great Britain, 1880–1940*, 1984. Inclusive comparative history placing undue emphasis on the study and industrial impact of business economics.

5.231 **Luffman**, G. A. and Reed, R., *The Strategy and Performance of British Industry, 1970–80*, 1985. Considers the diversification strategies pursued by British industry in the 1970s.

5.232 **Mackenzie**, D. A., *Statistics in Britain, 1865–1930. The Social Construction of Scientific Knowledge*, 1981.

5.233 **McCloskey**, D., ed., *Essays on a Mature Economy: Britain after 1840*, 1971. Mainly industrial, with a strong bias towards the 'new economic history', but includes a chapter on agriculture.

5.234 **Matthews**, R. C. O., Feinstein, C. H. and Odling-Smee, J. C., *British Economic Growth, 1856–1973*, 1983.

5.235 **Morgan**, K. O., *The People's Peace. British History, 1945–89*, 1990.

5.236 **Newton**, S. and Porter, D., *Modernisation Frustrated. The Politics of Industrial Decline in Britain since 1900*, 1988.

5.237 **Nicholas**, S., 'Total factor productivity growth and revision of post-1870 British economic history', *Ec.H.R.*, 2nd ser., XXXV, 1982, 83–98.

5.238 **O'Brien**, P. K., 'Britain's economy between the Wars: a survey of a counter-revolution in economic history', *P.P.*, 1987, 107–30.

5.239 **Owen**, G., *The Question of U.K. Decline: The Economy, State and Society*, 1993. Argues that the shortcomings of government, industrial capitalism and labour organisation account for Britain's declining economic performance.

5.240 **Phillips**, G. A. and Madocks, R. T., *The Growth of the British Economy, 1918–1968*, 1973.

5.241 **Pollard**, S., *The Development of the British Economy, 1914–1967*, 2nd ed., 1969.

5.242 —— *Britain's Prime and Britain's Decline. The British Economy, 1870–1914*, 1988. An examination of the declining rate of economic growth in Britain. The role of capital exports, shortcomings in the education of entrepreneurs and State intervention are considered. 50 page bibliography.

5.243 —— *Wealth and Poverty. An Economic History of the Twentieth Century*, 1990.

5.244 **Pope**, R. and Hoyle, B., *British Economic Performance, 1880–1980*, 1985.

5.245 **Read**, D., *England, 1868–1914*, 1979.

5.246 **Rubinstein**, W. D., *Elites and the Wealthy in Modern British History. Essays in Social History*, 1988. Based chiefly on income tax and probate evidence the book examines the slowly changing social structure of the rich since the Industrial Revolution.

5.247 **Saul**, S. B., *The Myth of the Great Depression, 1873–1896*, 1969. Excellent bibliography, 56–62.

5.248 **Saville**, J., ed., 'The British economy,

1870–1914', *Yorks B.*, XVII, No. 1, 1965, 1–112.

5.249 **Skidelsky**, R., ed., *The End of the Keynesian Era*, 1977.

5.250 **Southall**, H. R., 'The origins of the depressed areas: unemployment, growth and regional economic structure in Britain before 1914', *Ec.H.R.*, 2nd ser., XLI, 1988, 236–58.

5.251 **Stevenson**, J. and Cook, C., *The Slump. Society and Politics during the Depression*, 1977.

5.252 **Stewart**, M., *The Jekyll and Hyde Years. Politics and Economic Policy since 1964*, 1977.

5.253 **Supple**, B., 'Fear of failing: economic history and the decline of Britain', *Ec.H.R.*, 2nd ser., XLVII, 1994, 441–58.

5.254 **Warren**, K., *The Geography of British Heavy Industry since 1800*, 1976.

5.255 **Weiss**, L., *Creating Capitalism. The State and Small Business since 1945*, 1988.

5.256 **Williams**, L. J., *Britain and the World Economy, 1919–1970*, 1971.

5.257 **Worswick**, G. D. N. and Tipping, D. G., *Profits in the British Economy 1909–1938*, 1967.

5.258 **Youngson**, A. J., *Britain's Economic Growth, 1920–1966*, 2nd ed., 1968.

(d) Social conditions

5.259 **Beales**, H. L. and Lambert, R. S., *Memoirs of the Unemployed*, 1934.

5.260 **Beveridge**, W. H., *Unemployment: A Problem of Industry*, 1st ed., 1909, 2nd ed., with new material, 1930.

5.261 **Briggs**, A., ed., *They Saw It Happen: An Anthology of Eye-witnesses' Accounts of Events in British History, 1897–1940*, 1962.

5.262 **Calder**, A. and Sheridan, D., eds., *Speak for Yourself. A Mass Observation Anthology, 1937–49*, 1984.

5.263 **Hannington**, W., *The Problem of the Distressed Areas*, 1937.

5.264 —— *A Short History of the Unemployed*, 1938.

5.265 —— *Ten Lean Years: An Examination of the Record of the National Government in the Field of Unemployment*, 1940.

5.266 —— *Unemployed Struggles, 1919–1936*, 1937.

5.267 **Bedarida**, F., *A Social History of England, 1851–1975*, 1979. A lively and perceptive analysis of the principal forces –

economic, sociological, political and spiritual – which have moulded English society in the last century.

5.268 **Beevers**, R., *The Garden City Utopia. A Critical Biography of Ebenezer Howard*, 1987.

5.269 **Blythe**, R., *The Age of Illusion: England in the Twenties and Thirties, 1919–1940*, 1963.

5.270 **Bogdanov**, V. and Skidelsky, R., eds., *The Age of Affluence, 1951–1964*, 1970.

5.271 **Bourne**, J. M., *Patronage and Society in Nineteenth-Century England*, 1986. Makes much use of the archives of the East India Company and India Office to explore some of the ramifications of patronage as an ingredient of nineteenth-century society.

5.272 **Branson**, Noreen, *Britain in the 1920s*, 1976.

5.273 —— and Heinemann, Margot, *Britain in the 1930s*, 1971.

5.274 **Brown**, K. D., *Labour and Unemployment, 1900–1914*, 1971, bibliography, 203–13. *See* Harris (5.291).

5.275 **Bulmer**, M., Bales, K., and Kish Sklar, Kathryn, eds., *The Social Survey in Historical Perspective 1880–1940*, 1992. Considers the tensions in the development of social surveys between the agendas of social reformers and the empirical questions of academics. Booth, Rowntree, Bowley and the Webbs figure prominently.

5.276 **Carr-Saunders**, A. M. and Jones, D. C., *A Survey of the Social Structure of England and Wales*, 1927, 2nd rev. ed., 1937.

5.277 —— and Moser, C. A., *A Survey of Social Conditions in England and Wales as illustrated by Statistics*, 1958.

5.278 **Clarke**, Linda, *Building Capitalism. Historical Change and the Labour Process in the Production of the Built Environment*, 1991. Looks at the building process, especially housing design, brick-making and paving, and places this in a broader socio-economic context.

5.279 **Constantine**, S., *Unemployment in Britain between the Wars*, 1980.

5.280 —— *Social Conditions in Britain, 1918–39*, 1983.

5.281 **Cronin**, J. E. and Schneer, J., eds., *Social Conflict and the Political Order in Modern Britain*, 1982.

5.282 **Crowther**, M. A., *British Social Policy, 1914–1939*, 1988.

5.283 **Dellheim**, C., *The Face of the Past. The Preservation of the Medieval Inheritance in Victorian England*, 1983.

5.284 **Garside**, W. R., *The Measurement of Unemployment in Great Britain, 1850–1979. Methods and Sources*, 1981.

5.285 **Gilbert**, D., *Class, Community and Collective Action. Social Change in Two British Coalfields, 1850–1926*, 1992. Looks at mining communities in Wales and Nottinghamshire and combines sociological and historical approaches.

5.286 **Glynn**, S. and Oxborrow, J., *Interwar Britain. A Social and Economic History*, 1976.

5.287 **Goldring**, D., *The Nineteen Twenties: A General Survey and some Personal Memories*, 1945.

5.288 **Graves**, R. and Hodge, A., *The Long Weekend: A Social History of Great Britain, 1918–1939*, 1941, latest ed., 1971.

5.289 **Halsey**, A. H., ed., *Trends in British Society since 1900*, 1972.

5.290 **Harris**, José, *Private Lives, Public Spirit. A Social History of Britain, 1870–1914*, 1993. Reassesses the paradoxes and plurality of the period. Demography, property, family, household and the state come under review.

5.291 —— *Unemployment and Politics: A Study in English Social Policy, 1886–1914*, 1972. Better than Brown (5.274).

5.292 **Harrison**, J. F. C., *The Common People. A History from the Norman Conquest to the Present*, 1984. Principally a descriptive treatment which aims to document the authentic experience of people in the past.

5.293 **Hopkins**, H., *The New Look. A Social History of the Forties and Fifties in Britain*, 1963. Extensive bibliography, 493–504.

5.294 **Hynes**, S., *The Edwardian Turn of Mind*, 1968.

5.295 **Johnson**, P., 'Small debts and economic distress in England and Wales, 1857–1913', *Ec.H.R.*, 2nd ser., XLVI, 1993, 65–87.

5.296 **Laybourn**, K., *Britain on the Dole. A Social and Political History of Britain between the Wars*, 1990.

5.297 **Lynd**, Helen M., *England in the Eighteen-eighties: Towards a Social Basis for Freedom*, 1945. Reprinted 1968.

5.298 **McElwee**, W., *Britain's Locust Years, 1918–1940*, 1962.

5.299 **Marsden**, G., ed., *Victorian Values. Personalities and Perspectives in Nineteenth-century Society*, 1990. *See also* Sigsworth (5.314).

5.300 **Marsh**, D. C., *The Changing Social Structure of England and Wales, 1871–1961*, rev. ed., 1965.

5.301 **Marwick**, A., *The Explosion of British Society, 1914–62*, 1963, 2nd ed., 1971.

5.302 —— *British Society since 1945*, 1982.

5.303 **Mowat**, C. L., *Britain Between the Wars, 1918–1940*, 1955.

5.304 **Nicholas**, Kate, *The Social Effects of Unemployment on Teesside 1919–39*, 1987. Argues that living standards were worse in the 1920s than in the 1930s.

5.305 **Nowell-Smith**, S., ed., *Edwardian England 1901–1914*, 1964. Chapters on the economy (A. J. Taylor) and domestic life (Marghanita Laski).

5.306 **O'Day**, A., ed., *The Edwardian Age. Conflict and Stability, 1900–14*, 1979.

5.307 **Page**, N., *The Thirties in Britain*, 1990.

5.308 **Perkin**, H. J., *The Rise of Professional Society: England since 1880*, 1989. A continuation of Perkin (5.1907).

5.309 **Raymond**, J., ed., *The Baldwin Age*, 1960. A collection of essays on various topics of the interwar period.

5.310 **Read**, D., *Edwardian England, 1901–15: Society and Politics*, 1973. *See also* Read (5.182).

5.311 **Robertson**, A. J., *The Bleak Midwinter, 1947*, 1987.

5.312 **Rosenthal**, M., *The Character Factory. Baden Powell and the Origins of the Boy Scout Movement*, 1986. Stresses the personal vanity of the founder and the mindless militarism of the movement in its early days.

5.313 **Ryder**, Judith and Silver, H., *Modern English Society. History and Structure, 1850–1970*, 1970. 2nd ed. 1977. Attempts to marry history and sociology.

5.314 **Sigsworth**, E. M., ed., *In Search of Victorian Values. Aspects of Nineteenth-Century Thought and Society*, 1988. Includes chapters on attitudes to work and poverty, Crime, women religion and imperialism. There are specific chapters on J. S. Mill, Darwin and W. S. Gilbert *See also* (5.299) and (5.316).

5.315 **Sissons**, M. and French, P., eds., *The Age of Austerity, 1945–51*, 1963, 1986.

5.316 **Smout**, T. C., ed., *Victorian Values*, 1992. *See also* (5.299) and (5.314).

5.317 **Stevenson**, J., *British Society, 1914–45*, 1984. An insightful survey of a period dominated by the First World War and its aftermath.

5.318 —— *Social Conditions in Britain between the Wars*, 1977. A 'myth-breaking' book.

5.319 **Thane**, Pat and Sutcliffe, A., eds., *Essays in Social History, II, 1986.* A collection of reprinted articles predominantly on the nineteenth century. *See also* Flinn and Smout (1.327).

5.320 **Thompson**, P., *The Edwardians. The Remaking of British Society*, 1975.

5.321 **Thompson**, Thea, *Edwardian Childhoods*, 1981. Nine oral history case studies of people born between 1892 and 1904.

5.322 **Whiteside**, Noelle, *Bad Times. Unemployment in British Social and Political History*, 1991. Looks at the issue of unemployment over a long time period and its significance to politicians, social researchers and charity organisations.

5.323 **Williamson**, W., *The Temper of the Times. British Society since World War II*, 1990. Based squarely on both documentary research and oral history the book explores a changing variety of attitudes and sentiments.

(e) The world wars and their effects

5.324 **Abrams**, P., 'The failure of social reform, 1918–20', *P.P.*, 24, 1963, 43–64.

5.325 **Adams**, R. J. Q., and Poirier, P. P., *The Conscription Controversy in Great Britain, 1900–1918*, 1987. Mainly devoted to the wartime experience itself.

5.326 **Barker**, R., *Conscience, Government and War: Conscientious Objection in Great Britain, 1939–45*, 1982.

5.327 **Barnett**, L. Margaret, *British Food Policy during the First World War*, 1985. Considers how this essential element of the war effort was organised.

5.328 **Beckett**, I. and Simpson, P., eds., *A Nation in Arms. A Social History of the British Army in the First World War*, 1985. Examines the social composition, structure and organisation of the vastly increased First World War army, the tensions in it between new and traditional elements, and its accommodation to peacetime conditions after 1918.

5.329 **Beddoe**, D., *Back to Home Duty. Women between the Wars, 1919–39*, 1939.

5.330 **Bourne**, J., *Britain and the Great War 1914–18*, 1989. An accessible general account which includes chapters on men and munitions.

5.331 **Bowley**, A. L., *Some Economic Consequences of the Great War*, 1930. Mainly the effects on Great Britain.

5.332 **Braybon**, Gail, *Women Workers in the First World War: the British Experience*, 1981.

5.333 **Burk**, Kathleen, *Britain, America and the Sinews of War, 1914–18*, 1985. Considers how the First World War transformed Anglo-American relations and the relative importance of the two countries.

5.334 —— ed., *War and the State. The Transformation of British Government, 1914–1919*, 1982.

5.335 **Calder**, A., *The People's War: Britain 1939–45*, 1969. Critical bibliography, 624–39.

5.336 **Clarke**, R., *Anglo-American Economic Collaboration in War and Peace, 1942–49*, 1982.

5.337 **Crosby**, T. L., *The Impact of Civilian Evacuation in the Second World War*, 1986. Argues that evacuation did not significantly contribute to social levelling.

5.338 **Dakers**, Caroline, *The Countryside at War, 1914–18*, 1987. Principally a top-level view of rural society in crisis.

5.339 **Dewey**, P. E., *British Agriculture in the First World War*, 1989.

5.340 **Dobson**, A. P., *U.S. Wartime Aid to Britain, 1940–46*, 1986.

5.341 **Dwork**, Deborah, *War is Good for Babies and Other Young Children. A History of the Infant and Child Welfare Movement in England, 1898–1918*, 1987.

5.342 **Fitzgibbon**, C., *The Blitz*, 1970.

5.343 **Griffiths**, G., *Women's Factory Work in World War I*, 1991.

5.344 **Hardy**, D., 'War, planning and social change: the example of the garden city campaign, 1914–18', *Planning Perspectives*, IV, 1989, 187–206.

5.345 **Holdford**, J., *Re-shaping Labour. Organisation, Work and Politics in the Great War and After*, 1988.

5.346 **Horn**, Pamela, *Rural Life in England in the First World War*, 1984.

5.347 **Inglis**, R., *The Children's War. Evacuation, 1939–45*, 1989.

5.348 **Jackson**, C., *Who will take our Children? The Story of the Evacuation of Britain,*

1939–45, 1985.

5.349 **Johnson**, P. B., *Land Fit for Heroes: The Planning of British Reconstruction, 1916–1919*, Chicago, 1968.

5.350 **Kent**, Susan K., 'The politics of sexual difference: World War I and the demise of feminism', *J.Brit.Studs.*, XXVII, 1988, 232–53.

5.351 **Kohan**, C. M., *Works and Buildings* (History of the Second World War), 1952.

5.352 **Lang**, C., *Keep Smiling Through. Women in the Second World War*, 1989.

5.353 **Longmate**, N., *How We Lived Then: A History of English Life During the Second World War*, 1971.

5.254 **McDermott**, J., ' "A needless sacrifice": British businessmen and business as usual in the First World War', *Albion*, XXI, 1989, 263–82.

5.355 **Marwick**, A., *Britain in the Century of Total War*, 1968. Extensive bibliography.

5.356 —— *The Deluge: British Society and the First World War*, 1965.

5.357 —— *The Home Front. The British and the Second World War*, 1978.

5.358 —— *Women at War, 1914–18*, 1977.

5.359 **Merson**, E., *Children in the Second World War*, 1983.

5.360 **Milward**, A. S., *The Economic Effects of the World Wars on Britain*, 1970. Critical bibliography, 53–7.

5.361 **Mosley**, L., *Backs to the Wall*, 1971. Life in London, 1939–45.

5.362 **Parker**, P., *The Old Lie. The Great War and the Public School Ethos*, 1987.

5.362a **Simpkins**, P., *Kitchener's Armies. The Raising of the New Armies, 1914–16*, 1988. Shows how comradeship, local pride and organisation were exploited to create the mass volunteer army of the early stages of the First World War.

5.363 **Pelling**, H. M., *Britain and the Second World War*, 1970.

5.364 **Postan**, M. M., *British War Production* (History of the Second World War), 1952.

5.365 **Smith**, H., 'The problem of 'equal pay for equal work' in Great Britain during World War II', *J.M.H.*, LIII, 1981, 652–72.

5.366 —— ed., *War and Social Change. British Society in the First World War*, 1987. A collection of essays dealing with the War and the Welfare State, the effects of evacuation, the 1944 Education Act, the 'levelling of class', and the War's significance for women.

5.367 **Summerfield**, P., *Women Workers in the Second World War*, 1984.

5.368 **Thomas**, D., War, *Industry and Society: the Midlands, 1939–45*, 1989. Looks at a key region in the War effort. Employment patterns and wage levels are discussed.

5.369 **Thomas**, M., 'Rearmament and economic recovery in the late 1930s', *Ec.H.R.*, 2nd ser., XXXVI, 1983, 552–79.

5.370 **Thoms**, D., War, *Industry and Society: the Midlands, 1939–45*, 1989.

5.371 **Vellacott**, J., 'Feminist consciousness and the First World War', *H.Workshop*, XXIII, 1987, 81–101.

5.372 **Waites**, B., *A Class Society at War. England, 1914–18*, 1987.

5.373 **Winter**, J. M., 'Aspects of the impact of the First World War on infant mortality in Britain', *J.Europ.Ec.H.*, XI, 1982, 713–39.

5.374 —— *The Great War and the British People*, 1987. Largely demographic the book explores the paradoxical juxtaposition of high mortality and injury on the front and improved standards of living and life expectancy at home.

5.375 —— 'Britain's lost generation of the First World War', *Pop.Studs.*, XXXI, 1977, 449–66.

5.376 —— 'The impact of the First World War on civilian health in Britain', *Ec.H.R.*, 2nd ser., XXX, 1977, 487–503.

5.377 —— 'Military fitness and civilian health in Britain during the First World War', *J.Contemp.H.*, XV, 1980, 211–44.

5.378 —— *Socialism and the Challenge of War. Ideas and Politics in Britain, 1912–18*, 1974.

5.379 **Woodward**, L., *Great Britain and the War of 1914–1918*, 1967. Chapter XII deals with economic matters.

ECONOMIC FLUCTUATIONS

(a) 1700–1800

5.380 **Ashton**, T. S., *Economic Fluctuations in England, 1700–1800*, 1959.

(b) 1800–1913

5.381 **Aldcroft**, D. H. and Fearon, P., eds., *British Economic Fluctuations, 1790–1939*, 1972.

5.382 **Gayer**, A. D., Rostow, W. W. and Schwartz, Anna J., *The Growth and Fluctuation of the British Economy, 1790–1850*, 2 vols., 1953.

5.383 **Hughes**, J. R. T., *Fluctuations in Trade, Industry and Finance: A Study of British Economic Development, 1850–1860*, 1960.

5.384 **Layton**, W. T. and Crowther, G., *An Introduction to the Study of Prices*, 3rd rev. ed., 1938. Useful charts and tables of prices since 1820.

5.385 **Lewis**, W. A., *Growth and Fluctuations, 1870–1914*, 1978.

5.386 **Link**, R. G., *English Theories of Economic Fluctuations, 1815–1848*, 1959.

5.387 **Matthews**, R. C. O., *A Study in Trade-Cycle History: Economic Fluctuations in Great Britain, 1833–1842*, 1954.

5.388 **Rostow**, W. W., *British Economy of the Nineteenth Century*, 1948. A classic treatment.

5.389 **Tinbergen**, J., *Business Cycles in the U.K., 1870–1914*, Amsterdam, 1951.

5.390 **Ward-Perkins**, C. N., 'The commercial crisis of 1847', in Carus-Wilson, ed. (1.326), III, 263–79.

(c) 1918–1939

5.391 **Alford**, B. W. E., *Depression and Recovery?, British Economic Growth 1918–1939*, 1972.

5.392 **Rees**, G., *The Great Slump: Capitalism in Crisis, 1929–33*, 1970.

5.393 **Richardson**, H. W., *Economic Recovery in Britain, 1932–39*, 1967.

POPULATION

(a) General works

5.394 **Anderson**, Olive, 'Did suicide increase with industrialisation in Victorian England?' *P.P.*, 86, 1980, 149–73.

5.395 **Andrew**, D. T., 'Debate: the secularisation of suicide in England, 1660–1800, and reply by M. MacDonald', *P.P.*, CXIX, 1988, 158–70.

5.396 **Arkell**, T., 'Forename frequency in 1851', *Loc.Pop.Studs.*, XLVII, 1991, 65–76.

5.397 **Banks**, J. A., *Prosperity and Parenthood*, 1954. Family limitation among the late nineteenth-century British middle classes.

5.398 **Barker**, T. C. and Drake, M., eds., *Population and Society in Britain 1850–1980*, 1982.

5.399 **Brookes**, B., *Abortion in England, 1919–67*, 1988.

5.400 **Buer**, M. C., *Health, Wealth and Population in the Early Days of the Industrial Revolution*, 1926. *See also* Chambers (4.37).

5.401 **Connell**, K. H., 'Some unsettled problems in English and Irish population history, 1750–1845', *Irish H.Studs.*, VII, 1951.

5.402 **Crafts**, N. F. R., 'Illegitimacy in England and Wales in 1911', *Pop.Studs.*, XXXVI, 1982, 327–49.

5.403 **Davey**, Claire, 'Birth control in Britain during the interwar years: evidence from the Stopes correspondence', *J.Family Hist.*, XIII, 1988, 329–46.

5.403a **Drake**, M., ed., *Population in Industrialisation*, 1969. Reprints eight articles on the subject. Good bibliography.

5.403b **Dyhouse**, Carol, 'Working-class mothers and infant mortality in England, 1895–1914', *J.Soc.H.*, XII, 1978, 248–67.

5.404 **Eversley**, D. E. C., 'Population and economic growth in England before the 'Take Off'', *Communications of the First International Conference of Economic History, Stockholm*, Paris, 1960, 457–73.

5.405 **Flinn**, M. W., *British Population Growth, 1700–1850*, 1970. The best introduction to the study of this subject; critical bibliography, 59–64; glossary, 65.

5.406 **Glass**, D. V., 'Population and population movements in England and Wales, 1700–1850'. In Glass and Eversley, eds. (4.167), 221–46.

5.407 —— ed., *Introduction to Malthus*, 1953. Essays, bibliography (84–112) and reprints of two scarce Malthus items.

5.408 —— *Numbering the People. The*

Eighteenth-Century Population Controversy and the Development of Census and Vital Statistics in Britain, 1973.

5.409 **Griffith**, G. T., *Population Problems of the Age of Malthus*, 1926. Reprinted 1967, with new bibliographical introduction, V–XVII, and bibliography of recent work, 277–80.

5.410 **Habakkuk**, H. J., 'English population in the eighteenth century'. In Glass and Eversley, eds. (4.167), 269–84.

5.411 —— *Population Growth and Economic Development since 1750*, 1971.

5.412 **Hill**, Bridget, 'The marriage age of women and the demographers', *Hist.WorkshopJ.*, XXVIII, 1989, 129–47.

5.413 **Himes**, N. E., *Medical History of Contraception*, 1st ed., 1936. Reprinted N. Y., 1963.

5.414 **Joshi**, H., ed., *The Changing Population of Britain*, 1989.

5.415 **Krause**, J. T., 'Changes in English fertility and mortality, 1781–1850', *Ec.H.R.*, 2nd ser., XI, 1958, 52–70.

5.416 —— 'Some neglected factors in the English Industrial Revolution'. Reprinted in Drake (5.403a), 103–17.

5.417 —— 'Some aspects of population change, 1690–1790'. In Jones and Mingay (5.81), 187–205.

5.418 —— 'The changing adequacy of English registration, 1690–1837'. In Glass and Eversley, eds. (4.167), 379–93.

5.419 **Langer**, W. L., 'The origins of the birth control movement in England in the early nineteenth century', *J.Interdis.H.*, V, 1975, 669–86.

5.420 **Loudon**, I., 'Maternal mortality, 1880–1950: some regional and international comparisons', *Soc.Hist.Medicine*, I., 1988, 183–228.

5.421 **McKeown**, T. and Brown, R. G., 'Medical evidence related to English population changes in the eighteenth century'. In Glass and Eversley, eds. (4.167), 285–307.

5.422 —— and Record, R. G., 'Reasons for the decline of mortality in England and Wales during the nineteenth century', *Pop.Studs.*, XVI, 1962–3, 94–122. Covers mainly the period 1851–1900.

5.423 **McLaren**, A., *Birth Control in Nineteenth-Century England*, 1978.

5.424 **Marshall**, T. H., 'The population of England and Wales from the Industrial Revolution to the First World War',
Ec.H.R., V, 1934, 65–78.

5.425 —— 'The population problem during the Industrial Revolution: a note on the present state of the controversy'. In Carus-Wilson, ed. (1.326), I, 306–30.

5.426 **Mercer**, A., *Disease, Mortality and Population in Transition. Epidemiological-Demographic Change in England since the Eighteenth Century as part of a Global Phenomenon*, 1990.

5.427 **Mitchison**, Rosalind, *British Population Change since 1860*, 1977.

5.428 **Razzell**, P. E., 'Population change in eighteenth-century England: a re-interpretation'. *Ec.H.R.*, 2nd ser., XVIII, 1965, 312–32. Importance of mass inoculations against smallpox from 1760s.

5.429 —— 'Population growth and economic change in eighteenth and early nineteenth-century England and Ireland'. In Jones and Mingay (5.81), 260–81.

5.430 —— *Edward Jenner's Cowpox Vaccine. The History of a Medical Myth*, 1977.

5.431 —— *The Conquest of Smallpox. The Impact of Inoculation on Smallpox Mortality in Eighteenth-Century Britain*, 1977.

5.432 **Snell**, K. D. M., 'Settlement, Poor Law and the rural historian: new approaches and opportunities', *Rural Hist.*, III, 1992, 145–72.

5.433 **Sigsworth**, E. M., 'Gateways to death? Medicines, hospitals and mortality, 1700–1850'. In Mathias, ed. (5.97), 97–110.

5.434 **Tranter**, N. L., *Population and Industrialization*, 1973. Extracts from British writers on population problems between 1680 and 1967.

5.435 —— *Population since the Industrial Revolution: The Case of England and Wales*, 1973.

5.436 —— *Population and Society, 1750–1940. Contrast in Population Growth*, 1985. Looks at sources and methods, demographic trends and their impact on economic, social and political development.

5.437 **Woods**, R. and Hinde, P. R. A., 'Mortality in Victorian England: models and patterns', *J.Interdis.H.*, XVIII, 1988, 27–54.

5.438 **Wrigley**, E. A. and Schofield, R. S., *The Population History of England, 1541–1871*,

1981, 2nd ed., 1989. A mammoth study of sources, methods and trends. Appendices, 485–740. Valuable bibliography. *See* the reviews by M. W. Flinn, *Ec.H.R.*, 2nd ser., XXXV, 1982, 443–58, and by D. Gaunt et al., *Soc.Hist.*, VIII, 1983, 139–68.

(b) Regional studies

5.439 **Boyer**, G. R., 'Malthus was right after all: poor relief and birth rates in southeastern England', *J.Pol.Econ.*, XCVII, 1989, 93–114.

5.440 **Chambers**, J. D., 'Population change in a provincial town: Nottingham, 1700–1800'. *In* Pressnell (5.106), 97–124.

5.441 **Beckwith**, F., 'The population of Leeds during the Industrial Revolution', *Thoresby Soc.*, XII, 1948, 118–96.

5.442 **Daunton**, M. J., 'Inheritance and succession in the City of London in the nineteenth century', *Bus.H.*, XXX, 1988, 269–86.

5.443 **Lawton**, R., 'Population trends in Lancashire and Cheshire from 1801', *T.H.S.L.C.*, CXIV, 1962, 189–213

5.444 —— 'The population of Liverpool in the mid-nineteenth century', *T.H.S.L.C.*, CVII, 1956, 89–120.

5.445 **Martin**, J. M., *The Rise in Population in Eighteenth-Century Warwickshire*. Dugdale Soc.Occ.Papers, XXIII, 1976.

5.446 **Minchinton**, W. E., ed., *Population and Marketing. Two Studies in the History of the South West*, 1977.

5.447 **Reay**, B., 'Sexuality in nineteenth-century England: the social context of illegitimacy in rural Kent', *Rural Hist.*, I, 1990, 219–47.

5.448 **Sharpe**, P., 'Literally spinsters: a new interpretation of local economy and demography in Colyton in the seventeenth and eighteenth centuries', *Ec.H.R.*, 2nd ser., XLIV, 1991, 46–65.

5.449 **Sogner**, S., 'Aspects of the demographic situation in seventeen parishes in Shropshire, 1711–1760: an exercise based on parish registers', *Pop.Studs.*, XVII, 1963–4, 126–46.

5.450 **Thomas**, P., 'The population of Cornwall in the eighteenth century', *J.Roy.Inst.Cornwall*, X, 1990, 416–56.

(c) Internal migration

5.451 **Armstrong**, W. A., 'Some counter-currents of migration: London and the south in the mid-nineteenth century', *Southern H.*, XII, 1990, 82–113.

5.452 **Baines**, D., *Migration in a Mature Economy. Emigration and Internal Migration in England and Wales, 1861–1900*, 1985.

5.453 **Behlmer**, G. K., 'The gypsy problem in Victorian England', *Vict.Studs.*, XXVIII, 1985, 231–54.

5.454 **Cairncross**, A. K., 'Internal migration in Victorian England', *Manchester School*, XVII, 1949, 67–83. Reprinted in Cairncross (5.1262), 65–83.

5.455 **Grundy**, J. E., 'Population movements in nineteenth-century Herefordshire', *Trans.Woolhope Nat.Field Club*, XLV, 1986, 488–500.

5.456 **Mayall**, D., *Gypsy Travellers in Nineteenth Century Society*, 1988.

5.457 **Nicholas**, S. and Shergold, P. R., 'Internal migration in England, 1818–39', *J.Hist.Geog.*, XIII, 1987, 155–68.

5.458 **Redford**, A., *Labour Migration in England 1800–1850*, 1926, 3rd ed. 1976.

5.459 **Saville**, J., *Rural Depopulation in England and Wales, 1851–1951*, 1957.

5.460 **Southall**, H. R., 'The tramping artisan revisits: labour mobility and economic distress in early Victorian England', *Ec.H.R.*, 2nd ser., XLIV, 1991, 272–96.

5.461 **Stapleton**, B., 'Migration in pre-industrial southern England: the example of Odiham', *Southern H.*, X, 1988, 47–93.

(d) Immigration

5.462 **Alderman**, G., *Modern British Jewry*, 1992.

5.463 **Ashton**, Rosemary, *Little Germany. Exile and Asylum in Victorian England*, 1986. Chiefly biographical, the book concentrates on Germans moving to England in the 1840s and 50s.

5.464 **Black**, E. C., *The Social Politics of Anglo-Jewry, 1880–1920*, 1989.

5.465 **Buckman**, J., *Immigrants and the Class Struggle. The Jewish Immigrant in Leeds, 1880–1914*, 1983.

5.466 **Cesarani**, D., ed., *The Making of Modern*

Anglo-Jewry, 1989.

5.467 **Chevette**, B., *Constructions of the 'Jew' in English Literature and Society. Racial Representations, 1875–1945*, 1993.

5.468 **Cowen**, A. and R., *Victorian Jews through British Eyes*, 1986.

5.469 **Davis**, G., *The Irish in Britain, 1815–1914*, 1992.

5.470 **Endelman**, T. M., *Radical Assimilation in English Jewish History, 1656–1945*, 1990. A long range study of the social and economic interactions between the Jewish community and its English hosts.

5.471 **File**, N. and Power, C., *Black Settlers in Britain 1555–1958*, 1980. *See also* Shyllon (5.488) and Walvin (5.493).

5.472 **Finnegan**, Frances, *Poverty and Prejudice. A Study of Irish Immigrants in York, 1840–75*, 1983.

5.473 **Gainer**, B., *The Alien Invasion: The Origins of the Aliens Act of 1905*, 1972.

5.474 **Gartner**, L. P., *The Jewish Immigrant in England, 1870–1914*, 1960.

5.475 **Gerrard**, J. A., *The English and Immigration, 1880–1910*, 1971.

5.476 **Holmes**, C., ed., *Immigrants and Minorities in British Society*, 1978. Includes chapters on the German, Jewish, Irish and Chinese communities.

5.477 —— *John Bull's Island. Immigration and British Society, 1871–1971*, 1988.

5.478 **Jackson**, J. A., *The Irish in Britain*, 1963.

5.479 **Kerr**, Barbara M., 'Irish seasonal migration to Great Britain 1800–38', *Irish Hist.Studs.*, III, 1942, 365–80.

5.480 **Kushner**, T., *The Persistance of Prejudice. Anti-Semitism in British Society during the Second World War*, 1989.

5.481 **Lawton**, R., 'Irish immigration to England and Wales in the mid-nineteenth century', *Irish Goeg.*, IV, 1959, 35–54.

5.482 **Lees**, L. H., *Exiles of Erin. Irish Migrants in Victorian London*, 1979.

5.483 **Lorimer**, D. A., *Colour, Class and the Victorians. English Attitudes to the Negro in the Mid-Nineteenth Century*, 1978. *See also* File and Power (5.471), Shyllon (5.488) and Walvin (5.493).

5.484 **Lunn**, K., ed., *Hosts, Immigrants and Minorities. Historical Responses to Newcomers in British Society, 1870–1914*, 1980.

5.485 **O'Tuathaigh**, M. A. G., 'The Irish in nineteenth-century Britain: problems of integration', *T.R.H.S.*, 5th ser., XXXI, 1981, 149–75.

5.486 **Panayi**, P., *Immigration, Ethnicity and Racism, 1815–1945*, 1994. A general survey beginning with nineteenth-century Irish immigration and extending to influxes from the empire.

5.487 **Pollins**, H., *Economic History of Jews in England*, 1983. A wide-ranging study concentrating on Anglo-Jewish relations from the re-admission of the 1650s.

5.488 **Shyllon**, F. O., *Black People in Britain, 1555–1833*, 1977. *See also* File and Power (5.471) and Walvin (5.493).

5.489 **Sponza**, L., *Italian Immigrants in Nineteenth-Century Britain. Realities and Images*, 1988. Examines the social and geographical patterns of this small-scale immigration.

5.490 **Stacey**, C. P. and Wilson, B. M., *The Half Million. The Canadians in Britain, 1939–45*, 1987.

5.491 **Swift**, R. and Gilley, S., *The Irish in Britain, 1815–1939*, 1989.

5.492 —— eds., *The Irish in the Victorian City*, 1985.

5.493 **Walvin**, J., *The Black Presence. A Documentary History of the Negro in England, 1555–1860*, 1971. *See also* File and Power (5.471) and Shyllon (5.488).

5.494 —— *Passage to Britain. Immigration in British History and Politics*, 1984.

5.495 **Williams**, B., *The Making of Manchester Jewry, 1740–1875*, 1976.

(e) Emigration

5.496 **Constantine**, S., ed., *Emigrants and Empire. British Settlement in the Dominions between the Wars*, 1990.

5.497 **Dunae**, P. A., *Gentleman Emigrants. From the British Public Schools to the Canadian Frontier*, 1983.

5.498 **Ekirch**, A. R., *Bound for America. The Transportation of British Convicts to the Colonies, 1718–1775*, 1988. Concerned substantially with the growth of an emigration policy and with the geography and sociology of the deportees.

5.499 **Erickson**, Charlotte, ed., *Emigration from Europe 1815–1914, Select Documents*, 1976.

5.500 **MacDonagh**, O., ed., *Emigration in the Victorian Age*, 1974. Reprints articles from contemporary periodicals.

5.501 **Berthoff**, R. T., *British Immigrants in Industrial America, 1790–1850*, Cambridge, Mass., 1953.

5.502 **Boston**, R. J., *British Chartists in America*, 1971.

5.503 **Carrothers**, W. A., *Emigration from the British Isles, with Special Reference to the Development of the Overseas Dominions*, 1929.

5.504 **Coleman**, T., *The Atlantic Passage*, 1972.

5.505 **Cowan**, Helen I., *British Emigration to British North America: The First Hundred Years*, 2nd rev. and enlarged ed., Toronto, 1961.

5.506 **Duncan**, R., 'Case studies in emigration: Cornwall, Gloucestershire and New South Wales, 1877–1886', *Ec.H.R.*, 2nd ser., XVI, 1963, 272–89.

5.507 **Erickson**, Charlotte, 'The encouragement of emigration by British trade unions, 1850–1900', *Pop.Studs.*, III, 1949–50, 248–73.

5.508 **Erickson**, Charlotte J., 'Emigration from the British Isles to the U.S.A. in 1841. II: Who were the English emigrants', *Pop.Studs.*, XLIV, 1990, 21–40.

5.509 **Hitchins**, F. H., *The Colonial Land and Emigration Commission, 1840–78*, Philadelphia, 1931.

5.510 **Johnson**, S. C., *Emigration from the United Kingdom to North America, 1763–1912*, 1913. Reprinted 1966.

5.511 **Johnson**, H. J. M., *British Emigration Policy, 1815–1830*, 1972.

5.512 **Jones**, M. A., *Destination America*, 1976.

5.513 **Kennedy**, D., 'Empire migration in post-war reconstruction: the role of the Overseas Settlement Committee', *Albion*, XX, 1988, 403–20.

5.513a **Taylor**, P. A. M., *Expectations Westwards: The Mormons and the Emigration of their British Converts in the Nineteenth Century*, 1965.

5.514 **Thistlethwaite**, F., 'The Atlantic migration of the pottery industry', *Ec.H.R.*, 2nd ser., XI, 1958, 264–78.

5.515 **Thomas**, B., *Migration and Economic Growth: A Study of Great Britain and the Atlantic Economy*, 1954.

5.516 —— *Migration and Urban Development: A Reappraisal of British and American Long Cycles*, 1972.

(f) Marriage and the family

5.517 **Abbot**, Mary, *Family Ties. English Families, 1540–1920*, 1993. An introduction to family history and its methodologies with separate chapters on different social groups.

5.518 **Anderson**, M., *Family Structure in Nineteenth-Century Lancashire*, 1971. A sociological study of the impact of urban industrial life on the kinship system of the working classes.

5.519 **Anderson**, Olive, 'The incidence of civil marriage in Victorian England and Wales', *P.P.*, 69, 1975, 50–87. *See also* Floud and Thane (5.525).

5.520 **Banks**, J. A., *Victorian Values: Secularism and the Size of Families*, 1981.

5.521 **Barrett-Ducrocq**, F., *Love in the Time of Victoria. Sexuality, Class, and Gender in Nineteenth-Century London*, 1991.

5.522 **Bonfield**, L., 'Strict settlement and the family: a differing view', A response to Eileen Spring, 'The strict settlement: its role in family history', *Ec.H.R.*, 2nd ser., XLI, 1988, 461–6.

5.523 **Constable**, D., *Household Structure in Three English Market Towns, 1851–71*, 1977.

5.524 **Davies**, M., 'Corsets and conception: fashion and demographic trends in the nineteenth century', *Comp.Studs.Soc. & Hist.*, XXIV, 1982, 611–41.

5.524a **Davis**, R. W., ' "We are all Americans now". Anglo-American marriages in the later nineteenth century', *Proc.Am. Phil.Soc.*, CXXXV, 1991, 140–99.

5.525 **Floud**, R. and Thane, Pat, 'The incidence of civil marriage in Victorian England and Wales', *P.P.*, 84, 1979, 146–54. *See also* Anderson (5.519).

5.526 **Gittins**, Diana, *Fair Sex: Family Size and Structure 1900–39*, 1982.

5.527 **Holtzman**, E. M., 'The Pursuit of Married Love; women's attitudes towards sexuality in Great Britain, 1918–39', *J.Soc.H.*, XVI, 1982, 39–52.

5.528 **Levine**, D., 'Illiteracy and family life during the first Industrial Revolution', *J.Soc.H.*, XIV, 1980, 25–44.

5.529 —— 'Industrialisation and the proletarian family in England', *P.P.*, CVII, 1985, 168–203.

5.530 **Lewis**, J., *Labour and Love. Women's Experience of Home and Family, 1850–1940*, 1985.

5.531 **Loudon**, I., *Death in Childbirth. An International Study of Maternal Care and Maternal Mortality, 1800–1950*, 1992. A comparative study of trends in Britain, Holland, Scandinavia, North America, and Australasia.

5.532 **Macfarlane**, A., *Marriage and Love in England. Modes of Reproduction 1300–1840*, 1986. Using an adventurous methodology the author makes much use of diaries, autobiographies and treatises to explore the chronology and changing character of the marriage system.

5.533 **Menefee**, S. P., *Wives for Sale. An Ethnographic Study of British Popular Divorce*, 1981.

5.534 **Mintz**, S., *A Prisoner of Expectations. The Family in Victorian Culture*, New York, 1983.

5.535 **Montgomery**, M., *Gilded Prostitution. Status, Money and Transatlantic Marriages, 1870–1914*, 1989.

5.536 **Outhwaite**, R. B., 'Age at marriage in England from the late seventeenth to the nineteenth century', *T.R.H.S.*, 5th ser., XXIII, 1973, 55–70.

5.537 **Ruggles**, S., *Prolonged Connections. The Rise of the Extended Family in Nineteenth-Century England and America*, 1987.

5.538 **Seabrook**, J., *Working Class Childhood*, 1982.

5.539 **Shorter**, E., *The Making of the Modern Family*, 1976.

5.540 **Smart**, Carol, ed., *Regulating Motherhood. Historical Essays on Marriage, Motherhood and Sexuality*, 1992.

5.541 **Springhall**, J., *Coming of Age. Adolescence in Britain, 1860–1960*, 1986. A blend, not always a happy one, of history and sociology.

5.542 **Strathern**, Marilyn, *After Nature. English Kinship in the Late Twentieth Century*, 1992. An essay in social anthropology which places the family within its broader political, social and economic context.

5.543 **Tadmor**, N., ' "Family" and "friend" in Pamela: A case study in the history of the family in eighteenth-century England', *Soc.Hist.*, XIV, 1989, 289–307.

5.544 **Walvin**, J., *A Child's World. A Social History of English Childhood, 1800–1914*, 1982.

5.545 **Wohl**, A. S., ed., *The Victorian Family. Structures and Stresses*, 1978.

AGRICULTURE AND RURAL SOCIETY

(a) Bibliographies

5.546 **Fussell**, G. E., *More Old English Farming Books from Tull to the Board of Agriculture, 1731–1793*, 1950.

5.547 **Harvey**, N., ed., *G. E. Fussell: A Bibliography of his Writings on Agricultural History*, 1967.

See also Brewer (4.399).

(b) General works

5.548 **Jewell**, A., ed., *Victorian Farming: A Sourcebook*, 3rd ed. 1975. A useful condensation of H. Stephens, *The Book of the Farm*, 3rd ed., 1876.

5.549 **Mingay**, G. E., ed., *The Agricultural Revolution. Changes in Agriculture, 1650–1880*, 1977. A documentary collection.

5.550 —— *Arthur Young and his Times* 1975. A sourcebook culled from Young's travel and agricultural writings. The appendix gives a complete list of Young's publications.

5.551 **Pyne**, W. H., *Microcosm*, 1806. Reprinted N. Y. 1961. Well-known early nineteenth-century engravings of agriculture and rural labour.

5.552 **Abel**, W., *Agricultural Fluctuations in Europe*, 1980.

5.553 **Adams**, L. P., *Agricultural Depression and Farm Relief in England 1813–1852*, 1932, new impression, 1965.

5.554 **Allen**, R. C., 'Labour productivity and farm size in English agriculture before mechanisation: reply to Clark', *Expl.Ec.H.*, XXVIII, 1991, 478–92. *See* (5.565).

5.555 **Beckett**, J. V., *The Agricultural Revolution*, 1990.

5.556 —— 'Regional variation and the Agri-Agricultural Depression, 1730–50', *Ec.H.R.*, 2nd ser., XXXV, 1982, 35–51.

5.557 **Beer**, M., ed., *The Pioneers of Land Reform: Thomas Spence, William Ogilvie, Thomas Parrie*, 1920.

5.558 **Bonser**, K. J., *The Drovers: Who They Were and How They Went. An Epic of the English Countryside*, 1970. For other works on the drovers see Haldane (7.308), Colyer (6.126), Godwin (6.128) and Hughes (6.133).

5.559 **Brown**, J., *Agriculture in England. A Survey of Farming, 1870–1947*, 1987.

5.560 —— *Farm Machinery, 1750–1945*, 1989.

5.561 **Chambers**, J. D. and Mingay, G. E., *The Agricultural Revolution 1750–1880*, 1966.

5.562 **Chartres**, J. A., 'City and towns: farmers and economic change in the eighteenth century', *Hist.Res.*, LXIV, 1991, 138–55.

5.563 **Chase**, M., 'Out of Radicalism: the mid Victorian freehold land movement', *E.H.R.*, CVI, 1991, 319–45.

5.564 **Claire**, J. D., *Agricultural Change since 1750*, 1988.

5.565 **Clark**, G., 'Labour productivity and farm size in English agriculture before mechanisation: a note', *Expl.Ec.H.*, XXVIII, 1991, 248–57. *See* Allen (5.554).

5.566 **Collins**, E. J. T., 'Harvest technology and labour supply in Britain, 1790–1870', *Ec.H.R.*, 2nd ser., XXII, 1969, 453–73.

5.567 —— *The Economy of Upland Britain, 1750–1950. An Illustrated Review*, 1978.

5.568 **Collins**, K., 'Marx on the English Agricultural Revolution: theory and evidence', *H. & Theory*, VI, 1966, 351–81. Vigorous debunking.

5.569 **Cooper**, A. F., *British Agricultural Policy, 1912–36: A Study in Conservative Politics*, 1989.

5.570 **Crosby**, T. L., *English Farmers and the Politics of Protection, 1815–32*, 1977.

5.571 **Dewey**, P. E., 'Food production and policy in the United Kingdom, 1914–18', *T.R.H.S.*, 5th ser., XXX, 1980, 71–89.

5.572 **Douglas**, R., *Land, People and Politics. A History of the Land Question in the United Kingdom, 1878–1952*, 1976.

5.573 **Drescher**, L., 'The development of agricultural production in Great Britain and Ireland from the early nineteenth century', *Manchester School*, 1955, 153–83. Translation of an attempt to construct an index of agricultural production, first published in 1935.

5.574 **Evans**, E. J., *The Contentious Tithe: The Tithe Problem and English Agriculture, 1750–1850*, 1976. A neglected subject.

5.575 **Fletcher**, T. W., 'The Great Depression of English Agriculture 1873–96', in Minchinton (1.330), II, 239–58.

5.576 **Fussell**, G. E., *Jethro Tull: His Influence on Mechanized Agriculture*, 1973.

5.577 —— 'The size of English cattle in the eighteenth century', *Ag.H.*, III, 1929, 160–81. Criticises the view that the average weight of cattle and sheep increased considerably.

5.578 —— and Goodman, Constance, 'Eighteenth-century estimates of sheep and wool production', *Ag.H.*, IV, 1930, 131–51.

5.579 —— and Goodman, Constance, 'The eighteenth-century traffic in milk products', *Ec.J.Ec.H.Supp.*, III, 1937, 380–7.

5.580 **Galpin**, W. F., *The Grain Supply of England during the Napoleonic Period*, N. Y., 1925.

5.581 **Gould**, J. D., 'Agricultural fluctuations and the English economy in the eighteenth century', *J.Ec.H.*, XX, 1962, 313–33.

5.582 **Habakkuk**, H. J., *Marriage, Debt and the Estates System. English Landownership, 1650–1950*, 1994.

5.583 —— 'Economic functions of English landowners in the seventeenth and eighteenth centuries'. Reprinted in Carus-Wilson, ed. (1.326), I, 187–201.

5.584 **Holderness**, B., *British Agriculture since 1945*, 1985.

5.585 —— and Turner, M., eds., *Land, Labour and Agriculture, 1700–1920*, 1991. Includes chapters on the Bridgewater estate, the Anti-Corn Law League, the origins of high farming, farm buildings in the Midlands, and production problems in agriculture during the First World War.

5.586 **Horn**, Pamela, *The Changing Countryside in Victorian and Edwardian England*, 1984.

5.587 —— *The Rural World, 1780–1850. Social Change in the English Countryside*, 1980.

5.588 —— *The Victorian Country Child*, 1974.

5.589 —— *William Marshall (1745–1818). The Life and Work of an Agricultural Pioneer*, 1982.

5.590 **Howkins**, A., *Re-shaping Rural England. A Social History, 1850–1925*, 1991. A perceptive analysis of the underlying realities, often unpleasant, which lay behind prevailing myths of an idyllic rural England.

5.591 **James**, N. D. G., *A History of English Forestry*, 1982.

5.592 **Jeans**, D. N., 'Planning and the myth of the English countryside in the inter-war period', *Rural H.*, I, 1990, 249–64.

5.593 **John**, A. H., 'The course of agricultural change 1660–1760', reprinted in Carus-

Wilson, ed. (1.326), I, 221–53.

5.594 —— 'Farming in war-time: 1793–1815'. In Jones and Mingay (5.81), 28–47.

5.595 **Jones**, E. L., *The Development of English Agriculture 1815–73*, 1968. Useful pamphlet, with select bibliography, 35–7.

5.596 —— *Agriculture and the Industrial Revolution*, 1974. Collects together the author's essays on agricultural history from the mid-seventeenth to the late nineteenth centuries.

5.597 **Kain**, R. J. P. and Prince, H. C., *The Tithe Surveys of England and Wales*, 1985. Chiefly concerned to demonstrate the utility of this source for the study of mid nineteenth-century agriculture.

5.598 **Kirk**, J. H., *U.K. Agricultural Policy, 1870–1970*, 1979.

5.599 **Mills**, D. R., *Lord and Peasant in Nineteenth-Century Britain*, 1980. A useful survey of nineteenth-century social structure.

5.600 **Mingay**, G. E., ed., *The Agrarian History of England and Wales. VI: 1750–1850*, 1989. A massive study dealing with the changing rural landscape. Prices, productivity and output, marketing, farming techniques, servicing and processing industries, landownership and estate management, and labour receive extended treatment.

5.601 —— 'The agricultural depression 1730–1750', *Ec.H.R.*, 2nd ser., 1956, 323–38.

5.602 —— 'The "Agricultural Revolution" in English history: a reconsideration', *Ag.H.*, XXXVII, 1963, 123–33.

5.603 —— *Rural Life in Victorian England*, 1977.

5.604 —— ed., *The Victorian Countryside*, 2 vols, 1981. Forty-six chapters broadly divided into five sections dealing with (1) the land, (2) agriculture, (3) country towns and country industries, (4) landed society, (5) labouring life.

5.605 **Morris**, R. M., *The Tithe War*, 1989.

5.606 **Murray**, K. A. H., *Factors affecting the Prices of Livestock in Great Britain: A Preliminary Study*, 1931. Useful statistical summary of the period 1871–1931.

5.607 **Newby**, H., *Country Life. A Social History of Rural England*, 1987. Surveys the period from the eighteenth century to the present day. Rural craftsmen, women, and home life receive little attention.

5.608 **Offer**, A., 'Farm tenure and land values

in England, c.1750–1950', *Ec.H.R.*, XLVI, 1991, 1–20.

5.609 **Ormrod**, D., *English Grain Exports and the Structure of Agrarian Capitalism 1700–1760*, 1984.

5.610 **Orwin**, Christabel S. and Whetham, Edith H., *History of British Agriculture, 1846–1914*, 1964.

5.611 **Parker**, R. A. C., *Coke of Norfolk, a financial and agricultural study, 1707–1842*, 1975.

5.612 **Perry**, P. J., ed., *British Agriculture, 1873–1914*, 1973. A collection of essays on various aspects of this historical problem.

5.613 —— *British Agriculture in the Great Depression, 1870–1914: An Historical Geography*, 1974.

5.614 **Phillips**, A. D. M., *The Underdraining of Farmland in England during the Nineteenth Century*, 1989.

5.615 **Robinson**, J. M., *Georgian Model Farms*, 1984.

5.616 **Russell**, E. J., *A History of Agricultural Science in Great Britain 1620–1954*, 1966.

5.617 —— *British Agricultural Research: Rothamsted*, 1942, 2nd rev. ed., 1946.

5.618 **Short**, B., ed., *The English Rural Community. Image and Analysis*, 1992. A collection of essays exploring the social, moral and cultural values associated with and ascribed to the countryside. The contributors include Joan Thirsk and John Lowerson.

5.619 **Taylor**, D., 'The English dairy industry, 1860–1930', *Ec.H.R.*, 2nd ser., XXIX, 1976, 585–601.

5.620 **Thompson**, F. M. L., 'Landownership and economic growth in England in the eighteenth century'. In *Agrarian Change and Economic Development*, ed. E. L. Jones and S. J. Woolf, 1969, 41–60.

5.621 **Trow-Smith**, R., *A History of British Livestock Husbandry 1700–1900*, 1959.

5.622 **Turner**, M. and Mills, D., eds., *Land and Property. The English Land Tax, 1692–1832*, 1986. Deals with land tax records and their utility for studying village communities, the development of country towns and industrial development.

5.623 **Vamplew**, W., 'The protection of English cereal producers: the Corn Laws re-assessed', *Ec.H.R.*, 2nd ser., XXXIII, 1980, 382–95.

5.624 **Ward**, S., *Seasons of Change. Rural Life in Victorian and Edwardian England*, 1982.

5.625 **Weir**, R. B., 'Distilling and agriculture, 1870–1939', *Ag.H.R.*, XXXII, 1984, 49–63.

5.626 **Whetham**, Edith H., ed., *The Agrarian History of England and Wales. VIII: 1914–39*, 1978. Deals comprehensively with the period with chapters on types of farming, marketing, government policies, war-time emergency, scientific innovation, and on landowners and the rest of rural society.

(c) Regional and local studies

5.627 **Ambrose**, P., *The Quiet Revolution: Social Changes in a Sussex Village, 1871–1971*, 1974 (Ringmer).

5.628 **Ashby**, Mabel K., *Joseph Ashby of Tysoe, 1859–1919: A Study of English Village Life*, 1961.

5.629 **Barley**, M. W., ed., *History of Lincolnshire. XII: Twentieth Century Lincolnshire*, 1989.

5.630 **Beckett**, J. V., 'The decline of the small landowner in eighteenth and nineteenth century England. Some regional considerations', *Ag.H.R.*, XXX, 1982, 97–112.

5.631 —— *A History of Laxton. England's last Open Field Village*, 1989.

5.632 —— 'Regional variation and agricultural depression, 1730–50', *Ec.H.R.*, 2nd ser., XXXV, 1982, 35–51.

5.633 **Beastall**, T. W., *The Agricultural Revolution in Lincolnshire*, 1978.

5.634 **Crouch**, D. and Ward, C., *The Allotment: its Landscape and Culture*, 1988.

5.635 **Davey**, B. J., *Ashwell, 1830–1914. The Decline of a Village Community*, 1980.

5.636 **Davies**, C. Stella, *The Agricultural History of Cheshire, 1750–1850*, Chet.Soc., 3rd ser., 10, 1960.

5.637 **Dodd**, J. P., 'Aspects of the agriculture of Northamptonshire in the first half of the nineteenth century', *Northants.P.P.*, VII, 1988, 425–33.

5.638 **Everson**, P. L., Taylor, C. C., and Dunn, C. J., *Change and Continuity. Rural Settlement in North-West Lincolnshire*, 1991.

5.639 **Fletcher**, T. W., 'The agrarian revolution in arable Lancashire', *T.L.C.A.S.*, LXXII, 1965, 93–122.

5.640 —— 'Lancashire livestock farming during the Great Depression', in Perry, ed. (5.613).

5.641 **Garnett**, F. W., *Westmorland Agriculture, 1800–1900*, 1912.

5.642 **Gaut**, R. C., *A History of Worcestershire Agriculture and Rural Evolution*, 1939.

5.643 **Grigg**, D. B., *The Agricultural Revolution in South Lincolnshire*, 1966.

5.644 **Havinden**, M. A. and others, *Estate Villages: A Study of the Berkshire Villages of Ardington and Lockinge*, 1966. Study in depth of a Victorian landed estate.

5.645 **Hoskins**, W. G., ed., *History from the Farm*, 1970. Historical studies of a number of individual farms in Great Britain.

5.646 **Kain**, R. and Holt, H., 'Agriculture and land use in Cornwall, c. 1840', *Southern H.*, III, 1981, 139–82.

5.647 **Martin**, J. M., 'Village traders and the emergence of a proletariat in South Warwickshire, 1750–1851', *Ag.H.R.*, XXXII, 1984, 179–89.

5.648 —— 'The social and economic origins of the Vale of Evesham market gardening industry', *Ag.H.R.*, XXXIII, 1985, 41–51.

5.649 **Martins**, Susanna W., *Norfolk. A Changing Countryside, 1780–1914*, 1988.

5.650 **Minchinton**, W., ed., *Agricultural Improvement. Medieval and Modern*, 1981. Six essays extending from a discussion of Wiltshire agriculture in the later Middle Ages to regional variations in food consumption amongst nineteenth-century agricultural labourers.

5.651 **Mutch**, A., *Rural Life in South-West Lancashire, 1840–1914*, 1988.

5.652 **Perkins**, J. A., *Sheep Farming in Eighteenth- and Nineteenth-Century Lincolnshire*, 1977.

5.653 **Pickles**, May F., 'Agrarian society and wealth in mid Wharedale, 1664–1743', *Yorks.Arch.J.*, LIII, 1981, 63–78.

5.654 **Rawding**, C., *Society and place in nineteenth-century North Lincolnshire*, 1992.

5.655 **Riches**, Naomi, *The Agricultural Revolution in Norfolk*, 1937, 2nd ed., 1967, with bibliographical note.

5.656 **Robin**, Jean, *Elmdon: Continuity and Change in a North West Essex Village, 1861–1964*, 1980.

5.657 **Roper**, E. M. C., *Seedtime. The History of Essex Seeds*, 1989.

5.658 **Sturgess**, R. W., *The Rural Revolution in an English Village*, 1981.

5.659 **Virgoe**, Norma and Yaxley, Susan, eds., *The Banville Diaries. Journals of a Norfolk Gamekeeper, 1822–44*, 1986. Not the journals themselves but a book based on them.

5.660 **Ward**, J. T., *East Yorkshire Landed Estates in the Nineteenth Century*, 1967.

5.661 **Winter**, G., *A Country Camera, 1844–1914: Rural Life as Depicted in Photographs*, 1966.

(d) Enclosures

5.662 **Anscombe**, J. W., 'Parliamentary enclosure in Northamptonshire: process and procedures', *Northants.P.P.*, VII, 1988, 409–24.

5.663 **Chapman**, J., 'The extent and nature of Parliamentary enclosure', *Ag.H.R.*, XXXV, 1987, 25–35.

5.664 **Gonner**, E. C. K., *Common Land and Inclosure*, 1912, 2nd ed. with introduction by G. E. Mingay, 1966.

5.665 **Levy**, H., *Large and Small Holdings: A Study of English Agricultural Economics*, 1st ed. 1911, new impression, 1966.

5.666 **McCloskey**, D., 'The enclosure of open-fields: preface to the study of its impact on the efficiency of English agriculture in the eighteenth century', *J.Ec.H.*, XXXII, 1972, 15–35.

5.667 **Mingay**, G. E., *Enclosure and the Small Farmer in the Age of the Industrial Revolution*, 1968.

5.668 **Slater**, G., *The English Peasantry and the Enclosure of the Common Fields*, 1909. Inaccurate.

5.669 **Tate**, W. E., *The English Village Community and the Enclosure Movements*, 1967. *See* in particular Appendix II on the historiography of the enclosure movements.

5.670 —— *A Domesday of English Enclosure Acts and Awards* (ed. M. E. Turner), 1978.

5.671 **Turner**, M. E., *English Parliamentary Enclosure. Its Historical Geography and Economic History*, 1980. A useful study which provides significant revisions to the statistics and chronology offered by Gonner and Tate. *See also* Brewer (4.399).

5.672 —— 'Economic protest in rural society: opposition to Parliamentary enclosure in Buckinghamshire', *Southern H.*, X, 1988, 94–128.

5.673 —— *Enclosure in Britain, 1750–1830*, 1984.

5.674 —— 'English open fields and enclosures:

5.675 **Wordie**, J. R., 'The chronology of English enclosure, 1500–1914', *Ec.H.R.*, 2nd ser., XXVI, 1983, 483–505.

(e) Landed society

5.676 **Bateman**, J., *The Great Landowners of Great Britain and Ireland*, 4th ed., 1883, 5th ed., with introduction by D. Spring, 1971.

5.677 **Brodrick**, G. C., *English Land and English Landlords*, 1st ed., 1881. Reprinted 1968.

5.678 **Caird**, J., *The Landed Interest and the Supply of Food*, 1st ed., 1878, 5th ed., 1968, with introduction by G. E. Mingay.

5.679 **Beard**, M., *English Landed Society in the Twentieth Century*, 1989.

5.680 **Beastall**, T. W., *A North Country Estate. The Lumleys and Saundersons as Landowners, 1600–1900*, 1975.

5.681 **Beckett**, J. V., *The Aristocracy in England, 1660–1914*, 1986. Looks at the aristocracy's deployment of its landed and other wealth to exercise power.

5.682 —— 'The pattern of landownership in England and Wales, 1660–1880', *Ec.H.R.*, 2nd ser., XXXVII, 1984, 1–22.

5.683 **Cannadine**, D., *The Decline and Fall of the British Aristocracy*, New Haven, Conn., 1990. Though criticised for imprecisions in its social categorisation, this substantial book effectively documents the waning of the economic and social fortunes of the elite.

5.684 **Chalklin**, C. W. and Wordie, J. R., eds., *Town and Countryside. The English Landowner in the National Economy, 1660–1860*, 1989.

5.685 **Clay**, C., 'Property settlements, financial provision for the family and sale of land by the greater landowners, 1660–1790', *J.Brit.Studs.*, XXI, 1981, 18–38.

5.686 **Clemenson**, H. A., *The English Landed Estate*, 1981.

5.687 **McCahill**, M. W., 'Peers, patronage and the Industrial Revolution, 1760–1800', *J.Brit.Studs.*, XVI, 1976, 84–107.

5.688 **Martins**, Susanna W., *A Great Estate at Work. The Holkham Estate and its Inhabitants in the Nineteenth Century*, 1980.

5.689 **Massey**, D. and Catalano, A., *Capital and*

Land. Land Ownership in Great Britain, 1978.

5.690 **Mingay**, G. E., *English Landed Society in the Eighteenth Century*, 1963.

5.691 —— 'The eighteenth-century land steward'. In Jones and Mingay (5.81), 3–27.

5.692 —— *The Gentry. The Rise and Fall of a Ruling Class*, 1976.

5.693 **Spring**, D., *The English Landed Estate in the Nineteenth Century: Its Administration*, Baltimore, Md., 1963.

5.694 **Thompson**, F. M. L., *English Landed Society in the Nineteenth Century*, 1963. The final chapter deals with the period 1914–39; excellent bibliography.

5.695 **Thompson**, F. M. L., 'English Landed Society in the twentieth century: I', *T.R.H.S.*, 5th ser., XL, 1990, 1–24, II: *T.R.H.S.*, 6th ser., I, 1991, 1–20; III: *T.R.H.S.*, 6th ser., II, 1992, 1–23; *T.R.H.S.*, 6th ser., III, 1993, 1–22.

5.696 **Ward**, J. T. and Wilson, R. G., eds., *Land and Industry: The Landed Estate and the Industrial Revolution*, 1971.

(f) Farm labourers

5.697 **Archer**, J. E., *"By a Flash and a Scare"*. *Incendiarism, Animal Maiming and Poaching in East Anglia, 1815–70*, 1990. Examines social tensions in the countryside and their expression in community approval of arson, poaching and animal maiming in cases where owners were unpopular landlords.

5.698 **Armstrong**, A., *Farmworkers. A Social and Economic History, 1770–1980*, 1987. Explores demographic aspects, trade unionism, class consciousness, and standards of living.

5.699 **Barnett**, D. C., 'Allotments and the problem of rural poverty, 1780–1840'. In Jones and Mingay (5.81), 162–83.

5.700 **Bohstedt**, J., *Riots and Community Politics in England and Wales, 1790–1810*, Cambridge Mass., 1983.

5.701 **Brown**, A. F. G., *Meagre Harvest. The Essex Farm Workers' Struggle against Poverty, 1750–1914*, 1990.

5.702 **Charlesworth**, A., 'An agenda for historical studies of rural protest in Britain, 1750–1850', *Rural H.*, II, 1991, 231–40.

5.703 —— ed., *An Atlas of Rural Protest in*

Britain, 1548–1900, 1983.

5.704 **Chase**, M., *The People's Farm: English Agrarian Radicalism, 1775–1840*, 1988.

5.705 **Collins**, E. J. T., 'Migrant labour in British agriculture in the nineteenth century', *Ec.H.R.*, 2nd ser., XXIX, 1976, 38–59.

5.706 —— 'The rationality of "surplus" agricultural labour: mechanisation in English agriculture in the nineteenth century', *Ag.H.R.*, XXXV, 1987, 36–46.

5.707 **Cox**, G., Lowe, P. and Winter, M., 'The origins and early development of the National Farmers' Union', *Ag.H.R.*, XXXIX, 1991, 30–47.

5.708 **Danzinger**, R., *Political Powerlessness: Agricultural Workers in Post War England*, 1988.

5.709 **Donajgrodzski**, A. P., 'Twentieth-century rural England: a case for "peasant studies?" ', *J.Peasant Studs.*, XVI, 1988, 425–42.

5.710 **Dunbabin**, J. P. D., *Rural Discontent in Nineteenth-century Britain*, 1973 (with chapters by A. J. Peacock and Pamela Horn).

5.711 **Gash**, N., 'Rural unemployment, 1815–34', *Ec.H.R.*, VI, 1935, 90–3.

5.712 **Hammond**, J. L. and Barbara, *The Village Labourer, 1760–1832: A Study in the Government of England before the Reform Bill*, 1911. Reprinted, with an introduction by G. E. Mingay, 1978. Well-written, sentimental and misleading.

5.713 **Hobsbawm**, E. J. and Rudé, G., *Captain Swing*, 1969, 2nd ed., 1973 with new introduction. The agrarian riots of 1830. *See* bibliography, 367–71.

5.714 **Horn**, Pamela L., *Labouring Life in the Victorian Countryside*, 1976. Mainly about the Midlands and South.

5.715 **Horn**, Pamela, *Life and Labour in Rural England, 1760–1850*, 1987. A brief interdisciplinary study with chapters on change in the countryside, village life and labour, the post Napoleonic War world, and on the rural community.

5.716 **Howkins**, A., *Poor Labouring Men. Rural Radicalism in Norfolk, 1872–1923*, 1985.

5.717 **Kerr**, Barbara, M., *Bound to the Soil: A Social History of Dorset, 1750–1918*, 1968.

5.718 **King**, P., 'Gleaners, farmers and the failure of legal sanctions in England, 1750–1850', *P.P.*, CXXV, 1989, 116–50.

5.719 **Mingay**, G. E., ed., *The Vanishing*

Countryman, 1989.

5.720 **Morgan**, D. H., *Harvests and Harvesting, 1840–1900. A Study of the Rural Proletariat*, 1982.

5.721 **Neave**, D., *Mutual Aid in the Victorian Countryside, Friendly Societies in the Rural East Riding, 1830–1912*, 1991.

5.722 **Newby**, H., *The Deferential Worker. A Study of Farm Workers in East Anglia*, 1977. Though primarily sociological, the book opens with a lengthy section on the historical context.

5.723 **Peacock**, A. J., *Bread or Blood: The Agrarian Riots in East Anglia, 1816*, 1965.

5.724 **Reay**, B., *The Last Rising of the Agricultural Labourers. Rural Life and Protest in Nineteenth Century England*, 1990. Examines the disturbances in the Kentish countryside of 1838 and their wider social, demographic and economic context.

5.725 **Reed**, M., and Wells, R., eds., *Class, Conflict and Protest in the English Countryside, 1700–1800*, 1990.

5.726 —— 'The peasantry of nineteenth-century England: a neglected class?', *H.Workshop J.*, XVIII, 1984, 53–77.

5.727 **Samuel**, R., ed., *Village Life and Labour*, 1975.

5.728 **Seal**, G., 'Tradition and agrarian protest in nineteenth-century England and Wales', *Folklore*, XCIX, 1988, 146–69.

5.729 **Short**, B., 'The decline of living in servants in the transition to capitalist farming: a critique of the Sussex evidence', *Sussex Arch.Collns.*, CXXII, 1984, 147–64.

5.730 **Snell**, K. D. M., *Annals of the Labouring Poor. Social Change and Agrarian England, 1660–1900*, 1985. Based principally on Poor Law records, the book offers a quantitative and qualitative examination of the life of rural labourers.

5.731 **Springall**, L. Marion, *Labouring Life in Norfolk Villages, 1834–1914*, 1936. *See also* Hasbach (4.1160) and Fussell (4.1156).

(g) William Cobbett

5.732 **Cole**, G. D. H., *The Life of William Cobbett*, 1927. Includes a chapter on Rural Rides by F. E. Green.

5.733 **Spater**, G., *William Cobbett: the Poor Man's Friend*, 2 vols, 1982. Based on

much new and important material, this is now the definitive biography.

INDUSTRY

(a) Science and technology

5.734 **Alter**, P., *The Reluctant Patron. Science and the State in Britain, 1850–1920*, 1986.

5.735 **Buchanan**, R. A., *The Power of the Machine. The Impact of Technology from 1700 to the Present Day*, 1992.

5.736 **Cooter**, R., *The Cultural Meaning of Popular Science. Phrenology and the Organisation of Consent in Nineteenth-Century Britain*, 1984.

5.737 **Davenport**, A. N., *James Watt and the Patent System*, 1989.

5.738 **Dutton**, H. I., *The Patent System and Inventive Tradition, 1750–1852*, 1984. Deals with a neglected subject and documents the rapid growth of patenting from ten a year in 1750 to 500 in 1840. *See also* MacLeod (5.748).

5.739 **Greenhalgh**, P., *Ephemeral Vistas. A History of the Expositions Universelles, Great Exhibitions and World's Fairs, 1851–1939*, 1988.

5.740 **Habakkuk**, H. J., *American and British Technology in the Nineteenth Century: The Search for Labour-saving Inventions*, 1962.

5.741 **Harris**, J. R., 'Skills, coal and British industry in the eighteenth century', *Hist.*, LXI, 1976, 167–82.

5.742 **Hudson**, K., *The Archaeology of the Consumer Society. The Second Industrial Revolution in Britain*, 1983.

5.743 **Inkster**, I. and Morrell, J., eds., *Metropolis and Province. Science in British Culture, 1780–1850*, 1983. Essays which take a sociological approach to the development of scientific research in London and in the regions.

5.744 **Jeremy**, D. J., *Transatlantic Industrial Revolution. The diffusion of Textile Technologies between Britain and America, 1790–1830*, 1981.

5.745 **Kargon**, R., *Science in Victorian Manchester. Enterprise and Expertise*, 1977. Deals with the amateur scientific tradition in Manchester and the emergence of 'civic science' and university science in the second half of the century.

5.746 **Kenwood**, A. G. and Lougheed, A. L., *Technological Diffusion and Industrialisation before 1914*, 1982.

5.747 **Lea**, F. M., *Science and Building. A History of the Building Research Station*, 1971.

5.748 **MacLeod**, Christine, *Inventing the Industrial Revolution. The English Patent System, 1660–1800*, 1988. Explores the shift from patronage to legal protection. *See also* Dutton (5.738).

5.749 **MacLeod**, R. and Collins, P., eds., *The Parliament of Science. The British Association for the Advancement of Science, 1831–1981*, 1982.

5.750 **Mathias**, P., ed., *Science and Society, 1660–1900*, 1972. Essays by various hands.

5.751 **Musson**, A. E., ed., *Science, Technology and Economic Growth in the Eighteenth Century*, 1972. Assembles eight key articles.

5.752 —— 'Technological change and manpower', *Hist.*, LXVII, 1982, 237–51.

5.753 —— and Robinson, E. H., *Science and Technology in the Industrial Revolution*, 1969. Also contains important material on the rise of the British chemical industry.

5.754 **Robinson**, E. H., 'The Lunar Society: its membership and organisation', *Trans. Newcomen Soc.*, XXXV, 1964, 153–77.

5.755 **Saul**, S. B., ed., *Technological Change: The United States and Britain in the Nineteenth Century*, 1970. Six essays by H. J. Habakkuk, D. L. Burn and others.

5.756 **Schofield**, R. E., *The Lunar Society of Birmingham: A Social History of Provincial Science and Industry in Eighteenth-century England*, 1963.

5.757 **Singer**, S., Holmyard, E. J., Wall, A. R., and Williams, T. I., eds., *A History of Technology. The Industrial Revolution, c.1750–c.1850*, 1958. The various sections are very uneven.

5.758 **Sumida**, J. T., *In Defence of Naval Supremacy. Finance, Technology and British Naval Policy, 1889–1914*, 1989. Explores the rapid pace of change in the Royal Navy in the pre-First World War period.

5.759 **Williams**, T. I., ed., *A History of Technology. The Twentieth Century,* *c.1900–c.1950*. VI (Part I), VII (Part II), 1978.

(b) Power and light

(i) WIND AND WATER MILLS

5.760 **Bennett**, R. and Elton, J., *History of Corn Milling*, 4 vols., 1898–1904.

5.761 **Ellis**, C. M., 'A gazetteer of the water, wind and tide mills of Hampshire', *Proc.Hants.Field Club*, XXV, 1968, 119–40.

5.762 **Farriers**, K. G. and Mason, M. G., *The Windmills of Surrey and Inner London*, 1966.

5.763 **Hillier**, J., *Old Surrey Watermills*, 1951.

5.764 **Norris**, J. H., 'The water-powered corn mills of Cheshire', *T.L.C.A.S.*, LXXV and LXXVI, 1968, 33–71.

5.765 **Pelham**, R. A., *The Old Mills of Southampton*, 1963.

5.766 **Syson**, L., *British Water Mills*, 1965. Contains a good bibliography.

(ii) STEAM ENGINES

5.767 **Tann**, Jennifer, ed., *The Selected Papers of Boulton and Watt* I: *The Engine*, 1981. The first instalment of the published correspondence of the Birmingham firm that took the lead in supplying steam power in the Industrial Revolution.

5.768 **Barton**, D. B., *The Cornish Beam Engine*, 1965. 2nd ed., 1966.

5.769 **Cardwell**, D. S. L., *Steam Power in the Eighteenth Century*, 1963. The scientific background.

5.770 **Cule**, J. E., 'Finance and industry in the eighteenth century: the firm of Boulton and Watt', *Ec. J.*, *Ec.H.Supp.*, IV, 1940, 319–25.

5.771 **Dickinson**, H. W., *The Cornish Engine*, 1950.

5.772 —— *James Watt, Craftsman and Engineer*, 1935.

5.773 —— *Matthew Boulton*, 1936.

5.774 —— *A Short History of the Steam Engine*, 1st ed., 1938, 2nd ed., with corrections and new bibliographical introduction by A. E. Musson, 1963.

5.775 —— and Jenkins, R., *James Watt and the Steam Engine*, 1927.

5.776 —— and Titley, A., *Richard Travithick:*

The Engineer and the Man, 1934.

5.777 **Gale**, W. K. V., 'Soho Foundry: Some Facts and Fallacies', *Trans. Newcomen Soc.*, XXXIV, 1963, 73–87.

5.778 **Harris**, J. R., 'The employment of steam power in the eighteenth century', *Hist.*, LII, 1967, 133–48.

5.779 **Hills**, R. L., *Power in the Industrial Revolution*, 1970.

5.780 **Lord**, J., *Capital and Steam Power, 1750–1800*, 1st ed. 1923, 2nd ed., with corrections and bibliographical introduction by W. H. Chaloner, 1966.

5.781 **Musson**, A. E., 'Industrial motive power in the United Kingdom, 1800–70', *Ec.H.R.*, 2nd ser., XXIX, 1976, 415–39.

5.782 —— and Robinson, E. H., 'The early growth of steam power', *Ec.H.R.*, 2nd ser., XI, 1959, 418–39. Reprinted with additions in Musson and Robinson (5.753).

5.783 **Robinson**, E. H. and Musson, A. E., *James Watt and the Steam Revolution: A Documentary History*, 1969.

5.784 **Roll**, E., *An Early Experiment in Industrial Organisation: Being a History of the Firm of Boulton & Watt, 1775–1805*, 1930. Reprinted 1968.

5.785 **Rolt**, L. T. C., *Thomas Newcomen: The Pre-history of the Steam Engine*, 1963.

5.786 **Tunzelmann**, G. N. von, 'Technological diffusion during the Industrial Revolution: the case of the Cornish pumping engine'. In Hartwell, ed. (5.69), 77–98.

5.787 —— *Steam Power and British Industrialisation to 1860*, 1978.

5.788 **Watkins**, G., *The Stationary Beam Engine*, 1968.

5.789 —— *The Textile Mill Engine*, I, 1970, II, 1971.

(iii) LIGHT

(1) GENERAL

5.790 **O'Dea**, W. T., *The Social History of Lighting*, 1958.

(2) GAS

5.791 **Chandler**, D. and Lacey, A. D., *The Rise of the Gas Industry in Britain*, 1949.

5.792 **Everard**, S., *History of the Gas Light and Coke Company, 1812–1949*, 1949.

5.793 **Falkus**, M., 'The British gas industry before 1850', *Ec.H.R.*, 2nd ser., XX, 1967, 494–508.

5.794 —— 'The early development of the British gas industry, 1790–1815', *Ec.H.R.*, 2nd ser., XXXV, 1982, 217–34.

5.795 **Harris**, S. A., *The Development of Gas Supply on North Merseyside, 1815–1949*, 1956.

5.796 **Millward**, R. and Ward, R., 'The cost of public and private gas enterprises in late nineteenth-century Britain', *Oxford Ec. Papers*, XXXIX, 1987, 713–37.

5.797 **Nabb**, H., *The Bristol Gas Industry, 1815–1949*, 1987.

5.798 **Peebles**, M. W. H., *The Evolution of the Gas Industry*, 1980.

5.799 **Williams**, T. I., *A History of the British Gas Industry*, 1981.

(3) ELECTRICITY

5.800 **Ballin**, H. H., *The Organisation of Electricity Supply in Great Britain*, 1946. Covers the period 1879–1944.

5.801 **Byatt**, I. C. R., *The British Electrical Industry, 1875–1914*, 1979.

5.802 **Dunsheath**, P., *A History of Electrical Engineering*, 1962.

5.803 **Hannah**, L., *Electricity before Nationalisation. A Study of the Development of the Electricity Supply Industry in Britain to 1948*, 1979.

5.804 **Hinton**, C., *The Development of Heavy Current Electricity in the United Kingdom*, 1978.

5.805 **Luckin**, B., *Questions of Power. Electricity in Inter-War Britain*, 1990.

5.806 **Parsons**, R. H., *A Short History of the Power Station Industry*, 1939.

5.807 **Swale**, W. E., *Forerunners of the North Western Electricity Board*, 1963.

(c) Textiles

(i) GENERAL

5.808 **Harte**, N. B. and Ponting, K. G., eds., *Textile History and Economic History: Essays in Honour of Miss Julia de Lacy Mann*, 1973. Essays on aspects of the stocking-knitting, wollen, worsted, linen and cotton trades from 1500 to 1867.

(ii) COTTON

5.809 **Aspin**, C., *James Hargreaves and the Spinning Jenny*, 1964.

5.810 **Bamberg**, J. H., 'The rationalisation of the British cotton industry in the interwar years', *Textile H.*, XIX, 1988, 83–102.

5.811 **Bowker**, B., *Lancashire under the Hammer*, 1928.

5.812 **Boyson**, R., *The Ashworth Cotton Enterprise: The Rise and Fall of a Family Firm, 1818–1880*, 1970.

5.813 **Bythell**, D., *The Handloom Weavers: A Study in the English Cotton Industry During the Industrial Revolution*, 1969.

5.814 **Cairncross**, A. K. and Hunter, J. B. K., 'The early growth of Messrs J. P. Coats, 1830–83', *Bus.Hist.*, XXIX, 1987, 157–77.

5.815 **Catling**, H., *The Spinning Mule*, 1970.

5.816 **Chapman**, S. D., *The Early Factory Masters: The Transition to the Factory System in the Midlands Textile Industry*, 1967.

5.817 —— *The Cotton Industry in the Industrial Revolution*, 1972. Excellent summary.

5.818 —— 'Financial restraints on the growth of firms in the cotton industry, 1790–1850', *Ec.H.R.*, 2nd ser., XXXII, 1979, 50–69.

5.819 **Clapp**, B. W., *John Owens, Manchester Merchant*, 1965. Covers the period 1790–1846.

5.820 **Clark**, H., 'The design and designing of Lancashire printed calicoes during the first half of the nineteenth century', *Textile H.*, XV, 1984, 101–18.

5.821 **Dupree**, M., 'Fighting against fate. The cotton industry and the government during the 1930s', *Textile H.*, XXI, 1990, 101–17.

5.822 **Edwards**, M. M., *The Growth of the British Cotton Trade, 1780–1815*, 1967.

5.823 **Ellison**, Mary, *Support for Secession: Lancashire and the American Civil War*, Chicago, 1972.

5.824 **English**, W., *The Textile Industry: An Account of the Early Inventions of Spinning, Weaving and Knitting Machines*, 1969. Useful glossary of technical terms and bibliography, 225–35.

5.825 **Farnie**, D. A., 'The Cotton Famine in Great Britain', in Ratcliffe (5.107), 153–78.

5.826 —— *The English Cotton Industry and the World Market, 1815–96*, 1979.

5.827 **Fitton**, R. S. and Wadsworth, A. P., *The Strutts and the Arkwrights, 1758–1830*, 1958.

5.828 **Henderson**, W. O., *The Lancashire Cotton Famine, 1861–1865*, 1934, 2nd rev. and enlarged ed., 1969, with bibliography, 157–94.

5.829 **Howe**, A., *The Cotton Masters, 1830–60*, 1984. A study based on the biographies of over 350 Lancashire textile masters which delineates not simply the patterns of their economic activity but also their lifestyle and culture.

5.830 **Huberman**, M., 'The economic origins of paternalism: Lancashire cotton spinning in the first half of the nineteenth century', *Soc.H.*, XII, 1987, 177–92.

5.831 **Jenkins**, D. T., 'The cotton industry in Yorkshire, 1780–1900', *Textile H.*, X, 1979, 75–95.

5.832 **Lee**, C. H., *A Cotton Enterprise, 1795–1840: A History of McConnel and Kennedy, Fine Cotton Spinners*, 1972.

5.833 **Lloyd Jones**, R. and Lewis, M. J., *Manchester and the Age of the Factory. The Business Structure of 'Cottonopolis' in the Industrial Revolution*, 1987.

5.834 **Muir**, A., *The Kenyon Tradition: The History of James Kenyon and Son, Ltd., 1664–1964*, 1964.

5.835 **Pearson**, R., 'Collective diversification: Manchester cotton merchants and the insurance business in the early nineteenth century', *Bus.H.R.*, LXV, 1991, 379–414.

5.836 **Pigott**, S. C., *Hollins: A Study of Industry, 1784–1949*, 1949.

5.837 **Prest**, J., *The Industrial Revolution in Coventry*, 1960.

5.838 **Robson**, R., *The Cotton Industry in Britain*, 1957.

5.839 **Rose**, Mary B., *The Gregs of Quarry Bank Mill. The Rise and Decline of a Family Firm, 1750–1914*, 1986. Charts the fluctuating fortunes of this family business.

5.840 **Sandberg**, L. G., 'American rings and English mules: the role of economic rationality'. In S. B. Saul, ed., *Technological Change: The United States and Britain in the Nineteenth Century*, 1970, 120–40.

5.841 —— *Lancashire in Decline: A Study in Entrepreneurship Technology and International Trade*, Columbus, Ohio,

1974.

5.842 **Shapiro**, S., *Capital and the Cotton Industry in the Industrial Revolution*, Ithica, N. Y., 1967.

5.843 **Silver**, A., *Manchester Men and Indian Cotton, 1847–1872*, 1966.

5.844 **Singleton**, J., *Lancashire on the Scrapheap. The Cotton Industry, 1945–70*, 1991.

5.845 **Smelser**, N. J., *Social Change in the Industrial Revolution: An Application of Theory to the Lancashire Cotton Industry, 1770–1840*, 1959. Bibliography, 411–40.

5.846 **Temin**, P., 'Product quality and vertical integration in the early cotton textile industry', *J.Ec.H.*, XLVIII, 1988, 891–907.

5.847 **Tippett**, L. H. C., *A Portrait of the Lancashire Textile Industry*, 1969. Covers the period 1919–69.

5.848 **Unwin**, G., *et al.*, *Samuel Oldknow and the Arkwrights; The Industrial Revolution at Stockport and Marple*, 1924, 2nd rev. ed., 1968.

5.849 **Wells**, F. A., *Hollins and Viyella: A Study in Business History*, 1968.

(iii) WOOLLENS AND WORSTEDS

5.850 **Beckinsale**, R. P., 'The plush industry of Oxfordshire', *Oxoniensa*, XXVIII, 1963, 53–67.

5.851 **Coleman**, D. C., 'Growth and decay during the Industrial Revolution: the case of East Anglia', *Scand.Ec.H.R.*, X, 1962, 115–27.

5.852 **Crump**, W. B., *The Leeds Woollen Industry, 1780–1820*, 1931.

5.853 —— and Ghorbal, Gertrude, *History of the Huddersfield Woollen Industry*, 1935. Reprinted 1967.

5.854 **Hartley**, Marie and Ingilby, Joan, *The Old Hand-knitters of the Yorkshire Dales*, 1951.

5.855 **Hudson**, Pat, *The Genesis of Industrial Capital. A Study of the West Riding Wool Textile Industry, c.1760–1850*, 1986. Stresses the importance in the eighteenth century of the ploughing back of profits and, in the nineteenth, the increasing role of banks.

5.856 **Jenkins**, D. T., *The West Riding Wool Textile Industry, 1770–1835. A Study of Fixed Capital Formation*, 1975.

5.857 —— and Ponting, K. G., *The British Wool Textile Industry, 1770–1914*, 1982.

5.858 **Mann**, Julia de L., *The Cloth Industry in the West of England, 1640–1880*, 1971.

5.859 —— 'Clothiers and weavers in Wiltshire during the eighteenth century'. In Pressnell, ed. (5.106).

5.860 **Moir**, Esther, A. L., 'The gentlemen clothiers: a study of the organisation of the Gloucestershire cloth industry, 1750–1835'. In H. P. R. Finberg (4.109).

5.861 **Plummer**, A. and Early, R. E., *The Blanket Makers, 1669–1969. A History of Charles Early and Marriot (Witney) Ltd.*, 1969.

5.862 **Ponting**, K. G., *The Woollen Industry of South-West England*, 1971.

5.863 **Prichard**, M. F. Lloyd, 'The decline of Norwich', *Ec.H.R.*, 2nd ser., III, 1951, 371–7.

5.864 **Rogers**, K., *Wiltshire and Somerset Woollen Mills*, 1976.

5.865 **Sigsworth**, E. M., *Black Dyke Mills: A History*, 1958. Contains useful introductory chapters on the development of the worsted industry in the nineteenth century. *See also* Tann (4.502).

5.866 **Wilson**, R. G., *Gentlemen Merchants: The Merchant Community in Leeds, 1700–1830*, 1971.

(iv) CLOTHING INDUSTRY

5.867 **Lemire**, B., 'Developing Consumerism and the ready-made clothing trade in Britain, 1750–1800', *Textile H.*, XV, 1984, 21–44.

5.868 **Levitt**, S., *Victorians Unbuttoned. Registered Designs for Clothing, their Makers and Wearers, 1839–1900*, 1986.

5.869 **Sigsworth**, E. M., *Montague Burton. The Tailor of Taste*, 1990. A business biography of the Russian immigrant who built up one of the most succesful clothing businesses of the twentieth century.

5.870 **Thomas**, Joan, *A History of the Leeds Clothing Industry*, 1955.

5.871 **Wray**, Margaret, *The Women's Outerwear Industry*, 1957.

(v) SILK AND MAN-MADE FIBRES

5.872 **Chaloner**, W. H., 'Sir Thomas Lombe (1685–1739) and the British silk industry', In *People and Industries*, 1963,

8–20.

5.873 **Clapham**, J. H., 'The Spitalfields Acts, 1773–1824', *Ec.J.* XXVI, 1916, 459–71.

5.874 **Coleman**, D. C., *Courtaulds: An Economic and Social History*, 3 vols, 1969–80.

5.875 **Hertz** (later Hurst), G. B., 'The English silk industry in the eighteenth century', *E.H.R.*, XXIV, 1909, 710–27.

5.876 **Warner**, F., *The Silk Industry of the United Kingdom*, 1921.

5.877 **Weinstock**, Maureen, '*Portrait of an eighteenth-century Sherborne silk mill owner*'. In *Studies in Dorset History*, 1953, 83–102.

On rayon *see also* Buxton and Aldcroft (5.199).

(vi) LINEN AND FLAX

5.878 **Evans**, N., *The East Anglian Linen Industry*, 1984.

5.879 **Horner**, J., *The Linen Trade of Europe During the Spinning-Wheel Period*, 1920. Contains useful trade statistics.

5.880 **Rimmer**, W. G., *Marshalls of Leeds, Flax-Spinners, 1788–1886*, 1960. Excellent bibliography, 327–35.

(vii) HATTING

5.881 **Dony**, J. G., *A History of the Straw Hat Industry*, 1942. South Midlands, Essex and Suffolk in the period 1680–1939.

5.882 **Giles**, Phyllis M., 'The felt-hatting industry, c. 1500–1800, with particular reference to Lancashire and Cheshire', *T.L.C.A.S.*, LXIX, 1960, 104–32.

(viii) HOSIERY AND LACE

5.883 **Chapman**, S. D., 'Mergers and takeovers in the post-war textile industry: the experience of hosiery and knitwear', *Bus.H.*, XXX, 1988, 219–39.

5.884 **Oldfield**, G., 'The Nottingham lace market', *Textile H.*, XV, 1984, 191–208.

5.885 **Varley**, D. E., *A History of the Midland Counties Lace Manufacturers' Association, 1915–58*, 1959.

5.886 **Wells**, F. A., *The British Hosiery Trade*, 1935; 2nd rev. and enlarged edn., 1972.

(d) Iron and steel

5.887 **Addis**, J. P., *The Crawshay Dynasty: A Study in Industrial Organisation and Development, 1765–1867*, 1957.

5.888 **Andrews**, P. W. S. and Brunner, Elizabeth, *Capital Development in Steel: A Study of the United Steel Companies, Ltd.*, 1951.

5.889 **Ashton**, T. S., *An Eighteenth-century Industrialist: Peter Stubs of Warrington, 1756–1806*, 1939, 2nd ed., 1961. *See also* Dane (5.902).

5.890 —— *Iron and Steel in the Industrial Revolution*, 1st ed., 1924, 2nd rev. ed., 1951, 3rd ed., with new bibliographical introduction, 1963.

5.891 **Barraclough**, K. C., *Steelmaking before Bessemer. I: Blister Steel, the birth of an industry; II: Crucible Steel, the growth of technology*, 1985. A technical history of the changes which revolutionised the science and scale of steel-making.

5.892 **Benyon**, H., Hudson, R, and Sadler, D., *A Tale of Two Industries. The Contraction of Coal and Steel in the North East of England*, 1991.

5.893 **Birch**, A., *The Economic History of the British Iron and Steel Industry, 1784–1879*, 1967.

5.894 —— and Flinn, M. W., 'The English steel industry before 1856 with special reference to the development of the Yorkshire Steel Industry', *Yorks.B.*, VI, 1954, 163–77.

5.895 **Boswell**, J., 'Hope, efficiency or public duty? The United Steel Companies and West Cumberland, 1918–39', *Bus.H.*, XXII, 1980, 35–50.

5.896 **Burn**, D. L., *The Economic History of Steelmaking, 1867–1939*, 1940, 2nd rev. ed., 1961.

5.897 —— *The Steel Industry, 1939–1959*, 1961.

5.898 **Campbell**, R. H., *Carron Company*, 1961.

5.899 **Cantrell**, J. A., *James Nasmyth and the Bridgewater Foundry*, 1985.

5.900 **Carr**, J. C., Taplin, W. and Wright, A. E. G., *History of the British Steel Industry*, 1962.

5.901 **Chaloner**, W. H., 'Isaac Wilkinson, pot-founder'. In Pressnell (5.106).

5.902 **Dane** E. S., *Peter Stubs and the Lancashire Hand Tool Industry*, 1973.

5.903 **Elsas**, Madeleine, *Iron in the Making; Dowlais Iron Company Letters, 1782–1860*, 1960.

5.904 **Evans**, C., 'Failure in a new technology: smelting iron with coke in south Gloucestershire in the 1770s', *Trans.Bristol & Glouces.Arch.Soc.*, CIX, 1991, 199–206.

5.905 **Fereday**, R. P., *The Career of Richard Smith 1783 1868*, 1966. Smith was mineral agent to the Earl of Dudley.

5.906 **Flinn**, M. W., *Men of Iron. The Crowleys in the Early Iron Industry*, 1962.

5.907 **Gale**, W. K. V., *The Black Country Iron Industry: A Technical History*, 1966. Mainly 1700 to 1960s.

5.908 —— 'The Bessemer steelmaking process', *Trans. Newcomen Soc.*, XLVI, 1976, 17–24.

5.909 —— *The British Iron and Steel Industry: A Technical History*, 1967.

5.910 **Gloag**, J. and Bridgwater, D., *A History of Cast Iron in Architecture*, 1948.

5.911 **Hammersley**, G., 'Did it fall or was it pushed? The Foleys and the end of the charcoal iron industry in the eighteenth century', in Smout (5.116), 67–90.

5.912 **Harris**, A., *Cumberland Iron: The Story of Hodbarrow Mine, 1855–1968*, 1971.

5.913 **Harris**, J. R., *The British Iron Industry, 1700–1850*, 1988.

5.914 **Hey**, D., *The Rural Metalworkers of the Sheffield Region*, 1972.

5.915 **Hyde**, C. K., *Technological Change and the British Iron Industry, 1700–1870*, Princeton, N. J., 1977. Surveys all aspects of ironmaking in a period of gradual, continuous change.

5.916 **Johnson**, B. L. C., 'The Midland iron industry in the early eighteenth century: the background to the first successful use of coke in iron smelting', *Bus.H.*, II, 1960, 67–74.

5.917 **McCloskey**, D., *Economic Maturity and Entrepreneurial Decline: British Iron and Steel, 1870–1913*, 1974.

5.918 **Minchinton**, W. E., *The British Tinplate Industry: A History*, 1957.

5.919 **Musgrave**, P. W., *Technical Change, the Labour Force and Education: A Study of the British and German Iron and Steel Industries, 1860–1964*, 1967. Deals mainly with technical education. Should be used with great caution.

5.920 **Mutton**, N., 'The Marked Bar Association: Price Regulation in the Black Country Wrought Iron Trade', *W.Midland Studs.*, IX, 1976, 2–8.

5.921 **Page**, R., 'Richard and Edward Knight: iron-masters of Bringewood and Wolverley', *Trans.Woolhope Nat.Field Club*, XLIII, 1979, 7–17.

5.922 **Pollard**, S., *Three Centuries of Sheffield Steel: The Story of a Family Business* (Marsh Bros. & Co.), 1954.

5.923 **Raistrick**, A., *Dynasty of Ironfounders; The Darbys and Coalbrookdale*, 1953.

5.924 —— and Allen, E., 'The South Yorkshire iron-masters, 1690–1750', *Ec.H.R.*, IX, 1939, 168–85.

5.925 **Riden**, P., 'The output of the British iron industry before 1870', *Ec.H.R.*, XXX, 1977, 442–59.

5.926 —— 'The iron industry' in Church (5.47), 63–86.

5.927 **Robinson**, P., *The Smiths of Chesterfield: A History of the Griffin Foundry, Brampton, 1775–1833*, 1957.

5.928 **Roepke**, H., *Movements of the British Iron and Steel Industry, 1720–1951*, Urbana, Ill., 1956.

5.929 **Sanderson**, M., 'The Professor as industrial consultant: Oliver Arnold and the British steel industry, 1900–14', *Ec.H.R.*, 2nd ser., XXXI, 1978, 585–600.

5.930 **Stones**, F., *The British Ferrous Wire Industry, 1882–1962*, 1977.

5.931 **Tolliday**, S., *Business, Banking and Politics. The Case of British Steel, 1918–1939*, 1987. Looks at the steel industry in the N.E., Scotland, S.Wales, and at the role of the banks in restructuring the steel industry in the interwar period.

5.932 **Trinder**, B., ed., *'The Most Extraordinary District in the World'. Ironbridge and Coalbrookdale*, 1977.

5.933 **Tweedale**, G., *Sheffield Steel and America. A Century of Commercial and Technological Independence*, 1987.

5.934 **Warren**, K., *Consett Iron, 1840–1980. A Study in Industrial Location*, 1990. Examines what the author considers to be an improbable survival of an iron and steel company.

5.935 —— *The British Iron and Steel Sheet Industry since 1840*, 1970.

5.936 —— 'Iron and Steel' in Buxton and Aldcroft, 103–28. See also Allen (5.132), Raybould (5.119), and Schubert (2.279).

(e) Copper, brass and lead

5.937 **Burt**, R., ed., *Cornish Mining: Essays on the Organisation of the Cornish Mines and the Cornish Mining Economy*, 1969.

5.938 **Clough**, R. T., *The Lead Smelting Mills of the Yorkshire Dales: Their Architectural Character, Construction and Place in the European Tradition*, 1962; bibliography, 169–72.

5.939 **Day**, Joan, *Bristol Brass: The History of the Industry*, 1973.

5.940 **Ford**, T. D. and Nieuwerts, J. H., eds., *Lead Mining in the Peak District*, 1968; bibliography, 123–4.

5.941 **Hunt**, C. J., *The Lead Miners of the Northern Pennines in the Eighteenth and Nineteenth Centuries*, 1970.

5.942 **Jennings**, B., ed., *A History of Nidderdale*, 1967, 151–61, 266–325.

5.943 **Kirkham**, Nellie, *Derbyshire Lead-mining through the Centuries*, 1968.

5.944 **Raistrick**, A., *Miners and Miners of Swaledale*, 1955.

5.945 —— *Two Centuries of Industrial Welfare: The London (Quaker) Lead Company, 1692–1905*, 1938.

5.946 —— *The Lead Industry of Wensleydale and Swaledale*, 1975.

5.947 **Roberts**, R. O., 'Copper and economic growth in Britain, 1729–84', *Nat.Lib.Wales J.*, X, 1957, 1–10.

5.948 **Rowe**, D. J., *The British Lead Manufacturing Industry, 1778–1982*, 1983.

5.949 **Turnbull**, L., *The History of Lead Mining in the North East of England*, 1975. *See also* Hamilton (4.524), Jenkin (4.1163), and Raistrick and Jennings (4.538).

(f) Coal

5.950 **Benson**, J., comp., *Bibliography of the British Coal Industry*, 1981.

5.951 **Anderson**, D., 'Blundell's Wigan Collieries' (Parts, I, II, III), *T.H.S.L.C.*, CXVI, 1964, 69–115; 117, 1965, 109–43: 119, 1967, 113–79.

5.952 **Ashton**, T. S. and Sykes, J., *The Coal Industry of the Eighteenth Century*, 1929, 2nd rev. ed., 1964, with additions to the bibliography, 255–62.

5.953 **Ashworth**, W., *The History of the British Coal Industry. V: The Nationalised Industry, 1946–82*, 1986.

5.953a **Atkinson**, F., *The Great Northern Coalfield, 1700–1900. Illustrated Notes on the Durham and Northumberland Coalfield*, 1966.

5.954 **Banks**, A. G. and Schofield, R. B., *Brindley at Wet Earth Colliery: An Engineering Study*, 1968. Reconstruction of James Brindley's work at a colliery near Manchester.

5.955 **Benson**, J. and Neville, R. G., eds., *Studies in the Yorkshire Coal Industry*, 1976.

5.956 **Bulley**, J. A., ' "To Mendip for coal": A Study of the Somerset Coalfield before 1830', *Proc.Somerset Arch & Nat.H.Soc.*, Part I, XCVII, 1952, 46–78; Part II, XCVIII, 1953, 46–78.

5.957 **Bulmer**, M., ed., *Mining and Social Change. Durham County in the Twentieth Century*, 1977.

5.958 **Buxton**, N. K., *The Economic Development of the British Coal Industry from Industrial Revolution to the Present Day*, 1978.

5.959 **Church**, R. A. with Hall, A. and Kanefsky, J., *The History of the British Coal Industry. III: 1830–1913. Victorian Pre-eminence*, 1986. A statistical study which reassesses production, productivity, and profits. Less satisfactory on the social aspects. *See also* (5.953), (5.965), (5.973).

5.960 **Cromar**, P., 'The coal industry on Tyneside 1715–60', *Northern H.*, XIV, 1978, 193–207.

5.961 **Dintenfass**, M., 'Entrepreneurial failure reconsidered; the case of the interwar British coal industry', *Bus.H.R.*, LXII, 1988, 1–34.

5.962 **Down**, C. G. and Warrington, A. J., *The History of the Somerset Coalfield*, 1971.

5.963 **Duckham**, B. F. and H., *Great Pit Disasters: Great Britain 1700 to the Present Day*, 1973.

5.964 **Fine**, B., *The Coal Question. Political Economy and Industrial Change from the Nineteenth Century to the Present Day*, 1990. Considers some of the controversial aspects of this subject including amalgamations, cartels, mechanisation, the royalties debate, and the question of productivity.

5.965 **Flinn**, M. W. and Stoker, D., eds., *History of the British Coal Industry. II: 1700–1830*, 1984. *See also* (5.953), (5.959), (5.973).

5.966 **Fraser-Stephen**, Elspet, *Two Centuries in*

the London Coal Trade: The Story of Charringtons, 1950.

5.967 **Griffin**, A. R., *Mining in the East Midlands, 1550–1947*, 1971. Deals with production and unionism.

5.968 **Hughes**, E., 'The coal trade', in *North Country Life in the Eighteenth Century: The North East, 1700–1750*, 1952, 151–257.

5.969 —— 'The collieries' and 'The coal trade'. In *North Country Life in the Eighteenth Century: Cumberland and Westmorland, 1700–1830*, 1965, 133–99.

5.970 **Kirby**, M. W., *The British Coalmining Industry, 1870–1946: A Political and Economic History*, 1977.

5.971 **Mitchell**, B. R., *Economic Development of the British Coal Industry, 1800–1914*, 1984. Utilising evidence drawn from coal companies, inspectors' reports and royal commissions, the author surveys the growing scale and complexity of the coal industry.

5.972 **Mott**, R. A., 'The London and Newcastle chaldron for measuring coal', *Arch.Aeliana*, 4th ser., XL, 1962, 227–39.

5.973 **Supple**, B., *The History of the British Coal Industry. IV: 1913–1946*, 1987. Part of the official history. See also (5.953), (5.959), (5.965).

5.974 **Sweezy**, P. M., *Monopoly and Competition in the English Coal Trade, 1550–1850*, Cambridge, Mass., 1938.

5.975 **Taylor**, A. J., 'The coal industry'. In Aldcroft, ed. (5.184), 37–70.

5.976 —— 'Combination in the mid-eighteenth-century coal industry', *T.R.H.S.*, 5th ser., III, 1953, 23–39.

5.977 —— 'Labour productivity and technological innovation in the British coal industry, 1850–1914', *Ec.H.R.*, 2nd ser., XIV, 1961, 48–70.

5.978 —— 'The third marquis of Londonderry and the north-eastern coal trade', *Durham University J.*, 1955, 21–7.

5.979 —— 'The Wigan coalfield in 1851', *T.H.S.L.C.*, 106, 1954, 117–26.

5.980 **Waller**, R. J., *The Dukeries Transformed. The Social and Political Development of a Twentieth-Century Coalfield*, 1983. An excellent study of the new coalfield in East Nottinghamshire and its social ramifications.

5.981 **Warwick**, D. and Littlejohn, G., *Coal, Capital and Culture. A Sociological Analysis of Mining Communities in West Yorkshire*, 1992. Looks at the nature of community and social networks in the mining districts of West Yorkshire and draws on surveys and oral history.

5.982 **White**, A. W. A., *Men and Mining in Warwickshire*, 1970.

5.983 **Wood**, O., 'A Cumberland colliery during the Napoleonic War', *Economica*, XXI, 1954, 54–63.

(g) Engineering

5.984 **Armytage**, W. H. G., *A Social History of Engineering*, 1st ed. 1961, 3rd rev. ed., 1969.

5.985 **Baker**, E. C., *Sir William Preece F.R.S. Victorian Engineer Extraordinary*, 1976. Spans the era from railways to radio.

5.986 **Boucher**, C. T. G., *James Brindley, Engineer, 1716–1772*, 1968.

5.987 —— *John Rennie, 1761–1821: The Life and Work of a Great Engineer*, 1963.

5.988 **Bracegirdle**, B. and Miles, Patricia H., *Thomas Telford*, 1973.

5.989 **Clements**, P., *Marc Isambard Brunel, 1769–1849*, 1970.

5.990 **Dougan**, D., *The Great Gun Maker*, 1971. A biography of Sir William, later Lord, Armstrong.

5.991 **Farnie**, D. A., 'Platt Bros. & Co. Ltd. of Oldham, machine makers to Lancashire and to the World. An index of production of cotton spinning spindles, 1880–1914', *Bus.H.*, XXIII, 1981, 84–87.

5.992 **Floud**, R., *The British Machine Tool Industry, 1850–1914*, 1976. A quantitative approach which discusses the structure, efficiency and productivity of the industrry and its place in international trade.

5.993 **Harris**, T. R., *Arthur Woolf: The Cornish Engineer, 1766–1837*, 1966.

5.994 **McNeil**, I., *Joseph Bramah: A Century of Invention, 1749–1851*, 1968.

5.995 **Malster**, R., 'The rise of an industry. Suffolk agricultural machinery makers in the nineteenth century and after', *Suffolk Rev.*, XIII, 1989, 19–32.

5.996 **Rolt**, L. T. C., *Great Engineers*, 1962. Short studies of A. Darby, T. Newcomen, W. Jessop, M. Murray, H. Maudslay, J. Locke, J. Fowler, B. Baker, R. E. Crompton and F. W. Lanchester.

5.997 —— *Thomas Telford*, 1958.

5.998 —— *Tools for the Job: A Short History of Machine Tools*, 1965.

5.999 —— *Victorian Engineering*, 1970.

5.1000 —— *Waterloo Ironworks: A History of Taskers of Andover, 1809–1968*, 1969.

5.1001 **Ruddock**, T., *Arch Bridges and their Builders, 1735–1835*, 1979.

5.1002 **Saul**, S. B., 'The machine tool industry in Britain to 1914', *Bus.H.*, X, 1968, 22–43.

5.1003 —— 'The market and the development of the mechanical engineering industries in Britain, 1860–1914', *Ec.H.R.*, 2nd ser., XX, 1967, 111–30.

5.1004 **Scott**, J. D., *Siemens Brothers, 1858–1958: An Essay in the History of Industry*, 1958.

5.1005 **Semler**, E. G., ed., *Engineering Heritage*, 2 vols, 1963, 1966. Short biographies of eminent British engineers and industrial innovators.

5.1006 **Todd**, A. C., *Beyond the Blaze: A Biography of Davies Gilbert*, 1967.

5.1007 **Wilson**, C. and Reader, W. J., *Men and Machines: A History of D. Napier & Son, Engineers, Limited, 1808–1958*, 1958. *See also* Burstall (1.307).

(h) Chemicals, soap and salt

5.1008 **Barker**, T. C., 'Lancashire coal, Cheshire salt and the rise of Liverpool', *T.H.S.L.C.*, CIII, 1951, 83–101.

5.1009 **Bolitho**, H., *Alfred Mond, First Lord Melchett*, 1933.

5.1010 **Clow**, A. and Nan L., *The Chemical Revolution: A Contribution to Social Technology*, 1952.

5.1011 **Cohen**, J. M., *The Life of Ludwig Mond*, 1956.

5.1012 **Davenport-Hines**, R. P. T. and Slinn, J., *Glaxo. A History to 1962*, 1992.

5.1013 **Fieldhouse**, D. K., *Unilever Overseas. The Anatomy of a Multinational, 1895–1965*, 1978.

5.1014 **Haber**, L. F., *The Chemical Industry During the Nineteenth Century: A Study of the Economic Aspect of Applied Chemistry in Europe and North America*, 1958.

5.1015 —— *The Chemical Industry, 1900–1930: International Growth and Technological Change*, 1971.

5.1016 **Hardie**, D. W. F., *A History of the Chemical Industry in Widnes*, 1950.

5.1017 —— and Pratt, J. D., *A History of the Modern British Chemical Industry*, 1966.

5.1018 **Iredale**, D. A., 'John and Thomas Marshall and the Society for improving

the British Salt Trade', *Ec.H.R.*, 2nd ser., XX, 1967, 79–93.

5.1019 —— 'The rise and fall of the Marshalls of Northwich, salt proprietors, 1720–1917', *T.H.S.L.C.*, CXVII, 1965, 59–82.

5.1020 **Koss**, S. E., *Sir John Brunner, Radical Plutocrat, 1842–1919*, 1970.

5.1021 **Musson**, A. E., *Entreprise in Soap and Chemicals: Joseph Crosfield and Sons, Ltd., 1815–1865*, 1965. The soap industry in Warrington.

5.1022 **Padley**, R., 'The beginnings of the British alkali industry', *Birm.H.J.*, III, 1951, 64–78.

5.1023 **Pettigrew**, A., *The Awakening Giant. Continuity and Change in ICI*, 1985. Concentrates on the period 1960 to 1983 analysing changes in strategy, structure, technology and industrial relations.

5.1024 **Reader**, W. J., *Imperial Chemical Industries: A History. I: The Forerunners, 1870–1926*, 1970. Excellent bibliography, 524–34. II: *The First Quarter Century 1926–52*, 1975.

5.1025 —— *Fifty Years of Unilever, 1930–80*, 1980.

5.1026 **Warren**, K., *Chemical Foundations: The Alkali Industry in Britain to 1926*, 1980.

5.1027 **Wilson**, C., *The History of Unilever: A Study in Economic Growth and Social Change*, 2 vols, 1954.

5.1028 —— *Unilever, 1945–1965: Challenge and Response in the Post-war Industrial Revolution*, 1968.

5.1029 —— *Management and Policy in Large-Scale Enterprise. Lever Brothers and Unilever, 1918–38*, 1977. For other material on the salt industry *see* Calvert (5.543) and Chaloner (4.544).

(i) Pottery

5.1030 **Barton**, R. M., *A History of the Cornish China-clay Industry*, 1966.

5.1031 **Bladen**, V. W., 'The Potteries in the Industrial Revolution', *Ec. J.Ec.H.Supp.* I, 1926, 117–30.

5.1032 **Hower**, R. M., 'The Wedgwoods: ten generations of potters', *J.Ec. & Bus.H.*, IV, 1932, 281–313; 665–90.

5.1033 **Mackenzie**, C., *The House of Coalport, 1750–1950*, 1951.

5.1034 **Rolt**, L. T. C., *Potters' Field: A History of the South Devon Ball Clay Industry*, 1974.

5.1035 **Thomas**, J., 'The pottery industry and the Industrial Revolution', *Ec.J.Ec.H.Supp.*, III, 1937, 399–414.
5.1036 —— *The Rise of the Staffordshire Potteries*, 1971.
5.1037 **Weatherill**, Lorna, *The Pottery Trade and North Staffordshire, 1660–1760*, 1971.
5.1038 **Whiter**, L., *Spode: A History of the Family, Factory and Wares from 1733 to 1833*, 1970.

(j) Glass

5.1039 **Barker**, T. C., *The Glassmakers. Pilkington: The Rise of an International Company, 1826–1976*, 1977. A substantially enlarged and updated version of a business history first published in 1960. Almost half the book is devoted to the period after 1914.
5.1040 **Harris**, J. R., 'Origins of the St. Helens glass industry', *Northern H.*, III, 1968, 105–17.
5.1041 **Louw**, H., 'Window glass making in Britain, c.1660–1860 and its architectural impact', *Construction H.*, VII, 1991, 47–68.

(k) Rubber

5.1042 **Jones**, G., 'The growth and performance of British multinational firms before 1939: the case of Dunlop', *Ec.H.R.*, 2nd ser., XXXVII, 1984, 35–53.
5.1043 **Levitt**, S., 'Manchester mackintoshes. A history of the rubberised garment trade in Manchester', *Textile H.*, XVII, 1986, 51–70.
5.1044 **Payne**, P. L., *Rubber and Railways in the Nineteenth Century: A Study of the Spencer Papers*, 1961.
5.1045 **Schidrowitz**, P., and Dawson, T. R., eds., *History of the Rubber Industry*, 1952.
5.1046 **Woodruff**, W., *The Rise of the British Rubber Industry During the Nineteenth Century*, 1958.

(l) Paper

5.1047 **Hills**, R. L., *Papermaking in Britain, 1488–1988. A Short History*, 1988.
5.1048 **Reader**, W. J., *Bowater. A History*, 1981. Written to commemorate the centenery of this giant paper-making concern.
5.1049 **Shorter**, A. H., *Paper Making in the British Isles*, 1971. *See* Coleman (4.551) and Shorter (4.552).

(m) Printing and publishing

5.1050 **Black**, M. H., *Cambridge University Press, 1584–1984*, 1984.
5.1051 **Briggs**, A., *Essays in the History of Publishing*, 1974. Includes essays on copyright and on the paperback revolution.
5.1052 **Carter**, H., *A History of the Oxford University Press*. I: *To the Year 1780*, 1975.
5.1053 **Clair**, C., *A History of Printing in Britain*, 1965.
5.1054 **Handover**, P. M., *Printing in London from 1476 to Modern Times*, 1960.
5.1055 **Hunt**, C. J., *The Book Trade in Northumberland and Durham to 1860*, 1975.
5.1056 **Plant**, Marjorie, *The English Book Trade*, 1939. Reprinted 1974.
5.1057 **Roberts**, S. C., *The Evolution of Cambridge Publishing*, 1956.
5.1058 **St John**, J., *William Heinemann. A Century of Publishing, 1890–1990*, 1990.

(n) Shipping and shipbuilding

(i) GENERAL

5.1059 **Burton**, V., ed., *Liverpool Shipping, Trade and Industry. Essays on the Maritime History of Merseyside, 1780–1860*, 1989.
5.1060 **Coleman**, T., *The Liners*, 1976.
5.1061 **Davies**, P. N., *Sir Alfred Jones: Shipping Entrepreneur par excellence*, 1978.
5.1062 —— *The Trade Makers: Elder Dempster in West Africa, 1852–1972*, 1973.
5.1063 **Fisher**, H. E. S., ed., *West Country Maritime and Social History: Some Essays*, 1980.
5.1064 **Hyde**, F. E., *Cunard and the North Atlantic*, 1975.
5.1065 —— *Shipping Enterprise and Management 1830–1939: Harrisons of Liverpool*, 1967.
5.1066 —— and Harris, J. R., *Blue Funnel: A History of Alfred Holt and Company of Liverpool, 1865–1914*, 1956.
5.1067 **Jackson**, G., *The Trade and Shipping of Eighteenth-Century Hull*, E. Yorks.Loc.H.Soc., XXI, 1975.

5.1068 —— *The Whaling Trade*, 1978.
5.1069 **Jarvis**, R. C., 'Eighteenth-century London shipping'. In Hollaender and Kellaway (2.360).
5.1070 **John**, A. H., *A Liverpool Merchant House, Being the History of Alfred Booth and Company, 1863–1958*, 1959.
5.1071 **Kirkaldy**, A. W., *British Shipping; Its History, Organisation and Importance*, 1914. Excellent treatment; useful on shipping conferences, Lloyd's Register and marine insurance, bibliography, XIII–XX.
5.1072 **Marriner**, Sheila, *Rathbones of Liverpool, 1845–73*, 1961. The China trade.
5.1073 —— and Hyde, F. E., *The Senior: John Samuel Swire, 1825–98: Management in Far Eastern Shipping Trade*, 1967.
5.1074 **Matthews**, K. and Panting, G., eds., *Ships and Shipbuilding in the North Atlantic Region*, 1978.
5.1075 **Murray**, M., *Union Castle Chronicle, 1853–1953*, 1953.
5.1076 **Sturmey**, S. G., *British Shipping and World Competition*, 1962.
5.1077 **Syrett**, D., *Shipping and the American War, 1775–83: A Study of British Transport Organisation*, 1970.
5.1078 **Ville**, S. P., *English Shipowning during the Industrial Revolution. Michael Henley & Son, London Shipowners, 1770–1830*, 1987. A case study made possible by the rich archives of an individual company. Chapters deal with the emergence of professional shipowning, capital accumulation, ship construction, masters and crews.
5.1079 —— 'The growth of specialisation in English shipowning, 1780–1850', *Ec.H.R.*, 2nd ser., XLVI, 1993, 702–22.

(ii) PERSONNEL

5.1080 **Carew**, A., *The Lower Deck of the Royal Navy, 1900–39. Invergordon in Perspective*, 1982.
5.1081 **Course**, A. G., *The Merchant Navy: A Social History*, 1963.
5.1082 **Grandish**, S., *The Manning of the British Navy during the Seven Years' War*, 1980.
5.1083 **Kemp**, P., *The British Sailor: A Social History of the Lower Deck*, 1971.
5.1084 **Lewis**, M., *A Social History of the Navy (1793–1815)*, 1960.
5.1085 **Lloyd**, C., *The Nation and the Navy: A History of Naval Life and Policy*, 2nd rev. ed., 1961.
5.1086 **Rasor**, E. L., *Reform in the Royal Navy. A Social History of the Lower Deck, 1850–80*, Hamden, Conn., 1977.

(iii) STEAM

5.1087 **Hughes**, J. R. T. and Reiter, S., 'The first 1945 British steamships', *J.American Stat.Ass.*, 53, 1958, 360–81. *See* however, *T.L.S.*, 29 September, 13 and 27 October 1966.
5.1088 **Moyse Bartlett**, H., *From Sail to Steam*, Hist.Ass. pamphlet, 1946.
5.1089 **Spratt**, H. P., *The Birth of the Steamboat*, 1958.
5.1090 **Tyler**, D. B., *Steam Conquers the Atlantic*, N. Y. 1939.

(iv) SHIPBUILDING

5.1091 **Dougan**, D., *The History of North East Shipbuilding*, 1968.
5.1092 **Jones**, L., *Shipbuilding in Britain, Mainly Between the two World Wars*, 1957. Chapter I is on the nineteenth century, but contains a number of inaccuracies.
5.1093 **Lorenz**, E. H., *Economic Decline in Britain. The Shipbuilding Industry, 1890–1970*, 1991.
5.1094 **Morriss**, R., *The Royal Dockyards during the Revolutionary and Napoleonic Wars*, 1983.
5.1095 **Pollard**, S. and Robertson, P., *The British Shipbuilding Industry, 1870–1914*, Harvard, 1979. A comprehensive history dealing with the organisation and geography of the industry, with labour and labour relations, wages and productivity, and with state intervention.
5.1096 **Scott**, J. D., *Vickers: A History*, 1962.
5.1097 **Trebilcock**, C., *The Vickers Brothers. Armaments and Enterprise, 1854–1914*, 1977.

(o) Building

5.1098 **Bowley**, Marian, *The British Building Industry: Four Studies in Response to Resistance and Change*, 1969. Covers the twentieth century.
5.1099 —— *Housing and the State, 1919–1944*,

1946.

5.1100 —— *Innovations in Building Materials*, 1960.

5.1101 **Brown**, Joyce M., 'W. B. Wilkinson (1819–1902) and his place in the history of reinforced concrete', *Trans.Newcomen Soc.*, XXXIX, 1966–7, 129–42.

5.1102 **Cooney**, E. W., 'The origins of the Victorian master builders', *Ec.H.R.*, 2nd ser., VIII, 1955–6, 167–76.

5.1103 —— 'Long waves in building in the British economy of the nineteenth century'. In Aldcroft and Fearon (5.381), 220–35.

5.1104 **Davey**, N., *Building in Britain: The Growth and Organisation of Building Processes in Britain from Roman times to the Present Day*, 1964.

5.1105 —— *A History of Building Materials*, 1961.

5.1106 **Francis**, A. T., *The Cement Industry, 1796–1914. A History*, 1978.

5.1107 **Habakkuk**, H. J., 'Fluctuations in house-building in Britain and the United States in the nineteenth century'. In Aldcroft and Fearon (5.381), 236–67.

5.1108 **Hobhouse**, Hermione, *Thomas Cubitt, Master Builder*, 1971.

5.1109 **Lewis**, J. P., *Building Cycles and Britain's Growth*, 1965. Covers period from 1700 to the present.

5.1110 **Lloyd**, N., *A History of English Brickwork from Mediaeval Times to the End of the Georgian Period*, 1925.

5.1111 **Middlemas**, R. K., *The Master Builders: Thomas Brassey; Sir John Aird; Lord Cowdray; Sir John Norton-Griffiths*, 1963.

5.1112 **Powell**, C. G., *An Economic History of the British Building Industry, 1815–1979*, 1980. A popular approach combining the approaches of the architectural and social historian.

5.1113 **Richardson**, H. W. and Aldcroft, D. H., *Building in Britain Between the Wars*, 1968.

5.1114 **Saul**, S. B., 'House building in England, 1890–1914', *Ec.H.R.*, 2nd ser., XV, 1962–3, 119–37.

5.1115 **Skempton**, A. W., 'Portland cements, 1843–1887', *Trans.Newcomen.Soc.*, XXXV, 1964, 117–52.

(p) Fishing

5.1116 **Dunlop**, T., *The British Fisheries Society, 1786–1893*, 1978.

5.1117 **Gray**, M., 'Organisation and growth in the East-coast herring fishing, 1800–1885', in Payne (7.296), 187–216.

5.1118 **Lummis**, T., *Occupation and Society. The East Anglian Fishermen, 1880–1914*, 1985.

5.1119 **Robinson**, R., *A History of the Yorkshire Coast Fishing Industry, 1780–1914*, 1987.

5.1120 **Stern**, W., 'Fish supplies for London in the 1760s: an experiment in overland transport', parts I and II, *J.Roy.Soc. Arts*, CXVIII, 1970, 360–5, 430–5. *See also* Cutting (4.566).

(q) Food and drink

5.1121 **Blackman**, Janet, 'The food supply of an industrial town: a study of Sheffield's public markets, 1780–1900', *Bus.H.*, V, 1963, 82–97.

5.1122 **Briggs**, A., *Wine for Sale. Victoria Wine and the Liquor Trade, 1860–1984*, 1985. Has more to say about wine drinking than about the company.

5.1123 **Brown**, J., *Steeped in Tradition. The Malting Industry in England since the Railway Age*, 1983.

5.1124 **Chalmin**, P., *The Making of a Sugar Giant. Tate and Lyle, 1859–1989*, 1990.

5.1125 **Chivers**, K., 'Henry Jones *versus* the Admiralty', *H.Today*, X, 1960, 247–54. The invention of self-raising flour.

5.1126 **Corley**, T. E. B., *Quaker Enterprise in Biscuits: Huntley and Palmers of Reading, 1822–1972*, 1972.

5.1127 **Curtis-Bennett**, N., *The Food of the People: Being the History of Industrial Feeding*, 1949.

5.1128 **Deerr**, N., *The History of Sugar*, 2 vols., 1949–50.

5.1129 **Forrest**, D. M., *A Hundred Years of Ceylon Tea, 1867–1967*, 1967

5.1130 **French**, R. V., *Nineteen Centuries of Drink in England*, 1886.

5.1131 **Hugill**, A., *Sugar and All That. A History of Tate and Lyle*, 1978.

5.1132 **Mathias**, P., *The Brewing Industry in England 1700–1830*, 1959.

5.1133 **Perren**, R., 'Structural change and market growth in the food industry: flour milling in Britain, Europe and America, 1850–1914', *Ec.H.R.*, 2nd ser., XLIII, 1990, 420–37.

5.1134 **Sigsworth**, E. M., *The Brewing Trade During the Industrial Revolution: The Case of Yorkshire*, 1967.

5.1135 **Stuyvenberg**, J. H. van, ed., *Margarine; An Economic, Social and Scientific History, 1869–1969*, 1969.

5.1136 **Twining**, S., *The House of Twining, 1706–1956*, 1956. Tea and coffee.

5.1137 **Vaizey**, J., *The Brewing Industry, 1886–1951: An Economic Study*, 1960.

5.1138 **Webber**, R., *Covent Garden: Mud Salad Market*, 1969.

5.1139 **Whiteway**, E. V. N., *Whiteways Cider. A Company History*, 1990.

5.1140 **Williams**, K., *The Story of Typhoo and the Birmingham Tea Industry*, 1990.

(r) Miscellaneous

5.1141 **Alford**, B. W. E., *W. D. and H. O. Wills and the Development of the U.K. Tobacco Trade, 1786–1965*, 1973.

5.1142 **Bartlett**, J. N., *Carpeting the Millions. The Growth of Britain's Carpet Industry, c. 1740–1970*, 1978.

5.1143 **Brace**, H. W., *History of Seed Crushing in Great Britain*, 1960.

5.1144 **Bythell**, D., *The Sweated Trades: Outwork in Nineteenth-Century Britain*, 1978.

5.1145 **Chapman**, S. D., *Jesse Boot of Boots the Chemists*, 1974.

5.1146 **Hayward**, K., *The British Aircraft Industry*, 1989.

5.1147 **Hogg**, O. F. G., *The Royal Arsenal: its Background, Origin and Subsequent History*, 2 vols., 1963.

5.1148 **Jones**, G., 'The Gramophone Company: An Anglo-American Multinational, 1898–1931', *Bus.H.R.*, LIX, 1985, 76–100.

5.1149 **Satre**, L. J., 'After the matchgirls' strike. Bryant and May in the 1890s', *Victorian Studs.*, XXVI, 1982, 7–32.

5.1150 **Weiss**, L., *Watchmaking in England*, 1982.

THE FACTORY SYSTEM AND FACTORY LEGISLATION

5.1151 **Fielden**, J., *The Curse of the Factory System*, 1st ed., 1836, 2nd ed., 1969, with introduction by J. T. Ward. The introduction is the best life of Fielden.

5.1152 **Gaskell**, P., *Artisans and Machinery: The Moral and Physical Condition of the Manufacturing Population Considered with Reference to Mechanical Substitutes for Human Labour*, 1836. Reprinted 1968.

5.1153 **Taylor**, W. Cooke, *Notes of a Tour in the Manufacturing Districts of Lancashire*, 1841, 2nd ed., 1842, 3rd ed., 1968.

5.1154 **Ure**, A., *The Philosophy of Manufactures*, 1st ed., 1835, 3rd ed. 1961. Reprint of 1st ed., 1967.

5.1155 **Wing**, C., *Evils of the Factory System Demonstrated by Parliamentary Evidence*, 1837. Reprinted 1967. A summary of the Parliamentary Papers and debates.

5.1156 **Bartrip**, P., 'Success or failure? The prosecution of the early Factory Acts', *Ec.H.R.*, 2nd ser., XXXVIII, 1985, 423–27.

5.1157 **Blaug**, M., 'The classical economists and the Factory Acts – a re-examination'. In Coats (5.2526), 104–22.

5.1158 **Cowherd**, R. G., *The Humanitarians and the Ten Hour Movement in England*, Boston, Mass., 1956. Should be used with caution.

5.1159 **Djang**, T. K., *Factory Inspection in Great Britain*, 1942.

5.1160 **Driver**, C., Tory Radical: *The Life of Richard Oastler*, N. Y., 1946.

5.1161 **Henriques**, Ursula R. Q., *The Early Factory Acts and their Enforcement*, Hist.Ass. pamphlet, 1971.

5.1162 **Joyce**, P., *Work, Society and Politics. The Culture of the Factory in later Victorian England*, 1980. Relates the political power of the factory-owners to their economic and social leadership in the mill towns and explores the different ways in which this élite influenced the culture of their workforce.

5.1163 **Lee**, W. R., 'Robert Baker, the first doctor in the factory department' (Part I 1803–1858; Part II: 1958 onwards), *Brit.J.Indust.Med.*, XXI, 1964, 85–93, 167–79.

5.1164 **Martin**, Bernice, 'Leonard Horner: a portrait of an inspector of factories', *Internat.R.Soc.H.*, XIV, 1969, 412–43.

5.1165 **Muter**, W. G., *The Buildings of an Industrial Community: Coalbrookdale and Ironbridge*, 1979.

5.1166 **Richards**, J. M., *The Functional Tradition in Early Industrial Buildings*, 1958.

5.1167 **Sorenson**, L. R., 'Some classical economists, *laissez-faire* and the Factory Acts', *J.Ec.H.*, XII, 1952, 247–62.

5.1168 **Tann**, Jennifer, *The Development of the Factory*, 1970.

5.1169 **Thomas**, M. W., *The Early Factory Legislation: A Study in Legislative and Administrative Evolution*, 1948. Covers the period 1802–53 in some detail.

5.1170 **Walker**, K. O., 'The classical economists and the factory Acts', *J.Ec.H.*, I, 1941, 168–77. Takes the question to 1833.

5.1171 **Ward**, J. T., *The Factory Movement, 1830–1855*, 1962.

5.1172 **Winter**, J., *Industrial Architecture*, 1970. A study of early factories. *See also* Berg (5.28) and Chapman (5.816).

OVERSEAS TRADE AND OVERSEAS INVESTMENT

(a) General and statistical

5.1173 **Britton**, A., *The Trade Cycle in Britain, 1958–82*, 1986.

5.1174 **Clark**, G. N., *Guide to English Commercial Statistics, 1696–1782*, 1938.

5.1175 **Croft**, Pauline, 'The rise of the English stocking export trade', *Textile H.*, XVIII, 1987, 3–16.

5.1176 **Crowhurst**, P., *The Defence of British Trade 1689–1815*, 1877.

5.1177 **Davis**, R., 'English foreign trade, 1700–1774', *Ec.H.R.*, 2nd ser., XV, 1962.

5.1178 —— *The Industrial Revolution and British Overseas Trade*, 1978.

5.1179 **Donaldson**, Frances, *The British Council. The First Fifty Years*, 1984. Looks at the strengths and weaknesses of this well-known image-projecting organisation.

5.1180 **Ehrman**, J., *The British Government and Commercial Negotiations with Europe, 1783–1793*, 1962.

5.1181 **Fawcett**, T., 'Argonauts and commercial travellers: the foreign marketing of Norwich stuffs in the later eighteenth century', *Textile H.*, XVI, 1985, 151–82.

5.1182 **Fisher**, S., *Studies in British Privateering, Trading Enterprise and Seamen's Welfare,*

1775–1900, 1987.

5.1183 **Harley**, C., 'Ocean freight rates and productivity, 1740–1913: the primacy of mechanical innovation reaffirmed', *J.Ec.H.*, XLVIII, 1988, 851–76.

5.1184 **Heckscher**, E. F., *The Continental System: An Economic Interpretation*, 1922.

5.1185 **Henderson**, W. O., 'The Anglo-French Commercial Treaty of 1786', *Ec.H.R.*, 2nd ser., X, 1957, 104–12.

5.1186 **Hoon**, Elizabeth E., *The Organisation of the English Customs System, 1699–1786*, N. Y., 1938.

5.1187 **Olson**, M., *The Economics of the War-time Shortage: A History of British Food Supplies in the Napoleonic war and in World Wars I and II*, Durham, N. C., 1963.

5.1188 **Porter**, B., *Britain, Europe and the World, 1850–1982*, 1983.

5.1189 **Schlote**, W., *British Overseas Trade from 1700 to the 1930s*, 1952. English translation of a German book published in 1938; bibliography of books and articles since 1938, v–vi.

5.1190 **Schumpeter**, Elizabeth, *English Overseas Trade Statistics, 1697–1808*, 1960. With an introduction by T. S. Ashton.

5.1191 **Schuyler**, R. L., *The Fall of the Old Colonial System: A Study in British Free Trade, 1770–1870*, N. Y., 1945. Useful bibliography, 327–43.

5.1192 **Sherwig**, J. M., *Guineas and Gunpowder: British Foreign Aid in the Wars with France*, Cambridge, Mass., 1969.

5.1193 **Starkey**, D. J., *British Privateering Enterprise in the Eighteenth Century*, 1990.

5.1194 **Taylor**, P. M., *The Projection of Britain. British Overseas Publicity and Propaganda, 1919–39*, 1981.

5.1195 **Williams**, Judith B., *British Commercial Policy and Trade Expansion, 1750–1850*, 1972.

(b) Trade with specific areas up to 1815

5.1196 **Armytage**, Frances, *The Free Port System in the British West Indies: A Study in Commercial Policy, 1766–1822*, 1953.

5.1197 **Astrom**, S. E., 'Britain's timber imports from the Baltic, 1775–1830: some new figures and viewpoints', *Scand.Ec.H.R.*, XXXVII, 1989, 57–71.

5.1198 **Clendenning**, P., 'The Anglo-Russian

trade treaty of 1776 – an example of eighteenth century power group interests', *J.Eur.Ec.H.*, XIX, 1990, 475–520.

5.1199 **Crouzet**, F., *L'Economie britannique et le blocus continental (1806–13)*, 2 vols., Paris, 1958.

5.1200 **Davis**, R., *Aleppo and Devonshire Square: English Traders in the Levant in the Eighteenth Century*, 1967.

5.1201 **Farnie**, D. A., 'The commercial empire of the Atlantic, 1607–1783', *Ec.H.R.*, 2nd ser., XV, 1962, 205–18.

5.1202 **Fisher**, H. E. S., *The Portugal Trade: A Study of Anglo-Portuguese Commerce, 1700–1770*, 1971. Excellent bibliography, 153–62.

5.1203 **Gill**, C., *Merchants and Mariners in the Eighteenth Century*, 1961. Based on the papers of Thomas Hall, 1692–1748.

5.1204 **Kent**, H. S. K., *War and Trade in the Northern Seas. Anglo-Scandinavian Economic Relations in the mid-eighteenth Century*, 1973.

5.1205 **Marshall**, P. J., *East India Fortunes. The British in Bengal in the Eighteenth Century*, 1976.

5.1206 **Morgan**, K., 'Bristol and the Atlantic trade in the eighteenth century', *E.H.R.*, CVII, 1992, 626–50.

5.1207 **Pares**, R., *Merchants and Planters*, 1960. The anatomy of the colonial trade.

5.1208 —— *War and Trade in the West Indies, 1739–1763*, 1936. Reprinted 1963.

5.1209 —— *A West India Fortune*, 1950. The Pinneys of Bristol.

5.1210 **Parkinson**, C. N., *Trade in the Eastern Seas, 1793–1813*, 1937.

5.1211 **Price**, J. M. and Clemens, P. E., 'A revolution of scale in overseas trade: British firms in the Chesapeake trade, 1675–1775', *J.Ec.H.*, XLVII, 1987, 1–43.

5.1211a **Rediker**, M., *Between the Devil and the Deep Blue Sea. Merchant Seamen, Pirates, and the Anglo-American Maritime World, 1700–1750*, 1988. Analyses the social origins of the merchant navy and its plebeian culture.

5.1212 **Shillington**, V. M. and Chapman, A. B. W., *The Commercial Relations of England and Portugal*, 1907.

5.1212a **Sutherland**, Lucy S., *A London Merchant, 1695–1774*, (William Braund), 1933. Reprinted 1962.

5.1213 **Wilson**, C., *Anglo-Dutch Commerce and Finance in the Eighteenth Century*, 1941.

5.1214 **Yogev**, G., *Diamonds and Coral: Anglo-Dutch Jews and Eighteenth-Century Trade*, 1978.

(c) The repeal of the corn laws, the free trade era and after

(i) THE REPEAL OF THE CORN LAWS AND THE COMING OF FREE TRADE

5.1215 **Barnes**, D. G., *A History of the English Corn Laws from 1660–1846*, 1930. Useful statistical tables, 297–302, and excellent bibliography, 303–31.

5.1216 **Brown**, Lucy M., *The Board of Trade and the Free Trade Movement, 1830–42*, 1958.

5.1217 **Chaloner**, W. H., 'The agitation against the Corn Laws'. In Ward (5.2080), 135–48. Bibliographical notes, 149–51.

5.1218 **Grampp**, W. D., *The Manchester School of Economics*, 1960. Good bibliography, 139–49, inferior text.

5.1219 **Hyde**, F. E., *Mr Gladstone at the Board of Trade*, 1934.

5.1220 **Imlah**, A. H., 'The fall of protection in Britain'. In D. E. Lee and G. E. McReynolds, eds., *Essays in History and International Relations in Honor of G. H. Blakeslee*, Worcester, Mass., 1949, 306–20.

5.1221 **McCord**, N., *The Anti-Corn Law League, 1838–1846*, 1958. Important study based on private papers of Cobden and George Wilson.

5.1222 **Nye**, J. V., 'The myth of free trade Britain and fortress France: tariffs and trade in the nineteenth century', *J.Ec.H.*, LI, 1991, 23–46.

5.1223 **Prouty**, R., *The Tranformation of the Board of Trade, 1830–1855: A Study of Administrative Reorganization in the Heyday of Laissez-faire*, 1957.

5.1224 **Read**, D., *Cobden and Bright: A Victorian Political Partnership*, 1967.

(ii) THE FREE TRADE ERA AND AFTER, 1860–1939

5.1225 **McCord**, N., *Free Trade: Theory and Practice from Adam Smith to Keynes*, 1970. Documents, with commentary.

5.1226 **Turner**, B., *Free Trade and Protection*, 1971. Documents with commentary.

5.1227 **Abel**, D., *A History of British Tariffs, 1923–1942*, 1945.

5.1228 **Brown**, B. H., *The Tariff Reform Movement in Great Britain 1881–1895*, N. Y., 1943.

5.1229 **Dunham**, A. L., *The Anglo-French Treaty of Commerce of 1860 and the Progress of the Industrial Revolution in France*, Ann Arbor, Mich., 1930.

5.1230 **Hutchinson**, H. J., *Tariff-making and Industrial Reconstruction*, 1965. An account of the work of the Import Duties Advisory Committee.

5.1231 **McGuire**, E. B., *The British Tariff System*, 1939. Good on technical points of the working of tariffs.

5.1232 **Richardson**, J. H., *British Economic Foreign Policy*, 1936.

5.1233 **Saul**, S. B., *Studies in British Overseas Trade, 1870–1914*, 1960.

5.1234 **Snyder**, R. K., *The Tariff Problem in Great Britain, 1918–1923*, Stanford University Publications in History, Economics and Political Science, V, No. 2, Stanford, Calif., 1944.

(d) Trade with specific areas after 1815

5.1235 **Buck**, N. S., *The Development of the Organisation of Anglo-American Trade, 1800–1850*, New Haven, Conn., 1925.

5.1236 **Checkland**, Olive, *Britain's Encounter with Meiji Japan, 1868–1912*, 1989.

5.1237 **Davenport-Hines**, R. P. T. and Jones, G., eds., *British Business in Asia since 1860*, 1989.

5.1238 **Davies**, P. N., *Fyffes and the Banana. Musa Sapientum: A Centenary History*, 1990.

5.1239 **Greenberg**, M., *British Trade and the Opening of China, 1800–1842*, 1951.

5.1240 **Hoffman**, R. J. S., *Great Britain and the German Trade Rivalry, 1875–1914*, Philadelphia, 1933.

5.1241 **Hyde**, F. E., *Far Eastern Trade, 1860–1914*, 1973.

5.1242 **Munting**, R., 'Ransomes in Russia: An English Agricultural Engineering Company's trade with Russia to 1917', *Ec.H.R.*, 2nd ser., XXXI, 1978, 257–69.

5.1243 **Platt**, D. C. M., *Latin America and British Trade, 1806–1914*, 1972. Deals with the nature of Latin American markets, the changing pattern of British investment and with the extent of foreign competition.

5.1244 **Redford**, A., *et al.*, *Manchester Merchants and Foreign Trade 1794–1858*, 1934.

5.1245 —— and Clapp, B. W., *Manchester Merchants and Foreign Trade*, II: *1850–1939*, 1956.

5.1246 **Steeds**, D. and Nish, I., *China, Japan and Nineteenth-century Britain*, 1977.

5.1247 **Tolley**, B. H., *Liverpool and the American Cotton Trade*, 1978.

(e) The slave trade

5.1248 **Ashton**, T. S., ed., *Letters of a West African Trader, Edward Grace, 1767–70*, 1950

5.1249 **Richardson**, D., ed., *Bristol, Africa and the Eighteenth Century Slave Trade to America. I: The Years of Expansion, 1698–1729; II: The Years of Ascendancy, 1730–45*, Bristol Rec.Soc., XXXVIII, 1986 and XXXIX, 1987.

5.1250 **Anstey**, R., *The Atlantic Slave Trade and British Abolition, 1710–1810*, 1975.

5.1251 **Coupland**, R. G., *The British Anti-Slavery Movement*, 1933, 2nd ed., with new introduction, 1964.

5.1252 **Eltis**, D., *Economic Growth and the Ending to the Transatlantic Slave Trade*, 1987. Emphasises economic utilitarianism as a factor.

5.1253 **Klein**, H. S., *The Middle Passage. Comparative Studies in the Atlantic Slave Trade*, 1978.

5.1254 **Mackenzie-Grieve**, Averil, *The Last Years of the English Slave Trade. Liverpool, 1750–1807*, 1941. Reprinted with corrections 1968.

5.1255 **Mellor**, G. R., *British Imperial Trusteeship, 1783–1850*, 1951.

5.1256 **Temperley**, H., *British Antislavery, 1833–1870*, 1972.

5.1257 **Walvin**, J., ed., *Slavery and British Society, 1776–1846*, 1982.

5.1258 **Williams**, E., *Capitalism and Slavery*, Chapel Hill, N. C., 1944.

5.1259 —— *British Historians and the West Indies*, 1966. Attempts to rebut Coupland (5.1251) and Mellor (5.1255).

(f) Overseas investment

5.1260 **Bendana**, A., *British Capital and*

Argentine Dependence, 1816–1914, 1988.

5.1261 **Brewer**, J., *The Sinews of Power. War, Money and the English State, 1688–1783*, 1989.

5.1262 **Cairncross**, A. K., *Home and Foreign Investment 1870–1913: Studies in Capital Accumulation*, 1953.

5.1263 **Chapman**, S. D., *The Rise of Merchant Banking*, 1984. Uses the Rothschilds and Barings to open up the subject.

5.1264 **Cottrell**, P. L., *British Overseas Investment in the Nineteenth Century*, 1975.

5.1265 **Dawson**, F. G., *The First Latin American Debt Crisis. The City of London and the 1822–25 Loan Bubble*, New Haven, Conn., 1990.

5.1266 **Edelstein**, M., *Overseas Investment in the Age of High Imperialism*, 1982.

5.1267 **Feis**, H., *Europe, the World's Banker 1870–1914*. New Haven, Conn., 1930. Sections on British overseas investments.

5.1268 **Hall**, A. R., ed., *The Export of Capital from Britain 1870–1914*, 1969. A collection of articles.

5.1269 **Helton**, J. J. V. and Cassis, Y., *Capitalism in a Mature Economy. Financial Institutions, Capital Exports and British Industry, 1870–1939*, 1990. Considers how the long and short term financial needs of industry were served by the banks and by the Stock Exchange.

5.1270 **Jenks**, L. H., *The Migration of British Capital to 1875*, 1927.

5.1271 **Jones**, C. A., 'Great capitalists and the direction of British overseas investment in the late nineteenth century: the case of Argentina', *Bus.H.*, XXII, 1980, 152–69.

5.1272 **Jones**, G., 'Multi-national chocolate: Cadbury overseas, 1918–39', *Bus. H.*, XVI, 1984, 57–75.

5.1273 **Lowe**, R., *The British Treasury. Economic Depression and International Finance, 1916–43*, 1986.

5.1274 **Neal**, L., *The Rise of Financial Capitalism. International Capital Markets in the Age of Reason*, 1990.

5.1275 **Paterson**, D. G., *British Direct Investment in Canada, 1890–1914*, 1976.

5.1276 **Perkins**, E. J., *Financing Anglo-American Trade. The House of Brown, 1800–80*, 1976.

5.1277 **Platt**, D. C. M., *Britain's Investment Overseas on the Eve of the First World War. The Use and Abuse of Numbers*, 1987. Attempts – not altogether convincingly –

to quantify Britain's cumulative net overseas investment in 1913.

5.1278 **Price**, J. M., *Capital and Credit in British Overseas Trade*, Cambridge, Mass., 1980.

5.1279 **Stone**, I., *The Composition and Distribution of British Investment in Latin America, 1865–1913*, 1987.

5.1280 **Warner**, F., *Anglo-Japanese Financial Relations*, 1991.

(g) Imperialism

5.1281 **Ambirajan**, S., *Classical Political Economy and British Policy in India*, 1978.

5.1282 **Balachandran**, G., 'Gold and empire. Britain and India in the Great Depression', *J.Eur.Ec.H.*, XX, 1991, 239–70.

5.1283 **Banerji**, A. K., *Aspects of Indo-British Economic Relations, 1858–98*, 1982.

5.1284 **Bangura**, Y., *Britain and Commonwealth Africa. The Politics of Economic Relations, 1951–75*, 1983.

5.1285 **Barber**, W. J., *British Economic Thought and India, 1600–1858*, 1975.

5.1286 **Bartlett**, C. J., ed., *Britain Pre-eminent: Studies in British World Influence in the Nineteenth Century*, 1969. Essays by various authors.

5.1287 **Blakeley**, B. L., 'The Society for Overseas Settlement of British Women and the problem of empire settlement, 1917–36', *Albion*, XX, 1988, 421–44.

5.1287a **Blaug**, M., *Economic Theory in Retrospect*, 2nd rev. ed., 1968. Pages 261–71 contain the best short refutation of the theories of Marx and Lenin on imperialism.

5.1288 **Bolt**, Christine, *Victorian Attitudes to Race*, 1970.

5.1289 **Bowen**, H. V., 'Investment and empire in the later eighteenth century. East India stockholding, 1756–97', *Ec.H.R.*, 2nd ser., XLII, 1989, 186–206.

5.1290 **Broeze**, F., 'Distance tames. Steam navigation to Australia and New Zealand from its beginnings to the outbreak of the Great War', *J.Trans.H.*, X, 1989, 1–21.

5.1291 **Cain**, P. J., *Economic Foundations of British Overseas Expansion, 1815–1914*, 1980.

5.1292 —— 'J. A. Hobson, Cobdenism and the radical theory of economic imperialism, 1898–1914', *Ec.H.R.*, XXXI, 1978, 565–84.

5.1293 **Chamberlain**, Muriel E., *The New Imperialism*, 1970. A useful Hist.Ass. pamphlet on the period 1870–1914, with bibliography, 43–6.

5.1294 **Darwin**, J., *Britain and Decolonisation. The Retreat from Empire in the Post-War World*, 1988.

5.1295 **Davis**, L. and Huttenbach, R., *Mammon and the Pursuit of Empire. The Political Economy of British Imperialism, 1860–1912*, 1987. Considers the size of the British imperial commitment, the nature and variety of the investments, and the social composition of the investors. Imperial costs and benefits are also examined.

5.1296 **Drummond**, I. A., *British Economic Policy and the Empire, 1919–1939*, 1972. Contains useful extracts from original documents.

5.1297 —— *Imperial Economic Policy, 1917–39*, 1974.

5.1298 **Eldridge**, C. C., ed., *British Imperialism in the Nineteenth Century*, 1984.

5.1299 **Fieldhouse**, D. K., *Colonialism, 1880–1945. An Introduction*, 1981.

5.1300 —— *Economics and Empire 1830–1914*, 1973.

5.1301 **Galbraith**, J. S., *Crown and Charter. The Early Years of the British South Africa Company*, 1975.

5.1302 **Gallagher**, J., *The Decline, Revival and Fall of the British Empire*, 1982.

5.1303 **Gillard**, D., *The Struggle for Asia, 1828–1914. A Study of British and Russian Imperialism*, 1977.

5.1304 **Hobson**, J. A., *Imperialism: A Study*, 1902, 3rd rev. ed., 1938. Once influential, but now largely of historiographical interest; written in the shadow of the Boer War, 1899–1902.

5.1305 **Hyam**, R., *Britain's Imperial Century, 1815–1914. A Study of Empire and Expansion*, 1976. Looks at the foundations, dynamics and controls of British imperialism. Particularly useful on the cultural ramifications.

5.1306 —— and Martin, G., *Reappraisals in British Imperial History*, 1975.

5.1307 **Hynes**, W. G., *The Economics of Empire, Britain, Africa and the New Imperialism, 1870–95*, 1979.

5.1308 **Imlah**, A. H., *Economic Elements in the Pax Britannica: Studies in British Foreign Trade in the Nineteenth Century*, Cambridge, Mass., 1958.

5.1309 **Keay**, J., *The Honourable Company. A History of the English East India Company*, 1991.

5.1310 **Kent**, Marion, *Oil and Empire. British Policy and Mesopotamian Oil, 1900–20*, 1976.

5.1311 **Kesner**, R. M., *Economic Control and Colonial Development. Crown Colony Financial Management in the Age of Joseph Chamberlain*, 1981.

5.1312 **Koebner**, R. and Schmidt, H. D., *Imperialism: The Story and Significance of a Political Word, 1840–1960*, 1964.

5.1313 **Krozewski**, G., 'Sterling, the "minor" territories and the end of empire, 1939–58', *Ec.H.R.*, 2nd ser., XLVI, 1993, 239–65.

5.1314 **Lewis**, W. R., ed., *Imperialism. The Robinson and Gallagher Controversy*, 1976.

5.1315 **Mackenzie**, J. M., *Imperialism and Popular Culture*, 1986. Includes essays on Music Hall, popular art, juvenile literature, feature films, the BBC, and the scouting and girl guide movements.

5.1316 **Mangan**, J. A., ed., *Making Imperial Mentalities. Socialism and British Imperialism*, 1990.

5.1317 **Meredith**, D., 'The British government and colonial economic policy, 1919–39', *Ec.H.R.*, 2nd ser., XXVIII, 1975, 484–99.

5.1318 **O'Brien**, P., 'The costs and benefits of British imperialism, 1846–1914'. *P.P.*, CXX, 1988, 163–200.

5.1319 **Offer**, A., 'The British Empire, 1870–1914. A Waste of Money?., *Ec.H.R.*, XLVI, 1993, 215–38.

5.1320 **Platt**, D. C. M., *Finance, Trade and Politics in British Foreign Policy, 1815–1914*, 1968. The standard work; excellent bibliography, 418–33.

5.1321 —— ed., *Business Imperialism, 1840–1930*, 1977. Looks at the operations of British firms trading in South America.

5.1322 **Porter**, A. N. and Holland, R. F., eds., *Money, Finance and Empire, 1790–1850*, 1985.

5.1323 **Porter**, B., *Critics of Empire. British Radical Attitudes to Colonialism in Africa, 1895–1914*, 1968.

5.1324 **Ratcliffe**, B. M., 'Commerce and empire. Manchester merchants and West Africa, 1873–1905', *J.Imperial & Commonwealth H.*, VII, 1979, 293–320.

5.1325 **Rendell**, W., *The History of the Commonwealth Development Corporation,*

1948–72, 1976.

5.1326 **Semmel**, B., *Imperialism and Social Reform: English Social-Imperial Thought 1895–1914*, 1960.

5.1327 —— *The Rise of Free Trade Imperialism: Classical Political Economy, the Empire of Free Trade and Imperialism, 1750–1850*, 1970.

5.1328 **Shaw**, A. G. L., ed., *Great Britain and her Colonies, 1815–1865*, 1970. A collection of articles.

5.1329 **Smith**, T., *The Pattern of Imperialism. The United States, Great Britain and the Industrialising World since 1815*, 1981.

5.1330 **Stanley**, B., *The Bible and the Flag. Protestant Missions and British Imperialism in the Nineteenth and Twentieth Centuries*, 1990.

5.1331 **Tomlinson**, B. R., *The Political Economy of the Raj, 1914–47. The Economics of Decolonisation in India*, 1979.

5.1332 **Ward**, J. R., 'The Industrial Revolution and British Imperialism, 1750–1850', *Ec.H.R.*, XLVII, 1994, 44–65.

5.1333 **Winks**, R. W., *British Imperialism: Gold, God, Glory*, N. Y., 1966. Extracts from the literature on British Imperialism.

5.1334 **Wolff**, R. D., *The Economics of Colonialism: Britain and Kenya, 1870–1930*, New Haven, Conn., 1975.

5.1335 **Wood**, J. C., *British Economists and the Empire, 1860–1914*, 1983.

TRANSPORT, THE COASTING TRADE AND PORTS

Note: for books and articles on river navigation, see p. 81 above.

(a) General

5.1336 **Aldcroft**, D. H., *British Transport since 1914*, 1975.

5.1337 —— *Studies in British Transport History, 1870–1914*, 1974.

5.1338 —— and Freeman, M. J., eds., *Transport in the Industrial Revolution*, 1983. A collection of essays covering canals, turnpikes, road carriage, coastal shipping and ports.

5.1339 **Bagwell**, P. S., *The Transport Revolution from 1770*, 1974.

5.1340 **Barker**, T. C. and Savage, C. I., *An Economic History of Transport in Britain*, 3rd rev. ed., 1974.

5.1341 **Dyos**, H. J. and Aldcroft, D. H., *British Transport: An Economic Survey from the Seventeenth Century to the Twentieth*, 1969. Excellent bibliography, 401–38.

5.1342 **Freeman**, M. J. and Aldcroft, D. H., eds., *Transport in Victorian Britain*, 1988. A collection of essays which considers the contribution of railways to the Victorian economy and management structures. There are also chapters on the interlocking features of urban transport, on coastal shipping, and on ports and the shipping industry.

5.1343 **Jackman**, W. T., *The Development of Transportation in Modern England*, 1916, 2 vols., 2nd rev. ed., with new bibliographical introduction, 1962, 3rd ed., 1966.

5.1344 **Sherrington**, C. E. R., *One Hundred Years of Inland Transport in Great Britain*, 1934. Reprinted 1970.

5.1345 **Wrigley**, C. and Shepherd, J., eds., *On the Move. Essays in Labour and Transport History presented to Philip Bagwell*, 1991. A miscellaneous collection on topics ranging from the late eighteenth century to the mid twentieth. Railways, coastal shipping, labour organisation and unrest feature prominently.

(b) Roads

5.1346 **Albert**, W. A., *The Turnpike Road System in England, 1663–1840*, 1971. The indispensable work on the subject.

5.1347 **Austen**, B., 'The impact of the mail coach on public coach services in the East and West, 1784–1840', *J.Trans.H.*, 3rd ser., II, 1981, 25–38.

5.1348 **Earle**, J. B. F., *A Century of Road Materials: The History of the Roadstone Division of Tarmac Ltd.*, 1971.

5.1349 **Everitt**, A. M., 'Country carriers in the nineteenth century', *J.Trans.H.*, new ser., III, 1976, 179–202.

5.1350 **Freeman**, M. J., 'Road transport in the Industrial Revolution: an interim re-assessment', *J.Hist.Geog.*, VI, 1980,

17–28.

5.1351 **Hanson**, H., *The Coaching Life*, 1983.

5.1352 **Herbert**, N., ed., *Road Travel and Transport in Gloucestershire, 1722–1822*, 1985.

5.1353 **Jeffreys**, R., *The King's Highway: An Historical and Autobiographical Record of the Developments of the Past Sixty Years*, 1949.

5.1354 **Morgan**, K. O., *Country Carriers in the Bristol Region in the Nineteenth Century*, 1988.

5.1355 **Pawson**, E., *Transport and Economy. The Turnpike Roads of Eighteenth-Century Britain*, 1977.

5.1356 —— *The Turnpike Trusts of the Eighteenth Century. A Study of Innovation and Diffusion*, 1976. See also Albert (5.1346).

5.1357 **Reader**, W. J., *Macadam: The Macadam Family and the Turnpike Roads 1798–1861*, 1980.

5.1358 **Turnbull**, G. L., 'Provincial road carrying in the eighteenth century', *J.Trans.H.*, new ser., IV, 1977,17–39.

5.1359 —— *Traffic and Transport. An Economic History of Pickfords*, 1979.

5.1360 **Williams**, L. A., *Road Transport in Cumbria in the Nineteenth Century*, 1974.

5.1361 **Woodforde**, J., *History of the Bicycle*, 1970.

(c) The coasting trade

5.1362 **Armstrong**, J., 'The role of coastal shipping in U.K. transport: an estimate of comparative traffic movements in 1910', *J.Trans.H.*, 3rd ser., VIII, 1987, 164–78.

5.1363 —— and Bagwell, P. S., 'Coastal shipping's relationship to railways and canals', *J.Rly. and Canal H.Soc.*, XXIX, 1988, 214–21.

5.1364 **Read**, A., *The Coastwise Trade of the United Kingdom, Past and Present and its Possibilities*, 1925. *See* Willan (4.775).

(d) Ports and their trade

5.1365 **Andrews**, J. H., 'Two problems in the interpretation of the port books', *Ec.H.R.*, 2nd ser., IX, 1956, 119–22.

5.1366 —— 'The port of Chichester and the grain trade, 1650–1750', *Sussex Arch.Collns.*, XCII, 1954, 93–105.

5.1367 —— 'The Thanet seaports 1650–1750', *Arch.Cant.*, LXVI, 1953, 37–44.

5.1368 —— 'The trade of the port of Faversham, 1650–1750', *Arch.Cant.*, LXIX, 1955, 125–31.

5.1369 **Clark**, E. A. G., *The Ports of the Exe Estuary, 1660–1860: A Study in Historical Geography*, 1960.

5.1370 **Craig**, R., 'Shipping and shipbuilding in the port of Chester in the eighteenth and early nineteenth centuries', *T.H.S.L.C.*, CXVI, 1964, 39–68.

5.1371 **Davies**, G. J., 'Incentive payments and the sale of smuggled goods in Dorset in the eighteenth century', *Southern H.*, XIV, 1992, 29–45.

5.1372 **Hyde**, F. E., *Liverpool and the Mersey: An Economic History of a Port, 1700–1970*, 1971. *See also* Parkinson listed above and Harris listed below.

5.1373 **Swann**, .D., 'The pace and progress of port investment in England 1660–1830', *Yorks.B.*, XII, 1960, 32–44.

(e) Canals

5.1374 **Barker**, T. C., 'The Sankey Navigation', *T.H.S.L.C.*, 1948, 121–55. The first eighteenth-century canal in Great Britain, 1755–57.

5.1375 **Broadbridge**, S. R., *The Birmingham Canal Navigations I (1768–1846)*, 1974.

5.1376 **Denholm**, A. F., 'The impact of the canal system on three Staffordshire market towns, 1760–1850', *Midland H.*, XIII, 1988, 59–76.

5.1377 **Farnie**, D. A., *The Manchester Ship Canal and the Rise of the Port of Manchester, 1894–1975*, 1980.

5.1378 **Hadfield**, C., *British Canals: An Illustrated History*, 1950, 2nd ser., rev. and enlarged, 1959.

5.1379 —— *The Canals of South Wales and the Border*, 1960.

5.1380 —— *The Canals of the West Midlands*, 1966, 2nd rev. ed., 1969.

5.1381 —— *The Canals of the East Midlands*, 1966.

5.1382 —— *The Canals of Yorkshire and North-East England*, 2 vols., 1972–3.

5.1383 —— and Biddle, G., *The Canals of North-West England*, 2 vols., 1970.

5.1384 **Malet**, H., *Bridgewater, the Canal Duke, 1763–1803*, 1977.

5.1385 **Mather**, F. C., *After the Canal Duke: A*

Study of the Industrial estates Administered by the Trustees of the Third Duke of Bridgewater in the Age of Railway Building, 1825–1872, 1970. *See also Richards (7.234).*

5.1386 **Owen**, D. E., *The Manchester Ship Canal*, 1983.

5.1387 **Patterson**, A. T., 'The making of the Leicestershire canals, 1766–1814', *Trans.Leics.Arch.Soc.*, XXVII, 1951, 1–35.

5.1388 **Porteous**, J. D., *Canal Ports. the Urban Achievement of the Canal Age*, 1977. Based largely on case studies of Runcorn, Stourport, Ellesmere Port and Goole.

5.1389 **Rolt**, L. T. C., *The Inland Waterways of England*, 1950.

5.1390 **Turnbull**, G., 'Canals, coal and regional growth during the Industrial Revolution', *Ec.H.R.*, 2nd ser., XL, 1987, 537–60.

5.1391 **Ward**, J. R. *The Finance of Canal Building in Eighteenth-century England*, 1974.

(f) Postal history and telecommunications

5.1392 **Clear**, C. R., *John Palmer (of Bath), Mail Coach Pioneer*,1955.

5.1393 **Daunton**, M. J., *Royal Mail. The Post Office since 1840*, 1985. Looks at the ways in which the reformed postal service acquired the range of functions which made it the local representative of the state.

5.1394 **Ellis**, K. L., *The Post Office in the Eighteenth Century: A Study in Administrative History*, 1958.

5.1395 **Gregory**, D., 'The friction of distance? Information circulation and the mails in early nineteenth-century England', *J.H.Geog.*, XIII, 1987, 130–54.

5.1396 **Harcourt**, F., 'British oceanic mail contracts in the age of steam, 1838–1914', *J.Trans.H.*, IX, 1988, 1–18.

5.1397 **Hemmeon**, J. C., *The History of the British Post Office*, Cambridge, Mass., 1912.

5.1398 **Kieve**, J. L., *The Electric Telegraph: A Social and Economic History*, 1973.

5.1399 **Robertson**, J. H., *The Story of the Telephone: A History of the Telecommunications Industry of Britain*, 1948.

5.1400 **Robinson**, H., *The British Post Office: A History*, Princeton, N. J., 1948.

5.1401 **Staff**, F., *The Penny Post, 1680–1918*, 1964.

5.1402 **Vale**, E., *The Mail Coach men of the Late Eighteenth Century*, 1960.

(g) Railways

(i) BIBLIOGRAPHIES

5.1403 **Bryant**, E. T., *Railways: A Reader's Guide*, 1968.

5.1404 **Ottley**, G., *A Bibliography of British Railway History*, 1965. 2nd ed., 1983.

(ii) CONTEMPORARY ACCOUNTS

5.1405 **Acworth**, W., *The Railways of England*, 1st ed., 1889, 5th and best ed., 1900.

5.1406 **Chattaway**, E. D., *Railways: their capital and dividends*, 1855–6.

5.1407 **Dorsey**, E. B., *English and American Railroads Compared*, 1887.

5.1408 **Francis**, J., *A History of the English Railway*, 2 vols., 1852. Reprinted 1968.

5.1409 **Galt**, W., *Railway Reform: its importance and practicability*, 1865.

5.1410 **Lardner**, D., *Railway Economy. A Treatise on the New Art of Transport*, 1850.

5.1411 **Simmons**, E. J., *Memoirs of a Station Master (1879)*, ed. J. Simmons, 1974.

5.1412 **Simmons**, J.., ed., *The Birth of the Great Western Railway. Extracts from the Diary and Correspondence of George Henry Gibbs*, 1971. Shows at first hand the activities of a major promoter and director.

5.1413 —— *The Railway Traveller's Handy Book*, 1971. An assortment of hints, suggestions and advice first published in 1862.

5.1414 **Spencer**, H., *Railway Morals and Railway Policy*, 1855.

5.1415 **Williams**, F. S., *Our Iron Roads*, 1852.

(iii) GENERAL WORKS

5.1416 **Aldcroft**, D. H., *British Railways in Transition: The Economic Problems of Britain's Railways since 1914*, 1968.

5.1417 —— 'The efficiency and enterprise of British railways, 1870–1914', *Expl.Entrepren.H.*, 2nd ser., V, 1968, 157–74.

5.1418 **Alderman**, G., *The Railway Interest*, 1972. Examines the growth of the railway lobby in the nineteenth century.

5.1419 **Bagwell**, P. S., *The Railway Clearing House in the British Economy, 1844–1922*, 1968.

5.1420 **Baxter**, B., *Stone Blocks and Iron Rails*, 1966. Deals with the pre-steam railway.

5.1421 **Bell**, R., *History of the British Railways during the War, 1939–45*, 1946.

5.1422 **Bonavia**, M. R., *Railway Policy between the Wars*, 1981. Focuses attention on railway management and compares the managers' own assessment of their policies with the historians' verdicts.

5.1423 **Bosley**, P., *Light Railways in England and Wales*, 1990.

5.1424 **Broadbridge**, S. R., *Studies in Railway Expansion and the Capital Market in England, 1825–1873*, 1970. Deals mainly with the finances of the Lancashire & Yorkshire Railway Company.

5.1425 **Cain**, P., 'Private enterprise or public utility? Output, pricing and investment on English and Welsh railways, 1870–1914', *J.Trans.H.*, 3rd ser., I, 1980, 9–28.

5.1426 **Campbell**, C. D., *British Railways in Boom and Depression: An Essay in Trade Fluctuations and Their Effects, 1878–1930*, 1932.

5.1427 **Channon**, G., 'Railway pooling in Britain before 1900: the Anglo-Scottish traffic', *Bus.H.R.*, LXII, 1988, 74–92.

5.1428 **Cleveland-Stevens**, C., *English Railways: Their Development and Relation to the State*, 1915.

5.1429 **Ellis**, C. H., *British Railway History: An Outline from the Accession of William IV to the Nationalization of Railways*, 2 vols., 1954–59. The two volumes divide at 1876–7.

5.1430 **Gourvish**, T. R., *Railways and the British Economy, 1830–1914*, 1980.

5.1431 —— *British Railways, 1948–73. A Business History*, 1986. Looks at fluctuations in freight and passenger traffic, the declining size of the workforce, and at failures in investment policy.

5.1432 **Hawke**, G. R., *Railways and Economic Growth in England and Wales, 1840–1870*, 1970. The first large-scale attempt to apply the methods of the 'new economic history' to a British subject.

5.1433 **Irving**, R. J., 'The efficiency and enterprise of British railways, 1870–1914: an alternative hypothesis',

Ec.H.R., 2nd ser., XXXI, 1978, 46–66.

5.1434 **Lewin**, H. G., *Early British Railways: A Short History of Their Origin and Development, 1801–1844*, 1925.

5.1435 —— *The Railway Mania and its Aftermath, 1845–1852*, 1936.

5.1436 **Lewis**, M. J. T., *Early Wooden Railways*, 1970.

5.1437 **Marshall**, C. F. D., *A History of British Railways down to the Year 1830*, 1938, 2nd rev. ed., 1971.

5.1438 **Mitchell**, B. R., 'The coming of the railway and United Kingdom economic growth' in Reed (5.1441), 13–32.

5.1439 **Parris**, H., *Government and the Railways in Nineteenth-Century Britain*, 1965.

5.1440 **Perkin**, H. J., *The Age of the Railway*, 1970. Social and economic effects, c. 1780–1914.

5.1441 **Reed**, M. C., ed., *Railways in the Victorian Economy: Studies in Finance and Economic Growth*, 1969.

5.1442 —— *Investment in Railways in Britain, 1820–44*, 1975. A detailed analysis of the shareholders of eleven railway companies.

5.1443 **Richards**, J. and Mackenzie, J. M., *The Railway Station. A Social History*, 1986.

5.1444 **Robbins**, M. R., *The Railway Age*, 1962. An analytical study with useful 'Notes on Sources', 199–212.

5.1445 **Schivelbusch**, W., *The Railway Journey. Trains and Travel in the Nineteenth Century*, 1980.

5.1446 **Simmons**, J., *The Railways of Britain: An Historical Introduction*, 1961, 2nd ed., 1969. Includes a useful chapter on 'Literature and Maps'.

5.1447 —— *The Railway in England and Wales, 1830–1914. I: The System and its Working*, 1978.

5.1448 —— *The Railway in Town and Country, 1830–1914*, 1986.

5.1449 **Smith**, D., *The Railway and its Passengers. A Social History*, 1988.

5.1450 **Wooler**, N., *Dinner in the Diner. A History of Railway Catering*, 1987.

(iv) RAILWAY BIOGRAPHIES

5.1451 **Gourvish**, T. R., *Mark Huish and the London and North Western Railway*, 1972. Exhaustive survey of a general manager.

5.1452 —— 'A British business élite: the chief executive managers of the railway industry, 1850–1922', *Bus.H.R.*, XLVII, 1973, 289–316.

5.1453 **Lambert**, R. S., *The Railway King, 1800–71: A Study of George Hudson and the Business Morals of his Time*, 1934.

5.1454 **Marshall**, J. D., *A Biographical Dictionary of Railway Engineers*, 1978.

5.1455 **Rolt**, L. T. C., *George and Robert Stephenson: The Railway Revolution*, 1960.

5.1456 —— *Isambard Kingdom Brunel: A Biography*, 1957.

5.1457 **Webster**, N. W., *Joseph Locke: A Railway Revolutionary*, 1971. A neglected contemporary of the Stephensons.

(v) LOCOMOTIVES

5.1458 **Ahrons**, E. L., *The British Steam Railway Locomotive, 1825–1925*, 1927.

5.1459 **Clark**, E. K., *Kitson's of Leeds*, 1938.

5.1460 **Kidner**, R. W., *The Early History of the Locomotive, 1804–1876*, 1956.

5.1461 **Larkin**, E. J. and J. G., *The Railway Workshops of Britain, 1823–1986*, 1988.

5.1461a **Marshall**, C. F. D., *A History of Railway Locomotives down to the end of the Year 1831*, 1953.

5.1462 **Warren**, J. G. H., *A Century of Locomotive Building by Robert Stephenson and Company 1823–1923*, 1923. An account of the Stephensons' works at Newcastle upon Tyne.

(vi) INDIVIDUAL LINES AND REGIONAL STUDIES

The histories of individual lines are now so numerous – and of such varying quality – that it would be impossible here to list them all. A selection only is given below. For a fuller list *see* Ottley (5.1404).

5.1463 **Allen**, C. J., *The Great Eastern Railway*, 4th ed., 1967.

5.1464 **Barker**, T. C. and Robbins, R. M., *A History of London Transport: Passenger Travel and the Development of the Metropolis*, Vol. I, 1963, vol. II, 1974.

5.1465 **Barnes**, E. G., *The Rise of the Midland Railway, 1844–74*, 1966.

5.1466 **Carlson**, R. E., *The Liverpool and Manchester Railway Project, 1821–1831*, 1969.

5.1467 **Channon**, G., 'The Great Western Railway under the British Railways Act

of 1921', *Bus.H.R.*, LV, 1981, 188–216.

5.1468 **Christiansen**, R., *A Regional History of the Railways of Great Britain. VII: The West Midlands*, 1973.

5.1469 **Cocks**, J. V. S., 'The Great Western Railway and the development of Devon and Cornwall', *Devon and Cornwall N. and Q.*, XXXVI, 1987, 9–20.

5.1470 **Dow**, G., *Great Central*, 3 vols., 1959–65.

5.1471 **Irving**, R. J., *The North Eastern Railway Company, 1870–1914. An Economic History*, 1976.

5.1472 **MacDermot**, E. T., *History of the Great Western Railways*, 3 vols., 1964.

5.1473 **Robbins**, M. R., 'Transport and Suburban Development in Middlesex down to 1914', *Trans.London & Middx.Arch.Soc.*, XXIX, 1978, 129–36.

5.1474 **Thomas**, R. H. G., *The Liverpool and Manchester Railway*, 1980.

5.1475 **Webster**, N. W., *Britain's First Trunk Line: The Grand Junction Railway, 1972.*

(h) Motor transport

5.1476 **Alder**, T., *Vauxhall. The Postwar Years*, 1991.

5.1477 **Barker**, T. C., ed., *The Economic and Social Effects of the Spread of Motor Vehicles*, 1986.

5.1478 —— *The Transport Contractors of Rye. John Jempson and Son. A Chapter in the History of British Road Haulage*, 1982.

5.1479 **Church**, R. A., *Herbert Austin. The British Motor Car Industry to 1941*, 1979.

5.1480 **Cornwell**, E. L., *Commercial Road Vehicles*, 1960. Emphasis on technical history.

5.1481 **Dunnett**, P. J. S., *The Decline of the British Motor Industry. The Effects of Government Policy, 1945–79*, 1980.

5.1482 **Hibbs**, J., *A History of British Bus Services* 1970.

5.1483 —— ed., *The Omnibus. Readings in the History of Road Passenger Transport*, 1971.

5.1484 **Holding**, D., *A History of British Bus Services. The North-East*, 1979.

5.1485 **Knockolds**, H., *Lucas: The First Hundred Years*, 2 vols., 1976–8.

5.1486 **Lanning**, G., ed., *Making Cars. A History of Car Making in Cowley*, 1985.

5.1487 **Lloyd**, I., *Rolls Royce. I: The Growth of a Firm. II: The Merlin at War. III: The Years of Endeavour*, 3 vols., 1979.

5.1488 **Maxy**, G. and Silbertson, A., *The British

Motor Industry, 1959.

5.1489 **Overy**, R. J., *William Morris, Viscount Nuffield*, 1976.

5.1490 **Perkin**, H. J., *The Age of the Automobile*, 1976. A general survey which emphasises the social implications of the coming of the motor car for patterns of leisure and community life.

5.1491 **Plowden**, W., *The Motor Car and Politics, 1896–1970*, 1971. Contains an up-to-date bibliography, 421–4.

5.1492 **Saul**, S. B., 'The motor industry in Britain to 1914', *Bus.H.*, V, 1963, 23–44. *See* Aldcroft (5.1336) and Dyos and Aldcroft (5.1341).

(i) The Channel Tunnel

5.1493 **Slater**, H., Barnett, C. and Geneau, R. H., *The Channel Tunnel*, 1958; bibliography, 205–6.

5.1494 **Whiteside**, T., *The Tunnel under the Channel* 1962.

(j) Air travel

5.1495 **Aldcroft**, D. H., 'Britain's internal airways: the pioneer stage of the 1930s', *Bus.H.*, VI, 1964, 113–23.

5.1496 **Brooks**, P. W., 'A short history of London's airports', *J.Trans.H.*, III, 1957, 12–22.

5.1497 **Gardner**, C., *British Aircraft Corporation: A History*, 1981.

5.1498 **Higham**, R., *Britain's Imperial Air Routes, 1918–39*, 1960.

5.1499 **Pudney**, J., *The Seven Skies: A Study of B.O.A.C. and its Forerunners since 1919*, 1959. *See also* Dyos and Aldcroft (5.1341).

HOME MARKET, INCLUDING SHOPPING AND THE CO-OPERATIVE MOVEMENT

(a) Developments to 1850

5.1500 **Marshall**, J. D., ed., *The Autobiography of William Stout of Lancaster, 1665–1752*, 1967.

5.1501 **Vaisey**, D., *The Diary of Thomas Turner, 1754–65*, 1985. Chronicles the daily life of a Sussex shopkeeper and his local community.

5.1502 **Weatherill**, Lorna, ed., *The Account Book of Richard Latham, 1724–67*, 1990.

5.1503 **Adburgham**, Alison, *Shopping in Style, London from the Restoration to Edwardian Elegance*, 1979.

5.1504 **Alexander**, D., *Retailing in England during the Industrial Revolution*, 1970.

5.1505 **Atkins**, P. J., 'The retail milk trade in London, c. 1790–1914', *Ec.H.R.*, 2nd ser., XXXIII, 1980, 522–37.

5.1506 **Benson**, J. and Shaw, G., eds., *The Evolution of Retail Systems, c.1800–1914*, 1992.

5.1507 **Brewer**, J. and Porter, R., eds., *Consumption and the World of Goods*, 1993. Shifts the attention away from production towards consumerism. Britain takes its place in a broad international scenario.

5.1508 **Chapman**, S. D., 'British marketing enterprise: the changing roles of merchants, manufacturers and financiers, 1700–1860', *Bus.H.R.*, LIII, 1979, 205–34.

5.1509 **Davis**, Dorothy. *A History of Shopping*, 1965.

5.1510 **Eversley**, D. E. C., 'The home market and economic growth in England 1750–80'. In Jones and Mingay (5.81), 206–59.

5.1511 **Feather**, J., *The Provincial Book Trade in Eighteenth-Century England*, 1985.

5.1512 **Fine**, B. and Leopold, E., 'Consumerism and the Industrial Revolution', *Soc.H.*, XV, 1990, 151–80.

5.1513 **Gilboy**, Elizabeth W., 'Demand as a factor in the Industrial Revolution', in A. H. Cole, ed., *Facts and Factors in Economic History*, Cambridge, Mass., 1932. Reprinted in Hartwell, ed. (5.69), 121–38.

5.1514 **Lemire**, B., 'Consumerism in preindustrial and early industrial England: the trade in secondhand clothes', *J.Brit.Studs.*, XXVII, 1988, 1–24.

5.1515 **McKendrick**, N., 'Home demand and economic growth: a new view of the role of women and children in the Industrial Revolution' in McKendrick ed., *Historical Perspectives*, 1974, 152–210.

5.1516 —— Brewer, J. and Plumb, J. H., *The Birth of a Consumer Society: The Commercialisation of Eighteenth-Century England*, 1982.

5.1517 **Mokyr**, J., 'Demand *versus* supply in the Industrial Revolution', *J.Ec.H.*, XXXVII, 1977, 981–1008.

5.1518 **Mui**, Lorna and H. C., *Shops and Shopkeeping in Eighteenth-Century England*, 1989. Explores the retailing revolution of the eighteenth century. Entrepreneurial innovation and tea consumption are two of the topics discussed.

5.1519 **Robinson**, E. H., 'Eighteenth-century commerce and fashion: Matthew Boulton's marketing techniques', *Ec.H.R.*, 2nd ser., XVI, 1963, 39–60.

5.1520 **Shammas**, Carole, *The Preindustrial Consumer in England and America*, 1990. An ambitious transatlantic study which examines patterns of demand, standard of living, and distribution networks.

5.1521 **Weatherill**, Lorna, *Consumer Behaviour and Material Culture in Britain, 1660–1760*, 1988. Within the general context of a discussion of the factors promoting economic growth of consumerism, the author examines changing trends in the household, levels of comfort, and standards of living.

5.1522 **Willan**, T. S., *An Eighteenth-century Shopkeeper: Abraham Dent of Kirkby Stephen*, 1970.

(b) Co-operation

5.1523 **Barou**, N. I., ed., *The Co-operative Movement in Labour Britain*, 1948.

5.1524 **Carr-Saunders**, A. M., Florence, P. Sargant, and Peers, R., eds., *Consumers' Co-operation in Great Britain*, 1933, 3rd rev. ed., 1942 .

5.1525 **Cole**, G. D. H., *A Century of Co-operation*, 1945. A history of the co-operative movement in Great Britain and Ireland.

5.1526 **Flanagan**, D., *1869–1969: The Centenary Story of the Co-operative Union of Great Britain and Ireland*, 1969.

5.1527 **Musson**, A. E., 'The ideology of early co-operation in Lancashire and Cheshire', *T.L.C.A.S.*, LXVIII, 1959, 117–38. Reprinted in Musson (5.2203).

5.1528 **Pollard**, S., 'Nineteenth century co-operation: from community-building to shopkeeping'. In Briggs and Saville, 74–112.

5.1529 **Purvis**, M., 'Co-operative retailing in England, 1833–50: developments beyond Rochdale', *Northern H.*, XXII, 1986, 198–215.

5.1530 —— 'The development of co-operative retailing in England and Wales, 1850–1901: a geographical study', *J.Hist.Geog.*, XVI, 1990, 314–31.

5.1531 **Richardson**, W., *The C.W.S. in War and Peace, 1939–76*, 1977.

(c) Developments since 1850

5.1532 **Adburgham**, Alison, *Shops and Shopping, 1800–1914: Where and in What Manner the Well-Dressed Englishwoman Bought her Clothes*, 1964.

5.1533 **Benson**, J., *The Penny Capitalists. A Study of Nineteenth Century Working Class Entrepreneurs*, 1983. Looks at small scale, often part-time, working-class businessmen and women, those normally overlooked in general surveys of Victorian entrepreneurship.

5.1534 **Bradley**, K. and Taylor, S., *Business Performance in the Retail Sector. The Experience of the John Lewis Partnership*, 1992. Looks at the firm's organisation, productivity and profits, chiefly in the period 1970–1989.

5.1535 **Briggs**, A., *Friends of the People. The Centenary History of Lewis's*, 1956.

5.1536 **Corina**, M., *Fine Silks and Oak Counters: Debenham, 1778–1978*, 1978.

5.1537 —— *Pile it High, Sell it Cheap. The Authorised Biography of Sir John Cohen, Founder of Tesco*, 1971.

5.1538 **Fraser**, W. H., *The Coming of the Mass Market, 1850–1914*, 1981.

5.1539 **Grether**, E. T., *Reseale Price Maintenance in Great Britain*, University of Calfornia Publications in Economics, XI (for 1932–5), 1942.

5.1540 **Harrison**, G. and Mitchell, F. C., *The*

Home Market: A Handbook oif Statistics, 1936, 2nd rev. ed., 1939.

5.1541 **Hudson**, K., *Pawnbroking. An Aspect of British Social History*, 1982.

5.1542 **Jefferys**, J. B., *Retail Trading in Britain, 1850–1950*, 1954.

5.1543 **Lambert**, R. S., *The Universal Provider: A Study of William Whiteley and the Rise of the London Department Store*, 1938.

5.1544 **Mathias**, P., *Retailing Revolution: A History of Multiple Retailing in the Food Trades, Based on the Allied Suppliers Group of Companies*, 1967. Useful bibliography, 402–5. A history of the group built up around Maypole, Home and Colonial, and Lipton.

5.1545 **O'Brien**, P., 'Agriculture and the home market for British industry, 1660–1820', *E.H.R.*, C, 1985, 773–801.

5.1546 **Pound**, R., *Selfridge: A Biography*, 1960.

5.1547 **Rees**, G., *St. Michael: A History of Marks and Spencer*, 1969.

5.1548 **Scola**, R., *Feeding the Victorian City. The Food Supply of Manchester, 1770–1870*, 1992. Explores the networks and sources of supply needed to feed one of the fastest growing cities of the Industrial Revolution.

5.1549 **Tebbutt**, Melanie, *Making Ends Meet. Pawnbroking and Working-Class Credit*, 1983. Draws on evidence from Lancashire to explore the extent and organisation of the pawnbroking business and its place in working-class society.

5.1550 **Wild**, M. T. and Shaw G., 'Population distribution and retail provision: the Halifax–Calder Valley area during the second half of the nineteenth century', *J.H.Geog.*, I, 1975, 193–210.

5.1551 **Willcock**, H. D., ed., *Browns and Chester: Portrait of a Shop 1780–1946*, 1946.

5.1552 **Wilson**, C., *First with the News. The History of W.H. Smith, 1792–1972*, 1985. Examines the entrepreneurial exploitation of new printing technology and improved transport (stage coaches and railways).

5.1553 **Winstanley**, M. J., *The Shopkeeper's World, 1830–1914*, 1983. Partly an oral history which examines the range of retail activity and the social positions and social horizons of shopkeepers.

(d) Advertising

5.1554 **Darwin**, B., *The Dickens Advertiser*, 1930. A collection of the advertisements in the original parts of Dickens's novels.

5.1555 **Elliott**, Blanche B., *A History of English Advertising*, 1962.

5.1556 **Field**, E., *Advertising: The Forgotten Years*, 1959. The inter-war period.

5.1557 **Treasure**, J., *History of British Advertising Agencies, 1875–1939*, 1977.

5.1558 **Turner**, E. S., *The Shocking History of Advertising*, 1952.

5.1559 **Vries**, L. de, *Victorian Advertisements*, 1968.

BUSINESS HISTORY

5.1560 **Cain**, L. P. and Uselding, P. J., eds., *Business Enterprise and Economic Change*, Athens, Ohio, 1973.

5.1561 **Hannah**, L., ed., *Management Strategy and Business Development. A Historical and Comparative Study*, 1976. Deals with the British tobacco, glass, petroleum, pharmaceutical, electrical and service industries.

5.1562 **Marriner**, Sheila, ed., *Business and Businessmen: Studies in Business, Economic and Accounting History*, 1978. A miscellaneous collection which includes essays on marine insurance, business management, steel technology, and the use of company financial statements as a historical source.

5.1563 **Prais**, S. J., *The Evolution of Giant Firms in Britain*, 1976.

5.1564 **Supple**, B. E., ed., *Essays in British Business History*, 1977. Includes essays on the hardware, rayon and motor industries, and on the development of insurance services.

5.1565 **Tucker**, K. A., ed., *Business History*, 1977. Reprints twenty essays arranged under the following headings: (1) Aims and Methods in Business History; (2) Entrepreneurs, the firm and industrial structure; (3) Techniques of business management and organisation.

5.1566 **Williams**, P. L., *The Emergence of the Theory of the Firm from Adam Smith to Alfred Marshall*, 1979.

URBAN HISTORY

(a) General works

5.1567 Sutcliffe, A., ed., *The History of Urban and Regional Planning*, 1981. A bibliography on planners and planning in different countries and cities.

5.1568 Ashworth, W., *The Genesis of Modern British Town Planning: A Study in the Economic and Social History of the Nineteenth and Twentieth Centuries*, 1954. Excellent bibliography.

5.1569 Borsay, P., ed., *The Eighteenth Century Town. A Reader in English Urban History, 1688–1820*, 1990. Twelve reprinted essays with a substantial bibliographical introduction. London, Bath and Birmingham are looked at in particular. More general chapters address questions relating to the urban renaissance, provincial culture and social class and geography.

5.1570 —— *The English Urban Renaissance. Culture and Society in the Provincial Town, 1660–1770*, 1989. Examines the widening of provincial elites which underpinned the urban renaissance in this period. The architectural evidence is considered and cultural and philanthropic provision.

5.1571 Briggs, A., *Cities and Countrysides. British and American Experience, 1860–1914*, 1982.

5.1572 —— *Victorian Cities*, 1963, 2nd rev. ed., 1968. Includes London, Manchester, Leeds, Birmingham and Middlesbrough.

5.1573 Brown, J., *The English Market Town. A Social and Economic History, 1750–1914*, 1986. A profusely illustrated popular study concentrating chiefly on the nineteenth century.

5.1574 Cannadine, D., *Lords and Landlords. The Aristocracy and the Towns, 1774–1967*, 1980. A valuable study which deals with the aristocratic contribution to urban development both in general terms and by way of two case studies of Edgbaston and Eastbourne.

5.1575 —— ed., *Patricians, Power and Politics in Nineteenth-Century Towns*, 1982. Has chapters on the development of Cardiff, Dudley, Southport and Bournemouth.

5.1576 —— 'The Victorian cities: how different?', *Soc.H.*, IV, 1977, 457–482.

5.1577 —— and Reeder, D., eds., *Exploring the Urban Past. Essays in Urban History by H. J. Dyos*, 1982. Collects together twelve of Dyos's essays which are prefaced by the editors' evaluation of his contribution to the field.

5.1578 Carter, H. and Lewis, C. R., *An Urban Geography of England and Wales in the Nineteenth Century*, 1990. Examines the distribution of cities and the social and economic distributions within them. Individual chapters consider the dynamics of the urban demographic growth and the structure of city systems.

5.1579 Chalklin, C. W., *The Provincial Towns of Georgian England: A Study of the Building Process 1740–1820*, 1974.

5.1580 Clark, P., *Sociability and Urbanity. Clubs and Societies in the Eighteenth-Century City*, 1986.

5.1581 Coleman, B. I., *The Idea of the City in Nineteenth Century Britain*, 1973. A collection of documents with useful commentary, and good bibliography, 235–8.

5.1582 Corfield, Penelope J., *The Impact of English Towns, 1700–1800*, 1982. An invaluable, thematically structured survey.

5.1583 Cunningham, C., *Victorian and Edwardian Town Halls*, 1981. Discusses the financial, organisational, architectural and symbolic aspects of civic buildings.

5.1584 Dennis, R. J., *English Industrial Cities in the Nineteenth Century. A Social Geography*, 1984. Offers a distinctive reassessment of mobility, interaction and community building in the industrial towns of the Midlands and North.

5.1585 Dyos, H. J., ed., *The Study of Urban History*, 1968. The best introduction to the subject.

5.1586 —— and Wolff, M., *The Victorian City: Images and Reality*, 2 vols., 1973.

5.1587 Fraser, D., ed., *Municipal Reform and the Industrial City*, 1981. Has substantial chapters on Manchester, Leeds and Bradford.

5.1588 —— *Power and Authority in the Victorian City*, 1979. A general discussion exemplified with case studies of Liverpool, Leeds, Birmingham, Bristol, Leicester, Bradford and Sheffield.

5.1589 —— ed., *Municipal Reform and the Industrial City*, 1982.

5.1590 **Harrison**, M., *Crowds and History. Mass Phenomena in English Towns, 1790–1835*, 1989. Draws chiefly on Bristol evidence.

5.1591 **Hennock**, E. P., *Fit and Proper Persons. Ideal and Reality in Nineteenth-Century Urban Government*, 1973.

5.1592 **Johnson**, J. H. and Pooley, C. G., eds., *The Structure of Nineteenth-Century Cities*, 1982.

5.1593 **Keith-Lucas**, B., *Unreformed Local Government, 1800–35*, 1980.

5.1594 —— and Richards, P. G., *A History of Local Government in the Twentieth Century*, 1978.

5.1595 **Kellett**, J. R., *The Impact of Railways on Victorian Cities*, 1969.

5.1596 —— 'Municipal socialism, enterprise, and trading in the Victorian city', *Urban H.Yearbook*, 1978, 36–45.

5.1597 **Lees**, A., *Cities Perceived. Urban Society in European and American Thought, 1820–1940*, 1985. British towns are well represented in this study.

5.1598 **Lipman**, V. D., *Local Government Areas, 1834–1945*, 1949.

5.1599 **Marshall**, J. D., 'The rise and transformation of the Cumbrian market town, 1660–1900', *Northern H.*, XIX, 1983, 128–209.

5.1600 **Morris**, R. J., ed., *Class, Power and Social Structure in British Nineteenth-century Towns*, 1986.

5.1601 **Offer**, A., *Property and Politics, 1870–1914. Landownership, Law and Urban Development in England*, 1981.

5.1602 **Pfautz**, H., *Charles Booth on the City*, Chicago, 1967.

5.1603 **Sigsworth**, E. M., ed., *Ports and Resorts in the Regions*, 1982. Fifteen essays weighted particularly towards the North.

5.1604 **Sutcliffe**, A., *Towards the Planned City: Germany, Britain, the United States and France, 1780–1914*, 1981. Concentrates particularly on Germany and stresses its importance as a pioneer of the urban extension plan.

5.1605 —— ed., *British Town Planning: The Formative Years*, 1981. Includes chapters on suburban planning, housing and town planning in Manchester before 1914, and on the emergence of the town planning profession.

5.1606 **Thompson**, F. M. L., ed., *The Rise of Suburbia*, 1981. Has chapters on Bromley, Bexley, outer West London, and Leeds. *See also* Everitt (4.586) and Porteous (5.1388).

5.1607 **Walvin**, J., *English Urban Life, 1776–1851*, 1984. Discusses the variety of urban life, accentuated by the Industrial Revolution, and its economic, social, political and cultural expression.

5.1608 **Williamson**, J. G., *Coping with City Growth during the British Industrial Revolution*, 1990.

5.1609 **Wrigley**, E. A., 'City and country in the past: a sharp divide or a continuum?', *Hist.Res.*, LXIV, 1991, 107–20.

(b) Individual towns and cities

5.1610 **Andrew**, D. T., *Philanthropy and Policy. London Charity in the Eighteenth Century*, 1989.

5.1611 **Archer**, J. H. G., ed., *Art and Architecture in Victorian Manchester*, 1985. A well illustrated collection of essays dealing with the changing architectural appearance of the cottonopolis and with its self confident culture.

5.1612 **Armstrong**, W. A., *Stability and Change in a English County Town: A Social Study of York, 1801–51*, 1974. *See also* Feinstein (5.1638).

5.1613 **Aspden**, J. C., *A Municipal History of Eastbourne, 1938–74*, 1979.

5.1614 **Attfield**, C. E., ' Hereford in the 1850s', *Trans.Woolhope Nat.Field Club*, XLV, 1986, 347–70.

5.1615 **Bailey**, F. A., *History of Southport*, 1955.

5.1616 **Barker**, T. C. and Harris, J. R., *A Merseyside Town in the Industrial Revolution: St Helens, 1750–1900*, 1954.

5.1617 **Belchem**, J., ed., *Popular politics, Riots and Labour. Essays in Liverpool History, 1790–1940*, 1992.

5.1618 **Bradshaw**, D. L., *Visitors to Manchester. A Selection of Foreign Visitors' Descriptions of Manchester from c.1538 to 1865*, 1987.

5.1619 **Brown**, A. F. J., *Colchester, 1815–1914*, 1980.

5.1620 **Brown**, C., *Northampton, 1835–1985: Shoe Town, New Town*, 1990.

5.1621 **Carrick**, T. W., *History of Wigton* (1949).

5.1622 **Carson**, R., *A Short History of Middlesborough*, 1977.

5.1623 **Cave**, L. F., *Leamington Spa. Its History and Development*, 1988.

5.1624 **Chaloner**, W. H., *The Social and Economic Development of Crewe, 1780–1923*, 1950.

5.1625 **Church**, R. A., *Economic and Social Change in a Midland Town: Victorian Nottingham, 1815–1900*, 1966.

5.1626 **Corfield**, Penelope J., *Towns, Trade, Religion and Radicalism. The Norwich Perspective on English History*, 1980.

5.1627 **Cullingford**, C. N., *A History of Poole and Neighbourhood*, 1988.

5.1628 **Davies**, J., *Class Practices and Political Culture in Liverpool*, 1988.

5.1629 **Davis**, J., *Reforming London. The London Government Problem, 1885–1900*, 1988.

5.1630 **Daysh**, G. H. J., ed., *A Survey of Whitby and the surrounding areas*, 1958. Contains much historical information.

5.1631 **Dickinson**, H. W., *Water Supply of Greater London*, 1954.

5.1632 **Dyos**, H. J., *Victorian Suburb: A Study of the Growth of Camberwell*, 1961.

5.1633 —— ' The slums of Victorian London', *Vict. Studs.*, XI, 1967–8, 5–40.

5.1634 **Ede**, J. F., *History of Wednesbury*, 1962.

5.1635 **Elliot**, M., *Victorian Leicester*, 1979. *See also* Greaves (5.1649), Patterson (5.1686), and Simmons (5.1697).

5.1636 **Farrant**, S., *Georgian Brighton, 1740–1820*, 1980.

5.1637 **Faulkner**, T. E., ' The early nineteenth-century planning of Newcastle upon Tyne', *Planning Perspectives*, V, 1990, 149–67.

5.1638 **Feinstein**, C. H., ed., *York, 1831–1981. 150 Years of Scientific Endeavour and Social Change*, 1981. *See also* Armstrong (5.1612).

5.1639 **Feldman**, D. and Jones, G. S., eds., *Metropolis. Histories and Representations of London since 1800*, 1989. A collection of essays, both empirical and theoretical, which explore the connections between socio-economic forces and their representation.

5.1640 **Fieldhouse**, R., and Jennings, B., *A History of Richmond and Swaledale*, 1978.

5.1641 **Fissell**, Mary, *Patients, Power and the Poor in Eighteenth-Century Bristol*, 1992. Looks beyond the local medical milieu to wider issues of social formation.

5.1642 **Foster**, A. M., *Market Town, Hitchin in the Nineteenth Century*, 1987.

5.1643 **Foster**, D., ' Poulton le Fylde: a nineteenth-century market town', *T.H.S.L.C.*, CXXVII, 1978, 91–108.

5.1644 **Fraser**, D., ed., *A History of Modern Leeds*, 1980. A comprehensive history concentrating on post-1750 economic,

social and political developments. *See also* Wilson (5.866).

5.1645 **George**, M. Dorothy, *London Life in the Eighteenth Century*, 1925, 3rd corrected ed., 1951.

5.1646 **Gill**, C. and Briggs, A., *History of Birmingham*, 2 vols., 1952, vol I: *Manor and Borough to 1865*; vol. II: *Borough and City 1865 to 1938*. *See also* Stephens (5.1702).

5.1647 **Gillett**, E., *A History of Grimsby*, 1973.

5.1648 —— and Macmahon, M. A., *A History of Hull*, 1980. *See also* Jackson (5.1662).

5.1649 **Greaves**, R. W., *The Corporation of Leicester, 1689–1836*, 1st ed., 1939, 2nd ed., 1969. *See also* Elliot (5.1635), Patterson (5.1686), and Simmons (5.1697).

5.1650 **Grinsell**, L. V., *et al.*, *Studies in the History of Swindon*, 1950.

5.1651 **Harris**, J. R., ed., *Liverpool and Merseyside*, 1969. *See also* White (5.1711).

5.1652 **Heape**, R. G., *Buxton under the Dukes of Devonshire*, 1948.

5.1653 **Hill**, J. W. F., *Georgian Lincoln*, 1966.

5.1654 —— *Victorian Lincoln*, 1975.

5.1655 **Hinton**, M., *A History of the Town of Reading*, 1954; bibliography, 166–8.

5.1656 **Homeshaw**, E. J., *The Corporation of the Borough and Foreign of Walsall*, 1960.

5.1657 **Hopkins**, E., *Birmingham. The First Manufacturing Town in the World, 1760–1840*, 1989. Shows how rapid expansion preserved rather than destroyed the essential characteristics of Birmingham's earlier workshop economy.

5.1658 **Hoskins**, W. G., *Industry, Trade and People in Exeter, 1688–1800, with Special Reference to the Serge Industry*, 1935.

5.1659 **Humphries**, S. and Taylor, J., *The Making of Modern London*, 1986.

5.1660 **Hunt**, Edith M., *The History of Ware*, 1946. Reprinted 1949.

5.1661 **Jackson**, A. A., *Semi-detached London*, 1973.

5.1662 **Jackson**, G., *Hull in the Eighteenth Century: A Study in Economic and Social History*, 1971. *See also* Gillett and Macmahon (5.1648).

5.1663 **Jenkins**, S., *Landlords to London. The Story of a Capital and its Growth*, 1975.

5.1664 **Jones**, G. S., *Outcast London*, 1972. *See also* Dyos (5.1633).

5.1665 **Kennedy**, M., *Portrait of Manchester*, 1970. The best one-volume treatment.

5.1666 **Kidd**, A. J. and Roberts, K. W., eds., *City, Class and Culture. Studies of Social Policy and Cultural Production in Victorian Manchester*, 1985. Includes chapters on the police, philanthropy, anti-Semitism and on middle class and working-class culture.

5.1667 **Latimer**, C., *Parks for the People. Manchester and its Parks, 1846–1926*, 1987.

5.1668 **Little**, B., *The City and County of Bristol: A Study in Atlantic Civilisation*, 1954. *See also* Minchinton (5.1676).

5.1669 **Lloyd-Jones**, R. and Lewis, M. L., *Manchester and the Age of the Factory. The Business Structure of 'Cottonopolis' in the Industrial Revolution*, 1988.

5.1670 **Lowerson**, J., ed., *Cliftonville, Hove. A Victorian Suburb*, 1977.

5.1671 —— *Crawley. Victorian New Town*, 1980.

5.1672 **McInnes**, A., ' The emergence of a leisure town: Shrewsbury, 1660–1760', *P.P.*, CXX, 1988, 53–87.

5.1673 **Malmgreen**, G., *Silktown. Industry and Culture in Macclesfield, 1750–1835*, 1985. A reworked doctorial thesis which looks at the social and economic aspects of the Macclesfield silk industry. Religion, social order and social tension are also discussed.

5.1674 **Mason**, F., *Wolverhampton. The Town Commissioners, 1777–1848*, 1977.

5.1675 **Messinger**, G. S., *Manchester in the Victorian Age. The Half Known City*, 1985. A popular introduction.

5.1676 **Minchinton**, W. E., ' Bristol: metropolis of the west in the eighteenth century', *T.R.H.S.*, 5th ser., 4, 1954, 69–89. *See also* Little (5.1668).

5.1677 **Mingay**, G. E., *Georgian London*, 1975. *See also* George (5.1645) and Rudé (5.1694).

5.1678 **Money**, J., *Experience and Identity. Birmingham and the West Midlands, 1760–1800*, 1977. The centre of interest is politics but there is a full discussion of the social and economic community and its cultural provision.

5.1679 **Morgan**, J. B. and Peberdy, P., eds., *Collected Essays on Southampton*, 1968. Aspects of civic history from Anglo-Saxon times to the present.

5.1680 **Musgrave**, C., *Life in Brighton*, 1970.

5.1681 **Neale**, R. S., *Bath, 1680–1850. A Social History*, 1981. Looks at patterns in consumption, production and social consciousness.

5.1682 **Newton**, R., *Eighteenth-Century Exeter*, 1984.

5.1683 —— *Victorian Exeter, 1837–1914*, 1968. *See also* Hoskins (5.1658).

5.1684 **Olsen**, D. J., *Town Planning in London: The Eighteenth and Nineteenth Centuries*, 1967.

5.1685 **Owen**, C. C., *The Development of Industry in Burton upon Trent*, 1978.

5.1686 **Patterson**, A. T., *Radical Leicester: A History of Leicester, 1780–1850*, 1954.

5.1687 —— *A History of Southampton, 1700–1914*, vol. I, 1966 (covers 1700–1835); vol. II, 1972 (covers the period 1836–67), vol. III, (1868–1914), 1975.

5.1688 **Peacock**, S. E., *Borough Government in Portsmouth, 1835–1974*, 1975.

5.1689 **Redford**, A. and Russell, Ina S., *History of Local Government in Manchester*, 3 vols., 1939–40.

5.1690 **Richardson**, K., *Twentieth-century Coventry*, 1972.

5.1691 **Robson**, W. A., *The Government and Misgovernment of London*, 1939. Contains much historical material mainly from 1835 to date of publication.

5.1692 **Roebuck**, Janet, *Urban Development in Nineteenth-Century London: Lambeth, Battersea and Wandsworth, 1838–88*, 1979. Concentrates on local government administration.

5.1693 **Royle**, S. A., ' The development of Coalville, Leicestershire in the nineteenth century', *East Midlands Geog.*, VII, 1978, 32–42.

5.1694 **Rudé**, G., *The History of London: Hanoverian London, 1714–1808*, 1971.

5.1695 —— *Paris and London in the Eighteenth Century*, 1970. Concerned mainly with problems of public order and disorder. *See also* George (5.1645) and Mingay (5.1677).

5.1696 **Sheppard**, F. H. W., *London, 1808–70. The Infernal Wen*, 1971.

5.1697 **Simmons**, J., *Leicester Past and Present. II: The Modern Town*, 1975. Vol. I is listed above (2.371). On Leicester *see also* (5.1635), (5.1649), (5.1686).

5.1698 **Smith**, Doreen, ' Otley: a study of a market town during the late seventeenth and eighteenth centuries', *Yorks.Arch.J.*, LII, 1980, 43–56.

5.1699 **Smith**, J. H. and Simonds, J. V., eds., *New Mills. A short History including an Analysis of the Census of 1851*, 1977.

5.1700 **Smith**, V., ed., *The Town Book of Lewes, 1837–1901*, Sussex Rec.Soc., LXX, 1976.

5.1701 **Spiers**, M., *Victoria Park, Manchester. A Nineteenth-Century Suburb in its Social and Administrative Context*, Chet.Soc., 3rd ser., XXIII, 1976.

5.1702 **Stephens**, W. B., ed., *V.C.H. Warwickshire VII: The City of Birmingham*, 1964.

5.1703 **Stevenson**, J., ed., *London in the Age of Reform*, 1977. Includes chapters on the city opposition to Walpole and his successors and on the experience of 1848.

5.1704 **Stewart**, C., *The Stones of Manchester*, 1956. The Victorian buildings of the city.

5.1705 **Styles**, J., *Titus Salt and Saltaire. Industry and Virtue*, 1990.

5.1706 **Taylor**, R. P., *Rochdale Retrospect*, 1956. Useful summary; source references, 207–8.

5.1707 **Thompson**, F. M. L., *Hampstead: Building a Borough, 1650–1964*, 1974. *See also* Williams.

5.1708 **Tiratsou**, N., *Reconstruction, Affluence and Labour Politics: Coventry, 1945–60*, 1990.

5.1708a **Unwin**, R. W., ' Tradition and transition: market towns of the Vale of York, 1660–1830', *Northern H.*, XVII, 1981, 72–116.

5.1709 **Vigier**, F., *Change and Apathy: Liverpool and Manchester During the Industrial Revolution*, Cambridge, Mass., 1970.

5.1710 **Walker**, H. H., *History of Harrogate under the Improvement Commissioners, 1841–84*, 1986.

5.1711 **White**, B. D., *A History of the Corporation of Liverpool, 1834–1914*, 1951. On Liverpool *see also* (5.1617).

5.1712 **Williams**, G. R., *London in the Country: The Growth of Suburbia*, 1975. *See also* Thompson (5.1707).

5.1713 **Winter**, G., *Past Positive: London's Social History Recorded in Photographs*, 1971. Covers the period from 1840s to 1914.

5.1714 **Wood**, R., *West Hartlepool: The Rise and Development of a Victorian New Town*, 1967.

5.1715 **Young**, K. and Garside, P., *Metropolitan London. Politics and Urban Change, 1837–1981*, 1982.

BANKING, CURRENCY AND PUBLIC FINANCE

(a) Banking and the London money market

5.1716 **Anderson**, B. L. and Cottrell, P. L., *Money and Banking in England. The Development of the Banking System, 1694–1914*, 1974.

5.1717 **Gregory**, T. E., ed., *Select Statutes, Documents and Reports Relating to British Banking, 1832–1928*, 2 vols., 1929, 2nd ed., 1964 (vol. I: 1832–44: vol. II: 1847–1928).

5.1718 **Acworth**, A. W., *Financial Reconstruction in England, 1815–1822*, 1925.

5.1719 **Ashton**, T. S. and Sayers, R. S., eds., *Papers in English Monetary History*, 1953.

5.1720 **Bolitho**, H. and Peel, D., *The Drummonds of Charing Cross*, 1967.

5.1721 **Booth**, H. M., *The Commercial Crisis of 1847*, 1984.

5.1722 **Bowden**, S. and Collins, M., *The Bank of England, Industrial Regeneration and Hire Purchase between the Wars*, 1991.

5.1723 **Boyle**, A., *Montagu Norman*, 1967.

5.1724 **Broadberry**, S. N., ' Cheap money and the housing boom in interwar Britain: an economic appraisal', *Manchester School*, LV, 1987, 378–91.

5.1725 **Capie**, F. and Webber, E., *Profits and Profitability in British Banking, 1870–1939*, 1985.

5.1726 **Clapham**, J. H., *The Bank of England: A History*, 2 vols., 1944. Reprinted 1958 (Vol. I: *1694–1797*, Vol. II: *1797–1914*).

5.1727 **Clay**, H. *Lord Norman*, 1957, especially Chapter VIII on banks and the finance of industry.

5.1728 **Collins**, M., ' The banking crisis of 1878', *Ec.H.R.*, 2nd ser., XLII, 1989, 504–27.

5.1729 —— *Banks and Industrial Finance before 1939*, 1990.

5.1730 —— ' English bank lending and the financial crisis of the 1870s', *Bus.H.*, XXXII, 1990, 198–224.

5.1731 **Costigliola**, F. C., ' Anglo-American financial rivalry in the 1920s', *J.Ec.H.*, XXXVII, 1977, 911–34.

5.1732 **Cramp**, A. B., *Opinion on Bank Rate, 1822–1860*, 1962.

5.1733 **Dacey**, H. M., *The British Banking Mechanism*, 1951. Outlines the working of the financial system since 1931.

5.1734 **De Cecco**, M., *Money and Empire. The International Gold Standard, 1890–1914*, 1975.

5.1735 **Drummond**, I., *The Floating Pound and the Sterling Area, 1931–39*, 1981.

5.1736 —— *The Gold Standard and the International Monetary System, 1900–29*, 1987.

5.1737 **Duffy**, I. P. H., ' The discount poicy of the Bank of England during the suspension of cash payments, 1797–1821', *Ec.H.R.*, 2nd ser., XXXV, 1982, 67–82.

5.1738 **Eichengreen**, B., *Golden Fetters. The Gold Standard and the Great Depression, 1919–39*, 1992.

5.1739 **Fetter**, F. W., *The Development of British Monetary Orthodoxy, 1797–1875*, Cambridge, Mass., 1965.

5.1740 **Fletcher**, G. A., *The Discount Houses in London*, 1976.

5.1741 **Goetschin**, P., *L'Evolution du marché monétaire de Londres (1931–1952)*, Geneva and Paris, 1963.

5.1742 **Goodhart**, C. A. E., *The Business of Banking, 1891–1914*, 1972, 2nd ed. 1986.

5.1743 **Grady**, J., *British Banking, 1960–85*, 1986.

5.1744 **Grant**, A. T. K., *A Study of the Capital Market in Britain from 1919–1936*, 2nd ed., 1967, of book originally published 1937 under slightly different title.

5.1745 **Hawtrey**, R. G., *A Century of Bank Rate*, 1938.

5.1746 **Hennessy**, Elizabeth, *A Domestic History of the Bank of England, 1930–60*, 1992. Concerned with change in the Bank's organisation, staff and buildings.

5.1747 **Horsefield**, J. K., ' The orgins of the Bank Charter Act, 1844'. In Ashton and Sayers, eds. (5.1719), 109–25.

5.1748 **James**, H., Lindgren, H. and Teichova, A., eds., *The Role of Banks in the Interwar Economy*, 1991.

5.1749 **King**, W. T. C., *The History of the London Discount Market*, 1936.

5.1750 **Lavington**, E., *The English Capital Market*, 1921. Reprinted 1969.

5.1751 **Michie**, R. C., *The City of London. Continuity and Change, 1850–1990*, 1992. Looks at the trade and commodity markets, the banks, the stock exchange, and at insurance, accountancy and business law in the capital in the last 140 years.

5.1752 —— *The London and the New York Stock Exchanges, 1850–1914*, 1987.

5.1753 **Moggridge**, D. E., *The Return to Gold, 1925*, 1969.

5.1754 —— *British Monetary Policy, 1924–1931: The Norman Conquest of $4.86*, 1972.

5.1755 **Morgan**, E. V., *The Theory and Practice of Central Banking, 1797–1913*, 1st ed., 1943, 2nd ed., 1965.

5.1756 —— *Studies in British Financial Policy, 1914–1925*, 1952.

5.1757 —— and Thomas, W. A., *The Stock Exchange: Its History and Functions*, 1962.

5.1758 **Nishimura**, S., *The Decline of Inland Bills of Exchange in the London Money Market, 1855–1913*, 1971.

5.1759 **Pollard**, S., ed., *The Gold Standard and Employment Policies between the wars*, 1970. Seven essays by Keynes, R. S. Sayers and others.

5.1760 **Pressnell**, L. S., ' Gold reserves, banking reserves and the Baring Crisis of 1890'. In *Essays in Money and Banking in Honour of R. S. Sayers*, eds. C. R. Whittlesey and J. S. G. Wilson, 1968, 167–78.

5.1761 **Redish**, A., ' The evolution of the gold standard in England', *J.Ec.H.*, L, 1990, 789–806.

5.1762 **Rees**, J. F., *A Short Fiscal and Financial History of England, 1815–1918*, 1921.

5.1763 **Richards**, R. D., ' The first fifty years of the Bank of England, 1694–1744'. In J. G. van Dillen, *History of the Principal Public Banks*, 1934, 2nd ed., 1964, 201–72.

5.1764 **Rowland**, B. M., ed., *Balance of Power or Hegemony: The Inter-war Monetary System*, 1976.

5.1765 **Sayers**, R. S., *The Bank of England, 1891–1944*, 3 vols., 1976. Vol. I takes the study as far as the Macmillan Committee, vol. II covers the years 1931–44, and vol. III consists of appendices.

5.1766 —— *Central Banking after Bagehot*, 1957.

5.1767 —— *Gilletts in the London Money Market, 1867–1967*, 1968.

5.1768 **Sheppard**, D. K., *The Growth and Role of U.K. Financial Institutions, 1880–1962*, 1971.

5.1769 **Silberling**, N. J., ' Financial and monetary policy in Great Britain during the Napoleonic Wars', *Quarterly J.Economics*, LXXIII, 1924, 145–68.

5.1770 **Solomon**, R., *The International Monetary*

System, 1945–76, 1977.

5.1771 **Sutherland**, Lucy S., *Politics and Finance in the Eighteenth Century*, 1983. Looks at the ways in which politics in this period was underpinned by the City of London monied interest and by the East India Company.

5.1772 **Tew**, B., *The Evolution of the International Monetary System, 1945–77*, 1977.

5.1773 **Thomas**, S. E., *British Banks and the Finance of Industry*, 1931.

5.1774 **Winton**, J. R., *Lloyds Bank, 1918–69*, 1982.

5.1775 **Ziegler**, P., *The Sixth Great Power: Barings, 1762–1929*, 1988.

(b) The exchange equalisation account

5.1776 **Hall**, N. F., *The Exchange Equalization Account*, 1935.

5.1777 **Waight**, L., *The History and Mechanism of the Exchange Equalisation Account*, 1939.

(c) Country banking

(i) GENERAL WORKS

5.1778 **Horne**, H. O., *A History of Savings Banks*, 1947.

5.1779 **Pressnell**, L. S., *Country Banking in the Industrial Revolution*, 1956.

5.1780 **Sykes**, J., *The Amalgamation Movement in English Banking*, 1926.

5.1781 **Thomas**, S. E., *The Rise and Growth of Joint Stock Banking*, 2 vols., 1934.

(ii) REGIONAL AND LOCAL STUDIES

5.1782 **Allman**, A. H., *et al.*, *Williams Deacon's, 1771–1970*, 1971.

5.1783 **Ashton**, T. S., ' The bill of exchange and private banks in Lancashire, 1790–1830'. In Ashton and Sayers, (5.1719), 37–50.

5.1784 **Chandler**, G., *Four Centuries of Banking, as Illustrated by the Bankers, Customers, and Staff Associated with the Constituent Banks of Martins Bank Ltd.*, 2 vols., 1964–8. Vol. I: *The Grasshopper and the Liver-Bird-Liverpool and London*. Vol. II: *The Northern Constitutent Banks*.

5.1785 **Crick**, W. F. and Wadsworth, J. E., *A Hundred Years of Joint Stock Banking*, 1936. A history of the Midland Bank.

5.1786 **Duffy**, I. P. H., *Bankruptcy and Insolvency in London during the Industrial Revolution*, 1985.

5.1787 **Hoare**, H. P. R., *Hoare's Bank: A Record, 1673–1932*, 1932.

5.1788 **Hyde**, F. E. *et al.*, ' The port of Liverpool and the crisis of 1793', *Economica*, n.s., XVIII, 1951, 363–78.

5.1789 **Leighton-Boyce**, J. A. S. L., *Smiths the Bankers* [of Nottingham] *1658–1958*, 1958.

5.1790 **Miles**, M., ' The money market in the early Industrial Revolution: the evidence from West Riding attorneys, c.1750–1800', *Bus.H.*, XXIII, 1981, 127–47.

5.1791 **Moss**, D. J., ' The Bank of England and the country banks: Birmingham, 1827–33', *Ec.H.R.*, 2nd ser., XXXIV, 1981, 540–53.

5.1792 **Saunders**, P. T., *Stuckey's Bank*, 1926. A famous Somerset bank.

5.1793 **Sayers**, R. S., *Lloyds Bank in the History of English Banking*, 1957.

5.1794 **Taylor**, Audrey M., *Gilletts, Bankers at Banbury and Oxford: A Study in Local Economic History*, 1964.

5.1795 **Ziegler**, D., *Central Bank, Peripheral Industry. The Bank of England in the Provinces, 1826–1913*, 1990. *See* p. 219 on Welsh banking p. 231, on Scottish banking, and p. 246 on Irish banking.

(d) Currency

5.1796 **Cannan**, E., ed., *The Paper Pound of 1797–1821: A Reprint of the Bullion Report* (of 1810), 1919, 2nd ed., 1925, 3rd ed., with new introduction by B. A. Corry, 1969.

5.1797 **Tooke**, T., *An Inquiry into the currency Principle*, 2nd ed., 1844. Reprinted 1959.

5.1798 **Capie**, F. and Webber, E., *A Monetary History of the United Kingdom, 1870–1982*, 1985.

5.1799 **Challis**, C. E., ed., *A New History of the Royal Mint*, 1992.

5.1800 **Chaloner**, W. H., 'Currency problems of the British Empire, 1814–1914', in Ratcliffe (5.107), 179–208.

5.1801 **Coppieters**, E., *English Bank Note*

Circulation, 1694–1954, The Hague, 1955.

5.1802 **Dalton**, R. and Hamer, S. H., *The Provincial Token Coinage of the Eighteenth Century*, 4 vols., 1910–18. Reissued in one vol., 1967.

5.1803 **Holden**, J. M., *The History of Negotiable Instruments in English Law*, 1955.

5.1804 **Mathias**, P., *English Trade Tokens: The Industrial Revolution Illustrated*, 1962.

(e) Public finance

(i) THE NATIONAL DEBT

5.1805 **Carter**, Alice C., *The English Public Debt in the Eighteenth Century*, 1968.

5.1806 **Dickson**, P. G. M., *The Financial Revolution in England: A Study in the Development of Public Credit, 1688–1756*, 1967.

5.1807 **Hargreaves**, E. L., *The National Debt*, 1930, 2nd ed., 1966.

(ii) THE SOUTH SEA BUBBLE

5.1808 **Carswell**, J., *The South Sea Bubble*, 1960.

5.1809 **Hoppit**, J., 'Financial crises in eighteenth-century England', Ec.H.R., Ec.H.R., 2nd ser., XXXIX, 1986, 39–58.

5.1810 **Patterson**, M. and Reiffen, D., 'The effect of the Bubble Act on the market for joint stock shares', *J.Ec.H.*, L, 1990, 163–71.

5.1811 **Sperling**, J. G., *The South Sea Company: An Historical Essay and Bibliographical Finding List*, Boston, Mass., 1962.

(iii) TAXES

5.1812 **Langford**, P., *The Excise Crisis. Society and Politics in the Age of Walpole*, 1975.

5.1813 **Mathias**, P. and O'Brien, P., 'Taxation in Britain, 1715–1810', *J.Europ.Ec.H.*, V, 1976, 601–50.

5.1814 **O'Brien**, P. K., 'The political economy of British taxation, 1600–1815', *Ec.H.R.*, 2nd ser., XLI, 1988, 1–32.

(1) INCOME TAX

5.1815 **Farnsworth**, A., *Addington, Author of the Modern Income Tax*, 1951.

5.1816 **Hope-Jones**, A., *Income Tax in the*

Napoleonic Wars, 1939.

5.1817 **Sabine**, B. E. V., *A History of Income Tax*, 1966. Covers the modern period.

5.1818 **Shehab**, F. A., *Progressive Taxation: A Study of the Progressive Principle in the British Income Tax*, 1953.

(2) LAND TAX

5.1819 **Ginter**, D. E., *A Measure of Wealth. The English Land Tax in Historical Analysis*, 1992.

5.1820 **Ward**, W. R., *The English Land Tax in the Eighteenth Century*, 1953.

(3) SALT TAX

See Hughes (4.977).

(iv) ADMINISTRATION AND BUDGETARY CONTROL

5.1821 **Baker**, N., *Government and Contractors: The British Treasury and War Supplies, 1775–1783*, 1971.

5.1822 **Binney**, J. E. D., *British Public Finance and Administration, 1774–1792*, 1958.

5.1823 **Blaug**, M., *John Maynard Keynes. Life, Ideas, Legacy*, 1989.

5.1824 **Bleaney**, M., *The Rise and Fall of Keynesian Economics*, 1984.

5.1825 **Booth**, A., *British Economic Policy, 1931–49. Was there a Keynesian Revolution?*, 1989.

5.1826 **Clarke**, P., *The Keynesian Revolution in the Making, 1924–1936*, 1988. Considers the development of Keynes's economic thinking in the light of the changing context of the interwar period.

5.1827 **Dimand**, R., *The Origins of Keynesian Revolution. The Development of Keynes's Theory of Employment and Output*, 1988.

5.1828 **Fletcher**, G. A., *The Keynesian Revolution and its Critics*, 1986.

5.1829 **Harcourt**, G. C., ed., *Keynes and his Contemporaries*, 1985.

5.1830 **Hicks**, Ursula K., *British Public Finances: Their Structure and Development, 1880–1952*, 1954.

5.1831 —— *The Finance of British Government, 1920–36*, 1938.

5.1832 **Hillard**, J., ed., *J. M. Keynes in Retrospect. The Legacy of the Keynesian Revolution*, 1988.

5.1833 **Hirst**, F. W., *Gladstone as Financier and Economist*, 1931.

5.1834 **Howson**, Susan, *Domestic Monetary Management in Great Britain, 1919–38*, 1975.

5.1835 **Keynes**, M., ed., *Essays on John Maynard Keynes*, 1975.

5.1836 **Kindleberger**, C. P., *Keynesianism v. Monetarism and other Essays in Financial History*, 1985. Includes comparative essays on Britain and France in the nineteenth and twentieth centuries.

5.1837 **Middleton**, R., 'The constant employment budget balance and British budgetary policy, 1929–39', *Ec.H.R.*, 2nd ser., XXXIV, 1981, 266–86.

5.1838 **Minsky**, H. P., *John Maynard Keynes*, 1976.

5.1839 **Moggridge**, D. E., *Keynes*, 1976.

5.1840 **Morgan**, B., *Monetarists and Keynesians. Their Contribution to Monetary Theory*, 1978.

5.1841 **Morton**, W. A., *British Finance, 1930–1940*, Madison, Wis., 1943.

5.1842 **Murray**, B. K., *The People's Budget, 1909–10*, 1980.

5.1843 **Nevin**, E., *The Mechanism of Cheap Money: A Study of British Monetary Policy, 1931–39*, 1955.

5.1844 **O'Donnell**, R. M., *Keynes. Philosophy, Economics and Politics*, 1989.

5.1845 **Patinkin**, D., *Keynes's Monetary Thought: A Study of its Development*, 1976.

5.1846 **Roseveare**, H. G., *The Treasury, 1660–1870. The Foundations of Control*, 1973. A volume in the *Historical Problems: Studies and Documents* series.

5.1847 **Sabine**, B. E. V., *British Budgets in Peace and War, 1932–1945*, 1970.

5.1848 **Sayers**, R. S., *Financial Policy, 1939–45*, 1956. Part of the British official civil history of the war.

5.1849 **Skidlesky**, R., *John Maynard Keynes. I: Hopes Betrayed 1883–1920*, 1983; *II: The Economist as Saviour, 1920–1937*, 1992. The standard biography.

5.1850 **Thirlwall**, A. P., ed., *Keynes as a Policy Advisor*, 1982.

5.1851 **Tomlinson**, J., 'The Attlee government and the balance of payments, 1945–51', *Twentieth Century Brit.H.*, 1991, 47–66.

ACCOUNTANCY

5.1852 **Jones**, E., *Accountancy and the British Economy, 1840–1980. The Evolution of Ernst and Whinney*, 1982.

5.1853 **Littleton**, A. C. and Yamey, B. S., *Studies in the History of Accounting*, 1956. Contains a number of articles on various aspects of British accountancy history.

5.1854 **Stacey**, N. A. H., *English Accountancy: A Study in Social and Economic History, 1800–1954*, 1954.

INSURANCE

5.1855 **Cockerell**, H. A. L. and Green, E., *The British Insurance Business, 1547–1970. An Introduction and Guide to Historical Records in the United Kingdom*, 1976.

5.1856 **Dickson**, P. G. M., *The Sun Insurance Office, 1710–1960: The History of Two Hundred and Fifty Years of British Insurance*, 1960.

5.1857 **Drew**, B., *The London Assurance: A Second Chronicle*, 1949. Much enlarged version of a 'first chronicle' published in 1927.

5.1858 **Garnett**, R. G., *A Century of Co-operative Insurance: The Co-operative Insurance Society 1867–1967*, 1968.

5.1859 **Morrah**, D., *A History of Industrial Life Assurance* 1955.

5.1860 **Pearson**, R., 'Taking risks and containing competition: diversification and oligopoly in the fire insurance markets of the North of England in the early nineteenth century', *Ec.H.R.*, 2nd ser., XLVI, 1993, 39–64.

5.1861 **Supple**, B. E., *The Royal Exchange Assurance: A History of British Insurance*, 1970. The best treatment of the subject.

5.1862 **Trebilcock**, C., *Phoenix Assurance and the Development of British Insurance. I: 1787–1870*, 1985.

5.1863 **Withers**, H., *Pioneers of British Life Assurance*, 1951.

BUILDING SOCIETIES

5.1864 **Bellman**, H., *The Thrifty Three Millions: A Study of the Building Society Movement and the Story of the Abbey Road Society*, 1935.

5.1865 **Clearly**, E. J., *The Building Society Movement*, 1965. The best general history.

5.1866 **Hobson**, O. R., *A Hundred Years of the Halifax: The History of the Halifax Building Society, 1853–1953*, 1953.

5.1867 **Humphries**, J., 'Interwar house building, cheap money and building societies: the housing boom revisited', *Bus.H.*, XXIX, 1987, 325–45.

5.1868 **Mansbridge**, A., *Brick upon Brick*, 1934. History of the Co-operative Permanent Building Society from 1884.

5.1869 **Price**, S. J., *Building Societies: Their Origins and History*, 1958.

5.1870 —— *From Queen to Queen: The Centenary History of the Temperance Permanent Building Society, 1854–1954*, 1954.

quantitative with a qualitiative approach. Undue reliance on insurance records as indicators of firms' assets calls into question some of the findings.

5.1876 **Higgins**, J. P. R. and Pollard, S., eds. *Aspects of Capital Investment in Great Britain, 1750–1850: A Preliminary Survey*, 1971.

5.1877 **Minchinton**, W. E., ed., *Capital Formation in South-West England*, 1978.

5.1878 **Pollard**, S., 'Fixed capital in the industrial revolution in Britain', *J.Ec.H.*, XXIV, 1964, 299–314.

5.1879 **Richardson**, P., 'The structure of capital during the Industrial Revolution revisited: two case studies from the cotton textile industry', *Ec.H.R.*, 2nd ser., XLII, 1989, 484–503.

5.1880 **Thomas**, W. A., *The Provincial Stock Exchange*, 1973. Mainly 1800–1914.

5.1881 —— *The Finance of British Industry, 1918–76*, 1978. Deals, inter al., with internal funding, the capital market, the banks and industry, and with the public corporations.

CAPITAL FORMATION

5.1871 **Anderson**, B. L., ed., *Capital Accumulation in the Industrial Revolution*, 1974. Selected readings from Adam Smith to Giffen.

5.1872 **Black**, I., 'Geography, political economy and the circulation of capital in early industrial England', *J.Hist.Geog.*, XV, 1989, 366–84.

5.1873 **Cottrell**, P. L., *Industrial Finance, 1830–1914. The Finance and Organisation of English Manufacturing Industry*, 1980. Deals with the development of company law, with shares and shareholders, private companies and public combines, and with the role of the banks.

5.1874 **Crouzet**, F., intro. and ed., *Capital Formation in the Industrial Revolution*, 1972. A symposium of essays by various hands.

5.1875 **Feinstein**, C. H. and Pollard, S., eds., *Studies in Capital Formation in the United Kingdom, 1750–1920*, 1988. Combines a

JOINT STOCK COMPANIES

5.1882 **Cooke**, C. A., *Corporation, Trust and Company: An Essay in Legal History*, 1950.

5.1883 **Du Bois**, A. B., *The English Business Company After the Bubble Act, 1720–1800*, N. Y., 1938.

5.1884 **Evans**, G. H. *British Corporation Finance, 1775–1800*, Baltimore, 1936. The evolution of the preference share in the canal age.

5.1885 **Hunt**, B. C., *The Development of the Business Corporation in England, 1800–1867*, Cambridge, Mass., 1936.

5.1886 **Jefferys**, J. B., 'The denomination and character of shares, 1855–1885'. In Carus-Wilson, ed. (1.326), I, 344–57.

5.1887 **Shannon**, H. A., 'The coming of general limited liability'. In Carus-Wilson, ed. (1.326), I, 358–79.

5.1888 —— 'The first five thousand limited companies and their duration', *Ec.J.,Ec.H.Supp.*, II, 1932, 396–424.

5.1889 —— 'The limited companies of

1866–1883'. In Carus-Wilson, ed. (1.326), I, 380–405.

5.1890 **Welbourne**, E., 'Bankruptcy before the era of Victorian reform', *Cambridge H.J.*, IV, 1932, 51–62.

CLASSES AND SOCIAL GROUPS

(a) General works

5.1891 **Briggs**, A., 'The language of "class" in early nineteenth-century England', in Briggs and Saville (5.1987), I, 43–73.

5.1892 —— 'The language of "mass" and "masses" in nineteenth-century England', in Martin & Rubinstein (5.2024), 62–83.

5.1893 **Cannadine**, D., 'The theory and practice of the English leisure classes', (Review article), H.J., XXI, 1978, 445–67.

5.1894 **Cashmore**, E. E., *United Kingdom? Class, Race and Gender since the War*, 1989.

5.1895 **Donajgrodzki**, A. P., ed., *Social Control in Nineteenth-Century Britain*, 1977. *See also* Thompson (5.1911).

5.1896 **Gloversmith**, F., ed., *Class, Culture and Social Change. A New View of the 1930s*, 1980.

5.1897 **Hardy**, D., *Alternative Communities in Nineteenth-Century England*, 1979.

5.1898 **Kaye**, H. J., ed., *History, Classes and Nation States. Selected Writings of Victor Kiernan*, 1988. A lively collection of reprinted essays by this eminent Marxist historian with a useful introduction.

5.1899 **Kearns**, G. and Withers, C. W. J., eds., *Urbanising Britain. Essays on Class and Community in the Nineteenth Century*, 1991.

5.1900 **Mabey**, R., ed., *Class: A Symposium*, 1967.

5.1901 **Marshall**, G., Newby, H., Rose, D., and Vogler, Carolyn, *Social Class in Modern Britain*, 1988. Through social survey methods the book considers the extent to which class has become overshadowed by divisions of gender, race, region, occupation, and unemployment.

5.1902 **Marwick**, A., *Class: Image and Reality in Britain, France and the U.S.A. since 1930*, 1980.

5.1903 **Mason**, P., *The English Gentleman. The Rise and Fall of an Ideal*, 1982.

5.1904 **Morris**, R. J., *Class and Class Consciousness in the Industrial Revolution*, 1979. A general introduction with useful select bibliography.

5.1905 **Neale**, R. S., *Class in English History, 1680–1850*, 1981. Rehearses the author's well-known five-class model of English society and explores the theoretical and empirical problems involved in defining class and class consciousness.

5.1906 —— ed., *History and Class. Essential Readings in Theory and Interpretation*, 1983. An edited collection of readings in which key exponents, such as Briggs, Thompson, Perkin and Laslett, are represented.

5.1907 **Perkin**, H. J., *The Origins of Modern English Society 1780–1880*, 1969. Principally concerned with class and class consciousness and their relation to the Industrial Revolution and its consequences.

5.1908 —— *Professionalism, Property and English Society since 1880*, 1981.

5.1909 —— *The Structured Crowd. Essays in English Social History*, 1981. A curiously titled miscellany of essays. 'Land reform and class conflict in Victorian Britain' is the most substantial.

5.1910 **Phillips**, K. C., *Language and Class in Victorian England*, 1984. Chiefly a linguistic study weighted towards upper class usage.

5.1911 **Thompson**, F. M. L., 'Social control in Victorian Britain', *Ec.H.R.*, 2nd ser., XXXIV, 1981, 189–208. *See also* Donajgrodzki (5.1895).

(b) The entrepreneurial and professional middle classes

5.1912 **Aldcroft**, D. H., 'British industry and foreign competition, 1875–1914'. In Aldcroft (5.184), 11–36.

5.1913 **Armytage**, W. H. G., *The Rise of the Technocrats: A Social History*, 1965. Contains important material on connections between British industrialists and scientists.

5.1914 **Arnstein**, W. L., 'The myth of the triumphant Victorian middle class', *Historian*, XXXVII, 1975, 205–21.

5.1915 **Aylett**, P., 'Attorneys and clients in eighteenth-century Cheshire: a study in relationships, 1740–85', *Bull.J.Rylands Lib.*, LXIX, 1987, 326–58.

5.1916 **Baker**, M., *The Rise of the Victorian Actor*, 1978.

5.1917 **Beresford**, M. W., *The Leeds Chambers of Commerce*, 1951.

5.1918 **Bradley**, I., *The English Middle Classes are Alive and Kicking*, 1982. *See also* Lewis and Maude (5.1937).

5.1919 **Campbell**, R. H. and Wilson, R. G., eds., *Entrepreneurship in Britain, 1750–1939*, 1975.

5.1920 **Carr-Saunders**, A. M., and Wilson, P., *The Professions*, 1933.

5.1921 **Carter**, B., *Capitalism, Class Conflict and the New Middle Class*, 1985.

5.1922 **Checkland**, S. G., *The Gladstones. A Family Biography, 1764–1851*, 1971.

5.1923 **Crossick**, G., ed., *The Lower Middle Class in Britain, 1870–1914*, 1976. Includes chapters on values, politics, religion, culture and housing.

5.1924 **Crouzet**, F., *The First Industrialists: the Problem of Origins*, 1984. Shows that many came from relatively humble backgrounds.

5.1925 **Davidoff**, Leonore and Hall, Catherine, *Family fortunes. Men and Women of the English Middle Classes, 1780–1850*, 1987. Avowedly feminist approach to the structures of middle class life in Birmingham, Essex and Suffolk.

5.1926 **Duman**, D., 'The creation and diffusion of a professional ideology in nineteenth-century England', *Soc.R.*, XXVII, XXVII, 1979, 113–38. *See also* Perkin (5.1907).

5.1927 **Erickson**, Charlotte, *British Industrialists: Steel and Hosiery, 1850–1950*, 1959.

5.1928 **Erlich**, C., *The Music Profession in Britain since the Eighteenth Century. A Social History*, 1986. Places the nineteenth-century revolution in the profession of music in context.

5.1929 **Green**, E., *Debtors to their Profession. A History of the Institute of Bankers, 1879–1979*, 1979.

5.1930 **Gross**, J., *The Rise and Fall of the Man of Letters. Aspects of English Literary Life since 1800*, 1969.

5.1931 **Harries-Jenkins**, G., *The Army in Victorian Society*, 1977.

5.1932 **Hartwell**, R. M., 'Business management in England during the period of early industrialization: inducements and obstacles'. In Hartwell, ed. (5.71), 28–41.

5.1933 **Heeney**, B., *A Different Kind of Gentleman. Parish Clergy as Professional Men in Early and Mid-Victorian England*, 1977.

5.1934 **Howe**, E., *The British Federation of Master Printers, 1900–1950*, 1950.

5.1935 **Jeremy**, D. J., ed., *Dictionary of Business Biography*, 4 vols., 1984–5.

5.1936 —— 'The hundred largest employers in the U.K. in manufacturing and non-manufacturing industries in 1907, 1935, and 1955', *Bus.H.*, XXXIII, 1991, 93–111.

5.1937 **Lewis**, R. and Maude, A., *The English Middle Classes*, 1949. *See also* Bradley (5.1918).

5.1938 **Malchow**, H. L., *Gentleman Capitalists. The Social and Political World of the Victorian Businessman*, 1992. Examines the overlapping social, economic and political networks of the late nineteenth-century industrialists. Case studies illustrate the general themes.

5.1939 **Mayer**, A. J., 'The lower middle class as historical problem', *J.M.H.*, XLVII, 1975, 409–36.

5.1940 **Morris**, R. J., *Class Sect and Party. The Making of the British Middle Class: Leeds 1820–50*, 1990. A computer aided study which analyses the structure and complexities of the group's status, wealth, religious allegiance, political behaviour and cultural identities.

5.1941 —— 'Samuel Smiles and the Genesis of Self Help: the retreat to a petit bourgeois utopia', *H.J.*, XXIV, 1981, 89–110.

5.1942 **Munford**, W. A., *A History of the Library Association, 1877–1977*, 1977.

5.1943 **Parry**, N. and J., *The Rise of the Medical Profession. A Study of Collective Social Mobility*, 1976.

5.1944 **Payne**, P. L., *British Entrepreneurship in the Nineteenth Century*, 1974.

5.1945 **Perkin**, H. J., *Key Profession: The History of the Association of University Teachers*, 1969.

5.1946 **Pollard**, S., *The Genesis of Modern Management: A Study of the Industrial Revolution in Great Britain*, 1965.

5.1947 **Reader**, W. J., *Professional Men: The Rise of the Professional Classes in Nineteenth-century England*, 1966.

5.1948 **Robson**, R., *The Attorney in Eighteenth-century England*, 1959.

5.1949 **Rubinstein**, W. D., *Men of Property*, 1981. Surveys the propertied elite from the Industrial Revolution. Packed with statistical tables.

5.1950 —— 'The Victorian middle class: wealth, occupation and geography', *Ec.H.R.*, 2nd ser., XXX, 1977, 582–601.

5.1951 —— 'The size and distribution of the English middle classes in 1860', *Hist.Res.*, LXI, 1988, 65–89.

5.1952 **Schwarz**, L. D., 'Social class and social geography: the middle classes in London at the end of the eighteenth century', *Soc.H.*, VII, 1982, 167–86.

5.1953 **Skelly**, A. R., *The Victorian Army at Home*, 1977. *See also* Harries-Jenkins (5.1931).

5.1954 **Stephens**, J. R., *The Profession of the Playwright. British Theatre, 1800–1900*, 1992.

5.1955 **Thompson**, F. M. L., *Chartered Surveyors: The Growth of a Profession*, 1968. With the exception of the first two chapters the book is concerned with developments after 1700.

5.1956 —— 'Life after death: how successful nineteenth-century businessmen disposed of their fortunes', *Ec.H.R.*, 2nd ser., XLIII, 1990, 40–61.

5.1957 **Travers**, T. H. E., 'Samuel Smiles and the origins of Self Help: reform and the new enlightenment', *Albion*, IX, 1977, 161–87. *See also* (5.1941).

5.1958 **Tropp**, A., *The School Teachers: The Growth of the Teaching Profession in England and Wales from 1800 to the Present Day*, 1957.

5.1959 **Turner**, J., ed., *Businessmen and Politics. Studies of Business Activities in British Politics, 1900–1945*, 1984. Essays exploring the collective response of businessmen to economic trends and government policy.

5.1960 **Wolff**, Janet and Seed, J., eds., *The Culture of Capital. Art, Power and the Nineteenth-Century Middle Class*, 1988. A collection of seven essays which includes discussions of the 'failure' of the urban industrial middle class, the art world of Victorian Manchester, and exhibitions in Leeds.

(c) The working class

(i) BIBLIOGRAPHICAL STUDIES AND STATISTICS

5.1961 **Lee**, C. H., *British Regional Employment Statistics, 1841–1971*, 1979.

5.1962 **Maehl**, W. H., ' "Jerusalem deferred": recent writing in the history of the British labour movement', *J.M.H.*, 41, 1969, 335–67.

5.1963 **Wolfe**, W., 'A century of books on the history of Socialism in Britain. Part I: before 1950. Part II: after 1850', *Brit.Studs.Monitor*, X, 1 & 2, 1980, 46–65; X, 3, 1981, 18–46.

(ii) DOCUMENTARY COLLECTIONS AND CONTEMPORARY WORKS

5.1964 **Burnett**, J., ed., *Destiny Obscure. Autobiographies of Childhood, Education and Family from the 1820s to the 1920s*, 1982.

5.1965 **Bray**, J. F., *A Voyage from Utopia*, ed. M. F. Lloyd-Pritchard, 1957.

5.1966 —— *Labour's Wrongs and Labour's Remedy*, 1839. Reprinted 1931.

5.1967 **Coats**, A. W., ed., *Poverty in the Victorian Age*, 4 vols, 1974. Reprints articles from contemporary periodicals.

5.1968 **Cole**, G. D. H., and Filson, A. W., *British Working Class Movements: Select Documents, 1789–1875*, 1951. Reprinted 1965.

5.1969 **Engels**, F., *The Condition of the Working Class in England (1845)*, trans. and ed. W. O. Henderson and W. H. Chaloner, 1958 and 1971. Another edition ed. E. J. Hobsbawm, 1969. On Engels *see* Marcus (5.2023).

5.1970 **Ginswick**, J., ed., *Labour and the Poor in England and Wales 1849–51*, 3 vols., 1983. Collects together the Morning Chronicle's reports.

5.1971 **Hobsbawm**, E. J., ed., *Labour's Turning Point 1880–1900: Extracts from Contemporary Sources*, 1948.

5.1972 **Hodgskin**, T., *Labour Defended Against the Claims of Capital*, 1825. Reprinted 1922 and 1964, with introduction by G. D. H. Cole.

5.1973 **Hollis**, Patricia M., ed., *Class and Conflict in Nineteenth-century England, 1815–50*, 1973. A collection of documents largely from radical sources: guides to further reading are unsatisfactory.

5.1974 **Jefferys**, J. B., ed., *Labour's Formative Years 1849–1879: Extracts from Contemporary Sources*, 1948.

5.1975 **Mayhew**, H., *London Labour and the London Poor*, 1st ed. in 3 vols., 1851, 2nd enlarged ed. in 4 vols., 1861–2, new impression, 1967.

5.1976 —— *The Street Trader's Lot – London, 1851*, (ed. S. Rubinstein), 1947.

5.1977 —— *Mayhew's London, Being Selections from London Labour and the London Poor*, ed. P. Quennell, 1969.

5.1978 —— *London's Underworld: Selections from London Labour and the London Poor*, ed. P. Quennell, 1969.

5.1979 —— *The Unknown Mayhew: Selections from the Morning Chronicle, 1849–50*, eds. E. P. Thompson and Eileen Yeo, 1971. On Mayhew *see*:

5.1980 **Hughes**, J. R. T., 'Henry Mayhew's London', *J.Ec.H.*, XXIX, 1969, 526–36.

5.1981 **Humpherys**, Anne, *Travels into the Poor Man's Country. The Work of Henry Mayhew*, 1980.

5.1982 **Morris**, M., ed., *From Cobbett to the Chartists 1815–1848: Extracts from Contemporary Sources*, 1948.

5.1983 **Thompson**, E. P., 'The political education of Henry Mayhew', *Vict.Studs.*, XI, 1967–8, 41–62.

5.1984 **Wrigley**, C. J., ed., *The Working Classes in the Victorian Age. Debates on the Issue from Nineteenth-Century Critical Journals*, 4 vols., 1973.

(iii) GENERAL WORKS

5.1985 **Belcham**, J., *Industrialisation and the Working Class. The English Experience, 1750–1900*, 1900. A pessimistic view of the working class experience of industrialisation, displaying a keen awareness of regional variations.

5.1986 **Benson**, J., ed., *The Working Class in England, 1875–1914*, 1985.

5.1987 **Briggs**, A. and Saville, J., eds., *Essays in Labour History: In Memory of G. D. H. Cole*, 1960; rev. ed., 1967. Includes essays on the language of 'class', on the nineteenth-century Co-operative Movement, and on wages and workloads.

.1988 —— *Essays in Labour History, 1886–1923*, 1971. Includes essays on the Triple Industrial Alliance, on Clydeside, and on the foundation of the Co-operative Party.

5.1989 —— *Essays in Labour History. III: 1918–39*, 1977. The collection includes essays on the T.U.C. in 1926, and on the non-political trade union movement.

5.1990 **Brown**, K. D., *The English Labour Movement, 1700–1851*, 1982.

5.1991 —— ed., *Essays in Anti-Labour History. Responses to the Rise of Labour in Britain*, 1974. Includes essays on the New Liberalism, the Anti-Socialist Union, and on the Charity Organisation Society.

5.1992 **Calhoun**, C., *The Question of Class Struggle. Social Foundations of Popular Radicalism in the Industrial Revolution*, 1982.

5.1993 **Church**, R. A. and Chapman, S. D., 'Gravenor Henson and the making of the English working class', in Jones and Mingay (5.81), 131–61.

5.1994 **Cole**, G. D. H. and Postgate, R., *The Common People, 1746–1946*, 1946.

5.1995 **Cornforth**, M., ed., *Rebels and their Causes: Essays in Honour of A. L. Morton*, 1978. Includes essays on 'Lollards to Levellers', 'Robert Owen and the Family', and on the nineteenth-century working class.

5.1996 **Crafts**, N. F. R., 'Long-term unemployment in Britain in the 1930s', *Ec.H.R.*, 2nd ser., XLI, 1987, 418–32.

5.1997 **Cunningham**, H., 'The employment and unemployment of children in England c.1680–1851', *P.P.*, CXXVI, 1990, 115–50.

5.1998 **Day**, C., 'The distribution of industrial occupations in England 1841–1861', *Trans. Connecticut Academy of Arts and Sciences*, XXVIII, 1927, 79–235.

5.1999 **Donnelly**, F. K., 'Ideology and early English working-class history: Edward Thompson and his critics', *Soc.H.*, I, 1976, 219–38.

5.2000 **Eichengreen**, B., 'Unemployment in interwar Britain: dole or doldrums?', *Oxford Ec.Papers*, XXXIX, 1987, 597–623.

5.2001 —— 'Unemployment in interwar Britain: new evidence from London', *J.Interdis.H.*, XVII, 1987, 335–58.

5.2002 **Elbaum**, B., 'Why apprenticeship persisted in Britain but not in the United States', *J.Ec.H.*, XLIX, 1989, 337–50.

5.2003 **Emsley**, C. and Walvin, J., eds., *Artisans, Peasants and Proletarians*, 1985.

5.2004 **Foster**, J., *Class Struggle and the Industrial Revolution: Early Industrial Capitalism in Three English Towns* (Oldham, Northampton and South Shields), 1974.

5.2005 **Glen**, R., *Urban Workers in the Early Industrial Revolution*, 1983. Utilises evidence from the N.W. to rebut the thesis that an English working class had come into existence by 1832.

5.2006 **Hammond**, J. L. and Barbara, *The Skilled Labourer, 1760–1832*, 1919. Last reprinted 1965. The best of the 'labourer' trilogy.

5.2007 —— *The Town Labourer, 1760–1832: The New Civilisation*, 1917. Reprinted with an introduction by J. Rule, 1978.

5.2008 **Harrison**, B., 'Class and gender in modern British labour history', *P.P.*, CXXIV, 1989, 121–58.

5.2009 **Hearn**, F., *Domination, Legitimation and Resistance: The Incorporation of the Nineteenth-Century English Working Class*, Westport, Conn., 1978. Heavily sociological and theoretical treatment. Contains an extended historiographical discussion of the competing explanations of the nineteenth-century emergence of the working class.

5.2010 **Hopkins**, E., *The Rise and Decline of the English Working Classes, 1918–90. A Social History*, 1991.

5.2011 **Humphries**, S., *Hooligans or Rebels? An Oral History of Working-Class Childhood and Youth, 1889–1913*, 1982.

5.2012 **Jones**, G. S., *Languages of Class in English Working Class History, 1832–1982*, 1983. Collection of essays outlining the author's work in progress. The most important are those on 'Re-thinking Chartism' and on 'Working-class culture and politics in London 1870–1900'.

5.2013 **Johnson**, P., *Saving and Spending: the Working Class Economy in Britain, 1870–1939*, 1985.

5.2014 —— 'The employment and retirement of older men in England and Wales, 1881–1981', *Ec.H.R.*, XLVII, 1994, 106–28.

5.2015 **Joyce**, P., *Visions of the People. Industrial England and the Question of Class, 1840–1914*, 1991. Studies the social ramifications of language to examine popular values and beliefs. Politics, work, culture and the social order are examined using art and popular literature as sources.

5.2016 **Kiernan**, V. G., 'Working class and nation in nineteenth-century Britain' in Cornforth (5.1995), 123–40.

5.2017 **Kingsford**, P., *The Hunger Marches in Britain, 1920–39*, 1982.

5.2018 **Kirk**, N., 'In defence of class: a critique of recent revisionist writings upon the nineteenth-century English working class', *Internat.R.Soc.H.*, XXXII, 1987, 2–47.

5.2019 —— *The Growth of Working Class Reformism in Mid Victorian England*, 1985. Takes Foster (5.2004) as his starting point but demonstrates that the post Chartist shift from overt class conflict was more complex than that author recognised.

5.2020 **Kynaston**, D., *King Labour. The British Working Class, 1850–1914*, 1976.

5.2021 **Maccoby**, S., *English Radicalism*, 6 vols., 1935–61. I: *1762–1785*; II: *1786–1832*, 1955; III: *1832–1852*, 1935; IV: *1853–1886*, 1938; V: *1886–1914*, 1953; VI: *The End?*, 1961.

5.2022 **Malcolmson**, R. W., *Life and Labour in England, 1700–80*, 1981.

5.2023 **Marcus**, S., *Engels, Manchester and the Working Class*, 1974.

5.2024 **Martin**, D. E. and Rubinstein, D., eds., *Ideology and the Labour Movement. Essays presented to John Saville*, 1979. The collection includes essays on the language of 'class', working-class women and the reform of family law, and on the post Second World War government's policy of social welfare.

5.2025 **Meacham**, S., *A Life Apart. The English Working Class, 1890–1914*, 1977.

5.2026 **Nardinelli**, C., *Child Labour and the Industrial Revolution*, 1990.

5.2027 **Park**, J., *Profit Sharing and Industrial Co-Partnership in British Industry, 1880–1920. Class Conflict or Class Collaboration*, 1987.

5.2028 **Penn**, R., *Skilled Workers in the Class Structure*, 1984.

5.2029 **Pennington**, Shelley and Westover, Belinda, *A Hidden Workforce. Homeworkers in England, 1850–1985*, 1989. A book for the general reader which examines the ideology as well as the economics of domestic employment.

5.2030 **Richards**, P., 'The state and early industrial capitalism: the case of the handloom weavers', *P.P.*, 83, 1979, 91–115.

5.2031 **Rose**, L., '*Rogues and vagabonds*'. The

Vagrant Underworld in Britain,
1815–1985, 1988.

.2032 **Routh**, G., *Occupations of the people of*
Great Britain, 1801–1891, 1987.

.2033 **Rule**, J. G., *The Experience of Labour in*
Eighteenth-Century Industry, 1981.
Concentrates on adult male labour
outside the factory, and has sections on
wages, apprenticeship and industrial
relations.

.2034 —— *The Labouring Classes in Early*
Industrial England, 1750–1850, 1986.

.2035 **Saito**, O., 'Labour supply behaviour of
the poor in the English Industrial
Revolution', *J.Eur.Ec.H.,* X, 1981,
633–52.

.2036 **Saville**, J., ed., *Democracy and the Labour*
Movement, 1955.

.2037 **Stearns**, P. N., *Lives of Labour. Work in a*
Maturing Industrial Society, 1975.

.2038 **Tholfsen**, T., *Working-class Radicalism in*
Mid-Victorian England, 1976. Suggests
that after Chartism, the radical tradition
was preserved in a working-class sub-
culture.

.2039 **Thomis**, M. I., *The Town Labourer and*
the Industrial Revolution, 1974.

.2040 **Thompson**, E. P., *The Making of the*
English Working Class, 1963, 2nd ed.,
1980 with critical appendix, 916–39. A
major contribution to 'history from
below'. By attempting to present the
working-class – and by that the author
chiefly means the artisans – in the light
of their own experience, Thompson
seeks to rescue them from 'the enormous
condescension of posterity'.

.2041 —— 'The moral economy of the crowd
in eighteenth-century England', *P.P.,* 50,
1971, 76–136.

.2042 **Vincent**, D., 'Love and death and the
nineteenth-century working class',
Soc.H., V, 1980, 223–47.

.2043 **Weisser**, H., *British Working-Class*
Movements and Europe, 1815–48, 1976.

.2044 **Williams**, G. A., *Artisans and Sans*
Culottes. Popular Movements in France and
Britain during the French Revolution, 1968.

.2045 **Winstanley**, M., *Life in Kent at the Turn*
of the Century, 1978. An oral history
which examines both urban and rural
life and also the working patterns of
Kentish fishermen.

.2046 **Winter**, J., ed., *The Working Class in*
Modern British History. Essays in Honour of
Henry Pelling, 1983.

5.2047 **Woods**, R. L., 'Individuals in the rioting
crowd: a new approach', *J.Interdis.H.,*
XIV, 1983, 1–24.

5.2048 **Young**, J. D., *Socialism and the English*
Working Class. A Social History of English
Labour, 1883–1939, 1989.

(iv) MISCELLANEOUS

5.2049 **Childs**, M. J., *London's Apprentices.*
Working Class Lads in Late Victorian and
Edwardian England, 1992.

5.2050 **Hanson**, H., *The Canal Boatmen,*
1760–1914, 1975.

5.2051 **Hone**, J. A., *For the Cause of Truth.*
Radicalism in London, 1796–1821, 1982.

5.2052 **Koditschek**, T., *Class Formation and*
Urban Industrial Society. Bradford,
1750–1850, 1990.

5.2053 **Marriott**, J., *The Culture of Labourism.*
The East End between the Wars, 1991.
Deals chiefly with West Ham in the
years 1918 to 1922 and has interesting
material on the local Labour Party and
on the Co-operative Women's Guild.

5.2054 **Phillips**, G. and Whiteside, Noelle,
Casual Labour. The Unemployment
Question in the Port Transport Industry,
1880–1970, 1985.

5.2055 **Prior**, Mary, *Fisher Row: Fishermen,*
Bargemen and Canal Boatmen in Oxford,
1500–1900, 1981.

5.2056 **Randall**, A., *Before the Luddites. Custom,*
Community and Machinery in the English
Woollen Industry, 1776–1809, 1991.
Stresses the disruptive effects of the
introduction of textile machinery and
regional variations in resistance.

5.2057 **Rodger**, N. A. M., *The Wooden World. An*
Anatomy of the Georgian Navy, 1986.
Concentrates chiefly on the Seven Years
War and is over-optimistic in its view of
conditions of service.

5.2058 **Savage**, M., *The Dynamics of Working-*
Class Politics. The Labour Movement in
Preston, 1840–1940, 1988.

5.2059 **Smith**, D., *Conflict and Compromise. Class*
Formation in English Society. A
Comparative Study of Birmingham and
Sheffield, 1982.

5.2060 **Stern**, W., *The Porters of London,* 1960.

5.2061 **Williamson**, B., *Class, Culture and*
Community. A Biographical Study of Social
Change in Mining, 1982.

(v) LUDDISM AND POPULAR DISTURBANCES

(1) LUDDISM

5.2062 **Hobsbawm**, E. J., 'The Machine breakers', in Hobsbawm (5.2188).

5.2063 **Munby**, L. M., ed., *The Luddites and Other Essays*, 1971. Contributions by Marxist historians.

5.2064 **Thomis**, M. I., *The Luddites*, 1970.

5.2065 —— ed., *Luddism in Nottinghamshire*, 1972. A collection of documents of 1811–16 with short introduction.

(2) POPULAR DISTURBANCES

5.2066 **Bohstedt**, J., *Riots and Community Politics in England and Wales, 1790–1810*, 1984. An empirical analysis of 600 riots, many of them linked to food shortages.

5.2067 **Divine**, D., *Mutiny at Invergordon*, 1970. Includes new material, badly handled.

5.2068 **Dugan**, J., *The Great Mutiny, Spithead and the Nore, 1797*, 1966.

5.2069 **Edwards**, K., *The Mutiny at Invergordon*, 1937. *See also* (5.2067).

5.2070 **Gill**, C., *The Naval Mutinies of 1797*, 1913.

5.2071 **Manwaring**, G. E. and Dobrée, B., *The Floating Republic: An Account of the Mutinies at Spithead and the Nore in 1797*, 1935.

5.2072 **Read**, D., *Peterloo: The 'Massacre' and its Background*, 2nd ed., 1973. *See also* Walmsley (5.2079).

5.2073 **Rose**, A. G., 'The Plug Riots of 1842 in Lancashire and Cheshire', *T.L.C.A.S.*, LXVII, 1958, 75–112.

5.2074 **Rudé**, G., *The Crowd in History, 1730–1848: A Study of Popular Disturbances in France and England*, N. Y., 1964.

5.2075 **Shelton**, W. J., *English Hunger and Industrial Disorders*, 1973. Confined to the 1760s.

5.2076 **Stevenson**, J., and Quinault, R., *Popular Protest and Public Order: Six Studies in British History, 1790–1920*, 1975.

5.2077 **Thomis**, M. I., *Politics and Society in Nottingham 1785–1835*, 1969.

5.2078 **Thompson**, E. P., *Customs in Common*, 1991. Reprints Thompson's well-known articles on work discipline under early capitalism, food riots in eighteenth-century England, and on the structure of English society in that period. Three completely new essays are included.

5.2079 **Walmsley**, R., *Peterloo: The Case Reopened*, 1969. *See also* Read (5.2072), and Mather.

5.2080 **Ward**, J. T., ed., *Popular Movements c. 1830–1850*, 1970. Includes chapters on the factory movement, the anti-New Poor Law agitation, trade unionism, Chartism, the agitation against the Corn Laws, and the public health moveemnt. *See also* the section on *Law and Order* (pp. 192–94).

(vi) OWENISM, SOCIALISM AND UTOPIANISM

5.2081 **Owen**, R., *The Life of Robert Owen written by Himself*, vol. I, 1857. Reprinted 1971 with an introduction by J. Butt. A reprint of both volumes of the first edition (1857 and 1858) was issued in 1967.

5.2082 —— *A New View of Society and other Writings*, ed. J. Butt, 1974.

5.2083 —— *A New View of Society and Report to the County of Lanark*, ed. with introduction by V. A. C. Gatrell, 1969.

5.2084 —— *A New View of Society*, ed. with introduction by J. Saville, Clifton, N. J., 1972.

5.2085 **Armytage**, W. H. G., *Heavens Below: Utopian Experiments in England 1560–1960*. 1961. Includes Scotland, Wales and Ireland.

5.2086 **Beales**, H. L., *The Early English Socialists*, 1933.

5.2087 **Butt**, J. ed., *Robert Owen, Prince of Cotton Spinners*, 1971. Essays in honour of Owen's 200th anniversary.

5.2088 **Cole**, G. D. H., *The Life of Robert Owen*, 1925, 3rd ed., 1965, with new introduction by Margaret I. Cole.

5.2088a **Claeys**, G., *Machinery, Money and the Millenium. The New Moral Economy of Owenite Socialism, 1815–60*, 1987.

5.2089 **Garnett**, R. G., *Co-operation and the Owenite Socialist Communities in Britain, 1825–45*, 1972.

5.2090 **Goodwin**, B., *Social Science and Utopia: Nineteenth-Century Models of Social Harmony*, 1978.

5.2091 **Halvéy**, E., *Thomas Hodgskin*, ed. A. J. Taylor, 1956.

5.2092 **Harrison**, J. F. C., *Robert Owen and the*

Owenites in Britain and America: the Quest for the New Moral World, 1969. Detailed bibliography, 263–369.

5.2093 —— *The Second Coming. Popular Millenarianism, 1780–1850,* 1979.

5.2094 **Kimball,** Janet, *The Economic Doctrines of John Gray, 1799–1883,* Washington D. C., 1948.

5.2095 **Morton,** A. L., *The Life and Ideas of Robert Owen,* 1962. A Marxist view with extracts from Owen's writings.

5.2096 **Pankhurst,** R. K. P., *William Thompson, 1775–1833. Britain's Pioneer Socialist, Feminist and Co-operator,* 1954.

5.2097 **Podmore,** F., *The Life of Robert Owen,* 2 vols., 1906. Reprint in 1 vol., 1923.

5.2098 **Pollard,** S. and Salt, J., eds., *Robert Owen: Prophet of the Poor,* 1971. Essays in honour of Owen's 200th anniversary.

5.2099 **Taylor,** K., *The Political Ideas of the Utopian Socialists,* 1981.

(vii) CHARTISM

(1) GENERAL WORKS

.2100 **Harrison,** J. F. C. and Thompson, Dorothy, *Bibliography of the Chartist Movement, 1837–1976,* 1977.

.2101 **Gammage,** R. G., *History of the Chartist Movement,* 1854, 2nd ed., 1895, reprinted 1969 with introduction by J. Saville, 4–66.

.2102 **Mather,** F. C., ed., *Chartism and Society. An Anthology of Documents,* 1980.

.2103 **Thompson,** Dorothy, *The Early Chartists,* 1971. Covers the period 1837–41 only; documents, with commentary.

.2104 **Church,** R. A., 'Chartism and the miners: a reinterpretation', *Lab.H.R.,* LVI, 1991, 23–36.

.2105 **Cullen,** M., 'The Chartists and education', *New Zealand J.H.,* X, 1976, 162–77.

.2106 **Epstein,** J. and Thompson, Dorothy, eds., *The Chartist Experience. Studies in Working Class Radicalism and Culture, 1830–60,* 1982.

.2107 **Faulkner,** H. U., *Chartism and the Churches,* 1st ed., 1916. Reprinted 1970.

2108 **Hadfield,** Alice M., *The Chartist Land Company,* 1970.

2109 **Hammond,** J. L. and Barbara, *The Age of the Chartists, 1832–1854: A Study of Discontent,* 1930.

5.2110 **Haraszti,** Eva H., *Chartism,* 1978.

5.2111 **Harrison,** B., 'Teetotal Chartism', *Hist.,* 58, 1973, 193–217.

5.2112 **Hovell,** M., *The Chartist Movement,* 1918, 4th ed., 1970, with bibliographical additions (iii–ix, 318) which give details of literature up to 1970.

5.2113 **Jones,** D., *Chartism and the Chartists,* 1975. Extensive bibliography.

5.2114 —— 'Women and Chartism', *Hist.,* LXVIII, 1983, 1–21.

5.2115 **MacAskill,** Joy, 'The Chartist Land Plan'. In Briggs, ed. (5.2124), 304–41.

5.2116 **Mather,** F. C., *Public Order in the Age of the Chartists,* 1959.

5.2117 —— *Chartism,* Hist.Assoc. pamphlet, 1965, 3rd rev. ed., 1974. Sums up research since 1925.

5.2118 **Rosenblatt,** F. F., *The Chartist Movement in its Social and Economic Aspects,* 1916. Reprinted 1967.

5.2119 **Slosson,** P. W., *The Decline of the Chartist Movement,* 1916. Reprinted 1967.

5.2120 **Thompson,** Dorothy, *The Chartists,* 1983. Eschews hindsight and locates the Chartist experience within the unfolding conditions of the 1830s and 1840s.

5.2121 **Ward,** J. T., *Chartism,* 1973.

5.2122 **West,** J., *History of Chartism,* 1920.

5.2123 **Yeo,** Eileen, 'Christianity in Chartist struggle, 1838–42', *P.P.,* 91, 1981, 109–39.

(2) REGIONAL STUDIES

5.2124 **Briggs,** A., ed., *Chartist Studies,* 1959. Mainly essays on local aspects of the movement.

5.2125 **Cannon,** J., *The Chartists in Bristol,* 1964.

5.2125a **Goodway,** D., *London Chartism, 1838–48,* 1982.

5.2126 **Howell,** G., *A History of the London Working Men's Association from 1836 to 1850,* new ed., 1972.

5.2127 **Peacock,** A. J., *Bradford Chartism, 1838–1840,* 1969.

5.2128 **Rowe,** D. J., ed., *London Radicalism, 1830–1843: A Selection from the Papers of Francis Place,* London Rec.Soc., 1970. *See also* Thale (5.2330) and Wallas (5.2140).

5.2129 **Wells,** R., 'Southern Chartism', *Rural H.,* II, 1991, 37–60.

(3) BIOGRAPHIES

5.2130 **Cole**, G. D. H., *Chartist Portraits*, 1941, 2nd ed., 1965. Useful bibliography of Chartist literature, 359–66.

5.2131 **Conklin**, R. J., *Thomas Cooper the Chartist (1805–1892)*, Manila, 1935.

5.2132 **Epstein**, J. and Thompson, Dorothy, eds., *The Chartist Experience: Studies in Working-class Radicalism and Culture, 1830–60*, 1982.

5.2133 **Harrison**, B. and Hollis, Patricia M., eds., *Robert Lowery, Radical and Chartist*, 1979.

5.2134 **Kirby**, R. G. and Musson, A. E., *The Voice of the People: John Doherty, 1798–1854, Trade Unionist, Radical and Factory Reformer*, 1975.

5.2135 **Plummer**, A., *Bronterre: A Political Biography of Bronterre O'Brien, 1801–1864*, 1971.

5.2136 **Read**, D., and Glasgow, E. L. H., *Feargus O'Connor, Irishman and Chartist*, 1961.

5.2137 **Saville**, J., ed., *Ernest Jones, Chartist: Selections from the Writings and Speeches of Ernest Jones ...* 1952.

5.2138 **Schoyen**, A. R., *The Chartist Challenge: A Portrait of George Julian Harney*, 1958.

5.2139 **Smith**, F. B., *Radical Artisan: William James Linton, 1812–1897*, 1973.

5.2140 **Wallas**, G., *The Life of Francis Place*, 4th ed., 1951. *See also* Thale (5.2230), and Rowe (5.2128).

5.2141 **Williams**, D., *John Frost: A Study in Chartism*, 1939. Reprinted 1969.

(viii) FRIENDLY SOCIETIES, ETC.

5.2142 **Fuller**, Margaret, D., *West Country Friendly Societies*, 1964.

5.2143 **Gosden**, P. H. J. H., *The Friendly Societies in England, 1815–75*, 1961.

5.2144 —— *Self-Help: Voluntary Associations in the Nineteenth Century*, 1973.

(ix) TRADE UNIONISM AND LABOUR

(1) GENERAL WORKS

5.2145 **Bain**, G. S. and Woolven, Gillian B., *A Bibliography of British Industrial Relations, 1880–1970*, 1979.

5.2146 **Smith**, H., *The British Labour Movement to 1970: A Bibliography*, 1981.

5.2147 **Aspinall**, A., ed., *The Early English Trade Unions: Documents from the Home Office Papers in the Public Record Office*, 1949. Covers the period 1791–1825.

5.2148 **Bailey**, W. M., *Trade Union Documents: Compiled and Edited with an Introduction*, 1929. Documents and extracts ranging from 1841 to 1928 but mostly 1913–28.

5.2149 **Coates**, K. and Topham, T., *Workers' Control: A Book of Readings and Witnesses for Workers' Control*, 1970. Documents and extracts from books relative to anarchosyndicalism in the British labour movement from 1910 to 1969.

5.2150 **Frow**, Ruth and E. and Katanka, M., *Strikes: A Documentary History*, 1971. Collection of contemporary or near-contemporary accounts of strikes in Britain, 1812–1926.

5.2151 **Howell**, G., *Trade Unionism Old and New*. Reprint of 4th ed., 1907, with introduction by F. M. Leventhal, 1973.

5.2152 **Laybourn**, K., *British Trade Unionism, 1770–1990. A Reader in History*, 1991. An accessible collection of source material extending from the eighteenth century to the Thatcher period.

5.2153 **Pollard**, S., ed., *The Sheffield Outrages: Report Presented to the Trades Union Commissioners in 1867*, 1971.

5.2154 **Robertson**, N. and Sams, K. I., *British Trade Unionism: Select Documents*, 2 vols., 1972.

5.2155 **Saville**, J., ed., *Working Conditions of the Victorian Age*, 1974. Reprints articles from contemporary periodicals.

5.2156 **Ward**, J. T. and Fraser, W. H., eds., *Workers and Employers. Documents on Trade Unions and Industrial Relations since the Early Eighteenth Century*, 1980.

5.2157 **Bagwell**, P. S., *Industrial Relations*, 1974. Guide to British Parliamentary Papers on this subject.

5.2158 **Bellamy**, Joyce and Saville, J., eds., *Dictionary of Labour Biography*, I, 1972: II, 1974; III, 1976: IV, 1977; V, 1979; VI 1982; VII, 1984; VIII, 1987. A monumental reference work.

5.2159 **Bienefield**, M. A., *Working Hours in British Industry. An Economic History*, 1972. Deals with the period from 1820 and covers all major branches of industrial labour.

5.2160 **Boyer**, G. R., 'What did unions do in nineteenth-century Britain?', *J.Ec.H.*,

XLVIII, 1988, 319–32.

5.2161 **Browne**, H., *The Rise of British Trade Unionism, 1818–1914*, 1979.

5.2162 **Brown**, K. D., *The English Labour Movement, 1700–1951*, 1982.

5.2163 **Burgess**, K., *The Origins of British Industrial Relations: The Nineteenth-Century Experience*, 1975.

5.2164 —— *The Challenge of Labour. Shaping British Society, 1850–1930*, 1980.

5.2165 **Clegg**, H. A., Fox, A. and Thompson, A. F., *A History of British Trade Unions since 1889*, I (1889–1910), 1964; II, (1911–33), 1985. A scholarly discussion of syndicalism, shop stewards, and the General Strike; III, (1934–51), 1993. Elaborates the author's contention that this was the most impressive period of British trade unionism.

5.2166 **Clinton**, A., *Trade Union Rank and File. Trades Councils in Britain, 1900–40*, 1977.

5.2167 **Cole**, G. D. H., *Attempts at General Union: A Study in British Trade Union History, 1818–1834*, 1953. Should be used with caution; many inaccuracies.

5.2168 **Cox**, A., *History and Heritage. The Social Origins of the British Industrial Relations System*, 1985. Stresses the early non interventionism which allowed the unions to develop and their non revolutionary nature.

5.2169 **Cronin**, J. E., *Industrial Conflict in Modern Britain*, 1979. Deals with the period from the 1880s to c. 1970.

5.2170 **Cross**, G. S., *A Quest for Time. The Reduction of Work in Britain and France, 1840–1940*, 1989.

5.2171 **Cruikshank**, Marjorie, *Children and Industry. Juvenile Work and Welfare in the North West, 1800–1900*, 1981.

5.2172 **Department of Labour and Productivity**. *British Labour Statistics: Historical Abstract, 1886–1968*, 1971.

5.2173 **Dobson**, C. R., *Masters and Journeymen. A Pre-history of Industrial Conflict, 1717–1800*, 1980.

5.2174 **Durcan**, J. W. et al., *Strikes in Postwar Britain. A Study of Stoppages of Work due to Industrial Disputes, 1946–73*, 1983. Based chiefly on the records of the Department of Employment.

5.2175 **Eisenberg**, C., 'Old and new interpretations of the English and German labour movements before 1914', *Internat.R.Soc.H.*, XXXIV, 1989, 403–32.

5.2176 **Fitzgerald**, R., *British Labour Management and Industrial Welfare, 1846–1939*, 1989.

5.2177 **Fraser**, W. H., *Trade Unions and Society: The Struggle for Acceptance, 1850–1880*, 1974.

5.2178 **Frow**, Ruth and E. and Katanka, M., *The History of British Trade Unionism: A Select Bibliography*, Hist.Ass., 1969. Extremely useful, and should be used to supplement this section.

5.2179 **George**, M. Dorothy, 'The Combination Laws reconsidered', *Ec.J.Ec.H.Supp.*, I, 1927, 214–28. Essential for any real understanding of the laws relating to early trade unions.

5.2180 —— 'The Combination Laws', *Ec.H.R.*, VI, 1936, 172–8. *See* remarks on previous entry.

5.2181 **Goodrich**, C. L., *The Frontier of Control: A Study in British Workshop Politics*, 1920. 2nd rev. ed., 1975, with new foreward by R. Hyman.

5.2182 **Gupta**, P. S., *Imperialism and the British Labour Movement, 1914–64*, 1975.

5.2183 **Harrison**, R. and Zeitlin, J., eds., *Divisions of Labour. Skilled Workers and Technological Change in Nineteeenth-Century England*, 1985.

5.2184 **Haydu**, J., *Between Craft and Class. Skilled Workers and Factory Politics in the United States and Britain, 1890–1922*, Berkeley, CA, 1988. A comparative study, sociological in its foundations, focussing on engineers. Coventry and Bridgeport, Conn. are the chosen case studies.

5.2185 **Hedges**, R. Y., and Winterbottom, A., *The Legal History of Trade Unionism*, 1930.

5.2186 **Hinton**, J., *The First Shop Stewards' Movement*, 1973. *See also* Pribicevic (5.2206).

5.2187 —— *Labour and Socialism. A History of the British Labour Movement, 1867–1974*, 1983. Surveys the efforts of the Labour movement to achieve a socialist society.

5.2188 **Hobsbawm**, E. J., *Labouring Men: Studies in the History of Labour*, 1964. Reprints eighteen articles on working-class subjects.

5.2189 —— *Worlds of Labour. Further Studies in the History of Labour*, 1984. A collection of reprinted essays, wide-ranging geographically and with class consciousness foregrounded.

5.2190 **Holbrook-Jones**, M. R., *Supremacy and Subordination of Labour. Work and Control in the Early Labour Movement*, 1982.

5.2191 **Hopkins**, E., 'Working hours and conditions during the Industrial Revolution: a re-appraisal', *Ec.H.R.*, 2nd ser., XXXV, 1982, 52–66.

5.2191a **Hunt**, E. H., *British Labour History, 1815–1914*, 1981. A comprehensive, judicious study which explores the labour market, incomes and consumption, and the whole spectrum of working-class movements.

5.2192 **Jenkins**, M., *The General Strike of 1842*, 1980.

5.2193 **Kapp**, Y., *The Air of Freedom. The Birth of the New Unionism*, 1989.

5.2194 **Knowles**, K. G. J. C., *Strikes: A Study of Industrial Conflict, with Special Reference to British Experience between 1911 and 1947*, 1952.

5.2195 **Leeson**, R. A., *Strike. A Live History, 1887–1971*, 1973. Covers 150 strikes in twenty major industries from the strikers' point of view.

5.2196 —— *Travelling Brothers: The Six Centuries Road from Craft Fellowship to Trade Unionism*, 1979. A study of the tramping system.

5.2197 **Lovell**, J., *British Trade Unions, 1875–1933*, 1977.

5.2198 **Lunn**, K., *A Social History of British Labour, 1870–1970*, 1980.

5.2199 **McCord**, N., *Strikes*, 1980. A brief survey, with chapters on the 1871 engineers' strikes and on 1926.

5.2200 **Macdonald**, D. F., *The State and the Trade Unions*, 1960.

5.2200a **Mason**, S., *Trade Unions and Social Change, 1750–1980*, 1987.

5.2201 **Middlemas**, R. K., *Politics in Industrial Society. The Experience of the British System since 1911*, 1979. A study of the politics of industrial relations.

5.2202 **Musson**, A. E., *British Trade Unions, 1800–1875*, 1972. Excellent bibliography.

5.2203 —— *Trade Union and Social History*, 1974. Collected essays.

5.2204 **Orth**, J. V., *Combination and Conspiracy. A Legal History of Trade Unionism, 1721–1906*, 1991.

5.2205 **Pidduck**, W., *Conflict and Consensus in British Industrial Relations, 1916–48*, 1985.

5.2206 **Pribicevic**, B., *The Shop Stewards' Movement and Workers' Control, 1910–1922*, 1959. *See also* Hinton (5.2186).

5.2207 **Price**, R., *Labour in British Society. An Interpretative History*, 1986. Provocative.

5.2208 **Rule**, J., ed., *British Trade Unionism, 1750–1850. The Formative Years*, 1988.

5.2209 **Schneer**, J., *Ben Tillett. Portrait of a Labour Leader*, 1982.

5.2210 **Sharp**, I. G., *Industrial Conciliation and Arbitration in Great Britain*, 1950.

5.2211 **Tsuzuki**, C., *Tom Mann, 1856–1941. The Challenges of Labour*, 1991. A biography which is not always firmly contextualised. *See* (5.2213).

5.2212 **Webb**, S. and Beatrice, *The History of Trade Unionism*, 1894 (bibliography), 2nd enlarged ed., 1920 (no bibliography).

5.2213 **White**, J. L., *Tom Mann*, 1991. *See also* (5.2211).

5.2214 **Willman**, P., Morris, T., and Aston, B., *Union Business. Trade Union Organisation and Financial Reform in the Thatcher Years*, 1993. Takes both a macro and a micro approach.

5.2215 **Wrigley**, C. J., *The Government and Industrial Relations, 1910–21*, 1980.

5.2216 —— *A History of British Industrial Relations 1914–39*, 1987.

5.2217 **Young**, J., *Socialism and the English Working Class. A History of English Labour, 1883–1939*, 1989.

(2) WORKING-CLASS AUTOBIOGRAPHIES

5.2218 **Bamford**, S., *The Autobiography of Samuel Bamford*, ed., W. H. Chaloner, 2 vols., 1967.

5.2219 **Burnett**, J., ed., *The Autobiography of the Working Class*, 1984.

5.2220 —— ed., *Useful Toil: Autobiographies of Working People from the 1820s to the 1920s*, 1974.

5.2221 **Carter**, T., *Memoirs of a Working Man*, 1846.

5.2222 **Chancellor**, Valerie E., ed., *Master and Artisan in Victorian England: The Diary of William Andrews and the Autobiography of William Gutteridge*, 1969.

5.2223 **Herbert**, G., *Shoemaker's Window: Recollection of Banbury Before the Railway Age*, 1972.

5.2224 **Holloway**, J., ed., *The Journals of Two Poor Dissenters, 1786–1880*, 1970. A bricklayer and baker named Swan.

5.2225 **Hopkinson**, J., *Memoirs of a Victorian Cabinet Maker*, ed. Jocelyne B. Goodman, 1968.

5.2226 **Hudson**, Pat and Hunter, L., eds., 'The

autobiography of William Hart, cooper, 1776–1857. A respectable artisan in the Industrial Revolution', *London J.*, VII, 1981, 144–60.

5.2227 **Lovett**, W., *The Life and Struggles of William Lovett*, 1876, 2nd ed., introduction by R. H. Tawney, 1920.

5.2228 **Smith**, C. M., *The Working Man's Way in the World*, ed. E. Howe, 1968.

5.2229 **Somerville**, A., *The Autobiography of a Working Man*, 1848, 2nd ed., ed. J. Carswell, 1951.

5.2230 **Thale**, Mary, ed., *The Autobiography of Francis Place, (1771–1854)*, 1972. *See also* Rowe (5.2128) and Wallas (5.2140).

5.2231 **Thomson**, C., *The Autobiography of an Artisan*, 1847.

5.2232 **Vincent**, D., *Bread, Knowledge and Freedom: A Study of Nineteenth-Century Working-Class Autobiography*, 1981. A useful analysis of this substantial body of source material. Working-class family life and the pursuit of knowledge receive particular attention.

(3) THE LABOUR ARISTOCRACY

5.2233 **Banks**, J. A., 'Imperialism and the aristocracy of labour'. In *Marxist Sociology in Action*, 1970, 218–37.

5.2234 **Barbalet**, J. M., 'The "labour aristocracy" in context', *Sci. and Soc.*, LI, 1987, 133–53.

5.2235 **Chaloner**, W. H., *The Skilled Artisan During the Industrial Revolution, 1750–1850*, 1969.

5.2236 **Gray**, R., *The Aristocracy of Labour in Nineteenth-Century Britain, 1850–1914*, 1981.

5.2237 **Hobsbawm**, E. J., 'Artisan or labour aristocrat?', *Ec.H.R.*, XXXVII, 1984, 355–72.

5.2238 —— 'The labour aristocracy in nineteenth-century Britain'. In Hobsbawm (5.2188), 272–315.

5.2239 —— 'The tramping artisan'. In Hobsbawm (5.2188), 34–63.

5.2240 **Moorhouse**, H. F., 'The marxist theory of the labour aristocracy', *Soc.H.*, III, 1978, 61–82.

5.2241 **More**, C., *Skill and the English Working Class, 1870–1914*, 1980. Considers the nature of technology in various industries the growth of technical education and the implications for the labour aristocracy.

5.2242 **Pelling**, H. M., 'The concept of the labour aristocracy'. In *Popular Politics and Society in Late Victorian Britain*, 1968, 37–61.

5.2243 **Price**, R., *An Imperial War and the British Working Class: Working Class Attitudes and Reactions to the Boer War, 1899–1902*, 1972.

(4) THE T.U.C., THE LABOUR PARTY AND THE I.L.P.

5.2244 **Bealey**, F. and Pelling, H. M., *Labour and Politics, 1900–1906: A History of the Labour Representation Committee*, 1958.

5.2245 **Birch**, L., ed., *The History of the Trades Union Congress, 1868–1968*, 1968.

5.2246 **Brand**, C. F., 'The conversion of British trade unions to political action', *A.H.R.*, XXX, 1924, 251–70.

5.2247 **Brown**, E. H. P., *The Growth of British Industrial Relations from the Standpoint of 1906–14*, 1959.

5.2248 **Dowse**, R. E., *Left in the Centre*, 1966. History of the Independent Labour Party.

5.2249 **Duffy**, A. E. P., 'New Unionism in Britain, 1889–90: a reappraisal', *Ec.H.R.*, 2nd ser., XIV, 1961, 306–19.

5.2250 **Frow**, E. and Katanka, M., *1868: Year of the Unions*, 1968.

5.2251 **Garbati**, J., 'British trade unionism in the mid-Victorian era', *University of Toronto Quarterly*, XX, 1950–51, 69–84.

5.2252 **Gillespie**, F. E., *Labour and Politics in England, 1850–1867*, Durham, N. C., 1927.

5.2253 **Harrison**, M., *Trade Unions and the Labour Party since 1945*, 1960.

5.2254 **Harrison**, R., *Before the Socialists: Studies in Labour and Politics, 1861–1881*, 1965.

5.2255 **Howell**, D., *British Labour and the Independent Labour Party, 1888–1906*, 1983. A well researched study of the circumstances which cemented the relationship between the two.

5.2256 **Leventhal**, F. M., *Respectable Radical. George Howell and Victorian Working-class Politics*, 1971.

5.2257 **Lovell**, J. and Roberts, B. C., *A Short History of the T.U.C.*, 1968.

5.2258 **McKibbin**, R., *The Evolution of the Labour Party, 1910–1924*, 1975.

5.2259 **Musson**, A. E., *The Congress of 1868: The Origins and Establishment of the Trades Union Congress*, 1955, 2nd rev. ed., 1968.

5.2260 **Pelling**, H. M., *A Short History of the Labour Party*, 1961, 3rd rev. ed., 1968.

Useful guides to further reading at the end of each chapter.

5.2261 —— *The Origins of the Labour Party, 1880–1900*, 1954, 2nd ed., 1965, with excellent bibliographical essay, 234–45.

5.2262 —— *Social Geography of British Elections 1885–1910*, 1967.

5.2263 **Poirier**, P. P., *The Advent of the Labour Party*, 1958. History of the Labour representation Committee.

5.2264 **Roberts**, B. C., *The Trades Union Congress, 1868–1921*, 1958.

(5) HISTORIES OF UNIONISM IN PARTICULAR INDUSTRIES

Agriculture

5.2265 **Boyer**, G. R. and Hatton, T. J., 'Did Joseph Arch raise agricultural wages? Rural trade unions and the labour market in late nineteenth-century England', *Ec.H.R.*, 2nd ser., XLVII, 1994, 310–34.

5.2266 **Dunbabin**, J. P. D., 'The "Revolt of the Field": the agricultural labourers' movement in the 1870's', *P.P.*, 26, 1963, 68–97, (*see also P.P.*, 27, 1964, 109–13 for further discussion). *See also* Dunbabin (5.710).

5.2267 **Edwards**, G., *From Crow-scaring to Westminster: An Autobiography*, 1922, 2nd ed., 1957.

5.2268 **Fussell**, G. E., *From Tolpuddle to T.U.C.: A Century of Farm Labourers' Politics*, 1948.

5.2269 **Groves**, R., *Sharpen the Sickle! The History of the Farm Workers' Union*, 1949.

5.2270 **Horn**, Pamela L., *Joseph Arch (1826–1919), the Farm Workers' Leader*, 1971. A model biography with abundant documentation.

5.2271 **Marlow**, Joyce, *The Tolpuddle Martyrs*, 1972.

5.2272 **Russell**, R. C., *The 'Revolt of the Field' in Lincs.: The Origins and Early History of Farm Workers' Trade Unions*, 1956.

Engineering and metalworkers

5.2273 **Allen**, E., Clarke, J. F., McCord, N., and Rowe, D. J., eds., *The North-East Engineers' Strikes of 1871*, 1971.

5.2274 **Fyrth**, H. J., and Collins, H., *The Foundry Workers: A Trade Union History*, 1959.

5.2275 **Jefferys**, J. B., *The Story of the Engineers 1800–1945*, 1946. The Amalgamated Society of Engineers and the Amalgamated Engineering Union.

5.2276 **Kidd**, A. T., *History of the Tin-Plate Workers' and Sheet-Metal Workers' and Braziers' Societies*, 1949.

5.2277 **Mortimer**, J. E., *A History of the Association of Engineering and Shipbuilding Draughtsmen*, 1960.

5.2278 —— *History of the Boilermakers' Society*, I: *1834–1906*, 1973.

5.2279 **Owen**, J., *Ironmen: Short History of the National Union of Blastfurnacemen, 1878–1935*, 1935, 2nd rev. ed., 1953.

5.2280 **Pugh**, A., *Men of Steel, by One of Them: A Chronicle of Eighty-eight Years of Trade Unionism*, 1952.

Builders and woodworkers

5.2281 **Connelly**, T. J., *The Woodworkers, 1860–1960*, 1960.

5.2282 **French**, J. O., *Plumbers in Unity: History of the Plumbing Trades Union, 1865–1965*, 1965.

5.2283 **Hilton**, W. S., *Foes to Tyranny: A History of the Amalgamated Union of Building Trade Workers*, 1963.

5.2284 **Newman**, J. R., *The N.A.O.P. Heritage: A Short Historical Review of the Development of the National Association of Operative Plasterers 1860–1960*, 1961.

5.2285 **Postgate**, R. W., *The Builders' History*, 1923.

5.2286 **Price**, R., *Master, Unions and Men. Work Control in Building and the Rise of Labour, 1830–1914*, 1980.

Railway labour

5.2287 **Hudson**, K., *Working to Rule: Railway Workshop Rules: A Study of Industrial Discipline*, 1970.

5.2288 **Williams**, A., *Life in a Railway Factory*, 1915. Reprinted with a new introduction 1969. Deals with the Swindon works.

5.2289 **Bagwell**, P. S., *The Railwaymen: the History of the National Union of Railwaymen*, 1963. Vol. II: *The Beeching Era and After*, 1982.

5.2290 **Coleman**, T., *The Railway Navvies*, 1965, 2nd rev. ed., 1968. Excellent guide to sources and selected bibliography, 238–46 of 2nd ed.

5.2291 **Kingsford**, P. W., *Victorian Railwaymen: The Emergence and Growth of Railway Labour, 1830–1870*, 1970.

5.2292 **McKenna**, F., *The Railway Workers, 1840–1970*, 1980.

2293 **McKillop**, N., *The Lighted Flame: A History of the Associated Society of Locomotive Engineers and Firemen*, 1950.

Coal mining

2294 **Arnot**, R. P., *The Miners: A History of the Miners' Federation of Great Britain, 1889–1910*, 1949.

2295 —— *The Miners: Years of Struggle: A History of the Miners' Federation of Great Britain from 1910 onwards*, 1953.

2296 —— *The Miners in Crisis and War: A History of the Miners' Federation of Great Britain from 1930 onwards*, 1961.

2297 **Benson**, J., *British Coalminers in the Nineteenth Century: A Social History*, 1980. Has chapters on the miner at work, on earnings, domestic life, and on community and recreation.

2298 **Challinor**, R., *The Lancashire and Cheshire Miners*, 1972. A study in trade union history from the 1840s onwards.

2299 —— and Ripley, B., *The Miners Association: A Trade Union in the age of the Chartists*, 1969.

2300 **Church**, R., Outram, Q., and Smith, D. N., 'British coal mining strikes, 1893–1940: dimensions, distributions and persistence', *Br.J.Indust.Relations*, XXVIII, 1990, 329–49.

2301 —— 'The "isolated mass" revisited. Strikes in British coal mining', *Sociol.R.*, XXXIX, 1991, 55–87.

2302 —— 'The militancy of British miners, 1893–1986: interdisciplinary problems and perspectives', *J.Interdis.H.*, XXII, 1991, 49–66.

2303 **Colls**, R., *The Pitmen of the Northern Coalfield. Work, Culture, and Protest, 1790–1850*, 1987. A social history of the mining communities and of changes in the relations of production.

2304 **Daunton**, M. J., 'Down the pit: work in the Great Northern and South Wales coalfields, 1870–1914', *Ec.H.R.*, 2nd ser., XXXIV, 1981, 578–97.

2305 **Edwards**, C., *Management Control and Union Power. A Study of Labour Relations in Coal Mining*, 1989.

2306 **Garside**, W. R., *The Durham Miners, 1919–60*, 1971.

2307 **Gregory**, R., *The Miners and British Politics, 1906–14*, 1968.

2308 **Griffin**, A. R., *The Miners of Nottinghamshire. A History of the Nottinghamshire Miners' Association*, I, 1956.

5.2309 —— *The Miners of Nottinghamshire, 1914–1944: A History of the Nottinghamshire Miners' Union*, II, 1962.

5.2310 **Jaffe**, J. A., *The Struggle for Market Power. Industrial Relations in the Northern Coal Industry, 1800–40*, 1991.

5.2311 **McCormick**, B. J., *Industrial Relations in the Coal Industry*, 1979.

5.2312 **Machin**, F., *The Yorkshire Miners: A History*, I, 1958.

5.2313 **Samuel**, R., ed., *Miners, Quarrymen, and Salt Workers*, 1977. Has two chapters on the Durham miners. Slate quarrymen, Cheshire saltworkers, and mineral workers receive attention in the rest of the volume.

5.2314 **Taylor**, A. J., 'The Miners' Association of Great Britain and Ireland, 1842–48. *Economica*, XXII, 1955, 45–60.

5.2315 **Williams**, J. E., *The Derbyshire Miners: A Study in Industrial and Social History*, 1962.

Printing and publishing

5.2316 **Bundock**, C. J., *The National Union of Journalists: A Jubilee History, 1907–1957*, 1957.

5.2317 **Healey**, H. A. H. (pseud. T. N. Shane), *Passed for Press: A Centenary History of the Association of the Correctors of the Press*, 1954.

5.2318 **Howe**, E., ed., *The London Compositor: Documents Relating to Wages, Working Conditions and Customs of the London Printing Trade, 1785–1900*, 1947.

5.2319 —— and Waite, H. H., *The London Society of Compositors: A Centenary History*, 1948.

5.2320 —— and Child, J., *The Society of London Bookbinders, 1780–1951*, 1952.

5.2321 **Moran**, J., *Natsopa Seventy-five Years: The National Society of Operative Printers and Assistants, 1889–1964*, 1964.

5.2322 **Musson**, A. E., *The Typographical Association: Origins and History up to 1949*, 1954.

White-collar and service workers

5.2323 **Anderson**, G., *Victorian Clerks*, 1976. Deals with their status, work conditions and salaries, and with their involvement in voluntary associations, trade unions and commercial education.

5.2324 **Bain**, G. S., *The Growth of White Collar*

Unionism, 1970.

5.2325 **Dix**, B. and Williams, S., *Serving the Public. Building the Union. The History of the National Union of Public Employees. I: The Forerunners, 1889–1928*, 1987.

5.2326 **Hoffman**, P. C., *They also Serve: The Story of the Shop Worker*, 1950. *See also* Whitaker (5.2333).

5.2327 **Hughes**, F., *By Hand and Brain: The story of the Clerical and Administrative Workers' Union*, 1953.

5.2328 **Humphreys**, B. V., *Clerical Unions in the Civil Service*, 1958.

5.2329 **Radford**, F. H., *'Fetch the Engine …': The Official History of the Fire Brigades Union*, 1951.

5.2330 **Reynolds**, G. W., and Judge, A., *The Night the Police Went on Strike*, 1969.

5.2331 **Spoor**, A., *White-collar Union: Sixty Years of N.A.L.G.O.*, 1967. National Association of Local Government Officers.

5.2332 **Swift**, H. G., *A History of Postal Agitation from Fifty Years Ago till the Present Day*, 1900, 2nd ed., 1929.

5.2333 **Whitaker**, W. B., *Victorian and Edwardian Shopworkers: The Struggle to Obtain Better Conditions and a Half-holiday*, 1973.

Cotton unions

5.2334 **Hall**, R. G., 'The 1818 strike wave in the English cotton district', *Internat. R.Soc.H.*, XXXIV, 1989, 433–70.

5.2335 **Hopwood**, E., *A History of the Lancashire Cotton Industry and the Amalgamated Weavers' Association*, 1969.

5.2337 **Turner**, H. A., *Trade Union Growth Structure and Policy: A Comparative Study of the Cotton Unions*, 1962.

5.2338 **White**, J. L., *The Limits of Trade Union Militancy. The Lancashire Textile Workers, 1910–14*, Westport, Conn., 1978.

Dockers

5.2339 **Brown**, R., *Waterfront Organisation In Hull, 1870–1900*, 1972.

5.2340 **Haas**, J. M., 'Trouble at the workplace. Industrial relations in the Royal Dockyards, 1889–1914', *B.I.H.R.*, LVIII, 1985, 210–26.

5.2341 **Lovell**, J., *Stevedores and Dockers*, 1969. London waterside unionism c. 1870–1914.

5.2342 **McCarthy**, T., ed., *The Great Dock Strike, 1889*, 1988.

5.2343 **Pedlar**, Ann (pseud. Stafford), *A Match t Fire the Thames*, 1961. The London match-girls, dockers and gas workers' strikes of 1888–9.

5.2344 **Smith**, H. L., and Nash, V., *The Story of the Dockers' Strike*, 1889.

5.2345 **Taplin**, E., *The Dockers' Union. A Study of the National Union of Dock Labourers, 1889–1922*, 1986.

Footwear and clothing

5.2346 **Cuthbert**, N. H., *The Lace Makers' Society: A Study of Trade Unionism in the British Lace Industry, 1760–1960*, 1960.

5.2347 **Fox**, A., *A History of the National Union o Boot and Shoe Operatives, 1874–1957*, 1958.

5.2348 **Galton**, F. W., ed., *Select Documents, Illustrating the History of Trade Unionism. I: The Tailoring Trade*, 1896.

5.2349 **Kiddier**, W., *The Old Trade Unions: From Unprinted Records of the Brushmakers*, 1930, 2nd ed., 1932.

5.2350 **Stewart**, Margaret and Hunter, L., *The Needle is Threaded: The History of an Industry.* (National Union of Tailors and Garment Workers.) 1964.

Miscellaneous

5.2351 **Coates**, K. and Topham, T., *The History of the TGWU. I: The Making of the Transport and General Workers Union. The Emergence of the Labour Movement, 1870–1922*, 1991. The prehistory of the union. Enriched by much local and regional detail.

5.2352 **Hyman**, R., *The Workers' Union*, 1971.

5.2353 **Marsh**, A. and Ryan, Victoria, *The Seamen. A History of the National Union o Seamen*, 1989. A conventional account of a largely non-militant union.

5.2354 **Reid**, H., *The Furniture Makers. A History of Trade Unionism in the Furniture Trade, 1865–72*, 1986.

(6) LOCAL STUDIES

5.2355 **Barnsby**, G. J., *The Working-Class Movement in the Black Country, 1750–1867*, 1977.

5.2356 **Bennett**, A., *Oldham Trades and Labour Council 1867–1967*, 1967.

5.2357 **Corbett**, J., *The Birmingham Trades Council, 1866–1966*, 1966.

5.2358 **Crossick**, G., *An Artisan Elite in Victorian Society: Kentish London, 1840–80*, 1978.

5.2359 **Cullen**, M. J., 'The 1887 survey of the London working class', *Internat. R.Soc.H.*, XX, 1975, 48–60.

5.2360 **Dutton**, H. I. and King, J. E., *Ten Per Cent and No Surrender. The Preston Strike, 1853–4*, 1981.

5.2361 **Hambling**, W., *A Short History of the Liverpool Trades Council 1848–1948*, 1948.

5.2362 **Hone**, J. Ann, *For the Cause of Truth. Radicalism in London 1796–1821*, 1982.

5.2363 **Huberman**, M., 'How did labour markets work in Lancashire? More evidence on prices and quantities in cotton spinning, 1822–52', *Expl.Econ.Hist.*, XXVIII, 1991, 87–120.

5.2364 **Large**, D. and Whitfield, R., *The Bristol Trades Council, 1873–1973*, 1973.

5.2365 **Pollard**, S., *A History of Labour in Sheffield*, 1959.

5.2366 **Prothero**, I. T., *Artisans and Politics in Early Nineteenth-Century London*, 1978.

5.2367 **Tate**, G. K., *London Trades Council, 1860–1950: A History*, 1950.

5.2368 **Warburton**, W. H., *The History of Trade Union Organisation in the North Staffordshire Potteries*, 1931.

(7) WAGES

5.2369 **Brown**, E. H. P. and Browne, Margaret H., *A Century of Pay*, 1968.

5.2370 **Dorfman**, G. A., *Wage Politics in Britain, 1945–67*, 1974.

5.2371 **Hilton**, G. W., *The Truck System, Including a History of the British Truck Acts, 1465–1960*, 1960.

5.2372 **Hines**, A. G., 'Trade unions and wage inflation in the United Kingdom, 1893–1961', *R.Economic Studs.*, XXXI, 1964, 221–52.

5.2373 **Hobsbawm**, E. J., 'Custom, wages and workload', in Hobsbawm (5.2188).

5.2374 **Hunt**, E. H., *Regional Wage Variations in Britain, 1850–1914*, 1973.

5.2375 —— and Botham, F. W., 'Wages in Britain during the Industrial Revolution', *Ec.H.R.*, 2nd ser., XL, 1987, 380–99. See 5.2379.

5.2376 **Lipsey**, R. G., 'The relation between unemployment and the rate of change of money wage rates in the United Kingdom 1862–1957: a further analysis', *Economica*, XXVII, 1960, 1–31.

5.2377 **Phillips**, A. W., 'The relation between unemployment and the rate of change of money wages in the United Kingdom, 1861–1957', *Economica*, XXV, 1958, 283–99.

5.2378 **Routh**, G., *Occupational Pay in Great Britain, 1906–60*, 1965.

5.2379 **Schwarz**, L. D., 'Trends in real wage rates, 1750–90: a reply to Hunt and Botham', *Ec.H.R.*, 2nd ser., XLIII, 1990, 90–98. See (5.2375).

(8) THE GENERAL STRIKE OF 1926

5.2380 **Bullock**, A., *The Life and Times of Ernest Bevin*, I, 1960, 248–390.

5.2381 **Clegg**, H. A., 'Some consequences of the General Strike', *Proc.Manchester Stat.Soc.*, 1954, 1–29.

5.2382 **Crook**, W. H., *The General Strike: A Study Of Labour's Tragic Weapon in Theory and Practice*, Chapel Hill, N. C., 1931, 233–495.

5.2383 —— *Communism and the General Strike*, 1960.

5.2384 **Farman**, C., *The General Strike*, 1973.

5.2385 **Hills**, R. I., *The General Strike in York, 1926*, Borthwick, Papers, 57, 1980.

5.2386 **Hughes**, M., ed., *Cartoons from the General Strike*, 1968.

5.2387 **Laybourn**, K., *The General Strike of 1926*, 1993. Combines historiographical and historical perspectives on this unique moment in British industrial relations.

5.2388 **Mason**, A., *The General Strike in the North East*, 1970.

5.2389 **Morris**, Margaret, *The General Strike*, 1976.

5.2390 **Phillips**, G. A., *The General Strike. The Politics of Industrial Conflict*, 1976.

5.2391 **Renshaw**, P., *The General Strike*, 1975.

5.2392 **Skelley**, G., ed., *The General Strike*, 1976.

5.2393 **Symons**, J., *The General Strike: A Historical Portrait*, 1957.

(9) THE COMMUNIST PARTY

5.2394 **Collins**, H., and Abramsky, C., *Karl Marx and the British Labour Movement: The Years of the First International*, 1965.

5.2395 **Holton**, R., *British Syndicalism, 1900–14. Myths and Realities*, 1976.

5.2396 **Klugmann**, J., *History of the Communist Party of Great Britain*, Vol. I (*1919–1924*), 1968. Vol. II (*1925–1927: The General Strike*), 1969.

5.2397 **MacFarlane**, L. J., *The British Communist Party: Its Origin and Development until 1929*, 1966.

5.2398 **MacIntyre**, S., *Little Moscows: Communism and Working-Class Militancy* *in Inter-War Britain*, 1980.

5.2399 **Martin**, R., *Communism and the British Trade Unions, 1924–1933: A Study of the National Minority Movement*, 1969.

5.2400 **Pelling**, H. M, *The British Communist Party: A Historical Profile*, 1958.

STANDARDS OF LIVING

(a) Housing

5.2401 **Wall**, R., ed., *Slum Conditions in London and Dublin*, 1974. Reprints articles from the *Journal of the Royal Statistical Society*.

5.2402 **Brunskill**, R. W., *Illustrated Handbook of Vernacular Architecture*, 1970. Excellent bibliography, 212–24.

5.2403 **Burnett**, J., *A Social History of Housing, 1815–1970*, 1978.

5.2404 **Chapman**, S. D., ed., *The History of Working-Class Housing: A Symposium*, 1971.

5.2405 **Chesher**, V. M. and F. J., *The Cornishman's House: An Introduction to the History of Traditional Domestic Architecture in Cornwall*, 1968.

5.2406 **Clifton-Taylor**, A., *The Pattern of English Building*, 1962; bibliography, 343–7.

5.2407 **Cook**, O. and Smith, E., *English Cottages and Farmhouses*, 1954.

5.2408 —— *The English House through Seven Centuries*, 1968; bibliography, 313–16.

5.2409 **Daunton**, M. J., *House and Home in the Victorian City. Working Class housing, 1850–1914*, 1983. Examines the organisation of the market in working class housing, and rents, rates, and management.

5.2410 —— *Housing the Workers. A Comparative History, 1850–1914*, 1990

5.2411 **Dennis**, R., 'The geography of Victorian values: philanthropic housing in London, 1840–1900', *J.H.Geog.*, XV, 1989, 40–54.

5.2412 **Dickens**, P. and Gilbert, P., 'Interwar housing policy: a study of Brighton', *Southern H.*, III, 1981, 201–32.

5.2413 **Doughty**, M., ed., *Building the Industrial City*, 1986. Case studies of Huddersfield

and the West Riding, Liverpool, and of Scotland.

5.2414 —— 'Dilapidated housing and housing policy in Southampton, 1890–1914', *Southampton Rec.Ser.*, XXIX, 1986.

5.2415 **Dutton**, R., *The Victorian Home: Some Aspects of Nineteenth-Century Taste and Manners*, 1954.

5.2416 **Eden**, P. M., *Small Houses in England, 1520–1820: Towards a Classification*, 1969.

5.2417 **Emerson**, J., 'The lodging market in a Victorian city; Exeter', *Southern H.*, IX, 1987, 103–13.

5.2418 **Englander**, D., *Landlord and Tenant in Urban Britain, 1838–1918*, 1983. Concentrates on the advancement of rent control.

5.2419 **Fletcher**, V., *Chimney Pots and Stacks: An Introduction to Their History, Variety and Identification*, 1968.

5.2420 **Forrester**, H., *The Smaller Queen Anne and Georgian House, 1700–1840*, 1964.

5.2421 **Gauldie**, Enid M., *Cruel Habitations: A History of Working-class Housing, 1780–1918*, 1974.

5.2422 **Girouard**, M., *Life in the English Country House. A Social and Architectural History*, New Haven, Conn., 1978.

5.2423 —— *The Victorian Country House*, 1979.

5.2424 **Gloag**, J., *The English Tradition in Architecture*, 1963; bibliography, 241–7.

5.2425 —— *Victorian Comfort: A Social History of Design from 1830–1900*, 1961. Should be used with caution.

5.2426 —— *Victorian Taste: Some Social Aspects of Architecture and Industrial Design, from 1820 to 1900*, 1962; bibliography, 159–65.

5.2427 **Goodhart-Rendel**, H. S., *English Architecture since the Regency: An Interpretation*, 1953.

5.2428 **Hadfield**, M., *Landscape with Trees*, 1967; bibliography, 186–92.

5.2429 **Hartley**, Marie and Ingilby, Joan, *Life and Tradition in the Yorkshire Dales*, 1968.

5.2430 **Henderson**, A., *The Family House in England*, 1964.

5.2431 **Hitchcock**, H. R., *Architecture, Nineteenth and Twentieth Centuries*, 1958; bibliography, 473–83.

5.2432 **Hussey**, C., *English Country Houses: Early Georgian, 1715–1760*, 1955.

5.2433 —— *English Country Houses: Mid-Georgian, 1760–1800*, 1956.

5.2434 —— *English Country Houses: Late Georgian, 1800–1840*, 1958.

5.2435 —— *English Gardens and Landscapes*

1700–1750, 1967.

5.2436 **Iredale**, D., *This Old House*, 1968.

5.2437 **Jenkins**, F., *Architect and Patron*, 1961.

5.2438 **Jones**, S. R., *English Village Homes and Country Buildings*, 1936.

5.2439 **Kerr**, Barbara. *Dorset Cottages*, Dorset Monographs, 4, 1965.

5.2440 **Lees-Milne**, J., *English Country Houses: Baroque, 1685–1715*, 1970.

5.2441 **Lloyd**, N., *A History of the English House from Primitive Times to the Victorian Period*, 1931.

5.2442 **Lowe**, W. J., *A New Century of Social Housing*, 1991.

5.2443 **Melling**, J., ed., *Housing, Social Policy and the State*, 1980.

5.2444 **Pearson**, Lynn F., *The Architectural and Social History of Co-operative Living*, 1988. Looks at fifteen experiments in this form established between 1874 and 1925.

5.2445 **Pritchard**, R. M., *Housing and the Spatial Structure of the City. Residential Mobility and the Housing Market in an English City since the Industrial Revolution*, 1976. A case study of Leicester.

5.2446 **Roberts**, E., 'Working-class housing in Barrow and Lancaster, 1880–1930', *T.H.S.L.C.*, CXXVII, 1977, 109–32.

5.2447 **Rodger**, R., *Nineteenth-century housing, 1780–1914. Class, Capitalism and Construction*, 1989.

5.2448 **Rubinstein**, D., ed., *Victorian Homes*, 1974. A source collection dealing with the homes of all classes of Victorians.

5.2449 **Short**, J. R., *Housing in Britain. The Post War Experience*, 1982. Analyses the relationship between public housing and owner occupation and the changing framework in which they co-existed.

5.2450 **Simpson**, M. A. and Lloyd, T., eds., *Middle-Class Housing in Britain*, 1976.

5.2451 **Summerson**, J., *Architecture in Britain, 1530–1830*, 1953, 4th ed., 1963; bibliography, 363–70.

5.2452 —— *Heavenly Mansions and Other Essays on Architecture*, 1949.

5.2453 —— *The London Building World of the 1860s*, 1974.

5.2454 **Swenarton**, M., *Homes Fit for Heroes. The Politics and Architecture of Early State Housing in Britain*, 1981. Deals with the housing legislation which followed the First World War.

5.2455 **Tarn**, J. N., *Working-class Housing in Nineteenth Century Britain*, 1971.

5.2456 —— *Five Per Cent Philanthropy: An Account of Housing in Urban Areas, 1840–1914*, 1974.

5.2457 **Trowell**, F., 'Speculative housing development in the suburb of Headingley, Leeds, 1838–1914', *Thoresby Soc.Pub.*, LIX, 1985, 50–118.

5.2458 **White**, J., *The Worst Street in North London. Cambell Bank, Islington, between the Wars*, 1986. Partly based on oral history, the book examines the social and economic characteristics of the area and its reputation for poverty, violence and crime.

5.2459 **Wohl**, A. S., *The Eternal Slum. Housing and Social Policy in Victorian London*, 1977.

5.2460 **Woodforde**, J., *The Truth about Cottages*, 1969.

5.2461 **Yelling**, Joyce. A., *Slums and Slum Clearance in Victorian London*, 1986. Concentrates on the post-1875 demolitions and their atendant problems.

(b) Food and drink

5.2462 **Barker**, T. C., McKenzie, J. C. and Yudkin, J., *Our Changing Fare: Two Hundred Years of British Food Habits*, 1966. Contains chapters on marketing, bread, meat, fish and fruit consumption and Scots diet, with detailed references.

5.2463 —— Oddy, D. J. and Yudkin, J., *The Dietary Surveys of Dr Edward Smith, 1862–3: A New Assessment*, 1970.

5.2464 —— and Yudkin, J., eds., *Fish in Britain: Trends in its Supply, Distribution and Consumption During the Past Two Centuries*, 1971.

5.2465 **Burnett**, J., *Plenty and Want: A Social History of Diet in England from 1815 to the Present Day*, 1966.

5.2466 **Chaloner**, W. H., 'Trends in fish consumption', in Barker *et al.* (5.2462), listed above, 94–114.

5.2467 **Crawford**, W. and Broadley, H., *The People's Food*, 1938.

5.2468 **Filby**, F. A., *History of Food Adulteration and Analysis*, 1934.

5.2469 **Johnston**, J., *A Hundred Years Eating. Food, Drink, and the Daily Diet in Britain since the late Nineteenth century*, 1977.

5.2470 **Morris**, Helen, *Portrait of a Chef: The Life of Alexis Sayer*, 1938.

5.2471 **Oddy**, D. J. and Miller, D. S., eds., *The*

Making of the Modern British Diet, 1976. Eighteen essays grouped under three main headings: supply, consumption, and nutritional evaluation.

5.2472 —— and Miller, D., eds., *Diet and Health in Modern Britain*, 1985. Includes essays on meat consumption, war-time food rationing, and school meals.

5.2473 **Palmer**, A., *Movable Feasts*, 1952. Reprinted 1953. Changing English mealtimes.

5.2474 **Salaman**, R. N., *The History and Social Influence of the Potato*, 1949.

5.2475 **Shammas**, Carole, 'The eighteenth-century English diet and economic change', *Expl.Ec.H.*, XXI, 1984, 254–70.

5.2476 **Unwin**, Jane C., ed., *The Hungry Forties, or Life under the Bread Tax*, 1904.

5.2477 **Walton**, J. K., *Fish and Chips and the British Working Class, 1870–1940*, 1992.

(c) The standard of living controversy

5.2478 **Ashton**, T. S., 'The standard of life of the workers in England, 1790–1830'. In Hayek, ed. (1.130), 127–59.

5.2479 —— Changes in standards of comfort in eighteenth-century England', *Proc.Brit.Acad.*, XLI, 1955, 171–87.

5.2480 **Barnsby**, G. J., 'The Standard of living in the Black Country during the nineteenth century', *Ec.H.R.*, 2nd ser., XXIV, 1971, 220–33.

5.2481 **Chaloner**, W. H., *The Hungry Forties*, Hist.Ass. pamphlet, 1957, 3rd rev. ed., 1963.

5.2482 **Collier**, Frances, *The Family Economy of the Working Classes in the Cotton Industry, 1784–1833*, 1964.

5.2483 **Crafts**, N. F. R., 'Regional price variations in England in 1843. An aspect of the standard of living debate', *Expl.Ec.H.*, XIX, 1982, 51–71.

5.2484 **Gazeley**, I., 'The cost of living for urban workers in late Victorian and Edwardian England', *Ec.H.R.*, 2nd ser., XLII, 1989, 207–21.

5.2485 **Gilboy**, Elizabeth, W., *Wages in Eighteenth-Century England*, Cambridge, Mass., 1934.

5.2486 —— 'The cost of living and real wages in eighteenth-century England', *Review of Economic Statistics*, XVIII, 1936, 134–43.

5.2487 **Hartwell**, R. M., 'Interpretations of the

Industrial Revolution in England', *J.Ec.H.*, XIX, 1959, 229–49.

5.2488 —— 'The standard of living controversy: a summary'. In Hartwell, ed. (5.71), 167–79.

5.2489 —— 'The rising standard of living in England 1800–1850'. In Hartwell (5.71), 313–45.

5.2490 **Hobsbawm**, E. J., 'The British standard of living, 1790–1850', *Ec.H.R.*, 2nd ser., X, 1957, 46–48. Reprinted with additions in Hobsbawm (5.2188), 64–104.

5.2491 —— and Hartwell, R. M., 'The standard of living during the Industrial Revolution: a discussion', *Ec.H.R.*, 2nd ser., XVI, 1963, 120–46.

5.2492 **Inglis**, B., *Poverty and the Industrial Revolution*, 1971. Largely an attack on the Classical Economists.

5.2493 **Komlos**, J., 'The secular trend in the biological standard of living in the U.K., 1730–1860', *Ec.H.R.*, 2nd ser., XLVI, 1993, 115–44.

5.2494 **Lindert**, P. H. and Williamson, J. G., 'English workers' living standards during the Industrial Revolution: a new look', *Ec.H.R.*, 2nd ser., XXXVI, 1983, 1–26.

5.2495 **Mokyr**, J., 'Is there still life in the pessimist case? Consumption during the Industrial Revolution, 1790–1850', *J.Ec.H.*, XLVIII, 1988, 69–92.

5.2496 **Neale**, R. S., 'The standard of living, 1780–1844: a regional and class study', *Ec.H.R.*, 2nd ser., XIX, 1966, 590–606.

5.2497 **Pollard**, S., 'Investment, consumption and the Industrial Revolution', *Ec.H.R.*, 2nd ser., XI, 1958, 215–36.

5.2498 **Taylor**, A. J., ed., *The Standard of Living in Britain in the Industrial Revolution*, 1975. Reprints key contributions to the debate from Gilboy, Tucker, Ashton, Hartwell, Hobsbawm, Thompson and Neale.

5.2499 **Tucker**, R. S., 'Real wages of aritisans in London, 1729–1935', *J.American Statistical Assn.*, XXXI, 1936, 73–84.

5.2450 **Williams**, J. E., 'The British standard of living, 1750–1850', *Ec.H.R.*, 2nd ser., XIX, 1966, 581–9.

5.2501 **Wilsher**, P., *The Pound in Your Pocket, 1870–1970*, 1970.

5.2502 **Woodruff**, W., 'Capitalism and the Victorians: a contribution to the discussion on the Industrial Revolution', *J.Ec.H.*, XVI, 1956, 1–17.

ECONOMIC THOUGHT AND POLICY

5.2503 **Aldcroft**, D. H., *Full Employment. An Elusive Goal*, 1984. Examines the quadrupling of unemployment between 1972 and 1984 and the economic setting in which this occurred.

5.2504 **Allett**, J., *New Liberalism. The Political Economy of J. A. Hobson*, Toronto, 1981.

5.2505 **Arnon**, A., *Thomas Tooke. A Pioneer of Monetary Theory*, 1991.

5.2506 **Ashworth**, W., *The State in Business. 1945 to the mid 1980s*, 1991.

5.2507 **Backhouse**, R., *Economists and the Economy. The Evolution of Economic Ideas, 1600 to the Present Day*, 1988.

5.2508 **Bahmueller**, C. F., *The National Charity Company. Jeremy Bentham's Silent Revolution*, 1982.

5.2509 **Bartrip**, P. W. J., 'British government inspection, 1832–75. Some observations', *H.J.*, XXV, 1982, 605–26.

5.2510 —— 'State intervention in mid nineteenth Britain: fact or fiction?', *J.Brit.Studs.*, XXIII, 1984, 63–83.

5.2511 —— and Burman, S. B., *The Wounded Soldiers of Industry. Industrial Compensation Policy, 1833–97*, 1983.

5.2512 **Bellamy**, C., *Administering Central-Local Relations, 1871–1919. The Local Government Board in its Fiscal and Cultural Context*, 1988.

5.2513 **Berg**, Maxine, *The Machinery Question and the Making of Political Economy, 1815–48*, 1980. A major study of the politico-economic debate on the machinery question.

5.2514 **Booth**, A., 'Britain and the 1930s: a managed economy', *Ec.H.R.*, 2nd ser., XL, 1987, 499–522.

5.2515 **Bowley**, Marian, *Nassau Senior and Classical Economics*, 1937.

5.2516 **Brebner**, J. B., 'Laissez-faire and state intervention in nineeenth-century Britain' in Carus-Wilson ed. (1.326), III, 252–62.

5.2517 **Bristow**, E. J., *Individualism v. Socialism in Britain, 1880–1914*, 1987.

5.2518 **Browning**, P., *The Treasury and Economic Policy, 1964–85*, 1986.

5.2519 **Cairncross**, A., *Years of Recovery. British Economic Policy, 1945–51*, 1985. An astute analysis of post-War Labour government policy making.

5.2520 **Campbell**, R. H. and Skinner, A., *Adam Smith*, 1985.

5.2521 **Capie**, F., 'Effective protection and economic recovery in Britain, 1932–37', *Ec.H.R.*, 2nd ser., XLIV, 1991, 339–42.

5.2522 **Caravale**, G. A., ed., *The Legacy of Ricardo*, 1985.

5.2523 **Checkland**, S. G., *British Public Policy. An Economic, Social and Political Perspective*, 1983.

5.2524 **Cheyney**, E. P., *Modern English Reform, from Individualism to Socialism*, Philadelphia, 1931.

5.2525 **Clark**, G. K., 'Statesmen in disguise', *H.J.*, II, 1959, 19–39.

5.2526 **Coats**, A. W., ed., *The Classical Economists and Economic Policy*, 1971.

5.2527 **Cromwell**, Valerie, 'Interpretations of nineteenth-century administration: an analysis', *Vic.Studs*, IX, 1965–6, 245–58.

5.2528 —— *Revolution or Evolution? British Government in the Nineteenth Century*, 1977.

5.2529 **Cronin**, J. E., *The Politics of State Expansion. War, State, and Society in Twentieth-Century Britain*, 1991.

5.2530 **Cullen**, M. J., *The Statistical Movement in Early Victorian Britain. The Foundations of Empirical Social Research*, 1975.

5.2531 **Davidson**, R., *Whitehall and the Labour Problem in Late Victorian and Edwardian Britain*, 1984. Focusses on the Labour Department of the Board of Trade and its accumulation and use of statistical information.

5.2532 **Deane**, Phyllis, *The Evolution of Economic Ideas*, 1978.

5.2533 **Feinstein**, C., ed., *The Managed Economy. Essays in British Economic Policy and Performance since 1929*, 1983.

5.2534 **Fetter**, F. W., *The Economist in Parliament, 1780–1868*, 1980.

5.2535 **Fishbein**, W. H., *Wage restraint by Consensus. Britain's Search for an Incomes Policy Agreement, 1965–79*, 1984. Examines the evolution of government policy and the emergence of the concept of social contract.

5.2536 **Foreman-Peck**, J. S., 'Natural monopoly and railway policy in the nineteenth century', *Oxford Ec.Papers*, XXXIX, 1987, 699–718.

5.2537 **French**, D., *British Economic and Strategic Planning, 1905–15*, 1982.

5.2538 **Freyer**, T., *Regulating Big Business. Anti-Trust in Great Britain and America, 1880–1990*, 1992.

5.2539 **Furner**, M. O. and Supple, B., eds., *The State and Economic Knowledge. The American and British Experiences*, 1990.

5.2540 **Gamble**, A., *Britain in Decline. Economic Policy, Political Strategy and the British State*, 1981.

5.2541 **Garside**, W. R., *British Unemployment, 1919–39. A Study in Public Policy*, 1990. An account of the measures taken to alleviate unemployment in the interwar period.

5.2542 **Goldsmith**, M. M., *Private Vices, Public Benefits. Bernard Mandeville's Social and Political Thought*, 1985. Explores dimensions of Mandeville's defence of vice and its economic benefits.

5.2543 **Gordon**, B., *Economic Doctrine and Tory Liberalism, 1824–30*, 1980.

5.2544 —— *Political Economy in Parliament*, 1976.

5.2545 **Gore**, C., ed., *Property: Its Rights and Duties*, 1914, 2nd ed., 1915 with an additional essay.

5.2546 **Hall**, P., *Governing the Economy. The Politics of State Intervention in Britain and France*, 1986.

5.2547 **Hart**, Jenifer M., 'Nineteenth-century social reform: a Tory interpretation of history', *P.P.*, 31, 1965, 39–61.

5.2548 **Hausman**, W. J. and Newfield, J. L., 'Excise anatomised. The political economy of Walpole's 1733 tax scheme', *J.Eur.Ec.H.*, X, 1981, 131–45.

5.2549 **Hey**, J. D. and Winch, D., eds., *A Century of Economics. 100 Years of the Royal Economic Society and the Economic Journal*, 1990.

5.2550 **Hilton**, B., *Corn, Cash, Commerce: The Economic Policies of Tory Governments, 1815–30*, 1977.

5.2551 **Hollander**, S., 'Ricardo and the Corn Laws: A Revision', *Hist.Pol.Econ*, IX, 1977, 1–47.

5.2552 **Holmes**, C. J., 'Laissez faire in theory and practice: Britain, 1800–75', *J.Europ.Ec.H.*, V, 1976, 671–88.

5.2553 **Horne**, T. A., *The Social Thought of Bernard Mandeville. Virtue and Commerce in Early Eighteenth-Century England*, 1978.

5.2554 **Howson**, Susan, *British Monetary Policy, 1945–51*, 1993. Critically reviews Hugh Dalton's policies in the postwar Labour government.

5.2555 —— and Winch, D., *The Economic Advisory Council, 1930–39*, 1977.

5.2556 **Hume**, L. J., *Bentham and Bureaucracy*, 1981.

5.2557 **Hutchinson**, T., *Before Adam Smith. The emergence of Political Economy, 1662–1776*, 1988.

5.2558 **Hutchinson**, T. W., *A Review of Economic Doctrines, 1870–1929*, 1953.

5.2559 **Innes**, J., 'Parliament and the shaping of eighteenth-century English social policy', *TRHS.*, 5th ser., XL, 1990, 63–92.

5.2560 **James**, Patricia, *Population Malthus: His Life and Times*, 1979. *See also* Peterson (5.2583).

5.2561 **Jeffery**, K., *States of Emergency. British Governments and Strikebreaking since 1919*, 1983.

5.2562 **Jha**, N., *The Age of Marshall: Aspects of British Economic Thought, 1890–1915*, 2nd ed., 1973.

5.2563 **Jones**, G. and Kirby, M., eds., *Competitiveness and the State. Government and Business in Twentieth Century Britain*, 1991.

5.2564 **Jones**, G. G., *The State and the Emergence of the British Oil Industry*, 1980.

5.2565 **Jones**, R., *Wages and Employment Policy, 1936–85*, 1987.

5.2566 **Kennedy**, W. P., *Industrial Structure, Capital Markets and the Origins of British Economic Decline*, 1986.

5.2567 **Lekachman**, R., *The Age of Keynes: A Biographical Study*, 1967.

5.2568 **Levy**, S. L., *Nassau W. Senior, 1790–1864*, 1970.

5.2569 **Liesenfeld**, V. J., *The Licensing Act of 1737*, Madison, Wis, 1984.

5.2570 **Lubenow**, W. C., *The Politics of Government Growth: Early Victorian Attitudes Towards State Intervention, 1853–1848*, 1971.

5.2571 **MacDonagh**, O. *A Pattern of Government Growth 1800–60: The Passenger Acts and their Enforcement*, 1961.

5.2572 —— 'The ninteeeth-century revolution in government: a reappraisal', *H. J.*, I, 1958, 52–67.

5.2573 —— *Early Victorian Government, 1830–70*, 1977.

5.2574 **McGregor**, O. R., 'Social research and social policy in the nineteenth century', *Brit.J.Soc.*, VIII, 1957, 146–57.

5.2575 **McKibbin**, R., 'The economic policy of the second Labour government, 1929–31', *P.P.*, 68, 1975, 95–123.

5.2576 **Martin**, D., *John Stuart Mill and the Land Question*, 1981.

5.2577 **O'Brien**, D. P., *The Classical Economists*, 1975.

5.2578 **O'Brien**, P., Griffiths, T., and Hunt, P., 'Political components of the Industrial Revolution: Parliament and the English cotton textile industry, 1660–1774', *Ec.H.R.*, XLIV, 1991, 395–423.

5.2579 **Parris**, H., *Constitutional Bureaucracy: The Development of Central Administration since the Eighteenth Century*, 1969.

5.2580 —— 'The nineteenth-century revolution in government: a reappraisal reappraised', *H. J.*, III, 1960, 17–37.

5.2581 **Peden**, G. C., *British Re-armament and the Treasury, 1932–9*, 1979.

5.2582 **Pellew**, Jill, *The Home Office, 1848–1914: From Clerks to Bureaucrats*, 1982.

5.2583 **Peterson**, W., *Malthus*, 1979. See also James (5.2560).

5.2584 **Pollard**, S., *The Wasting of the British Economy. British Economic Policy, 1945 to the Present*, 1982.

5.2585 **Robbins**, L., *The Theory of Economic Policy in English Classical Political Economy*, 1952.

5.2586 —— *Political Economy: Past and Present. A Review of Leading Theories of Economic Policy*, 1976.

5.2587 **Rodgers**, T., 'Employers' organisations, unemployment and social politics in Britain during the interwar period', *Soc.H.*, XIII, 1988, 315–42.

5.2588 **Shelton**, G., *Dean Tucker and Eighteenth-Century Economic and Political Thought*, 1981.

5.2589 **Skinner**, A. S., and Wilson, T., eds., *Essays on Adam Smith*, 1976.

5.2590 **Stafford**, W., *Socialism, Radicalism and Nostalgia. Social Criticism in Britain, 1775–1830*, 1987. Framework chapters on social context and 'mental furniture' prepare the way for case studies of Godwin, Coleridge, Cobbett, Hodgskin, Owen, Spence and Ogilvie.

5.2591 **Stark**, W., ed., *Economic Writings of Jeremy Bentham*, 1952, I, (introduction).

5.2592 **Sturges**, R. P., *Economists' Papers, 1750–1950. A Guide to Archive and other Sources for the History of British and Irish Economic Thought*, 1975.

5.2593 **Sykes**, A., *Tariff Reform in British Politics, 1903–13*, 1979.

5.2594 **Taylor**, A. J., *Laissez-faire and State Intervention in Nineteenth Century Britain*, 1972.

5.2595 **Thompson**, N., *The Market and its Critics. Socialist Political Economy in Nineteenth Century Britain*, 1988. Discusses, inter al.,

the ideas of Charles Hall, William Godwin, Thomas Hodgskin, William Thompson, the Owenites, William Hyndman, Robert Blatchford, Sidney Webb and G. B. Shaw.

5.2596 **Tomlinson**, J., *Problems of British Economic Policy, 1870–1945*, 1981.

5.2597 —— *The Unequal Struggle? British Socialism and the Capitalist Enterprise*, 1982.

5.2598 **Turner**, M., ed., *Malthus and his time*, 1986.

5.2599 **Vickerstaff**, S. and Sheldrake, J., *The History of Industrial Training in Britain*, 1987.

5.2600 **Werhane**, P. H., *Adam Smith and his Legacy for Modern Capitalism*, 1991.

5.2601 **Wilson**, T. and Skinner, A. S., eds., *The Market and the State. Essays in Honour of Adam Smith*, 1976. See also Skinner and Wilson (5.2589).

5.2602 **Winch**, D., *Economics and Policy: An Historical Study*, 1970. Covers Britain 1900–60. See also Tucker (4.953).

5.2603 **Wright**, J. F., *Britain in the Age of Economic Management*, 1979.

POOR LAW, CHARITY AND SOCIAL PROTECTION, THE WELFARE STATE

(a) Poor Law

5.2604 **Checkland**, S. G. and E. Olive A., eds., *The Poor Law Report of 1834*, 1974.

5.2605 **Rose**, M. E., *The English Poor Law 1780–1930*, 1971. Select documents with commentary.

5.2606 **Watkin**, B., ed., *Documents on Health and Social Services, 1834 to the Present Day*, 1975.

5.2607 **Ayres**, G., *Social Conditions and Welfare Legislation, 1800–1930*, 1988.

5.2608 **Blaug**, M., 'The myth of the Old Poor Law and the making of the New', *J.Ec.H.*, XXIII, 1963, 151–84.

5.2609 —— 'The Poor Law Report re-examined', *J.Ec.H.*, XXIV, 1964, 229–45.

5.2610 **Boyer**, G. R., *An Economic History of the*

English Poor Law, 1750–1850, 1990. Concentrates chiefly on the provision of outdoor relief.

5.2611 **Boyson**, R., 'The New Poor Law in North East Lancashire, 1834–71', *T.L.C.A.S.*, LXX, 1960, 45–56.

5.2612 **Branson**, Noreen, *Poplarism, 1919–25. George Lansbury and the Councillors' Revolt*, 1979. See also Keith-Lucas (5.2633) and Postgate (5.2644).

5.2613 **Brundage**, A., *The Making of the New Poor Law. The Politics of Inquiry, Enactment and Implementation, 1832–79*, 1978.

5.2614 **Coats**, A. W., 'Economic thought and poor law policy in the eighteenth century', *Ec.H.R.*, 2nd ser., XIII, 1960, 39–51.

5.2615 **Cowherd**, R. G., 'The humanitarian reform of the English Poor laws from 1782–1815', *Proc.American Phil.Soc.*, CIV, 1960, 328–42.

5.2616 —— *Political Economists and the English Poor Laws*, Athens, Ohio, 1977. Appraises the influence of economists on social policy from Adam Smith to J. S. Mill.

5.2617 **Crocker**, R. H. C., 'The Victorian Poor Law in crisis and change: Southampton, 1870–95', *Albion*, XIX, 1987, 19–44.

5.2618 **Crowther**, M. A., *The Workhouse System, 1834–1929*, 1981.

5.2619 **Digby**, Anne, *Pauper Palaces*, 1978. A study of workhouses.

5.2620 —— *The Poor Law in Nineteenth Century England and Wales*, 1982.

5.2621 **Driver**, F., *Power and Pauperism. The Workhouse System 1834–84*, 1993.

5.2622 —— 'The historical geography of the workhouse system in England and Wales, 1834–83', *J.H.Geog.*, XV, 1989, 269–86.

5.2623 **Edsall**, N. C., *The Anti-Poor Law Movement, 1934–44*, 1971.

5.2624 **Ely**, J. W., 'The eighteenth-century Poor Laws in the West Riding of Yorkshire', *Am.J.Legal H.*, XXX, 1986, 1–24.

5.2624a **Finnegan**, Frances and Sigsworth, E. M., *Poverty and Social Policy. An Historical Study of Batley*, 1978.

5.2625 **Flinn**, M. W., 'The Poor Employment Act of 1817', *Ec.H.R.*, 2nd ser., XIV, 1961, 82–92.

5.2626 **Fraser**, D., ed., *The New Poor Law in the Nineteenth Century*, 1976. Has chapters on the working of the Poor Law in urban and rural areas, pauper education, medical provision under the Poor Law, and on the relationship between the Poor Law and philanthropy.

5.2627 **Hastings**, R. P., *Poverty and the Poor Law in the North Riding of Yorkshire, c.1780–1837*, Borthwick Papers, 61, 1982.

5.2628 **Hennock**, E. P., 'The movement of poverty: from the metropolis to the nation, 1880–1920', *Ec.H.R.*, 2nd ser., XL, 1987, 208–27.

5.2629 **Henriques**, Ursula R. Q., 'How cruel was the Victorian poor law?', *H.J.*, XI, 1968, 365–71. See also Roberts (5.2648).

5.2630 —— *Before the Welfare State. Social Administration in Early Industrial Britain*, 1979.

5.2631 **Hindle**, G. B., *Provision for the Relief of the Poor in Manchester, 1754–1826*, Chet.Soc., 3rd ser., 22, 1975.

5.2632 **Jones**, K., *The Making of Social Policy in Britain, 1830–1990*, 1991.

5.2633 **Keith-Lucas**, B., 'Popularism', *Public Law*, Spring 1962, 52–80.

5.2634 **Knott**, J., *Popular Opposition to the 1834 Poor Law*, 1986. Covers much of the same ground as Edsall (5.2623).

5.2635 **Lees**, L. H., *Poverty and Pauperism in Nineteenth-Century London*, 1988.

5.2636 **Marshall**, Dorothy, *The English Poor in the Eighteenth Century: A Study in Social and Administrative History*, 1926.

5.2637 —— 'The Old Poor Law, 1662–1795'. In Carus-Wilson, ed. (1.326), I, 295–305. Ineffectiveness of law of settlement and removal as a brake on mobility of labour.

5.2638 **Marshall**, J. D., *The Old Poor Law, 1795–1834*, 1968; Select bibliography, 47–8.

5.2639 —— 'The Nottinghamshire reformers and their contribution to the Old Poor Law', *Ec.H.R.*, 2nd ser., XIII, 1961, 382–96.

5.2640 **Miller**, A., *Poverty Deserved? Relieving the Poor in Victorian Liverpool*, 1988.

5.2641 **Mitchelson**, N., *The Old Poor Law in East Yorkshire*, 1953.

5.2642 **Oxley**, G. W., 'The relief of the permanent poor in S. W. Lancashire under the Old Poor Law'. In Harris, ed. (5.1651), 16–49.

5.2643 —— *Parish Relief in England and Wales, 1601–1834*, 1974.

5.2644 **Postgate**, R., *Life of George Lansbury*, 1951 Poplarism.

5.2645 **Poynter**, J. R., *Society and Pauperism;*

English Ideas on Poor Relief, 1795–1834, 1969.

5.2646 **Proctor**, Winifred, 'Poor law administration in Preston Union, 1838–1848', *T.H.S.L.C.*, 117, 1965, 145–66.

5.2647 **Radice**, Lisanne, *Beatrice and Sidney Webb. Fabian Socialists*, 1984. A timely reassessment of the Webbs' place in British socialism.

5.2648 **Roberts**, D., 'How cruel was the Victorian Poor Law?' *H.J.*, VI, 1963, 97–107.

5.2649 **Rose**, M. E., ed., *The Poor and the City. The English Poor Law in its Urban Context, 1834–1914*, 1985.

5.2650 —— *The Relief of Poverty, 1834–1914,* 1972.

5.2651 —— 'The allowance system under the New Poor Law', *Ec.H.R.*, 2nd ser., XIX, 1966, 607–20.

5.2652 —— 'The Anti-Poor Law agitation'. In Ward (5.2080), 78–94, with bibliographical note.

5.2653 —— 'The Anti-Poor Law Movement in the North of England', *Northern H.*, I, 1966, 70–91.

5.2654 **Searby**, P., 'The Relief of the Poor in Coventry, 1830–63', *Hist. Jnl.*, XX, 1977, 345–61.

5.2655 **Taylor**, J. S., 'A different kind of Speenhamland: non resident relief in the Industrial Revolution', *J.Brit.Studs*, XXX, 1991, 183–208.

5.2656 **Treble**, J. H., *Urban Poverty in Britain, 1830–1914*, 1979. Considers the relationship between poverty and the urban labour market, food and housing, and expedient remedies.

5.2657 **Vorspan**, R., 'Vagrancy and the New Poor Law in late Victorian and Edwardian England', *E.H.R.*, XCII, 1977, 59–81.

5.2658 **Wells**, R. A. E., *Dearth and Distress in Yorkshire, 1793–1802*, Borthwick Papers, 52, 1977.

(b) Charity and social protection

5.2659 **Binfield**, C., *George Williams and the Y.M.C.A.*, 1973.

5.2660 **Briggs**, A., *Social Thought and Social Action: A Study of the Work of Seebohm Rowntree, 1871–1954*, 1961.

5.2661 **Cohen**, P., *The British System of Social Insurance: A History and Description*, 1932.

5.2662 **Cunningham**, H., *The Children of the Poor. Representations of Childhood since the Seventeenth Century*, 1991.

5.2663 **Fried**, A., and Elman, R. M., *Charles Booth's London: Portrait of the Poor at the Turn of the Century, Drawn from his 'Life and Labour of the People of London'*, 1969.

5.2664 **Gilbert**, B. B., *The Evolution of National Insurance in Great Britain: The Origins of the Welfare State*, 1966.

5.2665 —— *British Social Policy, 1914–1939*, 1970. Better on the period 1914–31 than on the 1930s; critical bibliography, 325–36.

5.2666 **Hanes**, D. G., *The First British Workmen's Compensation Act, 1897*, 1968.

5.2667 **Harris**, R. W., *National Health Insurance in Great Britain, 1911–1946*, 1946.

5.2668 **Harrison**, B., 'Philanthropy and the Victorians', *Vict.Studs.*, IX, 1965–6, 353–74.

5.2669 **Himmelfarb**, Gertrude, *The Idea of Poverty. England in the Early Industrial Age*, 1984. Takes in accounts of Defoe, Wesley, Adam Smith, Malthus, Carlyle, the Chartists, and Engels. But the treatment of poverty was more contentious than the author apparently recognises.

5.2670 **Johnson**, P., 'Self Help versus State Help: Old Age pensions and personal savings in Great Britain, 1906–37', *Expl.Ec.H.*, XXI, 1984, 329–51.

5.2671 **Jones**, Helen, 'Employers' welfare schemes and industrial relations in interwar Britain', *Bus.H.*, XXV, 1983, 61–76.

5.2672 **Lewis**, J., *The Politics of Motherhood. Child and Maternal Welfare in England, 1900–39*, 1980.

5.2673 **Linsley**, C. A. and Christine L., 'Booth, Rowntree, and Llewelyn Smith: a reassessment of interwar poverty', *Ec.H.R.*, 2nd ser., XLVI, 1993, 88–104.

5.2674 **MacNicol**, J., *The Movement for Family Allowances, 1918–45. A Study in Social Policy Development*, 1980.

5.2675 **Meacham**, S., *Toynbee Hall and Social Reform, 1880–1914. The Search for Community*, 1987. The history of an institution designed to build bridges between social classes.

5.2676 **Moore**, M. J., 'Social work and social welfare: the organisation of philanthropic resources in Britain,

1900–14', *J.Brit.Studs.*, XVI, 1977, 85–104.

5.2677 **Mowat**, C. L., *The Charity Organisation Society, 1869–1913: Its Ideas and Work*, 1961.

5.2678 **Owen**, D., *English Philanthropy, 1660–1960*, Cambridge, Mass., 1965. Useful, although the time-span clearly hampered the author. *See also* Harrison (5.2668).

5.2679 **Pope**, R., Pratt, A. and Hoyle, B., eds., *Social Welfare in Britain, 1885–1985*, 1986.

5.2680 **Roberts**, D., *The Victorian Origins of the Welfare State*, New Haven, Conn., 1960.

5.2681 —— *Paternalism in Early Victorian England*, 1979.

5.2682 **Rober**, M. J. D., 'Re-shaping the gift relationship: The London Mendicity Society and the suppression of begging in England, 1818–69', *Int.R.Soc.H.*, XXXVI, 1991, 201–31.

5.2683 **Rooff**, M., *A Hundred Years of Family Welfare. A Study of the Family Welfare Association, 1869–1969*, 1972.

5.2684 **Seldon**, A., ed., *The Long Debate on Poverty*, 1972. Essays on the history of social welfare.

5.2685 **Simey**, Margaret B., *Charitable Effort in Liverpool in the Nineteenth Century*, 1951.

5.2686 **Simey**, T. S., and Margaret B., *Charles Booth, Social Scientist*, 1960.

5.2687 **Thane**, Pat, ed., *The Origins of British Social Policy*, 1978.

5.2688 **Tompson**, R., *The Charity Commission and the Age of Reform*, 1979. A detailed examination of the first major Royal Commission of Enquiry into social reform.

5.2689 **Waddilove**, L. E., *Private Philanthropy and Public Welfare. The A. J. Rowntree Memorial Trust, 1954–79*, 1983. A careful study of the activity of a remarkable organisation established by a Quaker chocolate manufacturer.

5.2690 **Whiteside**, Noelle, 'Welfare insurance and casual labour: a study of administrative intervention in industrial employment, 1906–26', *Ec.H.R.*, 2nd ser., XXXII, 1979, 507–22.

5.2691 **Woodroofe**, Kathleen, *From Charity to Social Work: A History of Social Work in England and the United States*, 1962.

5.2692 **Young**, A. F., and Ashton, E. T., *British Social work in the Nineteenth Century*, 1956.

(c) The welfare state

5.2693 **Bruce**, M., *The Coming of the Welfare State*, 1961, 4th rev. ed., 1968. Extensive bibliographical references from Tudor to modern times.

5.2694 **Finlayson**, G., 'A moving frontier; voluntarism and the state in British social welfare, 1941–49', *Twentieth Century Brit. H.*, I, 1990, 183–206.

5.2695 **Fraser**, D., *The Evolution of the British Welfare State: A History of Social Policy since the Industrial Revolution*, 1973.

5.2696 **George**, V. and Wilding, P., *The Impact of Social Policy*, 1984.

5.2697 **Gregg**, Pauline, *The Welfare State: An Economic and Social History of Britain, from 1945 to the Present Day*, 1967. Useful select bibliography, 368–76.

5.2698 **Harris**, José, *William Beveridge. A Biography*, 1977.

5.2699 **Hay**, J. R., *The Development of the British Welfare State, 1880–1975*, 1978.

5.2700 **Inglis**, F., *Radical Earnestness. English Social Theory, 1880–1980*, 1982.

5.2701 **Jeffreys**, M., ed., *Growing Old in the Twentieth Century*, 1989.

5.2702 **Lowe**, R., 'Welfare legislation and the unions during and after the First World War', *H.J.*, XXV, 1982, 437–42.

5.2703 **Thane**, Pat, 'The working class and state "welfare" in Britain, 1880–1914', *H.J.*, XXVII, 1984, 877–900.

LAW AND ORDER

5.2704 **Bailey**, V., *Delinquency and citizenship: Reclaiming the Young Offender, 1914–48*, 1987.

5.2705 —— ed., *Policing and Punishment in Nineteenth-Century Britain*, 1981.

5.2706 **Beattie**, J. M., *Crime and the Courts in England, 1660–1800*, 1986. Concentrates specifically on crime, trials, and punishment in Surrey.

5.2707 **Beloff**, M., *Public Order and Popular Disturbances, 1660–1714*, 1938, new imp., 1963.

5.2708 **Booth**, A., 'Food riots in the north west of England, 1790–1801', *P.P.*, 86, 1977, 84–107.

5.2709 **Browne**, D. G., *The Rise of Scotland Yard: A History of the Metropolitan Police*, 1956.

5.2710 **Cornish**, W. R., ed., *Crime and Law in Nineteenth-Century Britain*, 1979.

5.2711 **Darvall**, F. O., *Popular Disturbances and Public Order in Regency England*, 1934, 2nd ed., 1970, with new introduction.

5.2712 **Davies**, A., 'The police and the people. Gambling in Salford', *H.J.*, XXIV, 1991, 87–116.

5.2713 **De Lacy**, Margaret, *Prison Reform in Lancashire, 1700–1850. A Study in Local Administration*, Chet. Soc., 3rd ser., XXXIII, 1986.

5.2714 **Evans**, A., *Victorian Law and Order*, 1988.

5.2715 **Forsythe**, W. J., *Penal Discipline, Reformatory Projects and the English Prison Commission, 1895–1939*, 1991.

5.2716 —— *The Reform of Prisoners, 1830–1900*, 1987.

5.2717 **Geary**, R., *Policing Industrial Disputes, 1893–1985*, 1985. Looks at the surrounding attitudes and policies influencing the nature of police intervention.

5.2718 **Harding**, C., Hines, B., Ireland, R., and Rawlings, P., *Imprisonment in England and Wales. A Concise History*, 1986.

5.2719 **Hart**, Jenifer M., *The British Police*, 1951. Useful for administrative history.

5.2720 —— 'The reform of the borough police, 1835–1856', *E.H.R.*, LXX, 1955, 411–27.

5.2721 **Hay**, D. et al., *Albion's Fatal Tree. Crime and Society in Eighteenth-Century England*, 1975.

5.2722 —— 'War, dearth and theft in the eighteenth century: the record of the English courts', *P.P.*, 95, 1982, 117–60.

5.2723 —— and Snyder, F., eds., *Policing and Prosecution in Britain, 1750–1850*, 1989.

5.2724 **Hopkins**, H., *The Long Affray. The Poaching Wars, 1760–1914*, 1985. A meticulously researched study of widespread incidents of poaching in the English countryside and of the forms of retaliation devised by landowners and lawcourts.

5.2725 **Howard**, P. A., Smith, B. S., and Wrattan, N A., *Crime and Punishment in Gloucestershire, 1700–1800*, 1978.

5.2726 **James**, D. W., ed., *Crime and Punishment in Nineteenth-Century England*, 1975.

5.2727 **Jones**, D., *Crime, Protest, Community and Police in Nineteenth-Century Britain*, 1982.

5.2728 —— 'The poacher. A study in Victorian crime and protest', *H.J.*, XXII, 1979. 825–60.

5.2729 **Keith**, M., *Race, Riots and Policing. Law and Disorder in a Multi Racial Society*, 1993. Focusses on the criminalisation of black people in England, on riots, and on black/police conflict.

5.2730 **Langbein**, J. H., 'Albion's fatal flaws',, *P.P.*, XCVIII, 1983–120. A critique of Hay et al. (5.2721).

5.2731 **Linebaugh**, P., *The London Hanged. Crime and Civil Society in the Eighteenth Century*, 1991. A sociological analysis of the 1242 persons publicly hanged at Tyburn between 1703 and 1772 and, more generally, a reevaluation of the Tyburn phenomenon itself.

5.2732 **McLynn**, F. J., *Crime and Punishment in Eighteenth Century England*, 1989.

5.2733 **Melossi**, D. and Pavarini, M., *The Prison and the Factory. The Origins of the Penitentiary System*, 1981.

5.2734 **Midwinter**, E. C., *Law and Order in Early Victorian Lancashire*, 1968.

5.2735 **Morgan**, Jane, *Conflict and Order. The Police and Labour Disputes in England and Wales, 1900–1939*, 1987. Based on public records and local police archives. The author examines the use made of emerging law enforcement powers and the growth of administrative centralisation.

5.2736 **Munsche**, P. B., *Gentlemen and Poachers. The English Game Laws, 1671–1831*, 1982. The first full-length study of this subject. The author rejects the view that the Game Laws imposed unjustifiably high penalties, but agrees that they represented notorious examples of class legislation.

5.2737 **Musket**, P., 'Riotous Assemblies'. Popular disturbances in East Anglia, 1740–1822*, 1984.

5.2738 **Palmer**, S., *Police and Protest in England and Ireland, 1780–1850*, 1988.

5.2739 **Phillips**, D., *Crime and Authority in Victorian England. The Black Country, 1835–60*, 1977.

5.2740 **Priestley**, P., *Victorian Prison Lives. English Prison Biography, 1830–1914*, 1986. Constructed from many prison memoirs, the book builds up a telling picture of prison life subjectively experienced.

5.2741 **Richter**, D. C., *Riotous Victorians*, 1981.

5.2742 **Robb**, G., *White collar Crime in modern*

England. Financial Fraud and Business Morality, 1845–1929, 1992. Looks at fraud and its victims in railway promotion, banking, investment, company floatation, and management.

5.2743 **Rogers**, N., 'Policing the poor in eighteenth century London: the vagrancy laws and their administration', *Hist.Soc.*, XXVI, 1991, 127–48.

5.2744 —— 'Popular protest in early Hanoverian London', *P.P.*, 79, 1978, 70–100.

5.2745 **Rudé**, G., *Crime and Society in Early Nineteenth Century England*, 1985.

5.2746 **Rule**, J. G., ed., *Outside the Law. Studies in Crime and Order, 1650–1850*, 1992.

5.2747 —— 'Social crime in the rural South in the eighteenth and early nineteenth centuries', *Southern H.*, I, 1979, 135–54.

5.2748 **Shoemaker**, R. B., 'The "crime wave" revisited: crime, law enforcement and punishment in Britain, 1650–1900', *H.J.*, XXIV, 1991, 665–84.

5.2749 **Stead**, P. J., *The Police of Britain*, 1985. Looks – at times uncritically – at the growth of the service, its structure, and relations with the rest of the criminal justice system.

5.2750 **Steedman**, C., *Policing the Victorian Community. The Formation of English Provincial Police Forces, 1856–80*, 1984.

5.2751 **Stevenson**, J., *Popular Disturbances in England, 1700–1870*, 1979.

5.2752 **Swift**, R., *Police Reform in Early Victorian York, 1835–56*, Borthwick Papers, LXXIII, 1988.

5.2753 —— 'Urban policing in early Victorian England, 1835–86: a reappraisal', *Hist.*, LXXIII, 1988, 211–37.

5.2754 **Thomas**, J. E., *The English Prison Officer since 1850: A Study in Conflict*, 1972.

5.2755 **Thomis**, M. I. and Holt, P., *Threats of Revolution in Britain, 1789–1848*, 1977.

5.2756 **Thompson**, E. P., *Whigs and Hunters. The Origin of the Black Act*, 1975. 'History from below' challenging accepted orthodoxies about eighteenth-century stability.

5.2757 **Tobias**, J. J., *Crime and Industrial Society in the Nineteenth Century*, 1967.

5.2758 —— *Crime and Police in England 1700–1900*, 1979.

5.2759 **Townsend**, C., *Making the Peace. Public Order and Public Security in Modern Britain*, 1993. Takes a wide-ranging view of the subject, highlighting the Victorian

equipoise and the growth of formal security apparatus in the twentieth century.

5.2760 **Vamplew**, W., 'Ungentlemanly conduct. The control of soccer crowd behaviour in England, 1888–1914', in Smout (5.116), 139–54.

5.2761 **Wells**, R., *Insurrection. The British Experience, 1795–1803*, 1984. Presents the evidence relating to the growth of social unrest in the period in question.

5.2762 —— 'Popular protest and social crime: the evidence of criminal gangs in rural southern England, 1790–1860', *Southern H.*, 1991, 32–81.

5.2763 **Western**, J. R., 'The English Militia in the Eighteenth Century. The Story of a Political Issue, 1660–1802, *1965*.

See also Cockburn (4.1009), Hobsbawm and Rudé (5.713), and Mather (5.2116).

PUBLIC HEALTH AND MORALITY

(a) Public health

5.2764 **Brockington**, C. F., ed., *Papers relating to the Sanitary State of the People of England*, 1973. Reprints the study made by E. H. Greenhow for the General Board of Health.

5.2765 **Chadwick**, E., *Report on the Sanitary Conditions of the Labouring Population of Great Britain*, 1842, ed. M. W. Flinn, 1965.

5.2766 **Kay-Shuttleworth**, J. P., *The Moral and Physical Condition of the Working Classes employed in the Cotton Manufacture in Manchester*, 1832. Reprinted with a preface by W. H. Chaloner, 1970.

5.2767 **Abel-Smith**, B. and Pinker, R., *The Hospitals, 1800–1948: A Study in Social Administration in England and Wales*, 1964.

5.2768 **Allen**, P. and Jolley, M., eds., *Nursing, Midwifery and Health Visiting since 1900*, 1982.

5.2769 **Ayers**, Gwendoline M., *England's First*

State Hospitals and the Metropolitan Asylums Board, 1867–1930, 1971.

5.2770 **Baly**, M. E., *Florence Nightingale and the Nursing Legacy*, 1986.

5.2771 **Bayliss**, R. and Daniels, C., 'The physical deterioration report of 1904 and education in home economics', *Hist.Educ.Soc.Bull.*, XLI, 1988, 29–39.

5.2772 **Briggs**, A., 'Cholera and society in the nineteenth century', *P.P.*, 19, 1961, 76–96.

5.2773 **Brockington**, C. F., *Medical Officers of Health, 1848–1855*, 1957.

5.2774 —— *A Short History of Public Health*, 1956.

5.2775 **Bryder**, Linda, *Below the Magic Mountain. A Social History of T.B. in Twentieth Century Britain*, 1988.

5.2776 **Bullough**, V. L. and B., *The Care of the Sick: The Emergence of Modern Nursing*, 1979.

5.2777 **Bynum**, W. F., Porter, R., and Shepherd, M., eds., *The Anatomy of Madness. Essays in the History of Psychiatry. I: People and Ideas; II: Institutions and Society*, 1986. A scholarly collection of essays deriving from symposia and seminars at the Wellcome Institute.

5.2778 **Carpenter**, K. J., *The History of Scurvy and Vitamin C*, 1986. A long-range study of the disease from the fifteenth century onwards and of the discovery (and re-discovery) of the cure.

5.2779 **Cartwright**, F. F., *A Social History of Medicine*, 1977.

5.2780 **Davenport-Himes**, R., *Sex, Death and Punishment. Attitudes to Sex and Sexuality in Britain since the Renaissance*, 1990. Deals with venereal disease, prostitution, and homosexuality, and the changing social attitudes surrounding them.

5.2781 **Doerner**, K., *Madmen and the Bourgeoisie: A Social History of Insanity and Psychiatry*, 1981.

5.2782 **Durey**, M., *The Return of the Plague. British Society and the Cholera, 1831–2*, 1979. Comprehensive bibliography.

5.2783 **Finer**, S. E., *The Life and Times of Sir Edwin Chadwick*, 1952, 2nd ed., 1970.

5.2784 **Flinn**, M. W., *Public Health Reform in Britain*, 1968. Excellent bibliography, 69–70.

5.2785 **Hardy**, A., 'Urban famine or urban crisis? Typhus in the Victorian city', *Med.Hist.*, XXXII, 1988, 401–25.

5.2786 **Hodgkinson**, Ruth G., *The Origins of the National Health Service: The Medical Services of the New Poor Law 1834–1871*, 1967.

5.2787 **Jones**, Kathleen, *A History of the Mental Health Service*, 1972.

5.2788 **Lambert**, R. J., *Sir John Simon, 1816–1904, and English Social Administration*, 1963.

5.2789 —— 'A Victorian National Health Service: state vaccination, 1855–77', *H.J.*, V, 1962, 1–18.

5.2790 **Lewis**, R. A., *Edwin Chadwick and the Public Health Movement, 1832–1854*, 1952.

5.2791 **Longmate**, N., *King Cholera: The Biography of a Disease*, 1966.

5.2792 **Loudon**, I., *Medical Care and the General Practitioner, 1750–1850*, 1987. Concentrates on the rank and file of the medical profession.

5.2793 **Luckin**, B., *Pollution and Control. A Social History of the Thames in the Nineteenth Century*, 1986. Less of a social history than its title proclaims the book is chiefly concerned with the politics of the sanitary revolution.

5.2794 **McLeod**, R. M., 'The Alkali Acts Administration, 1863–84: the emergence of the civil scientist', *Vict.Studs.*, IX, 1965–66, 85–112.

5.2795 **Marland**, H., *Medicine and Society in Wakefield and Huddersfield, 1780–1870*, 1987.

5.2796 **Midwinter**, E. C., *Social Administration in Lancashire: 1830–1860: Poor Law, Public Health and Police*, 1969.

5.2797 —— *Victorian Social Reform*, 1968.

5.2798 **Morris**, R. J., *Cholera, 1832*, 1976.

5.2799 **Mort**, F., *Dangerous sexualities. Medico-Moral Politics in England since 1830*, 1987.

5.2800 **Navarro**, V., *Class Struggle, the State and Medicine: An Historical and Contemporary Analysis of the Medical Sector in Great Britain*, 1978.

5.2801 **Pickstone**, J. V., ed., *Health, Disease and Medicine in Lancashire, 1750–1950. Four Papers on Sources, Problems and Methods*, 1980.

5.2802 **Porter**, R., *Disease, Medicine and Society in England, 1550–1860*, 1987. A short survey which has most to say about the eighteenth century.

5.2803 —— *Health for Sale. Quackery in England, 1660–1850*, 1989. Sees the seventeenth and nineteenth centuries as the principal periods of change. The eighteenth century is presented as the heyday of the 'quack'.

5.2804 —— and Dorothy, *In Sickness and in Health. The British Experience, 1650–1850*, 1988. A well-organised survey concentrating on conceptions of health, the incidence of illness, and changing responses to disease.

5.2805 —— *Mind Forg'd Manacles. A History of Madness in England from the Restoration to the Regency*, 1987. Examines the changing cultural meanings of madness.

5.2806 **Povey**, W. P., 'The Manchester House of Recovery, 1796. Britain's first general fever hospital. The early years', *Trans.Lancs. and Ches.Antiq.Soc.*, LXXXIV, 1987, 15–45.

5.2807 **Poynter**, F. N. L., ed., *The Evolution of Hospitals in Britain*, 1964.

5.2808 **Richardson**, Ruth, *Death, Dissection and the Destitute*, 1988.

5.2809 **Riley**, J. C., *The Eighteenth-Century Campaign to Avoid Disease*, 1987. Looks particularly at contemporary texts.

5.2810 —— 'Ill health during the English mortality decline: the Friendly Societies' experience', *Bull.Hist.Medic.*, LXI, 1987, 563–88.

5.2811 **Scull**, A. T., *Museums of Madness. The Social Organisation of Insanity in Nineteenth-Century England*, 1979.

5.2812 **Sheail**, J., 'The South Downs and Brighton's water supplies – an interwar study of resource management', *Southern H.*, XIV, 1992, 93–111.

5.2813 **Smith**, F. B., *The People's Health, 1830–1910*, 1979.

5.2814 **Smith**, F. B., *The Retreat of Tuberculosis, 1850–1950*, 1988.

5.2815 **Smith**, J. R., *The Speckled Monster. Smallpox in England, 1670–1970, with particular reference to Essex*, 1987.

5.2816 **Spink**, W. W., *Infectious Diseases, Prevention and Treatment in the Nineteenth and Twentieth Centuries*, 1979.

5.2817 **Timms**, N., *Psychiatric Social Work in Great Britain, 1939–62*, 1964.

5.2818 **Uttley**, S., *Technology and the Welfare State: the Influence of Technological Change on the Development of Health Care in Britain and America*, 1991.

5.2819 **Vertinsky**, P., *The Eternally Wounded Woman. Women, Doctors, and Exercise in the Late Nineteenth Century*, 1990.

5.2820 **Webster**, C., ed., *Biology, Medicine and Society, 1840–1940*, 1981.

5.2821 **Whiteside**, Noelle, "Counting the cost". Sickness and disability among working people in an era of industrial recession, 1920–33', *Ec.H.R.*, 2nd ser., XL, 1987, 228–46.

5.2822 **Willcocks**, A. J., *The Creation of the National Health Service. A Study of Pressure Groups and a Major Policy Decision*, 1967.

5.2823 **Winnick**, W., ed., *Nutrition in the Twentieth Century*, 1984.

5.2824 **Woods**, R. and Woodward, J., eds., *Urban Disease and Mortality in Nineteenth-Century England*, 1984.

5.2825 **Woodward**, J., *To Do The Sick No Harm: A Study of the British Voluntary Hospital System to 1875*, 1974.

5.2826 —— and Richards, D., eds., *Health and Popular Medicine in Nineteenth-Century England. Essays in the Social History of Medicine*, 1977.

5.2827 **Youngson**, A. J., *The Scientific Revolution in Victorian Medicine*, 1979.

(b) Morality

5.2828 **Acton**, W., *Prostitution*, 2nd ed., 1870, 3rd abridged ed., 1968, with introduction by P. Fryer, 4th unabridged ed., 1972, with introduction by Anne Humphreys.

5.2829 **Neild**, K., ed., *Prostitution in the Victorian Age*, 1973. Reprints articles from contemporary periodicals.

5.2830 **Berridge**, Virginia and Edwards, G., *Opium and the People. Opiate Use in Nineteenth Century England*, 1982.

5.2831 **Bristow**, E. J., *Prostitution and Slavery. The Jewish Fight against White Slavery, 1880–1939* 1989.

5.2832 **Chaloner**, W. H., 'How immoral were the Victorians? A bibliographical reconsideration', *B. John Rylands Lib.*, LX, 1978, 362–75.

5.2833 **Chesney**, K., *The Victorian Underworld*, 1970. Chiefly about London.

5.2834 **Dingle**, A. E., *The Campaign for Prohibition in Victorian England: The United Kingdom Alliance, 1872–95*, 1980.

5.2835 **Finnegan**, Frances, *Poverty and Prostitution: A Study of Victorian Prostitutes in York*, 1979.

5.2836 **McHugh**, P., *Prostitution and Victorian Social Reform*, 1980.

5.2837 **Mahood**, L., *The Magdalenes. Prostitutes*

in the Nineteenth Century, 1990.

5.2838 **Mangan**, J. A. and Walvin, J., *Manliness and Morality. Middle Class Masculinity in Britain and America, 1800–1940*, 1987. Examines the diffusion of neo-Spartan models of masculinity and their ideological and sociological dimensions. Includes chapters on the promotion of character building amongst working class adolescents, the values of upper class education in late Edwardian and Victorian society, and on Baden Powell and the development of the scouting movement.

5.2839 **Marcus**, S., *The Other Victorians*, 1966.

5.2840 **Marsh**, P., *The Conscience of the Victorian State*, 1979.

5.2841 **Mosse**, G. L., 'Nationalism and respectability. Normal and abnormal sexuality in the nineteenth century', *J.Contemp.H.*, XVII, 1982, 221–46.

5.2842 **Pearsall**, R., *The Worm in the Bud: The World of Victorian Sexuality*, 1969. Excellent references, 529–44.

5.2843 —— *Public Purity, Private Shame: Victorian Sexual Hypocrisy Exposed*, 1976.

5.2844 **Pearson**, M., *The Age of Consent. Victorian Prostitution and its Enemies*, 1972.

5.2845 **Roberts**, M. J. D., 'The Society for the Suppression of Vice and its early critics, 1802–12', *H.J.*, XXVI, 1983, 159–76.

5.2846 **Seidman**, S., 'The power of desire and the danger of pleasure: Victorian sexuality reconsidered', *J.Soc.H.*, XXIV, 1991, 47–67.

5.2847 **Trudgill**, E., *Madonnas and Magdalens. The Origins and Development of Victorian Sexual Attitudes*, 1976.

5.2848 **Walkowitz**, Judith R., *Prostitution and Victorian Society. Women, Class and the State*, 1980.

5.2849 **Weeks**, J., *Sex, Politics and Society. The Regulation of Sexuality since 1800*, 1981.

(c) The Temperance Movement

5.2850 **Harrison**, B., *Drink and the Victorians: The Temperance Question in England 1815–1872*, 1971.

5.2851 —— *Dictionary of British Temperance Biography*, 1973.

5.2852 —— 'The British prohibitionists, 1853–1872: a biographical analysis', *Internat.R.Soc.H.*, XV, 1970, 375–467.

5.2853 **Longmate**, N., *The Waterdrinkers: A History of Temperance*, 1968.

5.2854 **Reid**, Caroline, 'Temperance, Teetotalism, and Local Culture', *Northern H.*, XIII, 1977, 248–64.

5.2855 **Shiman**, L. L., *Crusade against Drink in Victorian England*, 1986.

5.2856 **Wilson**, G. B., *Alcohol and the Nation, 1800–1935*, 1940.

LEISURE, CULTURE AND RECREATION

(a) General works

5.2857 **Bailey**, P., *Leisure and Class in Victorian England. Rational Recreation and the Contest for Control; 1830–85*, 1978.

5.2858 **Britain**, I., *Fabianism and Culture. A Study of British Socialism and the Arts, c.1884–1918*, 1982.

5.2859 **Chalklin**, C. W., 'Capital expenditure on building for cultural purposes in provincial England, 1730–1830', *Bus.H.*, XXII, 1980, 51–70.

5.2860 **Clark**, J. and Johnson, R., eds., *Working-Class Culture*, 1979.

5.2861 **Clarke**, J. and Critcher, C., *The Devil Makes Work. Leisure in Capitalist Britain*, 1985.

5.2862 **Collins**, B. and Robbins, K., eds., *British Culture and Economic Decline*, 1990.

5.2863 **Colls**, R. and Dodd, P., eds., *Englishness, Politics and Culture, 1880–1920*, 1986. A fascinating volume of essays which explores different facets of the ways in which 'Englishness' was invented in the nineteenth and early twentieth centuries.

5.2864 **Cross**, N., *The Common Writer*, 1985.

5.2865 **Cunningham**, H., *Leisure in the Industrial Revolution, c.1780–c.1880*, 1980. Analyses the processes of privatisation, institutionalisation and commercialisation of leisure.

5.2866 **Davidoff**, Leonore, *The Best Circles: Society, Etiquette and the Season*, 1973.

5.2867 **Dawes**, F., *A Cry from the Streets. The Boys' Club Movement in Britain from the 1850s to the Present Day*, 1975.

5.2868 **Easton**, S., *Disorder and Discipline. Popular Culture from 1550 to the Present*, 1988.

5.2869 **Elliott**, B. J., 'The social activities of the unemployed in an industrial city during the "Great Depression"', *Trans.Hunter Arch.Soc.*, XVI, 1991, 52–60.

5.2870 **Girling**, R., ed., *The Making of the English Garden*, 1988.

5.2871 **Jones**, S. G., *Workers at Play. A Social and Economic History of Leisure, 1918–39*, 1986.

5.2872 **Lemahieu**, D. L., *A Culture for Democracy. Mass Communication and the Cultivated Mind between the Wars*, 1988.

5.2873 **Mackenzie**, J. M., ed., *Imperialism and Popular Culture*, 1989.

5.2874 **MacMaster**, N., 'The battle for Mousehold Heath, 1857–84: "popular politics" and the Victorian public park', *P.P.*, CXXVII, 1990, 117–54.

5.2875 **Malcolmson**, R. W., *Popular Recreations in English Society, 1700–1850*, 1973.

5.2876 **Marwick**, A., *Culture in Britain since 1945*, 1991.

5.2877 **Meller**, Helen E., *Leisure and the Changing City, 1870–1914*, 1976. A case study of Bristol.

5.2878 **Minihan**, J., *The Nationalisation of Culture. The Development of State Subsidies to the Arts in Great Britain*, 1977.

5.2879 **Phillips**, J. and P., *Victorians Home and Away*, 1978.

5.2880 **Plumb**, J. H., *The Commercialisation of Leisure in Eighteenth-Century England*, 1973.

5.2881 **Rowntree**, B. S. and Lavers, G. R., *English Life and Leisure. A Social Study*, 1951.

5.2882 **Smith**, M. A., Parker, S., and Smith, C. S., eds., *Leisure and Society in Britain*, 1973.

5.2883 **Storch**, R. D., ed., *Popular Culture and Custom in Nineteenth-Century England*, 1982.

5.2884 **Thompson**, E. P., 'Patrician society, plebeian culture', *J.Soc.H.*, VII, 1974, 382–405.

5.2885 **Waites**, B., Bennett, T., and Martin, G., eds., *Popular Culture: Past and Present*, 1982.

5.2886 **Walton**, J. and Walvin, J., eds., *Leisure in Britain, 1780–1939*, 1983. Chapters on the London fairs, Oldham Wakes, cinema going, working-class reading habits, and on children's pleasures. Birmingham, Newcastle upon Tyne, Crewe, Blackpool, and Ilfracombe receive separate treatment.

5.2887 **Walvin**, J., *Leisure and Society, 1830–1950*, 1978.

5.2888 **Waters**, C., *British Socialists and the Politics of Popular Culture, 1884–1914*, 1990.

5.2889 **Yeo**, Eileen and S., *Popular Culture and Class Conflict, 1590–1914. Explorations in the History of Labour and Leisure*, 1981. A collection of essays dealing predominantly with the nineteenth century.

(b) Holidays

5.2890 **Bainbridge**, C., *Pavilions on the Sea. A History of the Seaside Pier*, 1986.

5.2891 **Black**, J., *The British and the Grand Tour*, 1985. Establishes the brutal facts of travel, the itineraries, and the variety of observations.

5.2892 —— *The British Abroad. The Grand Tour in the Eighteenth Century*, 1992. Examines the composition of the tourists – predominantly young men – and the range and organisation of their travels.

5.2893 **Brendon**, P., *Thomas Cook. 150 Years of Popular Tourism*, 1991.

5.2894 **Farrant**, S., 'London by the Sea. Resort development on the south coast of England, 1880–1939', *J.Contemp.H.*, XXX, 1987, 137–62.

5.2895 **Hern**, A., *The Seaside Holiday: The History of the English Seaside Resort*, 1967.

5.2896 **Lickorish**, J. and Kershaw, A. G., *The Travel Trade*, 1958.

5.2897 **Marsden**, C., *The English at the Seaside*, 1947.

5.2898 **Murfin**, Lyn, *Popular Leisure in the Lake Counties*, 1990. Predominantly an oral history which has chapters on domestic and family leisure and on public houses, sport, church and chapel, music, dancing, drama and cinema.

5.2899 **Pimlott**, J. A. R., *The Englishman's Holiday*, 1947.

5.2900 —— *The Englishman's Christmas. A Social History*, 1978.

5.2901 **Pudney**, J., *The Thomas Cook Story*, 1953.

5.2902 **Simmons**, J., *The Victorian Hotel*, 1984.

5.2903 **Walton**, J. K., *The Blackpool Landlady. A Social History*, 1978.

5.2904 —— *The English Seaside Resort. A Social*

History, 1750–1914, 1983.

5.2905 —— 'The demand for working-class seaside holidays in Victorian England', *Ec.H.R.*, 2nd ser., XXXIV, 1981, 249–65.

5.2906 —— 'Residential amenity, respectable morality and the rise of the entertainment industry: the case of Blackpool', *Lit. & Hist.*, I, 1975, 62–78.

5.2907 **Walvin**, J., *Beside the Seaside. A Social History of the Popular Seaside Holiday*, 1978.

5.2908 **Ward**, C. and Hardy, D., *Goodnight Campers! The History of the British Holiday Camp*, 1986.

(c) Entertainment

5.2909 **Aldgate**, A. and Richards, J., *Britain can take it. The British Cinema in the Second World War*, 1986.

5.2910 **Anderson**, P., *The Printed Image and the Transformation of Popular Culture, 1760–1860*, 1991.

5.2911 **Bailey**, P., *Music Hall. The Business of Pleasure*, 1986.

5.2912 **Booth**, M. R., *Theatre in the Victorian Age*, 1991.

5.2913 **Bradley**, D., *Understanding Rock 'n Roll. Popular Music in Britain, 1955–64*, 1992.

5.2914 **Bratton**, J. S., *Music Hall. Performance and Style*, 1986.

5.2915 —— *The Victorian Popular Ballad*, 1975.

5.2916 **Chanan**, M., *The Dream that Kicks. The Pre-history and Early Years of Cinema in Britain*, 1979.

5.2917 **Colls**, R., *The Collier's Rant. Song and Culture in the Industrial Village*, 1977.

5.2918 **Cunningham**, H., 'The metropolitan fairs: a case study in the social control of leisure', in Donajgrodzki (5.1895), 163–84.

5.2919 **Darcy**, C. P., *The Encouragement of the Fine Arts in Lancashire, 1760–1860*, Chet.Soc., 3rd ser., 24, 1976.

5.2920 **Ehrlich**, C., *The Piano: A History*, 1976. The history of a Victorian social symbol.

5.2921 **Elbourne**, R., *Music and Tradition in Early Industrial Lancashire, 1780–1840*, 1980.

5.2922 **Gaskell**, S. M., 'Gardens for the working class: Victorian practical pleasure', *Vict.Studs.*, XXIII, 1980, 479–501.

5.2923 **Herbert**, T., ed., *The Brass Band Movement in the Nineteenth and Twentieth Centuries*, 1991.

5.2924 **Hill**, C. R., *Horse Power. The Politics of the Turf*, 1987.

5.2925 **Hogwood**, C. and Luckett, R., eds., *Music in Eighteenth-Century England*, 1983.

5.2926 **Hollingsworth**, B., ed., *Songs of the People. Lancashire Dialect Poetry of the Industrial Revolution*, 1977.

5.2927 **Hudson**, K., *A Social History of Museums*, 1975.

5.2928 **Kuhn**, A., *Cinema, Censorship and Sexuality, 1909–25*, 1988.

5.2929 **Landy**, M., *British Genres. Cinema and Society, 1930–60*, 1991.

5.2930 **Low**, Rachel and Manvell, R., *History of the British Film*, 3 vols., 1948–50; 1985.

5.2931 **McKibbin**, R., 'Working class gambling in Britain, 1890–1939', *P.P.*, 82, 1979, 147–78.

5.2932 **Murphy**, R., *Realism and Tinsel. Cinema and Society in Britain, 1939–48*, 1989.

5.2933 **Richards**, J., *The Age of the Dream Palace. Cinema and Society in Britain, 1930–39*, 1984. An illuminating study of the cinema as a social institution.

5.2934 —— *Best of British. Cinema and Society, 1930–70*, 1983.

5.2935 **Rubinstein**, D., 'Cycling in the 1890s', *Vict. Studs.*, XXI, 1977, 47–71.

5.2936 **Scott**, H., *The Early Doors*, 1946. A social history of Music Hall.

5.2937 **Vamplew**, W., *The Turf. A Social and Economic History*, 1976.

5.2938 **Weber**, W., *Music and the Middle Classes. The Social Structure of Concert Life in London, Paris and Vienna between 1830 and 1848*, 1975.

5.2939 **Young**, P., *The Concert Tradition*, 1961.

(d) Sport

5.2940 **Cox**, R. W., ed., *Sport in Britain. A Bibliography of Historical Publications, 1800–1988*, 1991.

5.2941 **Arnold**, A. J., *A Game that Would Pay. A Business History of Professional Football in Bradford*, 1988.

5.2942 **Baker**, W. J., 'The making of a working-class football culture in Victorian England', *J.Soc.H.*, XIII, 1979, 241–52.

5.2943 **Bale**, J. R., 'Geographical diffusion and the adoption of professionalism in football in England and Wales', *Geog.*, LXIII, 1978, 188–97.

5.2944 **Blue**, A., *Grace Under Pressure. The Emergence of Women in Sport*, 1988.

5.2945 **Brailsford**, D., *Sport, Time and Society. The British at Play*, 1990.

5.2946 **Butler**, B., *The Football League, 1888–1988*, 1987.

5.2947 **Carr**, R., *English Fox Hunting: A History*, 1976.

5.2948 **Cashman**, R. I. and McKenna, M., eds., *Sport, Money, Morality and the Media*, Sydney, 1981. Includes a chapter on the earnings of professional sportsmen in England, 1870–1914.

5.2949 **Chandler**, T. J. L., 'Emergent athleticism; games in the English public schools, 1800–60', *Internat.J.H.Sport*, V, 1988, 312–30.

5.2950 **Dunning**, E. and Sheard, K., *Barbarians, Gentlemen and Players: A Sociological Study of the Development of Rugby Football*, 1979.

5.2951 —— Murphy, P., and Williams, J., *The Roots of Football Hooliganism. An Historical and Sociological Study*, 1988. Shows that crowd disorders accompanied the game since its emergence in the nineteenth century.

5.2952 **Eisenberg**, C., 'The middle class and competition: some considerations on the beginnings of modern sport in England and Germany', *Internat.H.Hist.Sport*, XVII, 1990, 265–82.

5.2953 **Fishwick**, N., *English Football and Society, 1910–50*, 1989. Considers the connections between football and the communities of town, nation, and class.

5.2954 **Halladay**, E., *Rowing in England. A Social History. The Amateur Debate*, 1990. Places the sport as practised both by the elite and by artisans within its social context. *See also* Wigglesworth (5.2975).

5.2955 **Hargreaves**, J., *Sport, Power and Culture. A Social and Historical Analysis of Popular Sports in Britain*, 1986.

5.2956 **Holland**, A., *Grand National. The Official Celebration of 150 Years*, 1988.

5.2957 **Holt**, A., 'Hikers and ramblers: surviving a thirties fashion', *Internat.J.Hist.Sport*, IV, 1987, 56–67.

5.2958 **Holt**, R., *Sport and the British. A Modern History*, 1989.

5.2959 **Huggins**, M., 'Horse-racing on Teesside in the nineteenth century: change and continuity', *Northern H.*, XXIII, 1987, 98–118.

5.2960 **Itykowitz**, D. C., 'Victorian bookmakers and their customers', *Vict.Studs.*, XXXII, 1988, 7–30.

5.2961 **Jones**, S. G., *Sport, Politics and the Working Class. A Study of Organised Labour and Sport in Interwar Britain*, 1988.

5.2962 —— 'State intervention in sport and leisure in Britain between the Wars', *J.Contemp.H.*, XXX, 1987, 163–82.

5.2963 **McCrone**, Kathleen E., *Class, Gender and English Women's Sport, c.1890–1914*, 1992.

5.2964 —— *Sport and the Physical Emancipation of English Women, 1870–1914*, 1988. Concentrates on the impact of girls' public schools and on the establishment of women's colleges at Oxford and Cambridge, and on the specialist physical training colleges.

5.2965 **Mason**, A., *Association Football and English Society, 1863–1915*, 1980. Examines the transformation of football to a mass working-class sport.

5.2966 —— *Sport in Britain. A Social History*, 1989.

5.2967 **Metcalfe**, A., 'Organised sport in the mining communities of south Northumberland, 1800–89', *Vict.Studs.*, XXV, 1982, 469–96.

5.2968 **Midwinter**, E., *Fair Game. Myth and Reality in Sport*, 1986.

5.2969 **Noel**, E. B. and Clark, J. O. M., *A History of Tennis*, 1991.

5.2970 **Schofield**, J. A., 'The development of first class cricket in England: an economic analysis', *J.Indust.Ec.*, XXX, 1982, 337–61.

5.2971 **Treadwell**, P., 'The Games mania; the cult of athleticism in the later Victorian public school', *Hist.Educ.Soc.Bull.*, XXXII, 1983, 24–31.

5.2972 **Vamplew**, W., *Pay Up and Play the Game. Professional Sport in Britain, 1875–1914*, 1989. Football, cricket, horseracing and rugby league provide the chief examples in this attempt to quantify the history of commercialised sport.

5.2973 **Wagg**, S., *The Football World. A Contemporary Social History*, 1984.

5.2974 **Walvin**, J., *The People's Game. A Social History of British Football*, 1975. A general survey weighted towards the nineteenth and twentieth centuries.

5.2975 **Wigglesworth**, N., *A Social History of English Rowing*, 1992. *See also* Halliday (5.2954).

(c) Reading habits (including the development of public libraries)

5.2976 **Altick**, R. D., *The English Common Reader: A Social History of the Mass Reading Public 1800–1900*, Chicago, Ill., 1957.

5.2977 **Blake**, A., *Reading Victorian Fiction. The Cultural Context and Ideological Content of the Nineteenth Century Novel*, 1989.

5.2978 **Hoggart**, R., *The Uses of Literacy*, 1958. A classic study of working-class reading habits.

5.2979 **James**, L, *Fiction for the Working Man, 1830–1850*, 1963.

5.2980 —— *Print and People, 1819–51*, 1975.

5.2981 **Kelly**, T., *Books for the People. An Illustrated History of the British Public Library*, 1977.

5.2982 —— *Early Public Libraries: A History of Public Libraries in Great Britain before 1850*, 1966.

5.2983 **McAleer**, J., *Popular Reading and Publishing in Britain, 1914–50*, 1992.

5.2984 **Neuburg**, V. E., *Popular Literature: A History and Guide*, 1977.

5.2985 **Rivers**, Isabel, ed., *Books and their Readers in Eighteenth-Century England*, 1982.

5.2986 **Rogers**, P., *Literature and Popular Culture in Eighteenth Century England*, 1985.

5.2987 **Shattock**, Joanne and Wolff, M., *The Victorian Periodical Press: Samplings and Soundings*, 1982.

5.2988 **Springhall**, J., 'Disseminating impure literature: the "penny dreadful" publishing business', *Ec.H.R.*, 2nd ser., XLVII, 1984, 567–84.

5.2989 **Suvin**, D., 'The social addressees of Victorian Fiction: a preliminary enquiry', *Lit.& H.*, VIII, 1982, 11–40.

5.2990 **Vincent**, D., *Literacy and Popular Culture: England, 1750–1914*, 1989. Casts doubt on some of the generalisations made about literacy levels and popular culture. Continuities are emphasised.

5.2991 **Webb**, R. K., *The British Working-Class Reader, 1790–1848: Literary and Social Tension*, 1955.

THE PRESS AND BROADCASTING

(a) The press

5.2992 **Adburgham**, Alison, *Women in Print*, 1972.

5.2993 **Aspinall**, A., *Politics and the Press, 1780–1850*, 1949.

5.2994 **Ayerst**, D., *Guardian: Biography of a Newspaper*, 1971.

5.2995 **Black**, J., *The English Press in the Eighteenth Century*, 1986. Concentrates on metropolitan and provincial newspapers, their political and economic role, and on subsidies and censorship.

5.2996 **Brown**, Lucy, *Victorian News and Newspapers*, 1985.

5.2997 **Cranfield**, G. A., *The Development of the Provincial Newspaper, 1700–1760*, 1962. Bibliography, 274–8.

5.2998 **Ewald**, W. B., *The Newsmen of Queen Anne*, 1956.

5.2999 **Hanson**, L., *Government and the Press, 1695–1763*, 1936.

5.3000 **Harris**, M., *London Newspapers in the Age of Walpole. A Study of the Origins of the Modern English Press*, 1987.

5.3001 —— and Lee, A., eds., *The Press in English Society from the Seventeenth to the Nineteenth Century*, 1987.

5.3002 **Hollis**, Patricia M., *The Pauper Press: A Study in Working-class Radicalism of the 1830s*, 1970.

5.3003 **Koss**, S., *The Rise and Fall of the Political Press in Britain. I: the Nineteenth Century*, 1981; II: *The Twentieth Century*, 1984. Painstakingly compiled this is probably the definitive study in this field.

5.3004 **Lee**, A. J., *The Origins of the Popular Press*, 1976.

5.3005 **Milne**, M., *Newspapers of Northumberland and Durham in the Nineteenth Century*, 1971.

5.3006 **Price**, R. G. G., *A History of Punch*, 1957.

5.3007 **Raven**, J., *Judging New Wealth. Popular Publishing and Responses to Commerce in England, 1750–1800*, 1992. Based chiefly on literary evidence. Criticisms of the social presumptions of businessmen are explored and questions raised about the implications of the consumer revolution.

5.3008 **Read**, D., *Press and People, 1790–1850: Opinion in Three English Cities*.

(Manchester, Leeds and Sheffield), 1961.

5.3009 **Seymour-Ure**, C., *The British Press and Broadcasting since 1945*, 1991.

5.3010 **Smith**, A. C. H., *Paper Voices. The Popular Press and Social Change, 1935–65*, 1975.

5.3011 **Weed**, K. K., and Bond, R. P., 'Studies of British newspapers and periodicals from their beginning to 1800: a bibliography'. In *Studies in Philology*, Durham, N. C., 1946.

5.3012 **White**, Cynthia L., *Women's Magazines, 1693–1968*, 1970.

5.3013 **Wiener**, J. H., *The War of the Unstamped: A History of the Movement to Repeal the British Newspaper Tax, 1830–1836*, 1970.

5.3014 **Wiles**, R. M., *Freshest Advices: Early Provincial Newspapers in England*, Columbus, Ohio, 1965.

(b) Broadcasting

5.3015 **Baker**, W. J., *A History of the Marconi Company*, 1970.

5.3016 **Briggs**, A., *A History of Broadcasting in the United Kingdom*, I: *The Birth of Broadcasting*, 1961; II: *The Golden Age of Wireless*, 1965; III: *The War of Words*, 1970; IV: *Sound and Vision*, 1979.

5.3017 —— *The BBC. The First Fifty Years*, 1985. A distillation of the author's multi-volume history of British broadcasting.

5.3018 **Burns**, R. W., *British Television. The Formative Years*, 1986.

5.3019 **Coase**, R. H., *British Broadcasting: A Study in Monopoly*, 1950.

5.3020 **Pegg**, M., *Broadcasting and Society, 1918–39*, 1982.

5.3021 **Scannell**, P. and Cardiff, D., *A Social History of British Broadcasting*, I: *1922–39, Serving the Nation*, 1991. Deals with the pioneering days of broadcasting and includes sections on the production of information and of entertainment and on audiences. Includes statistics on costs.

5.3022 **Sendall**, B., *Independent TV in Great Britain*. I: *Origin and Foundation, 1946–62*, 1982; II: *Expansion and Change, 1958–68*, 1983. A useful though somewhat indigestible survey of commercial TV in this country.

RELIGION, SOCIETY AND ECONOMIC LIFE

(a) General works

5.3023 **Briggs**, J. and Sellars, I., eds., *Victorian Nonconformity*, 1973. A documentary collection.

5.3024 **Thompson**, D. M., *Nonconformity in the Nineteenth Century*, 1972. A very useful collection of documents with an introduction and bibliography.

5.3025 **Bebbington**, D. W., *The Nonconformist Conscience. Chapel and Politics, 1870–1914*, 1982.

5.3026 **Binfield**, C., *So Down to Prayers. Studies in English Nonconformity, 1780–1920*, 1977.

5.3027 **Bradley**, I., *The Call to Seriousness. The Evangelical Impact on the Victorians*, 1976.

5.3028 **Brown**, C. G., 'Did urbanisation secularise Britain?', *Urban H. Yearbook*, 1988, 1–14.

5.3029 **Brown**, K. D., *A Social History of the Nonconformist Ministry in England and Wales, 1800–1930*, 1988.

5.3030 **Coleman**, B. I., *The Church of England in the mid Nineteenth Century. A Social Geography*, 1980.

5.3031 **Collins**, Irene, *Jane Austen and the Clergy*, 1994. A historian's contextualisation of Jane Austen's clergy which looks at their education, appointment, marriage, income and world view.

5.3032 **Englander**, D., 'Booth's Jews: the presentation of Jews and Judaism in *Life and Labour of the People in London*, *Vict.Studs*, XXXII, 1989, 551–72.

5.3033 **Everitt**, A. M., *The Pattern of Rural Dissent: The Nineteenth Century*, 1972.

5.3034 **Field**, C. D., 'The 1851 Religious Census: select bibliography of materials relating to England and Wales', *Proc.Wesley H.Soc.*, XLI, 1978, 175–82.

5.3035 **Gay**, J. D., *The Geography of Religion in England*, 1971. Deals mainly with the period after 1750. Useful on the Religious Census of 1851.

5.3036 **Haydon**, C. M., *Anti-Catholicism in Eighteenth Century England. A Political and Social Study*, 1993.

5.3037 **Heeney**, B., *The Women's Movement in the Church of England, 1850–1930*, 1988.

5.3038 **Lovegrove**, D. W., *Established Church, Sectarian People. Itinerancy and the transformation of English Dissent, 1780–1830*, 1988.

5.3039 **McLeod**, H., *Class and Religion in the Late Victorian City*, 1974. Compares and analyses the social organisation of religion in the East and West Ends and suburbs of London in a critical period of church history.

5.3040 **Norman**, E. R., *Church and Society in England, 1770–1970: A Historical Study*, 1976.

5.3041 **Studdert-Kennedy**, K., Dog Collar Democracy. *The Industrial Christian Fellowship, 1919–29*, 1982.

5.3042 **Taylor**, Anne, *Visions of Harmony. A Study in Nineteenth-Century Millenarianism*, 1986. A comparative study of New Lanark and Harmony, Indiana.

5.3043 **Wigley**, J., *The Rise and Fall of the Victorian Sunday*, 1980. Relates Sabbatarianism to the position and preferences of the middle classes.

(b) Nonconformity and economic development

5.3044 **Ambler**, R. W., *Ranters, revivalists and Reformers. Primitive Methodism and Rural Society. South Lincolnshire, 1817–75*, 1989.

5.3045 **Bradley**, J. E., *Religion, Revolution and English Radicalism. Nonconformity in Eighteenth-Century Politics and Society*, 1990.

5.3046 **Briggs**, J. H. Y., 'Charles Haddon Spurgeon and the Baptist denomination in nineteenth-century Britain', *Baptist. Q.*, XXI, 1986, 218–40.

5.3047 **Emden**, P. H., *Quakers in Commerce*, 1939.

5.3048 **Field**, C. D., 'The social structure of English Methodism: eighteenth to twentieth centuries', *Brit.J.Soc.*, XXVIII, 1977, 199–225.

5.3049 **Gilbert**, A. D., *Religion and Society in Industrial England. Church, Chapel and Social Change, 1740–1914*, 1976.

5.3050 **Green**, S. J. D., 'The death of pew rents, the rise of bazaars, and the end of the traditional political economy of voluntary religious organisations: the case of the West Riding of Yorkshire',

Northern H., XXVII, 1991, 198–235.

5.3051 **Grubb**, Isobel, *Quakerism and Industry before 1800*, 1930.

5.3052 **Hempton**, D., 'Methodism and the law, 1740–1820', *Bull.J.Rylands Lib.*, LXX, 1988, 93–107.

5.3053 —— *Methodism and Politics in British Society, 1750–1850*, 1984. Re-examines the impact of Methodism on trade unionism, education, Chartism, and other aspects of national life.

5.3054 **Hilton**, B., *The Age of Atonement. The Influence of Evangelicalism on Social and Economic Thought, 1795–1863*, 1988.

5.3055 **Hinchcliff**, P., 'Voluntary absolutism: British missionary societies in the nineteenth century', *Studs.Church H.*, XXIII, 1986, 363–80.

5.3056 **Hole**, R., *Pulpits, Politics and the Public Order in England, 1760–1832*, 1989.

5.3057 **Holt**, R. V., *The Unitarian Contribution to Social Progress in England*, 1938, 2nd rev. ed., 1952.

5.3058 **Isichei**, Elizabeth, *Victorian Quakers*, 1970.

5.3059 **Jeremy**, D. J., ed., *Business and Religion in Britain*, 1988.

5.3060 —— *Capitalists and Christians. Business Leaders and the Churches in Britain, 1900–60*, 1990. Looks at the religious background of middle class business leaders and at the impact this may have had on business policy and on social provision for workers.

5.3061 **Pratt**, D. H., *English Quakers and the First Industrial Revolution. A Study of the Quaker Community in Four Industrial Counties: Lancashire, Yorkshire, Warwickshire, and Gloucestershire, 1750–1830*, 1985.

5.3062 **Raistrick**, A., *Quakers in Science and Industry in the Seventeenth and Eighteenth Centuries*, 1950.

5.3063 **Snell**, K. D. M., *Church and Chapel in the North Midlands. Religious Observance in the Nineteenth Century*, 1991.

5.3064 **Urdank**, A. M., *Religion and Society in a Cotswold Vale. Nailsworth, Gloucestershire, 1780–1865*, 1990.

5.3065 **Wolffe**, J., *The Protestant Crusade in Great Britain, 1829–60*, 1991.

(c) Religion and the working class

5.3066 **Armstrong**, A., *The Church of England, the Methodists and Society 1700–1850*,

1973.

5.3067 **Bagwell**, P. S., *Outcast London. A Christian Response: the West London Mission of the Methodist Church, 1887–1987*, 1987.

5.3068 **Bailey**, V., 'In Darkest England and the Way Out': the Salvation Army, social reform and the Labour movement, 1885–1910', *Internat.R.Soc.H.*, XXIX, 1984, 133–72.

5.3069 **Bebbington**, D. W., 'The city, the countryside and the social gospel in late Victorian Nonconformity', *Studs.Church H.*, XVI, 1979, 415–26.

5.3070 **Billington**, L., 'Popular religion and social reform: a study of Revivalism and Teetotalism, 1830–50', *J.Rel.H.*, X, 1979, 266–93.

5.3071 **Clark**, G. K., *Churchmen and the Condition of England, 1832–1885*, 1973. *See also* Soloway (5.3086).

5.3072 **Coleman**, B. I., 'Southern England in the census of religious worship, 1851', *Southern H.*, V, 1983, 154–88.

5.3073 **Hargreaves**, J. A., 'Methodism and Luddism in Yorkshire, 1812–13', *Northern H.*, XXVI, 1990, 160–85.

5.3074 **Hart**, Jenifer M., 'Religion and social control in the mid nineteenth century' in Donajgrodzki (5.1895), 108–37.

5.3075 **Himmelfarb**, Gertrude, 'Postscript on the Halévy thesis', *Victorian Minds*, 1968, 292–9.

5.3076 **Hobsbawm**, E. J., 'Methodism and the threat of revolution in Britain'. In (5.2188), 23–33.

5.3077 **Inglis**, K. S., *Churches and the Working Classes in Victorian England*, 1963.

5.3078 **McEntee**, G. P., *The Social Catholic Movement in Great Britain*, N. Y., 1927.

5.3079 **McLeod**, H., *Religion and the Working Classes in Nineteenth-Century Britain*, 1984.

5.3080 **Mayor**, S. H., *The Churches and the Labour Movement*, 1967. Deals mainly with the period 1848–1914.

5.3081 **Moore**, R. S., *Pitmen, Preachers and Politics. The Effects of Methodism in a Durham Mining Community*, 1974. Focuses particularly on four mining villages in period 1870 to 1926.

5.3082 **Obelkevich**, J., *Religion and Rural Society. South Lindsey, 1825–75*, 1976.

5.3083 **Scotland**, N., *Methodism and the Revolt of the Field. A Study of the Methodist Contribution to Agricultural Trade Unionism in East Anglia, 1872–96*, 1981.

5.3084 **Semmel**, B., *The Methodist Revolution*, 1974. Reassesses the Methodist synthesis of liberty, order, and national mission.

5.3085 **Smith**, A., *The Established Church and Popular Religion, 1750–1850*, 1971. A collection of documents with commentary.

5.3086 **Soloway**, R. A., *Prelates and People: Ecclesiastical Social Thought in England 1783–1852*, 1969. *See also* Clark (5.3).

5.3087 **Taylor**, E. R., *Methodism and Politics 1791–1831*, 1935.

5.3088 **Valenze**, Deborah M., *Prophetic Sons and Daughters. Female Preaching and Popular Religion in Industrial England*, 1986. Examines the world of cottage evangelism between the 1790s and the 1850s and its links with cottage economy.

5.3089 **Wagner**, D. O., *The Church of England and Social Reform since 1854*, N. Y., 1930.

5.3090 **Ward**, W. R., *Religion and Society in England 1790–1850*, 1972. Based largely on unpublished sources.

5.3091 **Wearmouth**, R. F., *Methodism and the Common People of the Eighteenth Century*, 1945.

5.3092 —— *Methodism and the Working-class Movements of England, 1800–1850*, 1937.

5.3093 —— *Methodism and the Struggle of the Working Classes 1850–1900*, 1954.

5.3094 —— *Some Working Class Movements of the Nineteenth Century*, 1948.

5.3095 —— *The Social and Political Influence of Methodism in the Twentieth Century*, 1957.

5.3096 **Wickham**, E. R., *Church and People in an Industrial City*, 1957. A pioneer work on the social history of religion. The city is Sheffield.

5.3097 **Yeo**, S., *Religion and Voluntary Organisations in Crisis*, 1976. A case study (based on Reading) of the impact of capitalism and poverty on the churches between 1890 and 1914.

(d) Christian Socialism

5.3098 **Backstrom**, P. N., *Christian Socialism and Co-operation in Victorian England: Edward Vansittart Neale and the Co-operative Movements*, 1974.

5.3099 **Jones**, P. d'A., *The Christian Socialist Revival, 1877–1914: Religion, Class and Social Conscience in Late Victorian*

England, Princeton, N. J., 1968.

5.3100 **Masterman**, N. C., *John Malcolm Ludlow; The Builder of Christian Socialism*, 1963.

5.3101 **Norman**, E. R., *The Victorian Christian Socialists*, 1987.

5.3102 **Raven**, C. E., *Christian Socialism, 1848–1854*, 1920.

5.3103 **Saville**, J., 'The Christian Socialists of 1848'. In Saville (5.2036), 135–59.

(e) Freethought

5.3104 **Budd**, Susan, *Varieties of Unbelief: Atheists and Agnostics in English Society, 1850–1960*, 1977.

5.3105 **Gilbert**, A. D., *The Making of Post-Christian Britain. A History of the Secularisation of Modern Society*, 1980.

5.3106 **McCalman**, I., *Radical Underworld. Prophets, Revolutionaries and Pornographers in London, 1795–1840*, 1988.

5.3107 **Royle**, E., *Radicals, Secularists and Republicans*, 1980.

5.3108 —— *Victorian Infidels. The Origins of the British Secularist Movement, 1791–1866*, 1975.

EDUCATION

(a) Schooling

5.3109 **Digby**, Anne, and Searby, P., eds., *Children, School and Society in Nineteenth-Century England*, 1981. A sourcebook with sections on religion, social class and the economy, teachers, and girls' education. Bibliography.

5.3110 **Maclure**, J. S., *Educational Documents: England and Wales, 1816–1967*, 1968.

5.3111 **Allsobrook**, D. I., *Schools for the Shires. The Reform of Middle Class Education in mid Victorian England*, 1986. Deals with the changing pattern of schooling in Victorian England and the various reform schemes.

5.3112 **Archer**, R. L., *Secondary Education in the Nineteenth Century*, 1966.

5.3113 **Armytage**, W. H. G., *Four Hundred Years of English Education*, 1964.

5.3114 **Ball**, N., *Educating the People. A Documentary History of Elementary Schooling in England 1840–70*, 1983.

5.3115 **Banks**, Olive, *Parity and Prestige in English Secondary Education*, 1955.

5.3116 **Bardshaw**, D. C. A., ed., *Studies in the Government and Control of Education since 1860*, 1970.

5.3117 **Bergen**, B. H., 'Only a schoomaster: gender, class and the effort to professionalise elementary teaching in England, 1870–1910', *Hist.Educ.Q.*, XXII, 1982, 1–22.

5.3118 **Brown**, C. M., 'Lancashire industrialists and their schools, 1833–1902', *J.Educ.Admin. and Hist.*, XV, 1983, 10–21.

5.3119 **Bryant**, Margaret E., *The London Experience in Secondary Education*, 1986.

5.3120 **Clarke**, A., *Victorian Schools*, 1983.

5.3121 **Cruikshank**, Marjorie, *Church and State in English Education, 1870 to the Present Day*, 1964.

5.3122 **Davies**, W., *The Curriculum and Organisation of the County Intermediate Schools, 1880–1926*, 1989.

5.3123 **Dent**, H. C., *The Training of Teachers in England and Wales, 1800–1975*, 1977.

5.3124 **Elliott**, B., 'The effects upon education of the agricultural depression in Britain in the late nineteenth century', *Hist.Educ. Soc.Bull.*, XL, 1987, 54–60.

5.3125 **Ellis**, A., *Educating our Masters. Influences on the Growth of Literacy in Working Class Children*, 1985. Does not succeed in relating literacy to its wider social and economic context nor – in a convincing way – even to education.

5.3126 **Evans**, K., *The Development and Structure of the English Educational System*, 1975.

5.3127 **Gardner**, P., *The Lost Elementary Schools of Victorian England*, 1984.

5.3128 —— *The People's Schools in Victorian England*, 1984.

5.3129 **Goldstrom**, J. M., *The Social Content of Education, 1808–70. A Study of the Urban Working-Class Reader in England and Ireland*, 1972.

5.3130 **Gordon**, P., *The Victorian School Manager* 1974.

5.3131 **Gosden**, P. H. J. H., *The Development of Educational Administration in England and Wales*, 1966.

5.3132 —— *Education in the Second World War. A Study in Policy and Administration,* 1976.

5.3133 **Horn**, Pamela L., *Education in Rural England, 1800–1914,* 1978.

5.3134 —— *The Victorian and Edwardian Schoolchild,* 1989.

5.3135 **Hunt**, Felicity, ed., *Lessons for Life. The Schooling of Girls and Women, 1850–1950,* 1987. Considers how ideas about feminity and women's roles as wives and mothers influenced educational theory and practice.

5.3136 **Hurt**, J., *Education in Evolution: Church, State, Society and Popular Education, 1800–1870,* 1971.

5.3137 —— *Elementary Schooling and the Working Classes, 1860–1918,* 1979.

5.3138 **Johnson**, R., 'Educational Policy and social control in early Victorian England', *P.P.,* 49, 1970, 96–119.

5.3139 **Jones**, M. G., *The Charity School Movement: A Study of Eighteenth-Century Puritanism in Action,* 1938.

5.3140 **Judge**, H. A., *A Generation of Schooling. English Secondary Schools since 1944,* 1984.

5.3141 **Kazamias**, A. M., *Politics, Society and Secondary Education in England,* 1966.

5.3142 **Laqueur**, T. W., *Religion and Respectability. Sunday Schools and English Working-Class Culture, 1780–1850,* New Haven, 1976.

5.3143 **Lawn**, M., *Servants of the State. The Contested Control of Teaching, 1900–1930,* 1984.

5.3144 **Lawson**, J. and Silver, H., *A Social History of Education in England,* 1973. A general survey extending from the Middle Ages to the present day. The main emphasis is on the post-1760 period.

5.3145 **Lowndes**, G. A., *The Silent Social Revolution: An Account of the Expansion of Public Education in England and Wales 1895–1935,* 1950.

5.3146 **McCann**, P., ed., *Popular Education and Socialisation in the Nineteenth Century,* 1977.

5.3147 **McLachlan**, H., *English Education under the Test Acts,* 1931. Covers Dissenting Academies, 1663–1820.

5.3148 **McLoughlin**, M. G., *A History of the Education of the Deaf in England,* 1987.

5.3149 **Maclure**, J. S., *One Hundred Years of London Education, 1870–1970,* 1970.

5.3150 **Marsden**, W. E., *Unequal Educational Provision in England and Wales. The Nineteenth Century Roots,* 1987.

5.3151 **Mitch**, D. F., *The Rise of Popular Literacy in Victorian England. The Influence of Private Choice and Public Policy,* 1992. A cost benefit approach to the subject which argues that literacy levels rose in this period largely because of the perceived public benefits.

5.3152 **Muller**, D. et al., eds., *The Rise of the Modern Educational System. Structural Change and Social Reproduction, 1870–1920,* 1987.

5.3153 **Murphy**, J., *Church, State and Schools in Britain, 1800–1870,* 1971.

5.3154 **Musgrave**, P. W., *Society and Education in England since 1800,* 1968, 5th ed., 1972.

5.3155 **Neuburg**, V. E., *Popular Education in Eighteenth-Century England. A Study in the Origins of the Mass Reading Public,* 1971.

5.3156 **Pallister**, R., 'Urban school boards: some financial pressures', *Hist.Educ.Soc.Bull.,* XL, 1987, 41–53.

5.3157 **Pinchbeck**, Ivy and Hewitt, Margaret, *Children in English Society, Vol. 2: From the Eighteenth Century to the Children Act, 1948,* 1973. *See also* Vol. I (4.1140).

5.3158 **Rich**, E. E., *The Education Act, 1870,* 1970.

5.3159 **Roach**, J, *Public Examinations in England, 1850–1900,* 1971.

5.3160 —— *Secondary Education in England, 1870–1902. Public Activity and Private Enterprise,* 1991.

5.3161 **Robson**, D., *Some Aspects of Education in Cheshire in the Eighteenth Century,* 1966.

5.3162 **Sanderson**, M., *Education, Economic Change and Society in England, 1780–1870,* 1983.

5.3163 —— *Educational Opportunity and Social Change in England,* 1987.

5.3164 **Seaborne**, M. and Lowe, R., *The English School, its Architecture and Organisation. II: 1870–1970,* 1977. Vol. I of this work is listed above (4.1475).

5.3165 **Selleck**, R. J. W., *English Primary Education and the Progressives, 1914–1939,* 1972.

5.3166 **Sharp**, P. R., 'Victorian values and the private funding of education: the case of the School of Art in the 1860s', *J.Educ.Admin. and Hist.,* XXI, 1989, 18–27.

5.3167 **Sherington**, G. E., *English Education, Social Change and War, 1911–20,* 1981.

Places the 1918 Education Act firmly in context.

5.3168 **Silver**, H., *Education as History. Interpreting Nineteenth and Twentieth Century Education*, 1983. A collection of essays on the social history of education extending from Robert Owen's factory schools to post Second World War educational planning.

5.3169 **Simon**, B., *Studies in the History of Education: The Two Nations and the Educational Structure 1780–1870*, 1960.

5.3170 —— *Studies in the History of Education: Education and the Labour Movement, 1870–1920*, 1965.

5.3171 —— *Studies in the History of Education: The Politics of Educational Reform 1920–1940*, 1974.

5.3172 —— *Education and the Social Order, 1940–90*, 1991. The final volume of Brian Simon's social history of education and politics in modern Britain. The 1960s are seen as a kind of golden age for education.

5.3173 **Smith**, J. W. A., *The Birth of Modern Education: The Contribution of the Dissenting Academies, 1660–1800*, 1954.

5.3174 **Stephens**, W. B., *Education, Literacy and Society, 1830–70. The Geography of Diversity in Provincial England*, 1987. An exercise in comparative local history.

5.3175 **Sturt**, Mary, *The Education of the People*, 1967. The growth of English elementary education in the nineteenth century.

5.3176 **Sutherland**, Gillian, *Ability, Merit and Measurement. Mental Testing in English Education, 1880–1940*, 1984. A useful study divided into two parts, the first dealing with the beginnings of classification in state schools and the identification of mentally impaired children. Part two focusses on techniques such as the 11 plus to monitor intelligence levels in children.

.3177 —— *Policy-making in Elementary Education, 1870–1895*, 1974.

.3178 **Thornton**, A. H., *Samuel Smiles and Nineteenth Century Self Help in Education*, 1983.

.3179 **Tompson**, R. S., *Classics or Charity?: The Dilemma of the Eighteenth-century Grammar School*, 1971. A re-assessment of the condition and functions of the grammar schools. Useful bibliography, 144–64.

.3180 **Wardle**, D., *English Popular Education,*

1780–1970, 1970.

5.3181 —— *Education and Society in Nineteenth-Century Nottingham*, 1971.

5.3182 **West**, E. G., *Education and the Industrial Revolution*, 1975. Its interpretation differs markedly from Hurt (5.3137).

(b) The public schools

5.3183 **Allen**, E. A., 'Public School elites in early Victorian England: the boys at Harrow and Merchant Taylors Schools from 1825 to 1850', *J.Brit.Studs.*, XXI, 1982, 87–117.

5.3184 **Bamford**, T. W., *The Rise of the Public Schools*, 1967.

5.3185 **Chandos**, J., *Boys Together. English Public Schools, 1806–64*, 1984.

5.3186 **Custance**, R., ed., *Winchester College. Sixth Centenary Essays*, 1982.

5.3187 **Heward**, C., *Making a Man of Him. Parents and their Sons' Education at an English Public School, 1929–50*, 1988.

5.3188 **Mack**, E. C., *Public Schools and British Opinion, 1780–1860*, 1938.

5.3189 —— *Public Schools and British Opinion since 1860*, N. Y., 1941. Covers the period up to 1914.

5.3190 **Ollard**, R., *An English Education. A Retrospect of Eton*, 1982.

5.3191 **Simon**, B., and Bradley, I., eds., *The Victorian Public School*, 1975.

(c) Adult education

5.3192 **Blyth**, J. A., *English University Adult Education, 1908–58. The Unique Tradition*, 1983.

5.3193 **Devereux**, W. A., *Adult Education in Inner London, 1870–1980*, 1982.

5.3194 **Drodge**, S., 'Co-operative Society libraries and education in the nineteenth century: a preliminary assessment', *Studs. Educ.Adults*, XX, 1988, 49–59.

5.3195 **Harrison**, J. F. C., *Learning and Living, 1790–1860*, 1961.

5.3196 **Kelly**, T., *George Birkbeck, Pioneer of Adult Education*, 1957.

5.3197 **Marriott**, S., *Extramural Empires. Service and Self Interest in English University Adult Education, 1873–1983*, 1984.

5.3198 **Porter**, J., ed., *Education and Labour in the South-West*, 1975.

5.3199 **Rose**, J., 'The workers in the Workers' Educational Association, 1903–50', *Albion*, XXI, 1989, 591–608.

5.3200 **Stephens**, W. B., *Adult Education and Society in an Industrial Town: Warrington, 1800–1900*, 1980.

5.3201 **Stocks**, Mary D., *The Workers' Educational Association: The First Fifty Years*, 1953.

5.3202 **Tylecote**, Mabel, *The Mechanics Institutes of Lancashire and Yorkshire before 1851*, 1956.

(d) Technical education

5.3203 **Ahlström**, G., *Engineers and Industrial Growth*, 1982. Contrasts the education of engineers on the Continent and in England.

5.3204 **Argles**, M., *South Kensington to Robbins*, 1964. A survey of the development of technical education in the nineteenth and twentieth centuries.

5.3205 **Bagwell**, P. S., *The Polytechnic, 1838–1988. Meeting the Needs of London and Beyond*, 1989.

5.3206 **Cotgrove**, S. F., *Technical Education and Social Change*, 1958.

5.3207 **Katoh**, S., 'Mechanics' Institutes in Great Britain to the 1850s', *J.Educ.Admin. and Hist.*, XXI, 1989, 1–17.

5.3208 **Roderick**, G. and Stephens, M., eds., *Where did we go wrong? Industrial Performance, Education and the Economy in Victorian Britain*, 1981.

(e) The universities

5.3209 **Berdhal**, R. O., *British Universities and the State*, 1959.

5.3210 **Harte**, N. B., *The University of London, 1836–1986. An Illustrated History*, 1986.

5.3211 **Jones**, D. R., *The Origins of Civic Universities. Manchester, Leeds and Liverpool*, 1988. Shows how their development in the second half of the nineteenth century entailed the exclusion of non-degree, part-time and vocational students.

5.3212 **Sanderson**, M., *The Universities and British Industry, 1850–1870*, 1972. Excellent select bibliography, 398–419.

5.3213 —— *The Universities in the Nineteenth Century*, 1975.

5.3214 —— 'The English civic universities and the "industrial spirit", 1870–1914', *Hist.Res.*, LXI, 1988, 90–104.

5.3215 **Stewart**, W. A. C., *Higher Education in Post-War Britain*, 1989.

5.3216 **Sutherland**, Lucy and Mitchell, L. G., eds., *The History of the University of Oxford. V: The Eighteenth Century*, 1986. Strong on the religious, social and administrative aspects.

5.3217 **Ward**, W. R., *Georgian Oxford*, 1958. Excellent bibliography.

5.3218 —— *Victorian Oxford*, 1965.

WOMEN

(a) General

5.3219 **Barrow**, M., ed., *Women, 1870–1928*, 1981. A select guide to printed and archival sources in the U.K.

5.3220 **Hellerstein**, Erna O., Hume, L. P. and Offen, Karen M., eds., *Victorian Women. A Documentary Account of Women's Lives in Nineteenth-Century England, France and the United States*, 1981.

5.3221 **Adam**, R., *Women's Place, 1910–75*, 1975

5.3222 **John**, Angela V., *Unequal Opportunities. Women's Employment in England, 1800–1918*, 1985.

5.3223 **Jones**, F. L., 'Occupational statistics revisited: the female labour force in early British and Australian censuses', *Aust.Ec.H.R.*, XXVII, 1987, 56–76.

5.3224 **Jones**, M., *Women in Nineteenth-Century Britain*, 1987.

5.3225 **Lewis**, Jane, *Women and Social Action in Victorian and Edwardian England*, 1991.

5.3226 —— *Women in Britain since 1945. Women, Family, Work and the State in the Post-War Years*, 1992.

5.3227 —— *Women in England, 1870–1950*, 1984. Examines the framework of middle-class and working-class women' lives and the shifting sexual division of labour.

5.3228 **Malmgreen**, G., ed., *Religion in the Lives of English Women, 1760–1930*, 1986.

5.3229 **Need**, L., *Myths of Sexuality. Representations of Women in Victorian*

Britain, 1989.

.3230 **Perkin**, Joan, *Women and Marriage in Nineteenth-Century England*, 1989. Shows that childbearing and legal disabilities variously affected women of different social groups.

.3231 **Poovey**, Mary, *Uneven Developments. The Ideological Work of Gender in Mid-Victorian England*, Chicago, Ill., 1989. Drawing on parliamentary debates, medical journals, feminist tracts and novels, the author explores the binary opposites of gender representation in the mid-Victorian period.

.3232 **Roberts**, E., *Women's Work, 1840–1940*, 1989.

.3233 **Rose**, Sonya O., *Limited Livelihoods. Gender and Class in Nineteenth Century England*, 1992. Feminist cultural, social history.

.3234 **Scott**, Joan W., 'Women in History: the modern period', *P.P.*, CI, 1983, 141–57. A bibliographical essay.

.3235 **Shevelow**, K., *Women and Print Culture. The Construction of Feminity in the Early Periodical*, 1989.

.3236 **Thomis**, M. I. and Grimmett, J., *Women in Protest, 1800–50*, 1982.

.3237 **Uglow**, J. S., ed., *The Macmillan Dictionary of Women's Biography*, 1982.

.3238 **Vickery**, A., 'The neglected century: writing the history of eighteenth-century women', *Gender & Hist.*, III, 1991, 211–19.

(b) Middle class women

5.3239 **Anderson**, G., ed., *The White Blouse Revolution. Female Office Workers since 1870*, 1988.

.3240 **Ballaster**, R., Beetham, M., Frazer, E., and Hebron, S., *Women's Worlds. Magazines and the Female Reader*, 1990.

5.3241 **Basch**, Françoise, *Relative Creatures. Victorian Women in Society and the Novel, 1937–67*, 1975.

5.3242 **Bell**, E. M., *Octavia Hill. A Biography*, 1942.

5.3243 **Bott**, A. and Clephane, Irene, *Our Mothers. Late Victorian Women, 1870–1900*, 1932.

5.3244 **Branca**, Patricia, *Silent Sisterhood. Middle Class Women in the Victorian Home*, 1975.

5.3245 **Burston**, Joan N., *Victorian Education and the Ideal of Womanhood*, 1980.

5.3246 **Caine**, Barbara, 'Beatrice Webb and the "woman question"', *H. Workshop J.*, XIV, 1982, 23–44.

5.3247 **Crow**, D., *The Victorian Woman*, 1971.

5.3248 —— *The Edwardian Woman*, 1978.

5.3249 **Delemont**, Sarah, *Knowledgeable Women. Structuralism and the Reproduction of Elites*, 1989. Applying theoretical perspectives the book concentrates on middle class women's struggles in education and career development.

5.3250 —— and Duffin, L., eds., *The Nineteenth Century Woman. Her Cultural and Physical World*, 1978.

5.3251 **Dunbar**, Janet, *The Early Victorian Woman. Some Aspects of her Life, 1837–57*, 1953.

5.3252 **Dyhouse**, Carol, *Girls Growing Up in Late Victorian and Edwardian England*, 1981.

5.3253 **Elston**, M. A., *Women in the Medical Profession*, 1988.

5.3254 **Finch**, C., '"Hooked and buttoned together": Victorian underwear and representations of the female body', *Vict. Studs.*, XXXIV, 1991, 337–63.

5.3255 **Fletcher**, Sheila, *Women First. The Female Tradition in English Physical Education, 1880–1980*, 1984.

5.3256 **Gathorne-Hardy**, J., *The Rise and Fall of the English Nanny*, 1972.

5.3257 **Gerard**, J., 'Lady Bountiful: women of the landed classes and rural philanthropy', *Vict. Studs.*, XXX, 1987, 183–210.

5.3258 **Gorham**, D., *The Victorian Girl and the Feminine Ideal*, 1982.

5.3259 **Hill**, Bridget, ed., *Eighteenth Century Women. An Anthology*, 1984.

5.3260 —— *The Republican Virago. The Life and Times of Catherine Macaulay, Historian*, 1992. Looks at the place of this radical writer and her attempts to assail the man's world which surrounded her.

5.3261 **Holcombe**, Lee, *Wives and Property*, 1983. Deals chiefly with (eighteenth) century campaigns against legislation concerning married women's property.

5.3262 —— *Victorian Ladies at Work. Middle Class Working Women in England and Wales, 1850–1914*, 1974.

5.3263 **Horn**, Pamela, *Ladies of the Manor. Wives and Daughters in Country House Society, 1830–1918*, 1991.

5.3264 **Jailand**, Pat, *Women, Marriage and Politics, 1860–1914*, 1987. Argues that family life was less repressive than often supposed and throws light on the domestic sub-culture of high politics.

5.3265 **Jeffrys**, S., *The Spinster and her Enemies. Feminism and Sexuality, 1890–1930*, 1985.

5.3266 **Levy**, Anita, *Other Women. The Writing of Class, Race and Gender, 1832–98*, Princeton, N.J., 1991. Argues that Victorian social theorists reinforced middle class power and values and neglected working class and non white women.

5.3267 **McFeely**, M. D., *The Lady Inspectors*, 1988.

5.3268 **MacWilliams-Tullberg**, Rita, *Women at Cambridge*, 1975.

5.3269 **Myers**, S., *The Bluestocking Circle. Women, Friendship, and the Life of the Mind in Eighteenth Century England*, 1990.

5.3270 **Newton**, Stella M., *Health, Art and Reason. Dress Reformers of the Nineteenth Century*, 1975. Explores attacks on the tyranny of fashion.

5.3271 **Pedersen**, Joyce S., 'Schoolmistresses and headmistresses: elites and education in mid nineteenth-century England', *J.Brit.Studs.*, XV, 1975, 135–62.

5.3272 **Prentice**, Alison, 'The education of nineteenth-century British Women', *Hist.Educ.Q.*, XXII, 1982, 215–20.

5.3273 **Prochaska**, F. K., *Women and Philanthropy in Nineteenth-Century England*, 1980.

5.3274 **Rees**, B., *The Victorian Lady*, 1977.

5.3275 **Shilman**, Lilian L., *Women and Leadership in Nineteenth-Century England*, 1992. Considers the emergence of female leaders in the early nineteenth century, the struggles in the 1850s and 60s to maintain a feminist presence, and the phenomenon of the "women question" in the last quarter of the nineteenth century.

5.3276 **Staves**, Susan, *Married Women's Separate Property in England, 1660–1833*, Cambridge, Mass., 1990.

5.3277 **Steedman**, C., *Childhood, Culture and Class in Britain. Margaret Macmillan, 1860–1931*, 1990.

5.3278 **Vernon**, B. D., *Margaret Cole, 1893–1980*, 1986.

5.3279 **Vicinus**, Martha, *Independent Women. Work and Community for Single Women, 1850–1920*, 1985. Feminist approach to two generations of middle class career women and their employment.

5.3280 —— ed., *Suffer and be Still. Women in the Victorian Age*, Bloomington, Ind., 1972. Discusses the social position and sexuality of Victorian women.

5.3281 —— *A Widening Sphere. Changing Roles of Victorian Women*, Blommington, Ind., 1977.

(c) Suffragettes and feminists

5.3282 **Alberti**, J., *Beyond Suffrage. Feminists in War and Peace, 1914–28*, 1989.

5.3283 **Alexander**, S., *Studies in the History of Feminism, 1850s–1930s*, 1985.

5.3284 **Banks**, J. A. and Olive, *Feminism and Family Planning in Victorian England*, 1964.

5.3285 **Banks**, Olive, ed., *Biographical Dictionary of British Feminists*. I: 1800–1930, 1985. II: 1930–45, 1990.

5.3286 **Bennett**, D., *Emily Davies and the Liberation of Women, 1830–1921*, 1990.

5.3287 **Browne**, Alice, *The Eighteenth Century Feminist Mind*, 1987. Analyses changing attitudes by and to women on their place in society. Heavily laden with footnotes.

5.3288 **Brunt**, R. and Rowan, C., eds., *Feminism, Culture and Politics*, 1982.

5.3289 **Caine**, B., *Victorian Feminists*, 1992.

5.3290 **Crosby**, Christina, *The Ends of History. Victorians and the 'Woman Question'*, 1991.

5.3291 **Dinnage**, Rosemary, *Annie Besant*, 1987. A short, wide-ranging study of an intensely committed and varied career.

5.3292 **Dyhouse**, Carol, *Feminism and the Family in England, 1880–1939*, 1989. Focuses on middle class women. Working class feminists find no place here.

5.3293 **Fletcher**, Sheila, *Feminists and Bureaucrats. A Study in the Development of Girls' Education in the Nineenth Century*, 1980.

5.3294 **Fulford**, R., *Votes for Women. The Story of a Struggle*, 1957. 2nd ed., 1958. Bibliography, 273–83.

5.3295 **Garner**, L., *Stepping Stones to Women's Liberty. Feminist Ideas in the Women's Suffrage Movement, 1900–18*, 1983.

5.3296 **Harrison**, B., *Prudent Revolutionaries. Portraits of British Feminists between the Wars*, 1987.

5.3297 —— *Separate Spheres. The Opposition to Women's Suffrage in Britain*, 1978.

5.3298 **Helsinger**, E. K., Sheets, R. L., and Veeder, W., *The Woman Question. Society and Literature in Britain and America*,

1837–83, 1984. Wide-ranging and with much extended quotation.

5.3299 **Herstein**, Sheila, R., *A Mid Victorian Feminist, Barbara Leigh Smith Bodichon*, 1986. Looks principally at her public career and its context.

5.3300 **Hollis**, Patricia M., *Women in Public, 1850–1900. Documents of the Victorian Women's Movement*, 1979.

5.3301 **Kent**, Susan K., *Sex and Suffrage in Britain, 1860–1914*, 1987. Examines the moral dimension of the "Votes for Women, chastity for men" campaign.

5.3302 **Levine**, Phillipa, *Victorian Feminism*, 1988. Considers the different forms of Victorian feminist protest.

5.3303 **Lewis**, Jane, ed., *Before the Vote was Won. Arguments for and against Women's Suffrage, 1864–96*, 1987. A valuable collection of primary source material.

5.3304 **Mitchell**, D., *The Fighting Pankhursts. A Study of Tenacity*, 1967. Bibliography, 341–4.

5.3305 **O'Neill**, W., *The Woman Movement in Britain and America*, 1969.

5.3306 **Reed**, J. S., 'A "female movement": the feminisation of nineteenth-century Anglo-Catholicism', *Anglican and Episcopal Hist.*, LVII, 1988, 199–238.

5.3307 **Rendall**, Jane, ed., *Equal or Different? Women's Politics, 1800–1914*, 1987. Includes essays on eighteenth-century women preachers and philanthropists.

5.3308 —— *The Origins of Modern Feminism. Women in Britain, France and the United States, 1780–1860*, 1985. A useful compendium of information rather than a genuinely comparative sociological investigation.

5.3309 **Rogers**, Katherine M., *Feminism in Eighteenth Century England*, 1982. Principally a literary study.

5.3310 **Rosen**, A., *Rise up women! The Militant Campaign of the Women's Social and Political Union, 1903–14*, 1974.

5.3311 **Rover**, Constance, *Love, Morals and the Feminists*, 1970.

5.3312 —— *Women's Suffrage and Party Politics in Great Britain, 1866–1914*, 1967.

5.3313 **Rubinstein**, D., *Before the Suffragettes. Women's Emancipation in the 1890s*, 1987. Has chapters on love and marriage, legal struggles, salaried ladies, working class women's employment, higher education, and on leisure.

5.3314 **Shanley**, M. L., *Feminism, Marriage and*

Law in Victorian England, 1850–95, 1989.

5.3315 **Smith**, H. L., ed., *British Feminism in the Twentieth Century*, 1990. A collection of essays addressing feminism both as an ideology and as a reform movement.

5.3316 **Thom**, Deborah, *Feminism and the Labour Movement in Britain, 1850–1975*, 1988.

5.3317 **Vernon**, B. D., *Ellen Wilkinson, 1891–1947*, 1982.

(d) Working class women

5.3318 **Boston**, S., *Women Workers and the Trade Union Movement*, 1980.

5.3319 **Burman**, S., ed., *Fit Work for Women*, 1979.

5.3320 **Chinn**, C., *They Worked all their Lives. Women of the Urban Poor in England, 1880–1939*, 1988. Argues that working class married women exercised considerable influence in the family, a "hidden matriarchy" in fact.

5.3321 **Davidson**, C., *A Woman's Work is never done. A History of Housework in the British Isles, 1650–1950*, 1982.

5.3322 **Davies**, R., *Women and Work*, 1975.

5.3323 **Deem**, R., ed., *Schooling for Women's Work*, 1980.

5.3324 **Earle**, P., 'The female labour market in London in the late seventeenth and early eighteenth centuries', *Ec.H.R.*, 2nd ser., XLII, 1989, 328–53.

5.3325 **Ferguson**, N. A., 'Women's work: employment opportunities and economic roles, 1918–39', *Albion*, VII, 1975, 55–68.

5.3326 **Glucksmann**, Miriam, *Women Assemble. Women Workers and the New Industries in Inter War Britain*, 1990. Examines group cohesion and class relations of women assembly workers in light industries.

5.3327 **Hecht**, Jean J., *The Domestic Servant Class in Eighteenth-Century England*, 1956.

5.3328 **Hewitt**, Margaret, *Wives and Mothers in Victorian Industry*, 1958.

5.3329 **Higgs**, E., 'Women, occupations and work in the nineteenth-century census', *H. Workshop J.*, XXIII, 1987, 59–80.

5.3330 **Hill**, Bridget, *Women, Work and Sexual Politics in Eighteenth-Century England*, 1989. Influenced by, but critical of, Ivy Pinchbeck's study, the book explores the impact on women of industrialisation and the modernisation of agriculture.

5.3331 **Horn**, Pamela, *The Rise and Fall of the*

Victorian Servant, 1975. A general survey of recuitment to domestic service, conditions and pay, and employer-servant relations.

5.3332 —— *Victorian Countrywomen*, 1991.

5.3333 **Hudson**, Pat and Lee, W. R., eds., *Women's Work and the Family Economy in Historical Perspective*, 1990. A wide-ranging collection both chronologically and geographically which considers women's paid and unpaid labour. Chapters on the English experience focus on the Staffordshire potteries and the Liverpool dockland.

5.3334 **John**, Angela V., *By the Sweat of their Brow. Women Workers at Victorian Coal Mines*, 1984.

5.3335 —— *Coalmining Women. Victorian Lives and Campaigns*, 1984.

5.3336 **King**, P., 'Customary rights and women's earnings: the importance of gleaning to the rural labouring poor, 1750–1850', *Ec.H.R.*, 2nd ser., XLIV, 1991, 461–76.

5.3337 **Lown**, J., *Women and Industrialisation. Gender and Work in Nineteenth-Century England*, 1989.

5.3338 **McBride**, Theresa M., *The Domestic Revolution. The Modernisation of Household Service in England and France, 1820–1920*, 1976.

5.3339 **Malcolmson**, Patricia E., *English Laundresses. A Social History, 1850–1930*, Urbana, Ill., 1986. Looks at the extent of laundry work and the struggles to regulate it.

5.3340 **Marks**, L., *Working Wives and Working Mothers. A Comparative Study of Irish and East European Jewish Married Women's Work and motherhood in East London, 1870–1914*, 1990.

5.3341 **Marshall**, Dorothy, *The English Domestic Servant in History*, 1949. (Historical Association pamphlet).

5.3342 **Neff**, Wanda F., *Victorian Working Women. An Historical and Literary Study of Women in British Industries and Professions, 1832–50*, 1929, 2nd ed., 1966.

5.3343 **Nicholas**, S. and Oxley, Deborah, 'The living standards of women during the Industrial Revolution, 1795–1820', *Ec.H.R.*, XLVI, 1993, 723–49.

5.3344 **Pennington**, S. and Westover, B., *A Hidden Workforce. Women Homeworkers in Britain, 1850–1985*, 1989.

5.3345 **Pinchbeck**, Ivy, *Women Workers and the Industrial Revolution, 1750–1850*, 1930. A classic study taking an optimistic view of the benefits of industrialisation for working class women.

5.3346 **Prochaska**, F. K., 'Female philanthropy and domestic service in England', *B.I.H.R.*, LIV, 1981, 79–86.

5.3347 **Purvis**, June, 'Separate spheres and inequality in the education of working class women, 1854–1900', *H.Educ.*, X, 1981, 227–43.

5.3348 **Rendall**, Jane, *Women and Industrialisation. Work and Family, 1780–1880*, 1988.

5.3349 **Roberts**, E., *A Woman's Place. An Oral History of Working Class Women, 1890–1940*, 1985.

5.3350 **Ross**, Ellen, *Love and Toil. Motherhood in Outcast London, 1870–1918*, 1994. Examines the familial relations, community structures, and cultural patterns of working class women.

5.3351 **Simon**, Daphne, 'Master and servant' in Saville (5.2036), 160–200. Deals with the legal position.

5.3352 **Soldon**, N. C., *Women in British Trade Unions, 1874–1976*, 1978.

5.3353 **Taylor**, Barbara, *Eve and the New Jerusalem. Socialism and Feminism in the nineteenth Century*, 1983.

5.3354 **Thwaites**, W., 'Women in the market place. Oxfordshire, c.1690–1800', *Midland H.*, IX, 1984, 23–42.

5.3355 **Trustroom**, Myna, *Women of the Regiment. Marriage and the Victorian Army*, 1984. Considers wives, daughters and prostitutes in relation to the post-Crimean War army.

5.3356 **Waterson**, M., *The Servants' Hall. A Domestic History of Erdigg*, 1980. Makes full use of the portraits and other records relating to servants in this country house near Wrexham.

5.3357 **West**, J., ed., *Women, Work and the Labour Market*, 1982.

5.3358 **Whipp**, R., 'Women and the social organisation of work in the Staffordshire pottery industry, 1900–30', *Midland H.*, XII, 1987, 103–21.

5.3359 **Whitelegg**, E. et al., eds., *The Changing Experience of Women*, 1982. Includes chapters on working class families in the cotton industry, shopkeeping and the family in the Industrial Revolution, and on the need for women's labour in the First World War.

5.3360 **Williams**, B., *Women at Work*, 1991.

6

WALES

(A) WALES BEFORE 1700

GENERAL WORKS

(a) Bibliographies

6.1 **Jenkins**, R. T. and Rees, W., comps., *Bibliography of the History of Wales*, 2nd ed., 1962.

(b) Sources

6.2 **Jack**, I. R., ed., *Medieval Wales*, 1972. (Sources of History Series).

(c) Surveys

(i) MEDIEVAL

6.3 **Davies**, R. R., *Conquest, Co-existence and Change. Wales, 1063–1415*, 1987. Locates Wales within its British context and examines the country's changing economy, society and power structure.
6.4 ——*Lordship and Society in the Marches, 1282–1400*, 1978.
6.5 **Davies**, Wendy, 'Land and power in

early medieval Wales', *P.P.*, 81, 1978, 3–23.
6.6 **Denholm-Young**, N., *Collected Papers*, 1969. Covers a variety of medieval topics.
6.7 **Dodd**, A. H. *Life in Wales*, 1971. Extends from ancient to modern times.
6.8 **Jones**, G. R. J. 'Early territorial organisation in Gwynedd and Elmet', *Northern H.*, X. 1975, 3–27.
6.9 **Morgan**, P., *Wales. The Shaping of a Nation*, 1984.
6.10 **Owen**, D. H., 'The Englishry of Denbigh: an English colony in medieval Wales', *T.Hon.Soc.Cymmrod*, 1975, 57–76.
6.11 **Pierce**, T. J., *Medieval Welsh Society: Selected Essays*, 1973.
6.12 **Pugh**, T. B., ed., *Glamorgan County History Series. III: The Middle Ages*, 1971. Traces the history of the Marcher lordships of Glamorgan and Gower from the Norman Conquest to the Act of Union.
6.13 **Smith**, L. B., 'Disputes and settlements in medieval Wales: the role of arbitration', *EHR*, CVI, 1991, 835–60.
6.14 **Strayer**, J. R., and Rudishill, G., 'Taxation and community in Wales and Ireland, 1272–1327', *Speculum*, XXIX, 1954, 410–16.
6.15 **Walker**, D., *Medieval Wales*, 1990.

(i) EARLY MODERN

6.16 **Davies**, D. J., *The Economic History of Wales prior to 1800*, 1933.

6.17 **Davies**, E. and Howells, B., eds., *Pembrokeshire County History. III: Early Modern Pembrokeshire, 1536–1815*, 1987.

6.18 **Davies**, R. R., ed., *Welsh Society and Nationhood: Historical Essays presented to Glanmor Williams*, 1984.

6.19 **Dodd**, A. H. *Studies in Stuart Wales*, 1952.

6.20 ——*A History of Caernarvonshire, 1284–1900*, 1968.

6.21 **Herbert**, T. and Jones, G. E., eds., *Tudor Wales*, 1988.

6.22 **Johnson**, A. M., 'Wales during the Commonwealth and Protectorate' in Pennington and Thomas (4.80), 233–56.

6.23 **Jones**, G. D. *Wales in the Reign of James I*, 1988.

6.24 **Jones**, J. G., ed., *Class, Community and Culture in Tudor Wales*, 1989.

6.25 —— 'Concepts of continuity and change in Anglesey after the Acts of Union, 1536–1603', *Anglesey Antiq.Soc. & Field Club Trans.*, LVII, 1990, 22–57.

6.26 —— *Wales and the Tudor State. Government, Religious Change and the Social Order, 1534–1603*, 1989.

6.27 **Lynch**, A. L., *Pembrokeshire in the Civil War*, 1937.

6.28 **Phillips**, J. R. S., ed., *The Justices of the Peace in Wales and Monmouthshire, 1541–1689*, 1975.

6.29 **Thomas**, W. S. K., *Stuart Wales, 1603–1714*, 1988.

6.30 **Williams**, G., ed., *Glamorgan County History Series. IV: Early Modern Glamorgan*, 1974. Covers the period from 1536 to c.1700.

6.31 ——*Recovery, Reorientation and Reformation. Wales, 1415–1642.* (The History of Wales. III), 1987. Deals with a period in Welsh history whose boundaries are defined by the defeat of Owen Glendower and by the start of the English Civil War. The rise of the gentry is the central theme.

6.32 **Williams**, G. A., *The Welsh in their History*, 1982.

6.33 **Williams**, P., *The Council in the Marches of Wales under Elizabeth I*, 1958.

6.34 **Williams**, W. O., 'The social order in Tudor Wales', *T.Hon.Soc.Cymmrod.*, 1967, 167–78.

POPULATION

(a) MEDIEVAL

6.35 **Williams-Jones**, K., ed., *The Merioneth Lay Subsidy Roll, 1292–3*, 1976.

6.36 **Davies**, R., 'Race relations in post-Conquest Wales: confrontation and compromise', *T.Hon.Soc.Cymmrod, 1975, 32–56*.

6.37 **Meisal**, J., *Barons of the Welsh Frontier. The Corbet, Pantulf and Fitzwarin Families, 1066–1272*, 1981.

(b) Early modern

6.38 **Griffiths**, M., 'The Vale of Glamorgan in the 1543 Lay Subsidy Returns', *B.Bd.Celtic Studs.*, XXIX, 1982, 709–48.

6.39 **Owen**, L., 'The population of Wales in the sixteenth and seventeenth centuries', *T.Hon.Soc.Cymmrod.*, 1959, 99–113.

6.40 **Parry**, O., 'The Hearth Tax of 1662 in Merioneth', *J.Merion.H.Rec.Soc.*, II, 1953–4, 16–38.

6.41 **Richards**, T., *The Religious Census of 1676. An Enquiry into its Historical Value mainly in reference to Wales*, 1927.

AGRICULTURE AND RURAL SOCIETY

(a) Medieval

6.42 **Howells**, B., 'The distribution of customary acres in South Wales', *Nat.Lib.Wales J.*, XV, 1967, 226–35.

6.43 **Pierce**, T. J., 'Some tendencies in the agricultural history of Caernarvonshire during the later Middle Ages', *T.Caerns.H.Soc.*, I, 1939, 18–36.

6.44 —— 'The growth of commutation in Gwynedd during the thirteenth century', *B.Bd.Celtic Studs.*, X, 1941, 309–32.

6.45 **Smith**, L. B., 'The gage and the land market in late medieval Wales', *Ec.H.R.*, 2nd ser., XXIX, 1976, 537–50.

(b) Early modern

6.46 **James**, D. W., *St David's and Dewisland*, 1981. A comprehensive social history.

6.47 **Jones**, T. I. J., 'A study of rents and fines in South Wales in the sixteenth and early seventeenth centuries', in B. B. Thomas, ed., *Harlech Studies: Essays presented to Thomas Jones*, 1938, 215–44.

6.48 **Lloyd**, H. A., *The Gentry of South-West Wales, 1540–1640*, 1968.

6.49 **Pierce**, T. J., 'Landlords in Wales. Nobility and Gentry', in Thirsk (4.322), 357–80.

6.50 **Smith**, P., 'Rural housing in Wales' in Thirsk (4.322), 767–813.

6.51 **Williams**, G., 'Landlords in Wales. The Church' in Thirsk (4.322), 381–95.

6.52 —— 'The Dissolution of the Monasteries in Glamorgan', *Welsh H.R.*, III, 1966, 23–43.

6.53 **Williams**, W. O., 'The Anglesey gentry as businessmen in Tudor and Stuart times', *Anglesey Antiq.Soc. & Field Club*, 1948, 100–14.

INDUSTRY

(a) Medieval

6.54 **Carr**, A. D., 'The Welsh worker in the fourteenth century: an introduction to labour prehistory', *Llafur*, V, 1988, 5–13.

6.55 **Edwards**, J. G., 'Edward I's castle-building in Wales', *Proc.Brit.Acad.*, XXXII, 1946, 15–81.

6.56 **Jack**, I. R., 'The cloth industry in medieval Wales', *Welsh H.R.*, X, 1981, 443–60.

6.57 **Taylor**, A. J., 'Castle building in Wales in the late thirteenth century: the prelude to construction', in E. M. Jope, ed., *Studies in Building History*, 1961, 104–33.

(b) Early modern

6.58 **Jenkins**, J. G., *The Welsh Woollen Industry*, 1969.

6.59 **Lewis**, W. J., 'A Welsh salt-mining

venture of the sixteenth century', *Nat.Lib.Wales J.*, VIII, 1953–4, 419–25.

6.60 ——*Lead Mining in Wales*, 1967. The first four chapters deal with the pre-1700 period.

6.61 **Skeel**, Caroline A. J., 'The Welsh woollen industry in the sixteenth and seventeenth centuries', *Arch.Camb.*, seventh ser., II, 1922, 220–57.

6.62 **Williams**, L. J., 'A Welsh iron works at the close of the seventeenth century', *Nat.Lib.Wales J.*, XI, 1959–60, 266–84.

TOWNS

6.63 **Dodd**, A. H., ed., *A History of Wrexham, Denbighshire*, 1991.

6.64 **Griffiths**, R. A., ed., *Boroughs of Medieval Wales*, 1978. Has chapters on Aberystwyth, Brecon, Caernarvon, Cardiff, Camarthen, Denbigh, Newport, Oswestry, Ruthin, Swansea, and Tenby.

6.65 —— 'The making of medieval Cardigan', *Ceredigion*, XI, 1990.

6.66 **Howells**, J., 'Haverfordwest and the plague, 1652', *Welsh H.R.*, XII, 1985, 411–19.

6.67 **Jones**, J. G., 'Law and order in Merioneth after the Act of Union, 1536–43', *J.Merioneth H. and Rec.Soc.*, X, 1986, 119–47.

6.68 **Morgan**, R., 'The foundation of the borough of Welshpool', *Montgom.Collns.*, LXV, 1977, 7–24.

6.69 **Owen**, H., 'The two foundation charters of the borough of Denbigh', *B.Bd.Celtic Studs.*, XXVIII, 1979, 253–66.

6.70 **Pierce**, T. J., 'A Caernarvonshire manorial borough. Studies in the medieval history of Pwllheli', *T.Caerns.H.Soc.* (for 1941), 1942, 9–32, (for 1942–3), 1943, 35–50, (for 1944), 1945, 12–40.

6.71 **Sanders**, I. J., 'The boroughs of Aberystwyth and Cardigan in the early fourteenth century', *B.Bd.Celtic Studs.*, XV, 1952–4, 282–92.

6.72 **Soulsby**, I., *The Towns of Medieval Wales. A Study of their History, Archaeology and Topography*, 1983.

6.73   **Usher**, G., 'Holyhead as a fourteenth-century port', *B.Bd.Celtic Studs.*, XV, 1952–4, 209–92.

(B) WALES AFTER 1700

TRADE

(a) Medieval

6.74   **Lewis**, E. A., 'A contribution to the commercial history of medieval Wales with tabulated accounts from 1301 to 1547', *T.Hon.Soc.Cymmrod.*, 1913, 86–188.

(b) Early modern

6.75   **Lewis**, E. A., 'The toll books of some north Pembrokeshire fairs, 1599–1603', *B.Bd.Celtic Studs.*, VII, 1934, 283–318.
6.76   ——ed., *The Welsh Port Books, 1550–1603*, Cymmrodd.Rec.series., XII, 1927.

RELIGION

(a) Medieval

6.77   **Cowley**, F. G., *The Monastic Order in South Wales, 1066–1349*, 1977.
6.78   **Williams**, D. H., *The Welsh Cistercians. Aspects of their Economic History*, 1969.
6.79   **Williams**, G., *The Welsh Church from the Conquest to the Reformation*, 1952, 2nd ed., 1976.

(a) Early modern

6.80   **Williams**, G., *Religion, Language and Nationality in Wales*, 1979. Collected essays extending from late medieval to modern times.
6.81   —— *The Welsh and their Religion, 1991.*

GENERAL WORKS

6.82   **Morgan**, J., *A Select List of Parliamentary Papers relating to Wales, 1801–51*, 1974.
6.83   —— *A Breviate of Parliamentary Papers relating to Wales, 1868–1964*, 1975.
6.84   **Davies**, A. E., 'Some aspects of the operation of the Old Poor Law in Cardiganshire, 1750–1834', *J.Cardigan.Antiq.Soc.*, VI, 1968, 1–44.
6.85   **Evans**, D. G., *A History of Wales, 1815–1906*, 1989.
6.86   **Evans**, E. D., *A History of Wales, 1660–1815*, 1976.
6.87   **Gray-Jones**, A., *A History of Ebbw Vale*, 1970.
6.88   **Herbert**, T. and Jones, G. E., eds., *Wales 1880–1914*, 1988.
6.89   ——*Wales between the Wars*, 1988.
6.90   **Hignell**, A., *A 'Favourite' Game: Cricket in South Wales before 1914*, 1992.
6.91   **Jenkin**, P., *A History of Modern Wales, 1536–1990*, 1992.
6.92   **John**, Angela V., ed., *Our Mothers. Chapters in Welsh Women's History, 1830–1939*, 1991.
6.93   **John**, A. H. and Williams, G., eds., *Glamorgan County History Series. V: Industrial, Glamorgan*, 1980. One of the major industrial regions of the British Isles examined in its expansion, depression and recovery.
6.94   **Jones**, D., *Crime in Nineteenth Century Wales*, 1992.
6.95   **Jones**, E. D., ed., *Victorian and Edwardian Wales from Old Photographs*, 1972.
6.96   **Jones**, G. E., *Modern Wales. A Concise History, c.1485–1979*, 1984. Explores the dominance of landed gentry and the transforming effects of industrialisation.
6.97   **Jones**, I. G., *Communities. Essays in the Social History of Victorian Wales*, 1987.
6.98   ——*Mid Victorian Wales. The Observers and the Observed*, 1992.
6.99   ——*Explorations and Explanations: Essays*

in the Social History of Victorian Wales, 1981. Includes essays on the 1851 Religious Census and on the emergence of an independent middle class in the country towns.

6.100 ——*Health, Wealth and Politics in Victorian Wales*, 1979.

6.101 **Lambert**, W. R., *Drink and Sobriety in Victorian Wales, c.1820–95*, 1983.

6.102 **Moore**, D., ed., *Wales in the Eighteenth Century*, 1976.

6.103 **Morgan**, K. O., *Re-birth of a Nation: Wales 1880–1980*, 1981. Devotes three full chapters to economic issues.

6.104 **Peate**, I. C., *The Welsh House: A Study in Folk Culture*, 1940, 2nd ed., 1944.

6.105 **Price**, C., *English Theatre in Wales in Eighteenth and Early Nineteenth Centuries*, 1948.

6.106 **Pryce**, W. T. R., 'Industrialism, urbanisation and the maintenance of culture areas in North East Wales in the mid nineteenth century', *Welsh H.R.*, VII, 1975, 307–40.

6.107 **Smith**, D. and Williams, G., *Fields of Praise*, 1980. A social history of Welsh Rugby Union from 1881 placing the game firmly in the context of the Welsh economy and of working-class experience.

6.108 **Thomas**, B., ed., *The Welsh Economy: Studies in Expansion*, 1962.

6.109 **Williams**, D., *A History of Modern Wales*, 1950.

POPULATION

6.110 **Alderman**, G., 'The Jew as scapegoat? The settlement and reception of Jews in South Wales before 1914', *T. Jewish H.Soc.*, XXVI, 1979, 62–70.

6.111 **Beddoe**, D., *Welsh Convict Women: A Study of Women Transported from Wales to Australia, 1787–1852*, 1979.

6.112 **Conway**, A., *The Welsh in America*, 1961.

6.113 **Dodd**, A. H., *The Character of Early Welsh Migration to the United States*, 1953 2nd rev. ed., 1967.

6.114 **Jenkins**, J. P., 'The demographic decline of the landed gentry in the eighteenth

century: A South Wales study', *Welsh H.R.*, XI, 1982, 31–49.

6.115 **Jones**, D. J. V., 'The criminal vagrant in nineteenth-century Wales', *Welsh H.R.*, VIII, 1977, 312–43.

6.116 **Jones**, E., 'The Welsh in London in the seventeenth and eighteenth centuries', *Welsh H.R.*, X, 1981, 461–79.

6.117 **Jones**, P. E., 'The urban morphology and social structure of a working class district in the mid-nineteenth century', *Welsh H.R.*, XV, 1991, 562–91.

6.118 **Jones**, P. N., *Mines, Migrants and Residence in the South Wales Steam Coal Valleys. The Ogmore and Garw Valleys in 1881*, 1987.

6.119 **Pooley**, C. G., 'Welsh migration to England in the mid nineteenth century', *J.H.Geog.*, IX, 1983, 287–306.

6.120 **Roderick**, G. W., 'South Wales industrialists and the theory of gentrification, 1770–1914', *Trans.Cymmrodorion Soc.*, 1987, 65–83.

6.121 **Van Vught**, W. E., 'Welsh emigration to the U.S.A. during the mid nineteenth century', *Welsh H.R.*, XV, 1991, 545–61.

6.122 **Williams**, D., *Wales and America*, 1975.

AGRICULTURE AND RURAL SOCIETY

6.123 **Aitchison**, J. and Carter, H., 'Rural Wales and the Welsh language', *Rural H.*, II, 1991, 61–80.

6.124 **Colyer**, R. J., 'The gentry and the county in nineteenth-century Cardiganshire', *Welsh H.R.*, X, 1981, 497–535.

6.125 —— 'The Land Agent in nineteenth-century Wales', *Welsh H.R.*, VIII, 1977, 401–25.

6.126 ——*The Welsh Cattle Drovers*, 1976. *See also* Godwin (6.128) and Hughes (6.133).

6.127 **Davies**, J., 'The end of the great estates and the rise of freehold farming in Wales', *Welsh H.R.*, VII, 1974, 186–212.

6.128 **Godwin**, Fay and Toulson, Shirley, *The Drovers' Roads to Wales*, 1971. Well illustrated.

6.129 **Gray**, M., 'Crown property and the land market in S. E. Wales in the nineteenth century', *Ag.H.R.*, XXXV, 1987, 133–50.

6.130 **Howell**, D. W., 'The economy of the landed estates of Pembrokeshire, c. 1680–1830', *Welsh H.R.*, III, 1967, 265–86.

6.131 —— 'The impact of railways on agricultural development in nineteenth-century Wales', *Welsh H.R.*, VII, 1974, 40–62.

6.132 ——*Land and People in Nineteenth-Century Wales*, 1978.

6.133 **Hughes**, P. G., *Wales and the Drovers*, 1947.

6.134 **Jenkins**, D., *The Agricultural Community in South West Wales at the turn of the Twentieth Century*, 1971.

6.135 **Jenkins**, D. G., *Agricultural Transport in Wales*, 1962.

6.136 **Lowe**, J. B., *Welsh Country Workers' Housing, 1775–1875*, 1985

6.137 **Martin**, Joanna, 'Estate stewards and their work in Glamorgan, 1660–1760', *Morgannwg*, XXIII, 1979, 9–28.

6.138 —— 'Private enterprise *versus* manorial rights: mineral property disputes in mid eighteenth-century Glamorgan', *Welsh H.R.*, IX, 1978, 155–75.

6.139 **Riden**, P., *Farming in Llanblethian, 1660–1750*, 1980.

6.140 **Roberts**, R. O., ed., *Farming in Caernarvonshire around 1800*, 1973. Documents on the Vaenol estate.

6.141 **Thomas**, D., *Agriculture in Wales During the Napoleonic Wars*, 1963.

INDUSTRY

6.142 **Atkinson**, M. and Barker, C., *The Growth and Decline of the South Wales Iron Industry: An Industrial History*, 1987.

6.143 **Bevan-Evans**, M., 'Gadlys and Flintshire lead-mining in the eighteenth century', Parts I, II, III, *Flints.H.Soc.*, XVIII, 1960, 75–130; XIX, 1961, 32–60, XX, 1962, 58–89.

6.144 **Chappell**, E. L., *Historic Melingriffith: An Account of the Pentyrch Iron Works*, 1940.

6.145 **Daunton**, M. J., 'Miners' houses: South Wales and the Great Northern Coalfield, 1880–1914', *Internat.R.Soc.H.*, XXV,

1980, 143–75.

6.146 **Davies**, J. I., 'The history of printing in Montgomeryshire, 1789–1960', *Montgom.Collns.*, LXVIII, 1980, 7–28.

6.147 **Dodd**, A. H., *The Industrial Revolution in North Wales*, 1933, 3rd ed., with corrections and additions, 1971.

6.148 **Edwards**, I., 'John Wilkinson and the development of gunfounding in the late eighteenth century', *Welsh H.R.*, XV, 1991, 524–44.

6.149 **Egan**, D., *Coal Society. A History of the South Wales Mining Valleys, 1840–1980*, 1987.

6.150 **Elis-Williams**, M., *Bangor, Port of Beaumaris, the Nineteenth Century Shipbuilders and Shipowners of Bangor*, 1988.

6.151 **Evans**, J. D., 'The uncrowned Iron King (the first William Crawshay)', *Nat.Lib.Wales J.*, VII, 1951, 12–32.

6.152 **Harris**, J. R., *The Copper King: A Biography of Thomas Williams of Llanidan*, 1964.

6.153 **Hughes**, S. and Reynolds, P., *A Guide to the Industrial Archaeology of the Swansea Region*, 1988.

6.154 **Jenkin**, J. G., *From Fleece to Fleece. The Technological History of the Welsh Woollen Industry*, 1981.

6.155 ——and D., *Cardiff Shipowners*, 1986.

6.156 **John**, A. H., *The Industrial Development of South Wales, 1750–1850*, 1950. *See also* Davies (6.16).

6.157 **Jones**, J. R., *The Welsh Builder on Merseyside: Annals and Lives*, 1946.

6.158 **Jones**, R. M., *The North Wales Quarrymen, 1874–1922*, 1981.

6.159 **Lambert**, W. R., 'Drink and work discipline in industrial South Wales, c. 1800–1870', *Welsh H.R.*, VII, 1975, 289–306.

6.160 **Lerry**, G. G., *The Collieries of Denbigshhire*, 1946.

6.161 **Lewis**, E. D., *The Rhondda Valleys: A Study in Industrial Development, 1800 to the Present Day*, 1959.

6.162 **Lindsay**, Jean, *A History of the North Wales Slate Industry*, 1974.

6.163 **Minchinton**, W. E., ed., *Industrial South Wales, 1750–1914: Essays in Welsh Economic History*, 1969.

6.164 **Morris**, J. H. and Williams, L. J., *The South Wales Coal Industry, 1841–75*, 1958.

6.165 **Newell**, E., ' "Copperopolis": the rise and fall of the copper industry in the

Swansea district, 1826–1931', *Bus.H.*, XXXII, 1990, 75–97.

6.166 **North**, F. J., *The Slates of Wales*, 3rd rev. ed., 1946.

6.167 **Owen-Jones**, S., 'Women in the tinplate industry: Llanelli, 1930–50', *Oral H.*, XV, 1987, 42–49.

6.168 **Powell**, C. and Fisk, M., 'Early industrial housing in Rhondda, 1800–50', *Morgannwg*, XXV, 1991, 50–78.

6.169 **Rees**, E., *The Welsh Book Trade before 1820*, 1988.

6.170 **Roberts**, R. O., 'Enterprise and capital for non-ferrous metal smelting in Glamorgan, 1694–1924', *Morgannwg*, XXIII, 1979, 48–82.

6.171 **Tucker**, D. G., 'The leadmines of Glamorgan and Gwent', *Morgannwg*, XX, 1976, 37–52.

6.172 **Tucker**, Mary, 'The slate industry of Pembrokeshire and its borders', *Ind.Arch.R.*, III, 1979, 203–27.

6.173 **Walters**, R., 'Capital formation in the South Wales coal industry, 1840–1914', *Welsh H.R.*, X, 1980, 69–92.

6.174 **Williams**, H., *Davies the Ocean. Railway King and Coal Tycoon*, 1991.

6.175 **Williams**, L. J., 'The coal owners of South Wales, 1873–80: problems of unity', *Welsh H.R.*, VIII, 1976, 75–93.

6.176 —— 'A Carmarthenshire ironmaster and the Seven Years War', *Bus.H.*, II, 1959–60, 32–43.

TRADE, TRANSPORT AND COMMUNICATIONS

6.177 **Archer**, M. S., *The Welsh Post Towns before 1840*, 1970.

6.178 **George**, Barbara J., 'Pembrokeshire seatrading before 1900', *Field Studs.*, II, 1964, 1–39.

6.179 **Hadfield**, C., *The Canals of South Wales and the Border*, 1960.

6.180 **Jones**, P. N., 'Workmen's trains in the South Wales Coalfield, 1870–1926', *Trans.H.*, 1970, 21–35.

TOWNS

6.181 **Alban**, J. R., *Swansea, 1184–1984*, 1984.

6.182 **Carter**, H., *Merthyr Tydfil in 1851*, 1982.

6.183 ——and Wheatley, Sandra, 'Some aspects of the spatial structure of two Glamorgan towns in the nineteenth century', *Welsh H.R.*, IX, 1978, 32–56. Deals with Neath and Merthyr Tydfil.

6.184 **Daunton**, M. J., *Coal Metropolis: Cardiff, 1870–1914*, 1977.

6.185 **Davies**, J. I., *Cardiff and the Marquesses of Bute*, 1980. A case study of aristocratic participation in economic development concentrating on the Butes' contribution to the rise of the port of Cardiff and to the growth of the South Wales iron and coal trade.

6.186 **Evans**, N., 'The Welsh Victorian City: the middle class and civic and national consciousness in Cardiff, 1850–1914', *Welsh H.R.*, XII, 1985, 350–87.

6.187 **Jones**, P. E., *Bangor, 1883–1983. A Study in Municipal Government*, 1986.

6.188 **Kissack**, K., *Victorian Monmouth*, 1988.

6.189 **Oliver**, R. C. B., 'Holidays at Aberystwyth, 1789–1823', *Ceredigion*, X, 1987, 269–86.

6.190 **Sherwood**, M., 'Racism and Resistance: Cardiff in the 1930s and 40s', *Llafur*, V, 1991, 51–70.

6.191 **Williams**, H., ed., *Pontypridd. Essays on the History of an Industrial Community*, 1981.

BANKING

6.192 **Davies**, A. S., *The Early Banks of Mid-Wales*, 1935.

6.193 **Dodd**, A. H. 'The beginnings of banking in North Wales', *Economica*, VI, 1926, 16–30.

6.194 **Green**, F., 'Early banks in West Wales', *H.Soc. West Wales*, VI, 1916, 129–64.

LABOUR

6.195 **Arnot**, R. P., *The South Wales Miners. A History of the South Wales Miners Federation, 1898–1914*, 1967.

6.196 **Evans**, E. W., *Mabon: William Abraham, 1842–1922. A Study in Trade Union Leadership*, 1959. The leader of the South Wales miners.

6.197 **Greasley**, D., 'Wage rates and work intensity in the South Wales coalfield, 1874–1914', *Economica*, LI, 1985, 383–89.

6.198 **Jones**, D. J. V., *Before Rebecca: Popular Protests in Wales, 1793–1835*, 1973.

6.199 —— *The Last Rising. The Newport Insurrection of 1839*, 1986.

6.200 —— *Rebecca's Children. A Study of Rural Society, Crime and Protest*, 1989. A re-examination of the Rebecca riots in Wales in the 1830s and 40s, looking at the motivation and sociology of the participants and at their suppression.

6.201 **Pretty**, D. A., *The Rural Revolt that Failed. Farm Workers' Trade Unions in Wales, 1889–1950*, 1989.

6.202 **Smith**, D., ed., *A People and a Proletariat. Essays in the History of Wales, 1780–1980*, 1980. Some of the essays are local case studies, others range widely in considering the problems of 'locating' the working class in Wales and the links between language and community.

6.203 **Wilks**, I., *South Wales and the Rising of 1839*, 1983.

6.204 **Williams**, D., *The Rebecca Riots. A Study in Agrarian Discontent*, 1955.

6.205 **Williams**, G. A., ed., *Merthyr Politics. The Making of a Working-Class Tradition*, 1966.

6.206 —— *The Merthyr Rising*, 1978.

RELIGION AND EDUCATION

6.207 **Clement**, Mary, ed., *Correspondence and Minutes of the S.P.C.K. relating to Wales*, 1952. Covers the first half of the eighteenth century.

6.208 **Jones**, I. G. and Williams, D., eds., *The Religious Census of 1851. A Calendar of the Returns relating to Wales*. I: *South Wales*, 1976; II: *North Wales*, 1980.

6.209 **Williams**, A. H., *John Wesley in Wales, 1739–90*, 1971. Edited extracts from his journals and diaries.

6.210 **Bartle**, G. F., 'The role of the British and Foreign School Society in Welsh elementary education, 1840–76', *J.Educ.Admin. and H.*, XXII, 1990, 18–29.

6.211 **Davies**, E. T., *Religion in the Industrial Revolution in South Wales*, 1965.

6.212 **Enoch**, D. G., 'Schools and inspection as a mode of social control in S. E. Wales, 1839–1907', *J.Educ.Admin. and H.*, XXII, 1990, 9–17.

6.213 **Evans**, L. W., *Studies in Welsh Education. Welsh Educational Structure and Administration, 1800–1925*, 1975.

6.214 **Evans**, W. G., *Educational Development in a Victorian Community. A Case Study of Carmarthenshire's Response to the Welsh Intermediate Education Act, 1889*, 1990.

6.215 —— 'The centenary of the Welsh Intermediate and Technical Education Act, 1889, and the location of the intermediate schools in Merioneth'. *J.Merioneth H. and Rec.Soc.*, X, 1989, 325–46.

6.216 ——*Perspectives on a Century of Secondary Education in Wales, 1889–1989*, 1990.

6.217 **Harvest**, L., 'The Welsh Educational Alliance and the 1870 Elementary Education Act', *Welsh H.R.*, X, 1980, 172–206.

6.218 **Jones**, G. E., *Controls and Conflicts in Welsh Secondary Education, 1889–1944*, 1982.

6.219 **Lewis**, G. J., 'The geography of religion in the middle borderlands of Wales in 1851', *T.Hon. Soc.Cymmrod*, 1980, 123–42.

6.220 **Nash**, G. D., *Victorian Schooldays in Wales*, 1991.

6.221 **Randall**, P. J., 'The origins and establishment of the Welsh Department of Education', *Welsh H.R.*, VII, 1975, 450–71.

6.222 **Roberts**, H. P., 'Nonconformist Academies in Wales', *T.Hon.Soc. Cymmrod.*, 1928–9, 1–98.

6.223 **Seaborne**, M. V. J., 'The religious census of 1851 and early chapel building in North Wales: a sample survey', *Nat.Lib.Wales J.*, XXVI, 1990, 281–310.

6.224 **Williams**, J. G., *The University College of North Wales. Foundations, 1884–1927*, 1985.

7

SCOTLAND

(A) SCOTLAND BEFORE 1700

GENERAL WORKS

(a) Bibliographies

7.1 **Hancock**, P. D., *Bibliography of Works Relating to Scotland*, 2 vols., 1959–60.

7.2 **Marwick**, W. H., 'A bibliography of Scottish business history'. In Payne (7.296), 77–99.

7.2a —— 'A bibliography of Scottish economic history', *Ec.H.R.*, III, 1931–2, 117–37.

(b) Sources

7.3 **Dickinson**, W. C., *A Source Book of Scottish History to 1707*, 3 vols., 1952–4. Vol. I: *From the Earliest times to 1424;* Vol. II: *1424–1567* and Vol. III, *1567–1707*.

7.4 **Donaldson**, G., ed., *Scottish Historical Documents*, 1970. A useful source book covering the medieval and early modern periods. *See also* Browning, ed. (4.10), which contains a substantial section, 591–698, on Scotland.

(c) Surveys

(i) MEDIEVAL

7.5 **Barrow**, G. W. S., *The Kingdom of the Scots. Goverment, Church and Society from the Eleventh to the Fourteenth Century*, 1973.

7.6 ——*The Anglo-Norman Era in Scottish History*, 1980.

7.7 **Brown**, J. M., ed., *Scottish Society in the Fifteenth Century*, 1977.

7.8 **Campbell**, J., 'England, Scotland and the Hundred Years War in the fourteenth century'. In J. R. Hale, ed., *Europe in the Late Middle Ages*, 1965, 184–216.

7.9 **Dickinson**, W. C., *Scotland from the Earliest Times to 1603*, 1961. A useful textbook. Bibliography.

7.10 **Grant**, A., *Independence and Nationhood. Scotland, 1306–1469*, 1984. Principally a political study as the title suggests.

7.11 **Grant**, I. F., *Social and Economic Development of Scotland before 1603*, 1930, 2nd ed., Westport, Conn., 1971.

7.12 **Lythe**, S. G. E. and Butt, J., *An Economic History of Scotland, 1100–1939*, 1975. Primarily a thematic approach though with sections dividing at 1707 and 1870.

7.13 **Mackenzie**, W. C., *The Highlands and Isles of Scotland: An Historical Survey*, 1937, 2nd ed., 1949.

7.14 **Mackie**, J. D., *History of Scotland*, 1964.

7.15 **Nicholson**, R., *The Edinburgh History of Scotland. II. The Later Middle Ages*, 1974.

7.16 **Ritchie**, R. L. G., *The Normans in*

Scotland, 1954. *See also* Barrow (2.15), a general survey which devotes more space than usual to Scottish history, and Mitchinson (7.32).

(ii) EARLY MODERN

7.17 **Barrow**, G. W. S., ed., *The Scottish Tradition. Essays in Honour of R. G. Cant*, 1974. Includes essays on the Scottish advocates, aristocratic education, the management of forfeited estates and on the burghs.

7.18 **Bingham**, Caroline, *History of the Highlands of Scotland*, 1986.

7.19 **Brown**, K. M., *Bloodfeud in Scotland, 1573–1625. Violence, Justice and Politics in an Early Modern Society*, 1986.

7.20 **Buckroyd**, J. M., 'Bridging the gap. Scotland, 1659–60', *Scot.H.R.*, LXVI, 1987, 1–25.

7.21 **Butt**, J. and Ward, J. T., eds., *Scottish Themes. Essays in Honour of Professor S. G. E. Lythe*, 1976.

7.22 **Carstairs**, A. M., 'Some economic aspects of the union of the Parliaments', *Scot.J.Pol.Econ.*, II, 1955, 64–72.

7.23 **Donaldson**, G., *Scotland, James V to James VII*, 1965. Mainly of value on political and ecclesiastical aspects.

7.24 —— *Shetland Life under the Earl Patrick*, 1958.

7.25 **Dwyer**, J., Mason, R., and Murdoch, A., *New Perspectives on the Politics and Culture of Early Modern Scotland*, 1982.

7.26 **Houston**, R. A. and Whyte, I. D. eds., *Scottish Society, 1500–1800*, 1989.

7.27 **Knox**, S., *The Making of the Medieval Shetland Landscape*, 1985.

7.28 **Lythe**, S. G. E., *The Economy of Scotland in its European Setting, 1550–1625*, 1960.

7.29 —— 'The Union of the Crowns in 1603 and the debate on economic integration', *Scot.J.Pol.Econ.*, V, 1958, 219–28.

7.30 **Mason**, R. A., ed., *Scotland and England, 1286–1815*, 1987.

7.31 **Meikle**, H. W., *Some Aspects of Seventeenth Century Scotland*, 1947.

7.32 **Mitchison**, Rosalind, *A History of Scotland*, 1970. A general survey of Scottish history, particularly weighted, however, towards the seventeenth century – 'the key period for the understanding of modern Scotland' (ix). A useful critical

bibliography is appended, 430–42.

7.33 —— *Life in Scotland*, 1978.

7.34 —— *Lordship to Patronage. Scotland, 1603–1745*, 1983.

7.35 **Nobbs**, D., *England and Scotland, 1560–1707*, 1952.

7.36 **Pryde**, G. S., *Scotland from 1603 to the Present Day*, 1962.

7.37 **Shaw**, Frances J., *The Northern and Western Islands of Scotland: Their Economy and Society in the Seventeenth Century*, 1980.

7.38 **Simpson**, G. G., ed., *Scotland and Scandinavia, 800–1800*, 1990.

7.39 **Smout**, T. C., *A History of the Scottish People, 1560–1830*, 1969. Strong on economic and social aspects. Useful aids to further reading are appended to each chapter.

7.40 **Warrack**, J., *Domestic Life in Scotland, 1488–1688*, 1920. Deals mainly with furniture and household effects.

7.41 **Whittington**, G. and Whyte, I. D., eds., *An Historical geography of Scotland*, 1983. Essays of variable quality on the period extending from prehistoric times to 1914.

7.42 **Willson**, D. H., 'King James I and Anglo-Scottish unity'. In Aiken and Henning (4.1209), 41–56.

7.43 **Wormald**, Jenny, *Court, Kirk and Community. Scotland 1470–1625*, 1981.

POPULATION

(a) Medieval

7.44 **Barrow**, G. W. S., 'Rural settlement in central and eastern Scotland: the medieval evidence', *Scot.Studs.*, VI, 1962, 123–44.

7.45 **Stringer**, H. J., ed., *Essays on the Nobility of Medieval Scotland*, 1985.

(b) Early modern

7.46 **Adamson**, D., ed., *West Lothian Hearth Tax, 1691*. Scot.Rec.Soc., new ser., IX, 1981.

7.47 **Walton**, K., 'The distribution of population in Aberdeenshire, 1696', *Soc.Geog.Mag.*, LXVI, 1950, 17–25.

AGRICULTURE AND RURAL SOCIETY

(a) Medieval

7.48 **Anderson**, M. L., *A History of Scottish Forestry*, Vol. I: *From the Ice Age to the French Revolution*, ed. C. J. Taylor, 1967.

7.49 **Dodgshon**, R. A., *Land and Society in Early Scotland*, 1982.

7.50 **Franklin**, T. B., *A History of Scottish Farming*, 1952.

7.51 **Madden**, C. A., 'The Royal Demesne in Northern Scotland during the late Middle Ages', *Northern Scot.*, III, 1979, 1–24.

7.52 **Marwick**, H., *Medieval Lairds*, 1936, 2nd ed., 1939.

7.53 **Murray**, A., 'The crown lands in Galloway, 1455–1543', *Trans. Dumfriesshire and Galloway Nat.Hist. & Antiq.Soc.*, XXXVII, 1960, 9–25.

7.54 **Symon**, J. A., *Scottish Farming Past and Present*, 1959.

7.55 **Wormald**, Jenny, *Lord and Men in Scotland. Bonds of Manrent, 1442–1603*, 1985. A telling reappraisal of the late medieval Scottish nobility, of bond-making, violence and order.

(b) Early modern

7.56 **Donaldson**, G., 'Sources for Scottish agrarian history before the eighteenth century', *Ag.H.R.*, VIII, 1959, 82–90.

7.57 **Fenton**, A., ed., 'Skene of Hallyard's Ms. of Husbandrie', *Ag.H.R.*, XI, 1963, 65–81. A seventeenth-century account.

7.58 —— 'The rural economy of East Lothian in the seventeenth and eighteenth centuries', *Trans.East Lothian Antiq. and Field Naturalists' Soc.*, IX, 1963, 1–23.

7.59 —— *Scottish Country Life*, 1975.

7.60 **Mackerral**, A., *Kintyre in the Seventeenth Century*, 1948.

7.61 **Macinnes**, A. I., 'Repression and conciliation: the Highland dimension, 1660–88', *Scot.H.R.*, LXV, 1986, 167–95.

7.62 **Millman**, R. L., *The Making of the Scottish Landscape*, 1975.

7.63 **Murray**, J. E. L., 'The agriculture of Crail, 1550–1600', *Scot.Studs.*, VIII, 1964, 85–95.

7.64 **Sanderson**, M. H. B., *Scottish Rural Society in the Sixteenth Century*, 1982.

7.65 **Smout**, T. C., 'Problems of timber supply in later seventeenth-century Scotland', *Scottish Forestry*, XIV, 1960, 3–13.

7.66 —— 'Scottish landowners and economic growth 1650–1850', *Scot.J.Pol.Econ.*, XI, 1964, 218–34. *See also* Smout (7.239).

7.67 —— 'Goat keeping in the old highland economy: 4', *Scot.Studs.*, IX, 1965, 186–9. Assesses the significance of earlier contributions on this subject.

7.68 —— and Fenton, A., 'Scottish agriculture before the improvers – an exploration', *Ag.H.R.*, XIII, 1965, 73–93.

7.69 **Stevenson**, D., *Alasdair MacColla and the Highland Problem in the Seventeenth Century*, 1980.

7.70 **Whyte**, I. D., *Agriculture and Society in Seventeenth-Century Scotland*, 1979.

7.71 —— and K. A., *The changing Scottish Landscape, 1500–1800*, 1991.

7.72 —— 'Continuity and change in a seventeenth century Scottish farming community', *Ag.H.R.*, XXXII, 1984, 159–70.

7.73 —— 'Scottish rural communities in the seventeenth century', *Loc.H.*, XV, 1983, 456–63.

INDUSTRY

(a) Medieval

7.74 **Cochran-Patrick**, R. W., ed., *Early Records Relating to Mining in Scotland*, 1878.

7.75 **Adams**, I. H., 'The salt industry of the Forth Basin', *Scot.Geog.Mag.*, LXXXI, 1965, 153–62. *See also* Arnot (7.340).

(b) Early modern

7.76 **Knoop**, D. and Jones, G. P., *The Scottish Mason and Mason Word*, 1939.

7.77 **Lumsden**, H., ed., *The Records of the Trades House of Glasgow, 1605–1678*, 1910.

7.78 ——*History of the Skinners, Furriers and Glovers of Glasgow: Study of a Scottish Craft Guild in its Various Relations*, 1937.

7.79 **Marwick**, J. D., *Edinburgh Gilds and Crafts*, Scottish Burgh Record Society, 1909.

7.80 **Scott**, W. R., ed., *Records of a Scottish Cloth Manufactory at New Mills, Haddingtonshire, 1681–1703*, Scot.H.Soc., 1905.

7.81 **Smout**, T. C., 'The early Scottish sugar houses, 1660–1720', *Ec.H.R.*, 2nd ser., XIV, 1961, 240–53.

7.82 —— 'Lead-mining in Scotland, 1650–1850'. In Payne (7.296), 103–35. *See also* Nef (4.508), and Scott (4.726), vol. III of which deals with Scottish joint stock companies.

TOWNS

(a) Medieval

7.83 **Dickinson**, W. C., ed., *Early Records of Aberdeen, 1317, 1398–1407*, Scot.H.Soc., 1957.

7.84 **Ballard**, A., 'The theory of the Scottish burgh', *Scot.H.R.*, XIII, 1916, 16–29.

7.85 **Dunlop**, Annie I., *The Royal Burgh of Ayr*, 1953. An able account of the medieval period in particular.

7.86 **Ewan**, E., *Town Life in Fourteenth Century Scotland*, 1990.

7.87 **Lynch**, M., Spearman, M., and Stell, G., eds., *The Scottish Medieval Town*, 1988.

7.88 **Lythe**, S. G. E., 'The origin and development of Dundee', *Scot.Geog.Mag.*, LIV, 1939, 344–57.

7.89 **Mackenzie**, W. M., *The Scottish Burghs*, 1949. Covers both the medieval and early modern periods.

7.90 **Smith**, J. S., ed., *New Light on Medieval Aberdeen*, 1985.

(b) Early modern

7.90A **Roberts**, F. and MacPhail, I. M. M, eds., *Dumbarton Common Goods Accounts 1614–1660*, 1972.

7.91 **Shearer**, A., ed., *Extracts from the Burgh Records of Dunfermline in the Sixteenth and Seventeenth Centuries*, 1951.

7.92 **Taylor**, Louise B., ed., *Aberdeen Council Letters 1552–1681*, 6 vols., 1942–61.

7.93 —— ed., *Aberdeen Shore Works Accounts 1596–1670*, 1972. Lists ships and their cargoes entering and leaving the harbour.

7.94 **Dingwall**, Helen, 'The importance of social factors in determining the composition of the town councils in Edinburgh, 1550–1650', *Scot.H.R.*, LXV, 1986, 17–33.

7.95 **Lynch**, M., ed., *The Early Modern Town in Scotland*, 1987. A collection of new essays dealing with the political and economic organisation of towns, the Reformation in its urban context, mercantile investment, and occupational structure. Edinburgh, Perth, Aberdeen and Dumfries receive separate chapters.

7.96 **Lythe**, S.G. E., *Life and Labour in Dundee from the Reformation to the Civil War*, Abertay H.Soc., 5, 1958.

7.97 **Murray**, D., *Early Burgh Organisation in Scotland, as Illustrated in the History of Glasgow and of Some Neighbouring Burghs*, 2 vols., 1924.

7.98 **Smout**, T. C., 'Development and enterprise of Glasgow, 1556–1707', *Scot.J.Pol.Econ.*, VII, 1960, 194–212.

7.99 **Whyte**, I. D., 'Urbanisation in early modern Scotland: a preliminary analysis', *Scot.Ec. and Soc.H.*, IX, 1989, 21–37.

TRADE

(a) Medieval

7.100 **Dilley**, J. W., 'German merchants in Scotland, 1297–1327', *Scot.H.R.*, XXVII, 1948, 142–55.

7.101 **Reid**, W. S., 'Trade, traders and Scottish independence', *Speculum*, XXIX, 1954, 210–22.

(b) Early modern

7.102 **Dow**, J., 'Scottish trade with Sweden, 1512–80', *Scot.H.R.*, XLVIII, 1969, 64–79.

7.103 —— 'Scottish trade with Sweden, 1580–1622', *Scot.H.R.*, XLVIII, 1969, 124–50.

7.104 —— 'A comparative note on the Sound Toll registers, Stockholm customs accounts, and Dundee shipping lists 1589, 1613–1622', *Scand.Ec.H.R.*, XII, 1964, 79–85.

7.105 **Elder**, J. R., *Royal Fishery Companies of the Seventeenth Century*, 1912.

7.106 **Ferguson**, W., *Scotland's Relations with England. A Study to 1707*, 1977.

7.107 **Hart**, F. R., *The Disaster of Darien: The Story of the Scots Settlement, 1699–1701*, 1930.

7.108 **Insh**, G. P., *Scottish Colonial Schemes, 1620–86*, 1922.

7.109 —— *The Company of Scotland trading to Africa and the Indies*, 1932.

7.110 —— *The Darien Scheme*, Hist.Ass. pamphlet, 1947.

7.111 —— ed., *Darien Shipping Papers: Papers Relating to the Ships and Voyages of the Company of Scotland Trading to Africa and the Indies, 1699–1707*, Scot.H.Soc., 3rd ser., VI, 1934.

7.112 **Lythe**, S. G. E., 'Scottish trade with the Baltic 1550–1650'. In J. K. Eastham, ed., *Economic Essays in Commemoration of the Dundee School of Economics*, 1955, 63–84.

7.113 **Prebble**, J., *The Darien Disaster*, 1968.

7.114 **Scott**, W. W., 'The use of money in Scotland, 1124–1230', *Scot.H.R.*, LVII, 1979, 105–31.

7.115 **Smout**, T. C., *Scottish Trade on the Eve of the Union, 1660–1707*, 1963.

7.116 —— 'The overseas trade of Ayrshire, 1660–1707', *Ayrshire Arch.Collns.*, 2nd ser., VI, 1961, 56–80.

7.117 —— 'Scottish commercial factors in the Baltic at the end of the seventeenth century', *Scot.H.R.*, XXXIX, 1960, 122–8.

7.118 —— 'The foreign trade of Dumfries and Kirkcudbright, 1672–1696', *T.Dumfriesshire and Galloway Nat. H. & Antiq. Soc.*, XXXVII for 1958–9, 1960, 36–47.

7.119 —— 'The Glasgow merchant community in the seventeenth century', *Scot.H.R.*, XLVII, 1968, 53–71.

7.120 **Woodward**, D. M., 'Anglo-Scottish trade and English commercial policy during the 1660s', *Scot.H.R.*, LVI, 1977, 153–74.

7.121 **Zupco**, R. E., 'The weights and measures of Scotland before the Union', *Scot.H.R.*, LVI, 1977, 119–45.

PRICES, PUBLIC FINANCE AND BANKING

(a) Medieval

7.122 **Stewart**, I. H., *The Scottish Coinage*, 1955.

(b) Early modern

7.123 **Mitchison**, Rosalind, 'The movement of Scottish corn prices in the seventeenth and eighteenth centuries', *Ec.H.R.*, 2nd ser., XVIII, 1965, 278–91.

7.124 **Murray**, A., 'The procedure of the Scottish Exchequer in the early sixteenth century', *Scot.H.R.*, XL, 1961, 89–117.

7.125 —— 'The pre-Union records of the Scottish Exchequer', *J.Soc.Archivists*, II, 1961, 89–100.

7.126 —— 'The Scottish treasury, 1667–1708', *Scot.H.R.*, XLV, 1966, 89–104. See also Yamey, Edey and Thomson (4.956).

COMMUNICATIONS

7.127 **Hardie**, R. P., *The Roads of Medieval Lauderdale*, 1942.
7.128 **Taylor**, W, 'The Kings' mails, 1603–25', *Scott.H.R.*, XIII, 1963, 143–7. *See also* Haldane (7.309), for an introductory chapter on 'The early drovers' (i.e., before 1700).

POOR RELIEF

7.129 **Cormack**, A., *Poor Relief in Scotland: An Outline of the Growth and Administration of the Poor Laws in Scotland from the Middle Ages to the Present Day*, 1923.
7.130 **McPherson**, J. M., *The Kirk's Care of the Poor*, 1941.

EDUCATION

7.131 **Boyd**, W., *Education in Ayrshire through Seven Centuries*, 1961.
7.132 **Cant**, R. G., 'The Scottish universities in the seventeenth century', *Aberdeen University R.*, XLIII, 1970, 323–33.
7.133 —— *The College of St Salvator*, 1950.
7.134 **Devitt**, A. J., *Standardising Written English. Diffusion in the Case of Scotland, 1520–1659*, 1989.
7.135 **Durkan**, J., 'Education in the century of the Reformation'. In McRoberts (7.155), listed below, 145–68.
7.136 **Henderson**, G. D., *The Founding of Marischal College, Aberdeen*, 1947.
7.137 **Houston**, R., 'The literacy myth. Illiteracy in Scotland, 1630–1760', *P.P.*, XCVI, 1982, 81–103.
7.138 **Mackie**, J. D., *The University of Glasgow 1451–1951. A Short History*, 1954.
7.139 **MacQueen**, J., ed., *Humanism in Renaissance Scotland*, 1990.

7.140 **Scotland**, J., *The History of Scottish Education*, 1973.
7.141 **Simpson**, I. J., *Education in Aberdeenshire before 1872*, 1947.
7.142 **Withrington**, D. J., ed., 'List of schoolmasters teaching Latin, 1690', *Miscellany of the Scot.H.Soc.*, X, 1965, 121–42.

RELIGION AND LAW

(a) Medieval

7.143 **Cowan**, I. B., *The Parishes of Medieval Scotland*, Scot.Rec.Soc., XCIII, 1967.
7.144 **Easson**, D. E., *Medieval Religious Houses: Scotland*, 1957.
7.145 **Levy**, A., 'The origins of Scottish Jewry', *T. Jewish H.Soc.*, XIX, 1960, for 1955–9, 129–62.
7.146 **Morgan**, M., 'The organisation of the Scottish church in the twelfth century', *T. R.H.S.*, 4th ser., XXIX, 1947, 135–49.
7.147 **Stevenson**, Wendy B., 'The monastic presence in Scottish burghs in the twelfth and thirteenth centuries', *Scot.H.R.*, LX, 1981, 97–118.

(b) Early modern

7.148 **Cowan**, I. B., 'The Covenanters: a revision article', *Scot.H.R.*, XLVII, 1968, 35–52.
7.149 **Donaldson**, G., *The Scottish Reformation*, 1960.
7.150 —— 'The legal profession in Scottish society in the sixteenth and seventeenth centuries', *Juridical R.*, VII, 1976, 1–19.
7.151 **Foster**, W. R., *Bishop and Presbytery: The Church of Scotland 1661–1688*, 1958.
7.152 **Henderson**, G. D., *Religious Life in Seventeenth-Century Scotland*, 1937.
7.153 —— *The Scottish Ruling Elder*, 1935.
7.154 **Lee**, M., 'Revision article: the Scottish Reformation after 400 years', *Scot.H.R.*, XLIV, 1965, 135–47.
7.155 **McRoberts**, D., ed., *Essays on the Scottish Reformation, 1513–1625*, 1962.
7.156 **Mackay**, W., *The Church of the Covenant,*

1637–51: Revolution and Social Change in Scotland, 1979.

7.157 **Marshall**, G., *Presbyteries and Profits. Calvinism and the Development of Capitalism in Scotland, 1650–1707*, 1980. Suggests that Weber's thesis has something to recommend it in the case of Scotland. The connections between Calvinism and economic development are explored both in general terms and using empirical evidence.

7.158 **Trevor-Roper**, H. R., 'Scotland and the Puritan Revolution'. In H. E. Bell and R. L. Ollard, eds., *Historical Essays, 1600–1750, Presented to David Ogg*, 1963, 78–130.

(B) SCOTLAND AFTER 1700

GENERAL WORKS

7.159 **Brock**, W. R., *Scotus Americanus. A Survey of the Sources for Links between Scotland and America in the Eighteenth Century*, 1982.

7.160 **Brotherstone**, T., ed., *Covenant, Charter and Party. Traditions of Revolt and Protest in Modern Scottish History*, 1989.

7.161 **Campbell**, R. H. and Dow, J. B. A., *Source Book of Scottish Economic and Social History*, 1968.

7.162 **Campbell**, R. H., *Scotland from 1707: The Rise of an Industrial Society*, 1964.

7.163 **Devine**, T. M. and Mitchison, Rosalind, eds., *People and Society in Scotland. I: 1760–1830*, 1988.

7.164 **Dickson**, .T., ed., *Scottish Capitalism: Class, State and Nation from before the Union to the Present*, 1980.

7.165 **Dwyer**, J., *Virtuous Discourse. Sensibility and Community in Late Eighteenth-Century Scotland*, 1987.

7.166 **Hamilton**, H., *An Economic History of Scotland in the Eighteenth Century*, 1963.

7.167 **Harvie**, C., *No Gods and Precious Few Heroes. Scotland, 1914–80*, 1981.

7.168 **Hill**, C. W., *Edwardian Scotland*, 1976.

7.169 **Hook**, A., *Scotland and America: A Study of Cultural Relations, 1750–1835*, 1975.

7.170 **Leneman**, L, ed., *Perspectives in Scottish Social History. Essays in Honour of Rosalind Mitchison*, 1988.

7.171 **Lenman**, B., *An Economic History of Modern Scotland, 1660–1976*, 1977.

7.172 —— *Integration, Enlightenment and Industrialisation. Scotland, 1746–1832*, 1981.

7.173 **Levitt**, I., ed., *Government and Social Conditions in Scotland, 1845–1919*, 1988.

7.174 **MacLaren**, A., A., ed., *Social Class in Scotland: Past and Present*, 1976.

7.175 **Madden**, C. A. and Thompson, F. N., *Scotland in Change*, 1983.

7.176 **Marwick**, W. H., *Economic Developments in Victorian Scotland*, 1936.

7.177 —— *Scotland in Modern Times: An Outline of Economic and Social Development since the Union of 1707*, 1964.

7.178 **Mitchison**, Rosalind and Roebuck, P., eds., *Economy and Society in Scotland and Ireland, 1500–1939*, 1988.

7.179 **Niven**, D., *The Development of Housing in Scotland*, 1979.

7.180 **Orel**, H., Snyder, H. L. and Stokstad, M., eds., *The Scottish World. History and Culture of Scotland*, 1981.

7.181 **Phillipson**, N. T. and Mitchison, Rosalind, eds. *Scotland in the Age of Improvement: Essays in Scottish History in the Eighteenth Century*, 1970.

7.182 **Prattis**, J. I., *Economic Structures in the Highlands of Scotland*, 1977.

7.183 **Saville**, R., *The Economic Development of Modern Scotland, 1950–80*, 1985.

7.184 **Shaw**, J. S., *The Management of Scottish Society, 1707–64. Power, Nobles, Lawyers, Edinburgh Agents and English Influence*, 1983.

7.185 **Slaven**, A., *The Development of the West of Scotland, 1750–1960*, 1975.

7.186 **Smout**, T. C., *A Century of the Scottish People, 1830–1950*, 1986. Wide-ranging, well-organised study bringing out the variety of urban/rural, lowland/highland contrasts. Least effective on the last two decades of the survey.

7.187 —— *The Social Condition of Scotland in the 1840s*, 1981.

7.188 **Turnock**, D., *The Historical Geography of Scotland since 1707*, 1987. Takes a wide angled view of the economic, technological and social changes that have helped define modern Scotland.

7.189 **Withers**, C., *Gaelic Scotland. The Transformation of a Culture Region*, 1988.

POPULATION

7.190 **Britton**, Rachel, 'Wealthy Scots, 1876–1913', *B.I.H.R.*, LVIII, 1985, 78–95.

7.191 **Brock**, J., 'Spurious migration in the Scottish census'. *Scot.Ec. and Soc.H.*, IX, 1989, 80–87.

7.192 **Bumstead**, J. M., *The People's Clearance. Highland Emigration to British North America, 1770–1815*, 1982.

7.193 **Devine**, T. M., *The Great Highland Famine. Hunger, Emigration and the Scottish Highlands in the Nineteenth Century*, 1988.

7.194 —— ed., *Irish Immigrants and Scottish Society in the Nineteenth and Twentieth Centuries*, 1991.

7.195 **Donaldson**, G., *The Scots Overseas*, 1966. Excellent bibliography.

7.196 **Flinn**, M. W., ed., *Scottish Population History from the Seventeenth Century to the 1930s*, 1977.

7.197 **Harper**, M., *Emigration from North-East Scotland*, 1988.

7.198 **Hollingsworth**, T. H., *Migration: A Study based on Scottish Experience between 1939 and 1944*, 1970.

7.199 **Kelsall**, H. M., *Scottish Lifestyle 300 Years Ago. New Light on Edinburgh and Border Families*, 1986.

7.200 **Kyd**, K. D., *Scottish Population Statistics*, Scot.H.Soc., 1952.

7.201 **Lockhart**, D. G., 'Migration to planned villages in Scotland, 1725–1850', *Scot. Geog.Mag.*, CII, 1986, 165–80.

7.202 —— 'Patterns of migration and movement of labour to the planned villages of N.E. Scotland', *Scot.Geog.Mag.*, XCVIII, 1982, 35–47.

7.203 **McCaffrey**, J. F., 'Irish immigrants and radical movements in the west of Scotland in the early nineteenth century', *Innes R.*, XXXIX, 1988, 46–60.

7.204 **Macdonald**, D. F., *Scotland's Shifting Population, 1770–1850*, 1937.

7.205 **Macmillan**, D., *Scotland and Australia 1788–1850. Emigration, Commerce and Investment*, 1967.

7.206 **Mitchison**, Rosalind and Leneman, L., *Sexuality and Social Control. Scotland, 1660–1780*, 1989.

7.207 **Moody**, D., *Scottish Family History*, 1988.

7.208 **Osborne**, R. H., 'The movement of people in Scotland, 1851–1951', *Scot. Studs.*, II, 1958, 1–46.

7.209 **Withers**, C. W. J., 'Highland migration to Aberdeen, c.1649–1891', *Northern Scot.*, IX, 1989, 21–44.

AGRICULTURE AND RURAL SOCIETY

7.210 **Adam**, Margaret I., 'Eighteenth–century highland landlords and the poverty problem', *Scot.H.R.*, XIX, 1921–2, 1–20, 161–79.

7.211 **Adams**, D. G., *Bothy Nichts and Days. Farm Bothy Life in Angus and the Mearns*, 1991.

7.212 **Bil**, A., *The Shieling, 1600–1840. The Case of the Central Scottish Highlands*, 1990.

7.213 **Caird**, J. B., 'The creation of crofts and new settlement patterns in the Highlands and Islands of Scotland', *Scot.Geog.Mag.*, CIII, 1987, 67–75.

7.214 **Campbell**, R. H., *Owners and Occupiers. Changes in Rural Society in S. W. Scotland before 1914*, 1991.

7.215 **Carter**, I., *Farm Life in North East Scotland, 1840–1914: The Poor Man's Country*, 1979.

7.216 **Collier**, A., *The Crofting Problem*, 1953.

7.217 **Devine**, T. M., 'Social stability and agrarian change in the eastern lowlands of Scotland, 1810–40; *Soc.H.*, III, 1978, 331–46.

7.218 **Donaldson**, J. E., *Caithness in the Eighteenth Century*, 1938.

7.219 **Fenton**, A. and Walker, B., *The Rural Architecture of Scotland*, 1981.

7.220 **Gaskell**, P., *Morvern Transformed. A Highland Parish in the Nineteenth Century*, 1968. A comprehensive analysis of the problems of the west coast.

7.221 **Graham**, L, ed., *Shetland Crofters. A Hundred Years of Island Crofting*, 1987.

7.222 **Gray**, M., *The Highland Economy, 1750–1850*, 1957.

7.223 **Handley**, J. E., *Scottish Farming in the Eighteenth Century*, 1953.

7.224 **Houston**, R., *Records of a Scottish Village: Larswade, 1650–1750*, 1982.

7.225 **Hunter**, J., *The Making of the Crofting Community*, 1976.

7.226 —— *The Claim of Crofting, the Scottish Highlands and Islands, 1930–1990.*, 1991.

7.227 **Jones**, D. T., Duncan, J. F., Conacher, H. M., and Scott, W. R., *Rural Scotland During the War*, 1926.

7.228 **Leneman**, L., *Fit for Heroes? Land Settlement in Scotland after World War I*, 1989.

7.229 **MacArthur**, E. M., *Iona. The Living Memory of a Crofting Community, 1750–1914*, 1990.

7.230 **Mitchison**, Rosalind, *Agricultural Sir John*, 1962. Definitive biography of Sir John Sinclair.

7.231 —— 'Scottish landowners and communal responsibility in the eighteenth century'. *Brit.J.Eighteenth Century Studs.*, I, 1978, 41–5.

7.232 **Orr**, W., *Deer Forests, Landlords and Crofters. The Western Highlands in Victorian and Edwardian Times*, 1982.

7.233 **Richards**, E., *A History of the Highland Clearances. I: Agrarian Transformation and the Evictions, 1746–1886*, 1982; II: *Emigration, Protest, Reasons*, 1985. A dispassionate account of why the clearances took place and with what consequences.

7.234 —— *The Leviathan of Wealth: The Sutherland Fortune in the Industrial Revolution*, 1973.

7.235 —— and Clough, M., *Cromartie. Highland Life, 1650–1914*, 1989.

7.236 **Rosie**, J. and Kelly, L., *Agriculture in Lanarkshire, 1760–1840*, 1978.

7.237 **Selman**, P. H., ed., *Countryside Planning in Practice. The Scottish Experience*, 1988.

7.238 **Smith**, J. S. and Stevenson, D., eds., *Fermolk and Fisherfolk. Rural Life in Northern Scotland in the Eighteenth and Nineteenth Centuries*, 1989.

7.239 **Smout**, T. C., 'The landowner and the planned villages in Scotland, 1730–1830'. In G. Phillipson and Rosalind Mitchison, eds., *Scotland in the Age of Improvement*, 1970. *See also* Smout (7.66).

7.240 **Timperley**, L. R., ed., *A Directory of Landownership in Scotland c.1770*, Scot.Rec.Soc., new ser., V, 1976.

7.241 **Ward**, W. R., 'The land tax in Scotland, 1707–98', *B. John Rylands Lib*, XXXVII, 1954, 288–308.

7.242 **Wheeler**, P. T., 'Landownership and the crofting system in Sutherland since 1800', *Ag.H.R.*, XIX, 1971, 45–56.

7.243 **Whyte**, I. D., 'George Dundas of Dundas. The context of an early eighteenth century Scottish improving landowner', *Scot.H.R.*, LX, 1981, 1–13.

7.244 **Wordie**, J. R., *Estate Management in Eighteenth–Century Scotland. The Building of the Leveson–Gower Fortune*, 1982.

7.245 **Youngson**, A. J., *After the Forty–Five: The Economic Impact on the Scottish Highlands*, 1973. Covers the period up to 1840s.

INDUSTRY

7.246 **Butt**, J., *The Industrial Archaeology of Scotland*, 1968.

7.247 —— and Ponting, K., eds., *Scottish Textile History*, 1987.

7.248 **Buxton**, N. K., 'Economic growth in Scotland between the Wars: the role of production structure and rationalization'. *Ec.H.R.*, 2nd ser., XXXIII, 1980, 538–55.

7.249 —— 'The Scottish shipbuilding industry between the Wars', *Bus.H.*, X, 1968, 101–20.

7.250 **Cairncross**, A. K., ed., *The Scottish Economy*, 1954.

7.251 **Campbell**, R. H., *The Rise and Fall of Scottish Industry, 1707–1939*, 1980. Focuses on the key industries – textiles, coal, iron, engineering, and shipbuilding – in the principal phases of their expansion and stagnation.

7.252 **Cotterill**, M. S., 'The development of Scottish gas technology, 1817–1914: inspiration and motivation', *Ind.Arch.R..*, 1981, 19–40.

7.253 **Goull**, R., 'The engagement system during the Shetland herring boom, 1880–1914', *Scot.Ec. and Soc.R.*, VII,

1987, 55–64.

7.254 **Devine**, T. M., 'The rise and fall of illicit whisky making in northern Scotland, c.1780–1840', *Scot.H.R.*, LIV, 1975, 155–77.

7.255 **Donnachie**, I. L., *A History of the Brewing Industry in Scotland*, 1979.

7.256 **Donnelly**, T., 'Shipbuilding in Aberdeen, 1750–1914', *Northern Scot.* IV, 1981, 23–42.

7.257 **Duckham**, B. F., *A History of the Scottish Coal Industry I: 1700–1815*, 1970.

7.258 **Duncan**, W. R. H., 'Aberdeen and the early development of the whaling industry, 1750–1800', *Northern Scot.*, III, 1979, 47–59.

7.259 **Durie**, A. J., *The Scottish Linen Industry in the Eighteenth Century*, 1979.

7.260 **Gulvin**, C., *The Tweedmakers: A History of the Scottish Fancy Woollen Industry, 1600–1914*, 1973.

7.261 —— *The Scottish Hosiery and Knitwear Industry, 1680–1980*, 1984.

7.262 **Hamilton**, H., *The Industrial Revolution in Scotland*, 1932, 2nd ed., 1966.

7.263 **Hume**, J. R., *The Industrial Archaeology of Scotland. I; The Lowlands and Borders*, 1976; II: *The Highlands and Islands*, 1977.

7.264 —— and Moss, M. S., *Beardmore. The History of a Scottish Industrial Giant*, 1979.

7.265 **McClain**, N. E., 'Scottish lintmills, 1729–70', *Textile H.*, I, 1970, 293–308.

7.266 **McVeigh**, P., *Scottish East Coast Potteries, 1750–1840*, 1979.

7.267 **Michie**, R. C., 'North East Scotland and northern whale fishing, 1752–1893', *Northern Scot.*, III, 1979, 60–85.

7.268 **Moss**, M. S., and Hume, J. R., *A History of the Scotch Whisky Distilling Industry*, 1981.

7.269 —— *Workshop of the British Empire. Engineering and Shipbuilding in the West of Scotland*, 1977. A mixture of general surveys of the two industries together with case studies of individual firms.

7.270 **Nicholson**, M. and O'Neill, M., *Glasgow. Locomotive Builder to the World*, 1987.

7.271 **Payne**, P. L., *Colvilles and the Scottish Steel Industry*, 1979. Explores the heyday of this major Scottish company and its failure to adapt sufficiently to changing economic circumstances.

7.272 —— *The Early Scottish Limited Companies*, 1982.

7.273 —— *The Hydro. A Study of the Development of the Major Hydro–Electric Schemes undertaken by the North of Scotland Hydro–Electric Board*, 1988.

7.274 —— 'Rationality and Personality: A study of mergers in the Scottish iron and steel industry 1916–36', *Bus.H.*, XIX, 1977, 162–91.

7.275 **Perren**, R., 'Oligopoly and competition: price fixing and market sharing among timber firms in northern Scotland, 1890–1939', *Bus.H.*, XXI, 1979, 213–25.

7.276 **Robertson**, A. J., 'The decline of the Scottish Cotton Industry, 1800–1914', *Bus.H.*, XII, 1970, 116–28.

7.277 **Shaw**, J., *Water Power in Scotland, 1550–1870*, 1984.

7.278 **Thompson**, F. G., *Harris Tweed: The Story of a Hebridean Industry*, 1969.

7.279 **Thomson**, A. G., *The Paper Industry in Scotland, 1590–1861*, 1974. *See also* Coleman (4.551) and Shorter (4.552).

7.280 **Tucker**, G. D., 'The slate islands of Scotland: the history of the Scottish slate industry', *Bus.H.*, XIX, 1977, 18–36.

7.281 **Turner**, W. H. K., 'The development of flax spinning mills in Scotland, 1787–1840', *Scot.Geog.Mag.*, XCVIII, 1982, 4–15.

7.282 —— 'Flax weaving in Scotland in the early nineteenth century', *Scot.Geog. Mag.*, XCIX, 1983, 16–30.

7.283 —— 'The localisation of early spinning mills in the historic linen region of Scotland', *Scot.Geog.Mag.*, XCVIII, 1982, 77–86.

7.284 **Ward**, J. T., 'The Factory Reform Movement in Scotland', *Scot.H.R.*, XLI, 1962, 100–23.

7.285 **Weir**, R., 'Rationalisation and diversification in the Scotch whisky industry, 1900–39: another look at "old" and "new" industries', *Ec.H.R.*, 2nd ser., XLII, 1989, 375–95.

TRADE AND BUSINESS HISTORY

7.286 **Campbell**, R. H., 'The Anglo–Scottish Union of 1707: the economic consequences', *Ec.H.R.*, 2nd ser., XVI, 1964, 468–77.

7.287 —— 'The law and the joint stock company in Scotland'. In Payne (7.296), 136–51.

7.288 **Cochrane**, L. E., *Scottish Trade with Ireland in the Eighteenth Century*, 1985. *See also* Cullen (4.797).

7.289 **Devine**, T. M., 'An eighteenth–century business elite: Glasgow West India merchants c.1750–1815', *Scot.H.R.*, LVII, 1978, 40–67.

7.290 ——*The Tobacco Lords*, 1975. Deals with the merchant princes of Glasgow.

7.291 **Dupree**, M. W. and Crowther, M. A., 'A profile of the medical profession in the early twentieth century: the medical directory as a historical source', *Bull.Hist.Medic.*, LXV, 1991, 209–33.

7.292 **Haldane**, A. R. B., *The Great Fishmonger of the Tay. John Richardson of Perth and Pitfour, 1760–1821*, 1981.

7.293 **Kinloch**, J. and Butt, J., *History of the Scottish Co-operative Wholesale Society Ltd.*, 1981.

7.294 **Lenman**, B., *From Esk to Tweed: Harbours, Ships and Men of the East Coast of Scotland*, 1975.

7.295 **Morris**, A. S., 'The nineteenth-century Scottish carrier trade: patterns of decline', *Scot.Geog.Mag.*, XCVI, 1980, 74–82.

7.296 **Payne**, P. L., ed., *Studies in Scottish Business History*, 1967. Contains a copious bibliography of the subject, 79–99.

7.297 **Riley**, P. W. J., *The Union of England and Scotland*, 1978. Chapter six deals with trade and propaganda. *See also* Campbell (7.286).

7.298 **Scott**, J. and Hughes, M., *The Anatomy of Scottish Capital: Scottish Companies and Scottish Capital, 1900–79*, 1980.

7.299 **Smith**, H. D., *Shetland Life and Trade, 1550–1914*, 1984.

7.300 **Vamplew**, W., *Salvesen of Leith*, 1975. A case study of the nineteenth and twentieth-century trading operations of this major Norwegian-owned Scottish company.

See also Smout (7.39).

BANKING AND INVESTMENT

7.301 **Checkland**, S. G., *Scottish Banking: A History, 1695–1973*, 1975.

7.302 **Jackson**, W. T., *The Enterprising Scot: Investors in the American West after 1873*, 1968.

7.303 **Mepham**, M. J., *Accounting in eighteenth-century Scotland*, 1988.

7.304 **Michie**, R. C., *Money, Mania and Markets. Investment, Company Formation and the Stock Exchange in Nineteenth-Century Scotland*, 1982.

7.305 **Munn**, C. W., *The Scottish Provincial Banking Companies, 1747–1864*, 1981.

TRANSPORT AND COMMUNICATIONS

7.306 **Fyfe**, J., ed., *Autobiography of John McAdam (1806–83)*, Scot.H.Soc., 4th ser., XVI, 1980.

7.307 **Gordon**, A, *To Move with the Times. The Story of Transport and Travel in Scotland*, 1987.

7.308 **Haldane**, A. R. B., *The Drove Roads of Scotland*, 1952.

7.309 —— *New Ways through the Glens*, 1962. Telford's roadmaking in the Highlands.

7.310 —— *Three Centuries of Scottish Posts*, 1971.

7.311 **Lindsay**, Jean, *The Canals of Scotland*, 1968.

7.312 **Mellor**, R. E. H., ed., *The Railways of Scotland. Papers of Andrew O'Dell*, 1984.

7.313 **Riddell**, J. F., *Clyde Navigation: A History of the Development and Deepening of the River Clyde*, 1979.

7.314 **Turner**, J. R., *Scotland's North Sea Gateway. Aberdeen Harbour, 1136–1986*, 1986.

7.315 **Vamplew**, W., 'Railways and the transformation of the Scottish economy', *Ec.H.R.*, 2nd ser., XXIV, 1971, 37–54.

7.316 —— 'Scottish railways and the development of Scottish locomotive building in the nineteenth century', *Bus.H.R.*, XLVI 1972, 320–38.

7.317 **Weir**, M., *Ferries in Scotland*, 1988.

URBAN HISTORY

7.318 **Allen**, C. M., 'The genesis of British urban re-development with special reference to Glasgow', *Ec.H.R.*, 2nd ser., XXIII, 1965, 598–613. Deals with the urban renewal programme of the 1860s and '70s.

7.319 **Allison**, E. and Beaton, M., *Dumbarton, 1815–51*, 1979.

7.320 **Atherton**, C. M., 'The development of the middle class suburb: the west end of Glasgow', *Scot.Ec. and Soc.R.*, II, 1991, 19–35.

7.321 **Barke**, M. and Johnson, T., 'Emerging residential segregation in a nineteenth-century small town: the case of Falkirk', *Scot.Geog.Mag.*, XCVIII, 1982, 87–102.

7.322 **Brown**, J. L. and Lawson, I. C., *A History of Peebles, 1850–1990*, 1990.

7.323 **Checkland**, S. G., 'The British industrial city as history: the Glasgow case', *Urban Studs.*, I, 1964, 34–54.

7.324 **Dickson**, T. and Clarke, I. T., 'Social concern and social control in nineteenth-century Scotland. Paisley, 1841–3', *Scot.H.R.*, LXV, 1986, 48–60.

7.325 **Gibb**, A., *Glasgow. The Making of a City*, 1983. An evocative portrait of Scotland's great commercial centre.

7.326 **Gordon**, G., ed., *Perspectives on the Scottish City*, 1985.

7.327 —— and Dicks, B., eds., *Scottish Urban History*, 1983. A mixture of essays on individual towns and of thematic studies of urban planning, the merchant class, working class housing, and Victorian transport.

7.328 **Marwick**, W. H., *The River Clyde and the Clyde Burghs*, 1909. Useful for the burghs other than Glasgow.

7.329 **Meller**, H., *Patrick Geddes. Social Evolutionist and City Planner*, 1990.

7.330 **Smith**, J. S. and Stevenson, D., eds., *Aberdeen in the Nineteenth Century. The Making of the Modern City*, 1988.

7.331 **Stevenson**, D., ed., *From Lairds to Louns. Country and Burgh Life in Aberdeen, 1600–1800*, 1986.

7.332 **Walker**, W. M., *Juteopolis: Dundee and its Textile Workers, 1885–1923*, 1980.

7.333 **Worsdall**, F., *The Tenement: A Way of Life. A Social, Historical and Architectural Study of Housing in Glasgow*, 1979.

7.334 **Youngson**, A. J., *The Making of Classical Edinburgh*, 1966. The major study of the building of the new town.

HOUSING

7.335 **Horsey**, M., *Tenements and Towers. Glasgow Working Class Housing, 1890–1990*, 1990.

7.336 **Melling**, J., *Rent Strikes: People's Struggle for Housing in West Scotland, 1890–1916*, 1983.

7.337 **Morgan**, N. J. and Daunton, M. J., 'Landlords in Glasgow. A study of 1900', *Bus.H.*, XXV, 1983, pp. 264–86.

7.338 **Rodger**, R., *Scottish Housing. Policy and Politics, 1885–1985*, 1989.

LABOUR

7.339 **McDougall**, I., ed., *A Catalogue of Some Labour Records in Scotland and Some Scottish Records outside Scotland*, 1978.

7.340 **Arnot**, R. P., *A History of the Scottish Miners from the Earliest Times*, 1955.

7.341 **Buckley**, K. D., *Trade Unionism in Aberdeen, 1878–1900*, 1955.

7.342 **Cage**, R. A., *The Working Class in Glasgow, 1750–1914*, 1986.

7.343 **Carew**, A., *The Lower Deck of the Royal Navy, 1900–30. The Invergordon Mutiny in Perspective*, 1981.

7.344 **Devine**, T. M., ed., *Farm Servants and Labour in Lowland Scotland, 1770–1914*, 1984.

7.345 —— and Harnesk, B., 'The decline of farm service: a comparative study of Scotland and Sweden', *Scot.Ec. and Soc.H.*, II, 1991, 5–18.

7.346 **Fraser**, W. H., *Conflict and Class. Scottish Workers, 1700–1838*, 1988.

7.347 **Gillespie**, Sarah C., *A Hundred Years of Progress: The Record of the Scottish Typographical Association, 1853–1952*,

1953.

7.348 **Gourvish**, T. R., 'The cost of living in Glasgow in the early nineteenth century', *Ec.H.R.*, 2nd ser., XXV, 1972, 65–80.

7.349 **Gray**, R. Q., *The Labour Aristocracy in Victorian Edinburgh*, 1976.

7.350 **Handley**, J. E., *The Irish in Scotland, 1798–1845*, 2nd rev. ed., 1945.

7.351 —— *The Irish in Modern Scotland*, 1947.

7.352 —— *The Navvy in Scotland*, 1970.

7.353 **Levitt**, I. and Smout, T. C., eds., *The State of the Scottish Working Class in 1843*, 1980. A statistical and geographical investigation based on data collected for the Poor Law Commission Report of 1843.

7.354 **Logue**, K. J., *Popular Disturbances in Scotland, 1780–1815*, 1979.

7.355 **McDougall**, I., ed., *Essays in Scottish Labour History: A Tribute to W. H. Marwick*, 1978.

7.356 **Marwick**, W. H., *A Short History of Labour in Scotland*, 1967.

7.357 **Murray**, N., *The Scottish Handloom Weavers, 1790–1850. A Social History*, 1978.

7.358 **Trickett**, Ann, *The Scottish Carter: The History of the Scottish Horse and Motormen's Association, 1898–1960*, 1967.

7.358a **Wright**, L. C., *Scottish Chartism*, 1953.

7.359 **Young**, G. D., *The Rousing of the Scottish Working Class*, 1979.

POOR RELIEF

7.360 **Cage**, R. A., *The Scottish Poor Law, 1745–1845*, 1981.

7.361 **Checkland**, Olive, *Philanthropy in Victorian Scotland. Social Welfare and the Voluntary Principle*, 1980.

7.362 **Ferguson**, T., *Dawn of Scottish Social Welfare: A Survey from Medieval Times to 1863*, 1948.

7.363 —— *Scottish Social Welfare, 1864–1914*, 1958.

7.364 **Levitt**, I., *Poverty and Welfare in Scotland, 1890–1948*, 1989.

7.365 **Lindsay**, J., *The Scottish Poor Law. Its Operation in the North East from 1745 to 1845*, 1976.

7.366 **Mitchison**, Rosalind, 'East Lothian as innovator in the Old Poor Law', *Trans.E.Lothian Antiq. and Field Nat.Hist.Soc.*, XIX, 1987, 17–30.

7.367 —— 'The Making of the Old Scottish Poor Law', *P.P.*, 63, 1974, 58–93.

7.368 **Paterson**, Audrey, 'The Poor Law in nineteenth-century Scotland', in Fraser (5.2626), 171–93.

SOCIAL LIFE AND INTELLECTUAL DEVELOPMENT

7.369 **Anderson**, R. D., *Education and Opportunity in Victorian Scotland. Schools and Universities*, 1983. An exemplary analysis of the different sectors of the nineteenth-century Scottish system firmly grounded on statistical data.

7.370 —— 'Sport in the Scottish universities, 1860–1939', *Internat.J.H.Sport*, IV, 1987, 177–88.

7.371 —— *The Student Community at Aberdeen, 1860–1939*, 1988.

7.372 **Campbell**, R. H. and Skinner, A. S., eds., *The Origins and Nature of the Scottish Enlightenment*, 1982.

7.373 **Camil**, C., *Experience and Enlightenment. Socialisation for Cultural Change in Eighteenth Century Scotland*, 1983.

7.374 **Carter**, Jennifer J. and Withrington, D. J., eds., *Scottish Universities. Distinctiveness and Diversity*, 1992.

7.375 **Chitnis**, A., *The Scottish Enlightenment. A Social History*, 1976.

7.376 —— *The Scottish Enlightenment and Early Victorian Society*, 1985.

7.377 **Cowan**, R. M. W., *The Newspaper in Scotland, 1815–60*, 1946.

7.378 **Davie**, G. E., *The Democratic Intellect: Scotland and her Universities in the Nineteenth Century*, 1961.

7.379 —— *The Scottish Enlightenment*, 1981. Hist.Ass.pamphlet.

7.380 **Donaldson**, W., *Popular Literature in Victorian Scotland. Language, Fiction and the Press*, 1986.

7.381 **Fontana**, B., *Re-thinking the Politics of*

Commercial Society: the Edinburgh Review, 1802–32, 1985.

7.382 **Glaister**, R. T. D., 'Rural private teachers in eighteenth-century Scotland', *J.Educ.Admin. and Hist.*, XXIII, 1991, 49–61.

7.383 **Holiston**, R., *Scottish Literacy and the Scottish Identity*, 1985.

7.384 **Humes**, W. M. and Paterson, H. M., *Scottish Culture and Scottish Education, 1800–1980*, 1983.

7.385 **King**, E., *Scotland Sober and Free. The Temperance Movement, 1829–1979*, 1979.

7.386 **Littlejohn**, J. H., *The Scottish Music Hall, 1880–1990*, 1990.

7.387 **Lloyd**, J., 'Education and welfare during the Second World War', *Scot.Educ.R.*, XXIII, 1991, 93–103.

7.388 **McKinnon**, K. M., 'Education and social control: the case of Gaelic Scotland', *Scot.Educational Studs.*, IV, 1972, 125–37.

7.389 **Meikle**, H. W., *Scotland and the French Revolution*, 1912. Reprinted 1969.

7.390 **Minto**, C. S., *Victorian and Edwardian Scotland from Old Photographs*, 1970.

7.391 **Montgomery**, F. A., 'The unstamped press: the contribution of Glasgow, 1831–6', *Scot.H.R.*, LIX, 1980, 154–70.

7.392 **Moorehouse**, H. F., 'Scotland v. England: football and popular culture', *Internat.J.Sport*, IV, 1987, 189–202.

7.393 **Plant**, Marjorie, *The Domestic Life of Scotland in the Eighteenth Century*, 1952.

7.394 **Ralston**, A. G., 'The development of reformatory and industrial schools in Scotland, 1832–72', *Scot.Ec. and Soc.H.*, VIII, 1988, 40–55.

7.395 **Rendall**, Jane, *The Origins of the Scottish Enlightenment*, 1978. Chapters five and six cover social institutions and commerce and civilisation.

7.396 **Robertson**, P. L., 'The development of an urban university: Glasgow, 1860–1914', *Hist.Educ.Q.*, XXX, 1990, 47–78.

7.397 **Saunders**, L. J., *Scottish Democracy, 1815–40: The Social and Intellectual Background*, 1950.

7.398 **Tranter**, N. L., 'Popular sports and the Industrial Revolution in Scotland: the evidence of statistical accounts', *Internat.J.Hist. Sport*, IV, 1987, 21–38.

7.399 —— 'The social and occupational structure of organised sport in central Scotland in the nineteenth century', *Internat.J.Hist. Sport.*, IV, 1987, 301–14.

7.400 **Vamplew**, W., 'The economics of a sports industry: Scottish gate money football, 1890–1914', *Ec.H.R.*, 2nd ser., XXXV, 1982, 549–68.

7.401 **Withers**, C. W. J., *Gaelic in Scotland, 1698–1981, the Geographical History of a Language*, 1984.

RELIGION

7.402 **Brown**, C. G., *The Social History of Religion in Modern Scotland since 1730*, 1987. Particularly useful on the Highlands and on the place of religion in urbanisation.

7.403 **Chambers**, D., 'The Church of Scotland's Highlands and Islands Education Scheme, 1824–43', *J.Educ.Admin. & H.*, VII, 1975, 8–17.

7.404 **Cheyne**, A. C., *The Transforming of the Kirk. Victorian Religious Revolution*, 1983.

7.405 **Enright**, W. G., 'Urbanisation and the evangelical pulpit in nineteenth-century Scotland', *Church H.*, XLVII, 1978, 400–7.

7.406 **Gallagher**, T., *Glasgow: The Uneasy Peace. Religious Tension in Modern Scotland, 1819–1914*, 1987.

7.407 **Hillis**, P., 'Presbyterianism and social class in mid nineteenth-century Glasgow: a study of nine churches', *J.Eccles.H.*, XXXII, 1981, 47–64.

7.408 **Knox**, W. W., 'Religion and the Scottish labour movement c.1900–39', *J.Contemp.H.*, XXIII, 1988, 609–30.

7.409 **MacLaren**, A. A., *Religion and Social Class. The Disruption Years in Aberdeen*, 1974.

7.410 **McLeod**, R., 'The John Bunyan of the Highlands: the life and work of Robert Finlayson, 1793–1861', *Trans.Gaelic Soc.Inverness*, LIV, 1986, 240–68.

7.411 **Mechie**, S., *The Church and Scottish Social Development, 1780–1870*, 1960.

7.412 **Robb**, G., 'Popular religion and the christianisation of the Scottish Highlands in the eighteenth and nineteenth centuries', *J.Rel.H.*, XVI, 1990, 18–34.

7.413 **MacDougall**, N., *Church, Politics and Society. Scotland, 1408–1929*, 1983.

7.414 **Sher**, R., *Church and University in the Scottish Enlightenment*, 1985.

7.415 **Smout**, T. C., 'Born again at Cambuslang: new evidence on popular religion and literacy in eighteenth-century Scotland', *P.P.*, XCVII, 1982, 114–28.

WOMEN

7.416 **Fewell**, J. and Paterson, F., eds., *Girls in their Prime. Scottish Education Revisited*, 1990.

7.417 **Gordon**, E., *Women and the Labour Movement in Scotland, 1850–1914*, 1991.

7.418 —— and Brettenbach, E., eds., *The World is Ill Divided. Women's Work in Scotland in the Ninteeenth and Early Twentieth Centuries*, 1990.

7.419 **Leneman**, L. and Mitchison, Rosalind, 'Girls in trouble: the social and geographical setting of illegitimacy in early modern Scotland', *J.Soc.H.*, XXI, 1988, 483–98.

7.420 **Littlewood**, B. and Mahood, L., 'Prostitutes, magdalenes and wayward girls: dangerous sexualities of working class women in Victorian Scotland', *Gender & Hist.*, III, 1991, 160–76.

7.421 **Marshall**, Rosalind K., *Virgins and Viragos. A History of Women in Scotland, 1080–1980*, 1983. Freshly uncovered source material is the backbone of this entertaining attempt to revise the portrait of Scottish women since the eleventh century.

7.422 **Reynolds**, Sian, *Britannica's typesetters. Women Compositors in Edwardian Edinburgh*, 1989. A study of a group seen by their employers as a cheap source of labour and as rivals by the men who comprised the compositors' union.

8

IRELAND

(A) IRELAND BEFORE 1700

GENERAL WORKS

(a) Bibliographies

8.1 **Asplin**, P. W. A., *Medieval Ireland, c. 1170–1495. A Bibliography of Secondary Works*, 1970.

8.2 **Eager**, A. R., ed., *A Guide to Irish Bibliographical Material*, 1964.

8.3 **Edwards**, Ruth D., and Quinn, D. B., 'Thirty years' work in Irish history: sixteenth-century Ireland', *Irish H.Studs.*, XVI, 1969, 15–32. One of a series of very useful bibliographical articles.

8.4 **Johnston**, Edith M., ed., *Irish History: Select Bibliography*, Hist.Ass., 1969.

8.5 **Kavanagh**, M., ed., *A Bibliography of the County Galway*, 1965.

8.6 **Maclysaght**, E., ed., *Bibliography of Irish Family History*, 1981.

8.7 **Mulvey**, H. F., 'Modern Irish history since 1940: a bibliographical survey, 1600–1922', *Historian*, XXVIII, 1965, 516–59.

8.8 **Otway-Ruthven**, J., 'Thirty years' work in Irish history: medieval Ireland, 1169–1485', *Irish H.Studs.*, XV, 1967, 359–65.

8.9 **Povey**, K., 'The sources for a bibliography of Irish history', 1500–1700', *Irish H.Studs.*, 1, 1939, 393–403.

8.10 **Simms**, J. G., 'Thirty years' work in Irish history: seventeeth-century Ireland, 1603–1702', *Irish H.Studs.*, XV 1967, 366–75.

(b) Sources

8.11 **Edwards**, Ruth D., *An Atlas of Irish History*, 1973.

8.12 **Maxwell**, Constantia, *Irish History from Contemporary Sources, 1509–1610*, 1932. A useful collection, with sections on social and economic conditions and on Tudor efforts at colonisation. *See also* Browning (4.10). Part VIII, 701–83, deals with Ireland.

(c) Surveys

(i) MEDIEVAL

8.13 **Beckett**, J. C., *A Short History of Ireland*, 1952, 3rd ed., 1966.

8.14 **Bottigheimer**, K. S., *Ireland and the Irish. A Short History*, 1982.

8.15 **Chart**, D. A., *An Economic History of Ireland*, 1920. An elementary textbook.

8.16 **Cosgrove**, A., *Late Medieval Ireland, 1370–1541*, 1981.

8.17 —— ed., *A New History of Ireland. II:*

Medieval Ireland, 1169–1534, 1987.
Though a long time in the press this
book generally breaks new ground in its
account of the economy.

8.18 —— 'The writing of Irish medieval
history', *Ir.Hist.Studs.*, XXVII, 1990,
97–111.

8.19 **Curtis**, E., *A History of Ireland*, 1936, 6th
ed., 1950.

8.20 —— *A History of Medieval Ireland from
1086 to 1513*, 1923, enlarged ed., 1938.
Bibliography.

8.21 **Flanagan**, M. T., *Irish Society, Anglo-
Norman Settlers, Angevin Kingship.
Interactions in Ireland in the Twelfth
Century*, 1989.

8.22 **Frame**, R., *English Lordship in Ireland,
1318–61*, 1982.

8.23 —— 'Power and society in the lordship of
Ireland, 1272–1377', *P.P.*, 76, 1977, 3–33.

8.23A **Lydon**, J. F., *The Lordship of Ireland in the
Middle Ages*, 1972.

8.24 —— *Ireland in the Later Middle Ages*, 1973.

8.25 —— *England and Ireland in the Later
Middle Ages. Essays in Honour of Jocelyn
Otway-Ruthven*, 1981.

8.26 **McNeill**, T. E., *Anglo-Norman Ulster. The
History and Archaeology of an Irish Barony,
1177–1400*, 1980.

8.27 **Nicholls**, K., *Gaelic and Gaelicised Ireland
in the Middle Ages*, 1972.

8.28 **Nolan**, W., ed., *The Shaping of Ireland.
The Geographical Perspective*, 1986.

8.29 **O'Brien**, Maire and C. C., *A Concise
History of Ireland*, 1972.

8.30 **O'Domhnall**, S., 'Magna Carta
Hiberniae', *Irish H.Studs.*, III, 1942, 31–8.

8.31 **Orpen**, G. H., *Ireland under the Normans,
1169–1333*, 4 vols., 1911–20.

8.32 **O'Sullivan**, M. J. D., *Old Galway: The
History of a Norman Colony in Ireland*, 1942.

8.33 **Otway-Ruthven**, J., *A History of Medieval
Ireland*, 1968, 2nd ed. 1980. Mainly
political. Good bibliography.

8.34 **Ranelagh**, J., *A Short History of Ireland*,
1983.

8.35 **Richardson**, H. G. and Sayles, G. O., *The
Administration of Ireland, 1172–1377*, 1963.

8.36 **Richter**, M., *Medieval Ireland. The
Enduring Tradition*, 1988.

(ii) EARLY MODERN

8.37 **Beckett**, J. C., *The Making of Modern
Ireland, 1603–1923*, 1969. Mainly

political but some coverage of economic
and social aspects is attempted.
Bibliography.

8.38 **Cullen**, L. M., *Life in Ireland*, 1968. A
useful social history, although the weight
is on post-1700 developments.

8.39 **Edwards**, Ruth D., *Ireland in the Age of
the Tudors. The Destruction of Hiberno-
Norman Civilisation*, 1977.

8.40 **Hinton**, E. M., *Ireland through Tudor
Eyes*, Philadelphia, 1935.

8.41 **MacCurtain**, Margaret, *Tudor and Stuart
Ireland*, 1972.

8.42 **Maclysaght**, E., *Irish Life in the
Seventeenth Century*, 1939, 2nd ed.
enlarged and revised 1950. Has chapters
on rural and urban life, communications,
recreations. Documentary appendices
and bibliography.

8.43 **Moody**, T. W., Martin, F. X. and Byrne,
F. J., eds., *A New History of Ireland. III:
Early Modern Ireland, 1534–1691*, 1976.
Economic and social developments are
well covered. There is a separate chapter
on the Irish coinage.

8.44 **Quinn**, D. B., *The Elizabethans and the
Irish*, Ithaca, N. Y., 1966.

8.45 **Simms**, J. G., *Jacobite Ireland, 1685–91*,
1969.

8.46 **White**, D. G., 'The reign of Edward VI
in Ireland: some political, social and
economic aspects', *Irish H.Studs.*, XIV,
1964–5, 197–211. *See also* Salaman
(5.2474).

POPULATION

(a) Medieval

8.47 **Crawford**, E. M., ed., *Famine. The Irish
Experience, 900–1900. Subsistence Crises
and Families in Ireland*, 1989.

8.48 **Graham**, B. J., 'Anglo-Norman
settlement in County Meath',
Proc.Roy.Irish.Acad., LXXV, Sect. C,
1975, 223–48.

8.49 **Gwynn**, A., 'The Black Death in
Ireland', *Studies*, XXIV, 1935, 25–42.

8.50 **Russell**, J. C., 'Late thirteenth-century
Ireland as a region', *Demography*, III,
1966, 500–12.

(b) Early modern

8.51 **Carleton**, S. T., ed., *Heads and Hearths. The Hearth Money Rolls and Poll Tax Returns for Co. Antrim, 1660–69*, 1991.

8.52 **Pender**, S., ed., *A Census of Ireland, c. 1659*, 1939.

8.53 **Attreed**, Lorraine C., 'Preparation for death in sixteenth-century northern Ireland', *Sixteenth-Century Jnl.*, XIII, 1982, 37–66.

8.54 **Bladen**, B. S., 'English villages in the Londonderry Plantation', *Post. Med. Arch.*, XX, 1986, 256–69.

8.55 **Butlin**, R. A., 'The population of Dublin in the late seventeenth century', *Irish Geog.*, V, 1965, 51–66.

8.56 **Cairney**, C. T., *Clans and Families of Ireland and Scotland. An Ethnography of the Gael, AD 500–1750*, 1989.

8.57 **Lee**, Grace L., *The Huguenot Settlements in Ireland*, 1936.

8.58 **MacCarthy-Morrogh**, M., *The Munster Plantation. English Migration to Southern Ireland, 1583–1641*, 1986. Raises questions not only about migration but about the development and character of colonial society in Ireland.

8.59 **Maclysaght**, E., 'Seventeenth-century hearth money rolls with full transcript relating to County Sligo', *Analecta Hibernica*, XXIV, 1967, 1–89.

8.60 **O'Sullivan**, H., 'The landed gentry of the county of Louth in the age of the Tudors', *Co.Louth.Arch and Hist.J.*, XXII, 1989, 67–81.

8.61 **Paterson**, T. G. F., 'County Armagh house-holders, 1664–5', *Seanchas Ardmhacha*, III, 1958, 92–142.

8.62 **Percival-Maxwell**, M., *The Scottish Migration to Ulster in the Reign of James I*, 1973.

8.63 **Robinson**, P., 'British settlement in County Tyrone, 1610–66', *Irish Ec. & Soc.H.*, V, 1978, 5–26.

AGRICULTURE AND RURAL SOCIETY

8.64 **Aalen**, F. H. A., 'Enclosures in eastern Ireland: report of a symposium', *Irish Geog*, V, 1965, 29–39.

8.65 **Canny**, N. P., *The Formation of the Old English Elite in Ireland*, 1975.

8.66 **Crawford**, W. H., 'Landlord–tenant relations in Ulster, 1609–1820', *Irish Ec. & Soc.H.*, II, 1975, 5–21.

8.67 **Fitzpatrick**, H. M., ed., *The Forest of Ireland: An Account of the Forests of Ireland from Early Times until the Present Day*, 1966.

8.68 **Nicholls**, K., *Land, Law and Society in Sixteenth-Century Ireland*, 1976.

8.69 **O'Donovan**, J., *The Economic History of Livestock in Ireland*, 1940.

8.70 **Otway-Ruthven**, J., 'The organisation of Anglo Irish agriculture in the Middle Ages', *J.Roy.Soc. Antiquaries of Ireland*, LXXXI, 1951, 1–13.

See also McCracken (8.243).

INDUSTRY

8.71 **Boyle**, E., 'Irish embroidery and lace-making, 1600–1800', *Ulster Folk Life*, XXI, 1966, 52–65.

8.72 **Breathnach**, B., 'The Huguenots and the silk weaving industry in Ireland, *Eire–Ireland*, II, 1967, 11–18.

8.73 **Longfield**, Ada K., 'History of tapestry making in Ireland and in the seventeenth and eighteenth centuries', *J.Roy.Soc., Antiquaries of Ireland*, LXVIII 1938, 91–105.

8.74 **McCracken**, Eileen, 'Charcoal-burning iron-works in seventeenth- and eighteenth-century Ireland', *Ulster J.Arch.*, XX, 1957, 123–38.

8.75 **O'Sullivan**, D., 'The exploitation of the mines of Ireland in the sixteenth century', *Studies*, XXIV, 1935, 442–52. *See also* Gill (8.273), 1–30, on the linen industry in Stuart Ireland.

ANGLO-IRISH RELATIONS IN THE SIXTEENTH AND SEVENTEENTH CENTURIES

76 **Hogan**, J., ed., *Letters and Papers relating to the Irish Rebellion Between 1642–6*, Irish Manuscripts Commission, 1936.

77 **Moody**, T. W., ed., 'Ulster Plantation Papers, 1608–13', *Analecta Hibernica*, VIII, 1938, 179–297.

78 **Barnard**, T. C., *Cromwellian Ireland: English Government and Reform in Ireland, 1649–60*, 1975.

79 **Brady**, C. and Gillespie, R., eds., *Natives and Newcomers. The Making of Irish Colonial Society, 1534–1641*, 1986. Has chapters on the Irish towns, Gaelic economy and society, native culture, and the English presence in Ireland.

80 **Bottigheimer**, K. S., *English Money and Irish Land: The 'Adventurers' in the Cromwellian Settlement of Ireland*, 1971.

81 **Butler**, W. F. T., *Confiscation in Irish History*, 1917.

82 **Canny**, N. P., *Kingdom and Colony. Ireland in the Atlantic World, 1650–1800*, 1989.

83 —— *The Upstart Earl. A Story of the Social and Mental World of Richard Boyle, First Earl of Cork, 1566–1643*, 1982.

84 **Carlin**, N., 'The Levellers and the conquest of Ireland in 1649', *H.J.*, XXX, 1987, 269–88.

85 **Clarke**, A., *The Old English in Ireland, 1625–42*, 1966.

86 **Ellis**, S. G., *Tudor Ireland. Crown, Community and the Conflict of Cultures, 1470–1603*, 1985.

87 **Hickey**, N. M., 'The Cromwellian settlement in Balyna parish, 1641–88', *J.Co.Kildare Arch.Soc.*, XVI, 1986, 496–509.

88 **Kearney**, H. F., *Strafford in Ireland, 1633–41: A Study in Absolutism*, 1959.

89 —— 'The Court of Wards and Liveries in Ireland, 1622–24', *Proc.Roy. Irish Acad.*, C, 1956, 29–68.

90 **Mayes**, C. R., 'The early Stuarts and the Irish peerage', *E.H.R.*, LXXIII, 1958, 227–51.

91 **Moody**, I. W., *The Londonderry Plantation*, 1939. The main work on the subject.

8.92 —— 'The treatment of the native population under the scheme for the plantation in Ulster', *Irish H.Studs.*, 1938, 59–63.

8.93 **Morton**, R. G., 'The enterprise of Ulster', *H.Today*, 17, 1967, 114–21. Deals with Elizabethan efforts at plantation.

8.94 **O'Sullivan**, H., 'The plantation of the Cromwellian soldiers in the barony of Ardee, 1652–56', *Co.Louth.Arch. and Hist.Soc.*, XXI, 1988, 415–52.

8.95 **Ranger**, T. O., 'Strafford in Ireland: a revaluation', *P.P.*, 19, 1961, 26–45. Reprinted in Aston (4.30), 271–94.

8.96 **Robinson**, P. S., *The Plantation of Ulster. British Settlement in an Irish Landscape, 1600–70*, 1985.

8.97 **Simms**, J. G., *The Williamite Confiscation in Ireland, 1609–1703*, 1956.

8.98 —— 'The Civil Survey, 1654–56', *Irish H.Studs.*, IX, 1954–5, 253–63.

8.99 **Treadwell**, V., 'The Irish Court of Wards under James I', *Irish H.Studs.*, XII, 1960, 1–27.

PRICES AND PUBLIC FINANCE

(a) Medieval

8.100 **Dolley**, R. H. M., *Medieval Anglo-Irish Coins*, 1972.

8.101 **Lydon**, J. F., 'Edward II and the revenues of Ireland in 1311–12', *Irish H.Studs.*, XIV, 1964, 39–57.

8.102 —— 'Survey of the memoranda rolls of the Irish Exchequer, 1294–1509', *Analecta Hibernica*, XXII, 1966, 49–134.

8.103 **McDowell**, J. M., 'The devaluation of 1460 and the origins of the Irish pound', *Irish.H.Studs.*, XCVII, 1986, 19–28.

8.104 **Nolan**, D., *A Monetary History of Ireland*, 2 vols., 1926. Vol. 2 covers the period from the Anglo-Norman invasion to the death of Elizabeth.

8.105 **O'Brien**, A. F., 'The royal boroughs, the seaport towns and royal revenue in medieval Ireland', *J.R.Soc.Antiq.Ireland*, CXVIII, 1988, 13–26.

8.106 **O'Sullivan**, M. D., *Italian Merchant Bankers in Ireland in the Thirteenth*

Century: *A Study in the Social and Economic History of Medieval Ireland*, 1962.

8.107 **O'Sullivan**, W., *The Earliest Anglo-Irish Coinage*, 1950. Reprinted 1964.

8.108 **Richardson**, H. G. and Sayles, G. O., 'Irish revenue, 1278–1384', *Proc.Roy.Irish Acad.*, LXII, 1961–3, 87–100.

(b) Early modern

8.109 **Quinn**, D. B., 'Guide to English financial records for Irish history, 1461–1558, with illustrative extracts, 1461–1509', *Analecta Hibernica*, X, 1941, 1–69.

TRADE

8.110 **Kearney**, H. F., ed., 'The Irish wine trade, 1614–15' (document), *Irish H.Studs.*, IX, 1955, 400–42.

8.111 **Nash**, R. C., 'Irish Atlantic trade in the seventeenth and eighteenth centuries', *Will. and Mary Q.*, XLII, 1985, 329–56.

8.112 **O'Brien**, G., 'The Irish staple organisation in the reign of James I', *Ec.J.Ec.H.Supp.*, I, 1920, 42–56.

8.113 **Treadwell**, V., 'The establishment of the farm of the Irish customs, 1603–13', *E.H.R.*, XCIII, 1978, 580–602.

8.114 —— 'The Irish customs administration in the sixteenth century', *Irish H.Studs.*, XX, 1978, 384–417.

8.115 **Woodward**, D. M., 'The Anglo-Irish livestock trade in the seventeenth century', *Irish H.Studs.*, XVIII, 1973, 489–523.

See also Cullen (4.797), and Longfield (4.811).

TOWNS

8.116 **Butlin**, R. A., ed., *The Development of the Irish Town*, 1977.

8.117 **Camblin**, G., *The Town in Ulster: An Account of the Origin and Building of the Towns of the Province and the Development of their Rural Setting*, 1951. Illustrated.

8.118 **Clarke**, H., ed., *Medieval Dublin. The Living City*, 1990. Has chapters on local government and its socio-economic activity.

8.119 —— *Medieval Dublin. The Making of a Metropolis*, 1990. Includes sections on the town walls and on the city's water supply.

8.120 **Gillespie**, R., 'The small towns of Ulster 1600–1700', *Ulster Folklife*, XXXVI, 1990, 23–31.

8.121 **Graham**, B. J., 'Secular urban origins in erly medieval Ireland', *Irish Ec. and Soc. H.*, XVI, 1989, 5–22.

8.122 —— 'Urban genesis in early medieval Ireland', *J.H.Geog.*, XIII, 1987, 3–16.

8.123 **Harkness**, D. and O'Dowd, M. eds., *The Town in Ireland, H.Studs.*, XIII, 1979. Includes essays on medieval plantation boroughs, the social structure of fifteenth-century Dublin and early seventeenth-century urban development.

8.124 **Lennon**, C., *The Lords of Dublin in the Age of Reformation*, 1989.

8.125 **O'Sullivan**, W., *The Economic History of Cork City from the Earliest Times to the Act of Union*, 1937. One of the best of Irish urban studies. Documentary and statistical appendices. Good bibliography.

8.126 **Simms**, J. G., 'Dublin in 1685', *Irish H.Studs.*, XIV, 1965, 212–26.

RELIGION AND EDUCATION

8.127 **White**, N. B., ed., *Extracts of Irish Monastic Possessions, 1540–41*, Irish Manuscripts Commission, 1943.

8.128 **Barnard**, T. C., *Reforming Irish Manners. The Religious Societies in Dublin in the 1690s*, 1992.

8.129 **Beckett**, J. C., *Protestant Dissent in Ireland, 1687–1780*, 1948.

8.130 **Brady**, C., Gillespie, R., and O'Dowd, M., eds., *Politics, Religion and Society in Ireland, 1515–1641*, 1990. A sourcebook chronologically divided at 1558 and 1603. Each major section contains a sub-section on society and economy.

8.131 **Connolly**, S. J., *Religion, Law and Power. The Making of Protestant Ireland, 1660–1760*, 1992. A well-researched study which shows the strength of Protestant society in Ireland.

8.132 **Coonan**, T. L., *The Irish Catholic Confederacy and the Puritan Revolution*, 1954. Bibliography. Needs to be used with great care.

8.133 **Corish**. P. J., *The Catholic Community in the Seventeenth and Eighteenth Centuries*, 1981.

8.134 **Douglas**, J. M., 'Early Quakerism in Ireland', *J.Friends' H.Soc.*, XLVIII, 1956, 3-32.

8.135 **Edwards**, Ruth D., *Church and State in Tudor Ireland: A History of the Penal Laws against Irish Catholics, 1534–1603*, 1935. Bibliography.

8.136 **Fitzpatrick**, P., *Seventeenth-century Ireland. The War of Religions*, 1988.

8.137 **Hughes**, K., *Church and Society in Ireland, AD 400–1200*, 1987.

8.138 **McGrath**, F., *Education in Ancient and Medieval Ireland*, 1979.

8.139 **Miller**, D. W., 'Presbyterianism and 'modernisation' in Ulster', *P.P.*, 80, 1978, 66–90.

LXXXIX, 1959, 1–15.

8.144 —— 'The medieval county of Kildare', *Irish H.Studs.*, XI, 1959, 181–99.

8.145 **Richardson**, H. G. and Sayles, G. O., *The Irish Parliament in the later Middle Ages*, Philadelphia, 1952. Reprinted 1964.

(b) Early modern

8.146 **Gleeson**, D. F., *The Last Lords of Ormond: A History of the 'Countrie of the three O'Kennedys' During the Seventeenth Century*, 1938.

8.147 **Goodbody**, O. C., 'Anthony Sharp, wool merchant, 1643–1707, and the Quaker community in Dublin', *J.Friends' H.Soc.*, XLVIII, 1956, 38–50.

8.148 **Knox**, S. J., *Ireland's Debt to the Huguenots*, 1959.

8.149 **MacCurtain**, M. and O'Dowd, M., eds., *Women in Early Modern Ireland*, 1991.

8.150 **Ranger**, T. O., 'Richard Boyle and the making of an Irish fortune, 1588–1614', *Irish H.Studs.*, X, 1956–57, 257–97.

(B) IRELAND AFTER 1700

MISCELLANEOUS

(a) Medieval

8.140 **Hand**, G. J., 'The status of the native Irish in the Lordship of Ireland, 1272–1331', *The Irish Jurist*, n.s., I, 1966, 93–115.

8.141 **Lydon**, J. F., 'The problem of the frontier in medieval Ireland', *Topic*, XIII, 1967, 5–22.

8.142 **O'Keeffe**, P. and Simington, T., *Irish Road Bridges, AD 100–1830*, 1990. Examines the strategies of building, their financing and design. Part Two of the book consists of a gazetteer.

8.143 **Otway-Ruthven**, J., 'Knight service in Ireland', *J.Roy.Soc. Antiquaries of Ireland*,

GENERAL WORKS

8.151 **Public Record Office of Northern Ireland** (H. M. Stationery Office. Belfast), *Irish Economic Documents*, 1967.

8.152 **Bannon**, M. J., *A Hundred Years of Irish Planning. I: The Emergence of Irish Planning, 1880–1920; II: The Irish Planning Experience, 1920–80*, 1984.

8.153 **Blake**, R., ed., *Ireland after the Union*, 1990.

8.154 **Boyce**, D. G., *Nineteenth-Century Ireland. The Search for Stability*, 1990.

8.155 **Brophy**, S. A., *The Strategic Management of Irish Enterprise, 1834–84*, 1985.

8.156 **Clare**, J. D., *Northern Ireland, 1920–82,*

1990.

8.157 **Cullen**, L. M., *Economic History of Ireland since 1660*, 1972.

8.158 —— *The Emergence of Modern Ireland, 1600–1900*, 1981. Weighted heavily towards the eighteenth century, the book examines the juxtaposition of 'modern' and 'archaic' elements in Irish society.

8.159 —— (ed.), *The Formation of the Irish Economy*, 1969.

8.160 —— 'Problems in the interpretation and revision of eighteenth-century Irish economic history', *T.R.H.S.*, 5th ser., XVII, 1967, 1–22.

8.161 —— 'The value of contemporary printed sources for Irish economic history in the eighteenth century', *Irish H.Studs.*, XIV, 1964, 142–55.

8.162 —— and Smout, T. C., eds., *Comparative Aspects of Scottish and Irish Economic and Social History, 1600–1900*, 1978.

8.163 **Devine**, T. M. and Dickson, D., eds., *Ireland and Scotland, 1600–1850. Parallels and Contrasts in Economic and Social Development*, 1983.

8.164 **Drudy**, P. J., ed., *Ireland and Britain since 1922*, 1986.

8.165 —— *Ireland. Land, Politics and People*, 1982.

8.166 **Fitzpatrick**, D., 'Was Ireland special? Recent writing on the Irish economy and society in the nineteenth century', *H.J.*, XXXIII, 1990, 169–76.

8.167 **Freeman**, T. W., *Pre-Famine Ireland*, 1957.

8.168 **Girvin**, B., *Between Two Worlds. Politics and Economy in Independent Ireland*, 1989.

8.169 **Griffiths**, K., and O'Grady, E., *Curious Journey. An Oral History of Ireland's Unfinished Revolution*, 1982.

8.170 **Harris**, R. I. D., *Regional Economic Policy in Northern Ireland, 1945–88*, 1991.

8.171 **Hoppen**, K. T., *Ireland since 1800. Conflict and Conformity*, 1989.

8.172 **Johnson**, D. S., 'The economic history of Ireland between the Wars', *Irish Ec. & Soc.H.*, I, 1974, 49–61.

8.173 **Johnston**, Edith M., *Eighteenth-Century Ireland*, 1989.

8.174 **Kearney**, H., 'The Irish and their history', *H.Workshop*, XXXI, 1991, 149–55.

8.175 **Kennedy**, L., and Ollerenshaw, P., eds., *An Economic History of Ulster, 1820–1940*, 1985. Places the Ulster economy in a broad perspective. Useful chapters on

socio-economic change in the countryside and on capital/labour relations.

8.176 **Lee**, J. P., *The Modernisation of Irish Society, 1848–1918*, 1973.

8.177 **Lyons**, F. S. L., *Ireland since the Famine*, 1971.

8.178 —— *Culture and Anarchy in Ireland, 1890–1939*, 1979.

8.179 —— and Hawkins, R. A. J., eds., *Ireland under the Union. Varieties of Tension. Essays in Honour of T. W. Moody*, 1980.

8.180 **McCartney**, D., *The Dawning of Democracy. Ireland, 1800–1870*, 1987.

8.181 **MacDonagh**, O., Mandle, W., and Travers, P., *Irish Culture and Nationalism, 1750–1950*, 1983.

8.182 **McDowell**, R. B., ed., *Social Life in Ireland, 1800–45*, 1952.

8.183 —— *Ireland in the Age of Imperialism and Revolution, 1760–1801*, 1979.

8.184 **Maxwell**, Constantia, *Country and Town in Ireland under the Georges*, 1940.

8.185 —— *The Stranger in Ireland from the Reign of Elizabeth to the Great Famine*, 1954.

8.186 **Meenan**, J., *The Irish Economy since 1922*, 1970.

8.187 **Mokyr**, J., *Why Ireland Starved. A Quantitative and Analytical History of the Irish Economy, 1800–50*, 1983. Looks at the reasons why Ireland failed to participate in the economic growth and capital formation of this period.

8.188 **Moody**, T. W. and Beckett, J. C., eds., *Ulster since 1800: A Political and Economic Survey*, 1954.

8.189 —— *Ulster since 1800, Second Series: A Social Survey*, 1957. Bibliography, 236–40.

8.190 —— and Martin, F. X. (eds.), *The Course of Irish History*, 1967.

8.191 **O'Brien**, G., ed., *Parliament, Politics and People. Essays in Eighteenth-Century Irish History*, 1990. Includes chapters on the free trade crisis and on the eclipse of the Irish language, 1780–1880.

8.192 **O'Grada**, C., *Ireland Before and After the Famine. Explorations in Economic History, 1800–1925*, 1988.

8.193 **Opel**, H., ed., *Irish History and Culture, Aspects of a People's Heritage*, Lawrence, Kansas, 1976.

8.194 **O'Tuathaigh**, G., *Ireland before the Famine, 1798–1848*, 1972.

8.195 **Philpin**, C. H. E., ed., *Nationalism and Popular Protest in Ireland*, 1987.

8.196 **Raymond**, R. J., 'A reinterpretation of

Irish economic history, 1730–1850', *J.Europe.Ec.H.*, XI, 1982, 651–65.

8.197 **Roebuck**, P., ed., *Plantation to Partition. Essays in Ulster History in Honour of J. L. McCracken*, 1981. A valuable *festschrift* which includes essays on Ulster's population, 1660–1760, economic diversification, agricultural development, the industrial structure of Belfast in 1900, and on cross-border trade in the 1920s.

8.198 **Vaughan**, W. E., ed., *A New History of Ireland. V: Ireland under the Union, 1801–70*, 1989.

8.199 **Wichert**, S., *Northern Ireland since 1945*, 1991.

8.200 **Wilson**, T., ed., *Ulster Under Home Rule: A Study of the Political and Economic Problems of Northern Ireland*, 1955.

POPULATION

8.201 **Adams**, W. F., *Ireland and Irish Emigration to the New World from 1815 to the Famine*, New Haven, Conn., 1932.

8.202 **Barrington**, R., *Health, Medicine and Politics in Ireland, 1906–1970*, 1987.

8.203 **Black**, R. D. C., *Economic Thought and the Irish Question, 1817–1870*, 1960.

8.204 **Caldicott**, C. E. J., ed., *The Huguenots and Ireland. Anatomy of an Emigration*, 1987.

8.205 **Collins**, Brenda, 'Proto-industrialisation and pre-famine emigration', *Soc.H.*, VII, 1982, 127–46.

8.206 **Connell**, K. H., *The Population of Ireland, 1750–1845*, 1950.

8.207 —— *Irish Peasant Society*, 1968.

8.208 **Connolly**, S. J., 'Illegitimacy and pre-nuptial pregnancy in Ireland before 1864: the evidence of some Catholic parish registers', *Irish Ec. & Soc.H.*, VI, 1979, 5–23.

8.208A **Costello**, C., *Botany Bay. The Story of the Convicts transported from Ireland to Australia, 1791–1853*, 1987.

8.209 **Drake**, M., 'The Irish demographic crisis of 1740–41', *H.Studs.*, VI, ed. T. W. Moody, 1968, 101–24.

8.210 —— 'Marriage and population growth in Ireland, 1750–1845', *Ec.H.R.*, 2nd ser.,

XVI, 1963, 301–13.

8.211 **Edwards**, R. D. and Williams, T. D., eds., *The Great Famine: Studies in Irish History, 1845–1852*, 1956.

8.212 **Ellis**, P. B., *A History of the Irish Working Class*, 1972.

8.213 **Fitzpatrick**, D., 'Divorce and separation in modern Irish history', *P.P.*, CXIV, 1987, 172–96.

8.214 **Goldstrom**, J. M. and Clarkson, L. A., eds., *Irish Population, Economy and Society: Essays in Honour of the late K. H. Connell*, 1982.

8.214a **Hogan**, D. and Osborough, W. N., eds., *Studies in the History of the Irish Legal Profession*, 1990. Includes essays on the different branches of the legal profession in Ireland and the different aspects of their roles.

8.215 **Kennedy**, R. E., *The Irish. Emigration, Marriage, and Fertility*, Berkeley, Cal., 1973.

8.216 **Malcolmson**, A. P. W., *The Pursuit of the Heiress. Aristocratic Marriage in Ireland, 1750–1820*, 1982.

8.217 **Miller**, K. A., *Emigrants and Exiles. Ireland and the Irish Exodus to North America*, 1985.

8.218 **Mokyr**, J. and O'Grada, C., 'Emigration and poverty in pre-famine Ireland', *Expl.Ec.H.*, XIX, 1982, 360–85.

8.219 —— 'Poor and getting poorer? Living standards in Ireland before the Famine', *Ec.H.R.*, 2nd ser., XLI, 1988, 209–35.

8.220 **O'Brien**, G., 'The establishment of Poor Law unions in Ireland, 1838–43', *Irish Hist.Studs.*, XXIII, 1982, 97–120.

8.221 —— 'The new Poor Law in pre-famine Ireland: a case history', *Irish Ec. and Soc.H.*, XII, 1985, 33–49.

8.222 **O'Grada**, C., *The Great Irish Famine*, 1989.

8.223 **Robins**, J., *The Lost Children. A Study of Children in Ireland, 1700–1900*, 1980.

8.224 **Wall**, Maureen, 'The rise of a Catholic middle class in eighteenth-century Ireland', *Irish H.Studs.*, XI, 1958, 91–115.

8.225 **Walsh**, B. M., *Ireland's Changing Demographic Structure*, 1989.

8.226 **Woodham-Smith**, Cecil, *The Great Hunger: Ireland, 1845–9*, 1962.

AGRICULTURE AND RURAL SOCIETY

8.227 **Aalen**, F. H. A., 'The re-housing of rural labourers in Ireland under the Labourers (Ireland) Acts, 1883–1919', *J.H.Geog.*, XII, 1986, 287–306.

8.228 **Armstrong**, D. L., *An Economic History of Agriculture in Northern Ireland, 1850–1900*, 1989.

8.229 **Beames**, M. R., 'Rural conflict in pre-Famine Ireland', *P.P.*, 81, 1978, 75–91.

8.230 **Bew**, P., *Land and the National Question in Ireland, 1858–82*, 1978.

8.231 **Bric**, M. J., 'The tithe system in eighteenth-century Ireland', *Proc.Roy.Irish Acad.*, LXXXVI, section C, 1987, 271–88.

8.232 **Brody**, H., *Irish Killane, change and Decline in the West of Ireland*, 1986.

8.233 **Casey**, D. J. and Rhodes, R. E., eds., *Views of the Irish Peasantry, 1800–1916*, Hamden, Conn., 1977.

8.234 **Clark**, S. and Donnelly, J. S., eds., *Irish Peasants*, 1983.

8.235 **Cohen**, M., 'Peasant differentiation and proto industrialisation in the Ulster countryside, 1690–1825', *J.Peasant Studs.*, XVII, 1990, 413–32.

8.236 **Crawford**, W. H., 'The significance of landed estates in Ulster, 1600–1820', *Irish Ec. and Soc.H.*, XVII, 1990, 44–61.

8.237 **Crotty**, R. D., *Irish Agriculture. Its Volume and Structure*, 1976.

8.238 **Curtis**, L. P., 'Incumbered wealth. Landed indebtedness in post-Famine Ireland', *A.H.R.*, LXXXV, 1980, 332–67.

8.239 **Donnelly**, J. S., 'The Irish agricultural depression of 1859–64', *Irish Ec. & Soc.H.*, III, 1976, 33–54.

8.240 —— *The Land and People of Nineteenth-Century Cork*, 1925, 2nd ed., 1985.

8.241 **Fitzpatrick**, D., 'Irish farming families before the First World War', *Comp.Studs. Soc. and H.*, XXV, 1983, 339–74.

8.242 **Kennedy**, L., 'Farm succession in modern Ireland: elements of a theory of inheritance', *Ec.H.R.*, XLIV, 1991, 477–99.

8.243 **McCracken**, Eileen, *The Irish Woods since Tudor Times: Their Distribution and Exploitation*, 1971.

8.244 **Maguire**, W. A., *The Downshire Estates in Ireland, 1801–45. The Management of Irish Landed Estates in the Early Nineteenth Century*, 1972.

8.245 **McKillop**, D. G. and Glass, J. C., 'The structure of production: Northern Ireland agricultural industry, 1955–86', *Scot.J.Pol.Ec.*, XXXVIII, 1991, 192–205.

8.246 **Malcolmson**, A. P. W., 'Absenteeism in eighteenth-century Ireland', *Irish Ec. & Soc.H.*, I, 1974, 15–35.

8.247 **Nolan**, W., *Fassadinin: Land Settlement and Society in South-East Ireland, 1600–1850*, 1979.

8.248 **Nunan**, D., 'Price trends for agricultural land in Ireland, 1801–86', *Irish J.Ag.Ec. and Rural Sociol.*, XII, 1987, 51–77.

8.249 **O'Conner**, R. and Guiomard, C., 'Agricultural output in the Irish Free State area before and after independence', *Irish Ec. and Soc. H.*, XII 1985, 31–47.

8.250 **O'Flanagan**, P., 'Markets and fairs in Ireland, 1600–1800: index of economic and regional growth', *J.H.Geog.*, XI 198? 364–78.

8.251 —— Ferguson, P., and Whelan, K., eds. *Rural Ireland, 1600–1900. Modernisation and Change*, 1987.

8.252 **O'Grada**, C., 'The beginnings of the Irish creamery system, 1880–1914', *Ec.H.R.*, 2nd ser., XXX, 1977, 284–305.

8.253 —— 'Primogeniture and ultimogeniture in rural Ireland', *J.Interdis.H.*, X, 1980, 491–7.

8.254 **O'Rourke**, K., 'Rural depopulation in a small open economy: Ireland, 1856–76', *Expl.Ec.H.*, XXVIII, 1991, 409–32.

8.255 **Shiel**, M. J., *The Quiet Revolution. The Electrification of Rural Ireland, 1946–76*, 1984.

8.256 **Solow**, Barbara L., *The Land Question and the Irish Economy, 1870–1903*, 1971.

8.257 **Steele**, E. D., *Irish Land and British Politics. Tenant Right and Nationality, 1865–70*, 1974.

8.258 **Turner**, M., 'Towards an agricultural prices index for Ireland, 1850–1914', *Ec. and Soc.R.*, XVIII, 1987, 123–36.

8.259 **Vaughan**, W. E., *Landlords and Tenants in Ireland, 1848–1904*, 1984.

8.260 **Warwick-Haller**, Sally, *William O'Brien and the Irish Land War*, 1990. Explores this key individual's contribution to the successive phases of the Land League's campaigns.

.261 **Winstanley**, M., *Ireland and the Land Question, 1800–1922, 1984.*

TRANSPORT AND INDUSTRY

.262 **Barker**, T. C., 'The beginnings of the canal age in the British Isles' (the Newry Canal). In Pressnell, ed. (5.106), 1–22.

.263 **Bianconi**, M. A. and Watson, S. J., *Bianconi, King of the Irish Roads, 1962.*

.264 **Boyd**, A., *The Rise of the Irish Trade Unions, 1729–1970, 1972.* Should be used with caution.

.265 **Casserley**, H. C., *Outline of Irish Railway History, 1974.*

.266 **Coe**, W. E., *The Engineering Industry of the North of Ireland, 1969.*

.267 **Conroy**, J. C., *A History of Railways in Ireland, 1928.* Needs revision.

.268 **Cullen**, L. M., 'Eighteenth-century flour milling in Ireland', *Irish Ec. & Soc.H.,* IV, 1977, 5–25.

.269 **Delany**, R., *The Grand Canal of Ireland, 1973.*

.270 **Delany**, V. T. H. and D. R., *The Canals of the South of Ireland, 1966.*

.271 **Geary**, F., 'The Belfast cotton industry re-visited', *Irish Hist.Studs.,* XXVI, 1989, 250–67.

.272 —— and Johnson, W., 'Shipbuilding in Belfast, 1861–1986', *Irish Ec. and Soc.H.,* XV, 1989, 42–64.

.273 **Gill**, C., *The Rise of the Irish Linen Industry, 1925.* Reprinted 1964.

.274 **Green**, E. R. R., *The Industrial Archaeology of County Down, 1963.*

.275 —— *The Lagan Valley, 1800–50: A Local History of the Industrial Revolution, 1949.*

.276 **Gribbon**, H. D., *The History of Water Power in Ulster, 1969.*

.277 **Irvine**, H. S., 'Some aspects of passenger traffic between Britain and Ireland, 1820–1850', *J.Trans.H.,* IV, 1960, 224–41.

.278 **Jacobson**, D. S., 'The motor industry in Ireland', *Irish Ec. and Soc.H.,* XII, 1985, 109–16.

.279 **Kelleher**, P., 'Familism in Irish capitalism in the 1950s', *Ec. and Soc. R.,* XVIII, 1987, 75–94.

.280 **Lee**, J. P., 'The constructional costs of early Irish railways, 1830–52', *Bus.H.,*

IX, 1967, 95–109.

8.281 —— 'The provision of capital for early Irish railways', *Irish H.Studs.,* XVI, 1968, 33–63.

8.282 **Lynch**, P. and Vaizey, J., *Guinness's Brewery in the Irish Economy, 1759–1876, 1960.*

8.283 **McCabe**, C., *History of the Town Gas Industry in Ireland, 1823–1980, 1992.*

8.284 **McCutcheon**, W. A., *The Canals of the North of Ireland, 1968.*

8.285 —— *The Industrial Archaeology of Northern Ireland, 1981.*

8.286 **McGuire**, E. B., *Irish Whisky. A History of Distilling, the Spirit Trade and Excise Controls in England, 1974.*

8.287 **McNeil**, D. B., *Irish Passenger Steamship Services. I: North of Ireland, 1969.*

8.288 **Moss**, M. S., *Shipbuilders to the World. 125 Years of Harland and Wolff, Belfast, 1861–1986, 1986.*

8.289 **Murray**, K. A., *The Great Northern Railway (Ireland), 1944.*

8.290 **Nowlan**, K. B., *Travel and Transport in Ireland, 1973.*

8.291 **O'Mahoney**, C., 'Shipbuilding and repairing in nineteenth-century Cork', *J.Cork. H. and Arch.Soc.,* XCIV, 1989, 74–87.

8.292 **Patterson**, E. M., *The Belfast and County Down Railway, 1982.*

8.293 **Petree**, J. F., 'Charles Wye Williams (1780–1866) a pioneer in steam navigation and fuel efficiency', *Trans.Newcomen Soc.,* XXXIX, 1966–7, 35–46. Steam navigation in Irish waters.

8.294 **Press**, J., *The Footwear Industry in Ireland, 1922–73, 1989.*

8.295 **Swift**, J., *History of the Dublin Bakers, 1949.*

TRADE

8.296 **Bourke**, P. M. A., 'The Irish grain trade, 1839–48', *Irish H. Studs.,* XX, 1976, 156–69.

8.297 **Crawford**, W. H., 'The evolution of the linen trade in Ulster before industrialisation', *Irish Ec. and Soc.H.,* XV, 1988, 32–53.

8.298 **Kennedy**, L., 'Traders in the Irish rural

economy, 1880–1914', *Ec.H.R.*, 2nd ser., XXXII, 1979, 201–10.

8.299 —— 'Retail markets in rural Ireland at the end of the nineteenth century', *Irish Ec. & Soc.H.*, V, 1978, 46–63.

8.300 **Murray**, Alice E., *A History of the Commercial and Financial Relations Between England and Ireland from the Period of the Restoration*, 1907.

8.301 **Solar**, P. M., 'The Irish linen trade, 1820–52', *Textile H.*, XXI, 1990, 57–85.

8.302 —— 'The reconstruction of Irish external trade statistics for the nineteenth century', *Irish.Ec. and Soc.H.*, XVII, 1986, 27–38.

8.303 **Truxes**, T. M., *Irish-American Trade, 1660–1783*, 1989.

8.304 **Wall**, Maureen, 'The Catholic merchants, manufacturers and traders of Dublin, 1778–1782'. *Reportorium Novum: Dublin Diocesan Historical Record*, II, 1959–60, 298–323.

TOWNS

8.305 **Beckett**, J. C., and Glasscock, R. E., *Belfast, the Origin and Growth of an Industrial City*, 1967.

8.306 **Beilenberg**, A., *Cork's Industrial Revolution, 1780–1880. Development or Decline?*, 1992.

8.307 **Chart**, D. A., *A History of Dublin*, 1932.

8.308 **Clarkson**, L. A., 'An anatomy of an Irish town: the economy of Armagh, 1770', *Irish Ec. & Soc.H.*, V, 1978, 27–45.

8.309 **Craig**, M., *Dublin, 1660–1860*, 1952.

8.310 **Daly**, M. E., 'Irish urban history: a survey', *Urban H. Yearbook*, 1986, 61–72.

8.311 **Daly**, S., *Cork, A City in Crisis. A History of Social Conflict and Misery, 1870–2*, 1978.

8.312 **Devlin**, P., *Yes, we have no bananas. Outdoor Relief in Belfast, 1920–39*, 1981.

8.313 **Dickson**, D., ed., *The Gorgeous Mask. Dublin, 1700–1850*, 1987.

8.314 **Gilligan**, H. A., *A History of the Port of Dublin*, 1988.

8.315 **Gribbon**, S., *Edwardian Belfast*, 1982.

8.316 **Harvey**, J., *Dublin: A Study in Environment*, 1949.

8.317 **Maxwell**, Constantia, *Dublin under the Georges, 1714–1830*, 1936, 2nd rev. ed., 1956. *See also* Harkness and O'Dowd (8.123).

8.318 **Munck**, R., *Belfast in the Thirties. An Oral History*, 1987.

8.319 **O'Brien**, J. V., *'Dear Dirty Dublin'. A City in Distress, 1899–1916*, 1982.

FINANCE AND BANKING

8.320 **Barrow**, G. L., *The Emergence of the Irish Banking System, 1820–45*, 1974.

8.321 **Fetter**, F. W., ed., *The Irish Pound, 1797–1826: A Reprint of the Committee of 1804 of the British House of Commons on the Condition of the Irish Currency*, 1955.

8.322 **Hall**, F. G., *History of the Bank of Ireland 1783–1946*, 1949.

8.323 **McGowan**, P., *Money and Banking in Ireland. Origins, Development and Future*, 1990.

8.324 **Moynihan**, M., *Currency and Central Banking in Ireland, 1922–60*, 1975.

8.325 **O'Kelly**, E., *The Old Private Banks and Bankers of Munster*, 1959.

8.326 **Ollerenshaw**, P., *Banking in Nineteenth Century Ireland. The Belfast Banks, 1825–1914*, 1987.

8.327 **Robinson**, H. W., *A History of Accountants in Ireland*, 1964.

8.328 **Rowe**, D., ed., *The Irish Chartered Accountant*, 1988.

8.329 **Ryder**, M., 'The Bank of Ireland, 1721. Land, credit, and dependency', *H.J.*, XXV, 1982, 557–82.

8.330 **Simpson**, N., *The Belfast Bank, 1827–1970*, 1975.

8.331 **Stewart**, J. C., *Corporate Finance and Fiscal Policy in Ireland*, 1987.

8.332 **Tanning**, R., *The Irish Department of Finance, 1922–58*, 1978.

8.333 **Thomas**, W. A., *The Stock Exchanges of Ireland*, 1986.

RELIGION AND EDUCATION

8.334 **Akenson**, D. H., *The Irish Education Experiment. The National System of Education in the Nineteenth Century*, 1970.

8.335 **Atkinson**, N., *Irish Education. A History of Educational Institutions*, 1969.

8.336 **Barnes**, J., *Irish National Schools, 1868–1908. Origins and Development*, 1989.

8.337 **Burns**, R. E., 'The Catholic Relief Act in Ireland, 1778', *Church H.*, XXXII, 1963, 181–206.

8.338 **Casteleyn**, M., *A History of Literacy and Libraries in Ireland. The Long Traced Pedigree*, 1984.

8.339 **Connolly**, S. J., *Priests and People in Pre-Famine Ireland, 1780–1845*, 1982.

8.340 —— *Religion, Law and Power. The Making of Protestant Ireland, 1660–1760*, 1992.

8.341 —— *Religion and Society in Nineteenth-Century Ireland*, 1985.

8.342 **Corish**, P. J., 'Irish catholics before the Famine: patterns and questions', *J.Wexford H.Soc.*, II, 1987, 59–66.

8.343 **Hill**, J. R., 'Popery and Protestantism, civil and religious liberty: the disputed lessons of Irish history', *P.P.*, CXVIII, 1988, 96–129.

8.344 **Keenan**, D. J., *The Catholic Church in Nineteenth-Century Ireland. A Sociological Study*, 1983. Concentrates on the church's social ramifications.

8.345 **Larkin**, E., *The Consolidation of the Roman Catholic Church in Ireland, 1860–70*, 1987.

8.346 **MacElligott**, T. J., *Secondary Education in Ireland, 1870–1921*, 1981.

8.347 **Macourt**, M. P. A., 'The religious enquiry in the Irish census of 1861', *Irish H.Studs.*, XXI, 1979, 167–87.

8.348 **O'Brien**, J. B., *The Catholic Middle Classes in Pre-Famine Cork*, 1980.

8.349 **O'Buachalla**, S., *Education Policy in Twentieth-Century Ireland*, 1988.

8.350 **Parkes**, S. M., *Irish Education in British Parliamentary Papers in the Nineteenth Century and After, 1801–1920*, 1978.

8.351 **Power**, T. P. and Whelan, K., eds., *Endurance and Emergence. Catholics in Ireland in the Eighteenth Century*, 1990. Includes chapters on catholics' land and the Popery Acts of the early eighteenth century, catholic social classes under the penal laws, and on catholics and trade.

8.352 **Quane**, M., 'The Diocesan Schools, 1570–1870'. *J.Cork H. and Arch.Soc.*, LXVI, 1961, 26–50.

8.353 **Stevenson**, J., 'The beginnings of literacy in Ireland', *Proc.Roy.Irish Acad.*, LXXXIX, section C, 1989, 127–65.

LABOUR

8.354 **Beames**, M., *Peasants and Power. The Whiteboy Movements and their Control in Pre-Famine Ireland*, 1983.

8.355 **Bradley**, D., *Farm Labourers. Irish Struggle, 1900–76*, 1988.

8.356 **Broeker**, G., *Rural Disorder and Police Reform in Ireland, 1812–36*, 1970.

8.357 **Buckley**, J. D., ' "On the club": friendly societies in Ireland', *Irish Ec. and Soc.H.*, XIV, 1987, 39–58.

8.358 **Clark**, S., *Irish Peasants. Violence and Political Unrest, 1780–1914*, 1988.

8.359 **Crossman**, V., 'Emergency legislation and agrarian disorder in Ireland, 1821–41', *Irish H.Studs.*, XXVII, 1991, 309–23.

8.360 **Crotty**, R., *The Irish Land Question and Sectarian Violence*, 1981.

8.361 **Gailey**, A., *Ireland and the Death of Kindness. The Experience of Constructive Unionism, 1890–95*, 1986.

8.362 **Gray**, J., *City in Revolt. James Larkin and the Belfast Dock Strike of 1907*, 1985.

8.363 **Greaves**, C. D., *The Irish Transport and General Workers' Union: The Formative Years, 1909–23*, 1982.

8.364 **Hepburn**, A. C., 'The Belfast riots of 1935', *Soc.H.*, XV, 1990, 75–96.

8.365 **Keogh**, D., *The Rise of the Irish Working Class*, 1982.

8.366 **O'Conner**, E., *Syndicalism in Ireland, 1917–23*, 1988.

8.367 **O'Dowd**, A., *Spalpeens and Tattie Hokers: History and Folklore of the Irish Migratory Agricultural Worker in Ireland and Britain*, 1991.

WOMEN

8.368 **Bourke**, J., 'Women and poultry in Ireland, 1891–1914', *Irish Jurist*, XIX, 1984, 107–14.

8.369 —— 'Working women: the domestic labour market in rural Ireland, 1890–1914', *J.Interdis.H.*, XXI, 1991, 479–99.

8.370 **Murphy**, C., *The Women's Suffrage Movement and Irish Society in the Early Twentieth Century*, 1989.

8.371 —— *The Women's Suffrage Movement and Irish Society in the Early Twentieth Century*, 1988.

8.372 **Owens**, R. C., *Smashing Times. A History of the Irish Women's Suffrage Movement, 1889–1922*, 1984.

MISCELLANEOUS

8.373 **Curtis**, L. P., *Apes and Angels. Irish in Victorian Caricature*, 1971.

8.374 **Ditch**, J., *Social Policy in Northern Ireland between 1939 and 1950*, 1988.

8.375 **Finnane**, M., *Insanity and the Insane in Pre-Famine Ireland*, 1981.

8.376 **Inglis**, B., *The Freedom of the Press in Ireland, 1784–1841*, 1954.

8.377 **Lysaght**, P., ' "When I makes tea, I I makes tea" . . . Innovation in food: the case of tea in Ireland', *Ulster Folk*, XXXIII, 1987, 44–71.

8.378 **Malcolm**, Elizabeth, *Ireland Sober, Ireland Free. Drink and Temperance in Nineteenth-Century Ireland*, 1986.

8.379 **Menton**, W. A., *The Golfing Union of Ireland, 1891–1991*, 1991.

8.380 **Munter**, R., *The History of the Irish Newspaper, 1685–1760*, 1967.

8.381 **O'Brien**, G., 'Workhouse management i pre-famine Ireland', *Proc.Roy.Irish Acad.* LXXXVI, 1986, section c., 113–34.

8.382 **Sheehy**, Jeanne, *The Rediscovery of Ireland's Past. The Celtic Revival, 1830–1930*, 1980.

INDEX OF AUTHORS AND EDITORS

Numbers refer to items in the bibliographical guide

Aalen, F.H.A., 8.64, 8.227
Abbot, Mary, 5.517
Abel, D., 5.1227
Abel, W., 5.552
Abelove, H., 1.1
Abel-Smith, B., 5.2767
Abrams, P., 1.2, 4.575, 5.324
Abramsky, C., 5.2394
Ackrill, M., 5.183
Acton, W., 5.2828
Acworth, A.W., 5.1718
Acworth, W., 5.1405
Adam, I.H., 7.75
Adam, Margaret I, 7.210
Adam, R., 5.3221
Adams, C., 3.578
Adams, D.G., 7.211
Adams, J.W.R., 3.280
Adams, L.P., 5.553
Adams, R.J.Q., 5.325
Adams, W. F., 8.201
Adamson, D., 7.46
Adamson, J.W., 4.1441–3
Adburgham, Alison, 5.1503, 5.1532, 5.2992
Addison, W., 3.506
Adler, M., 2.397
Ahlstrom, G., 5.3203
Ahrons, E.L., 5.1458
Aitken, H.G.J., 1.3
Akenson, D.H., 8.334
Aiken, W.A., 4.1209
Aitchison, J., 6.123
Alban, J.R., 6.181
Albert, W.A., 5.1346
Alberti, J., 5.3282
Albion, R.G., 4.557
Alcock, N.W., 4.8
Aldcroft, D.H., 4.697, 5.114, 5.184–6, 5.199, 5.381, 5.1113, 5.1336–8, 5.1341–2, 5.1416–7, 5.1495, 5.1912, 5.2503
Alder, T., 5.1476
Alderman, G., 5.462, 5.1418, 6.110
Aldgate, A., 5.2909
Aldred, D., 3.144

Alexander, D., 5.1504
Alexander, H., 4.596
Alexander, M.V.C., 3.552
Alexander, S., 5.3283
Alford, B.W.E., 4.460, 5.187, 5.391, 5.1141
Allan, D.G.C., 4.1001
Alldridge, H.J., 4.597
Allen, C.J., 5.1463
Allen, C.M., 7.318
Allen, D.G., 4.778
Allen, E., 5.2273
Allen, E.A., 5.3183
Allen, G.C., 5.132, 5.188
Allen, P., 5.2768
Allen, R.C., 4.337, 4.386, 4.1147, 5.554
Allett, J., 5.2504
Allison, E., 7.319
Allison, K.J., 3.232–4, 4.148, 4.296, 4.420, 4.485–6
Allman, A.H., 5.1782
Allmand, C.T., 3.512
Allsobrook, D.I., 5.3111
Alsop, J.D., 4.909
Alter, P., 5.734
Altick, R.D., 5.2976
Altschul, M., 2.1, 2.85
Ambirajan, S., 5.1281
Ambrose, P., 5.627
Ames, E., 3.356
Anderson, B.L., 4.355, 5.1716, 5.1871
Anderson, D., 5.951
Anderson, G., 5.2323, 5.3239
Anderson, M., 4.229, 5.518
Anderson, M.L., 7.48
Anderson, Olive, 5.394, 5.519
Anderson, P., 5.2910
Anderson, R.D., 7.369–71
Andréades, A.M., 4.935
Andreano, R., 1.4
Andrew, D.T., 5.395, 5.1610
Andrews, C.B., 4.515
Andrews, C.M., 4.779–80
Andrews, J.H., 5.1365–8
Andrews, K.R., 4.694, 4.794
Angerman, A., 1.5

Anscombe, J.W., 5.662
Anstey, R., 5.1250
Appleby, A.B., 4.157, 4.207
Appleby, Joyce O., 4.28
Archer, I., 4.598
Archer, J.E., 5.697
Archer, J.H.G., 5.1611
Archer, M.S., 6.177
Archer, R.L., 5.3112
Argles, M., 5.3204
Arkell, T., 4.1111, 5.396
Armitage, Susan M.H., 5.189
Armstrong, A., 5.698, 5.3066
Armstrong, D.L., 8.228
Armstrong, J., 5.1362–3
Armstrong, W.A., 4.451, 5.1612
Armytage, Frances, 5.1196
Armytage, W.H.G., 5.984, 5.1913, 5.2085, 5.3113
Arnold, A.J., 5.2941
Arnold, C.J., 2.139
Arnold, G., 5.190
Arnon, A., 5.2505
Arnot, R.P., 5.2294–6, 6.195, 7.340
Arnstein, W.L., 1.6, 5.1914
Ashby, Mabel K., 5.628
Ashley, M., 4.29, 4.957
Ashley, W.J., 1.7–8, 2.163
Ashmore, O., 4.1183, 5.133
Ashplant, T.G., 1.9
Aspinall, A., 5.2993
Asplin, P.W.A., 8.1
Ashton, E.T., 5.2692
Ashton, R., 4.910–13, 4.936, 4.1210–11, 4.1343
Ashton, Rosemary, 5.463
Ashton, T.S., 1.10, 5.1, 5.23–4, 5.380, 5.952, 5.1248, 5.1783, 5.2478–9
Ashworth, W., 1.11, 5.191, 5.953, 5.1568, 5.2506
Asmussen, Susan D., 4.1524
Aspden, J.C., 5.1613
Aspin, C., 5.134, 5.809
Aspinall, A., 5.2147
Astill, G., 3.109
Aston, B., 5.2214

249